WHY VIET NAM?

CHINA
SOUTHEA
ASIA

0   200
Miles

WHY VIET NAM?

PRELUDE TO AMERICA'S ALBATROSS

Archimedes L. A. Patti

UNIVERSITY OF CALIFORNIA PRESS
Berkeley   Los Angeles   London

University of California Press
Berkeley and Los Angeles, California

University of California Press, Ltd.
London, England

Copyright © 1980 by Archimedes L. A. Patti

First Paperback Printing 1982

ISBN 0–520–04783–4

Library of Congress Cataloging in Publication Data:

Patti, Archimedes L. A.
  Why Viet Nam?

  Bibliography: p. 571
  Includes index.
  1. United States—Foreign relations—Vietnam.
2. Vietnam—Foreign relations—United States.   3. Vietnam—History—1945-1975.   4. United States—
Foreign relations—1954-   I. Title.
E183.8.V5P3   327.730597   80-51242

Designed by Graphics Two, Los Angeles

Printed in the United States of America

1   2   3   4   5   6   7   8   9

CONTENTS

v

PART THREE: HANOI

LIST OF ABBREVIATIONS
AND TERMS

ABCD powers   American, British, Chinese, Dutch powers
ABDACOM   American, British, Dutch, Australian Theater of Operations
                     covering the area from the Bay of Bengal to Australasia,
                     created at the ARCADIA Conference
ACofS (or AC/S)   Assistant Chief of Staff
AFHQ   Allied Force Headquarters
AFNS   Army for National Salvation
AG   Adjutant General
AGAS   Air Ground Aid Section—China
AGD   Adjutant General Department
AGFRTS   Air Ground Force Resources Technical Staff (Provisional),
                     5329th
ALUSNA   U.S. Naval attaché with the American Embassy in France
AMB   Ambassador
AMCONSUL   American Consul
AMEMBASSY   American Embassy
ANZUS   Australia, New Zealand, United States (Security Treaty)
AP   Associated Press (American news agency)
APO   Army Post Office
ARCADIA   Washington conferences, 22 December 1941–1 January 1942
                     (FDR–Churchill)
ARVN   Army of the Republic of [South] Vietnam
ATC   Air Transport Command

BAAG   British Army Aid Group (counterpart to AGAS)
BBC   British Broadcasting Corporation
BCRA   Bureau Central de Renseignements et d'Action (Militaire)
BELIEF   French clandestine operations in Indochina

xi

BIS	Bureau of Investigation and Statistics of the National Commission of Military Affairs of the Government of the Republic of China. See also: CISB
BOQ	Bachelor Officers' Quarters
Br	British
Brig. Gen. (or B/G)	Brigadier General
C-119	U.S. transport aircraft
CARBONADO	Revised plan to take the Canton-Hong Kong area
CBI	China-Burma-India
CBS	Columbia Broadcasting System
CCC	Chinese Combat Command
CCP	Chinese Communist Party
CCS	Combined (U.S.-Br) Chiefs of Staff
CEFEO	Corps Expéditionnaire Français d'Extrême-Orient (French Far East Expeditionary Corps)
CFLN	Comité Français de la Libération Nationale (French Committee of National Liberation)
CG (or COMGEN)	Commanding General
CI	Civilian Internee
CIA	Central Intelligence Agency
CIAC	Copy (ies) in author's collection
CICEI	Compagnie (Societé) Indochinoise de Commerce et d'Industrie
CIDIM	Compagnie (Societé) Indochinoise d'Industrie Minière (Japanese)
CinC	Commander in Chief
CISB	Central Investigation and Statistics Bureau (KMT intelligence organization under General Tai Li; also known as BIS)
CLI	Corps Légèr d'Intervention
CN	Chinese national currency
CO	Commanding Officer
CofS or C/S	Chief of Staff
COI	Coordinator of Information
Col	Colonel
colon	French generic term applied to non-Vietnamese residents of the colony engaged in the local economy, e.g., merchants, bankers, planters, shippers, bureaucrats, public officials, etc.
COMECON	Council of Mutual Economic Assistance (Russian)
COS	British Chiefs of Staff
CT	China Theater
Dai Viet	Dai Viet Quoc Dan Dang (Great Viet Nam Nationalist Party) (see Appendix III)
DCofS or DC/S	Deputy Chief of Staff
DET or Det.	Detachment (a military unit)
DGER	Direction Générale des Études et Recherches (French counterpart to OSS)
DGSS	Direction Générale des Services Speciaux
Disp.	Dispatch

DIXIE Mission	U.S. Army Observation Group at Yenan
DMH	Dong Minh Hoi, short for Viet Nam Cach Menh Dong Minh Hoi (Viet Nam Revolutionary League) (see Appendix III)
DMZ	Demilitarized Zone separating North and South Vietnam
Doc.	Document
DOD or DoD	Department of Defense
Domei	Japanese news agency
DOS	Department of State
DRV (N)	Democratic Republic of [North] Viet Nam
E	East
ECA	Economic Cooperation Administration
EDC	European Defense Community
EMBANKMENT	OSS operation south of the 16th parallel
ERP	European Recovery Plan
EUREKA	Teheran Conference, 28 November–1 December 1943 (FDR-Churchill-Stalin)
FFI	Forces Françaises de l'Intérieur (French Forces of the Interior)
FIC	French Indochina
FIR	Fortnightly Intelligence Report
FMM	French Military Mission
Force 136	British unit under SOE control in SEAC
FRUS	Foreign Relations of the United States, diplomatic papers
G-1	Personnel Officer of division or higher staff
G-2	Intelligence
G-3	Plans and operations
G-4	Logistics and supply
G-5	Civil affairs/military government section
GBT (Group)	Gordon-Bernard-Tan (intelligence unit)
GHQ	General Headquarters
G.M.T. or GMT	Greenwich mean time
GO	General Order
G.P.R.F.	Gouvernement Provisoire de la République Française (Provisional Government of the French Republic)
GRV	Government of the Republic of [South] Vietnam (also abbreviated GVN)
GS(C)	General Staff (Corps)
GVN	Government of [South] Vietnam (also abbreviated GRV)
HQ or Hqrs	Headquarters
Hump	The India-China air ferry route
IBT	India-Burma Theater
ICP	Indochinese Communist Party
IGHQ	Imperial General Headquarters (Japanese)
INDIV	Intelligence Division, OSS-CT
info	Information

JCS	Joint Chiefs of Staff (U.S.)
JICA	Joint Intelligence Collecting Agency
JWS	General Joseph W. Stilwell
kempeitai	Japanese Army Military Police
KMT	Kuomintang, the ruling party of the Nationalist Chinese government
Lieut. or Lt.	Lieutenant (may also prefix the ranks of Commander [Navy], General and Colonel [Army])
LST	Landing Ship, Tank (U.S. Navy vessel)
Ltr	Letter
M.5	French intelligence unit in Kunming, an element of DGER/ SLFEO
MA	Military Attaché
MAAG	Military Assistance Advisory Group
MACV	Military Assistance Command [U.S.] Vietnam
Maj.	Major (may also prefix the rank of General)
M/C	Message Center
MDAP	Mutual Defense Assistance Program
MI-5	British Security Service (counterintelligence)
MI-6	British Secret Intelligence Service (espionage)
MI-9	British intelligence unit charged with the mission of Evasion and Escape of POWs and CIs in enemy control. BAAG was its field unit in China.
MIS-X	War Department intelligence unit, counterpart to British MI-9
MO	Morale Operations unit of OSS engaged in "black" propaganda
MRP	Mouvement Républicain Populaire (Catholic Party)
Msg	Message
N	North
NATO	North Atlantic Treaty Organization
NCO	Non-commissioned officer
NE	Northeast
no.	Number
NSC	National Security Council
NW	Northwest
OB	Order of Battle
OCMH	Office of the Chief of Military History, U.S. Army
OCTAGON	Second Quebec conference (FDR-Churchill) 10 September 1944
OG	Operational Group(s), OSS unit trained in commando-type operations, adept at sabotage and guerrilla activity
OIR	Office of Intelligence Research (DOS)
ONI	Office of Naval Intelligence, U.S. Navy
OPD	Operations and Plans Division, WD General Staff

OSS	Office of Strategic Services
OVERLORD	Code name for the plan to invade northwest Europe, begun on 6 June 1944
OWI	Office of War Information
PAOVN	Political Alignments of Vietnamese Nationalists
para.	Paragraph
PAVN	People's Army of [North] Viet Nam
P.M.	Prime Minister (Churchill)
POW	Prisoner-of-war
Prov.	Provisional
QUADRANT	First Quebec conference (FDR-Churchill) 17–24 August 1943
QUAIL	OSS plan for clandestine operations in Indochina north of the 16th parallel
R&A	Research and Analysis, OSS
RAF	Royal Air Force (British)
REUR	Reference your
Reuters	British news agency
RIC	Régiment d'Infanterie Coloniale (French Colonial Infantry Regiment)
R.N.	Royal Navy (British)
RPF	Rassemblement du Peuple Français (De Gaulle's "mass" movement of 1947–53)
Rpt.	Report
S	South
SAC	Supreme Allied Commander
SACO	Sino-American (Special Technical) Cooperative Organization
SE	Southeast
SEAC	Southeast Asia Command
SEATO	Southeast Asia Treaty Organization
SecState	Secretary of State (U.S.)
Sec'y	Secretary
SHAEF	Supreme Headquarters, Allied Expeditionary Force
SI	Secret Intelligence, OSS
SIS	Secret Intelligence Service (British)
SLFEO	Section de Liaison Française en Extrême Orient (Far Eastern French Liaison Section)
SO	Special Operations unit of OSS
SOE	Special Operations Executive, British counterpart to OSS
SOS	Services of Supply
SRV	Socialist Republic of Viet Nam
SSO	Strategic Services Officer
S.S.U.-W.D.	Strategic Services Unit, War Department—the transitional agency following the termination of the OSS on 1 October 1945
Sûreté	French security police (criminal and political)

SVN	South Vietnam
SW	Southwest
SWNCC	State, War, Navy Coordinating Committee
T/	Prefix indicating Technician, grade level of enlisted personnel
TORCH	Code name for the Allied landings operation on the coasts of N. Africa, begun on 8 November 1942
TRIDENT	Third Washington Conference, 11–27 May 1943 (FDR-Churchill)
UN	United Nations
UNO	United Nations Organization
UNRRA	United Nations Relief and Rehabilitation Administration
UP	United Press (American news agency)
USA	United States Army
USAAF	United States Army Air Force
USAF	United States Army Forces
USFCT	United States Forces, China Theater
USF-IBT	United States Forces, India-Burma Theater
USGPO	United States Government Printing Office
USIA	United States Information Agency
USIS	United States Information Service
USMA	United States Military Academy at West Point, N. Y.
USN	United States Navy
USN Group–China	Naval Intelligence unit in China
USNR	United States Naval Reserve
USSR	Union of Soviet Socialist Republics (Russia)
VM	Viet Minh (see Appendix III)
VML	Viet Minh League (see Appendix III)
VN	Viet Nam
VNA	Vietnamese National Army [South]
VNQDD	Viet Nam Quoc Dan Dang (Viet Nam Nationalist Party) (see Appendix III)
VPA	Viet Nam People's Army [North]
W	West
WAC	Women's Army Corps
WD	War Department
WDGS	War Department General Staff
WH	White House
X-2	OSS unit engaged in counterespionage

PREFACE

This is an attempt to answer for many concerned Americans two most perplexing questions—"Why Viet Nam?" and concomitantly the collateral query, "What happened in Indochina in 1945?" Unquestionably there is a glaring gap in the history of the period which hopefully this work will help to fill. French and Vietnamese accounts, albeit partisan and fragmented, fail to present objectively America's role in that tragic episode of Franco-Vietnamese-American history.

Persistent questions about our involvement in Viet Nam have been met over the years by official Washington with a plethora of answers, each proving unsatisfactory and being gradually abandoned as it failed to stand the test of credulity—until all that remained was the argument that we were there to attain "peace with honor," and that too failed on 30 April 1975. Official pronouncements from the White House, subsequent memoirs from presidents and their close advisers, voluminous proceedings of Congressional hearings, culminating in the "all-revealing" Pentagon Papers—all tried to justify our deepening enmeshment but succeeded only in obfuscating our underlying objectives with vague rationalization, apologia, and protestations for our misadventure.

Why Viet Nam?, a first-hand account of our earliest presence in Indochina, provides at least a partial answer as to why we were there and what far-reaching decisions in the mid-1940s brought us to forget the sentiments so nobly expressed in the Atlantic Charter—the right of all people to choose the form of government under which they will live and to see sovereign rights and self-government restored to those who have been forcibly deprived of them. It is neither an acquittal nor a condemnation of anyone, but a straightforward presentation of events as they occurred, chronologically recorded by the author. From the documented facts the reader can derive his own conclusions.

Because of the passage of a whole generation, it has become necessary in the first of this four-part narrative to include relevant background information beginning with the year 1942 and progressing rapidly to the critical year 1945. The second part covers my experiences in China with

xvii

the French, Chinese, and Vietnamese, including my first meeting with Ho Chi Minh. The third part describes the arrival of my mission in Hanoi, my role in dealing with Japanese, French, and Vietnamese. It includes the tumultuous period of August–October 1945, with the birth of the first independent Democratic Republic of Viet Nam, the abortive French effort to regain control, the devastating Chinese occupation, the death of Lieutenant Colonel A. Peter Dewey, America's first casualty in Viet Nam, and the formal Japanese surrender. The fourth part—"Aftermath"—highlights the salient points of American post-World War II policy leading to our direct involvement and summarizes the outstanding issues still confronting us.

In recounting the many private conversations I had with Ho Chi Minh, I have tried to convey to the reader some of the more intimate thoughts of that enigmatic revolutionary regarding his ambitions for the people of Viet Nam and for the future of his new nation. The eventual withdrawal of American military intervention appeared to many Vietnamese the final defeat of colonialism in their nation. But Ho Chi Minh in 1945 already understood very well how difficult it would be for his nation to escape domination by its ancient enemy, China, or by the Soviet Union if used as a counterforce. His hope then that the United States would play a peaceful, stabilizing role in his nation's development is as relevant today as it ever was. As we move very gradually and hesitantly toward regularizing our relations with the Socialist Republic of Viet Nam it is very timely to review basic considerations and find where our own best interests lie.

The reader may properly ask why I have not come forward with my story until now. In 1946 I drafted a much shorter account of the period but other commitments precluded me from completing that manuscript. After the French collapse at Dien Bien Phu, my manuscript was ready for publication, but it was too late. Our nation was embroiled in the era of McCarthyism. Sensitive to adverse criticism of American foreign policy by members of the military establishment, the Department of the Army decreed that any public disclosure of information or opinion by me on the question of American involvement in Viet Nam would be regarded with official displeasure and I would be subject to disciplinary action. Under protest I acceded to the Department's injunction.

Only after our troops were finally withdrawn from Viet Nam in March 1973 did I once more undertake to assemble my wartime notes and reconstruct the events and circumstances of our early policy and operations in Indochina. The task of assembling the material was complicated by the dispersion of my many dispatches and reports throughout the archives of the Departments of State and the Army, and of the Central Intelligence Agency. Efforts to retrieve them within the Department of the Army proved futile; but those stored with the Department of State and the Central Intelligence Agency were almost intact and were made available to me. For this I am gratefully indebted to Robert M. Blum, formerly a staff member of (Senator Fulbright's) Committee on Foreign Relations, U.S. Senate; to Dr. Ronald Spector of the U.S. Army Center of Military History; and to Gail F. Donnalley, former Archivist of the Central Intelligence Agency. Their assistance in locating and obtaining original and critical documents, manuscripts, and dispatch files, including the "U.S.-Vietnam Relations," the Romanus-Saunderland series on the China-Burma-India operations, and the OSS/SSU files was invaluable in updating my 1946 manuscript.

This book would not have been possible had it not been for the generous assistance and support provided by my many colleagues in the Federal Government, the academia, and old Indochina hands, too many to single out, but to each my deep appreciation. I have made extensive use of the United States National Archives, the Library of Congress, the facilities of the Washington National Records Center at Suitland, Maryland, and the Mills Memorial Library at Rollins College in Winter Park, Florida. I am particularly grateful to John E. Taylor, Archivist, Modern Military Branch, U.S. National Archives, for his invaluable assistance in identifying and locating key military documents; to Patricia Dowling, Archivist, Diplomatic Branch, U.S. National Archives, for her knowledgeable and patient assistance in searching pertinent Department of State files indispensable to this work; and to Carolyn J. McFarland, Head Reference Librarian at the Mills Memorial Library, for her resourcefulness and professional know-how in securing rare and out-of-print references from the Library of Congress and other repositories.

To my very good friends Mai Van Elliott, Gareth Porter, Ngo Vinh Long, and Truong Dinh Hung, who tactfully but accurately guided me in unravelling the intricacies of Vietnamese politics and social mores, I extend my sincere thanks. I would be remiss were I not to express my personal appreciation and gratitude to three very special individuals whose advice and continued support I have relied on—Elizabeth McD. McIntosh, my China colleague and comrade-in-arms, who waded through my first draft; Charles E. Cuningham who, when Editor-in-Chief, University of Washington Press, in a few well-chosen words advised me wisely in the problems of managing large volumes of material more effectively; and Arthur Wang, Editor-in-Chief, Hill and Wang, who generously reviewed my third draft and encouraged me greatly.

Finally, it is a great pleasure to acknowledge the outstanding assistance of the University of California Press staff in seeing this project through to its ultimate conclusion. I am particularly indebted to its Assistant Director, Stanley Holwitz, whose personal interest, professional advice, and friendly support have eased the pain attendant to the publication of a book.

Above all, thanks to my wife, Margaret, who typed and edited the entire manuscript from the first draft through the fifth and final version, with her usual penchant for clarity, substance, and style, and to our daughter, Julie, who devoted her summer vacation to indexing the fourth draft. To these two ladies who cheerfully accepted the inconveniences of a household besieged with books, papers, maps, and charts and constant upheaval, I lovingly and gratefully dedicate this book.

PART ONE

WASHINGTON

CHAPTER 1

THE BEGINNING
OF AN ERA

I was in Kunming, China, on 6 August 1945 when the electrifying news flashed around the world that the United States had dropped a "super-bomb" on Hiroshima. Two days later the Soviet Union declared it would enter the war against Japan on 9 August and on that date we dropped a second "super-bomb" on Nagasaki. To those of us who were preparing extensive military operations against Japan, it was a stunning realization that this was the end of the war in the Far East. The next day, 10 August, the world received the news that the State Department had acknowledged receipt of a Japanese offer to accept the Potsdam terms of surrender, without prejudice to the Emperor's position.

In the great feeling of rejoicing, we believed the war was over for the Americans and for all Asians, and so it was for many. We did not realize that new struggles for power, dominion, or independence would come to a rapid boil almost at once and that the lives of millions of people would be immediately and deeply involved in these struggles—in China, in India, in Indonesia, in Manchuria, to name only a few.

The last battle of World War II which cost, roughly, 1.5 million lives[1] and which became the longest conflict in modern history began at once —not in the great capitals of the world but in a tiny, unknown jungle village called Tan Trao, where an informal congress of Vietnamese political

3

parties met from 13 August to 16 August. They proclaimed a determination to achieve national independence and elected Ho Chi Minh as their leader. By circumstance I was placed at the center of events to come.

While American and Chinese troops in Kunming celebrated their victory over Japan, Allied headquarters in China was already undertaking some major postsurrender operations. A China Theater directive to the Office of Strategic Services (OSS) required among other tasks the liberation of Allied prisoners-of-war (POWs) held by the Japanese in various camps of China, Manchuria, and Korea, but none for Indochina. On the night of 10 August Colonel Richard P. Heppner, Strategic Services Officer, China Theater,[2] directed the activation of previously prepared OSS contingency plans for the liberation and protection of Allied prisoners-of-war. Several OSS "Mercy Teams" were to be airdropped into Japanese POW camps to protect our POWs and return them to Allied control. During the next few days teams left as rapidly as possible for Mukden (where General Wainwright was held), for Peking (where the Wake Island Marines and the Doolittle Raid fliers were held), and for other camps.

After considerable discussion Heppner convinced General Albert C. Wedemeyer, Commanding General, U.S. Forces, China Theater,[3] that a Mercy Team should also be sent to Hanoi, Indochina, where several thousand Allied POWs (American, British, Australian, Indian, Dutch, and French) were interned. I took charge of the Hanoi team, with the added tasks of making preliminary arrangements for the Japanese surrender in Indochina, investigating charges of war crimes, and reporting politicomilitary and economic intelligence.

When Ho Chi Minh spoke to me a few weeks later of his premonition of a "scorched earth" policy for Viet Nam, little did he or I foresee the magnitude of the coming conflict or the ramifications it would have in American lives and the American body politic.

It was a hot and humid summer afternoon, and we had met to discuss the safety of the French populations in Hanoi, Haiphong, and other northern cities, but he steered the conversation, as he often had on earlier occasions, to his urgent need for American support for Vietnamese independence. And I, again, had to reply that the issue could not be resolved at that time but had to be a matter for postwar consultation between Hanoi and Paris or, perhaps, at the United Nations. Ho was silent for a moment, then in a soft voice but with deep conviction said that if the French intended to return to Viet Nam "as imperialists to exploit, to maim and kill my people," he could assure them "and the world" that Viet Nam from north to south would be reduced to ashes, even if it meant the life of every man, woman, and child, and that his government's policy would be one of "scorched earth to the end." This statement from a man who was a master of understated diplomacy was, I knew, not an idle threat and I still remember it vividly.

Our conversation took place in Hanoi when hostilities had ended but before the Japanese in Indochina had surrendered and before the arrival of the Chinese military forces who were to accept the Japanese surrender and handle the repatriation of Japanese troops.

During the previous six months I had been chief of the OSS Secret Intelligence (SI) operations for Indochina in Kunming. I had noted with some distress French intransigence on the status of Indochina, an attitude that seemed to make future trouble inevitable. There had been moments when a small step in the direction of moderation might well have changed the course of history.

CHAPTER 2

"...IF CHINA GOES UNDER..."

I n retrospect it seems odd that I received the first hint of my assignment to Indochina in complete darkness on the cold deck of a pitching and tossing LST nearing the Anzio beaches in Italy. At the time, however, it was not at all unusual for important discussions to take place in the middle-of-no-place—in a desert, in desolate bombed-out buildings, in seas of mud, or what have you. It was war.

On the night of 21 January 1944 a group of us were squatting around Major General William J. ("Wild Bill") Donovan, head of the OSS. The group included several OSS specialists in clandestine operations, Colonel John T. Whitaker,[1] and me. Donovan had been discussing operations in Italy, the Balkans, and France and had briefed us generally on OSS's plans for Operation OVERLORD, the cross-channel invasion of France. He suggested that Whitaker and I forego OVERLORD for a special mission in the Far East. He was having very little difficulty in filling the European teams but what he had in store for us, he said, was unique and challenging. We agreed to accept but wanted to know more. "After we take Rome," was Donovan's only reply. An hour after midnight, on the morning of the twenty-second, we waded ashore at Anzio.

What had been expected to be a brief twenty-five mile jaunt to Rome developed instead into a five-month bloody trek to the Italian capital. Our

6

troops did not march down the streets of Rome until 4 June, just two days before the invasion of France. However, by late June I had cleared the Mediterranean Theater and was on my way to Washington.

Whitaker met me at the station and we drove straight to Harvey's Restaurant, where General Donovan was waiting for us at an out-of-the-way table. He had arranged the luncheon meeting to get away from office interruptions. It was there that I first learned that I had been selected by Donovan to lead an OSS mission in Indochina.

During the summer of 1944 the war in Europe was hard fought and there were many battles still to be won, but there was a strong common purpose and the air was filled with optimism. The picture in the Far East was very different. A multifaceted conflict of interests militated against Allied unity. Frustration was the mood in Washington, London, and Chungking. In China, the Japanese controlled the lines of communications on land and at sea as well as in most of the urban-industrial complexes, but not the vast rural areas lying between. There, a separate war was being waged between Chiang Kai-shek's so-called Nationalist forces and Mao Tse-tung's Communists. This internecine struggle was further complicated by powerful warlords who tended to shift sides from time to time and who, in any case, were unwilling to submit themselves wholly to the authority of the central government of Chiang. For these reasons the armed forces of China could not be compared to the well-organized and disciplined forces of the Western world.

The lack of unity among the Allied nations in the Far East had surfaced very early. The fall of Singapore in February 1942, followed by a catastrophic debacle in Burma, had cut Britain's national pride to the quick. Churchill, an avowed champion of British primacy in the Southeast Asian colonial sphere, was concerned for the security of India. He considered Burma as the last bastion to be held if at all possible. Nevertheless, his top priorities were always for the survival of Britain and a "Europe-first" strategy.

Chiang Kai-shek was more immediately concerned with the struggle in Burma as a matter of defending his borders and insuring for himself a flow of Lend-Lease supplies from America.

ROOSEVELT-CHURCHILL-CHIANG

President Roosevelt sympathized with Britain's "Europe-first" strategy but wanted Churchill to take a more effective stand in the Far East. For several years we had been committed to support Chiang in the struggle against Japan's pan-Asiatic ambitions, and China was very hard pressed. Roosevelt feared that if Japan consolidated its effort in China and assumed military control, China would collapse, with unpredictable strategic consequences.

The President voiced his concern early in 1942 to his son, Elliott, when he asked:

. . . if China goes under, how many divisions of Japanese troops do you think will be freed—to do what? Take Australia, take India—and it's as ripe as a plum for the picking. Move straight on to the Middle East . . . a giant pincer movement by the Japanese and the Nazis, meeting somewhere in the Near East, cutting the Russians off completely, slicing off Egypt, slashing all communications lines through the Mediterranean? . . . How do we [supply] China? . . . the Burma Road. And if it falls? . . . India? That's it.

Later in his discussion with Elliott, Roosevelt added, "What we know is this: the Chinese are killing Japanese, and the Russians are killing Germans. We've got to keep them doing just that, until our armies and navies are ready to help."[3]

Churchill's concern that Japan's attack on Pearl Harbor might adversely draw away American support from the Allies in Europe prompted him to spend the Christmas holidays of 1941 with Roosevelt at the White House. The question of a unified Allied command in the Far East was discussed and an American-British-Dutch-Australian Command (ABDACOM) under General Sir Archibald P. Wavell was soon established. The new command structure excluded China because Roosevelt and Churchill agreed that Chiang Kai-shek would oppose any foreign control on Chinese territory.

Nonetheless, Roosevelt was anxious for strategic and political reasons to retain China in the war and convinced Churchill that the Generalissimo should be given formal status among the Allies. The British yielded to the President's suggestion on condition that the Chinese not be included in the Combined Chiefs of Staff (CCS) organization. The upshot was the creation of a separate China Theater under the Generalissimo, to include also such parts of Thailand and Indochina as were then occupied by the Allies, but not Burma. Chiang was invited to serve as Supreme Allied Commander, assisted by an Allied staff.

Recognizing the political and strategic advantages, Chiang accepted the unique role of "independent" Allied commander responsible only to himself and requested that the United States send a high-ranking American officer to serve as Chief of the Allied staff in Chungking.

Within weeks, however, Wavell and Chiang were at odds over control and allocation of Lend-Lease supplies in Burma and over central direction of Allied strategy in the Far East. Their animosity weakened Allied unity and threatened disaster for American military objectives in both the Far East and the Pacific.

Almost immediately rapid Japanese military advances against the British and the Chinese suggested to the three powers that their command structure should *again* be realigned. In less than two months Wavell's ABDACOM was deactivated[4] and, in line with Churchill's earlier comment that he clearly understood the American President would have primary responsibility in dealing with China in all cases, the whole Pacific (including China) came under American direction, though operational control in China would be with Chiang. Wavell was made "Supreme Commander, India" with responsibility for operations in Burma. The British sphere of responsibility ranged from Singapore to and including the Middle East.

ENTER STILWELL

In response to Chiang's request for an American chief of the Allied staff, General Marshall nominated Major General Joseph W. Stilwell.[5] With the newly-acquired rank of Lieutenant General, Stilwell reported to Chiang on 6 March 1942. He was cordially received by the Generalissimo and Mme. Chiang in Chungking where he learned of Chiang's concern about command in Burma and the difficulties of Sino-British relations. His first surprise came when Chiang announced that he, Stilwell, would be Chief of Staff only of the Allied (i.e., Anglo-American) forces, and *not* of the Chinese forces.

This placed Stilwell from the very start in an awkward position. Chiang chose to retain his old friend and confidant, General Ho Ying-chin, as chief of staff of the Chinese forces. Stilwell, sent to China to aid the Generalissimo in discharging the duties of Supreme Commander of an Allied theater, found his authority greatly curtailed. He also found himself assistant to a commander who was a free agent and whose conceptions of China's interest did not always coincide with those of the British and Americans. When differences arose, Stilwell would be in the middle between the wishes of Chiang as an independent Allied theater commander and the military directives of the Joint (U.S.) and Combined (British-American) Chiefs of Staff.

Stilwell also held three other roles: Commanding General of the American forces in China, Burma, and India (CBI); Military Representative of the President of the United States in Chungking; and the overall allocator of Lend-Lease materiel for the United States. The allocation of Lend-Lease supplies was a hot bone of contention at all times.

This confusing and overlapping situation prevailed until August 1943 when the President, the Prime Minister, and their Chiefs of Staff met at Quebec for the QUADRANT Conference. The conferees for the first time addressed themselves to a coordinated plan for the defeat of Japan. They concluded that China offered an excellent base for aerial attacks on Japanese strongholds, communications to the South Seas, and for an invasion of the Japanese homeland.

Their plan envisaged a two-pronged attack from the east and west to seize the Canton-Hong Kong area. From the east the advance was to be in stages from island to island with air, land, and sea forces culminating in an amphibious assault on the China coast. From the west Chiang's forces were to drive overland to meet the Allied landing parties. The two forces would then move to north China. The target date for operations against the Japanese homeland was set for 1947.

As on earlier occasions, disagreements between the British and Americans emerged over operations in Burma, a key to the successful execution of the newly-proposed strategy. The Americans maintained that once the Japanese had been driven from north Burma, a drive south was essential to open the port of Rangoon to augment the supply routes to China. The British, intent on regaining Sumatra as a jumping-off point to recapture Singapore and the Malay Peninsula, preferred to bypass Rangoon.

The American Joint Chiefs, although agreeing that the general lines of advance in the British plan were sound, privately feared the British might consider a negotiated peace with Japan which would have left the Americans fighting alone in the Pacific. The Americans countered with a proposal urging the development of an accelerated plan for driving the Japanese out of Burma, protecting the supply lines in northern Burma, securing the port of Rangoon, and setting a date for the defeat of Japan for twelve months after the fall of Germany. The American bid for an accelerated campaign directed always toward the Japanese homeland was bitterly challenged by the British. To them an early victory in Europe and salvaging their colonial empire in the Far East were more important than an actual defeat of the Japanese.

The heat engendered over these differences is well illustrated in the personal diary of Lord Alanbrooke, Chief of the Imperial General Staff, who made this entry on 1 October 1943:

A rushed morning with C. O. S. till 12 noon; then meeting with P. M., Chiefs of Staff, Dickie Mountbatten and Pownall. This resulted in an hour's pitched battle between me and the P. M. on the question of withdrawing troops from the Mediterranean for the Indian Ocean offensive. I was refusing to impair our amphibian potential power in the Mediterranean in order to equip Mountbatten for ventures in Sumatra. P. M., on the other hand, was prepared to scrap our basic policy and put Japan before Germany. However, I defeated most of his intentions in the end![6]

A new thrust in the Far East interested Churchill, particularly operations in the Indian Ocean and northern Sumatra, but he remained unconvinced of Roosevelt's arguments that China was essential to the defeat of Japan and that Burma operations were critical to that end.

In another important discussion at the QUADRANT Conference, Churchill steered the talks toward the establishment of a new Southeast Asian Command (SEAC) for Allied operations in Asia. Roosevelt was aware of Churchill's ambitions to regain Singapore and his desire to set up a key command post for Lord Louis Mountbatten, who was the King's cousin and the son of Churchill's old colleague, Prince Louis of Battenberg. The

President agreed to the formation of SEAC; and he, the Prime Minister, and their respective Chiefs of Staff endorsed the designation of Vice Admiral Mountbatten (former chief of Combined Operations) as Supreme Commander, Southeast Asian Theater. The appointment of a Royal Navy Vice Admiral merely confirmed the suspicions of the American staff at the conference that Churchill considered SEAC an amphibious rather than a land theater of operations, a command from which he would launch his cherished Sumatra campaign for retaking Singapore, the symbol of Britain's imperial power and authority in Asia.

Once more Stilwell's command position, such as it was, had to be adjusted to the changing summit maneuvering. In a detailed radiogram of 27 August 1943 General Marshall patiently and diplomatically explained Stilwell's position under Mountbatten. He emphasized that Burma strategy remained unchanged but that the scheduling of operations had to be accelerated by increasing the capabilities of the Burmese supply routes, both overland and by air. However, Marshall went on, the command relationships within SEAC were of the greatest complexity. Creation of SEAC meant there were to be four theaters, three geographic and one operational, representing, respectively, the interests of three nations and the three services, all operating in the same area. SEAC was to be an Anglo-American command which included Burma, Ceylon, Sumatra, and Malaya—but not India. India was under the India Command with responsibilities toward the Middle East where Indian divisions were fighting, as well as to the Far East. In China was, of course, Chiang's China Theater. The American operational theater, CBI, operated in all three geographical areas. It was not subordinate to SEAC.

The Chinese army in India commanded by Stilwell was based on the India Command for logistic support but was to fight in SEAC's area under Mountbatten's command. The U.S. Fourteenth Air Force under General Claire L. Chennault was based in China for operations, was supplied from India, but was formally under the Generalissimo. SEAC received logistic support from the India Command. The administration, defense, and internal security of the India Command were under General Sir Claude J. E. Auchinleck who was, in turn, responsible to the Government of India. As representative of the British War Cabinet and as Viceroy of India, Field Marshal Wavell was arbiter of priorities between the India Command and SEAC, but each could appeal Wavell's decisions to the British Chiefs of Staff. Liaison between SEAC and the Generalissimo was attempted by nominating Stilwell as Deputy Supreme Allied Commander, SEAC, and it was his task to see that the Chinese played their part. Marshall called the mission "no easy one."

It is easy to see that in this command tangle there would be no Allied unity, that dissensions would arise at every level and in every area. However, Stilwell and Mountbatten began their relationship on good terms. Marshall had predicted that Stilwell would find the Admiral "a breath of fresh air" and Stilwell agreed, noting in his diary, "Louis is a good egg, . . . full of enthusiasm and also disgust with inertia and conservatism."[7] So Stilwell could approach his work as Deputy Supreme Allied Commander with obedience to a little homily from Marshall that there had to be genuine cooperation with the British, who were the United States' principal ally. Anything that tended to split the two nations had repercussions around the globe. As General Thomas T. Handy[8] put it, if the British played "God Save the King," Stilwell did not have to join in the singing, but he might at least stand up.[9]

Before Mountbatten's arrival, Stilwell's open contempt for the British and Chinese "do-nothing" attitude on driving the Japanese out of Burma and China had earned him the appellation "Vinegar Joe." He was unrelenting in his criticism of the Chinese Kuomintang's corruption and mismanagement of our Lend-Lease supplies and of the Generalissimo's predilection for waging his personal campaign against Mao's Communists. Stilwell was gradually becoming the bête noire of the Far East. Chiang was only too aware of Stilwell's antagonism and by September 1943 differences between them had reached a critical stage. Chennault attributed his inability to achieve air superiority to the lack of fighter aircraft and supplies originally promised and blamed Stilwell as allocator of Lend-Lease. Chinese commanders also accused Stilwell of refusing their requests for troops and logistic supply.

When Mountbatten arrived in Chungking on 16 October 1943 to meet with Chiang Kai-shek, he learned from General Brehon B. Somervell[10] that the Generalissimo had formally expressed his desire to have Stilwell recalled. This was Mountbatten's rude initiation into the problems of his new command. After some reflection he concluded that he had no desire to use Chinese troops if the officer who had commanded them for two years was to be removed on the eve of active operations and he authorized Somervell to so inform the Generalissimo. The crisis was for a time resolved with Stilwell's pledge to the Generalissimo of full cooperation and more humility in the future.

Another thorny issue was raised at the Chungking meeting. Afterward no one could remember just how the question of boundaries between SEAC and the China Theater had been raised. But the question had come up at the QUADRANT Conference, and one of the conferees recalled that the Chinese had been told that Indochina and Thailand were in the China Theater. The fact that the Combined Chiefs of Staff wanted them transferred to SEAC was to be conveyed tactfully to the Generalissimo. Chiang protested vigorously. The question was ultimately settled by Mountbatten's proposal of a gentlemen's agreement which was to have long-range repercussions: Thailand and Indochina would remain in the China Theater on condition that both Mountbatten and Chiang would have the right to operate in them, with any area occupied automatically coming under the authority of the occupying command. The two commanders agreed, but their agreement was neither accepted nor rejected by the President, the Prime Minister, nor the CCS, all of whom preferred to let this touchy problem rest.

The creation of SEAC and the forced truce between Stilwell and Chiang brought no improvement to the situation. A strong opponent to Stilwell's concept that wars are fought and won on the ground and that air power is only a support-arm was General Chennault, the senior American air officer in China. He contended that Stilwell, by stressing reforms in the Chinese army and devoting his meager resources to it, was missing a chance for an early victory over Japan. Chennault won the support of the President and the Generalissimo and received priority on supplies flown into China by the U.S. Air Transport Command. This flow of supplies to Chennault's air war greatly hindered Stilwell's effort to equip and retrain the Chinese forces for his campaign in Burma.

Chennault used the increased tonnage with great success and intensified his air attacks on Japanese strongholds in east China to a point where the Japanese feared the Americans would base their newly-developed long-range bombers in east China where they could easily attack the Japanese homeland. The direct result was vigorous Japanese counterattacks against the forward American airfields from which Chennault operated. Their offensive opened in April 1944 and drove deep into China with little resistance on the ground. The Generalissimo refused to send arms of any sort, either Chinese or Lend-Lease, to the Chinese defenders of Chennault's airfields. Intelligence reports from American observers indicated that Chiang's refusal reflected an understanding between some local Chinese commanders and the Japanese that the Japanese would leave the Chinese undisturbed in southwest China if the Chinese did not interfere while the Japanese took the airfields which menaced their homeland.

The United States was understandably anxious to retain control of the airfields for land-based air support of American operations in the Western Pacific and tried to salvage the situation. The American Joint Chiefs concluded that if Stilwell took command of all forces in the China Theater, both Nationalist and Communist, he might be able to keep the Japanese from seizing the airfields. The President agreed.

EXIT STILWELL, ENTER WEDEMEYER

The entire postwar history of China indicates that any effort to persuade the Nationalists and Communists to join in a common operation against the Japanese would have failed in any case. But the proposal was never close to acceptance. From July to September 1944 the President's special representative, Major General Patrick J. Hurley,[11] tried to persuade Chiang to make Stilwell the field commander in the China Theater. Chiang first agreed in principle, later reversed himself, charged that Stilwell had shown himself unqualified, and finally again asked that Stilwell be recalled. The President ultimately had to acknowledge Chinese sovereignty in the matter and ordered Stilwell home, but he refused to accept Chiang's request that another American take command of the Chinese forces in China.

During the final phases of these unsuccessful negotiations, the Allied situation in the Pacific improved considerably. The American Navy decisively defeated the Imperial Japanese Navy in the Battle of Leyte Gulf. General MacArthur firmly reestablished American power in the Philippines. And on 15 October Marshal Stalin announced to American representatives in Moscow and to the British Prime Minister that the Soviet Union would throw sixty divisions against Japan, beginning about three months after Germany's defeat.

In this climate, saving the Chinese airfields was less critical to the war against Japan, but there remained a very real danger that Chiang's government might sign a separate peace with Japan or that Chiang himself might be removed through a coup by pro-Japanese elements. Either event would release substantial Japanese forces to strengthen the garrisons of the Japanese homeland.

With these possibilities in the air, the President changed his mind and nominated Major General Wedemeyer to be senior U.S. officer in the China Theater and chief of staff to the Generalissimo. On the last day of October 1944, with a promotion to lieutenant general, Wedemeyer arrived in Chungking. Four days earlier General Stilwell had left Karachi for the United States. Chennault remained.

Wedemeyer's orders from the War Department and the resources at his disposal were very different from those given to Stilwell two and a half years earlier; yet his problems, as he himself saw, were very similar: "Create conditions for the effective employment of maximum U.S. resources in the area. . . . The Chinese must be required to play an active role in this war." *Plus ça change, plus c'est la même chose.*

Since the summer of 1944, the War Department had contemplated splitting the China-Burma-India Theater in two. The plan survived, and Wedemeyer assumed command in a separate China Theater consisting of mainland China, Manchuria, and Indochina, plus all the offshore islands, except Taiwan.

The ambiguous agreements between high commands and theater commands as to Indochina would prove later to be of vital importance to French plans for the reoccupation of their former colony.

MODERN BABYLON

Wedemeyer's new assignment in China defied doctrinal concepts and school solutions of command and control in an irrational political scene.

In north China, Mao Tse-tung had established a state within a state where the Chinese Communists were in full control of a sizeable segment of China's mainland with its own economy and military apparatus, independent of Allied control or of Chiang's dubious authority.

In Chungking the Kuomintang (KMT), known popularly as the Nationalist government, was fragmented. Dissension among its military commanders was rampant. Its bad economic situation was exacerbated by the Japanese blockade and spiraling inflation, which threatened the dissolution of Nationalist China into a group of warring factions. As for Chiang Kai-shek, Wedemeyer put it succinctly to General Marshall, "I have now concluded that the Generalissimo and his adherents realize [the] seriousness of [the] situation but they are *impotent and confounded* . . . ."[12]

The American Joint Chiefs of Staff, reflecting past experience with Chiang, had appointed Wedemeyer Commanding General, United States Forces, China Theater, and had merely authorized him to "accept" the additional role of Chief of Staff to the Generalissimo. Thus the United States avoided repeating the impossible situation in which Stilwell had found himself. As it developed, the new arrangement worked out very well. Wedemeyer and Chiang struck a smooth and cordial personal relationship.

Our own command structure, however, left much to be desired. In China Wedemeyer found American personnel of the Army, the Navy, and the Army Air Force attached to various units which were completely or partially independent of him as Theater Commander. The U.S. Naval Group, China, reported to the Navy Department; the OSS reported to its headquarters in Washington; the Joint Intelligence Collection Agency (JICA) and the XX Bomber Command were directly under the Joint Chiefs of Staff; and the Air Transport Command (ATC) was independent of control by either the India-Burma or the China Theaters. There was also a myriad of Allied missions and clandestine organizations operated by the British and the French in Chungking.

Our Ambassador in China, Clarence E. Gauss, described the scene very well:

... there seems to be much confusion. . . . Correspondence shown us by our Army Hdqs here indicates that OSS, as well as Miles [U.S. Naval Group] and Taili [head of Chiang's Secret Service] are interested in Indo-China matters; that "OSS operating through AGFARTS [sic] . . . a Fourteenth Airforce Installation" is setting up communications with Indo-China French independently of the French Military Mission here and that "Chinese and OSS operate through the Gordon group, a setup not at all to the liking of the French Mission." . . . Thus we have Miles and Taili, OSS and Gordon, the United States Army; we have the French Military Mission going to the Army and the French Delegation coming to us with problems; and no one seems to know what anyone else is doing or what should be done.[13]

From a command and control point of view it was a modern Babylon, and the new Theater Commander promptly asked Marshall to define his relationship to the several organizations and to General Hurley, the President's personal representative. The reply, however, was noncommittal and referred Wedemeyer to his initial instructions. In effect, Wedemeyer was not being limited in his command role by new and detailed directives, nor were the independent agencies restricted in their activities to formal command channels, so long as they kept the Theater Commander "informed." The arrangement was apparently convenient to all concerned. Wedemeyer was free to select his own team and undertook to reorganize the command structure and make personnel changes to meet his particular operational needs. Wisely, he took his time and moved cautiously in dealing with the various intelligence agencies.

Among the first politico-military problems which confronted him as Theater Commander were the Chinese Communists at Yenan and the French military missions at Kunming and Chungking. The former, basically a Chinese matter, had to be resolved with the Generalissimo. The latter, however, was a different story. The international implications of the French presence in China impinged on Allied interests and were of immediate and serious concern to the United States.

CHAPTER 3

INDOCHINA: PRESSURE POINT

FDR AND COLONIALISM

President Roosevelt had long since formulated his basic policy regarding the postwar French role in the Far East. He regarded colonialism as a major cause of World War II. In discussing the French with his son, at Casablanca, he held them partially responsible for the Japanese attack on Pearl Harbor. "Don't think for a moment, Elliott, that Americans would be dying in the Pacific tonight [22 January 1943] if it hadn't been for the short-sighted greed of the French and the British and the Dutch. Shall we allow them to do it all, all over again? ... The United Nations—when they're organized—they could take over these colonies, couldn't they? Under a mandate, or as trustee—for a certain number of years."[1] Roosevelt had pressed the question of trusteeship at Cairo, Teheran, and Yalta and had received the endorsement of Chiang Kai-shek and Stalin. But Churchill had balked.

Cordell Hull's memoirs, published in 1948, are even more specific. The President, he wrote,

entertained strong views on independence for French Indo-China. That French dependency stuck in his mind as having been the springboard for the Japanese attack on the Philippines, Malaya, and the Dutch East Indies. He could not but remember the devious conduct of the Vichy Government in granting Japan the right to station troops there, without any consultation with us but with an effort to make the world believe we approved.[2]

17

On the subject of trusteeship Hull said,

> From time to time the President had stated forthrightly to me and to others his view
> that French Indo-China should be placed under international trusteeship shortly
> after the end of the war, with a view to its receiving full independence as soon as
> possible.[3]

Hull also quoted a January 1944 memorandum from the President expressing the opinion that . . . "Indo-China should not go back to France but that it should be administered by an international trusteeship . . . "[4] Despite the President's strong views, no official statement of American policy or Allied understanding was issued by the United States Government or the Allied high command.

THE FRENCH POSITION

The French, on the other hand, were never less than determined to "liberate" their former colony. Their goal had some degree of legitimacy, as they had in three instances been given official assurance of American support. Acting Secretary of State Welles had written on 13 April 1942 in a letter to Henri-Haye, the French Ambassador to Washington: "The Government of the United States recognizes the sovereign jurisdiction of the people of France over the territory of France and over French possessions overseas . . . [and] fervently hopes that it may see the reestablishment of the independence of France and of the integrity of French territory."[5] And in November our senior State Department officer in North Africa, Robert Murphy, had written to Giraud, "It is thoroughly understood that French sovereignty will be reestablished as soon as possible throughout all the territory, metropolitan and colonial, over which flew the French flag in 1939."[6] The Clark-Darlan Agreement concerning our invasion of North Africa had also stated a mutual agreement that French forces would "aid and support" the Allies "to restore integrally the French Empire."[7]

Thus a year later the "Free French" under General Charles de Gaulle decided the time had come to show the Tricolor and secure for postwar France a seat among the Allies at the peace table. To that end the French submitted to Allied Force Headquarters (AFHQ) in October 1943 their requirements to equip the Corps Expéditionnaire Français d'Extrême-Orient (CEFEO) to be ready for action by autumn 1944. Concurrently the French representative in Washington[8] indicated to General Marshall that the French military authorities intended to petition for representation in the Pacific War Council.

To the American planners in Washington these French demands were superfluous because the Anglo-American Far Eastern strategy was progressing quite well without French encumbrance. Furthermore, the underlying French intent of regaining their prewar colonial empire was obvious and ran counter to Roosevelt's policy for subject peoples.

As late as August 1944 no high-level decision had been communicated to the French with respect to their intention to participate in the Far East operations, especially in Indochina. The truth was that no decision had been reached because of the Anglo-American differences on the colonial question. In this situation there could be no agreed upon decision and none was reached throughout the war.

When Wedemeyer assumed command, the French problems of equipping the CEFEO and of attaining membership in the Pacific War Council were still in abeyance. Continued pressure by de Gaulle was met with stiff opposition by the administration in Washington and by General Eisenhower in Europe. In an attempt to circumvent the American resistance, de Gaulle sent a large military mission, headed by Lieutenant General Roger C. Blaizot, to Ceylon. There the French claimed American approval and official recognition and said they were to have the same status as other Allied missions accredited to SEAC. These claims were not true.

Nevertheless it must be noted that the French received some ill-advised encouragement from several American military and diplomatic officials in Europe. Understandably, Americans who had shared many wartime experiences with their French colleagues in Europe did not find it difficult to accept the French argument that the "Free French" should participate in Allied action in the Far East and that France should "liberate" Indochina from the common enemy. It must not have occurred to these Americans in Paris that they were abetting a French design to reestablish colonial sovereignty over Indochina contrary to the principles of the Atlantic Charter and American anticolonial policy.

TUG OF WAR

It was at this juncture in Franco-American relations that I first became aware of the complexities of my new assignment to the Far East. I had been in Washington for several months preparing for my mission to Indochina. The OSS had made available to me many State, War, and JCS files for background information. In late December 1944 I learned from those files that Samuel Reber, a senior State Department officer with SHAEF,[9] had by chance discovered that the French were organizing in the south of France a corps of two divisions for use in the Far East. This was being done with the tacit approval of SHAEF, provided that it did not interfere with Allied operations and that it was clearly understood the French would use their own equipment.

I noted for General Donovan obvious fallacies in the French plan which could not but interfere with Allied operations because shipping for two French divisions would have to be diverted from other planned operations. Further, the French had no logistical capability to support this sizeable contingent without Allied aid. To sanction an unplanned augmentation of troops in the Far East would have placed a severe strain on the resources of the SEAC and China Theater commanders to the detriment of their approved operations.

Reber also reported that a Commandant Bouheret was recruiting French for a Far Eastern clandestine service. With the help of Lieutenant Colonel Carlton-Smith of SOE,[10] as teams were recruited in France they were sent to London for special training. The sponsor of this venture was called the "Coordinating Committee on Far Eastern Affairs" functioning within the French "Shaef Mission" in Paris. It included, in addition to representatives from the French intelligence services, members of the British SOE and the American OSS.

The matter had been brought to the attention of Secretary of State Stettinius by Joseph W. Ballantine[11] emphasizing that the "attitude on the part of our military authorities in France would appear inconsistent with the position of the President . . . forbidding American activity . . . in relation to Indochina."[12]

Several days later (22 December) Stettinius wrote to Donovan noting that as late as 16 October "the President stated that in his judgment at that time we should do nothing in regard to resistance groups or in any other way in relation to Indochina. More recently, he has informed the Department that American approval must not be given to any French Military Mission being accredited to the Southeast Asia Command."[13] Stettinius pointed out that sending a French Expeditionary Force to participate in the liberation of Indochina and a light intervention force for clandestine operations in Indochina were all closely connected with the French Military Mission. He asked Donovan to consider whether the American participation reported by Reber was consistent with the instructions from the President.

The Secretary's letter was referred to me for comment on which to base a reply. Searching for background material in the Far East files I ran across several documents which at the time startled me. The first was a lengthy cable from Ambassador Gauss dated 26 July 1944 asking the Secretary of State "whether [the] time has now come for [the] American Government to formulate clear and definite policy in re to Indo-China."

My inquiry showed that the question had been brought to the President's attention on 26 August in connection with an aide-mémoire from Lord Halifax, the British Ambassador in Washington. Halifax also had emphasized that the matter was of the utmost urgency because Anthony Eden, British Secretary of State for Foreign Affairs, under pressure from the French in London, wanted to give them an affirmative reply. The points in question were the attachment to SEAC of the Blaizot mission and the establishment in India of a Corps Léger d'Intervention, which apparently had already been formed in Algiers.

Roosevelt had not allowed himself to be steamrolled into a decision by either the French or the British Foreign Office. On 28 August he had suggested that the matter be deferred until after he had met with Churchill in Quebec early in September.[14] But after the Quebec meeting there was still no word from the White House.

My State Department liaison told me in early October that the American Consul in Ceylon had reported a British intent to support Blaizot's mission at SEAC where they would collaborate and facilitate French operations in Indochina. However, as no American agreement had been obtained, the mission would be ostensibly unofficial and would be housed at first in a nearby hotel.

The British had raised still another question—that of French political warfare activities in Indochina—not a military matter. Their position was that it was an internal matter to be handled between Mountbatten's headquarters and the political branch of the French Military Mission. In Washington our people at State and JCS found the arrangement inconsistent with theater jurisdictions, because Indochina lay in the China Theater, not in SEAC.

Entirely too many extraneous problems were being injected into the Allied strategy for the Far East by French pertinacity and British countenance for recouping their lost colonial empires. Moreover, lacking a clear-cut policy directive regarding the current and postwar status of Indochina, our State Department officials were not always in agreement intrastaff. Wedemeyer and Mountbatten were having jurisdictional differences regarding operations in Indochina, and both commanders were being pressured by the French in Chungking and in Ceylon. The OSS was caught in the middle of this French cabal.

The OSS staff, since late 1942 and with JCS approval, had been planning to use resistance groups (Chinese Communists, Koreans, Indochinese, and Japanese puppet troops) against the Japanese forces. Although these plans were militarily advantageous, they were fraught with political implications. On 10 October 1944 Donovan had queried Abbot Moffat, Chief, Southwest Pacific Affairs, as to the State Department's views. The question was forwarded to the White House and on the sixteenth the President's flat reply had been, "Do nothing in regard to resistance groups or in any other way in relation to Indochina. . . ." Donovan was so advised on 20 October by Hull.[15]

Throughout the months of November and December the State Department was in a troubled ferment to secure an acceptable policy statement. Finally, in late December, Stettinius, provoked by the Reber report, had posed the question to the Secretaries of War and the Navy and to General Donovan of the propriety of American participation in Indochina operations. OSS took the position that it should not inject itself into French political warfare operations, nor should its operations serve French colonial aspirations. OSS saw no conflict with the President's stand in availing itself of French resources if they were used exclusively in the Allied effort against the Japanese.

Apparently the President did discuss some of these matters with Churchill at the Quebec conference, for he wrote a note to Stettinius on New Year's Day 1945 (in response to a second aide-mémoire from Lord Halifax) which said in part: "I do not want to get mixed up in any military effort toward the liberation of Indo-China from the Japanese.—You can tell Halifax that *I made this very clear to Mr. Churchill.* From both the military and civil point of view, action at this time is premature."[16] (Emphasis added)

But whatever may have been said at Quebec did not diminish in any way the French determination to position French personnel for quickly taking control of Indochina when the moment should be right.

CHAPTER 4

THE UNINTELLIGIBLE INTELLIGENCE COMMUNITY

W hen I undertook the Indochina mission in the fall of 1944 I was thoroughly baffled by the interlocking interests and unrelated operations in SEAC and the China Theater. The overlapping command structures, conflicting national objectives, inter-Allied and interagency jealousies, and intraagency power struggles militated against effective operations and resulted in enormous waste of human effort and national funds.

As I attempted to acquaint myself with the OSS operation in Asia, I came across a jumble: Detachment 101 at Nazir, India; Detachment 202 in Chungking; OSS/SACO working with the Chinese Nationalists; OSS/ AGFRTS, a joint OSS-Fourteenth Air Force group at Kunming; Detachment 303 at New Delhi; Detachment 404 at Kandy, Ceylon; plans for a Detachment 505 at Calcutta; DIXIE Mission at Yenan, and so forth.

I spent long hours trying to unravel the maze of seemingly duplicative yet unrelated units. Inquiries of the OSS staff only confused me more. A few would explain the role of one or possibly two units; others would simply say, "Sorry, it's classified"; and still others, more honest, would throw up their hands and admit they did not know and could not find out. Eventually I pieced it all together.

The evolution of OSS in Asia was traceable to three major segments: OSS/Pacific Ocean Areas, which never got off the ground and was limited to a liaison office in Hawaii; OSS/China; and OSS/SEAC (later, OSS/India-Burma). Soon after Pearl Harbor, General Donovan with the President's approval asked several of his associates to survey the possibility of establishing clandestine operations in Asia. Their findings indicated that intelligence and guerrilla operations could be conducted in Southeast Asia and China against Japanese units on the mainland and against targets in Japan. In the summer of 1942 General Stilwell accepted the first composite SI/SO[1] group for China. However, for "military necessity" Stilwell diverted the group from its original clandestine mission in China to a tactical mission in Burma. He designated it "U.S. Experimental Station, Detachment 101, OSS." It was commanded by Major (later Colonel) Carl Eifler.

Stilwell's real purpose in altering Donovan's plans was that he felt he could put the team to better use in his upcoming Burma campaign. He foresaw difficulties for OSS operations in China with the Chiang government and with the United States Navy which had started clandestine and paramilitary activities of its own in China and which was only nominally under Stilwell's authority.

The naval activities were conducted by U.S. Naval Group, China, under the command of Captain (later Rear Admiral) Milton E. Miles, a protégé of Admiral Ernest J. King, Chief of Naval Operations. From the start Miles had formed a strange relationship with Chiang Kai-shek's chief of internal security and counterintelligence service (Bureau of Investigations and Statistics, the BIS),[2] one General Tai Li, the archetype of oriental inscrutability. As I was to learn firsthand, the Miles-Tai Li alliance was a disastrous venture for the United States. The intelligence produced was of questionable value to the Allies, and the paramilitary exploits claimed were generally accepted on faith alone. The proven fact was that Tai Li took all that he could of American supplies without an accounting of any sort to the American Theater Commander.

Donovan's attempts to gain a foothold in China were frustrated by Tai Li's refusal to allow an independent foreign clandestine service in China. Miles's Navy resources were limited, compared to OSS's bonanza, and without supplies for the Chinese intelligence services Miles's position in China was in jeopardy. To save his own situation, Miles proposed to OSS a centralization of clandestine activities in China, with official status for himself. At the insistence of Secretary of the Navy Frank Knox, who was under pressure from Chiang's "China Lobby" in Washington, Donovan acceded to the proposal.

Thus in January 1943 Donovan entered into partnership with Miles and Tai Li to extend their arrangement into a Sino-Navy-OSS organization named Sino-American Cooperative Organization (SACO), one of history's greatest misnomers. Tai Li was designated Director and Miles became his Deputy Director. Again at the Navy's prodding in Washington, Captain Miles was also designated Chief of OSS Activities, Asiatic Theater. However, since Stilwell had already established Detachment 101 in Burma, Miles's authority over OSS personnel and operations in China was nominal. Nonetheless, Miles and the Navy were satisfied with the SACO arrangement. With only a handful of OSS personnel, Miles was assured of American supplies totaling 150 tons monthly and the control of their distribution.

The next problem in establishing OSS in the Far East had to do with OSS-British relations. By the middle of 1943, Detachment 101 had proven its worth to Stilwell and he approved plans for expansion of the organization and its operations. The British SOE became alarmed at the burgeoning American clandestine agency, totally free of British control, and tried to check expansion plans. In the summer of 1943 0SS-British relations had deteriorated to the point of open hostility, seriously hampering Stilwell's Burma campaign and the operations of Detachment 101. The situation was, of course, aggravated by SOE's strong misgivings as to American anticolonial sentiment and the implications of a rival organization conducting political warfare activities among "subject peoples" of Southeast Asia.

In August 1943 at the Quebec Conference Donovan found the solution to this problem when the discussion led to the creation of SEAC. With the approval of our Joint Chiefs of Staff, Donovan entered into agreement with Mountbatten and Stilwell which limited Detachment 101 to a tactical role in northern Burma and established a new OSS unit, OSS/SEAC, under the operational control of SEAC headquarters for operations "elsewhere" in the theater.

In China, meanwhile, OSS-SACO relations had come to a standstill. OSS operatives were not permitted to function. OSS reports to Washington plainly stated that, while SACO worked well as a Lend-Lease organization on behalf of Tai Li's secret police and unquestionably facilitated special activities for the Navy in the Pacific, it was producing very little useful intelligence for the Allies in the China Theater. Furthermore, the OSS personnel assigned to SACO were unable to do much more than mark time and strive patiently to break down the intangible but consistent opposition of the Chinese.

Thwarted in initiating his own intelligence operations through SACO and impeded by both Tai Li and the U.S. Naval Group, China, which consistently sided with Tai Li, Donovan modified the situation by relieving Miles as Strategic Services Officer, CBI, on 5 December 1943. He then activated Detachment 202 in Chungking and transferred several men from Detachment 101 to the new unit. Captain Miles remained at SACO as Tai Li's deputy but was replaced by Colonel John Coughlin as SSO-China Theater. Coughlin, a regular army officer, had served as Executive Officer to Eifler in Detachment 101 since its inception.

While he was in Chungking making these changes, Donovan was determined to achieve operational independence for his OSS/China operation, and he approached General Chennault, the only senior American officer in China (other than Stilwell), about entering into a joint clandestine venture. At the time the commander of the Fourteenth USAAF lacked effective tactical ground-air intelligence and needed an underground or behind-the-lines rescue system for downed pilots. Donovan's OSS was made to order for these operations. Conversely, Donovan needed someone close to the Generalissimo to offset the hostility of both Tai Li and Captain Miles, as well as a cover for his OSS unit entirely independent of SACO, all of which Chennault could provide. They reached an agreement, and on 26 April 1944 the arrangement was made official when Stilwell activated a new unit with the purposely obscure title, "Air Ground Force Resources Technical Staff (Provisional)" (AGFRTS), 5329th, with headquarters in Kunming.

After all the maneuvering with Tai Li's obstructionism and Miles's ambitious partisanship, the Donovan-Chennault venture succeeded where SACO had failed. The combination worked extremely well until early 1945, and it survived military reverses, Chinese political considerations, changes in Allied strategy, and theater reorganizations.

By the time Wedemeyer replaced Stilwell, OSS's expansion and success in clandestine activities in the China Theater had placed it in a position of preeminence in the intelligence community of the Far East vis-à-vis the U.S. Naval Group, China, Tai Li's BIS, British SOE, French and Dutch intelligence services, and the unofficial Soviet representation. Donovan, anxious to retain maximum and continued control of American interests in the field of unorthodox warfare, addressed a memorandum in the autumn of 1944 to the President to the point that it was time to make OSS/China directly responsible to the American Theater Commander and proposing that, if desired, OSS/China could also serve General MacArthur and Admiral Nimitz in the Pacific.

Anticipating White House approval, Donovan flew to China in January 1945 to meet his old friend, Wedemeyer. The new Theater Commander had in 1942 helped draft the original JCS directive establishing the OSS, had followed from SEAC headquarters the successful exploits of Detachment 101 in Burma, and was well disposed toward Donovan and his organization. Their meetings resulted in a major reorganization of the Theater's intelligence services. OSS was made responsible for all clandestine programs (except Chinese). Captain Miles (then Commodore) was relieved of control. Both U.S. Naval Group, China, and AGFRTS were placed under Wedemeyer. OSS was elevated to the status of an independent command responsible for broad policy to Wedemeyer but operationally answerable to the SSO/China.

Donovan then flew to Mountbatten's SEAC headquarters at Kandy where, with the Admiral's concurrence, OSS/SEAC was abolished and replaced by OSS/India-Burma Theater (OSS/IBT) headquartered at Kandy at Detachment 404. Lieutenant Colonel Richard P. Heppner, who had headed OSS/SEAC, was designated Strategic Services Officer for China and simultaneously promoted to the rank of colonel.

By the time I was ready to leave for China in March, most of the organizational problems seemed to be resolved. Donovan had achieved integration and control of clandestine activities and independent American intelligence procurement authority—his major objective for OSS/China. On the surface there appeared to be no obstacles to my mission in Indochina. I was assured of complete support by General Donovan and I was proceeding with clear and specific policy directives straight from the White House. Wedemeyer and Heppner were fully advised and I anticipated clear sailing. That was in the United States. But nothing in China was ever that simple.

CHAPTER 5

OSS: THE FRENCH INDOCHINA DESK

POLICY: GET THE JOB DONE

After reorganizing the OSS in Chiang's and Mountbatten's areas, Donovan returned to Washington. Whitaker and I met with him to discuss our new assignment in the Far East and learned that Wedemeyer was expecting us and that Heppner had been briefed on American policy, to wit: the President wanted the OSS to keep out of French efforts to reoccupy their former colony. He regarded the future status of Indochina a question for postwar determination and of no concern to the American military. Under no circumstances were we to give arms or supplies to the French except in furtherance of approved Allied objectives against the Japanese.

I was aware of French clandestine activities in Indochina from bases in SEAC and China, and I raised the question of collaboration with the French military missions at Kandy, Chungking, and Kunming. I was told there was "no objection," provided we did nothing that could be construed as "assistance" to French military or political goals for reoccupying Indochina.

Donovan probed my feelings toward the French, particularly the North African French, my personal views of their colonial policies toward the Algerians, and of de Gaulle's attitude toward the United States and his antagonism for President Roosevelt. I was surpised and a little taken aback at the direction our conversation had suddenly taken. I voiced my sympathy for the plight of France and her role under the Vichy regime notwithstanding that France as a nation had not presented the valiant image of Britain's "last ditch" stand. Still, I observed, many French men and women had acquitted themselves well in North Africa and Europe. I allowed that I had some reservations on the French colonial policies toward the Arabs in North Africa and believed the French would lean toward a status quo ante policy in Indochina.

Donovan appeared reassured by my remarks and went on to comment that French attitudes, aspirations, or even postwar objectives were not our business but warned me to anticipate considerable pressure to depart from our neutral stance from other quarters, aside from the French. There were, he said, many procolonial supporters among American oil and rubber interests, there were ideological enthusiasts for a return of France to its colonial empire, and there was British and Dutch support for French colonialist policies in Southeast Asia. If I encountered serious opposition, "Let John [Whitaker] know."

For well over six months I had been holding down the "French Indochina Desk" in OSS Washington, developing plans, monitoring correspondence, screening candidates for the field team and reviewing available files. Initially this mass of material was in total disarray, intermingled with unrelated files in other sections of OSS. Slowly, with the help of Austin Glass,[1] Duncan Lee[2] and others, I was able to form a composite of what was happening in that part of the world. The files were notably devoid of meaningful intelligence on Indochina itself but contained extensive information on Japanese intentions and capabilities in China and Southeast Asia. I found reports from the U.S. Naval Group, China; from an OSS team in the communist area of Yenan with the American Observation Group under Colonel David D. Barrett; and from the Joint Intelligence Collection Agency. When I raised the question of Chinese contribution to the intelligence efforts, particularly in Southeast Asia, our "old China hands" always wanted to know, "Which Chinese?" It did not take long for me to distinguish between the Nationalists, the Communists, the puppet Chinese groups set up by the Japanese, and the so-called Chinese "bandits." The last were independent forces who preyed on targets of opportunity, political causes not being part of their equipment.

I was also looking for French reports because our files already showed Free French collaboration with the British SOE, but OSS had no hard information from that source. There was a meager file on an organization operating in Indochina called "GBT." It contained no substantive intelligence but betrayed an ongoing British-French-Chinese clandestine operation of considerable potential to my upcoming mission.

The only other item of note pertaining to possible sources of clandestine collaboration was a letter from the League for the Independence of

Indochina. It was reasonably current, dated 18 August 1944, from Kunming, China, addressed to the American Ambassador. The writers appealed for American support in their struggle for independence, offering in return to fight with the Americans against "Japanese fascism." I pursued with the OSS staff the possibility of using this group. Their opinion was divided, the "old China hands" recommending strongly against working with "revolutionary elements," while some of the newcomers felt we had little to lose by using such resources against the Japanese anywhere in the Pacific. I was advised to get OSS's position from Donovan.

At the first opportunity I brought up the idea of using local guerrillas with General Donovan. He said that he and Wedemeyer's deputy, Major General Robert B. McClure, had agreed on a tentative policy for clandestine operations in the China Theater, particularly in using Mao Tsetung's guerrillas. When I pressed the point of using Indochinese agents, Donovan's answer was, "Use anyone who will work with us against the Japanese, but do not become involved in French-Indochinese politics." He assured me that by the time I got to China Heppner would have a clearcut directive from Wedemeyer on the use of guerrilla units. Donovan's words seemed clearly a broad directive to get the job done the best way possible and at the same time to avoid being drawn into French schemes in conflict with American policy.

FRENCH *ESCAMOTAGE* CASTS SHADOWS

Donovan's instructions regarding the French notwithstanding, I had misgivings about French efforts to use and manipulate American resources in the Far East in a secret and designing way. I had learned in mid-November 1944, long after the fact and only through the alertness of an American officer at SEAC, that a project undertaken by the British on behalf of the French military mission in Ceylon had all the earmarks of an unauthorized political warfare operation.

The project was important politically, and the details of its inception and execution are worth noting as an example of British-French collaboration to "end-run" American policy. On 21 February 1944, Force 136 submitted to the joint Anglo-American SEAC staff a French proposal for staff coordination. It was code-named Operation BELIEF and involved infiltrating a team into northern Indochina. Its objectives were: to lay the foundation for a clandestine organization in Indochina to be controlled from the outside, and to sabotage shipping facilities in Indochinese ports.

The original French proposal as presented to SOE called for the parachuting of "an officer or officers of the French military mission" from a China-based airfield into northern Tonkin. All air operations out of China required Chennault's approval and independent French missions were not authorized, so the British rephrased the mission objective to read: "the dropping of agents and supplies in North Tonkin for the development of an operation by one of the British Clandestine Services." The drop was made on the night of 4–5 July by a British aircraft staging at Kunming.

The French operation might have gone completely unnoticed, had there not been a request by Force 136 to obtain "special permission for operation BELIEF II, considered as an integral part of BELIEF I, to be launched on 13 July." This second mission was also approved at SEAC and at Chennault's headquarters.

In the meantime Lieutenant Commander Taylor,[3] the senior American officer of "P" Division, was informed on 7 July that it would probably be necessary to stage a third BELIEF operation to pick up the French officer dropped in BELIEF I, because that officer had carried a manuscript letter from General de Gaulle and had to come out of Indochina with the answer. This obvious circumvention of American policy by the French with SOE's assent and connivance aroused Taylor's indignation and prompted him to inform General Wedemeyer (at that time Deputy Chief of Staff, SEAC) about the whole affair.

Taylor's memorandum, suitably styled for the joint British-American staff, stated:

The military value and importance of operation BELIEF seems very great, and if it is not considered prejudicial to American National Policy it is the view of P Division that it should be strongly supported. On the other hand the information at present available to P Division does not provide any basis for a recommendation either favourable or unfavourable on the request of Force 136 that American Military assistance in the execution of their plan be solicited.[4]

Wedemeyer, entirely aware of the policy conflicts involved, discussed the matter with Mountbatten who, in turn, held a conference on 24 July with his Chief of Staff, the Director of Intelligence, Mr. John Keswick of SOE/SEAC and political adviser on Chinese affairs, Major General R. A. Wheeler representing Wedemeyer, and Brigadier General R. T. Maddocks, Wheeler's assistant. At the meeting Mountbatten revealed that the French agent was a Major de Langlade who appeared to be carrying a handwritten letter from de Gaulle. Further, in his opinion "the letter was not in a form calculated to incite the French in Indo-China to rise against the Japanese but was apparently merely an introductory letter."[5]

General Maddocks allowed that that might very well be the case but cannily noted that it was impossible to know what instructions de Langlade had been given to deliver verbally. Obviously the incident had far-reaching implications. It involved de Gaulle personally and conflicted with Allied policy and strategy. General Wheeler suggested the matter be referred to London and Washington, and Mountbatten directed that Mr. Keswick hand-carry a full report to the Foreign Office.

Naturally as I reviewed four months later the American memoranda concerning this incident, I could not but be aware of French intentions and the rather insidious methods displayed to secure support and transport. I also speculated on the effect they might have on my plans.

FROM CATROUX TO DECOUX

The French determination to mount an unauthorized scheme in Indochina obviously stemmed from de Gaulle who was at the time of the de Langlade airdrop a new ingredient in French-Japanese relations in Indochina. The fall of France in June 1940 had given the Japanese a free hand to move into Southeast Asia; the day after Marshal Pétain asked Germany for an armistice the Japanese had handed an ultimatum to the Governor General of French Indochina, General Georges Catroux. Within forty-eight hours Catroux had accepted[6] the Japanese terms, closed the Tonkin-Chinese frontier, and agreed to allow a Japanese military mission to supervise the suspension of all aid to China.

Paradoxically the Pétain-Darlan government while submitting at home to humiliating German demands castigated Catroux for accepting less harsh terms from the Japanese and replaced him with a Darlan protégé, Vice Admiral Jean Decoux. Abandoned by a government he was prepared to serve, humiliated and alone, Catroux threw in his lot with the French refugee in London, Charles de Gaulle.

It was not to be thought, however, that Japanese demands would stop there. Their plans were purposefully laid and methodically executed. Japan needed Dutch and French critical and strategic resources in Southeast Asia. Not Vichy, not London, not Washington could have stopped them in 1940. Britain and the United States, concerned with Hitler's drive in Europe, lacked the means to defend Far Eastern colonial empires.

The initial appeasement in Indochina only served to encourage Japan to levy more substantive demands on the new Governor General. On 22 September 1940, with Vichy's approval, Admiral Decoux and General Issaku Nishihara concluded a second agreement allowing Japanese occupation of key sites in northern Tonkin. Ten months later the Vichy government granted the Japanese the additional right to occupy portions of southern Indochina. After Pearl Harbor, Indochina became a base for Japanese attacks against the Allies.

The Japanese situation was ideally served. Despite the presence of some fifty thousand French troops in Indochina, Japan acquired a strategic base in Southeast Asia without bloodshed or a wasteful investment of occupational forces. On the contrary, Japan was conveniently able to leave the administration of the country to the French, even to the point of tolerating their colonial army. The "war years" were relatively comfortable for the French colon, and French entrepreneurs profited well from their trade with the enemy. Japan, in turn, found a ready and willing source of supply for its domestic economy.

During the period of collaboration, Decoux exploited with considerable success the so-called "Pétain myth" among the French who were by and large *pétainistes* and among such of the Vietnamese as were affluent and prospering in the new war economy. To counter the Japanese Greater East Asia Co-Prosperity Sphere propaganda which had a certain attraction in European-dominated colonies, Decoux instituted a series of meager reforms to "win the hearts of the Annamite," such as the prohibition of using the patronizing *"tu"* to a Vietnamese or of whipping him in public. Unwittingly Decoux also provided the upcoming revolutionary movement with a cadre of trained administrators and bureaucrats by doubling the number of middle and upper level Vietnamese officials in the civil service.

"CALL TO ARMS"—DE GAULLE

Only a handful in Indochina heard de Gaulle's initial appeal on the BBC for a rallying of the "Free French," broadcast on 18 June 1940 London time (19 June in Indochina). Of those who heard, only a very small number of senior French officers recognized Colonel Charles de Gaulle as the speaker. Catroux was one of them; yet not until he had been irrevocably dismissed by Pétain did he finally turn to "Gaullism." In any case, Indochina stood with Vichy well into 1944 and was not to move toward Gaullism until the eventual outcome of the war in Europe was unmistakable.

In China de Gaulle's appeal was heard by other Frenchmen and one of them, Jean Escarra, an expert in international law who had been serving as an adviser to the Kuomintang, answered the call and left for London. There, in association with Lapie, former Governor of Chad, and M. Hackin, de Gaulle's embryo foreign office staff was formed to keep "in touch with the various departments of the [British] Foreign Office and with the European governments-in-exile."[7]

Escarra traveled to Chungking in mid-1941 to contact Chiang Kai-shek on behalf of de Gaulle and arrange to set up official relations between the Kuomintang and "Free France." With help from the French explorer André Guibaut, then in Chungking, and several officers of the French army who had fled Indochina, Escarra formed the cadre of what was later to be known as the French Military Mission in China.

According to de Gaulle's own account, he had "representatives" of Free France operating at many capitals of the world who reported directly to him. Among many names mentioned in his memoirs were Schompré, Baron, and François de Langlade at Singapore, and Guibaut and Béchamp at Chungking. Of these, de Langlade stands out as a pioneer in the Far Eastern French clandestine apparatus. A former manager of rubber plantations in Malaya, he had offered his services to British intelligence in 1940 and collaborated with the Free French Intelligence Service in Singapore under Lieutenant Colonel Tutenges. When Singapore fell in 1942, the Tutenges-de Langlade team fled to China where they joined Escarra's unofficial French military mission.

The new French presence in China did not escape the ever-vigilant

Tai Li, nor would he tolerate any independent French intelligence operations. Escarra interceded for the group with Chiang and obtained a quasiofficial status for the Free French on condition that they were to deal only with Tai Li's BIS. The arrangement was nonproductive. Tutenges and de Langlade, while free to travel, were under constant Chinese surveillance. But the agreement had one redeeming feature for the French: Tai Li, using Captain Miles's resources obtained from the OSS, provided the French agents with funds, radio transmitters, and special supplies. The Free French set up a workable network in Indochina and repaid the Chinese with information on Japanese troop dispositions and target information for Chennault's air force, including occasional aid to downed American pilots.

Captain Miles's resources were only one source of support for Tai Li's vast and expensive secret operations. A more important source of revenue was the lucrative opium trade and black market routes from Malaya, Burma, and Thailand, which passed through Indochina. Tai Li needed uninterrupted access to this trade, and early in the Sino-Japanese war he had entered into partnership with the two powerful warlords who presided over the southwest gateway to China: General Chang Fa-kwei in Kwangsi province and General Lu Han in Yunnan province. Both provinces abut Indochina.

To protect himself against American interference, which he considered too puritanical, Tai Li had insisted early in the war that the Americans be kept out of Indochina. He later appeased the Americans by authorizing OSS operations in Indochina on condition that French rather than American personnel be used.

GIRAUDISTES AND GAULLISTES

To meet Tai Li's terms, Donovan approached the French in North Africa and suggested they assign several French officers to OSS for intelligence operations in Indochina. The French were receptive and Donovan instructed Miles, about to return to China from Washington, to discuss the matter with General Giraud.[8] That was in May 1943, when Miles was deputy to Tai Li in the newly-formed SACO.

Miles obtained the services of a celebrated and much decorated French naval officer, Commandant Robert Meynier, a young giraudiste submarine commander. He had not only distinguished himself in successful attacks against German shipping but in November 1942 had also made a dramatic escape from France with his ship and crew to Casablanca.

According to OSS records, it appeared that Meynier recruited several French officers with experience in Indochina and some Vietnamese soldiers from the French army then in France. The group was trained in an OSS area near Algiers and shipped to China in July 1943 for further training at a SACO base while awaiting Meynier. The official records become very unclear at that point, especially as to why Meynier passed through Washington in proceeding to China.

Meynier was married to an attractive Eurasian, allegedly an Annamese princess, niece of the former Khâm-sai (viceroy) of Tonkin and member of Bao Dai's privy council, Hoang Truong Phu. In 1943, Mrs. Meynier was in custody in occupied France. Meynier's plan evidently was to use his wife's knowledge and influence fully, a fact he did not divulge until the team was ready to leave for China. With the aid of SOE and elements of the French resistance, an OSS commando-type operation liberated Mrs. Meynier from a German concentration camp, but only at the cost of several British and French lives. She was escorted to a deserted field, put aboard a British plane for London, and then flown to Algiers for a reunion with her husband.

The liberation of Mrs. Meynier created a minor tempest in the intelligence community and exposed the conflicts caused by the ongoing power struggle between de Gaulle and Giraud, which de Gaulle was eventually to win. OSS had concealed from SOE the true objective of the Meynier giraudiste mission because of SOE's known support for the de Gaulle faction's rival intelligence apparatus, the BCRA.[9] OSS also mounted an elaborate deception in which Meynier was ostensibly to head a special OSS-USN operation in the Philippines to be launched from the China coast and Mrs. Meynier was to be an American WAC officer assigned to a "highly classified mission," for all of which reasons the Meyniers were flown from Algiers to Washington.

However, according to a cryptic comment in a message from OSS-Algiers to OSS-Washington, Meynier had been entrusted by Giraud's intelligence service with very special codes to use in an intelligence operation in Indochina, and it was necessary that the special codes be correlated with the codes of the Office of Naval Intelligence in Washington.

When Meynier finally arrived at Chungking in August 1943 to undertake his giraudiste mission, he found a newly established and *official* French Military Mission headed by de Gaulle's personal representative to Chiang Kai-shek, General Zinovi Pechkov[10] (also known as Pechkoff and Petchkoff). General Pechkov demanded that Meynier turn over his special codes and place himself under the Mission's control. Not wanting to openly defy Pechkov, Meynier lodged a complaint with Colonel Emblanc, successor to Tutenges, to the effect that his mission was being ill treated. He maintained that he had been selected by Giraud to conduct a most "critical mission for France," that the plan had the approval of de Gaulle, and that he, Meynier, intended to carry it out, even if that meant working outside the French Military Mission. Meynier suggested, perhaps as a veiled threat, that he might have to seek the support of Miles and Tai Li to get the job done. But Emblanc was not impressed and refused to endorse the Meynier mission.

This encounter developed into a major split among the French in the Far East. The Meynier group was identified as giraudistes and referred to by the French in Indochina as "l'Etat Major," while the Pechkov-Emblanc group were known as gaullistes who represented in Indochina the civil resistance group operating from China.

Even with official recognition the French Military Mission in Chungking continued to meet with strong opposition from Tai Li, who accused it of spying on the Chinese government. The Mission countered that Tai Li was resorting to murder of French nationals to insure unimpeded Chinese subversion of the Vietnamese in Tonkin.

Meanwhile Meynier's group with help from Miles and Tai Li was recruiting Vietnamese agents in China and had made contact with a wealthy relative of Mrs. Meynier and with French colonial officials in Hanoi. Through Mrs. Meynier's commercial connections, the Meyniers succeeded in establishing a liaison with anti-Gaullist officials in the Decoux government.

It was not long before the Emblanc group at the Mission cried "foul." Emblanc himself declared "l'Etat Major" an instrument of Vichy, working for foreign interests inimical to the future of France and one which every loyal Frenchman should therefore obstruct. The Emblanc and Meynier factions carried on their bitter feud throughout the war in the Far East.

As a protege of Captain Miles, Meynier was presented in a most favorable light to Tai Li, who welcomed his contacts with the Decoux regime in facilitating the BIS "import" traffic through Indochina. Meynier was also able to convince Tai Li that the French Military Mission was antagonistic to the BIS. Presumably this would have taken very little persuasion in view of the mutual sniping which had been going on. As a result, in early 1944 Tai Li decreed that the French Military Mission had to close down its communications facilities with Indochina, which crippled the operations of the gaullistes until the very end of the war.

The Meynier mission, which took on so much importance in splitting the French, was a disappointing failure to OSS. It made little progress in penetrating Indochina and OSS did not receive the military information Donovan had anticipated and Miles had promised. In December 1943 Miles was relieved as head of OSS operations in the Far East and of its supplies. At the same time the French political complexities appeared overwhelming and Donovan requested that the Meynier group be transferred to the full control and authority of General Pechkov's Mission.

MORDANT'S *"RÉSISTANCE"*

In Algiers, Indochina was not being ignored. De Gaulle in his memoirs recalled that

certain French authorities in Indochina gradually turned toward the Algiers government. M. François, a bank director, came from Saigon to tell us so; M. de

Boisanger, head of the Political Office of the Government General [the Decoux government], extended discreet antennae toward General Pechkoff, our ambassador [sic] to Chungking; General Mordant, high commander of the troops, secretly made contact with Colonel Tutenges . . . .[11]

Late in 1943, M. François[12] had relayed a message to General Giraud in Algiers from General Mordant that he wished to collaborate with the French Government (CFLN) in Algiers. The message was passed to BCRA and eventually to de Gaulle, who said in his memoirs, "On February 29, 1944, I wrote General Mordant to confirm him in the good intentions I knew were his and to stipulate what the government expected of him and his troops in the extraordinarily difficult situation in which he found himself."[13] De Gaulle's letter was to be delivered to Mordant by M. François but his return to Indochina was delayed and the letter was held at BCRA in Algiers until other arrangements were made four months later.

De Gaulle, anticipating American approval of French participation in the Far East, had by that time designated Blaizot to be commander of the Corps Expéditionnaire Français d'Extrême-Orient (CEFEO) with the principal mission of liberating Indochina. Concurrently plans were laid for merging Giraud's intelligence services into the BCRA organization. The merged services formed a new organization, the Direction Générale des Services Speciaux, using the acronym DGSS. All unorthodox warfare would be conducted by DGSS, including political warfare activities in the Far East to be headed by Lieutenant (later Major) François de Langlade.

De Langlade, who had been working in Ceylon with SOE/SEAC, arrived in Algiers in the spring of 1944 to report on his activities in Southeast Asia to Colonel Escarra, then with the National Defense Staff and in charge of all military missions abroad, and to brief his old colleague, Colonel Tutenges, on the Indochina situation. Tutenges, an expert on Southeast Asia, was to head General Blaizot's deuxième bureau (intelligence section).

In accepting the post of Chief, DGSS-Far East, de Langlade requested de Gaulle's personal support and the authority to exercise sole control over all French clandestine operations for Indochina. Both de Gaulle and René Pleven, Commissioner of Colonies, granted it. However, before de Langlade assumed his new post, de Gaulle wanted him to personally deliver highly classified instructions to General Mordant in Indochina. This was the reason for de Langlade's airdrop into Tonkin in BELIEF I. What de Gaulle's instructions for Mordant were was not known to the Americans. However, prior to my departure for the Far East in March 1945 we learned part of the story from our Military Attaché at New Delhi.[14]

Shortly after the Allied landings in North Africa, Mordant, who had commanded French forces in Indochina since 1940, perceived a new alignment in France and turned to the French provisional government in Algiers; hence his message to Giraud in 1943 via M. François. Having received the nod from de Gaulle through de Langlade, Mordant requested retirement from the active list on 23 July 1944. Admiral Decoux approved his request and appointed the second-in-command, General Aymé, to be the new commander-in-chief. De Gaulle's verbal instructions relayed by de Langlade designated Mordant leader of the French resistance in Indochina; his retirement was to free him for this new undertaking in preparation for "an Allied landing" against the Japanese in Indochina. After a Mordant-Aymé-de Langlade meeting in Hanoi, de Langlade went to Calcutta, where the gaullistes had set up the Section de Liaison Française en Extrême-Orient[15] (SLFEO), and arranged with the British to parachute arms, ammunition, supplies, and "Free French" agents to Mordant. So we knew roughly what the French were attempting from bases in Ceylon and India.

In Indochina the changes brought troubles. Mordant, essentially a military man, was not adept at clandestine methods; he conducted his activities as normal military operations and with little secrecy. He saw the resistance movement narrowly as a military operation and gave no thought to support from the civil population. When the SLFEO parachuted its trained civilian agents into Indochina and they suggested enlisting Vietnamese cooperation, the Army balked and stubbornly rejected political or operational advice from the civilian experts. Mordant's group went about their work with total disregard for security and it was not long before everyone, including the Japanese, knew of their activities. At bars and cafes the main topic of conversation was the myth that the Americans were coming, as they had in North Africa. The more the fiction was repeated the more convinced they became that it would happen momentarily. Visions were conjured of Allied landing operations on the Indochina coast, being greeted by the French waving the Tricolor, joining in a mass attack on the Japanese. Admonitions from the SLFEO to be more discreet and less euphoric did not dampen the overconfident spirit of the French who for the first time since 1940 felt they, too, were part of France.

All the loose talk of Allied landings, ousting the Japanese, and resistance worried Admiral Decoux and his supporters in the French commercial-industrial community. After the liberation of Paris in August 1944 it had become difficult to rule in the name of the defunct Vichy government. But de Gaulle, anxious for parity among the Allies, had wasted no time in declaring his "new France" at war with Japan. It placed Decoux in an especially tenuous position—neither friend nor foe of the occupying Japanese, nor a legitimate representative of the "new France." The old Admiral cautioned the Paris government and the French representative at Chungking that only through continued collaboration with the Japanese could Indochina retain its French sovereignty. And he protested all the turmoil Mordant was generating with his ill-concealed resistance movement.

Decoux's protests must have fallen on deaf ears, for on 12 September de Gaulle secretly designated Mordant his Delegate General for Indochina with full powers to make political and military decisions, becoming in effect the representative of the French government in Paris. When Decoux learned of it, he offered to resign. Once more, on 19 November 1944, de Langlade was dispatched to Hanoi, this time to dissuade Decoux from resigning and to induce him to collaborate with de Gaulle. Under instructions from Paris to be firm with the vacillating Governor General, de Langlade ordered Decoux in the name of the French Provisional Government to remain at his post, to alter in no way his attitude or relationship with the Japanese authorities, so as not to alert them to France's plans for Indochina, and to ignore the resistance movement. The proud and egotistical Admiral, taking stock of the situation and his own political future, acquiesced to the Paris *dictat* and agreed to all.

Less than ten days later (28 November) de Langlade was again back in Indochina to advise Decoux that the Paris government had set up a secret Indochinese Council to handle all French political and military matters. Decoux was designated "president" of the Council. Serving with him were Mordant as "vice president," General Aymé, and five other loyal gaullistes. Decoux thus found himself stripped of all authority in Indochina and simply a "front man" for Mordant.

JAPANESE REACTION

It was at just that point that France's final months of colonial preeminence in Southeast Asia began, for the Japanese who had been quite content to leave administrative and commercial controls with the French so long as there was no external interference now found the situation changed. One had only to listen to the careless and defiant boasts of French officers, government officials, and colons to perceive that something dramatically disquieting was afoot.

The Japanese had suffered reverses in Burma and in the Pacific and were alert to internal unrest and political agitation in Indochina; and they began to take precautions. They replaced their Garrison Army in Indochina with the tactical 38th Imperial Army under the command of Lieutenant General Yuitsu Tsuchihashi. As I was to learn firsthand some months later in Hanoi, the General had anticipated trouble with the gaullistes and the "Etsumei (Viet Minh) army" and had sought permission from Tokyo in December 1944 to take appropriate measures to forestall a French attack, but Tokyo had turned down his request.

Lieutenant Colonel Tateki Sakai, a senior officer on Tsuchihashi's staff, gave me in August 1945 his recollections of the Japanese mood during the preceding winter:

> As a result of the Philippines operation [by] the United States Army . . . the entire French Indochina coast was exposed to . . . enemy landings. . . . Our communications with Japan proper were expected to be intercepted by the superior United

States Air and Naval forces and native inhabitants of French Indochina were expected to be agitated by the enemy [U.S.] bombardment.... French Indochina which hitherto had been merely a line of communications zone was now converted into an operational theater.

Further:

The strengthening of the defensive preparations in the area could not be neglected. As the unfavorable operational progress on both western and eastern fronts was acknowledged, the French Indochina Army appeared to have planned an operational preparation against Japan, commencing to secretly conscript native inhabitants into the Army. In conscripting they especially avoided Annamese who were docile and pro-Japanese and took the savage Moi and Laos tribes into the Tonkin Division. This action caught our attention as it predicted their future relationship with China.

About the situation, specifically in January, Colonel Sakai said:

Meanwhile our Army continuously received such noteworthy intelligence reports as the following: "French spies are entering French Indochina through the air-route"; "They are conducting wireless communications with India and China"; "The FFI Group is responsible for underground activities"; "Governor Decoux made a speech reproaching Japan and praising the de Gaulle Government"; "Native inhabitants are being enlisted"; "The French Indochina Army is scattering in the suburbs and rural districts and is concentrating on constructing defensive fortifications." At this time French Indochina clearly showed their hostility toward Japan and yet tried to conceal their outward feelings until the arrival of the Allied forces.[16]

But in December 1944 Tokyo was not ready to upset the status quo. The newly reorganized 38th Imperial Army lacked its combat units, still enroute from areas outside Indochina, and they would not be in position until April 1945. From long-range political motives it was argued in Tokyo that in the event of a Japanese defeat it would be best not to add France to the powers claiming retribution. And what would be gained by provoking the French at that juncture? Supporting Vietnamese aspirations for independence, as Tsuchihashi once suggested, would serve no useful purpose because, in the end, Indochina would revert to France, be absorbed by China, or become a Soviet dependency. Whatever happened, Japan had incurred the enmity of the French, and in Tokyo it was concluded that it would be wise to avoid local political entanglements and perhaps be in the position of handing over Indochina intact to France. But in its reply to Tsuchihashi IGHQ in Tokyo cautioned extreme care and directed him to wait until his army was combat ready.

So the weeks went by with the Japanese army in Indochina seriously concerned about the problem of the gaulliste underground. From its inception in August 1944 to January 1945 it had grown vociferous, if not effective. From every quarter there were indications that plans for resistance were based on a minimum-risk operation: the French made no pretense that their resistance would be an independent French action to liberate the country; on the contrary, it was common knowledge that they would attack the Japanese only after Allied landings had begun. The Japanese in Indochina were thoroughly aware of these French plans and gave serious thought to their own safety. They also did not discount a further possibility that if no landings took place before Japan's defeat and the French were thus denied a modicum of heroics the French would still take their revenge. Thus the Japanese in Indochina saw no alternative to immobilizing the French army before Japan's defeat if a postceasefire massacre were to be avoided.

More experienced clandestine operatives among the French would have perceived Japanese military reorganization, troop augmentations, and diplomatic reassignments[17] as positive indicators that the resistance movement was being carefully watched. Yet Mordant and the SLFEO took extraordinary steps which only multiplied Japanese suspicions.

In January and February Mordant ordered the relocation of the French army from the cities and suburbs to the mountainous regions of Tonkin and Laos. The move was based on the rationale that in the event of an Allied attack the army would not be trapped in peacetime garrisons and could function as guerrillas in less populated areas. How they were going to assist in Allied landings on the distant coastal plains had not been thoroughly discussed. Furthermore, their troop movements were followed by the Japanese; as the French commanders moved troops from their regular posts, Japanese units followed and stationed themselves within watching distance.

In February the SLFEO in Calcutta foolishly revived the myth of an Allied landing in May, and feverish activities got under way—always under the watchful eyes of the *kempeitai*, the Japanese security police.[18]

By an unlucky coincidence of war, nine American airmen were forced to bail out over Indochina during this period, and four were taken into custody by the French. The Japanese demanded that they be surrendered into Japanese custody, but Admiral Decoux refused to comply.

The Japanese had had enough. The decision was made to put a stop to the French activities. On 9 March 1945 at 6:00 P.M., Saigon time, Ambassador Matsumoto handed Admiral Decoux at his palace in Saigon an ultimatum demanding that the French armed forces be placed under Japanese command. Receiving no satisfactory answer within the two hours stipulated, the Japanese assumed that Decoux had rejected the ultimatum.

Within the following forty-eight hours all French officials from Admiral Decoux down to the lowest functionary were stripped of authority and either imprisoned or confined to quarters. Generals Mordant and Aymé were placed under arrest. The French flag was lowered from all public buildings and military installations. Key industrialists and known gaullistes were arrested and interned as political prisoners. And all French officers and military units were disarmed and interned. The only French to escape the Japanese dragnet were several thousand troops deployed in northern Tonkin and Laos. And those who escaped began a long retreat on foot to China.

CHAPTER 6

THE AMERICANS DISCOVER HO CHI MINH

W hile the great powers were getting involved in clandestine activities in Indochina, other less conspicuous groups were already operating there. One represented Western oil interests—the GBT or the "Gordon Group." Another was the Vietnamese nationalist movement—the Viet Minh. The OSS was involved to some degree with both groups and, before leaving Washington, I looked into their activities.

GBT: THE GORDON GROUP

My interest in GBT was first aroused by a report from the Air Ground Aid Section (AGAS) China[1] giving a GBT account of an Allied raid over Saigon. GBT advised that nine American flyers had been forced down by enemy fire and three had been captured by the Japanese. As indicated earlier, the others had been rescued by the French who would not turn them over to the Japanese.[2]

Within a week the GBT report was confirmed when Hurley advised the Secretary of State that the French in Chungking anticipated a crisis in French-Japanese relations over several demands made by Ambassador Matsumoto of Admiral Decoux. One of the Japanese demands was that the French turn over to the Japanese military "four [sic] American fliers who had been grounded in Indo-China and who had fallen into French hands."[3]

The prompt GBT report on the American airmen reminded me also of the message Ambassador Gauss had sent six months before:

"Chinese and OSS operate through the Gordon group, a set-up not at all to the liking of the French mission." (Gordon is a British subject, local manager of the Texas Company who spends most of his time in interior on some kind of intelligence work for OSS and the United States Army; when in Chungking he resides with our Military Attaché.)[4]

I wanted to know more about this GBT, but my inquiries with the OSS staff were unproductive until Major Duncan Lee suggested I check with our New York office.[5] There in February 1945 I learned somewhat of the odd duality of the group.

GBT stood for Gordon-Bernard-Tan, under the direction of Laurence Laing Gordon, a British subject born in Canada. Formerly a coffee plantation owner in Kenya, Gordon had sold his coffee interests to venture into the oil industry and had managed several oil-drilling operations in Egypt, China, and Madagascar.

At the outbreak of the war (1939–40) Gordon was director of operations for Cal-Texaco at Haiphong. After the Japanese occupied the area, Gordon and his family settled in California where he reestablished contact with officials of Cal-Texaco. In 1941 he was encouraged by the company to return to Southeast Asia and look after the firm's interests. However, the arrangements for his departure were overtaken by the Japanese attack on Pearl Harbor, so a plan was devised by Cal-Texaco officials to infiltrate Gordon into Indochina under semiofficial cover.

The cover was provided by Sir William Stephenson,[6] the head of the British Security Coordination Office. Gordon was recruited into the British Secret Service and ordered to New Delhi, where on instructions from the War Office in London he was secretly commissioned a captain in military intelligence. His assignment was to work with the French military mission in Chungking in setting up an intelligence network in Indochina.

At first Gordon looked to the French mission for support but soon concluded that it was not only ineffectual because of Tai Li's restrictions but also hopelessly split by political rivalry. Casting about for official backing he found our Military Attaché,[7] who willingly introduced him to Admiral Yang Hsuan-cheng.[8] The Chinese authorized Gordon to operate in the province of Kwangsi,[9] with the understanding that he would not cooperate with the French intelligence services.

Gordon initially confined his activities to maintaining a company presence among former employees of Cal-Texaco. Later, under the guise of a free-lancing oil agent, he traveled through Tonkin, Annam, and Cochinchina, renewing old contacts, regrouping loyal Frenchmen and Vietnamese, and purchasing quantities of gasoline and other commodities for the Chinese black market, while at the same time organizing a network of informers in the interest of salvaging company assets. What at first may have been a casual arrangement soon began to assume the characteristics of an amateur intelligence organization.

Before his first year of operations had elapsed, Gordon, using British funds, radios and equipment, and Chinese personnel, was joined by two American associates. One was Frank ("Frankie") Tan, a Bostonian of Chinese extraction who had known Gordon in Haiphong, and the other was Harry V. Bernard, a former Cal-Texaco employee from Saigon.

In full operation by 1943, GBT made itself indispensable to the Chinese and to Chennault's Fourteenth Air Force. Using their French and Vietnamese contacts to the best advantage, they covered Indochina with a lively network of radio stations and listening posts. Although its agents were not trained observers, in 1942 and 1943 they were the major source of information from Indochina.

After the OSS/AGFRTS merger in April 1944 the British urged Donovan to use GBT and, of course, also to subsidize it. At first Gordon was adamant about wanting to retain his operational independence, unfettered by national interests and bureaucratic red tape. But recognizing British support limitations and OSS's resources and growing influence in the China Theater, he finally agreed to cooperate with OSS/AGFRTS and even to assist OSS in Morale Operations (MO).[10] By September 1944, OSS had assigned an officer to GBT to serve as liaison, one Lieutenant Charles Fenn.[11] As OSS later expanded its operations, efforts were again made to bring the freewheeling GBT under closer OSS supervision. Gordon would not have it and finally he disassociated himself from OSS/AGFRTS and joined AGAS. But in February 1945 Fenn was reassigned to AGAS as OSS liaison officer and he once more reestablished contact with the GBT organization, which collaborated with AGAS. Lieutenant Fenn continued to monitor Gordon for the OSS.

The disastrous Japanese coup a month later resulted in the inevitable disintegration of Gordon's operation.

THE CASE OF "MR. HO"

GBT reports often credited the successful escape of Allied personnel from behind Japanese lines to the effective organization and cooperation of Vietnamese "rebels." These "rebels" were from a well-established political movement for Vietnamese independence, allegedly Moscow-oriented and generally referred to by the Japanese, the Chinese, and the French as "communist." Department of State, AGAS, and OSS/AGFRTS reports frequently referred to them as "pro-Allied," "anti-Japanese," and "anticolonial." Personally, I sensed that this group, as a counterpart of the antifascist partisans in Europe, could be of valuable assistance to the war effort in Southeast Asia.

Searching the files I found a number of dispatches from our diplomats at Chungking, Saigon, and Kunming dating back to 1940 describing the activities of the nationalist movement. Early reports reflected French views and characterized the Vietnamese as "politically immature, apathetic, and pro-French." As the movement gained momentum and the resistance to French and Japanese authority became more open and belligerent, the French, the Japanese, and some of our Foreign Service officers began to label its members as "communists."

Admittedly there were Moscow-oriented elements among the nationalist leaders, but most of the instigators of popular unrest for national independence were a mix which included every element of the political spectrum, from religious zealots to monarchist followers of the pro-Japanese Prince Cuong De, and from pro-Chinese, noncommunist Vietnamese exiles in southern China to out-and-out communist followers of the Soviet delegate, Ho Chi Minh.

I found the first mention of Ho Chi Minh in a cable from Ambassador Gauss dated 31 December 1942.[12] It referred to an earlier dispatch reporting the arrest of a Vietnamese leader by the Chinese, "an Annamite named Ho Chih-chi(?)" (sic) reportedly detained at Liuchow, Kwangsi, on 2 September.

A year later our Embassy at Chungking sent to the Department of State two letters from Le Comité central de la Séction Indochinoise de l'Association Internationale Anti-Invasion.[13] One, in French, was addressed to the American Ambassador and the other, in Chinese, to Generalissimo Chiang. Both were dated 25 October 1943, Hanoi, but bore the postmark 25 November 1943, Tsingsi (Ch'ing-Hsi).* The letter to our Ambassador requested that he assist the "Association" in obtaining the release of "our delegate Ho Chi Minh." The letter to Chiang asked that he grant Ho Chi Minh freedom so that he might lead the members of the "Association" in activities against the Japanese.

The only other references to Ho Chi Minh in our OSS files were in a report from Powell of OWI[14] dated 28 August 1944 and in a cable from William R. Langdon, our Consul General at Kunming, requesting guidance from the State Department on the matter of a visa for Ho Chi Minh to come to the United States.

The persistence with which the name of Ho Chi Minh surfaced annually in our files aroused my interest, and I queried my good friend and adviser on Indochinese matters, Austin Glass. He knew of the "friendly Annamite" but was not sure what name he would be using nor where I would find him, since he had no fixed location. Glass said, "Look for him in Tonkin."

Through other associates at the OSS I learned that the Office of Far Eastern Affairs in the Department of State was quite agitated about "Mr. Ho," as they had come to call him and his case. My counterpart there

---

*Ch'ing-Hsi, also spelled Tsingsi, is approximately 275 air miles SE of Kunming and approximately 30 air miles N of the Indochina border.

pledged me to absolute secrecy before allowing me to read the departmental files for "background information only" and not for attribution.[15] The State Department files amplified the situation greatly.

Ho Chi Minh had first come to the notice of the Americans in China about four months after his arrest in Kwangsi (now known to have occurred on 28 August 1942). In a clever move to draw the attention of the Americans, Ho had used the help of several associates to plant an article in the Chungking daily, Ta Kung Pao, intended to embarrass the Kuomintang by revealing the existence of a Chinese-backed "provisional government" for Indochina. The article appeared on 18 December 1942 and was promptly picked up by United Press for relay to New York and Washington.

The UP dispatch had provoked considerable dismay among Chinese, French, and American diplomats in Chungking. Within hours of publication in the United States, our Ambassador in Chungking instructed one of his bright young Foreign Service officers, Philip D. Sprouse,[16] to look into the matter. Sprouse reported back that the story had been written by a Ta Kung Pao reporter named Hsu Ying, based on information from an unidentified Indochinese considered to be a communist. His inquiries also led him to a J. Fishbacher, the Chungking representative of the gaulliste "Fighting French." Fishbacher had disclaimed any knowledge of a Kuomintang-backed "provisional government" for Indochina, but he had shown Sprouse a letter[17] addressed to the local Reuters correspondent protesting the arrest on "September 2, 1942" by the Chinese authorities at Liuchow of an Annamese named "Ho Chih-chi(?)" characterized as the leader of the Indochina Section of the International Anti-Invasion Association. Fishbacher appeared eager to discount both the newspaper story and the letter to Reuters and hoped the American Embassy staff would forget the whole matter.

Neither Gauss nor Sprouse was completely put off. Gauss routinely advised the Department on 31 December of his findings, adding the Fishbacher account, and commented that he tended to agree with the French view that no such "provisional government" existed, but still he could not be sure; and his doubts stemmed from the hasty suppression of the story by the Chinese authorities[18] and by French sensitivity to American interest in Sino-Vietnamese affairs.

Gauss did not let the matter drop. As he left Chungking for consultations in Washington he asked the Chargé d'Affaires, George Atcheson, Jr., to follow up. Accordingly, John S. Service[19] and Sprouse arranged for a dinner on 20 May 1943 with George Wang, UP's Chungking correspondent, and with staff writers of Ta Kung Pao, including the original reporter, Mr. Hsu Ying. During the evening's conversation Hsu Ying elaborated on the original news story, revealing that two separate but related organizations existed among the Vietnamese exiles in China, and overseas Chinese, respectively.

One group had been established at Liuchow under the auspices of General Chang Fa-kwei[20] and was known as the "Indochina Revolutionary Alliance." Its leaders were all overseas Chinese but they were said to have approximately two thousand Annamite soldiers under training by the Chinese military.

The second group consisted of the Provisional Government of Indochina, an organization composed totally of Vietnamese, which had the backing of the Kuomintang. The leader of this group was a Vietnamese named Wu Fei, who had visited Chungking to consult with Dr. Chu Chiahua.[21] The so-called Provisional Government had been organized by two parties—one called the Kuomintang (not related to the Chinese central government) and the other the Pao Huang Tang or Protect-the-Emperor Party. Their "government" was allegedly backed by some twenty thousand guerrillas operating in northern Tonkin close to the China border.

Atcheson forwarded the Service-Sprouse report to the Department on 28 May where it was referred to John Carter Vincent.[22] He professed no knowledge of the organizations but was aware of a group from Indochina which, "while not under arrest or detention, was under close observation by the Chinese authorities and which did not have freedom of movement" at Liuchow. Vincent understood the group was suspected by the Chinese of having communist sympathies and of planning the establishment on Chinese soil of a provisional government for Indochina. He believed that the Chinese were not favorably disposed toward the project.[23]

Vincent, however, who had been Acting Counselor at our Embassy, thought that the French in Chungking also suspected the Chinese of "fostering a movement for the establishment of a provisional government in Indochina" and surmised that the Vietnamese at Liuchow were being held there with that idea in mind. He recalled that Boncour,[24] former Counselor at the French Embassy at Chungking, and other French officials were supersensitive to any suggestion that the Chinese had plans which might dispute French sovereignty in Indochina.

Secretary Hull, not satisfied with the drifting attitude of the Department in the Ho case, cabled our Embassy at Chungking on 30 June that the situation was "not entirely clear" and that he "would appreciate receiving by airmail a more detailed review thereof, together with the Embassy's comments."[25] The response prepared by Sprouse on 21 July made no mention of Ho's arrest or detention but merely confirmed previous reports and reflected the French view that the Vietnamese movement *had no particular importance at that time*. There the matter rested in July 1943.

Ho's first attempt at gaining release from detention and official recognition from the Allies in China had come to nothing. The planted *Ta Kung Pao* story had made some ripples in the diplomatic pond, but they had eventually subsided in the bureaucratic sea of the Department of State.

OSS AND "MR. HO"

Not so, however, in Chungking, where OSS was trying to establish an effective clandestine system. The OSS officers[26] with SACO (the Miles-Tai Li organization) had been approached by Mao Tse-tung's representative in Chungking with a suggestion that the Vietnamese leader could be induced with proper arrangements to join the Allied cause. Was this a second attempt originating with Ho to secure his own freedom?

1942 and 1943 had been difficult years for American clandestine operations in Southeast Asia, as we have seen. Both the French and Chinese—for different reasons—had been wary of American policy toward Indochina and had refused to confide or collaborate and, in fact, had actively conspired to insulate the Americans from their plans. The French were courting the sympathetic support of their colonial counterpart, the British, to the exclusion of the Americans.[27] The Chinese, anxious to deal from a position of strength at the peace table on the question of French extraterritorial rights and concessions in China, plotted with Vietnamese nationalists to eventually oust the French from their former colony.

With other avenues closed to them, the Chinese Communist suggestion had appealed to our OSS representatives in Chungking. Excluding Miles and Tai Li altogether, they discussed the matter with OWI and Embassy staffs, and it was agreed that an attempt would be made to officially secure Ho Chi Minh's release and arrange for his collaboration.

We know now that during the summer and fall of 1943 while OSS was negotiating through diplomatic and military channels for Ho's release, General Chang Fa-kwei had already pressed him into service for the Kuomintang. Chang had a tiger by the tail in the Vietnamese exile groups in southern China whose common goal of national independence was blurred by their diverging approaches to achieving it and by power struggles among the party leaders. Chang reasoned that if they were to be useful to the Kuomintang, either in war or peace, they had to be unified and organized into a homogeneous pro-Chinese bloc. Ho Chi Minh[28] was seen as the man for the job, and was therefore "drafted" to help reorganize the Chinese-sponsored nationalist front, the Dong Minh Hoi.[29]

It was in November of that year, as Ho was sought by the Americans, "drafted" by the Chinese, and missed by his communist friends in Viet Nam who were largely unaware of his fate in Kwangsi, that the two petitions for his release had been received from the International Anti-Invasion Association. The Department of State files revealed that the ever-alert Sprouse had promptly brought the petition to our Ambassador's attention, with the suggestion that it be forwarded to Washington, with a letter of transmittal prepared by Sprouse.[30] The buck-passing procedure relieved the Embassy of the onerous task of dealing with the distasteful business of Indochinese-French politics. The letter noted that "The Annamite . . . is apparently the person whose alleged arrest" had been reported almost a year earlier. Gauss advised the Secretary that in the face of emphatic French denials that they knew of such an "association," he would make "no reply to the letter from the Annamite organization."

At that time the Ambassador himself was preoccupied with Sino-American relations and critical command problems involving Lord Mountbatten and Chiang Kai-shek on the one hand and with the Stilwell-Chennault feud on the other. Lesser matters, such as Indochina, were delegated to the staff. But the staff, especially Sprouse, was constantly monitored and counselled on Indochinese affairs by the gaulliste French Military Mission, whose leading officials devoted much of their time and energy to convincing the Americans that all Vietnamese were pro-French and awaiting the arrival of the gaullistes, that there were no serious independence movements, and that only the Chinese were encouraging a few disaffected Vietnamese to make trouble for the French. Reflecting the French influence through Sprouse, the letter of transmittal to Hull had concluded that there "seemed to be no grounds" for believing that Indochinese nationalist organizations represented anything more than an attempt by the Chinese to make a show of their friendly attitude toward subject people of Asia and possibly to have at hand a nucleus organization for "possible eventualities." The letter-report had reached Washington on 12 January 1944 and had been circulated to various divisions "for information and file."[31]

Several days later our Consul at Kweilin[32] had reported that the leader of the Communist Party "is a certain Mr. Wang, long associated with the Chinese Communist Party . . . . The headquarters of this movement is in southern Yunnan."[33] This was almost certainly another allusion to Ho, but the name went unrecognized; it was not then known that Ho had been known at various times in Canton, Liuchow, and Kunming as "Comrade Wuong."

The State Department files were highly informative about the Powell/Langdon matter of a visa for Ho Chi Minh which occurred six months later. Powell of OWI had approached Langdon, the American Consul General at Kunming, China, to ask if he would issue a visa to one "Indochina-born Chinese, Ho Ting-ching." Powell indicated that for a long time OWI officials in New York had considered hiring this individual to broadcast Annamese translations of OWI material from San Francisco.

Langdon replied that he would issue the visa if OWI requested it and provided that "Ho Ting-ching" could obtain from the Chinese government a passport to proceed to the United States, a document which Langdon doubted "Ho Ting-ching" could get. Langdon had also noted that the French in any case would be "greatly disquieted" if "Ho Ting-ching," who was presumed to be also a French subject, went to the United States to enter American government employment without first consulting them. In view of the many possible complications, Langdon had sought departmental advice. The question reached Washington in December 1944 and had been referred to Sprouse[34] who, in turn, had prepared a memorandum on "Mr. Ho" describing his activities and relationships with OWI-Kunming. But the visa had not been granted.

This matter, like the *Ta Kung Pao* story and the petitions for Ho's release, had quietly died in the State Department's files. In hindsight and in view of our tragic casualty lists of later decades, one may only lament the lost opportunities for bending the direction of events that lay ahead. As far as I was concerned at the time, there were at least a few clues in early 1945 of an organized resistance among the Vietnamese, a fact which I felt might be useful to me in China. I did not then recognize that those dormant files and the OSS negotiations in Chungking represented a determined effort by Ho Chi Minh to bring his "cause" to official American notice.

Ho Chi Minh was a "guest" of Chang Fa-kwei at the Tienpao prison when Wendell Willkie visited China in October 1942. Through discarded newspapers and occasional radiocasts, Ho had kept up with world events and Willkie's public statements. He had noted Willkie's anti-imperialist stand and had detected a strain in American-British-French relations on the question of colonialism. Willkie had reported on returning to this country that Asians were demanding the application of the principles of the Atlantic Charter to their particular situations. In ensuing months the Chinese dailies carried news items and editorials of the Churchill-Roosevelt exchange on the application of the Atlantic Charter, which Ho had followed as best he could. In one of his rare moments of cynicism, Ho asked me in 1945 if "the Atlantic Charter is a companion piece to Wilson's Fourteen Points, applicable only to white European nations and excluding Asian and African colonials."[35]

The question of freedom for all dependent peoples became a major issue during the years 1942 to 1944, and the Americans championed the cause. Roosevelt and Cordell Hull insisted that the European colonial powers follow our example in the Philippines in laying the foundations for ultimate independence for their colonies. Roosevelt went out of his way to single out France in Indochina and often cited French rule there as a flagrant example of onerous and exploitative colonialism.

This prompted Lord Halifax[36] to call on Hull on 3 January 1944 to get a clearer understanding of President Roosevelt's intentions. According to the Foreign Office the President had made "rather definite" statements during his trip to Cairo and Teheran[37] to the effect "that Indochina should be taken away from the French and put under an international trusteeship."[38] Halifax added that he himself had on several occasions heard the President make such remarks, but he was not sure if the President's utterances represented final conclusions. The British feared the President's remarks might reach the French, giving rise to considerable embarrassment.

Hull assured Halifax that he knew no more about the matter than the Ambassador and suggested that perhaps the President and Mr. Churchill would find it desirable to talk it over at some future stage.

The conversation with Halifax opened a Pandora's box. Two days later the State Department's Political Adviser, S. K. Hornbeck, advised Hull that Chinese officials had on several occasions stated that China, though willing to see Indochina restored to France, would not wish to see that happen without some safeguards against France's using Indochina for activities inimical to Chinese rights and interests. In short, the future of Indochina was not to be settled without China at the peace table.[39] It was in the context of this new awareness of Indochina's import that the Chinese and OSS used Ho Chi Minh in 1944-45.

After a "demotion"[40] in the Dong Minh Hoi, Ho found himself in a comfortable position of relative freedom and recognized leadership among his compatriots, both friendly and unfriendly, and he used his new status to good advantage. The Allies were clearly going to win in Europe and he foresaw that the full strength of their war machine would then be directed against Japan. Ho also saw that his time was limited. He had to be ready to present a de facto, if not de juris, authority in Indochina to the conquering Allies if he were to gain and retain control of an independent Viet Nam. In fact, his time was much more limited than he imagined because of the atomic bomb.

Ho's analytic mind, pragmatic nature, and keen understanding of international power politics led him to conclude very early on that he had to enlist American sympathy. He saw conclusively that China could not be counted an ally and must not, therefore, so far as was possible, be antagonized. He anticipated no active support from "heroic" Russia; even in victory, Russia would be too exhausted from the war to be of assistance in his plans for Vietnamese independence. Among the Allied western bloc, the colonial powers—Great Britain, France, and the Netherlands—would be uniformly and irreversibly opposed to his anticolonial movement. From them he could anticipate only resistance. There was no question in his mind that, given the opportunity, France would reclaim Indochina as a colony.

That left the United States, his last possibility and an enigma to his Moscow-trained political mentality. He had to undergo some fancy mental gymnastics to reconcile his philosophical and practical needs. He felt the Americans were unquestionably anticolonialist; their historical background, past performance, and recent pronouncements all attested to that. But they were also capitalist. Their socio-economic reforms were not truly "democratic." Their proletariat was not really "free" and "emancipated," as in Russia. Yet the Americans were the only ones who might lend his movement a sympathetic ear.

In the late spring of 1944 as the burden of the Dong Minh Hoi was lifted from him, Ho became more than ever anxious to obtain American interest. His sense of timing and recognition of the *thoi co* (opportune moment) played an important part in the events that followed. He had learned that OSS was organizing teams of Chinese agents[41] to harass the Japanese all along the China coast and in the provinces of Yunnan and Kwangsi. Ho's assets in the field of intelligence and guerrilla warfare were well known by then to the OSS in China, but the French and Chinese in Chungking militated against the American desire to use the Viet Minh. Despite these obstacles, Ho, who had been cooperating with the Americans in propaganda activities on a part-time basis, was approached in mid-1944 by OSS and AGAS in a vain attempt to organize an intelligence network in Indochina.

The wily "old man" (he was only fifty-four) was opposed to being "used" as just another Chinese agent. He wanted official recognition and at the highest possible level. He did not, of course, have the diplomatic credentials necessary to deal with a foreign power. He was recognized by Moscow but the Communists were barely tolerated in Chungking. He had a loyal and effective political base in Indochina, but it was outlawed there by the French and repressed in China in favor of their "puppets," whom they hoped to use in postwar manipulations. If the Americans wanted to avail themselves of his help—and they wanted to—they were forced to deal with him sub rosa. An arrangement was reached between Ho and his OSS contacts.

HO SEEKS OFFICIAL RECOGNITION

In August 1944, with the help of several OSS and OWI officers in Kunming,[42] a letter was drafted from La Ligue de l'Independance de l'Indochine[43] to the American Ambassador. The writers pleaded for American help in their struggle for independence and for the opportunity to fight alongside the Allies against the Japanese. On 18 August one of the OSS officers delivered the letter to Langdon, our Consul General, with the comment that the "Annamite revolutionaries . . . are presently in high spirits . . . [and] take American support of their cause for granted" and that he anticipated "considerable trouble in Indochina after the war if at least a substantial measure of self-government is not put into effect in that country at an early date."

Prodded by the OSS, Langdon met with the writers of the letter on 8 September. According to Langdon's account,[44] Mr. Pham Viet Tu, acting as spokesman, said they were "calling to enlist the sympathy . . . of the United States." To this Langdon replied that it was

quite right for them to make known to American representatives the views and aspirations of the Annamite people, inasmuch as the highest spokesmen of the American Government had in numerous declarations given assurances of the interest of their government in the political welfare and advancement of oppressed peoples in the Orient, among whom the Annamite people might believe themselves to be included.

And Langdon had assured his callers that he would relay their views to his government. However, Langdon continued,

the Annamite people are citizens of France, who is fighting side by side with the United States . . . against the Axis. It would not make sense . . . if America with one hand at great expenditures of life and treasure rescued and delivered France from German slavery and with the other hand undermined her Empire. . . .

Pham Viet Tu replied that

Annamites are well aware of the long-standing Franco-American friendship and that his League had no intention of fighting the French but wished to range its members on the side of the Allies to fight the Japanese; also that the League had a plan of action for this purpose, if the United States would provide arms and assistance.

At that point Langdon interrupted to say that the question was a military matter and the League ought properly to discuss it with the Allied military command.

Pham Viet Tu said he would confine his remarks to the political aspects and asked Langdon to recommend to the American government that it insist upon autonomy for the Annamite people. Here, Langdon had pulled back again and replied that he hoped the League would view this request from a practical standpoint and realize that it connoted possible coercion of allied France. Langdon pointed out that if the Annamites had complaints against France, the normal course would be to deal directly with the French.

Pham Viet Tu countered that in theory that was the proper course, "but to advocate it in the case of Indochina was fatuously to ignore the realities of the situation, as there was only repression and no democracy in Indochina."

Again Langdon tried to soothe his visitors by saying that "the Annamite people ought not to take too pessimistic a view of their future. . . . General de Gaulle in Washington last July [1944] had told the press that France's policy was to lead all peoples of the French Empire toward self-government. . . ."

The conversation continued in the same vein to its obvious conclusion.

When Pham Viet Tu and his colleagues reported back to Ho, they were dejected and could only say that they had been given a cordial reception but no promise of political endorsement. The best they could hope for would be limited military support and only in payment for services rendered. To everyone's amazement, including the OSS-OWI officers, Ho was not discouraged; on the contrary, he was elated. His "League" had gained recognition from a highly-placed official of the American government and a promise that their cause would come to the attention of the highest authority in Washington, perhaps even the "great President Roosevelt."

The outcome in Washington was to be very different. The French had been anticipating, without any basis in fact, an Allied landing operation in China against Japanese strongholds. Not wanting to be omitted from the Pacific Theater of Operations and hoping to earn the right of sovereignty in Indochina, they were besieging the governments in Washington and London with their demands to participate in military plans for the Far East.

The issue of formal participation was further muddled by French demands for authority to conduct "prelanding" clandestine operations in Indochina itself. The matter came to the personal attention of both Churchill and Roosevelt. Churchill was not opposed to the French scheme but did not want to openly overrule Roosevelt's publicly-stated position that the French should not seize Indochina by force. The issue was widely debated and was the subject of voluminous diplomatic notes and correspondence both within and between the Foreign Office and the Department of State.

Roosevelt became thoroughly exasperated by French and British insistence and instructed Hull to "do nothing in regard to resistance groups or in any other way in relation to Indochina. . . ." That closed the matter on 16 October 1944 as it pertained to French activities, which Roosevelt specifically had in mind. But it also closed the matter to other "resistance groups." This point was later clarified in the spring of 1945, when authority was ultimately granted to aid only those resistance groups prepared to fight the Japanese.

HO MEETS CHENNAULT

In the meantime accommodations were being made in the field with Ho Chi Minh. Ho's new arrangements with Chang Fa-kwei provided him with relative freedom of action in southern China which resulted in his part-time work with OSS and OWI officials in conducting Allied propaganda. In Kunming, Kweilin, and Liuchow he made good use of OWI's facilities to improve his English and knowledge of American history, customs, and current world events. Betweentimes he provided the BIS with Japanese military information from Indochina, carried out his Viet Minh organization work, and proselyted among rival nationalist groups. For Ho it was a period of improving his opportunities, but he was in fact a very little fish in a big pond and it is much to be doubted if any American descried the importance of his future role in Viet Nam.

Ho's followers in Indochina, especially in Tonkin and northern Annam, unknown to the Americans in China, felt emboldened by his release from Chinese custody and by the Allied victories in Europe and the Pacific. Under the able leadership of Vo Nguyen Giap,[45] they carried out forays against French and Japanese military outposts. The inevitable French reprisals and "White Terror" followed. Vietnamese were arrested, their houses burned, their property confiscated. Villages and hamlets were razed. Some identifiable communists were summarily shot, beheaded, or had their arms cut off for display in market places. The Decoux administration was offering money and measures of salt as bounties for the heads of revolutionary leaders.

The Vietnamese terrorist attacks and the savage French reprisals were raging in August 1944 when the news of de Gaulle's entry into Paris reached the Viet Minh. Giap became impatient and wanted to unleash an armed insurrection against both the French and the Japanese, but his zeal was checked by more cautious leaders, and the insurrection was delayed. Nonetheless, French repressions continued and threatened the extermination of the revolutionary movement. From Kunming Ho sent word to "hold everything" until he could return to Pac Bo, his field headquarters in the mountainous village of Cao Bang province.

In late November Ho met with Giap and other militants in Tonkin. He discussed with them their situation, chided their impatience, and persuaded them that an armed insurrection at that moment would be premature and doomed. To keep up their spirits while discouraging any rash course which would jeopardize the whole movement, Ho created the Propaganda Brigade for the Liberation of Viet Nam[46] and placed Giap in full charge. Initially the Brigade concentrated on the dissemination of propaganda and instructions to the general population on resistance tactics, but it became the precursor of the present-day People's Army with Giap as its national commander and hero.

After setting a wise course and calming his supporters, Ho began his long journey back to Kunming. In crossing the Cao Bang region near the Chinese frontier, he met with another trusted lieutenant, Pham Van Dong,[47] who earlier had originated the petitions to Gauss and Chiang Kai-shek for Ho's release from prison. Ho learned from Dong, rather incidentally, that a downed American pilot was with one of Giap's guerrilla units nearby. This pilot, as it happened, was one of the nine airmen reported by GBT as having bailed out after a raid on Saigon.

Learning that an American flyer was being given safe haven, Ho instantly grasped the usefulness to him of this lucky circumstance (thoi co) and sent for the American. After a friendly chat, and feeling quite assured that the American had found the Vietnamese helpful, Ho instructed Dong to see that the flyer was escorted not merely to the border but to the American authorities in China. It was another opportunity to emphasize his revolutionary movement with the Americans and to bring it to official American notice.

It was during the unusually cold month of February that Ho again reached Kunming where he promptly contacted his OSS and OWI friends. He was anxious to report recent French and Japanese troop movements. To Ho it seemed odd that the French army was deploying its forces in the mountainous areas of Tonkin and Laos and that the Japanese forces were doing the same thing. He was unable to account for these maneuvers but he was certain something important was taking place, perhaps, he speculated, a joint French-Japanese drive toward Yunnan-fu (Kunming) to the north or to Nanning to the east.

What he did not know was that his new Propaganda Brigade was about to be the target of a French Army mop-up operation in which the "rebels" were to be decisively eliminated. The operation had been scheduled for the week of 10 March. In preparation, the French army in Tonkin had deployed a number of units to the north pointed toward the sanctuaries of the Vietnamese guerrillas. Actually, it was part of General Mordant's great master plan to position his entire force in the north and wait for the "Allied landings." The mop-up operation was his cover plan, but also his answer to "a handful of traitorous Annamites."

If Ho and Giap were ignorant of the intended eradication of their little force, the French were taken even more unaware by the Japanese, who struck on the evening of 9 March, before the French operation could begin. As described earlier, the Japanese disarmed and confined the French military forces and their leaders, including Mordant and Aymé, and stripped French officials of all authority—from Decoux to the lowest clerk. As noted earlier, the only French to escape the Japanese dragnet were the troops deployed in northern Tonkin and Laos[48] whose task had been to clear the mountains of Viet Minh guerrillas and wait for the "arrival of the Allies."

Thus Ho Chi Minh and his Viet Minh became double beneficiaries of a great stroke of good fortune. They were saved from their would-be French exterminators, whom they subsequently protected and sheltered in their retreat to China,[49] and the Vietnamese people were temporarily "liberated" from their French "masters."

Limited as it had been, the flow of intelligence from Indochina was cut off overnight. The Japanese coup de force blacked out all channels of political and military information from the SACO and GBT networks. Chennault needed target intelligence, and the Chinese were hard put to deploy their meager and ill-equipped forces along the Indochina border or to organize defense positions without information on Japanese troop dispositions. It was imperative that clandestine communications and operations be reopened if Allied plans against the Japanese in China and the Pacific were to prosper.

With the situation critical, OSS was directed to do everything possible to reestablish the flow of information and was authorized to use "any and all resistance groups."[50] This was, of course, a change in policy from the Presidential prohibition of the previous October, and meant that the OSS was at liberty to contact Ho Chi Minh.

Our Marine lieutenant, Fenn, then on loan to AGAS, had heard of an "Annamite named Hu Tze-ming" who had helped the downed flyer, "Lt Shaw," make his way back to China. Fenn learned that "Hu Tze-ming" was in Kunming and "occasionally could be found at the offices of OWI."

He arranged to meet him on the afternoon of 17 March. It was Ho Chi Minh, of course.

On my arrival in April 1945 some of the first field reports I had occasion to read were from Lieutenant Fenn and concerned the organization of "native intelligence networks in the interior of Indochina." Those reports, however, did not give the many details he described later in his book[51] published in 1973. A few of those details (which I have since confirmed from official records) are very relevant to Ho's political successes a few months later.

Fenn described their first meeting: "Ho came along with a younger man named Fam. . . . It seems he has already met . . . Glass and de Sibour, but got nowhere with any of them. I asked him what he wanted of them. He said—only recognition of his group (called Vietminh League or League for Independence)."[52] They met again three days later and worked out details for Ho to return to Indochina where intelligence listening posts would be set up with OSS radios and OSS-trained Vietnamese operators.

Ho suggested to Fenn that he would like to meet General Chennault. Fenn agreed to arrange it but only if Ho "agreed not to ask him for anything: neither supplies nor promises about support. Ho agreed."[53] On 29 March Fenn, Mr. Bernard, and Ho Chi Minh were shown into General Chennault's office and introduced to him. Fenn recalled:

Chennault told Ho how grateful he was about the saved pilot. Ho said he would always be glad to help the Americans and particularly to help General Chennault for whom he had the greatest admiration. They exchanged talk about the *Flying Tigers*. Chennault was pleased the old man knew about this. We talked about saving more pilots. Nothing was said about the French, or about politics. I heaved a sigh of relief as we started to leave. Then Ho said he had a small favour to ask the general. . . . But all Ho wanted was the general's photograph. . . . In due course . . . a folder of eight by ten glossies [were produced]." "Take your pick" says Chennault. Ho takes one and asks would the general be so kind as to sign it? . . . Chennault writes across the bottom, "Yours Sincerely, Claire L. Chennault."[54]

To be received by Chennault was very important in Ho's mind as official American notice. But the inscribed photograph turned out to be of vital importance to him only a few months later when he was badly in need of tangible evidence to convince skeptical Vietnamese nationalists that he had American support. It was a ruse which lacked foundation, but it worked.

While Fenn, Bernard, and Tan were arranging with AGAS to have Ho flown to the border area of Ch'ing-Hsi, where he would proceed on foot to Pac Bo, I was flying over the "Hump"[55] to Kunming to take over the Indochina operations.

PART TWO

✿ ✿ ✿

KUNMING

CHAPTER 7

WHAT WASHINGTON
DID NOT KNOW

CHAOS

M y flight to Kunming, some thirteen thousand air miles from New York, took in those days about a week. It was late in the evening of 13 April 1945 when our C-47 slipped into Kunming airport, unnoticed and unheralded. I was met by a Chinese driver who drove me to the OSS Staff House. There the billeting clerk handed me a note from Lieutenant Colonel Paul L. E. Helliwell.[1] "Welcome to China—see you at breakfast."

Next morning in the Officers' Mess a tall, pleasant-looking officer ambled across the dining room, extending his hand in welcome. He introduced himself as "Paul," adding with a wry smile, "Am I glad to see you!" He minced no words in letting me know that everything was "really fouled up" and that Washington was "of no help at all." After breakfast we drove to the OSS compound, a walled area with some six or seven buildings scattered around a dusty parade ground. The huge post flag was at half-mast—President Roosevelt had died two days before. We headed straight for a long two-story building and up to the office of Colonel Heppner. Heppner usually conducted business from his Chungking office, close to Wedemeyer's headquarters, the American Embassy, and Chiang Kai-shek's center of government. At the time of my arrival he had come to Kunming to chair a policy-planning conference regarding OSS operations in Indochina.

The recent Japanese coup and troop movements suggested a possible Japanese drive toward Kunming and other points along Chiang's southern flank. OSS had been instructed by Wedemeyer's headquarters to interdict Japanese advances and the conference was to clarify American-French relations and OSS's authority to operate in Indochina. Heppner wanted me to sit in, and the meeting was my introduction to the operating level in China, quite a descent from the lofty, rarified air of Washington. It was like a cold plunge.

Heppner opened the meeting by stating that the situation called for immediate action but that U.S. policy was unclear. Specifically, could the OSS assist the retreating French in Tonkin in either resisting the Japanese or helping the French escape into China? Neither the Embassy nor the Theater spokesmen present could answer the question. Chennault's representative took the position that both actions could be taken and introduced two messages to support his view.

The first message was from General Marshall to Chennault and was dated 19 March. It read, in part: "new attitude U.S. Government is to help French provided such aid does not interfere with planned operations. The 14th Air Force may undertake operations against the Japanese in Indochina to assist the French within the limitations imposed by the above policy."[2]

The second message was from the Joint Chiefs to Wedemeyer and was more current, dated 9 April. It asked that Wedemeyer "consider dropping such token supplies" (for humanitarian purposes), and that the "decision rests with China Theater."[3] It was evident the JCS was skirting the issue and passing the buck to Wedemeyer for a command decision, for which Heppner would seek Theater approval upon his return to Chungking. The conference adjourned at noon.

Helliwell took a sadistic delight in having large stacks of folders placed on my desk in my absence, with his note, "For a better appreciation of the muddled FIC Affair—Helliwell." The titles were straightforward enough: "U.S. Policy—FIC"; "QUAIL Plan"; "The French in FIC"; "French Military Mission—M.5"; "Annamites for SI-SO Operations"; and so on. But it became plain to me as I carefully reviewed the material that many policy issues were in limbo, that international relations on our local scene were filled with internecine political struggles and divergent war objectives, and that operational matters required command decisions at the highest levels. Before I could undertake operations there would have to be an indepth discussion of the issues and resolutions reached at the Chungking and Washington levels.

The next day Helliwell called a meeting of key staff officers to discuss the recently-approved "Project QUAIL," a major SI operation in Indochina. Among those present were Captain (later Major) Robert E. Wampler, Chief of the SO Branch, Mr. Roland Dulin representing the MO Branch, a representative from X-2 (Counterespionage), a briefer from the Research and Analysis Branch (R&A), and Major (later Colonel) A. R. Wichtrich representing AGAS.

Mainly for my benefit, since I was to be in charge of "Project QUAIL," Helliwell suggested a review of developments since his arrival in the Theater (the previous 25 January) and consideration of the problems already encountered and progress made, before discussing present problems.

The R&A briefer capsulized the Indochina intelligence activities. He stated that from the early days of Japanese occupation, French, British and Chinese interests had from time to time set up listening posts, courier systems, and radio networks to meet their individual needs—efforts generally uncoordinated with Allied objectives and in most instances in competition with each other. An exception was the GBT group which did provide considerable military information to the Allied commands. But even that element was at best an amorphous organization with questionable objectives and subject to dubious official Allied control. In any case, since the coup all intelligence sources out of Indochina, including GBT, were silent.

The R&A briefer revealed that early in November 1944 General Wedemeyer had decided on a vigorous program of clandestine operations in the China Theater and had asked Donovan to make arrangements.

An anticipation of Japanese reaction to Allied successes in the Pacific and to French agitation in Indochina prompted Helliwell on 1 March (before the coup) to seek policy guidance from Theater headquarters. The reply had been that he could not deal with "native individuals or revolutionary groups," and that "under no circumstances [was he to] give anyone in FIC supplies; . . . [nor] deal with the French except through high-level contacts in Chungking." He was further advised by Heppner "that by direct Presidential order OSS had been forbidden to make any policy decisions regarding FIC."[4]

The coup on 9 March had precipitated a state of utter confusion in China. At that moment, both General Wedemeyer and Ambassador Hurley were in Washington conferring with the President, the JCS, and officials of the Departments of State and War. General Chennault was in charge, in Wedemeyer's absence, and the Chargé d'Affaires, Atcheson, was running the Embassy. Without concrete information from Indochina, Japanese intentions were a strategic imponderable. Chiang feared a Japanese drive north into China; the French clamored to be rescued; and Chennault was without instructions.

Chennault, although second only to Wedemeyer, was not always privy to high-level policy discussions. His role as senior air officer in

China was considered more tactical than strategic from the viewpoint of policy-making. Hence, when the coup occurred, Chennault found himself in a most tenuous position.

He had not been apprised of a 26 January discussion among Counselor Clarac of the French Embassy, Wedemeyer, and Hurley regarding Japanese-French relations "coming to a crisis," nor of the Japanese demand to position a new division on the Tonkin-China border, etc.[5] Nor was Chennault aware that Wedemeyer was in direct communication with Lieutenant General John E. Hull,[6] then at the Yalta Conference, nor that Wedemeyer had been informed by Hull that General Marshall had discussed with the President the question of intelligence operations in Indochina. Specifically:

The President indicated [to Marshall] that he had no objection to [Wedemeyer's] carrying out intelligence and subversive operations in Indo-China, . . . that [the President] was in favor of anything that was against the Japs provided that we do not align ourselves with the French. The President has not changed his attitude concerning dealing with the French authorities in such a way as to give French interests in the Far East official recognition.[7]

This background information was not available to General Chennault and, when the French called for help after the coup, Chennault exercised his command prerogative and answered the call. He took his guidance from a vague State Department message which authorized Wedemeyer to be "helpful to the French" in the event they had to flee to China by "arranging for supplying medicines," provided the Chinese were informed.[8]

Chennault had approached Chiang Kai-shek on the morning of 10 March in the company of General Ho Ying-chin. Chennault asked the Generalissimo if the French would be disarmed should they enter China and offered no serious resistance to the Japanese. Chiang would only say that the French "may be permitted to remain in China at a specified area. . . . " To the question of what to do should the French put up a stiff resistance, would they "be left to their fate by themselves or shall we send troops to assist them?" Chiang replied, "If stiff resistance is put up, assistance may be rendered."[9]

Still lacking a clear-cut policy, Chennault interpreted the vague State Department directive and Chiang's ambiguous statements as a green light to help the French. He sent his intelligence officers (OSS/AGFRTS) into Indochina to contact the fleeing French and arranged for airdrops of arms, ammunition, medical supplies, and food. Then on 20 March the War Department put a stop to Chennault's delivery of arms and ammunition but permitted him to bomb and strafe the Japanese in Indochina.

Four years later Chennault gave his evaluation of the situation:

> The American government was interested in seeing the French forcibly ejected from Indo-China so the problem of postwar separation from their colony would be easier. The British, on the other hand, were determined then to uphold the colonial system in the Orient and regarded a French defeat in Indo-China as injurious to their own imperial prestige. While American transports in China avoided Indo-China, the British flew aerial supply missions for the French all the way from Calcutta, dropping tommy guns, grenades, and mortars.
>
> I carried out my orders to the letter but I did not relish the idea of leaving Frenchmen to be slaughtered in the jungle while I was forced officially to ignore their plight.[10]

To return to our briefing, Helliwell's problems had been very different from General Chennault's. On the very same date that Chennault was directed to stop sending arms and ammunition to the French in Indochina, OSS was directed to set up new intelligence channels. Two orders had been issued to OSS, both signed by General Marvin E. Gross, Acting Chief of Staff, China Theater, on behalf of General Chennault as Theater Commander.

The first ordered the establishment of intelligence networks in Indochina and authorized rendering aid to any and all "resistance groups whose active opposition to Japanese forces will accrue to the military advantage of United States and Chinese operations." There were two important caveats: the aid was limited "to such as will not interfere with current and planned operations in the China Theater"; and extreme care was to be exercised in carrying out operations so that "all groups will be dealt with impartially and irrespective of any particular governmental or political affiliations."[11] The second directive required OSS to set up several radio stations to serve both OSS and the French Military Mission.[12]

These Theater directives put OSS in business, but they also placed OSS in a sensitive and embarrassing position with the French. Helliwell explained that the French were pressing for the type of support (arms and war equipment of all sorts) which would interfere with current Theater operational plans in terms of massive displacement of air power or "Hump tonnage." At the same time, under the new directives OSS was at liberty to help the Vietnamese nationalists, who were also seeking arms and equipment but to such a small degree that no massive logistical support or rearrangement of planned operations would be involved.

I raised the question of whether there had been in the past month any evidence that the French were engaged in any organized resistance. Helliwell's reply was immediate and sharp in tone, "Hell, no. We have dropped tons of weapons and ammunition, but from nowhere are there any reports of French resistance. In fact, we suspect that the Japs are picking up our stuff while the French scurry toward the border."[13]

Helliwell said that with the two new directives he could have started infiltrating agents in Indochina, except for the arrival the next day of a cable from the War Department directing OSS to "do nothing about FIC." This message, the message prohibiting Chennault from further arms drops to the fleeing French, and the two Theater directives ordering intelligence operations directed at Indochina all bore the same date—20 March.

In the midst of the confusion caused by this flurry of messages, Helliwell received on 23 March Theater approval of "Project QUAIL" which he had been impatiently awaiting for weeks. But the next day he had received a message from Heppner's deputy, Colonel Willis S. Bird, to "do nothing about establishing the radio stations" which had been directed to serve both OSS and the French. It was a further irritant in the touchy American-French relations.

Helliwell had felt himself harassed by the combination of high-level demands for information on Japanese activities in Indochina and the chaotic orders and counterorders. He had sent several officers and Vietnamese radio operators to the border to meet the retreating troops of General Sabattier[13] and to send back Japanese intelligence. All they could report was that "the French were on the run with the Japs in hot pursuit." In fact, Helliwell said, they could furnish no information on the Japanese units chasing them.

Helliwell was also exasperated by a recent incident between the French, the British, the Americans, and the Chinese. It had been reported by GBT to Colonel Bird in Chungking and relayed to Helliwell. According to GBT, the Chinese military at Tung Hing[14] had on 20 March observed two Allied planes circle over Mong Cai[15] and drop British arms and ammunition. There being no one to receive the drop, the Chinese had picked it up. Within minutes GBT had received a radio message from the French that they had retreated to China and that the Japanese had occupied Tung Hing, Mong Cai, and Tien Yen.[16] The French requested that all three locations be bombed.

Obviously the French, unwilling to risk exposing themselves to the Japanese by backtracking to Mong Cai but not wanting the Chinese to collect the precious drop, requested a bombing mission on the Chinese. It was all too evident that the French were trying to dupe the Americans into bombing areas where Chinese troops were present, and it had been fortunate that GBT had been in radio contact with the intended victims.

Helliwell said that Gordon felt the French were "completely unreliable" and any action the United States took should take that into consideration. Gordon had also cautioned that in his opinion "the British have taken the bit in their teeth and are going into FIC on their own hook, without Theater coordination."[17]

WHAT ABOUT "MR. HO"?

This brought the discussion to how to proceed in a patchwork of do's and don'ts. It was evident from the briefing and from what I had learned in Washington that very little could be expected from the French at that point, so I asked, "What about the Vietnamese? Has anyone been in contact with them?"

Major Wichtrich said that AGAS had had numerous contacts with them and with very good results. Mr. Dulin supported Wichtrich and was of the opinion that, contrary to French disclaimers of Annamese worth and the China Theater's views of "political entanglements," the Vietnamese had an on-going organization which if properly approached could be extremely useful. But, he added, "the boys at the Embassy don't like to deal with them. They are supposed to be communist, and anti-French." Helliwell replied, "Bull. If they are any good we ought to use them. We have the OK from Washington and Chungking to use any and all resistance groups."

The R&A representative volunteered that they had reports of Vietnamese active opposition to the Japanese in the area of Tuyen Quang-Thai Nguyen-Lang Son-Bac Can[18] and that their operations smacked of paramilitary tactics. And numerous reports furnished by the Vietnamese to OSS/AGFRTS and GBT gave reliable order of battle information.

Dulin, an expert in political warfare, said that OWI had been using several members of the Viet Minh, led by an "old man" known as Ho Chi Minh, and that as a matter of fact Mr. Ho had been doing some psychological warfare work for the Chinese propaganda office in conjunction with OWI. Then Wichtrich admitted that AGAS had struck a deal with Mr. Ho to set up an air rescue operation in Indochina. With a sheepish smile he said to Helliwell, "Your man, Fenn, has had him in tow for several weeks." But Helliwell was not to be outdone and said, "I know. I gave him some weapons for protection."[19]

I told them that I had come across Ho's name in the Washington files dating back to 1942 and more recent ones from Sprouse and Langdon of the Embassy and from Powell of OWI. As a matter of fact I had read only the day before Fenn's report of an agreement with Ho to assist OSS and AGAS in organizing an intelligence network throughout Indochina. My desire was, if no one objected, to look into the Vietnamese organization with a view to "Project QUAIL," but I wanted first their informed opinion on the probable reaction of the French.

Helliwell did not think we should discuss it either with the French or with our own Embassy people, that Heppner's concurrence was all we needed. Wichtrich was visibly upset, and I addressed myself to him. What was his opinion? He said that he was not concerned with the French or the diplomatic staff, but he wanted assurances that SI would do nothing to interfere with his AGAS operation. Helliwell reassured him that Ho's services to AGAS would benefit from our SI support, both in funds and communications.

So we ended the meeting with the understanding that I would as soon as possible make a field inspection at Szemao[20] and along the Indochina border, make a start at reestablishing the intelligence flow, determine the condition of the French military, and possibly arrange to contact Viet Minh leaders.

Other aspects of my first few days in Kunming proved less enlightening. I had no news of the specially selected staff I had recruited in Washington; there was no indication that they were even on the way.

My first visit to the French Military Mission (M.5)[21] was also very disappointing. The Mission was undergoing a change of command and was in total disarray. The new Chief of Mission was out of town and no one appeared to be in charge. Nor was my visit returned in succeeding days.

At the Kunming offices of Tai Li's BIS, the reception was totally cordial and totally unrewarding—large quantities of tea, polite smiles, and much conversation in Chinese among the interpreters. But my hosts would only say that they had recently come from Szechwan[22] and were not familiar with intelligence activities in Yunnan and Indochina.

Helliwell and Dulin had given me a list of Vietnamese exiles Father Jean Tong,[23] a Chinese Catholic priest, had left. After fruitless attempts to locate them I had to give it up.

All the while Theater headquarters continued to clamor for intelligence and insist that OSS start harassing the Japanese along the Hanoi-Nanning-Canton corridor. And in the reigning confusion several OSS teams in southern China and northern Indochina were out of communication with Kunming and a source of serious concern.

"GENERAL" HO'S EMISSARY

Only one event of a positive nature occurred during these first days. My inquiries about Father Tong's exiles apparently were noised about among the Vietnamese in Kunming, and I received a visit from one Vuong Minh Phuong who introduced himself as a member of the League for the Independence of Indochina, amidst profuse apologies for intruding on my Sunday morning. His name was not new to me. I had encountered it in the Langdon report of his conversation with the members of the League in August 1944.

Phuong, in his early thirties, spoke French fluently. He had been, he said, a student at the University of Hanoi and had come to Kunming in the fall of 1943. He lived near the OSS compound at the Quang Lac Restaurant, 39 Tai Ho Gai. He said he knew M. Glass of OSS, had collaborated with M. Powell of OWI, had met Commandant Stevens[24] in Chungking, and was known to M. Langdon of our Kunming Consulate. Obviously he knew the right people. I awaited with interest the reason for his visit.

Phuong explained that he had come to let me know that the people I had been asking for were not the "best Annamites" in Kunming but were members of two French-sponsored societies[25] associated with the Chinese Annamite Revolutionary Alliance. According to him they were former employees of the Hanoi-Yunnan-fu Railroad in the pay of the French and no longer interested in Indochina. They had relocated with their families to China and considered themselves Chinese nationals. The only Vietnamese interested in fighting the "Japanese fascists," he said, were the members of his League, better known as the Viet Minh, whose leader was "General" Ho Chi Minh.

Phuong wore western clothes, appeared to be well educated, and was quite conversant with the war in general and, of course, with Indochinese affairs. He was more familiar with OSS and AGAS than I was with his League or the Viet Minh, and he knew more about me than I about him. I listened as he tactfully veered the conversation toward the real purpose of his visit.

With a touch of pride Phuong recounted how his colleagues in Indochina and China had been working "very closely" with a number of General Chennault's and OSS's Americans, providing Japanese order of battle and target information. He alluded to OSS-AGAS operations in which the Viet Minh had contributed to the evasion and escape of "many" Army and Navy flyers by giving them shelter and guiding them to safety.

Then Phuong slipped into the political arena, commenting that the Vietnamese were very grateful to the Americans for their understanding, interest, and concern in the colonial question and had noted that the late President Roosevelt[26] had on several occasions publicly supported their cause for independence. I interrupted to remind him that I was neither a diplomat nor a politician, that my mission was a military one. With an understanding smile, Phuong defensively admitted he had been carried away by his enthusiasm and the opportunity to express to an American official his people's sentiments toward the United States. But he returned to the subject of the Viet Minh's military capabilities.

The Viet Minh, he claimed, although a political front was also an armed force, organized into guerrilla units and actively engaged in unorthodox warfare against the Japanese. Phuong emphasized that aside from the bombings by the Fourteenth Air Force there were no other forces but the Viet Minh resisting the "common enemy." The French "who had never resisted the fascists in Indochina were no longer there." But the Viet Minh had a force on the ground willing and able to "fight side by side" with the United States and its Allies.

As noon approached, I invited Phuong to continue our conversation over lunch at the OSS mess. He seemed pleased to talk further but suggested a local Chinese restaurant as less conspicuous. So we drove to a modest restaurant in the vicinity of Yunnan University and the American and British Consulates. During lunch I kept encouraging him to talk about the Viet Minh, what it stood for, its aims, how it could in his opinion help the Allies against Japan, and what it might expect from the Allies.

His remarks (which I summarized for the record on the same day) were to this effect: the Viet Minh, a coalition party of Vietnamese nationalists under the leadership of the Indochinese Communist Party (ICP), was organized along party lines with the immediate objective of ousting the Japanese and preventing the return of the French. Ultimately the Viet Minh hoped to establish an "independent Indochinese democratic republic." Phuong was confident that it could furnish the Allies with useful information on the Japanese, French, and Indochinese quislings in Viet Nam. It would collaborate with the Americans in acts of sabotage, commando raids, and other attacks against the Japanese and it would urge and instruct the Vietnamese to continue their assistance to downed Allied airmen and lead them to safety. In return, the Viet Minh only wished for the United States to recognize La Ligue de l'Independance de l'Indochine as the sole legal and authorized organization representing the people of Viet Nam[27] in the struggle against the "fascists" and for the United States to provide them with the means to fight the war alongside the Allies. When I asked what they needed, he replied, "Weapons, ammunition, advisers, instructors, and communications with Allied headquarters."

Phuong waited. I thanked him and said his offer was generous and interesting but had to be discussed with my colleagues. In the meantime, how could one reach "General" Ho? Phuong said he had been in Kunming a few days earlier but was on his way back to Viet Nam and would be stopping at Ch'ing-Hsi. He could get word to him that I would be coming and felt sure Ho would be happy to meet with me. I told Phuong I could arrange to visit Ch'ing-Hsi but to confirm it with me the next morning. We parted at the restaurant late in the afternoon.

I discussed my meeting with Phuong that same afternoon with Helliwell and Wampler. The general proposition of working with Vietnamese which we had agreed to look into only a few days before took on a different aspect in the specifics of Phuong's statements. Their insistence on official recognition was a major stumbling block. And Helliwell shared a view held by Heppner that any weapons supplied by OSS would eventually be used against the French. Helliwell, however, still held to his view that since AGAS was going to use the Viet Minh for their operations we could perhaps expand the network to include intelligence collection and guerrilla warfare.

Heppner came in from Chungking that night and we presented the proposal to him. At first, he dismissed the idea as politically impracticable. He was already in serious difficulties with General Hurley[28] about the Chinese Communists. He told us then in strictest confidence that his deputy, Colonel Bird,[29] was working in Yenan with Colonel David D. Barrett[30] attempting to arrange a coalition between Chiang's Nationalists and Mao's Communists and that Hurley was indignant with OSS for involving itself in what he considered a State Department matter. Heppner was also sure the Chinese would raise all sorts of objections to any collaboration with the Vietnamese communists, as would our Embassy staff. And we were not to forget the French Military Mission—they would certainly be very unhappy if they discovered we were negotiating with the Viet Minh.

However, when Heppner heard how the French and Chinese had received me, he, too, took the position that we were left with no alternatives. He cautioned me not to antagonize either the Chinese or the French because he and Whitaker would be working with them in Chungking and General Donovan was committed by the White House to collaborate with both. So the matter of dealing with the Viet Minh was left open for further consideration as matters developed.

Phuong called punctually at my office the next morning to let me know that he had sent word to "General" Ho, but he was not sure his message would arrive before Ho left for the border. He suggested that if I were to go to Ch'ing-Hsi I should stop at a certain teahouse and ask for an English-speaking Chinese named Wang Yeh-li who would help me contact Ho if he were still there.

CHAPTER 8

THE NEW
FRENCH PROBLEM

THE 9 MARCH COUP

Before leaving for Szemao I had the benefit of a report put together on a crash basis by our R&A staff from fragmentary accounts of French civilian and military refugees and from OWI monitoring of Japanese broadcasts. It formed a composite of the 9 March coup de force and its aftermath and was of immense help to me during my field inspection.

I learned from the report that on the afternoon of 9 March the Japanese Ambassador, Shunichi Matsumoto, and Consul General Kono had called on Governor General Decoux to press for greater French cooperation and good will. Kono demanded a sizeable increase in the French contribution to Japan's "war fund," an easing of restrictions on the purchase of rice for the Japanese military, and assurance that the French-Japanese Joint Defense Agreement for Indochina would not be abrogated. Decoux demurred, saying that he needed time to consult with his government in Hanoi.

Suspecting Decoux of stalling, the Ambassador again called on the Governor General at six that same day with an ultimatum. This time the Japanese demands were broadened to include: that the French join the Japanese in the defense of Indochina in the event of an Anglo-American incursion; that all French military and police forces be placed under the command and control of the Japanese military authorities; and that the French surrender to the Japanese all communications, transportation, banking systems and administrative services. The terms of the ultimatum were to be unconditionally accepted within two hours.

When at 10:15 P.M., more than two hours past the hour specified in the ultimatum, the Japanese received a note from Decoux that he needed more time for "consultation," Matsumoto ordered the military to take over and placed Decoux under "protective custody."

At 2 a.m. (Tokyo time) on 10 March the Imperial Headquarters in Tokyo issued a communique announcing the takeover and placing the initiative for the coup with the Japanese military command in Indochina. Later that morning, at 9 a.m. (Tokyo time), after a special cabinet meeting at the Imperial Palace, the Tokyo government publicly endorsed the military decision and suggested a policy which encouraged Vietnamese independence. "As soon as Indochina shows signs of rising into an independent state the Japanese Government will assist that nation in attaining its *true racial independence* based on the principles enunciated in the Joint Declaration of the Greater East Asia Nations."[1]

While the Japanese on the afternoon of the ninth had been exerting pressure on the French for more support, Emperor Bao Dai of Annam, in a New Year (Tet) message to the Vietnamese, had lauded the French, remarking that "France had suffered greatly to restore herself and that the restoration is the forerunner of a period of peace and prosperity, through which all the countries living under the protectorate of France will profit." He said, "We eagerly thank Admiral Jean Decoux who is piloting the Indochinese ship through the world storm. Thanks to him, Indochina is enjoying conditions of peace and security. . . ."[2]

Two days later in a shameless about-face Bao Dai abrogated the French-Annamite Treaty of Protectorate of 1884, proclaimed the independence of the kingdom of Annam, and joined the Greater East Asian Nations. The Emperor promised to cooperate with Japan with his kingdom's total power, trusting in the sincerity and good will of the Japanese Empire.[3]

On the thirteenth Prince Norodom Sihanouk of Cambodia followed suit and declared his country's independence. His public statement announced that "the kingdom of Cambodia no longer feels the need of French protection and hereby declares the Treaty of Protectorate concluded with France null and void. . . . Placing implicit confidence in the Japanese Empire, . . . Cambodia will cooperate with Japan. . . ."[4]

A month later King Sisavang Vong of Luang Prabang in Laos joined his princely neighbors and declared Laos free of French entanglements and welcomed the Japanese as friends and allies.

In Indochina, the Japanese had quickly and effectively declared martial law, disarmed and interned the military and police forces, arrested and confined key military and civilian officials, imposed strict curfew and travel regulations, and had taken over all administrative services. The High Command announced on 11 March the names of some of those arrested, including Decoux, Generals Aymé and Mordant, and the famous Chief of the Indochinese police, Louis (Paul) Arnoux, who had been tracking Ho Chi Minh since 1919.

OSS analysts attributed the French debacle to poor planning on the part of the Mordant resistance organization, to their total disregard for secrecy, and to the lack of coordination between the military and civilian elements of the so-called resistance movement. This was particularly evident when a Vietnamese police official, an agent of the SLFEO, had on 8 March warned Mordant that the Japanese were planning to neutralize the French Army at some time between 8 and 10 March.

In Hanoi Mordant and Aymé had discounted the SLFEO agent's warning. After all, Mordant reasoned, the military intelligence services had no such indications and civilians were prone to exaggeration. General Gabriel Sabattier, in command of the French forces in Tonkin and chief of the resistance movement in the north, took the warning seriously. Without consulting Mordant or Aymé he declared a practice "state of alert" on 8 March and left Hanoi for his field headquarters. On the morning of the ninth Aymé learned of the practice "alert" and promptly cancelled Sabattier's order as unnecessary and unduly alarming to the Japanese. But Sabattier's action had alerted Alessandri who broke camp and moved his troops across the Black and Red Rivers to the northern and western mountainous region of Tonkin.

On the night of the ninth, when the Japanese attacked the French wherever they were, Mordant and Aymé found themselves prisoners of the Japanese and their troops unprepared to offer any resistance. Out of approximately ninety-nine thousand French officers and men in Indochina,[5] less than five thousand troops (under Sabattier and Alessandri) managed to stage any kind of rear-guard action and make their way to the Laotian and Chinese frontiers.[6]

Throughout the days and nights of 10 and 11 March radio reports announced the "peaceful" surrender of major French strongholds. Even in far-off outposts such as Kwang Chou-Wan (a French-leased territory in southern China) and Shanghai, which had a garrison of 1,200 French soldiers and 797 French policemen, French troops were disarmed without resistance.[7]

There were exceptions in which acts of great heroism and gallantry were displayed. At Lang Son (northeast of Hanoi near the China border) the fortified garrison of some twelve thousand troops fought bravely and with determination for two full days. Hopelessly outnumbered and out of water and ammunition, the surviving force of several hundred men surrendered to elements of the 37th Japanese Division whose commander, infuriated by the losses he had sustained at the hands of the stubborn French garrison, massacred every last Frenchman. At Dang Dong (another border town just north of Lang Son) the French garrison met an identical fate after the same Japanese commander, reinforced by a regiment of the 22nd Division, conducted a punitive expedition.

But they were the exceptions. In Hanoi, the Citadel offered some resistance, suffering several dead and many wounded, but it was considered by the Japanese to be a face-saving action, only several hours of uncoordinated rifle fire. At the royal city of Hué units of the French Peace Preservation Corps stationed at the 10th RIC barracks held out until mid-afternoon of 10 March. In central Annam and Cochinchina only token opposition was offered to the Japanese.

As to the unfortunate plight of the French, the R&A report commented that in view of the yearlong preparations for resistance and the well-known fact that all French posts, forts, and garrisons were fully manned and their arsenals amply stocked,[8] the only plausible explanation for the precipitous capitulations was a lack of central organization and direction. An additional consideration could have been a lack of popular support from the oppressed Vietnamese.

The R&A report included excerpts of a dispatch from Consul General Langdon[9] in which he stated that the French in Kunming agreed with the Japanese contention that their action against the French was triggered by a fear of French-American collaboration in the event of American landings in Indochina. Langdon noted that " ... if the French had any concrete plan, the evidence is that they did not coordinate it with American or Chinese plans and waited too long and too late to set it in motion; ... the Japanese outsmarted the French."[10]

The latest information before I left for the border area originated with one of the SI teams parachuted among the retreating French. Sabattier's and Alessandri's troops were moving westward from Hanoi toward Son La and Dien Bien Phu. After searching for the generals, one of our officers found Alessandri at Phong Saly in Laos on 3 April, but found no trace of Sabattier. He reported that the French troops were poorly equipped and were suffering from fatigue and low morale; to lighten their burden they had discarded their heavy weapons and several tons of ammunition, not even bothering to destroy them.

CHANGING IMAGES

The R&A report also contained some observations on the relationships of the French with the Vietnamese, the Chinese, and the Americans, observations which deserve comment based in some cases on facts which did not fully emerge for a period of weeks or months.

On the Vietnamese

Point: Langdon said, "The reaction of the Annamite population to the Japanese coup seems to have disappointed the French. Although a large body of the troops remained loyal, many of them went over to the Japanese, while the civilian population [Vietnamese] has remained generally passive and indifferent."[11]

Counterpoint: In actuality well over ninety percent of the Vietnamese troops surrendered their arms and went home when it became apparent that China was their destination. Many did rally to Indochinese political movements for national independence, but only a very small number, certainly not more than several hundred, joined the Japanese. Most of the political activists in the military threw in their lot with the anti-French, anti-Japanese movements.

In Hanoi, Hué, and Saigon a few Vietnamese were seen wearing the "Rising Sun" armband and collaborating with the local kempeitai. They were in the main members of pro-Japanese secret organizations associated with the Cao Dai,[12] Hoa Hao,[13] and other religious and royalist elements in Indochina.

Vietnamese political activists belonged to three principal nationalist movements: the Indochina Kuangfu Society, a pro-Japanese secret society advocating the return of a monarchical dynasty; the Indochina Kuomintang Party backed by the Chungking Nationalist government, favoring Chinese support and influence; and the Indochina Independence Party, a Moscow-oriented communist front.

The French disappointment in the Indochinese was not in their apathy, but in what the French considered their ingratitude. For over eighty years the French colon, and for that matter virtually every French person associated with Indochina, had developed a myth that visualized France as the great civilizer, benefactor, and protector of the "poor, helpless and inferior" Vietnamese. The myth included a strong desire by the Frenchman living in Indochina to be loved and served by his "native" dependent, coupled with the right to punish him when he failed in his servile duties. With the passing of time this myth became a reality in the minds of the French and therefore governed their daily lives. It was too deeply ingrained in the French character to dispel, even after the events of 9 March.

In their "tragic hour" of flight from the Japanese, the French were thoroughly perplexed and confounded by the paternalistic and protective attitude of the "natives," who were courteous but not solicitous toward them. The Vietnamese helped their former masters evade and escape the pursuing enemy, guided them through the jungle trails toward China, and even sheltered them in their homes for brief periods. Yet it was all too evident to the fleeing French that this was not done out of a sense of loyalty or concern for their safety but with the knowledge that they, the Vietnamese, were on the threshold of a new era. Their roles had suddenly reversed. The Vietnamese were no longer the colonial dependents but free and independent citizens of their own land. They were not moved by a spirit of revenge in those early days, only by a desire to rid the country of the French burden.

In April 1945 the French could not comprehend the Annamite reaction; they could only feel disappointment.

On the Chinese

Point: Chinese-French relations were not entirely cordial. At best they could be characterized only as tolerant and correct. Consul General Langdon reported the Chinese reaction to the coup "as being one of alarm for Yunnan's safety and the measures taken so far [March 1945] reflect a defensive attitude."[14]

Counterpoint: The Generalissimo was altogether displeased with the turn of events in Southeast Asia, for they affected his military position in Burma and China. He was particularly annoyed with the French who after precipitating the Japanese coup failed to put up what he considered a creditable resistance which might have drawn some Japanese forces from the Chinese fronts in Burma and China. Instead, they had unsettled the status quo and unnecessarily exposed the Chinese army to a Japanese attack on its weak southwestern flank. Further, the French had complicated matters by moving into China, risking a Japanese overrun into Yunnan and Kwangsi, and creating political and logistical problems.

Their relations were also aggravated by Chinese antagonism at the highest level of the Kuomintang. Many influential Chinese during the war years had been clashing with members of the Decoux administration and were in conflict with the political activism of the gaulliste elements in China and Indochina. For example, General Ho Ying-chin resented the coming of a foreign armed force to China and considered the retreating French an intrusion on his relationship with Wedemeyer, whose sympathies might be influenced in favor of the French. Although on the surface General Ho played the role of the sympathetic humanitarian and personally issued all _huchaos_ (permits and passes) for the relief of the French refugees, his solicitude served to slow down the process and provide the secret police with an opportunity to screen and segregate "undesirable" elements.

Governor Lung Yün of Yunnan, through whose province the French were passing, had many old scores to settle with the French. His "cousin," General Lu Han, particularly disliked General Alessandri, who was held responsible by many Chinese as one of the principal advisers to Catroux (and later Decoux) for allowing the entry of Japanese troops into Indochina. And Tai Li had for a long time been at odds with the French in China and Indochina on matters of clandestine activities and smuggling. An illustration of Chinese hostility to the French was reported to OSS by its agents on the frontier. One French military unit had lost its Annamite contingent of approximately three thousand which had disbanded and joined the local Viet Minh, leaving their French officers and NCOs to fend for themselves. When the French finally reached the Chinese crosspoint at the frontier near Lao Cai,[15] they were made to wait in the wilderness until authority was received to let them pass into Chinese territory.

On the Americans

Point: In the first weeks following the coup the French were highly criti-cal of the American response to their demands for assistance. They had asked for ammunition, but our ammunition did not fit their weapons. They had asked for weapons, but our weapons were earmarked for the Chinese. They had asked for air support and, although that was not in the Allied plans in China, the Fourteenth Air Force had supplied more than it should have. They had asked for transportation to Chungking on Army planes, but the Chinese would not grant permission.

Counterpoint: Somewhat later the French, both civil and military, began to appreciate the American supply position and the physical difficulties of aiding their compatriots in Indochina. They appreciated what our com-manders had done for their civilian and military refugees in providing quantities of blankets, cots, medicines, and clothing. They later acknowl-edged that our Air Force, with the help of AGAS, had evacuated hundreds of women and children to safety in India, including a daring mission to rescue French civilians in the Gulf of Haiphong.

But at the official level there still lingered national resentment. For example, by mid-April there were some twenty-four hundred French refugees gathered at various locations in Yunnan being assisted by UNRRA.[16] General Pechkov protested, stating that he felt there was a stigma attached to being assisted by what he considered a charitable or-ganization rather than being treated as gallant military allies. Our Embassy staff, very well acquainted with the always tight supply situa-tion, were obliged to explain to him that UNRRA was an international re-lief organization sponsored by the United Nations, of which France was a member, and that in extending assistance through UNRRA France was only helping herself.

Under the surface of the many lesser French complaints, though, what the French high echelon most resented was General Wedemeyer's insistence that Indochinese and French activities emanating from China, overt as well as covert, were under the authority of the Chinese.

CHAPTER 9

A TOUR OF THE
CHINA BORDER

DISARRAY

My introductory tour of southern China started at Szemao. At its busy airfield[1] Lieutenant William A. Pye of our station there greeted me with a depressing story of Chinese obstructionism, French complaints, and an "imminent" Japanese attack. He was thoroughly discouraged with the lack of progress in setting up an intelligence network and attributed his problem to the uncooperative attitude of the Chinese under Tai Li's direction and to the apathy of the French refugees who wanted to put distance between themselves and the Japanese at the Indochina border, about forty miles to the south.

We drove to the OSS House where a French Major de Monpezat[2] was waiting for me. He described the situation in Szemao as utterly chaotic. The "Annamite" troops were deserting in droves. The Chinese were making no effort at all to care for or evacuate French refugees to India as had been agreed by Generals Pechkov and Ho Ying-chin. Military and civilian refugees, many of whom were barefoot and in rags, were suffering from dysentery, malaria, and exhaustion, and in dire need of medical attention. The refugee population had reached the "astronomical figure of thirty-five hundred and many more on the way." De Monpezat wanted to know what I could do about the situation. The only thing I could do was to take a cursory look and advise Chungking, but I did suggest that he and Pye prepare a comprehensive report outlining the needs and detailing numbers of refugees and types of relief required. The major seemed satisfied.

The wizened magistrate of Szemao, Chao Cha-fung, was also waiting to see me. He had learned that another four hundred French refugees and military personnel would be arriving in four days and expressed his fear that they would be armed. He asked me to advise the French authorities to collect the weapons of these refugees before their arrival and place them in safekeeping with the Chinese military. I informed him that this was a French-Chinese matter which did not involve the Americans. I added, however, that it was my understanding that the French military were not to be disarmed and were to be directed by the Chinese to assembly areas pending final disposition from Chungking. The magistrate was manifestly unhappy with this information and foresaw unpleasantness between the French and Chinese military if the matter were not resolved. He complained that the large influx of refugees had created housing and food shortages, with the situation being aggravated by the language barrier. Soldiers were threatening the local merchants with bodily harm over availability and prices of merchandise. For all these problems I had to suggest he seek advice from Chungking. He thanked me for my "understanding" and left.

Matters at the OSS station were a mess. Several OSS officers had been on the border for a month, but no one knew their exact whereabouts. Urgent requests for supplies from various OSS outposts were stacked up at Szemao without action. I asked Pye to put things in order as best he could and radioed Helliwell to send someone to relieve him so that he could return to Kunming with a report on the French situation and an accounting of the station's affairs

The next morning I boarded my plane for the three hundred-mile flight to Ch'ing-Hsi. Enroute we stopped at our outpost at Muong Sing, a village in a mountainous area of Indochina about 125 miles south of Szemao. We landed on an airstrip with only a windsock to qualify it as a landing field and were met by Lieutenant Charles D. Ambelang.[3] He had been moving for three weeks from hilltop to dusty trail to hilltop, setting up listening posts, only to dismantle them as Japanese troops moved within sight. It was an impossible task. The French would not stay and local Vietnamese could not be trained fast enough in radio operations. I asked him to leave the area, join General Sabattier's group at Phong Saly, and then proceed with them to Szemao, where I would rejoin him.

My next stop was at Meng Tzu, in China, another OSS outpost, where things were less hectic. The team there had succeeded in gathering a respectable amount of Japanese order of battle information and some political intelligence on French-Japanese relations in Hanoi and Haiphong.

AGAS HOUSE

Finally, an hour before dusk I landed at Tepao, just north of Ch'ing-Hsi, and went to the AGAS House. We were joined at dinner by several French officers who had been working with GBT and collaborating with AGAS. Warmed by excellent French cognac, our conversation was casual shoptalk, with the French lamenting their misfortunes and blaming "the politicians." As a guest I avoided the controversial until someone referred to the "Annamites" as "unreliable" and a "problem" in general. To keep the conversation on that topic, I told them I had been approached by a member of the League for the Independence of Indochina who said it was not anti-French, only antifascist. This provoked discussion, and I sat back and listened.

The Americans took the position that the Vietnamese could be extremely useful. They knew the terrain, were inconspicuous, and easily trainable. And they were not all anti-French, as witness the many loyal Vietnamese serving in the ranks of the French colonial army. In any case, as matters stood, they saw little choice but to recruit Vietnamese agents where possible.

The French officers would only concede that as individual agents, properly screened by the French M.5, perhaps a few could be used under French supervision, but only with careful planning and tight security. They recommended to me that I look more carefully into the League and its Moscow-oriented organization, the Viet Minh. I would be interested to know, one said, that "a number of Russian Legionnaires in Alessandri's division had been court-martialed for seditious activities among the Annamite independence movement in the past several years." He said the Viet Minh in Indochina had been agitating the local populace for a long time and large segments of the people were "racists and pro-Japanese." If "they" gained a foothold in Indochina, it would spell the end of the white man's influence in Southeast Asia. They reminded me that had it not been for almost eighty years of French "benevolence" the "Annamite" would still be subservient to the Chinese without the benefits of French-western culture.

Not wanting to alienate the French guests, I agreed that France certainly had contributed to the westernization of Indochina, but the question at hand was how best to reestablish contact with the interior and engage our common enemy, the Japanese. One of the AGAS men returned to his premise of using Vietnamese where feasible and the French conceded it was one way but still maintained it would be risky. The conversation then drifted to other topics.

When the guests left, the AGAS team wanted to know what I had in mind regarding the Viet Minh. I only mentioned that SI and AGAS might be considering a joint venture with the Viet Minh and that I hoped to meet some of the Viet Minh people but would not want the French to know and would need AGAS's help in finding a certain Chinese. They agreed.

The next day I looked into the GBT establishment. With the help of Colonel Emblanc and several French officers of the Kunming military mission Gordon had reestablished some radio nets on the northeastern border.[4] He also had succeeded in organizing several "courier systems" between Haiphong and Hanoi and was feeding occasional information to OSS-Kunming and the U.S. Naval Group, China.

MR. WANG YEH-LI

My next business was to find Wang Yeh-li. A Chinese-speaking AGAS associate helped me locate the obscure teahouse I was seeking. It was on a narrow street lined with open shops and filled with a stream of humanity, including many smiling, half-naked children shouting a friendly *"ting hao."* Mrs. Wang welcomed us; her husband, she said, was out for a short while. We waited and ordered tea, noticing the several Chinese who came in. They neither ate nor drank but went directly to a room in the rear. Some soon returned and left; others were either members of the household or used another exit. We speculated on it and concluded the teahouse was more than a place for tea and cookies.

A youngish Chinese came in, walked straight to our table without hesitation, and introduced himself in English. He said his name was Wang and he was expecting me. I introduced my friend as Lieutenant "Karl."* Wang dispensed with the usual oriental formalities and launched a probing inquiry in his Hong Kong English into my impressions of China, of its army, and of what would happen to the KMT now that the United States had a new president. He was not sure that Japan could be defeated for several years, perhaps not until 1947 or 1948, and then only if Russia entered the war. He supposed that I was with General Chennault in some kind of intelligence work. He was sizing me up, forming an opinion of my political leanings, and looking for the real purpose of my visit. Slowly I helped him get the information I wanted him to have. Yes, I was in intelligence with the OSS. Under Wedemeyer, not Chennault. No, I was not interested in Chinese politics but in Japanese activities in Southeast Asia. I wanted to organize a network of clandestine operators in Indochina, preferably with the help of the Vietnamese.

Finally Wang observed that only the Chinese and the Vietnamese could succeed in such an undertaking and that perhaps he had just the man who could help us. Would I be interested in meeting him? Yes, I answered, but who was the man? He would only say he was an "Annamite

---

*AGAS personnel seldom revealed their true identities.

of influence and resources." After all that had gone before, it was apparent to me that he was speaking of Ho, but neither of us mentioned his name and, in a sense, it was a test of confidence. I would trust Wang and Wang would perhaps produce the right person. I was willing to gamble and agreed to meet Wang for that purpose the next day in the late afternoon. I was to come alone.

"Karl" was not so trusting. Back in our jeep he expressed his uneasiness. Tai Li's agents were everywhere and no one knew with certainty which side a particular Chinese was on. Would I mind if he made some inquiries about Wang? I told "Karl" just who I planned to meet and why, and he felt reassured, being convinced that perhaps Wang was a Chinese Communist, necessarily very cautious, and could be trusted. Nevertheless, he said he would look into Wang's file.

Late that evening I received a radio message from Helliwell letting me know the pressure was still on. G-2 was asking for OSS operations in Hanoi and Saigon. Headquarters wanted information about the arrival of new Japanese combat units and confirmation of aerial sighting of new airfields and military installations. They were even urgently requesting a propaganda campaign against Japanese troops of the 37th Division to lower morale and induce desertions.[5] They wanted everything and they wanted it right away. It was perfectly obvious that we had to enlist the help of anyone—Chinese, Vietnamese, or French—to get operations under way.

To make sure I could find the teahouse in the maze of lanes and alleys, we drove by it again in the early afternoon while "Karl" told me that Wang was indeed a Chinese Communist who had been active in the Dong Minh Hoi, organizing Vietnamese exiles at Liuchow and Kweilin. The previous fall he had been suspected of anti-Kuomintang leanings because of his close association with the Viet Minh, so the Dong Minh Hoi had ousted him and now he was waiting for an opportunity to head north to join Mao's group in Yenan.

A VILLAGE TEAHOUSE

The sun was setting when Wang and I drove into a small village called Chiu Chou Chieh. It had taken forty-five minutes to drive the six miles from Ch'ing-Hsi on the narrow (and only) road. At the end of the day all the traffic—human, animal and drayage—was against us, with innumerable delays from squeezing around water buffalo and overloaded carts. The village was nothing but a cluster of fifteen or twenty small buildings surrounded by a low wall and debris. Wang pointed to a low building in the center.

As we parked at the rear, two men came out to meet us.[6] They were not Chinese. Wang walked ahead and spoke a few words in what I believed was Chinese. The elder of the two, a slender, short man, fifty or sixty years old, approached me with a warm smile and extended hand. Perfectly at ease and in English he said, "Welcome, my good friend." I took Ho's thin, almost fragile, hand and expressed my pleasure in meeting a man who had so many American friends in Kunming. Ho then introduced the other Vietnamese, Mr. Le Tung Son,[7] as his close associate in the League.

Wang led the way into a dimly lit room which seemed to have an upper level where people could be heard moving about. Mr. Son came in last and closed the door and window shutter securely. Ho walked to the only table and invited us to sit down. Pouring tea for us, Ho explained that Mr. Son spoke neither English nor French, but understood some French. Ho preferred, he said, to use English because he needed the practice.

Wang got right to the point. The Kunming branch of the League hoped to collaborate with the Allies and we had come to make arrangements. Without hesitation Ho replied that collaboration would be possible, that Mr. Pham Viet Tu had been in contact with the American Consulate since the previous August and that Mr. Langdon was favorably disposed toward the Vietnamese. (This was a great overstatement of the Consul General's position, as I knew.) In fact, Ho went on, AGAS and the Viet Minh were presently working to organize a clandestine operation in the interior to assist downed airmen, but he considered that another matter.

Ho wanted, he said, to talk about our friends first. He was curious to know how I had come to know about the Viet Minh and, more to the point, about him. I told him frankly but highlighted only the main points that I had learned in Washington of his "detention" by the Kuomintang, of his work in the Dong Minh Hoi, his collaboration with the Allies in helping downed pilots, and, of course, my recent conversation with Phuong.

I could see Ho's intense interest in what I was revealing and, for only a moment, a glint of surprise and satisfaction in learning that the name of Ho Chi Minh was not unknown to official Washington, but this he quickly suppressed. He asked if I knew Major Glass, and I told him how Glass had suggested I look for a "friendly Annamite" in Tonkin and wondered aloud if perhaps he was the man.

The thin, curious little man smiled broadly and launched into several minutes of praise for Austin Glass, the "American Vietnamese." Ho recalled with apparently genuine affection how the Vietnamese of Haiphong esteemed Glass, who had married a Vietnamese lady and lived in Indochina for more than thirty years. According to Ho, Glass spoke Vietnamese fluently and had an intimate and sympathetic understanding of Vietnamese social, economic, and political problems. He recalled that when the Japanese occupied Tonkin in 1940 Glass was among the first westerners to come under the unpleasant scrutiny of the kempeitai, not because he was pro-French but because he shared with the Vietnamese a strong feeling for their spirit of independence and antifascism. He vividly recalled the accounts of Glass's many friends among the Vietnamese in

Haiphong who had turned out to say goodbye when Glass left in the first American-Japanese exchange of civilians. Having never met Glass personally, Ho was recounting what he knew thirdhand.

Ho was chain-smoking a brand of local cigarettes, which were very strong and acrid. When he ran out of them and asked Son to see if he could find more, I offered him a Chesterfield. His eyes lit up with pleasure as he reached with his long delicate fingers for one, adding apologetically that smoking was one of his more serious vices. And that, I found later, was the truth. When his state of health was precarious in the tense days of August and September, he was still enjoying my Chesterfields. Even with a racking cough, he smoked. It seemed to be his one indulgence and I never had the heart to preach as he enjoyed my cigarettes.

But to return to our conversation, some of Ho's reservations about me seemed to have been dispelled, but he was a veteran revolutionary, master of intrigue and clandestine operations, and he continued to delve with gentle, tactful probing. I realized he was searching my motives and trying to discover my attitude toward the Vietnamese as a people and, in particular, whether I represented colonial interests or Roosevelt's anti-colonialism. I wanted to gain his confidence and willingly participated in his dialectical jousting.

Ho also described at considerable length how difficult life had been for the Vietnamese during the previous winter in northern Viet Nam. The October crops in Tonkin had been devastated by typhoons, weakened dikes, and widespread flooding. The winter shortages of food, medicine, clothing, and transportation, coupled with a total absence of relief measures, had resulted in the end in one of the most calamitous famines in the entire history of their people.

Food shortages had been accompanied by the hoarding of rice and unbridled speculation, which became critical in January when the health of the Tonkinese and northern Annamese deteriorated rapidly. Many were too sick or too weak to work. Livestock died in the fields from lack of care and feeding. The intricate system of dikes developed and maintained by the French began to fall into disrepair during the fall because of budgetary cutbacks in public works. French workers were laid off and the untrained Vietnamese could not replace them. Huge tracts of farmlands ultimately became flooded.

When I asked what the French administration had done to alleviate the situation, Ho spread his hands wide with a sigh, "What they have always done—suited their personal interests." He characterized the Decoux regime as greedy, supportive of vested interests, and insensitive to the plight of the Vietnamese population. Instead of instituting a plan for distributing huge stores of foodstuffs in the south, the Decoux government had imposed harsh penalties, including death, on those attempting to survive.

The Viet Minh had taken the lead in this crisis. Its guerrilla units struck at village warehouses[8] throughout Annam and Tonkin, seizing quantities of foodstuffs, especially rice, which they distributed among those in need. Many had been helped, but still the famine grew. In only a few months between 1.5 and 2 million Vietnamese had died of starvation. No French or Japanese had died of starvation, only the Vietnamese. The French cities had survived; it was only in the villages and hamlets that the streets, ditches, canals, and rice paddies were littered with bodies, the living being too weak and emaciated to collect and bury them. Many villages had lost a third to a half of their populations.

Ho had been describing his people's catastrophe in a voice full of emotion, and as he came to its end he looked sad and tired. He offered to send me an "album of photographic evidence" and a detailed account entitled "The Black Book" which had been prepared by some of his people. I told him I would like to have a copy and believed it would be of special interest to my headquarters.[9]

Ho expressed the view that things would be different after the war. "We are making preparations for an independent democratic government, to be run by the Vietnamese for the Vietnamese." In a reflective mood, Ho admitted that it would be a large task. The French would undoubtedly oppose such a move. The Chinese had their reasons to support the French but perhaps could be won over to the side of the Vietnamese. And the British certainly did not want to upset the colonial structure of Southeast Asia; there would be a serious problem if they came to the help of the French.

Despite my studied objectivity and purposeful awareness of not allowing myself to become involved in the political aspects of the Indochina question, Ho's sincerity, pragmatism, and eloquence made an indelible impression on me. He did not strike me as a starry-eyed revolutionary or a flaming radical, given to cliches, mouthing a party line, or bent on destroying without plans for rebuilding. This wisp of a man was intelligent, well-versed in the problems of his country, rational, and dedicated. I also felt he could be trusted as an ally against the Japanese. I saw that his ultimate goal was to attain American support for the cause of a free Viet Nam and felt that desire presented no conflict with American policy. From a practical viewpoint, Ho and the Viet Minh appeared to be the answer to my immediate problem of establishing operations in Indochina.

It was almost midnight and Wang suggested we start back to Ch'ing-Hsi, but Ho insisted we stay on as there was still much to talk about—unless, he added, I was tired or had to get back right away. We stayed.

I inquired into the whereabouts of the Viet Minh headquarters and details of its apparatus. Wang broke in immediately, in Chinese, and appeared to caution Ho. But Ho raised his hand in disapproval of Wang's remarks and answered my questions.

The headquarters was located in some natural caves outside Cao Bang.[10] The Viet Minh was not a special unit that could be moved about, but rather comprised a very large segment of Vietnamese. It was everywhere among the industrial workers and the peasants of the countryside. Units of workers and peasants were organized in small manageable groups under a trained "cadre" (leader); each unit could operate independently or collectively according to the need. For example, if information were desired on Japanese troops stationed at Bien Hoa (near Saigon), units in the area would be requested to provide the information, which would be passed to Da Nang (Tourane) and eventually to Cao Bang. Admittedly the process was slow and by the time the information reached Kunming it would be stale. Similarly, if a particular commando raid were ordered against a Japanese unit at Son Tay (northwest of Hanoi), the Viet Minh's paramilitary organization in the area could execute the operation.

Ho saw it as a matter of time and distance. His people were poorly equipped with a wide assortment of French, Belgian, British, and Japanese weapons with little ammunition, no vehicles, and only a limited number of radios. They had to depend on captured equipment, which was substantial but required specialized training and instructors. If an arrangement were reached with the Allies for communications equipment and a limited number of small weapons for arming a few small units, using American instructors, then the situation would be entirely changed.

In this very brief presentation, Ho had conveyed to me what he could do with what he had and what he needed if we wanted more. In carefully couched terms, he had dangled a tempting proposition which he felt sure we would consider seriously. In his astuteness, Ho had asked for nothing; he had merely exposed me to the potential value of his political-military organization. And he would bide his time, asking no commitments.

As we got down to these particulars, however, I felt impelled to say that I was not prepared to make any commitments. The sly "old man," feigning surprise at my alarm, smiled mischievously and protested that he was not asking for any, only replying to my questions about the Viet Minh. No matter, he said, he understood perfectly. He was ready to align himself with the Americans whenever they were ready. All I had to do was let his people in Kunming know what was wanted, and he would see that it was provided.

It was very late as Wang and I started back, but the return trip on the now-deserted road was a fast one. Wang managed to exchange pleasantries in parting, but my impression was that he still regarded me with suspicion.

Back at my billet I felt sensible of the contrast between this meeting and the way these sessions were conducted in the war in Europe and Africa. There, underground representatives often made big claims of what they could accomplish (usually exaggerated) if only they were supplied with arms and money (large amounts). Ho had not even mentioned funds. And he had frankly revealed that his people had captured weapons. In Yugoslavia OSS officers knew that the underground buried quantities of captured German weapons and pretended to be short of arms, a device to prepare for the end of the war when they meant to settle their internal disputes with the largest possible cache of weapons. For that matter, such things were happening in China, to the dismay of American commanders. Ho had revealed his weapons, such as they were, and had not asked for any funding. OSS was accustomed to paying for intelligence. My conclusion was that much good would come of that night's meeting.

SABATTIER'S ARMY

Next morning I boarded my plane for Poseh, thirty minutes by air north of Ch'ing-Hsi. Our one-man outpost there was working with elements of GBT and the U.S. Naval Group and doing well. Poseh was another assembly point for the retreating French forces, but there was no need to linger, and I flew back to Szemao that same afternoon.

I learned on landing that one of our two SO teams sent to General Sabattier's forces in Indochina had been ambushed by a Japanese advance unit, owing to faulty French intelligence. Under heavy Japanese fire at Don Chai* Major Summers's team[11] had held its ground while the radios, codes, and special equipment were destroyed and had then dispersed northward. Helliwell and Davis asked me to look for them. I found them on 2 May after several daylight reconnaissance flights over mountainous trails and jungle terrain. They were on the Chinese side of the border at Chengtung (Keng Tung) and safe, after suffering severe hardships wandering through the jungle. I arranged for their evacuation to Kunming.

General Sabattier, still making his way to Szemao, had sent word ahead by de Monpezat that he wanted to discuss French resistance plans with me. I advised Helliwell and was instructed to "make no commitments since any dealing with [the] French must be cleared with Theater." However, if the plans looked good, Helliwell said, he "would press for immediate action."

We met on 2 May in Szemao, and General Sabattier expressed gratitude for the support the French had received from OSS and the Fourteenth Air Force in their "tragic hour" and voiced the hope that the Americans would continue their "generous and sympathetic" help. He informed me, so there would be no misunderstanding, that he was the "supreme commander of all the French troops in the Far East" and that he operated under direct instructions from the Provisional Government of France. He intended to establish his headquarters at Kunming where he would direct all future French operations "in collaboration" with the Allies. His plan was to reorganize his forces in China under the commands of General Alessandri and Colonel Seguin[12] and place them at the disposal of General Wedemeyer.

*Near Muong Ou Tay.

As to clandestine operations, he had on hand several hundred specially trained officers and men willing and ready to return to Indochina and reestablish communications with French agents left behind. I asked if the agents were part of General Mordant's network, and the general seemed surprised that I knew of their clandestine organization. With some embarrassment he said they were but quickly added that he also had his own network among the Man[13] people, who were "absolutely loyal" to him. We discussed further details of his plan which he had outlined on several maps and agreed to continue discussions in Kunming. The general observed that he would have to rely on the Americans for logistical support and training and would have to insist that the training be given at Szemao to avoid exposing French-Annamite cadres to the Chinese.

The weather in Szemao had turned. Heavy cloud cover and intermittent rains made flying impossible and road transport hazardous and slow. It also added to the misery of the refugees. The French trickling into China were in a deplorable state. Tired, hungry, sick, and barefoot, they were impatient with everyone in authority. They demanded quarters which were not even available to the Chinese army. They tried to requisition private vehicles and foodstuffs without authority, which resulted in acrimonious confrontations. When they learned there were Americans in the area, our office was besieged with requests from junior officers that we "order" the Chinese to meet their demands. We kept explaining that we were without authority but that the French Embassy would provide for them. They found this a very unsatisfactory answer.

I was deeply moved by the wretched sight of a defeated Western army, humbled by the Japanese and straggling to China's door for protection and refuge. I had seen Germans and Italians in huge numbers, both POWs and civilians, retreating to the rear of our lines in Africa and Europe, but they had been Westerners in a Western world. In Asia, the situation took on a different dimension, unspoken but real. The racial and cultural differences which for decades had been masked in diplomatic and social niceties were suddenly brought to the fore. The French, a symbol of European culture and military might in Asia, were broken by one oriental power and were at the uncomfortable mercy of another oriental people. The Chinese, on the surface, were sympathetic, helpful, and humane; underneath they indulged in the distasteful practice of polite procrastination, political rectitude, and strict adherence to real or imaginary local customs and international agreements. There was a spirit of "now the shoe is on the other foot and we Asiatics are in charge."

On the French side, there were also racially related problems: language difficulties, personal needs, and loss of face all contributed to the growing frustrations of the French, manifested in their unreasonable demands and outright arrogance toward all Asiatics. The result was constant friction with insidious racial overtones.

A PORTRAIT OF THE COLON

In the eight days since I had first landed at Szemao, it had become a center of French concentration. I saw a good opportunity to gather information from the refugees and to recruit Frenchmen for clandestine operations, so I asked Helliwell to send a qualified French-speaking officer with a supporting staff. He sent Lieutenant John P. Spaulding and several enlisted personnel, and I decided to stay on for a while myself. Over a period of ten days I interviewed perhaps a dozen officers and twice that number of senior NCOs and personnel from lower ranks, both French and Vietnamese, in addition to a number of civilian officials and businessmen. These conversations elicited an unattractive picture of indifference, vengefulness, and selfish interest.

The attitudes of the evacuees basically reflected French national policies as well as their experience with the civil or military establishment since 1940 under Decoux. They felt their present plight would soon end and they would return to Indochina to pick up just exactly where they had left off. There would be no change.

It appeared to me that most evacuees had spent their years in Indochina without ever leaving their French environment. Their knowledge of the native population and its language, ethnic characteristics and political aspirations was that of the casual traveler. They saw Vietnamese personnel in their army as "common soldiers and coolies," although many Frenchmen received faithful support from "native" troops and civilians during clashes with the Japanese. This was considered "normal and their duty." To them the "native resistance" was not a movement with a momentum of its own but rather a proof of successful French liberalism and leadership.

Almost to a man, the French I interviewed considered the Vietnamese incapable of political responsibility. They admitted that nationalists existed, but they were "rabble to be dealt with by the Sûreté or the Army." The French attitude at its best was paternal. At its worst but only among a few it was pure contempt, as epitomized in the sentiment of one field-grade officer that there was "not one honest Annamese."

In attitudes toward the Western Allies, I found greater variation of attitude, but the predominant feeling was suspicion of Allied intentions. I personally observed members of the French Military Mission at Szemao exerting themselves to instill this suspicion in new arrivals before they came into contact with my staff. The safeguarding of French interests against purported British and American covetousness was apparent as a rationalization for past collaboration with the Japanese.

Very few French officials were so frank as the one who, after evading my questions on transportation in Indochina, finally asked me, "Do the Americans intend to run the Indochinese railroads after the war?" A few apologized for the official obstructionism and offered full cooperation on intelligence questions if their collaboration were not revealed to the French authorities. One businessman expressed a willingness to see the country developed by foreign capital and initiative if French sources were not able to meet the needs. But he was the only one to make such a statement to me.

Although the French attitude toward the Western Allies seemed strange to many Americans in China, I did not find it so. On the contrary, I interpreted it as a natural extension of the official position in Paris under the new de Gaulle administration. French government spokesmen were publicly blaming France's severe political troubles in Syria and Lebanon on the activities of British agents and were also accusing the British of designs to supplant the French in their Middle Eastern possessions. French ministers addressing the Consultative Assembly had charged the United States with scheming for the acquisition of New Caledonia and bases in Indochina. American press criticism of French colonial policy was contemptuously dismissed by Foreign Minister Bidault with the emphatic statement that "France has no lessons to learn from anyone in such matters."[14] The bad feeling toward America in view of our general anticolonial policy one could understand, but attacking Britain, their only powerful ally in propping up the sagging ideal of "Empire," was shortsighted and splenetic.

In any case, I reported to Theater and Embassy staff upon my return to Kunming that the suspicious and resentful attitudes of the government in Paris and of the colonial authorities could not fail to reenforce each other. In both it was the aim of French officials to restore the French prewar position without compromise, which might call for methods certain to provoke criticism and weaken the combined Allied war effort. Allied opposition was to be met and disarmed by assuming an attitude of injured righteousness and a determination to settle matters rapidly and thoroughly by the use of French troops before questions could be asked. As will be seen in the events which followed, the mandate of the French authorities who embarked upon this policy was limited and the exact measure of support from their own countrymen questionable. But they wanted to present France, and the rest of the world, with an accomplished fact—an impossible task.

My discussions in those early days with Generals Sabattier and Alessandri and with Colonel Emblanc and Major de Monpezat also revealed a less publicized inter-Allied problem of which only a few Frenchmen were cognizant. It concerned the many open and clandestine contacts between China and Indochina.

Chinese residents of Indochina were in general hostile to the Japanese. Their open cooperation with the Japanese military was not then considered disloyal by the French—merely an exigency of war, a pragmatic arrangement. The French with whom I spoke were of the opinion that the Chinese community in Indochina would welcome the return of French rule, if for no other reason than for economic stability.

Responsible French officials, however, were very much concerned about the attitude of the Chinese Kuomintang. They had been alarmed by articles in the Chinese media, passed by the Chungking censorship, calling for Indochina's reincorporation into China while other semiofficial Chinese journals endorsed one or another of the Vietnamese revolutionary groups. The revolutionaries variously supported everything from a union with China to complete independence for Viet Nam. While their numbers were small, they constituted focal points of anti-French propaganda, the only sentiment on which the revolutionaries agreed, and were therefore a source of trouble in the "colony." The Chinese government made little distinction among these revolutionary groups, tolerating them all, but cooperating most closely with the Annamese branch of the Kuomintang. Moreover, responsible French officials also knew that Tai Li maintained throughout Indochina an active network of agents who had eluded both the Sûreté and the kempeitai.

French military leaders readily admitted to me that Decoux, like his predecessors, had been unable to stamp out the various Indochinese opposition parties or to prevent Chinese clandestine penetrations, both of which were directed from China. Moreover, after the coup, the Japanese had granted official status to some nationalist groups in Indochina. But French military leaders still saw the Viet Minh as the greatest threat to French sovereignty. It had continued its underground activities against the Japanese and the French throughout the war but had nevertheless been treated with contempt by all the anticommunists in Viet Nam.

The Decoux administration made little effort to court the support of the man in the street, which was not surprising in view of the low esteem in which the Vietnamese were held. French propaganda had been entirely in terms of the cultural blessings bestowed upon Indochina by French civilization. Little publicity was given to the various colonial reform statements emanating from the de Gaulle government during French-British-American negotiations. Strangely enough, the Japanese had used those same statements to contrast the paucity of the promised reforms and a supposed threat of postwar Anglo-American exploitation with the wonderful rewards the Vietnamese would find in Japan's program for a Greater East Asia Co-Prosperity Sphere.[15]

After the coup, the French propaganda line, which proved ineffective, merely centered on France's determination to free Indochina from the Japanese yoke. The disintegration of their propaganda machinery and Japanese surveillance made it impossible for the French to reach the Vietnamese, who would not have believed them in any case. Nevertheless, in April the French were placing their hopes on an adverse Vietnamese reaction to the Japanese occupation, contrasted to what they saw as their own benevolent rule. They seemed confident the Japanese would eventually drive the Vietnamese back into the arms of the French. This hope was also sustained by an illusion of native goodwill reflected by the royal families of Annam, Cambodia, and Laos. There was a false sense of confidence which took no account of the common Vietnamese and his desire for total independence.

Yet while the French as a whole blithely took for granted a Vietnamese acquiescence to the return of French rule, there were still French officials who were determined to reestablish that French rule by the use of European French troops. No Vietnamese were represented on the councils of the exiled colonial leaders. Deliberate limitations were imposed upon the participation of "native" troops in the "liberation" of the country. Vietnamese had been kept at the fringe of the de Langlade-Mordant-Sabattier underground, and French military leaders had resisted the issuance of arms to its so-called "native guerrillas." The policy was continued even with respect to "native" troops who fought in the French army in the recent engagements and whose continued loyalty was not in doubt.

This policy of exclusion was obviously not inspired by the requirements of winning the war against Japan but was designed for unilateral French interest. It was to give the French forces a completely free hand in dealing with the issues bound to arise after the expulsion of the Japanese. It would have assured that only European troops under French officers retaining control of supplies and weapons would be used when France moved back into the "colony" by force of arms.

I included all this in my report on the French in southern China, which generally was well received, but there were some on our Embassy staff who felt I had been too harsh in my interpretation of French motives. This gave rise in Kunming and Chungking to a belief that I was anti-French. However, my future collaboration with French authorities in China proved me to be not anti-French, but only pro-Allied.

We Americans in the Pacific and Asia had one overriding goal—to defeat Japan—even if we had to go it alone, knowing that among our Allies were those who would willingly let someone else win the war while they prepared to reap the fruits of victory.

THE FREE FRENCH DIG IN

I sent General Sabattier's plan to Kunming on 2 May. Helliwell succeeded in obtaining limited approval from Theater for joint French-American operations and on 6 May radioed, "OK to try Sabattier in Szemao territory first," but he also cautioned me to keep in mind "our limitations on equipment and personnel" and to take a "firm stand with [the] French to ensure that in no way do we get involved in anything of a political nature." There was a stern admonition that "no arms and ammo" were to be provided to the French except for limited self-defense and then only if "OSS has full operational control."[16]

Taking for granted that Generals Sabattier and Alessandri were in close collaboration, I was not surprised when Alessandri called on me on the afternoon of 6 May to inquire into my OSS plans for French personnel in clandestine activities. I told him enthusiastically that I had just then received the go-ahead from Kunming on General Sabattier's plan. Alessandri started in his chair and with undisguised irritation commented that "French resistance in Indochina is not a matter which should concern the high command." I mistook his remark to refer to our American high command and observed that as far as I was concerned my orders came from Theater Headquarters. Quickly Alessandri recovered his poise and said, *"Naturellement."* He had alluded, of course, to Sabattier and the "temporary" French command arrangement, and it was the first hint I had that all was not well in that matter.

Alessandri abruptly dropped the subject of clandestine activities, turning to what he said was the more pressing question of supplies for his troops. He conveyed in a conciliatory tone his anxiety to assemble his troops, then scattered over southern China from Szemao to Fangch'eng with more still crossing the border. He had hoped the Americans would provide regrouping areas, transportation, and supplies for refurbishing his troops. I expressed my full appreciation of his problems but was obliged to tell the General that OSS was in no position to help and that the matter had to be resolved in Chungking between the French Embassy and Chiang Kai-shek. He impatiently reminded me that he was very well aware of normal channels but was merely trying to facilitate an urgent Allied command function—the emergency requirements of his troops, "an element of the Allied forces in China." Hoping to calm him, I suggested that I would be more than happy to arrange for him or his representative to meet with Mr. Snyder of UNRRA, then at Szemao, who was empowered by the United Nations to assist the French.

But Alessandri was thoroughly exasperated with my insistence that he deal in other quarters and apparently never forgot this encounter. Later he was compelled to sit in at Theater-level conferences at which I sometimes represented OSS interests in Indochina, but he never addressed me directly in these meetings. In September in Hanoi he displayed his pique still further by refusing to attend a meeting with General Lu Han[17] which he himself had requested, but to which General Gallagher[18] had invited me as head of the U.S. Military Mission, because, in his words, "Commandant Patti is not friendly to the French."

General Sabattier had gone on to Kunming, anticipating a warm welcome as the senior commander of French forces in China and Delegate General for Indochina. It must have been a disappointment to him when he found no one of rank to greet him. Kunming was only the headquarters of the Rear Echelon. The seat of power was four hundred miles away at Chungking; there he would find Chiang Kai-shek and his close advisers, the French Military Mission, General Wedemeyer and his staff, and the American Ambassador. The so-called French Military Mission in Kunming was really M.5 and had already been purged by the SLFEO of "old

China hands" and had become the center of the gaulliste faction in China. Sabattier found no friends there.

The gaullistes in Kunming had hoped for a more distinguished figure to represent the "new France"—someone of the stature of Leclerc, Catroux, or even Blaizot. Sabattier was a poor second. His credentials as a gaulliste were at best circumstantial. His politics were those of the typical French regular army officer, loyal to France, supportive of the regime in power, and a strict adherent to the traditional code of military honor. With Aymé's arrest, Sabattier as senior on the scene assumed the post of Commander in Chief of all French forces in Indochina. Then with the "disappearance"[19] of Mordant, Sabattier had been appointed in his stead.

Agents of the SLFEO in Kunming, apparently under orders from Calcutta, launched a campaign to discredit Sabattier in the eyes of the French troops and the French Military Mission in Chungking by leaking portions of a classified message of 10 April from de Gaulle to Sabattier which read, "It is understood that you will prolong resistance on Indochina soil whatever the difficulties. It is equally necessary that you remain personally in Indochina to the utmost limit. . . ."[20] The same agents then circulated accusations that Sabattier had always been the first to leave areas threatened by the Japanese—first from Dien Bien Phu four days before his first troops moved out, from Phong Saly three days before the French evacuated the sector, and from Muong Ou Tay three days before the retreat.

Advance departures are normal security measures for a commander in chief but these were exaggerated out of all proportion and therefore produced the desired demeaning effect. The gaullistes considered Sabattier a "pompous accident of fate," doubting his capacity to gallantly carry the *croix de Lorraine* into the political arena of Chungking.

Despite the antagonism displayed by M.5, Sabattier decided to establish a headquarters in Kunming for the French forces and ordered Alessandri to take over the organization and training while he proceeded to Chungking to discuss utilization of French troops with Wedemeyer and Ho Ying Chin. Sabattier appeared confident and seemed very supportive of Allied goals, but the gaulliste faction had their eyes only on Indochina, and Sabattier's days in China were numbered.

CHAPTER 10

A "THINK TANK" SESSION

THE OSS TEAM

By the time I left Szemao on 12 May, Spaulding with a team of twenty was handling six listening posts along the frontier, much to my satisfaction. Returning to Kunming I was thinking in terms of extending our operations into the interior with the help of Sabattier's and Ho's resources, already in place.

In the meantime my staff in Kunming had been augmented by new arrivals from the United States: First Lieutenant (later Captain) Roger P. Bernique, U.S. Army; Lieutenant (later Lieutenant Commander) Carleton Swift, Jr., U.S. Navy; and several highly qualified enlisted personnel trained in French and Vietnamese. With this team and the assistance of other specialists on the OSS staff, we began a full-scale SI operation for Indochina.

Just prior to my flight back, a new Theater directive had instructed OSS to "disrupt traffic and destroy the road and railroad from Chen Nan Kuan to Hanoi." It had an unusual note of urgency:

. . . in the case of all railroads in operation, that rails be removed wherever possible and when it is not practicable to remove them . . . destroyed and bridges and tunnels destroyed. A minimum of ten-mile stretches of road and/or railroads will be rendered inoperable. Use of the line of communication will be denied the Japanese, . . . all ditches and spoil piles [will] be booby-trapped, . . . [and you will] effect the destruction of stores of Japanese supplies in or near the vicinity of Hanoi: . . . demolition teams will whenever practicable take prisoners.[1]

Helliwell and I discussed the message. It was strange—overdetailed but lacking a definition of the broad objective; and we wondered what headquarters dilettante had drafted it.

This was an SO/OG not an SI mission, but I asked Helliwell if he had any instructions for me. The "terrible tempered Colonel," as Helliwell had come to be known in some quarters, shot back, "Well, it's your area—go to it." It was absolutely the first intimation I had that my assignment ranged farther than secret intelligence. Helliwell with some acerbity announced to me that my job included the total spectrum of clandestine operations and political warfare. Helliwell said that General Donovan's instructions to Heppner had specifically stated that Whitaker and I would be responsible to him (Heppner) for Indochina operations. As I was barely getting started in SI, all this was a rather a large surprise, but Helliwell went on to assure me access and full support from all staff sections and said he would see that they cooperated.

The next day Heppner, Whitaker, and Quentin Roosevelt[2] came in from Chungking for a short stay. They joined Helliwell, Duncan Lee, and me in a rare feast—a specially prepared Chinese dinner of many courses —and we sat over Chinese vodka and British scotch long into the night. Frequent visits among our small and trusted circle served as our only means of secure and candid exchange of information and views on American policy and operations and reenforced our working relationships with a personal rapport.

Heppner had a cool head and we learned to rely with confidence on his solid judgment. He was diplomatic and strongly supportive of his staff but could be tough when necessary. Being in the full confidence of General Donovan and privy to White House discussions, he was dealing constantly with the most delicate problems with the Chinese leaders, but he never assumed an overburdened air of being too weary to hear or consider our problems; quite the contrary, he was always cheerful and available.

Whitaker had been assigned by Donovan to establish himself in French circles in Chungking in order to keep Washington informed of French plans. To his assignment he brought the advantages of having spent twenty years in Europe as an American writer and journalist. He had friends all over Europe, especially among the French, and he had urbanity, an outgoing personality, and an understanding in depth of European politics. He had been on the scene as a journalist at the decline and death of the League of Nations, had traveled to Moscow in search of the "truth" and come away disillusioned, and had covered as war correspondent the full cycle from Ethiopia to Spain and from the Hitler purge of 1934 to the Vienna putsch. He felt a deep personal commitment to the war against Germany and Japan and hoped the United Nations would eventually overcome the weaknesses which had destroyed the old League.

Helliwell was a decisive person and suffered like a man in pain when policy decisions delayed his plans and operations. He had a low boiling point, but his occasional angry outbursts spent themselves in high temper; he was not one to indulge in pettiness or grudges. When the air cleared, he was still pushing every operation, giving support and encouragement, driving all about him, but driving himself hardest.

Quentin Roosevelt was a grandson of President Theodore Roosevelt. He was doubtlessly named for his uncle killed in World War I. He was twenty-five or so at the time and was commonly called "Q" by his friends. He seemed very much at ease in a Chinese environment and had some facility in the language. His father, Theodore Roosevelt, Jr., was an old and intimate friend of Generalissimo and Mme. Chiang. Very important to us were his insights into the thinking of Chiang's advisers, but he was also good company and a fine raconteur.

Duncan Lee was a sinologist, born in China of missionary parents and fluent in Chinese, including some degree of literacy in the language. In civilian life he was an attorney, as were some of the others, and was also an Oxford graduate. Lee had already served as Chief of the Far East Branch of OSS in Washington, where I first met him, and his background was very helpful to us. He, too, was well liked and easy to get on with.

CARBONADO

The big news of the evening was top secret from Heppner. Wedemeyer (just back from Washington) was preparing the first major Allied offensive in China, code-named CARBONADO. It was to be an overland drive, along the Kweilin-Luichow-Nanning line, to secure the Canton-Hong Kong area, thus opening major seaports in southern China to receive the armies from Europe and the Philippines. The target date for starting the operation was only three and a half months away, 1 September, with a final assault by 1 November.

As a prelude to CARBONADO, Wedemeyer wanted to open the small seaport of Fort Bayard (Chanchiang) located on the Luichow Peninsula (Leichou Pantao), about 250 miles southwest of Canton, as a forward supply base to sustain the CARBONADO drive.

Heppner underscored the importance of our OSS operations, for Wedemeyer and his staff depended on us to provide the bulk of intelligence and harassment of the Japanese in the area of the projected drive. General McClure[3] had also asked OSS to spearhead the operation with guerrilla (SO), sabotage (OG), and morale (MO) activities. It was partic-

ularly important to prevent Japanese troops in Indochina from reenforc-
ing their positions lying within the CARBONADO area of operations. This, of
course, explained the peculiarities of the directive which Helliwell and I
had sneered at. Whitaker said that the Hanoi-Chen Nan Kuan sector
would be my "baby" and that the Chen Nan Kuan-Nanning line would be
cut by the U.S. Navy Group.

Still addressing me, Whitaker said he had met with Generals Pechkov and Sabattier in Chungking and was impressed with their offer to
help us and asked my opinion. Helliwell grimaced, I noticed, as Heppner
and Lee sat back with serious faces and Q put on a beatific smile. I
thought a moment and then said, "Sure, why not? As long as we have
plenty of time and logistical support and if the French do not object to
fighting in China." But I told him that from what I had seen of their condition and heard of their plans I doubted that fighting in China was high on
their list of priorities. And, moreover, my opinion was that their only objective at the moment was to get away as far as possible from the Japanese. In fact, since he was asking me, I would suggest they be sent to a
recuperation and rehabilitation center for at least six months. For a moment Whitaker maintained a stoical silence, betraying some disappointment with me. Then he asked, "How do you expect to operate in Indochina without the French?" I began to lose patience and, with everyone
else remaining so silent, said, "Look here, John are you serious? Have you
seen the evacuees? Why, these troops haven't seen a modern
weapon or learned new tactics since 1940. They are still living in World
War I." Whitaker couldn't hold his pose any longer. They all broke up in
howls of laughter at my expense as I discovered I was the butt of
Whitaker's little joke—he had been pulling my leg the whole time. It took
me a moment to unruffle my feathers.

When their hoots and guffaws finally subsided, Q told us that Pechkov had been a serious problem to General Ho Ying-chin, demanding all
sorts of supplies and transportation and wanting to equip "four thousand
Fighting French" to fight the Japanese in Indochina. M. Jean Daridan,
Chargé d'Affaires of the French Embassy in China, had made persistent
requests of the American Embassy staff to use their influence with the
Generalissimo toward the organization of French clandestine operations
for Indochina. General Chen Cheng, the Chinese Minister of War, had
twice refused to see either Pechkov or Sabattier when the subject for discussion had been the utilization of French forces in China. He had referred them politely to General Ho.

Heppner speculated on the number of troops Sabattier could, in fact,
muster. He had heard different figures, all the way from one to six thousand. However many, his opinion was that they could best be used as support troops in the rear areas with the Services of Supply (SOS).[4]
Whitaker thought a few could be used in intelligence work, provided OSS
retained control of operations. Helliwell suggested that if Sabattier could

raise several hundred willing and able men they could be used in guerrilla and sabotage operations. Obviously there was a role for some French troops in Allied plans if they were willing to accept Allied direction and control.

Taking my cue from Whitaker and Helliwell, I proposed approaching M.5 in Kunming to arrange for the selection and training of a small contingent for SI, SO, and OG operations. Heppner said no. Instead he asked me to develop a plan which he and Whitaker could take up with Sabattier in Chungking. Wedemeyer and Donovan were very sensitive about dealing with the French and it would be better, he said, to handle it at Theater and Embassy levels initially. McClure was already discussing with General Sabattier the possible use of a limited number of French troops in conjunction with the Chinese in northeastern China.

Whitaker agreed that we in Kunming should not get involved until the air had cleared in Chungking, especially in view of the bickering between the gaullistes in M.5 and the French General Staff (l'État Major) in Chungking. He, too, had become aware of personality clashes between Sabattier, Alessandri, and Pechkov. The latter two, both Legionnaire officers, were in collaboration with the gaullistes of SLFEO/Calcutta in a campaign to have Sabattier recalled to France, he said.

I raised the question of the Vietnamese, describing my recent contacts, and said I favored using that untapped reserve. The first reaction among our Chungking visitors was negative. Whitaker and Roosevelt both felt the French and Chinese would take umbrage at our working with the Vietnamese communists. Heppner foresaw the same problem but thought we still had no alternative for the moment and he could see no harm in it as long as we stayed out of politics and operated quietly, maintaining a low profile. Lee and Helliwell were in favor of using Ho Chi Minh's people, but very cautiously. With an air of skepticism, Lee wondered how we proposed to keep Tai Li from finding out. I said, "Leave it to me," and Whitaker backed me up and told them I had succeeded in Italy in working simultaneously with the communists, monarchists, and fascists without their finding out about the concurrent operations.

The conversation shifted to events in Chungking. Whitaker told us that six weeks before the Japanese coup Colonel Jacques Guillermag[5] had personally informed Wedemeyer that the Japanese were acting tough in Indochina and that as a consequence the French anticipated being disarmed and shorn of power. Still, when it happened, the French had expressed surprise and called for American help. After the coup Pechkov made preposterous claims regarding the nonexistent resistance movement and attempted to place the blame for the debacle on the United States, just as Vichy and Catroux had done in 1940. Their lack of foresight and determination to resist left Japan in undisputed strategic control of Southeast Asia and exposed China's soft underbelly. Both the Generalissimo and Wedemeyer were sorely disappointed with the French.

DE GAULLE AND THE RUSSIAN ORBIT

Three days after the coup the French Ambassador in Washington, Henri Bonnet, had painted for our Secretary of State a glowing picture of French resistance in Indochina and the "large number of native partisans." He had asked American support for the French *maquisards* (underground resistance fighters), for the formation of a joint civil affairs organization, and for accreditation of General Blaizot to General Wedemeyer for liaison purposes. Bonnet was told that there were no maquisards in Indochina, that plans for civil affairs were premature, and that Wedemeyer, when queried, had replied that he did not at the time need a French officer on his staff.

Whitaker had also learned that heavy pressure was still being applied. General de Gaulle had told our ambassador, Jefferson Caffery, in Paris that the French in Indochina were putting up a "real fight" but had been denied aid by both the Americans and the British. De Gaulle's information was that the Americans were under instructions not to give any aid and the British were following the American lead. De Gaulle had said he did not understand American policy. What were we trying to do, drive France into the Russian orbit? France did not want to become communist, but if our policy did not change he feared it would, even though against his will.

Ten days after the coup, as the French were beginning to cross the China border, Bonnet was still trying to convince the White House and the State Department that maquisards were "valiantly holding out in Indochina," that only lack of American aid was keeping them from making a good showing. Whitaker told us that we had sent hundreds of tons to the French during their retreat, only to have the Japanese pick them up. I could not help remarking that to see the destitute condition of the French troops one could hardly believe that we had dropped any supplies to them at all.

Heppner warned us then that we would be hearing rumors from French sources that American policy on Indochina had been modified, that our Secretary of State in private conversations with high French officials at the UN San Francisco Conference had said that the United States had never questioned French sovereignty over Indochina. Heppner said he had checked it out with Hurley and Wedemeyer and that American policy remained unchanged. Turning to me, he said, "Your instructions from Donovan still stand. We do not collaborate in any way with French reentry plans. In other words, until you hear differently from 109,* carry on as agreed." Whitaker added that when and if the policy were changed, 109 would change my assignment to stateside.

Interspersed with these discussions on Indochina were conversa-

---

*General Donovan's code name.

tions about other issues, including the Chinese Communist-OSS operation in Yenan, Helliwell's special project ("Eagle") for the penetration of Korea, and the SEAC-OSS project in southern Indochina and Thailand. The meeting broke up very late.

HO'S FIRST REPORT

I had received an interesting intelligence report from Ho Chi Minh, together with two political pamphlets for the American delegation at the UN Conference. I showed the pamphlets to Whitaker who decided to pass them along to the American Embassy. One was addressed to the leadership of America, China, Great Britain, and the Soviet Union and the other was an open letter to the UN.[6] Both appealed for support for Vietnamese independence.

These documents were authored by the "National Party of Indo-China (Annam)." The name connoted Kuomintang affiliation, but it was my opinion that its real origin was the Viet Minh. The National Party of Indo-China was one of a group of five parties that merged into the Dong Minh Hoi in 1942 but later formed La Ligue de l'Independance de l'Indochine. As they came from Ho I had no doubt he was using the old name so as not to reveal the true identity of the Viet Minh. Even in the English versions, his party line came through loud and clear.

The intelligence report which accompanied the pamphlets consisted of several typed pages laced with anecdotes of cordial French-Japanese relations and Vietnamese shrewdness in deceiving both, all of which we discounted as politically motivated. However, it also gave useful information identifying some units of the Japanese 37th Division, their location only a few days earlier, and the names of some senior officers. For a starter it was not bad, and our Order of Battle Section confirmed part of it and tentatively accepted the remainder. I was pleased and Whitaker was impressed.

Several days later I received by courier a second report from Ho with more military information, this time giving details of new Japanese construction and improvements to existing French-built defenses in the Cao Bang sector and on the road to Hanoi. The identification for the first time of units of the 38th Japanese Army and particularly elements of the 22d Division in the Cao Bang border area aroused considerable interest in our Order of Battle Section and at Theater level.

Ho had attached a short handwritten note in English asking if his two political documents had been of sufficient interest to forward to San Francisco. I told the bearer who awaited an answer that they had been sent to the proper authorities at Chungking but I could not be sure they would reach the delegation at San Francisco. As far as I can determine this was Ho's first attempt to bring his cause to the attention of the United Nations. It was, of course, to be thirty-two years before an independent Vietnamese government would be admitted to membership.

CHAPTER 11

THE RELUCTANT
ALLY

EURO-ASIATIC CONFLICT

I n retrospect one thing about what was going on in Asia stands out above all others: the view of postwar Asia differed widely among the Allies, depending on national interests. America's goal simplistically stated was to defeat Japan and, with some reservation, restore the status quo ante in the Far East. Our staunchest ally, Britain, was concerned mainly with preserving its empire intact. France's ambition was to regain her "rightful" position among the great powers by reclaiming her lost colonies. Chiang's China faced the dual task of resolving its conflict with the Japanese invader and securing its Nationalist regime from Mao's communist threat.

In the midst of that Euro-Asiatic conflict a third-world interest emerged to unbalance the status quo. The Vietnamese, kindled by the lofty declarations of the Atlantic Charter which promised that the Allies would "respect the right of all peoples to choose the form of government under which they will live," sensed the coming of a new era for them and they entered the fray.

This multiplicity of goals made coordination of Allied plans extremely difficult and sometimes chaotic—each national group mistrusting the others and each intranational group competing with its opposition party as adversaries. The subtleties of the struggle seemed endless.

The Americans in China, though few in number, were the only ones truly concerned with putting an end to the war with Japan. Our military advisers with the Chinese troops had to exert the full force of their leadership to convince the Chinese commanders to stay and fight. Chennault depended largely on his American flyers to hold the Japanese ground forces in check. And the massive American Lend-Lease supplies ferried in American planes over the Hump and in American trucks over the Burma Road kept China from collapsing under Japanese force. Neither the British nor the French contributed materially to the war effort in China.

In the field of clandestine operations and unorthodox warfare only the American OSS had an active and effective program. Within the context of my operation in Indochina, during the period of May to August 1945 we succeeded in setting up five major and twelve satellite clandestine nets, from which we gathered intelligence, conducted raids on key enemy installations, and carried out numerous acts of sabotage within the Japanese lines of communications.

This was accomplished in the end with very little assistance from our French, British, and Chinese allies, and in spite of their repeated attempts to subvert American efforts. The French particularly, with their overriding desire for an early reoccupation of their colony, withheld critical political and military intelligence. They appropriated to themselves arms and supplies intended for Allied operations and wherever they could obstructed American attempts to function within Indochina.

During the final months of the war, and continuing up to the present era, some of the French most deeply involved in impeding the war effort against Japan loudly proclaimed themselves mistreated, abused, neglected, and the victims of "conspiracy"—quite in line with their studied policy of injured righteousness.

A QUID PRO QUO ARRANGEMENT

The 10 May directive made it imperative that OSS get on with the job of disrupting the Japanese corridor from Hanoi to Nanning, in preparation for CARBONADO. It entailed the use of demolition teams and guerrilla units with some familiarity with the area and a working knowledge of Vietnamese or French. Wampler had a number of new arrivals from Europe trained in SO and OG operations but only a few spoke French. While Heppner and Whitaker approached Generals Sabattier and Pechkov in Chungking, I contacted the M.5 group in Kunming.

After my initial call in late April, I had been preoccupied with other pressing matters and had made no further attempt at personal contact, nor had my visit been returned. However, Bernique and Ettinger had established unofficial, but friendly, relations with the group and had learned that Lieutenant Commander Flichy[1] had been replaced as Chief of M.5 by a Major Jean Sainteny.[2]

I called on 18 May and was received by Sainteny and members of his staff. The major was a pleasant man in his early thirties, very earnest, reserved, and not totally at ease. He explained away his own omissions by referring to the pressure of his new duties which had prevented him from meeting me sooner. Since his arrival a month before he had been reorganizing the "Mission" and was looking forward, he said, to working with OSS. He asked Flichy to describe to me the role of M.5, and for the first time I learned officially that his predecessors[3] had established a respectable network of intelligence units along the China border and a small naval patrol in the northern sector of the Gulf of Tonkin. The meeting went well and we agreed to collaborate in the immediate future.

During our meeting Sainteny mentioned that he and Lieutenant Colonel Wichtrich of AGAS were working on a joint project having to do with rescue operations in the Pakhoi area.[4] He would be flying down in a few days and suggested that I might want to send along one of my French-speaking officers to survey the area for future joint operations. I thanked him and agreed to let him know. In the meantime we designated liaison officers[5] for day-to-day operations.

I advised Whitaker that M.5 was agreeable to joint ventures with OSS on a quid pro quo basis but suspected they wanted more. On the surface Sainteny had been frank in asking for American arms, equipment, and transportation in exchange for French-Annamite manpower, but underneath I detected that he hoped for exclusive recognition as the sole French agency in charge of clandestine operations in the China Theater. This implied M.5 independence from Sabattier and Pechkov, and direction and control of M.5 from SLFEO/Calcutta. I emphasized that this was my first impression and we would need to explore Sainteny's intent further. However, if my suspicions proved correct, we could anticipate problems.

TRIAL RUN

Awaiting word from Chungking to proceed with M.5, I moved out unilaterally on two Theater-directed operations. One was interrupting the rail line and road from Chen Nan Kuan to Hanoi; the other was a coast-watch patrol at the seaports of Haiphong and Fort Bayard. The first entailed only the time it would take for Major Gerald W. Davis's[6] men to walk into Indochina and do the job. The coastal watch, however, required navy-trained men and a small fleet of junks and sampans. With time I could procure them, but Wedemeyer was impatient for quick results and the only adequate naval craft in the area were those of the French, but I had no authority to use them. I kept thinking of the AGAS project with M.5 and its "naval fleet" in the Pakhoi area.

Bending the rules somewhat, I rationalized that as AGAS was authorized to cooperate with the French there was no reason why I could not work with AGAS and jointly use the French naval craft. In discussing the idea with Wichtrich we agreed that I would provide AGAS with OSS radio facilities for rescue operations in exchange for Japanese shipping information obtained by OSS-AGAS personnel through the facilities of the French naval units.

While I was negotiating with AGAS, I received word[7] from Chungking that Sabattier and Chiang Kai-shek had entered into an understanding that "all regular French troops fighting against the Japanese in French Indo-China are placed under the command of the Generalissimo," that Sabattier was recognized as the "supreme French commander" of *those* troops, and that General Alessandri had been designated "local French commander." It was an odd arrangement. All French resistance against the Japanese in Indochina had long since been suppressed, so Alessandri actually became commander of all *effective* French forces in China. What, then, was Sabattier commanding? Was it a quiet way of easing Sabattier out of the chain of command and giving Alessandri full operational control of the only French troops not in Japanese prisons? We found this new twist confusing and troublesome in our relations with the FMM, DGER, SLFEO, and M.5.

On 24 May, with still no word from Heppner on the use of French troops, we received a radio message from Major Davis that a sizeable contingent of French troops had arrived unannounced at Poseh under the command of a Major Revol who indicated that they were to be equipped and trained by the OSS for operations in Indochina.

Finally, on the twenty-sixth, Heppner notified us that he had concluded a tentative agreement[8] with the SLFEO. Again I called on Sainteny to work out details and, again, the reception was warm and friendly. The first sour note was struck by Sainteny when he assured me that we could work out a plan "to our mutual advantage." This remark did not sit well with me, and I answered pointedly that the only "advantage" the United States sought was to obtain Japanese intelligence and to conduct special operations behind their lines. Sainteny, of course, acquiesced, but his remark had put me on the qui vive.

My arrangements with AGAS now coincided with headquarters' approval to work with M.5, and I was at liberty to deal also with Sainteny on the Pakhoi project. Earlier in the month I had reassigned Ambelang to Maoming[9] to carry out coast-watching activities in connection with the Fort Bayard operation. On the twenty-seventh I sent Ettinger to Pakhoi to join Lieutenant James W. Jordan.[10] With Ettinger and Jordan at Pakhoi and Ambelang at Maoming, I had decided to establish a base station in the area and suggested to Sainteny that with the ongoing OSS-AGAS project and with his help we could jointly extend the operation to obtain maximum results in minimum time. He agreed and offered to work out a plan.

By 30 May Project PAKHOI was in operation. The French minifleet of two patrol boats, the *Crayssac* and the *Frézouls,* supported by several motor-junks, all manned by French crews, began to transmit (with OSS radios) valuable Japanese shipping information and assisted our naval coastal team in taking soundings along the Fort Bayard inlets and Mandarin Bay. Ettinger, Ambelang, and Jordan with the help of French agents provided by M.5 did splendid work, not only in reporting Japanese troop dispositions and naval operations (particularly from the Fort Bayard-Haiphong area) but also obtained some information from the interior of Indochina.

THE FRENCH STAGE A SIT-DOWN STRIKE

The day after Project PAKHOI was launched we concluded with the French in Chungking a second agreement for the use of one hundred Vietnamese troops and ten or twelve European French officers. Sabattier and Pechkov agreed that OSS would have full control of this group and the intelligence gathered would be shared. We worked out a plan to train the unit at Ch'ing-Hsi. Wampler selected Captain (later Major) Charles M. Holland and Major Allison K. Thomas to head two teams code-named, respectively, "Cat" and "Deer." We advised Davis at Poseh and asked him to send Holland and Thomas to Ch'ing-Hsi to receive the French, due on 12 June to begin training.

The new French group[11] arrived on schedule but refused to undergo training as agreed in Chungking. The senior French officer, a Major Courthlac, demanded that OSS pay his troops and also provide funds for their rations. This was not part of the agreement. The French should have drawn their rations from the Chinese SOS prior to their departure, the normal procedure, and the pay of French troops was the responsibility of the French government in Chungking. Major Thomas had no funds to satisfy the French demands and so advised Major Courthlac, whereupon the French staged a sit-down strike pending instructions from M.5. So from the fourth to the seventeenth of June the training program at Ch'ing-Hsi had come to a full stop.

The next clinker came to light on the morning of 12 June when Heppner received an undated letter from Sainteny, signed by Flichy, indicating that Sabattier had directed M.5 to take charge of a guerrilla operation in collaboration with American units. "In view of the preponderance of French forces" and the risk involved, Sainteny wanted to know the purpose of the operation, the orders issued to the Americans, and what had been accomplished thus far. Until he received an answer to his questions, Sainteny wrote, he had ordered the Chief of the French detachment to suspend operations. Heppner took immediate issue with Sainteny's order as a unilateral and arbitrary action and a breach of the Sabattier-Heppner agreement of 31 May and so informed General Wedemeyer. Obviously there was a breakdown in communications between the gaulliste M.5 in Kunming and "l'État Major" in Chungking. The question for us was, with whom among the French were we to deal?

The third phase of what was becoming a minor revolt on the part of the French came on 14 June when the entire PAKHOI communications net fell silent. I learned soon enough through Jordan that the French had ordered the flow of intelligence to the Americans stopped under threat of "court martial."

With every French-American operation at a standstill and the Americans in a mood of extreme exasperation, Brigadier General Douglas L. Weart[12] called a meeting in Kunming on 15 June[13] to straighten things out and in particular to have Sainteny's letter withdrawn and operations resumed under OSS control. Weart opened the meeting by reminding Alessandri that the French military were under the operational and supply control of General Ho Ying-chin and the OSS and that the use of French troops had been authorized at Theater level. Weart said he could not understand where M.5 entered the picture, noting for General Alessandri that "General Ho's operational control does not recognize the French Military Mission as a channel; all contacts are directly and solely with General Sabattier . . ."[14] General Alessandri apologetically explained that M.5 had acted in ignorance of the agreement between Wedemeyer and Sabattier and that Sainteny's letter would be withdrawn. The French detachment at Ch'ing-Hsi would be ordered to resume operations under the control of OSS. And so it was that on the seventeenth everything returned to normal, or so we thought.

SAINTENY'S M.5

At the Weart-Alessandri meeting Flichy had tried to stress the role of M.5 in clandestine operations, but he had been overruled and Sainteny was not happy. The day after the meeting Sainteny asked me to stop in at the French villa; he wanted to clear up several misunderstandings. He felt that I should know that SLFEO/Calcutta had charged M.5 with full responsibility for clandestine operations in the China Theater; and he, as Chief of M.5, had been authorized to deal directly with OSS. As for manpower, he had been delegated by Calcutta to use Sabattier's troops to complement DGER specialists then on their way from France and India. Regarding the question of command and control of M.5 in Kunming, Sainteny emphasized that he would accept only the instructions and directions of General Passy[15] in Paris and Colonel Roos[16] in Calcutta, who were answerable only to General de Gaulle.

I asked where the French Military Mission in Chungking fitted in, and Sainteny made it quite clear that General Pechkov did not enter the DGER picture at all. He was under instructions of the Ministry of Foreign Affairs, while the DGER operated under de Gaulle's personal directives.

Quite unintentionally Sainteny revealed to me that SLFEO/Calcutta had made certain definite agreements with British SOE to operate in Indochina. These agreements were to continue even after an OSS-DGER agreement had been concluded. They were to be separate and distinct: French-British, French-American. I commented that to me the arrangement smacked of opportunism and apparently was aimed at getting the maximum return from two separate parties. Sainteny replied that the British had contributed considerable material in terms of arms and transportation to the French cause in Indochina, adding, "Yes, we are opportunists in this case—it is toward the same end, isn't it?" I was about to reply that I thought not, but Sainteny continued that the British had offered help long before the Americans and had several teams in the field which were producing good results and he did not wish to discontinue their operations.

I then posed the question of Theater jurisdiction. The French in China were, after all, under the Generalissimo's command and Indochina fell in the China Theater of Operations. But Sainteny threw up his hands in a gesture of not wanting to be bothered with all that and said we could not ratify the ABCD agreement at our level, which led me to suggest that perhaps he should take the matter up with the Chief of Staff and Colonel Heppner. We were at an impasse and tabled the questions of jurisdiction for future discussions.

The British-French operations from SEAC gave me much concern. I was not sure how they could be integrated in my overall plan. Sainteny said he did not have many details but assured me the product of those teams would be shared with M.5 which, in turn, would pass it on to Sabattier who could then relay it to the "usual intelligence channels." Because I knew of the secret French prohibition imposed on the British not to release information to the Americans, I was more than skeptical. Without divulging my knowledge of the secret prohibition, I called Sainteny's attention to the agreement between Chiang Kai-shek and Sabattier that the only channel for the French in the China Theater for dissemination of intelligence was through OSS, who would pass it to Sabattier. To this Sainteny replied, "All right, then I'll pass it on to you, but on condition that it not be delayed through the usual bureaucratic procedures as was the case in Europe." Accepting his easy answer with considerable uneasiness, I assured him there would be no delays. And, of course, my concerns were justified: we never received such information at all.

We moved on to the final issue, his plan for operations. Sainteny said he would have it ready on 18 June. In parting, he asked if it were possible to be informed on Theater plans for Indochina, with specific reference to anticipated landings. I suggested he discuss that with Heppner.

M.5 GETS OFFICIAL STATUS

The plan Sainteny produced on the eighteenth was an extensive one for land and sea operations. It involved some one thousand French-Vietnamese officers and men, all to be armed and equipped by OSS. Helliwell and I were perhaps overimpressed and recommended that Heppner accept the plan with conditions: that the units be placed under OSS's control; that a senior American officer be in command of each unit; that only

OSS's radio codes be used; and that each unit operate only in OSS-sponsored missions against Japanese objectives.

To each condition Sainteny and Flichy objected. Sainteny said he could not in good conscience ask French officers to serve under the command of non-French officers, even if they were allies. Heppner observed that it was not an unusual procedure; after all were we not under the command of the Generalissimo in the China Theater? We had come to a standoff. So as not to waste more time, the target date for CARBONADO being upon us, I suggested we work one project at a time and resolve the question of command on the basis of objective and availability of qualified officers for each project. Reluctantly Sainteny agreed, but he wanted to arm and equip all the one thousand troops right away. Heppner held on that point. Each unit would be provided what it needed when it was actually committed to an OSS-approved mission.

Sainteny did raise the question of projected Allied landings and asked if he would be informed on what was being planned. Heppner told him that Sabattier would have the information when General Ho Ying-chin made it available.

It had been another thoroughly unsatisfactory meeting. The French felt rebuffed and we Americans came away with a clear sense of the ambiguity of the French position. Helliwell and I, along with Heppner, knew that Sainteny was not being candid. Too much was left unsaid and too many questions went unanswered.

During the next four weeks we spent a lot of time meeting, consulting, conferring, and discussing, without reaching an operable arrangement. Meanwhile the French were thrashing about the southern coast of China in aimless confusion. Our base at Pakhoi reported that a French commando unit was being organized and trained in the area, for what operations we knew not. M.5 was cluttering the intelligence systems of the Fourteenth Air Force, AGAS, the Chinese Combat Command (CCC), and OSS with a shower of unconfirmed reports of Japanese troop dispositions and movements.[17] When the Theater planning staff inquired of OSS as to the authenticity of these reports, we of course could not substantiate them nor vouch for their reliability because we were not being consulted by M.5.

The local Chinese papers in Kunming published a report, attributed to the French Military Mission, that a French unit in China had "invaded and captured" the Chinese island of Weichow.[18] The incident is hardly worthy of note, except that General Ho Ying-chin and Theater Headquarters flared up at the unauthorized French action. As the story was later unraveled, the Japanese in a planned withdrawal to mainland China had abandoned the island. M.5 on learning the Japanese had left Weichow ordered their patrol boats* to take it with a small French detachment. Sainteny proudly sent a message to General Chennault announcing

---

*The Frézouls and the Crayssac

"the destruction of the Japanese airfield and capture of the island in the name of the Allies." Several days later Sainteny was ordered by the Chinese high command to get off the island and to cease and desist from future unauthorized operations which greatly jeopardized Theater plans.

While still extricating M.5 from the ridiculous Weichow escapade, Sainteny sent word with Lieutenant Fauchier-Magnon that he was preparing a team to "occupy" Nightingale Island[19] with an intelligence unit and a radio to be provided by AGAS. General Wedemeyer himself called a halt to these plans.

I interpreted these juvenile melodramatics as Sainteny's way of attracting attention because the DGER and, in particular, Sainteny's M.5 were still not recognized at the China Theater level.

Completely disenchanted with French performance, I advised Heppner to consider dropping DGER's questionable support. The problem as a whole was the subject of a conference in Chungking on 29 June between General Paul W. Caraway,[20] Colonel Joseph Dickey,[21] Heppner, Whitaker, Helliwell, and myself. I outlined the OSS-DGER (M.5) arrangements, accomplishments, and failures. I conceded that the French had a tremendous potential for clandestine operations provided we accepted the DGER as a coequal agency in the Theater and made them privy to Theater plans. However I cautioned that, if we followed that route, General Sabattier's role as commander-in-chief would have to be subordinated to the authority of the DGER and we would lose control over French operations in the Theater.

Dickey and Whitaker agreed with my evaluation and observed that General Alessandri had met in Kunming with General Gross on the twenty-second and with Major General Ray T. Maddocks[22] on the twenty-seventh to reach an agreement on exactly those points—recognition for the DGER and Sabattier's role in clandestine operations. General Caraway remarked that, although this was strictly a French matter, we had a moral and legal responsibility to support the duly appointed commander, Sabattier.

Heppner, formerly a key staff member of Lord Mountbatten's headquarters, pointed out that official recognition of the DGER implied that SLFEO under SEAC would be permitted to operate in the China Theater; this was a serious jurisdictional matter requiring the Generalissimo's consent. Heppner also noted that the French were not the only source of trouble in the China Theater. He had on his desk several reports that the British Army Aid Group (BAAG) under Colonel Ride was operating in the Hong Kong–Canton area, arming Chinese guerrillas for the purpose of being ready to control Hong Kong in the event of an Allied landing. Both the French and British operations in the China Theater were without the Generalissimo's consent and could therefore have had serious repercussions for OSS operations. Heppner had advised General Wedemeyer on the BAAG activities, and he had called it to the attention of Major General E. C. K. Hayes, General Officer Commanding, British Troops, China.

Hayes promised to investigate the matter and furnish a full report. (Seven weeks later as the war ended, General Hayes still had not done so.)

We concluded that a firm stand had to be taken. Nevertheless, the French presence in China could not be ignored, despite political and logistical problems, and should be put to use. General Caraway observed that Wedemeyer had advised General Marshall "that as soon as these [French] forces are physically fit they will be used as airfield guards, border patrols, intelligence agents, and SOS troops."[23] We were therefore committed to making a concerted effort to employ them to some useful purpose. Thus far they had been used in all the areas indicated except intelligence. Perhaps, if we stretched a point or two, M.5 could be induced to accept a modicum of supervision. General Caraway would take the matter up with General Maddocks, and I was to prepare for Heppner a memorandum for the record specifying French violations of the 6 June DGER-OSS agreement.

Out of these considerations, a new operating agreement with the French was drawn up on 5 July between General Weart and General Alessandri.[24] Everyone present expressed understanding and satisfaction with the main points:

A weekly report was to be made to General Wedemeyer of all DGER operations in the China Theater.

M.5 was to secure intelligence gained by India-based DGER and pass it to Wedemeyer.

DGER was to receive its instructions directly from Paris and/or the Ministry of Colonies, not necessarily through Sabattier.

DGER was recognized as the French intelligence agency for Indochina interested in knowing the what, where, and why of all clandestine operations involving French personnel.

Any objections raised by DGER to specific intelligence operations were subject to being overruled by Sabattier.

In planning or directing intelligence operations for Indochina, OSS was to deal through normal French command channels, specifically, for intelligence operations through DGER and for military operations through Sabattier.

We had stretched a point or two in officially recognizing DGER as an arm of the Paris government and granting it a degree of autonomy, but we had not relinquished supervisory control nor surrendered Sabattier's role as the final authority. When I asked Sainteny what he thought of the new agreement, he gruffly remarked, "What is new?"

A CASE OF LEGERDEMAIN

During our weeks of agreements and disagreements I had been urging M.5 to get on with a project called COMORE.[25] It was a part of the preparation for CARBONADO to augment our information on how much the Japanese knew of U.S.-China plans, what forces were concentrated in the Hanoi-Haiphong area and in the Lang Son-Lao Cai corridor, which airfields and seaports showed unusual activity, and what troop movements were in progress.

I had assigned the mission to an ex-Jedburgh,[26] Captain Lucien E. Conein, an expert in demolition and guerrilla tactics, fluent in French, trustworthy, and not entirely in accord with French politics regarding Indochina. The team had about one hundred French-Vietnamese troops and five American officers and men. COMORE went off well in simultaneous raids on several Japanese installations in operations which began on the night of 28–29 July and continued through 8 August, suffering only one casualty. Despite strong Japanese opposition, COMORE personnel set fires and destroyed fuel and ammunition dumps, a battalion headquarters, and several barracks. They brought back two Japanese prisoners (one an officer) for interrogation and a quantity of documents, as many as they could carry.

The success of COMORE would have been a measure of reassurance as to the outlook for collaborating with the French had it not been for new difficulties developing simultaneously during the same period. Very much to my surprise while Sainteny was en route to Paris I received from M.5 on 20 July an entirely new plan code-named MAROC, a naval operation for gathering intelligence from mainland China and off-shore areas. It called for a number of subordinate units involving an undetermined number of French troops—anywhere from several hundred to several thousand. MAROC, according to the French, was to be serviced by an OSS base radio station, to which subordinate units would forward their information in OSS codes. "The existing French communications net is to be used exclusively for emergency traffic." The plan seemed feasible on the surface, except for the number of French troops to be armed and equipped by OSS.

A close examination of the MAROC plan, however, revealed that its command post was to be in the French Consulate at Pakhoi, manned by French personnel exclusively. Crews of its two junks (*Bluebird* and *Vieux Charles*) were to be under the command of French officers. In addition, two subunits (*Oise* and *Bach Long Vi*), also under French control, would be in liaison with the Chinese and AGAS. OSS personnel would participate *only* with the full concurrence of the French commander. Lieutenant Jordan, then at Pakhoi, was to be detailed to MAROC to receive airdrops of American supplies to be allocated by the French.

I was incensed. It was obvious that OSS was expected to fund and provide arms for operations which lacked any element of American control. At that point I frankly was tired of M.5's "cooperation" and intrigues and immediately demanded from M.5 clarification of the question of command and control. Copies of my letter went to Heppner and Helliwell with the notation, "Unless these changes are made, OSS's control over FIC activities will be reduced to a nullity, and we will become largely a supply service for independent DGER activities." The abrupt end of the war fortunately saved me from all but one of the aggravations and contentions which the MAROC plan would undoubtedly have engendered.

French troops in the field were suffering neglect during the protracted period of differences and negotiations. At K'ai-yuan, Poseh, Ch'ing-Hsi, and other areas of French concentration they were badly in need of clothing, shoes, medicines, and other personal items. The question of training and using these troops in OSS operations was contingent on their being armed and equipped by Theater. As we equipped a unit for a specific mission, a large portion of the unit's personnel would be transferred out of OSS control and a new group of derelict troops would replace them. It was understandable that this simple ruse would clothe many more men, but the training program naturally went forward but slowly. A much more serious aspect of this ruse was not so simple when we became aware that supplies such as weapons and radios were not always left behind during these personnel switches but were being cached for future French operations for the reconquest of Indochina. I gave Heppner a list of supplies, all duly receipted by French officers, which were no longer with French troops assigned to OSS missions, and Heppner took the matter up with General Olmsted.[27]

Once more General Alessandri met with Generals Maddocks, Caraway, and Olmsted. Immediately taking the offensive, Alessandri asked if we had received instructions from Washington to supply the French with Lend-Lease materiel. Olmsted replied in the affirmative, that the French were eligible for such aid, but it did not mean they would start drawing American equipment at once, explaining that it took about six months to procure equipment and ship it to China. Furthermore, Olmsted could not agree with Alessandri's premise that any provisions existed to provide equipment to French troops who were not engaged in Theater-directed operations: "We have no special set-up for separate French combat forces as such."[28]

Alessandri expressed surprise at this information; he had been told all he had to do was ask. Patiently Olmsted explained that only a few items of a housekeeping nature were available. Combat equipment would have to be obtained from the United States and it generally took six months. Alessandri looked crestfallen. Six months might be too long, he said. Caraway asked how many troops Alessandri expected to have in the China Theater, to which he replied, "Five thousand." Olmsted tried to ease the blow but frankly said he knew of no way to speed up the process.

General Alessandri then proposed to buy the equipment elsewhere and fly it in with French planes. And again he had to be reminded that the airfields were already operating at peak capacity. Alessandri tried one more time: could he buy the equipment in India and buy trucks to bring it in over the Burma Road? He had to be told that the supply of gasoline for such trucks was critically limited and that many convoys waited for space on the road; and in case he was not aware of it, it would require twenty-five hundred trucks to maintain five thousand troops from resources in India.[29]

Thoroughly dejected, Alessandri reiterated that the French troops might not be able to take part in operations if equipment for them arrived too late. Maddocks diplomatically stated that he recognized what the General wanted to do. It was obvious to all that Alessandri's anxiety was not for the defeat of Japan but for being ready to secure Indochina for France. The matter of the diversion of OSS supplies was not even mentioned at the meeting, but the message came through loud and clear— French troops would only be armed and equipped for OSS-controlled and Theater-directed missions.

Alessandri tried desperately to salvage the situation by expressing his disappointment with the assignment of French troops to guard airfields and participate in SOS operations. He said he would have liked to find a way to assign them to a combat mission. General Maddocks gently suggested he take it up with General Ho Ying-chin who could make appropriate recommendations to the Generalissimo. We all knew that the French had already been offered combat assignment in the northeastern sector of China, which they had refused, ostensibly because the troops were not physically fit for combat duty. Actually the French preferred to remain conveniently close to the Indochina border rather than accept combat assignment in other parts of China.

It was about ten days later, during Sainteny's continued absence,[30] that Flichy sent to me appropriate remarks and revisions of the MAROC plan and it appeared that we might make some progress on it when the flow of information from PAKHOI again came to a sudden and abrupt halt. The lame explanation from the French was that since we were working on the MAROC plan it was pointless to have men and equipment in the same area duplicating one another's work. The rationalization was totally unconvincing. MAROC was not yet in existence and OSS was left with absolutely nothing coming in from PAKHOI. That is where the OSS-M.5 "collaboration," already failing, became bankrupt.

We fortunately had other intelligence resources. Three major intelligence systems were successfully launched by putting people into the field with French and Vietnamese personnel under the control of regular French officers loyal to Sabattier. We also had five special-purpose missions completely independent of the French. Altogether there were about three hundred agent-teams and guerrilla units, with an extensive communications net operating without any DGER support. We were also receiving a steady flow of reliable intelligence from Ho Chi Minh's apparatus and from individuals in various localities who were not associated with any organized intelligence network.

With the sudden end of the war only days away, my task of securing intelligence from Indochina in support of our military operations would abruptly end, but the end of the hostilities with Japan would have no effect on Sainteny's operations; his campaign was only beginning.

CHAPTER 12

"TRUSTEESHIP" REDEFINED

T he indirect Roosevelt approach to the Indochina problem, proposing that it be resolved after the war, did not in mid-1945 face up either to the fast-changing situation in Southeast Asia or to the exigencies of the war. Ad hoc directives from Washington only complicated and confused critical command decisions and exacerbated the contentious Franco-Sino-American position.

The secrecy that surrounded the Yalta Conference in February, the Japanese coup in March, and the death of Roosevelt in April on the eve of the San Francisco Conference[1] accentuated the French role in the Far East beyond its true proportions. Our war plans in China, projected into mid-1946, did not include French participation. Still, the French in early 1945 had become a factor in Allied Theater considerations. Ambassador Hurley, General Wedemeyer, and Colonel Heppner constantly queried the Departments of State and War and the OSS in Washington regarding a possible change in policy or, at least, a clarification of the existing one.

DE GAULLE PRESSURES TRUMAN

Within two weeks of Roosevelt's death, de Gaulle's government launched an intensive propaganda effort to mold world opinion in favor of the status quo in Indochina, even to the extent of suggesting without basis in fact that American policy on Indochina had changed under the new Truman administration. The propaganda barrage was opened simultaneously in China and the United States on 25 April as General (Ambassador) Pechkov set the theme in a press conference timed with the opening of the San Francisco conference:

France is fighting in the Pacific where cruises the Richelieu, one of the most powerful battleships in the world, and in Indochina where the French guerrillas harass the Japanese, preventing them from attacking Yunnan and Kwangsi. . . .

In this conflict, the Indochinese are showing themselves faithful to the cause of France. The real "trusteeship," said the Ambassador, is in our hearts. . . .[2]

There is some question as to whether the Richelieu was actually in the Pacific at the time; I can only rely on the U.S. Navy's word that during 15-30 April 1945 it was in the Indian Ocean. Allegations of "French guerrillas" harassing the Japanese in Indochina and preventing attacks on southern China are already shown to be pathetic exaggerations. The Vietnamese would soon speak for themselves.

With Roosevelt dead, French spokesmen at San Francisco found their best weapons in the 1942 statement of Sumner Welles[3] and the 1944 American plan for dependent peoples which had been presented at the Dumbarton Oaks Conference.[4] On 2 May M. Georges Bidault, French Minister of Foreign Affairs, then attending the Conference, emphatically declared to the world that the decision for Indochina's future would rest with France and France alone. He was referring to the question of trusteeship as defined at Dumbarton Oaks, and he proclaimed that the principle was applicable to certain areas but not to Indochina.

Later M. Bonnet complained to Secretary of State Stettinius that "although the French Government interprets Mr. Welles's statement of 1942 concerning the restoration of French sovereignty over the French Empire as including Indochina, the American press continues to imply that a special status will be reserved for this colonial area."[5] To avoid discord in the Conference proceedings, Stettinius assured Bidault "that the record was entirely innocent of any official statement of this government questioning, even by implication, French sovereignty over Indochina but that certain elements of American public opinion condemned French policies and practices in Indochina."[6]

Having tested the water and finding it calm, de Gaulle applied pressure on the new Washington administration from a different direction. In a personal note he asked President Truman to receive his Foreign Minister who would discuss the participation of French forces "at the side of American forces in the decisive campaign against Japan."[7]

Bidault called at the White House on 17 May. The President, after expressing his appreciation of de Gaulle's offer of assistance, told Bidault that it was his policy to leave to the Commander-in-Chief in the field (MacArthur) the determination as to whether it would be practicable and helpful to have French forces join in the operations against Japan. The President thought it would depend largely on transportation, a problem involving three times the tonnage used in the war in the Atlantic.[8]

The next day Mr. Grew and M. Bidault went over exactly the same ground, except that the Minister mentioned that there were two French divisions ready for immediate transportation to the Far East. Perhaps to reassure Grew of France's motives, Bidault quickly added that they could be utilized anywhere in the Far East and there was no intention of limiting their contribution to attacking the enemy in Indochina. Grew replied that he would place the matter before our military authorities immediately.[9]

While the French diplomatic machinery churned, the political warfare arm of the DGER in Calcutta and Chungking circulated rumors attributed to "highly placed individuals" that Washington had dropped the trusteeship concept and no longer objected to the return of the French to Indochina.

WHAT HAPPENED AT YALTA?

The China Theater was the "end-of-the-line" in the global war, and news of events in Washington, London, and Paris reached that terminus mainly by personal correspondence among knowledgeable friends. Official communications between the decision-makers in the world capitals and the military and diplomatic leaders in China generally were limited to piecemeal guidance designed to preclude individual interpretation or independent action. Basic policies laid down for General Wedemeyer and Ambassador Hurley when they were first assigned to China underwent constant metamorphosis in Washington, but the alterations became evident only after the fact. Fortunately, that situation was not unique to the Americans in China; in varying degrees the British, French, and even the Chinese policies suffered similarly.

Faced with bold French demands and conflicting rumors of policy changes, those of us directly involved in coping with the French military looked to the American Embassy for support and guidance. Ambassador Hurley was familiar with the American trusteeship plan presented at the 1944 Dumbarton Oaks Conference and was also aware that the plan had been discussed by the "Big Three" at Yalta. However, he had not been informed that the plan had been either approved or modified. Either action would have had a bearing on his relationship, and that of the military, with the French in China. He wanted the latest thinking in Washingon and he radioed Washington on 10 May, referring to Pechkov's press statement:

It would be helpful in view of the fact that the future status of that area will doubt-less be subject to increasing interest and discussion here, if the Department would telegraph me for my secret information the substance of the Yalta decisions (or any other decision on policy) in that regard. (I know the Roosevelt policy toward Indochina but seek to ascertain whether there has been any change.)[10]

Eight days later he received a terse answer:

No Yalta decision (SFAMB) relating to Indochina known to Dept. (URTEL 750, May 10) Military and political policy papers now under consideration which will be transmitted for your secret information when approved. Grew (acting).[11]

Grew's cryptic reply added to the confusion. If no decision had been reached at Yalta, why didn't the Department know it? The implication was that a decision had been reached but that the Department was unwilling to divulge it. Personal correspondence between staff members at Yalta and Chungking indicated that Indochina *had* been discussed, at the very least between Roosevelt and General Marshall, and perhaps in one form or another with Churchill and Stalin.

Several days later Hurley sent by cable a long personal message to President Truman regarding British interests and manipulations in Asia. Using explicit language he expressed the fear that Mountbatten was using American Lend-Lease supplies and other American resources to invade Indochina, with the objective of defeating what Hurley believed to be American policy and to reestablish French imperialism. He wanted the President to know that there was a growing opinion throughout Asia that America favored imperialism rather than democracy in Asia. This, he observed, was unjustified and needed correcting. He had gathered the impression from what he could learn at his remote post that the American delegation at San Francisco seemed to support the theory of imperial control of colonies and dependent nations by the separate or combined imperialist nations and not a United Nations trusteeship.

NO CHANGE, SAYS TRUMAN

Hurley's message was referred by the White House on 29 May to the State Department for an appropriate reply, which was sent eight days later[12] and which dealt both with French control in Indochina and the British desire to reoccupy Hong Kong:

. . . The President has asked me to say that there has been no basic change in the policy . . . and that the present position is as follows:

The President assumes that you are familiar with the statement made by the Secretary of State on April 3, 1945, with the approval of President Roosevelt in which Mr. Stettinius declared that as a result of the Yalta discussions the "trusteeship structure, it was felt, should be defined to permit placing under it of such of the territories taken from the enemy in this war, as might be agreed upon at a later date, and also such other territories as might voluntarily be placed under trusteeship." The position thus publicly announced has been confirmed by the conversations which are now taking place in San Francisco in regard to trusteeships.

Throughout these discussions the American delegation has insisted upon the necessity of providing for a progressive measure of self-government for all dependent peoples looking toward their eventual independence or incorporation in some form of federation according to circumstances and the ability of the peoples to assume these responsibilities. Such decisions would preclude the establishment of a trusteeship in Indochina except with the consent of the French Government. The latter seems unlikely. Nevertheless it is the President's intention at some appropriate time to ask that the French Government give some positive indication of its intentions in regard to the establishment of civil liberties and increasing measures of self-government in Indochina before formulating further declarations of policy in this respect.

The message then related the President's conversation with Bidault, already described, and outlined the criteria provided to the Joint Chiefs for the possible utilization of French forces:

(a) While avoiding so far as practicable unnecessary or long-term commitments with regard to the amount or character of any assistance which the United States may give to French resistance forces in Indochina, this Government should continue to afford such assistance as does not interfere with the requirements of other planned operations. Owing to the need for concentrating all our resources in the Pacific on operations already planned, large-scale military operations aimed directly at the liberation of Indochina cannot, however, be contemplated at this time. American troops should not be used in Indochina except in American military operations against the Japanese.

(b) French offers of military and naval assistance in the Pacific should be considered on their military merits as bearing on the objective of defeating Japan as in the case of British and Dutch proposals. There would be no objection to furnishing of assistance to any French military or naval forces so approved, regardless of the theater of operations from which the assistance may be sent, provided such assistance does not involve a diversion of resources which the Combined or Joint Chiefs of Staff consider are needed elsewhere.

Sometime in mid-June Heppner was given the opportunity to see the full text of this message and was authorized to divulge pertinent passages to selected members of his staff, of whom I was one, on a need-to-know basis.

To Heppner and me it was obvious that the Truman administration had capitulated to de Gaulle's insistence that Indochina could be placed in trusteeship only with the consent of France. Whether or not Indochina came under the trusteeship system, however, was not of great moment to the military. What mattered was the question of providing the French in China with logistical support and to what purpose. We had hoped for a more definitive statement, one that dispelled the ambiguities we were trying to cope with. The specifics for us were the political parameters within which OSS could collaborate with the French, the British, and the Vietnamese, the geographical limits of its areas of operation, and the extent of its non-paramilitary activities.

Heppner set up a conference in the hope of clarifying those points. It included Embassy representatives, Theater planners, and OSS branch chiefs.

THE BIG FOUR BECOME FIVE

According to the Embassy briefer, Roosevelt's main objective had been to secure and keep the peace through the mechanism of an international organization (UNO). He had pictured the leadership of the organization as a quadrumvirate, the principal participants in the war: America, Great Britain, the Soviet Union, and China. But after the Dumbarton Oaks and Yalta Conferences it had become apparent that Britain needed the cooperation of France in Europe, and Roosevelt had to accept a "Big Five" concept.

It may have been de Gaulle's visit to the United States in July 1944 which influenced Roosevelt. De Gaulle had promised that France would grant Indochina a degree of autonomy after the war, and he may have asked Roosevelt not to press the trusteeship idea. Roosevelt was also very aware of Churchill's aversion to tampering with the colonial structure in Southeast Asia, although Stalin and Chiang were in favor of abolishing it. (Quentin Roosevelt, as a matter of fact, had disclosed to us that as of mid-March 1945 the President may have moderated his stance but had not altogether given up the idea of trusteeship. According to "Q," Roosevelt had said that if France pledged to assume for herself the role of trustee, then he would not object to France's retaining her colonies on the understanding that total independence would be assured.)

As far as our Embassy in China was aware, according to our briefer, Indochina first became a subject of presidential messages in November 1944 when Wedemeyer reported to the President that British, Dutch, and French interests were making an intensive effort to ensure recovery of their prewar political and economic positions in the Far East. He referred to Blaizot's military mission in India which was preparing to infiltrate Indochina and asked for policy guidance because, according to his understanding, Indochina was in the China Theater. The President had instructed Hurley on 16 November 1944 to inform Wedemeyer that American policy with regard to Indochina could not be formulated until after consultation with Allies at a forthcoming Combined Staff conference and asked Hurley to keep him posted on British, French, and Dutch activities in Southeast Asia. But Hurley had no additional information to pass to the President, nor did the Joint Chiefs know what our Allies proposed to do there.

In March 1945 when both Hurley and Wedemeyer were in Washington the President told Wedemeyer that he must watch carefully to prevent British and French political activities in the area and give only such support as would be required in direct operations against the Japanese.

In a related matter the Prime Minister had cabled the President that he understood there had been occasional difficulties between Wedemeyer and Mountbatten about activities in Indochina and proposed they direct the CCS to arrange for a full and frank exchange of intentions, plans, and intelligence between the two theater commanders. Roosevelt replied on 22 March that he and Churchill should agree to let Wedemeyer coordinate all Anglo-American-Chinese operations.

Churchill did not respond until 11 April after Wedemeyer, enroute from Washington to China, stopped to see Mountbatten at SEAC headquarters. There a "misunderstood agreement" had been reached between the two commanders. Wedemeyer came away believing that SEAC would not carry out operations in Indochina until they had been approved by him as Chief of Staff to Chiang. Mountbatten's interpretation of the same agreement was that all he had to do was "inform" Wedemeyer of proposed SEAC operations in Indochina. Churchill's subsequent message to the President reflected Mountbatten's understanding. The reply made by President Truman on 14 April did not take issue with Churchill but was carefully worded to reflect Wedemeyer's understanding of the agreement.

By mid-May the two commanders had come into open disagreement when Mountbatten informed Wedemeyer he intended to fly twenty-six sorties into Indochina in support of French "guerrilla" groups. Noting that the French government had placed all such units under the command and control of Chiang, Wedemeyer asked Mountbatten what arrangements had been made to insure that the equipment would be used against the Japanese. Mountbatten had not answered the question. After a rapid exchange of messages in which Mountbatten gave neither the numbers nor the locations of the French units he intended to supply, Mountbatten had abruptly ordered his planes to carry out the sorties without waiting for consent from either Wedemeyer or Chiang. Wedemeyer had protested vigorously on 25 May to Mountbatten and had informed our Joint Chiefs. The command relationship between the two had remained strained.

With the briefing over, Heppner asked us to assess the situation in the light of our current guidance but with extreme care not to violate publicly stated American policy.

Helliwell opened the discussion with an examination of our relationships with the British, French, and Vietnamese. We all agreed that OSS need not be too concerned with American-British interaction except where it directly affected Indochina, which would have to await higher-level resolution. The French and Vietnamese were quite another matter. In the long State Department message, Acting Secretary Grew had pointedly stated that there had been no basic change in policy. Therefore, we could reasonably assume a status quo situation. OSS would simply ignore French efforts to reoccupy Indochina; it would do nothing either to assist or to deter them but, where feasible, would use French troops in clandestine operations. That would be always in conjunction with or part of Theater-coordinated plans. As for the Vietnamese, there were no restrictions provided we did not contribute to their political aspirations.

One of the conferees questioned how that could be done since it was obvious that the Vietnamese apparatus was political, anti-French, and militantly struggling for national independence. It was suggested that the use of Vietnamese individuals for Theater-coordinated clandestine activities did not constitute either political or military endorsement. That stimulated considerable discussion, with the conferees about evenly divided. Finally, one of the Theater planners contended that so long as the Vietnamese contributed to the Allied effort against the Japanese and we did not provide them with more weapons than needed for individual protection, no one could accuse us of being partisan.

The next point was SEAC incursions into Indochina. It was emphasized that Indochina, that is, Viet Nam, Laos, and Cambodia, was part of the China Theater and under the command and control of Chiang. Someone raised the question of legality regarding areas of operation, because there existed only a "gentlemen's agreement" between Mountbatten and the Generalissimo. His opinion was that informal agreements were utterly unreliable. Heppner supported that view and referred to recent correspondence from OSS-SEAC disclosing that they had been excluded from Force 136 operations in Laos and southern Indochina. And there was, of course, the absence of coordination of clandestine operation plans between SEAC and the China Theater.

One of the Theater planners then announced that the Joint Chiefs were considering submitting to the Combined Chiefs a proposal that would divide Indochina into two parts, one giving SEAC full control of the area south of the 15th or 16th parallel north. It was, he said, only in the talking stage and would require CCS approval and Chiang's consent. He suggested, however, that OSS might want to keep the proposal in mind in planning future activities in Indochina, to which Heppner agreed. That was the first occasion on which I heard of the idea of splitting Viet Nam in two and we viewed it as a jurisdictional problem between theaters.

The conference was helpful to those of us struggling with operations. In the absence of detailed guidelines from Washington, we were able to extract a few nuggets on how the issues were being treated at higher levels and come to some sensible, agreed upon decisions at our own level. At the time we did not perceive the proposal in Washington to split Indochina in half as being deeply significant; however, it was to be a decisive factor before the year was out.

CHAPTER 13

THE "DEER" TEAM
AT KIM LUNG

As the months of laborious negotiation with the French went aimlessly by, Ho Chi Minh kept his word and furnished OSS with extremely valuable information and assistance in many of our clandestine projects. I kept in touch with him through his agents in Kunming, Poseh, and Ch'ing-Hsi.

Ho had returned to his headquarters in Indochina through Pac Bo, his first location, to Tan Trao,[1] where he established his political and military base for directing Viet Minh operations until he moved into Hanoi four months later.

By mid-June I had developed a certain rapport with select members of the Vietnamese community in Kunming. I spent many informative hours, and to me very pleasant ones, listening to the exploits of the Viet Minh in Indochina and the "wisdom" of their leader, Ho Chi Minh. The story that I had met with Ho gave rise to many rumors regarding our association and the role of OSS in the Viet Minh movement. Those rumors, a sort of self-important "puffing," originated with the Viet Minh itself in Kunming, but they proved very useful in establishing good working relations with its membership.

We spoke in French, but at times they would lapse into a *patois* I did not understand. They also spoke of individuals who, though undoubtedly important to the movement, were unknown to me. They spoke, too, of places in Indochina of which I had never heard and which I would later diligently try to locate on my maps. Despite all this, I learned much about the Vietnamese movement for independence and faithfully kept Chung-king and Washington informed of events and prognostications.

Theater headquarters and the American Embassy were unim-pressed with my early reports on the nature and significance of the Viet Minh. In fact, Whitaker questioned both my sources and my conclusions. He had been advised by the Embassy staff that I had been taken in by a few communist fanatics and was wasting my time. However, Whitaker, Helliwell, and Heppner could not ignore the quality of the intelligence produced by the Viet Minh or the effectiveness of the several Vietnamese agents I used in sabotage operations against Japanese targets. Naturally the Chinese on the Theater staff and the French Military Mission officers in contact with the American Embassy did not like the Vietnamese collab-oration, but we in OSS agreed to continue our unofficial cooperation.

THE ONLY ALTERNATIVE—THE VIET MINH

Facing a Franco-Sino cabal to thwart OSS's efforts to obtain independent results and recognizing our American penchant for substantive evidence, I assigned a member of my staff to develop a case file on the Viet Minh accomplishments since the March coup. Within two days I presented Heppner with a respectable box score: six provinces in northern Tonkin[2] under the military and administrative control of the Viet Minh, an estab-lished Army of Liberation with self-defense and guerrilla units, an effec-tive propaganda organization with limited press and radio capability, a political-social and military program, and that all-important ingredient, popular support from the Vietnamese people—an ingredient which we totally ignored in the sixties and seventies, much to our sorrow.

Heppner saw no advantage in pressing the issue with the American Embassy. Instead, he discussed it privately with Generals Wedemeyer and Gross and forwarded the study to Washington for the personal atten-tion of General Donovan. After that my activities and relationships with the Vietnamese were not questioned during my assignment in the China Theater.

During the first week of June Ho Chi Minh let me know he was pre-pared to make available up to one thousand "well-trained" guerrillas for any plan I might have against the Japanese. The guerrillas were in an as-sembly area in the Cho Chu-Ding Hoa sector, and I sent word to Ho that I was grateful for the offer and would give it serious consideration.

His offer came at a propitious moment when the French contingent under Courthlac (intended for the operation of disrupting the Chen Nan Kuan-Hanoi lines of communication) had just refused to go into training or participate in the mission. Helliwell, Wampler, and I had already been forced to the conclusion that French participation in OSS operations would be slow and fraught with obstructionism. Wampler and I favored substituting the Vietnamese for the French in the sabotage operation, but Helliwell was doubtful. The original plan for the mission was for "Cat" (under Holland) and "Deer" (under Thomas) to receive and train fifty French troops each at Ch'ing-Hsi.

Helliwell worried about the political repercussions if we substituted Vietnamese guerrillas and he also disliked the necessity of withdrawing arms and equipment already provided to the French contingent so as to equip the Vietnamese. I argued that if we used Ho's unit at Cho Chu we would eliminate the problem of walking or transporting the French a distance of 25 miles to the border, plus the additional 150 miles to Hanoi. On existing jungle trails the actual distance would have been closer to 250 miles, ten to fifteen days' travel time. Other important considerations favoring the use of the Viet Minh base and personnel for the operation were that we would have local native support and excellent terrain cover. These practical advantages weighed heavily, and Helliwell at last concurred. The French contingent under Courthlac was never used.

At that time GBT had one of its principals, Frankie Tan, at Ho's headquarters gathering Japanese intelligence and concurrently (working with AGAS) expanding the escape and evasion net. He was also looking for certain Americans evading capture in the Tuyen-Quang, Thai Nguyen, Bac Can triangle—all in the heart of Ho's anti-Japanese operations. AGAS was setting up a country-wide radio net from Hanoi to Saigon, which was in line with OSS's plans. We proposed to AGAS's Wichtrich that we jointly collaborate with Ho Chi Minh and set up operations independent of the French. He agreed and assigned a young lieutenant named Phelan to undertake the AGAS mission and to act as liaison between OSS and the Viet Minh until our "Deer" and "Cat" teams arrived at Ho's base.

After Sainteny ordered the complete suspension of French collaboration with OSS and after the PAKHOI radio silence, I asked Truong Quoc Anh,[3] one of my several Viet Minh contacts, to let Ho know that I was interested in his offer and, if agreeable to him, an American team headed by a senior American officer would be parachuted into the Tuyen-Quang area.

During our talk, M. Anh informed me that Major Sainteny had been consorting with Nguyen Tuong Tam.[4] I found it hard to believe that Sainteny would have dealings with an ultranationalist, much less the leader of a Chinese-sponsored revolutionary movement. Yet less than three weeks later this fact was confirmed by a French-Vietnamese member of the "Deer" team.

On 30 June I received Ho's reply agreeing to receive our team and asking to be informed when the Americans would arrive. In the meantime Phelan had been dropped into the Tuyen-Quang sector and had been met by Frankie Tan.

We advised Major Davis at Poseh of our change in plan and suggested he send the "Deer" and "Cat" cadres to the Tuyen-Quang area by plane where AGAS and GBT would have prepared drop zones. I asked Davis to caution Thomas and Holland to reconsider the original plan of taking French troops on their mission and informed him we had reliable information from the Viet Minh that a sizeable contingent of Vietnamese guerrillas was available in the drop area and that, although their political orientation was Marxist, their immediate concern was to fight the Japanese, the major consideration in our operation. After some confusion and a flurry of radiograms between Poseh and Kunming, Thomas concluded that a combined French-American operation might not be welcomed by the Vietnamese.[5]

HO'S JUNGLE LAIR

Thomas decided to make a personal reconnaissance of the situation before committing his team to Vietnamese or French participation. He organized an advance party of himself, Lieutenant Montfort of the French army, two American enlisted men, and two Vietnamese represented to be sergeants in the French army. In the late afternoon of 16 July the group parachuted into the vicinity of the village of Kim Lung, about twenty miles east of Tuyen-Quang. The drop was uneventful except that Thomas, Montfort, and one enlisted man landed unceremoniously in trees and had to be helped down. Then, according to Thomas, he received a welcoming salute from about two hundred men[6] armed with "French rifles, a few Brens, a few tommies, a few carbines, and a few stens." Thomas described it as "a very impressive reception committee."

Thomas's first report gave some of the flavor of his arrival:

I was then escorted to Mr. Hoe, one of the big leaders of the VML (Viet Minh League) Party. He speaks excellent English but is very weak physically as he recently walked from Tsingsi [Ch'ing-Hsi]. He received us most cordially. We then were shown our quarters. They had built for us a special bamboo shelter, consisting of a bamboo floor a few feet off the ground and a roof of palm leaves. We then had supper consisting of beer (recently captured), rice, bamboo sprouts and barbecued steak. They freshly slaughtered a cow in our honor.[7]

Very early the next day an M.5 officer came to me and announced that Major Thomas and Lieutenant Montfort had been captured by the Viet Minh guerrillas. I assured him that that was not the case and that we had word from Thomas that the drop had been completed as planned. The officer would not be reassured and with some embarrassment revealed that Montfort and the two Vietnamese, Logos and Phac by name, were M.5 agents on a "special mission." He was concerned for their safety and voiced the expectation that OSS would guarantee their safe return to French control with the least practicable delay.

I soon learned that M.5 had been interested in contacting Ho Chi

Minh and had asked Gordon of GBT to arrange a meeting. M.5 had instructed Major Revol, its agent at Ch'ing-Hsi, to follow up on GBT's arrangement, and he had sent Montfort with Thomas to Ho's headquarters. Unfortunately, M.5 had a proclivity for backdoor operations, and Montfort arrived at Kim Lung camouflaged as an American officer, a futile deception, as he was recognized almost immediately by one of the Viet Minh guerrillas who had served under him in the French colonial army at some earlier time.

In his first report, Thomas wrote, "Held long conference with Mr. Hoo . . . on the subject of the French." Ho told Thomas in no uncertain terms that "it would be impossible for Lt. Montfort, the French Officer, to stay, nor would any more French be welcome." As for the Vietnamese soldiers, Thomas reported, "Mr. Hoo consented to their staying on, however [he] doubted if the French would release them. This turned out to be the case."

While waiting to be returned to Poseh, "Sergeant" Phac was identified several days later by a Viet Minh guerrilla as a member of the pro-Chinese nationalist party, the VNQDD. He admitted under questioning that he had been instrumental in arranging the meeting (already mentioned) in Kunming between the Chief of M.5 and Nguyen Tuong Tam. To justify his present predicament, he told his Vietnamese interrogators that he had accompanied Montfort in the hope that the Viet Minh would let him stay and fight the Japanese. They evidently had a different interpretation and "Sergeant" or "Lieutenant" Phac was kept under close observation until his departure.

Montfort and the two Vietnamese left on 31 July to join twenty French refugees collected at a nearby village under the auspices of AGAS. They had been liberated on 4 July by Viet Minh guerrillas from a Japanese civilian concentration camp at Tam Dao.[8] Montfort then led on foot all the able-bodied men in the long trek back to the frontier, while the women and children were flown to China.

On the day after Thomas's arrival Ho, always in search of the "propitious moment," took the opportunity of the American presence to communicate with the French in China. He asked Thomas to let the American authorities know that the "VML would be willing to talk to some High Ranking French officer (General Sebotier, eg) [sic] and see what the French would have to offer." Several days later AGAS in Kunming advised me they were in receipt of a message from Ho intended for the French authorities stating that Ho would welcome a talk with a senior French official, especially on the subject of de Gaulle's proclamation concerning Indochina[9] which he considered contained some very vague points. I advised AGAS to convey the message to M.5 where I later learned it was coolly received.

Thomas again reported on 25 July that Ho had once more expressed a desire to talk with the French, either at Kunming or in Tonkin, and had included a five-point request to the French Government for reforms. These read:

> We the V.M.L. request the following points be made public by the French and incorporated into the future policy of French Indo-China.
> 1. That there be universal suffrage to elect a parliament for the governing of the country, that there be a French Governor-General as President until such time as independence be granted us, that he choose a cabinet or group of advisors acceptable to that parliament. Exact powers of all these officers may be discussed in the future.
> 2. That independence be given this country in not less than five years and not more than ten.
> 3. That natural resources of the country be returned to the people of the country by just payment to the present owners, and that France be granted economic concessions.
> 4. That all freedoms outlined by the United Nations will be granted to the Indochinese.
> 5. That the sale of opium be prohibited.
> We hope that these conditions may be acceptable to the French government.

Thomas forwarded Ho's message to Davis at Poseh for transmission to AGAS-Kunming. Since they had delivered the first, they also handled the second transmission, delivering it to the French Military Mission.

Insofar as I could determine Ho's messages went unanswered and unacknowledged. Our role had been simply one of service, avoiding any implications of partisan support for either side. It is interesting to reflect, however, that the modest demands of the Viet Minh, though obviously not acceptable to the French, might have served as a convenient basis for negotiation. Indeed these two appeals for meeting together on a serious basis were only the first of many attempts by the Vietnamese to negotiate with the French on behalf of their nation's future. The overwhelming evidence is that French intransigence made attempts at negotiation quite vain.

Any further consideration of French participation in the "Deer" mission was dropped, and Major Thomas's team remained with the Viet Minh guerrillas until they reached Hanoi on 9 September. During those seven weeks, Thomas and his American specialists spent four weeks in training about two hundred handpicked future leaders of the armies of Generals Chu Van Tan and Vo Nguyen Giap in the use of the latest American weapons and guerrilla tactics. Some of us may have suspected that in the future the weapons and training might be used against the French, but no one dreamed that they would ever be used against Americans.

CHAPTER 14

HISTORIC DECISIONS

O n the day that Ho Chi Minh and Major Thomas met in the jungles of Tonkin, I was in Kunming listening to General Alessandri receive the painful news that American Lend-Lease was not available to him for arming a French force to reconquer Indochina.

Major Sainteny was on the other side of the world, in Paris in a futile attempt to interest his government in the Indochina dilemma. He arrived in the French capital on the eve of Bastille Day (14 July) and hoped to alert the "*chef du* G.P.R.F."[1] (de Gaulle) and other national officials of the perilous course the Allies were following in the Far East regarding France's interests in Indochina. But General de Gaulle was *"très pris"* to see him at the moment and French officialdom too preoccupied with more urgent matters of state to be concerned with colonial problems in the Far East.[2] Sainteny returned to China empty-handed.

DECISION AT POTSDAM—16TH PARALLEL

Not far away, in a suburb of Berlin,[3] a full array of the political and military leaders of the United States, Great Britain, and the Soviet Union were meeting at the Conference of Berlin (Potsdam). They were beginning their long series of discussions which would end in many decisions of lasting significance, not the least of which concerned Indochina. The American Joint Chiefs were discussing, among other matters, the realignment of command boundaries in the Southeast Asia and Southwest Pacific areas. The realignment was intended to release American resources and commanders from the responsibility for containing and mopping up the Japanese forces in the areas of colonial interest to the British, Dutch, and French, freeing the American commanders to concentrate on the main effort—operations against the Japanese homeland.

Among the several boundaries under discussion one affected Indochina. Initially a line at the fifteenth degree North parallel had been selected by the Joint Chiefs but, after discussions with the British Joint Chiefs and Lord Mountbatten, the line was readjusted to the sixteenth parallel. That was to give Mountbatten greater latitude for clandestine operations in southern Indochina. All the area north of that line was to remain in the China Theater under the operational control of Chiang and Wedemeyer.

A week later, on 24 July, the proposed division was submitted to Truman and Churchill, who approved it with instructions that an approach to Chiang be made by both governments to secure his agreement. On 1 August Hurley delivered the message from the President advising the Generalissimo of the decision at Potsdam and expressing the hope that he would concur. Truman's message, carefully worded and emphasizing that the division was "for operational purposes," implied it had no other connotations. Ten days later Chiang replied with a conditional concurrence.

A THIRD FORCE IN TONKIN

Unnoticed by the power structure in Potsdam, Paris, and Chungking, Ho Chi Minh in his remote domain in Tonkin was feverishly propagandizing, organizing, training, and directing political and military leaders for a new nation.

After meeting Ho in April I had examined carefully the Viet Minh movement and by mid-June was convinced that it was real, dynamic, and bound to succeed. I had determined from solid evidence that it was well organized and had specific objectives and popular endorsement. In my reports to Heppner, Wedemeyer, and Hurley, I emphatically refused to accept the French allegations that there was no real movement for independence in Indochina, that a few agitators fomenting discord were "communist expatriates" aided and abetted by Moscow, Yenan, and Chungking or that the "natives" were loyal, dependent people waiting patiently for the return of the French to shelter and protect them from Chinese and Thai overlordship. On the contrary, I had concluded that the independence movement was only a medium for a first cause—the instinct for survival. If national independence could assure a Vietnamese of survival, he saw the Viet Minh as the answer. It mattered not to him whether the medium was democratic, socialistic, or communistic. The question was to be free from want, to enjoy the fruits of one's labor, and to exist unmolested.

I confirmed in my reports that French colonialism in Indochina had been one of the worst possible examples of peonage, disregard for human rights, and French cupidity and that for more than three-quarters of a century the Vietnamese had been cruelly exploited, brutally maltreated, and generally used as French chattel. They had protested, fought back, and revolted, but the French colonial army and the Sûreté had always prevailed. The most aggressive "natives" had been either murdered or relegated to penal colonies. The socioeconomic conditions generated by the French colonial system fostered discontent and rebellion, spawning numerous national movements and patriotic leaders, among whom Ho Chi Minh was one of the most influential and effective.

I knew from the Vietnamese in Kunming that Ho, after having spent twenty-five years abroad where he had adopted Marxist-Leninist philosophies and tactics, had returned to his homeland in 1940 and had set himself the task of gathering together the diverse nationalist groups into the Viet Nam Independence League.[4] Aware of the Vietnamese socioeconomic weakness, it being strictly a rural agrarian society, Ho first proposed that they set aside regional and class interests in favor of national independence and freedom from colonialism. Then he urged his followers to prepare for armed uprising to drive out the French and Japanese and seize power for the Vietnamese people.

During the war years, the Viet Minh had followed a program of education, organization, and forays against French and Japanese strongholds in Tonkin. With each victory the local populace rallied to the Viet Minh and the number of adherents increased in geometric proportions. Frightened by the revolutionary movement, the French had instituted a reign of terror in late 1943–44. Conversely, the Viet Minh intensified its educational campaign in both urban and rural areas, prodding the city workers and farmers alike to resist French and Japanese demands.

Then the unprecedented famine of 1944–45 had begun in northern Tonkin, triggering a fantastic increase in the cost of living. The price of rice rose from one hundred and fifty piastres per ton in October 1944, to five hundred piastres in December, to eight hundred in February. Although the shortage of food in Tonkin was caused by a general crop failure, the direct cause of starvation was the brutal application by the French and Japanese of impossible quotas in requisitioning foodstuffs. In addition to depriving the Vietnamese of rice for their table by exporting it to foreign markets and converting it to alcohol for French commercial interest, the quota system reduced the Vietnamese farmer to destitution. Normal production cost for a ton of paddy (rice in the husk) was about eighty piastres and the market price about two hundred, of which the farmer received perhaps twenty-five piastres. With the crop failure of 1944 the farmer was nevertheless obliged to meet his quota, which forced him to buy the necessary amount at the inflated market price, only to meet his quota at the much lower requisition price. He was left starving and without resources. All of this was related to me by Ho Chi Minh in April 1945.

When Ho told me of the famine, I had not grasped the full import of that disaster and its long-range effects. With the passing months I came to a better understanding of Ho's concern and grief. Aside from the loss of nearly two million people—many of them children—the famine had seriously affected the health of the surviving Tonkinese. It had also fanned their hatred for the Japanese and French oppressors and strengthened the people's determination to fight and win back the *right to live*.

The right to live—survival—that was the first cause of the revolution. Accordingly, the Indochinese Communist Party adopted the slogan, "Seize paddy stocks to save the people from starvation." They regarded it as the central task for mobilizing the masses in the preinsurrection period.

The resulting seizures of paddy stocks had several unplanned results: relief of the famine as the price of rice fell; identification of the Japanese and the French as the common enemy, focusing the people's grievances toward a specific target; encouragement of the people to organize for self-defense as well as for political power; highlighting the importance of organized resistance and unifed action; and drawing hundreds of thousands to the revolutionary movement—the Viet Minh.

At the time I met Ho at Chiu Chou Chieh I was not aware that he was returning to Indochina to assume personal leadership of a dynamic movement on the verge of exploding. I learned later that he had gone straight to Tan Trao, where he had established a mini-nation of six provinces and parts of three more, which he called the "Viet Bac Liberated Area." He then had consolidated the armed bands of Chu Van Tan and Vo Nguyen Giap into a unified Liberation Army. Finally he had laid down a ten-point program for the Liberated Area:

Drive out the Japanese.
Confiscate the properties of invaders and traitors and distribute them to the poor.
Proclaim universal suffrage and democratic freedoms.
Arm the people and urge them to support the guerrillas and join the Liberation Army.
Organize land reclamation, encourage production, achieve a self-supporting economy in the Liberated Area.
Put into effect social insurance and give relief to victims.
Redistribute communal lands, reduce land rents and debt interest, and order a moratorium on debts.
Abolish taxes and *corvées*.[5]
Fight illiteracy and give military and political training to the people.
Ensure equality among the various ethnic groups and between men and women.

Although each goal was important to Ho, he felt more strongly about some than others. The high rate of Vietnamese illiteracy and the existence of the corvées were sources of particular grief to him, as I was to learn later in Hanoi.

The points above, however, represented in Ho's mind a revolutionary base for the entire country, a miniature image of the Viet Nam to come, and they inspired and impelled vigorously the movement for national independence. In mid-July he had his first opportunity to unveil his dream to a few Americans. Thomas, Phelan, Defourneaux, Hoaglund, Squires, and other members of the "Deer" team were thoroughly impressed, even to the point of accepting Ho's assertion that it was not a communist movement.

THE PARTY CONVENTION AT TAN TRAO

On 6 August* the end of the war was heralded at Hiroshima. Ho was not ready for this, but when he learned from Thomas of Japan's collapse he acted decisively and moved rapidly because he had to secure a foothold where it counted—in Hanoi, Hué, and Saigon. Ho knew that to retain leadership and momentum for his movement he had to demonstrate both legitimacy and strength. Although much weakened by a recent bout with malaria and other complications, he nevertheless sent out a call for a meeting of the Viet Minh party delegates and political leaders and convened a party convention.

By 13 August the delegates began to arrive at Tan Trao. They were not all well disposed toward Ho. Many questioned his implied primacy in the nationalist movement. Some doubted the rumors of his alleged support from the Allies. Others coveted the position of leadership for themselves. Despite his very poor health Ho was on hand, bright and cheerful, to greet each new arrival personally and warmly. He circulated among them and exchanged news, views, and old stories. In his combined "quarters-office" he displayed several pictures, Lenin, Mao, and General Chennault with all his ribbons and stars, among others. Many of the conferees asked who the foreign officer was, and Ho was delighted to enlighten them.

By afternoon a sizeable number of the delegates had arrived for the convention—representatives of party headquarters from each of the three regions of Viet Nam—North, Central, and South—and a number from abroad. Heavy rains and poor road conditions were probably responsible for the absence of some; others very likely had not received the call.

The first order of business was the question of insurrection. On the evening of 13 August a National Insurrection Committee[6] was formed. The Committee agreed that the time had come for a general uprising and

*Tokyo date. It was 5 August in Washington.

an immediate call to arms. That very night the Committee issued Military Order Number 1, ordering the launching of a general insurrection. The next day the Viet Minh General Committee issued an appeal to the people to rise and fight for their independence. On the same day the National Insurrection Committee prepared a Plan of Action outlining four basic principles: merging all political and military actions; concentrating all forces under a unified command; consolidating civil and military ranks; and maintaining contact with the leadership. The Plan of Action then detailed how the principles were to be put into action.

THE PEOPLE'S NATIONAL CONGRESS

Immediately after the Party convention, the first People's National Congress was convened on 16 August. Under the chairmanship of Ho Chi Minh, it was attended by well over sixty delegates representing most of the political parties forming the Viet Minh Front, mass organizations, nationalities (ethnic groups), and religious communities in Indochina and overseas.

As the Congress met at Tan Trao, they were treated to discreet glimpses of well-uniformed, well-armed and well-disciplined troops coming and going in the area of their meetings. These were soon observed to be Vietnamese and members of the Liberation Army. Their American equipment and arms were new, of identical make and caliber. Ho was modestly silent but pleased at the delegates' curiosity and interest. What with Chennault's autographed photograph in Ho's hut and these well-equipped guerrillas, rumors were rampant that the Viet Minh, and "Uncle Ho" in particular, had "secret" Allied support. Ho must have rejoiced inwardly that the "Deer" team had arrived so opportunely and that, by spreading it thinly, everything could seem much more than it actually was.

The Congress got down to business and approved the resolution for a general insurrection and sanctioned Military Order Number 1. In the two-day session it adopted a ten-point program, a national flag with a five-point yellow star centered on a red field, and a national anthem,[7] and elected the Viet Nam Committee for National Liberation,[8] headed by Ho Chi Minh as President, to act as the provisional government pending national elections.

Ho, ever pragmatic, steered the Congress into advocating a realistic policy "to wrest power from the hands of the Japanese and the puppet government before the arrival of the Allied troops in Indochina, so that we, as masters of the country, would welcome these troops coming to disarm the Japanese."[9] This Congressional resolution was an expression of Ho's apprehensions as to Franco-Sino interests and the known danger to their cause from the French-British-Dutch bloc for the full recovery of their colonial empires. He perceived the Allies as not allies in fact, but only to the extent of preserving colonial interests in Southeast Asia. Ho, based on past experience, wisely foresaw that China would not easily abandon an opportunity to exploit Viet Nam.

At the conclusion of that memorable Congress, Ho issued an eloquent appeal to the entire Vietnamese people, which read in part:

> The decisive hour for the fate of our nation has struck. Let the people of the whole country rise up, using our own force to liberate ourselves. Many oppressed peoples in the world are emulating each other to advance and win independence. We cannot lag behind.
>
> Forward! Forward! Under the banner of the Viet Minh, let our people bravely march forward![10]

Ho signed his appeal using for the last time a name he had adopted at the beginning of his revolutionary struggle—Nguyen Ai Quoc. His appeal was to Vietnamese patriotism, and he wanted them to know who he was—"Nguyen who considers love of the fatherland as the supreme virtue."

The first day of the Congress was also a day of departure for the "Deer" team. Following the instructions of the National Insurrection Committee, a unit under the command of Vo Nguyen Giap (previously trained by the "Deer" team) was leaving Tan Trao to attack the Japanese garrison at Thai Nguyen in order to open the route south to Hanoi. When all was ready, Ho, the new President, called all the delegates, party leaders, and guests to watch the Vietnamese unit march out of camp, with the "Deer" team accompanying them.

Major Thomas was a fine young officer but understandably unsophisticated in the way of international power struggles. He and his team, along with scattered Americans all over China and Indochina, were disappointed and displeased when they were forbidden by a Theaterwide policy from demanding the surrender of any local Japanese troops, or even accepting such surrenders if offered. As Thomas put it, "This was indeed extremely disheartening to me as we all felt that we had risked our lives in coming here and now when the going was to be easy we were not allowed . . ."[11] And so on and so on. Some of the teams, being hundreds of miles from any military authority, were much more vociferous and defied their orders.

In the case of the "Deer" team, they assuaged their displeasure by accompanying the Viet Minh troops all the way to Hanoi, but only as observers. They probably were totally oblivious to the impression they undoubtedly gave of Ho's "secret" Allied support. But after the Congress concluded, the delegates scattered back to their homes all over Viet Nam, carrying their impressions with them.

CHAPTER 15

UNSCHEDULED PEACE

A VERITABLE PANDORA'S BOX

The abrupt end of the war took everyone by surprise. Final preparations for taking Fort Bayard were well advanced, our clandestine operations independent of French support were moving along well, and Major Sainteny had been back from Paris about a week when the stunning news of the Hiroshima bomb reached us. Two days later, on 9 August, Russia declared war on Japan and the second atomic strike was made at Nagasaki. All the preparations for CARBONADO ground to a halt, troops were held in place, and ships lying off Fort Bayard kept to their offshore positions—all awaiting developments that were not long in coming. On 10 August (China date) we received unofficial word that Japan had accepted the Potsdam terms for surrender.

Early in August the end of the war in Asia had been nowhere in sight. There were, we thought, many battles to be fought before V-J day; we therefore felt locked in a conventional time sequence. But as the aftershock of the atomic explosions spent itself, everyone in Asia came to the realization that this was a new ball game. Chiang Kai-shek and his China Theater took on a new dimension. The Generalissimo, as Supreme Commander, would be in full charge of accepting the Japanese surrender in the China Theater—a matter of utmost concern to the British, the Russians, and the French alike.

The British instantly regretted their recent approval of the theater boundary realignment. The Soviet Union wasted no time in moving its troops to protect its interests in Manchuria. And the French, who had not been consulted at Potsdam, were completely dismayed by their own impotence.

Just before the end of hostilities, Jean Daridan, the French Chargé d'Affaires, had approached Wedemeyer to request French participation in the reoccupation of Indochina and air transportation for Alessandri's troops. It being a military matter, Wedemeyer discussed it with General Alessandri but noted that planes and fuel were in short supply. The best he could do, he said, was to authorize one French plane to operate between the Kunming-Meng-tzu area and Hanoi for key French personnel and to agree to consult with the Generalissimo regarding the other matters. It was a useless gesture because Chiang had already decided that the French troops would proceed overland from Meng-tzu to the border city of Lao Cai, a distance of seventy-five miles, and then on to Hanoi, an additional one hundred miles. Wedemeyer was in no position to countermand Chiang's orders. To the French this was tantamount to being frozen in China while the Chinese occupied Indochina alone.

Having failed with the military, Daridan called on Ellis O. Briggs, Counselor of our Embassy. He told Briggs that he had discussed the French position with Dr. K. C. Wu, China's Acting Foreign Minister, stressing that it would have a "very bad effect" and might "gravely prejudice" Sino-French relations if the French troops were not allowed to proceed to Indochina and predicting "serious trouble" if the Chinese troops entered alone. To give more weight to the French position, Daridan reminded Briggs that there were some ten thousand French POWs in Indochina and Alessandri's troops should be the ones to minister to their needs. Briggs's answer was that under the surrender terms the Japanese would be responsible for the safe transportation of POWs to places designated by the Allied command. Daridan came away frustrated and discouraged.

At the moment there were two Chinese divisions near Nanning tentatively scheduled for shipment to Indochina to facilitate repatriation and disarmament and to receive the surrender of Japanese forces. Anticipating potential conflict in the situation, Ambassador Hurley advised the Department of State:

... France is urgently desirous of complete reestablishment of her authority in Indochina at the earliest possible moment and views with disfavor having any Chinese troops enter Indochina. . . . The French desire to save face by accepting Japanese surrender themselves [in Indochina].[1]

This was not possible, Hurley continued, under existing instructions and neither he nor Wedemeyer had any authority to change the surrender terms. Unless directed otherwise by the Department, he would suggest to the Generalissimo that arrangements be made directly between the Chinese and French governments to allow French representatives to participate in receiving the Japanese surrender in Indochina.[2]

The question as to who was to accept the Japanese surrender in Indochina also aroused considerable concern in other quarters. Secretary Byrnes instructed Ambassador Caffery in Paris to let Bidault know that the Japanese would surrender only to Chiang in the north and to Mountbatten in the south, bearing in mind that the "division" at the sixteenth degree North parallel was "purely an operational matter . . . and has no political significance whatever."[3] He added that we were suggesting to the British and Chinese governments that they invite French representatives to the surrender ceremonies and that the French might wish to take the question up directly with those governments.[4]

The sudden Japanese collapse brought into the open the intense disagreements over colonial possessions which had been simmering on the back burner throughout the war. The British advised the Chinese government that the United Kingdom was dispatching British troops to reoccupy and restore the administration of Hong Kong and, at the same time, was sending a force to Saigon to secure control of the Japanese headquarters there. With the same disregard they had often displayed toward the Chinese, the British simply announced to them that events had overtaken the negotiations over command boundaries in Indochina and there was no point in discussing it further. Therefore the British would assume that the Chinese government would agree that the common British-Chinese objective in Indochina should be to restore the French administration and to facilitate the return of French forces and administrative officers for that purpose as soon as they were available.

The Chinese were indignant and attempted to match British imperiousness with disapprobation. Chiang bluntly let the British know that they were in conflict with the agreed surrender procedure specified in General Order No. 1[5] and that the Chinese could not agree with the British proposal. Dr. Wu called on Hurley on 18 August and delivered a copy of the Chinese reply enjoining the British from landing troops anywhere in the China Theater without authority from General MacArthur and Chiang Kai-shek but assuring that the Chinese government would respect all legitimate British interests and accord them every protection.

Chiang wired President Truman on the same day, relating the British proposal and his own position. He concluded by stating that if the British took the steps contemplated it would be a matter of "great misfortune to the Allies" and by suggesting that the President urge the British to "refrain from taking any unwarrantable action."

Daridan's request to the Chinese to move French troops into Indochina from China had precipitated a separate crisis but one Chiang could deal with on his own terms. He agreed with Daridan that the

French should return south of the border. At the moment the Chinese had no transportation to spare, he said, but if the French wished they could walk, hand-in-hand as it were, with the Chinese occupation forces under the "direction" of his commander. Then, as an afterthought, Daridan was advised that as soon as the time and place for the surrender was fixed and as soon as the Chinese commander to receive the surrender was designated General Alessandri would be invited to go with him. This turned out to be a veritable Pandora's box, as will be seen.

The British proposal and its rejection by the Chinese government placed President Truman squarely in the middle of two allies. Prime Minister Attlee had cabled the President to alter his instructions to MacArthur to allow the Japanese to surrender Hong Kong to the British. He argued that the British colony could not be construed as being "within China," since it was in effect a sovereign British territory, having no relation to the military theater boundaries. However, the British would inform Chiang that the presence of a Chinese representative at the surrender would be "welcome."

Whatever the logic or illogic of the British reasoning, Hurley was in a huff. He had been handed a copy of the British reply to the Chinese indicating that at the time the British Embassy made its initial proposal they had not seen General Order No. 1,[6] but in good faith had let Chiang known their intentions in advance. Later the same morning (19 August) our Embassy was informed that London insisted on Hong Kong's being surrendered to the British but were willing to give in on Indochina and would follow the provisions of General Order No. 1 on condition that the senior Japanese commander at Saigon surrender to the British, with the Chinese receiving at Hanoi the surrender of subordinate Japanese commanders covering the northern area in the China Theater. As a palliative the British would invite a Chinese representative to the ceremony in Saigon.

The last I heard of the fracas before leaving for Hanoi was that the President had pressured Chiang into submitting to the British demand. He wired Chiang on 21 August that the question of Hong Kong was "primarily a military matter of an operational character" and that no question of British sovereignty had been raised by the Chinese. After handing Chiang a few bouquets for his understanding and cooperation, the President concluded by saying that the revised procedure "provides a reasonable solution."

Two days later Chiang replied that he had "agreed to delegate" his authority to a British commander, and concluded, "Mr. President, I have done so out of my great desire to cooperate with you in every way possible. Chiang Kai-shek."

Truman acknowledged Chiang's bowing to the realities of the situation: "Please accept this expression of my appreciation of your considerate action in regard to the surrender of the Japanese in Hong Kong to a British commander, by which action you eased a difficult situation."[7]

THE MERCY TEAMS

When the war ended, some twenty thousand American and Allied POWs and about fifteen thousand civilian internees were in Japanese hands. OSS had located them at scattered points from Manchuria and Korea south to Indochina. Allied authorities were concerned that the defeated Japanese might take reprisals on their captives or even discontinue their provisions and medicine, leaving them to die when they withdrew. OSS had been directed to prepare plans for a rescue operation, and by late July we had organized a number of commando-type teams generally referred to as Mercy Teams.[8] Their mission was to parachute in to the POW camps before the end of hostilities, provide for the prisoners' safety, prevent any maltreatment, and clear nearby airfields for quick air evacuation. For the OSS the teams would also provide opportunities to cover intelligence objectives and postsurrender political warfare activities. No one could predict Japanese reaction so the operation was staged in five steps: first, secret contact was to be made with the selected camps to find out the number and physical condition of the prisoners; second, our MO unit was to print leaflets to be dropped advising the Japanese that an OSS team would arrive for humanitarian reasons only; next, the teams would be parachuted into the camp sites, followed by airdrops of supplies; finally, the prisoners or internees would be rapidly evacuated.

When word was received that Japan had capitulated, OSS was ready. The Fourteenth Air Force had provided planes and staging facilities for four sorties out of Hsian (Sian) for Peking, Weihsien, Harbin, and Mukden. On 15 August three of the four teams were dispatched, but the flight for Harbin had to be cancelled, because we had failed to clear it with the Russians. The Mukden team landed but were told by the Japanese that future landings and operations had to be prearranged with them first. During the next seven days three additional teams were to be sent to Shanghai, Hainan Island, and Hanoi. I was to head the team bound for Hanoi.

In the midst of our preparations we were bombarded with radio messages from scattered OSS units wanting to play the role of victor to the hilt. The question of Japanese surrender anywhere in the theater was a touchy matter to the American command. Under no circumstances could we permit U.S. troops to accept even a unit surrender without Chinese approval. And that we did not have. With our American troops so irritated and defiant about the surrender terms, one can imagine how much more galling the terms were to the gaullistes in China and how desperate their attempts to circumvent the existing orders might become.

SELF-APPOINTED DELEGATE

Several days after the bombing of Nagasaki, Sainteny asked to see me on an urgent matter. I had not heard from him since his return from Paris, but I was neither surprised nor elated at his request. We met in my office on 12 August, and he was accompanied by Flichy, who was now less inflexible than formerly.

Sainteny with some humility got right to the point. He admitted ruefully that the war was coming to an end ahead of the French schedule, necessitating modification of French plans to meet the changing situation. According to Sainteny, the French government was not prepared to establish a military government nor to set up an interim Vietnamese administration under French tutelage, principally because France "had not been allowed" to muster her forces in the Far East.

I asked him what instructions he had from Paris on the question of French reentry into Indochina. He started to answer, "None," but instead explained that he was getting his instructions from Colonel Roos in India who was in direct contact with Paris. French policy, he said, was "to adopt a passive attitude toward the reoccupation of Indochina because of French inability to make a reentry with a powerful show of arms."

His immediate plans were to "feel out the various elements" in Indochina prior to attempting a French reentry, for which a "commission" of three had been appointed by the Paris government: himself as Chief of DGER-Kunming; the Inspector General of the Colonies (no name mentioned), then in Chungking; and the Chief of Administrative Services for Civil Affairs, Pierre Messmer, then in Calcutta awaiting transportation to China. They would proceed to Hanoi immediately to contact the local Vietnamese leaders and negotiate with them on "terms favorable to the Indochinese." The "commission" was empowered, he said, to negotiate and make commitments for the French government. Its findings and recommendations would be relayed to de Gaulle, the Ministers of Foreign Affairs and of the Colonies, and to the French Government. He had been "assured" that commitments made by the "commission" would be honored by the French government or, if necessary, with only slight modifications.

In the meantime, Sainteny reiterated, it was to be the policy of the French government to "soft pedal" the reentry of the French under the circumstances. He told me he wanted to make a preliminary flight to Hanoi, taking four or five members of his staff. He also wanted to contact his agent, Lieutenant Commander Blanchard, who had been in the Haiphong-Hanoi area since 8 August and through whom Sainteny would have made some contacts with the local leaders. He planned a forty-eight hour stay in Hanoi, then a return to Kunming to report his findings to the other two members of the "commission" and to the Military Delegate General for Indochina, General Alessandri. The "commission" would then report their joint findings and recommendations to the government in Paris, whereupon all three would go to Hanoi to establish an "interim French administration" with Indochinese endorsement.

Sainteny expanded at some length on the French position. Should the proposed negotiations fail completely, the French government would take no action and leave it entirely to the United States and Great Britain to "reestablish order" in Indochina. The "commission," he said, felt certain that neither the Americans nor the British were prepared or willing to maintain occupation forces in Indochina, which left only the Chinese and the French.

If the Chinese were chosen, Sainteny said, the French were sure that the Generalissimo would select General Chang Fa-kwei as his representative to accept the Japanese surrender in Hanoi. He thought him preferable to Governor Lung Yün's generals, but the French still feared wide-scale looting and pillaging and eventually a clash with the Vietnamese.

Then there was the possibility of the Japanese surrendering to the Vietnamese. That would be both a disaster and a blessing in disguise. Sainteny was certain in that case that the "Annamites" would not be able to cope and chaos would follow, resulting in a strong desire for the return of the French, for a while at least.

Sainteny also spoke at length of the statement on Indochina made by the Ministry of Colonies on 24 March promising, he alleged, "democratic freedoms" and complete economic independence from French interests and controls. Over and over he repeated that the French government's policy was to be one of "liberal administration, far and beyond the wildest dreams of even the most radical Annamites." Sainteny concluded with a question, "Would OSS provide me with a plane for my mission to Hanoi?" And, oh, yes, he said, the French would wear either American uniforms or civilian clothing.

Obviously the French were in a bind. They were neither equipped nor prepared for a military takeover of their former colony.[9] It was also clear, despite his bravado, that Sainteny lacked instructions from his government, although he would not admit it. Under the circumstances all that he could do would be to quickly establish some sort of French presence pending support and instructions from Paris. His hope of setting up a pro-French interim Vietnamese administration with the help of friendly Kuomintang (pro-Chinese) nationalists would have been a strong holding action, but he appeared unaware that anti-French feeling among the Vietnamese had already coalesced in a strong political front, the Viet Minh.

As to the request for OSS transportation and American cover, I told Sainteny I understood his problem and under similar circumstances might have tried the same approach but that American cover was completely out of the question and would bring about serious diplomatic consequences. His concern over a Japanese surrender to the Indochinese was unfounded. The Japanese would be ordered to surrender only to designated Allied commanders, and the Vietnamese did not fall into that category. I told him I doubted that Theater would divert an aircraft from the Mercy Team project but that I would submit his request. Before leaving, Sainteny thanked me for my sympathetic hearing and suggested that perhaps he and his men could be included in the Mercy Team for Hanoi. I assured him I would suggest this to Headquarters, and that very same afternoon I relayed the request to OSS-Chungking. Two days later Wedemeyer's headquarters replied that there was no useful purpose in the French going to Hanoi on the Mercy Team flight and that arrangements were being made for a French presence in Hanoi "at the proper time."

A SLIGHT DELAY DUE TO RAIN

Practically overnight the walled city of Kunming had changed from a military command center to a politically-oriented outpost. Foreign elements—French, Dutch, British and Chinese—previously very undercover, surfaced at OSS headquarters for postwar arrangements or special handling of one case or another. Our OSS staff was busier even than in the days of hostilities.

Then came the rains. They started gently during the first days of August and steadily increased in intensity each day. By mid-August it was a deluge which produced the worst flood in a generation. The canals flooded the low-lying roads, buildings were inundated, rice paddies submerged. Kunming became a huge lake. The OSS compound resembled a well-fortified lagoon with military debris floating aimlessly between the buildings.

The flood did not stop the frantic Mercy Team preparations, nor did it deter Koreans, Burmese, Thais, and Vietnamese from wading in with "secret" reports, schemes, and proposals for their various causes. Most prominent were the Vietnamese, all clamoring for preferential treatment and Allied support, especially American.

The Viet Minh spokesmen seriously proposed making Indochina an American protectorate and urged the United States to intercede in the UN for the exclusion of both the French and Chinese in Allied plans for the reoccupation of Indochina. Ho Chi Minh's representatives were very concerned with Chinese occupation plans. They feared that their neighbors to the north would become squatters in Indochina, living off the land, pillaging, raping, and looting. The French concurred in that concern and, in addition, wanted exclusive administrative rights for themselves.

The Viet Minh's Central Committee of Hanoi sent a note making their position clear. It read in part:

Should the French attempt to return to Indochina with the intention of governing the country and to act once more as oppressors, the Indochinese people are prepared to fight to the end against any such reoccupation. On the other hand, if they come as friends to establish commerce, industry, and without aspirations to rule, they will be welcomed the same as any other power.

The Central Committee wishes to make known to the United States Government that the Indo-Chinese people desire first of all the independence of Indo-China, and are hoping that the United States, as a champion of democracy, will assist her in securing this independence in the following manner:

1. Prohibiting or by not assisting the French from reentering Indo-China by force.

2. Keeping the Chinese under control, in order that looting and pillaging will be kept to a minimum.

3. Sending technical advisors to assist the Indo-Chinese to export the resources of the land.

4. Develop[ing] those few industries that Indo-China is capable of supporting.

In conclusion, the Indo-Chinese would like to be placed on the same status as the Philippines for an undetermined period.

This was the first semiofficial communication addressed to the United States, and I felt it was of sufficient import to forward to General Donovan, to whom it was dispatched by Helliwell on 18 August.

In the meantime, as the rains worsened and these other matters came to the fore, Sainteny and I had a second meeting (on the morning of 15 August) to discuss Chungking's rejection of his proposed trip to Hanoi. He was very upset and accused the OSS of working hand in glove with the Chinese to sabotage French reentry plans. He became exasperatingly unreasonable and impolitic, threatening to ignore Theater policy and pursue his own course, come what may. I calmed him down and offered to try again with Chungking if he promised to confine himself to nonpolitical activities, such as assisting in the administration of French POWs in Hanoi. Reluctantly he agreed to my proposal that he and four members of his staff in French uniform go to Hanoi as part of my mission.

That same day I received a conditional clearance from Theater. Sainteny and his staff of four could be added to the manifest provided they limited their activities to humanitarian tasks in the French community. However, the rains prevented our departure for the time.

Impatient to get to Hanoi to carry out his "secret mission," Sainteny found a French plane, a C-47 recently in from Calcutta. It had been flown in by a civilian pilot named Fulachier, working for Air France, who was to reestablish flights between India and China, with the French Embassy and the Chinese government working out the details. Late that evening Helliwell told me that Sainteny was planning to parachute into Hanoi from a French plane. Alessandri had asked General Ho Ying-chin for permission to send the French plane to Hanoi. The request had been denied, and the Chinese had posted guards around the French plane with instructions that no one was to emplane for Hanoi. The order was all-inclusive: "All planes, irrespective of origin or nationality, leaving for French Indo-China are grounded until further notice."

The next day there was another scene with Sainteny. He assailed me with wide-ranging accusations: the Americans were betraying the French; General Wedemeyer personally had been hindering the French activities in the Theater; the Americans in China had right along been playing the Chinese game, although unwittingly. He expressed his personal belief that Wedemeyer had not been honest with the French right from the start. When I inquired what he planned to do next, Sainteny reluctantly stated there was nothing for him to do but sit and wait for instructions from Chungking.

Then, by chance, I learned that Sainteny had infiltrated a ten-man team under Blanchard into Haiphong to contact the Japanese in Hanoi and work out a deal with a Lieutenant Colonel Kamiya, a former liaison officer between the Japanese Military Headquarters in Hanoi and the Decoux administration. But Kamiya had detained the French team in Haiphong and confined their activities to transmitting weather data to the French in Kunming.

Just as we had feared, the Japanese reception of Allied aircraft on other Mercy Missions had been mixed. Moreover, an Allied plane flying over Hanoi on 19 August had met antiaircraft fire, so Theater headquarters decided to hold up our Hanoi team until the Japanese command in Hanoi could be notified that we were coming. In any event the rains still precluded a takeoff.

The vexing difficulties with the French in China had been the subject of considerable correspondence between Chungking and Washington, and General Donovan had directed Heppner to coordinate closely all OSS plans regarding French reentry into Indochina with Theater headquarters and the American Embassy. In final response to Donovan's instruction, Helliwell radioed:

REUR 642, we are proceeding as instructed. Sainteny leaves with Patti on Sunday. It is thoroughly understood the French are under complete U.S. command, with only French those who have operated with OSS. French flag will not be used.[10]

Before the message was dispatched, I was briefed by Heppner on its significance and asked to indicate concurrence on the file copy. In short, under no circumstances were we to assist the French in a forced takeover of Indochina, or even to give the appearance of partisanship in their plans.

During the weather delays I met with several members of the Kunming branch of the Viet Minh League on the evening of 19 August at the residence of Pham Viet Tu. They had just received exhilarating news from Hanoi and were in high spirits when I came in. Tong Minh Phuong[11] had heard from a friend at Thai Ha Ap, a suburb of Hanoi, that Hanoi was in revolt. Their account, though sketchy, was that on 17 August the local Vietnamese administration of the Bao Dai regime had called for a demonstration in support of the central government of Tran Trong Kim.[12] The Central Committee of Civil Servants (Comité Central des Functionnaires) was the local sponsor, and a crowd of twenty-five thousand had gathered in front of the Théâtre Municipal. It was not clear just what had happened, except that members of the Viet Minh's Armed Propaganda Group had taken over the meeting and appealed to the crowd to reject the "puppet" government, join the Viet Minh, and seize power for the people. According to their news, the Japanese had not interfered and the Hanoi City Committee had seized the opportunity presented by the large meeting to set the wheels in motion for a city-wide uprising.

After the first high excitement the Kunming group also became apprehensive. Some thought the Hanoi City Committee's action might have been premature. What if the Japanese decided to quell the uprising? What if the Allies, particularly the Chinese, moved the French into Indochina with Kuomintang puppets? What if the Liberation Army was not ready to cope with the situation? These were some of the incertitudes which began to intrude on their elation, yet they did not hide their pride and high hopes. Tu and his colleagues looked to me for reassurance, but I could give none. My only suggestion was a caution not to let the situation get out of hand and result in needless bloodshed, whether Vietnamese or French.

The same evening I told Helliwell and Heppner what I had learned and suggested that General Wedemeyer be informed. Helliwell ventured that the Generalissimo was not going to be happy if his troops were to be tied up in Viet Nam for very long keeping order in Indochina. Heppner was more concerned with the evacuation of Allied POWs and getting the Japanese to surrender without complications. My concern was mainly about the French. If they were allowed to enter Indochina with the Chinese, there certainly would be clashes with the Vietnamese, and the Chinese would inevitably become involved. There was no question in our minds that this new development, if true, merited Theater consideration. However, when Heppner discussed the Hanoi situation the next morning with General Gross, it was not given much importance, and the Mercy Team was directed to proceed to Hanoi the moment weather permitted.

The torrential rains continued. With runways damaged and deeply flooded, with fuel contaminated by the floodwaters, and with low ceilings and poor visibility, there were no takeoffs. But Sainteny was still champing at the bit and had not lost his proclivity for backdoor operations. He could not resist divulging to me (what I had learned elsewhere) that Blanchard was in Haiphong and in contact with the Japanese and that he had alerted the Japanese that the French were coming on an American plane and not to fire on them. Therefore, said Sainteny, it would be entirely safe for us to go in. The whole idea of overriding our Theater orders was too ridiculous even to discuss, not to mention the fact that the Japanese had not agreed to Blanchard's "proposition."

So we waited in Kunming. It was not until the twenty-first that a few flights of the highest priority were cleared for takeoff. By then the Chinese had arranged with the Japanese liaison office in China for our team to land at the Bach Mai airfield outside Hanoi, and we were alerted for departure on the morning of the twenty-second. And this time nothing interfered.

Kim Lien, Ho Chi Minh's birthplace, and his revolutionary bases, Pac Bo and Tan Trao.

PART THREE

❧ ❧ ❧

HANOI

CHAPTER 16

UNINVITED GUESTS

FLIGHT TO HANOI

The main airport at Kunming was still awash, so takeoff was to be from Chanyi,[1] a field on higher ground. As our convoy moved slowly along the submerged roads in the early morning hours, our headlights revealed flooded rice paddies and overflowing canals littered with the bloated carcasses of animals and occasional human bodies, and the air reeked. We rode in silence except for the noise of the motors and the splashing of the floodwaters. In the shadows of first light we saw small groups of Chinese, hip high in the murky water, prodding oxen and water buffalo out of our path.

The airfield was asleep when we reached it; the Chinese guards leaning against stacked crates just waved us toward the control tower, the only lighted building. I was told that our plane was on the field but the crew would not arrive from Kunming for several hours. At about eight o'clock the morning mist lifted and the field came to life, flight crews arrived, and refueling vehicles rushed to and fro, but our plane sat idly in a far corner of the field. It was a C-47 Army cargo aircraft, and we had ample leisure to study its outlines and its number—5908. The flight crew finally arrived about nine. While they prepared the plane for takeoff, we loaded gear, checked weapons and parachutes, looked over the manifest, and posed for photographs. Quickly then, the engines started, the doors slammed shut, and we were taxied down the runway. My team of twelve[2] and Sainteny's four Frenchmen[3] sat silently facing each other.

We were airborne at 11:35 on 22 August and climbed steeply through the clouds. Suddenly over the clouds, the brilliant sunlight after the prolonged rains of Kunming lifted our spirits and seemed a good omen. The preflight tension left us. The pilot was announcing we would be flying at eight thousand feet and might run into some bad weather. He estimated the time of arrival at 1:30. Americans and French exchanged cigarettes, candy, and conversation, and broke into song from time to time.

As a group the French gave every appearance of confidence. Sainteny was sure we would have no difficulty and would be met by French and Vietnamese joyfully welcoming us as liberators. My own expectations were based on the sober reality that, even though the Tokyo High Command was negotiating a complete surrender, field commanders scattered over Asia might stubbornly refuse to accept Japan's defeat. Nor did I anticipate that the presence of uniformed Frenchmen, though only five in number, would enhance security. It was conceivable that if the Vietnamese objected to their presence, they might also interfere with my mission.

The pilot called me forward just before 1:30. He had Bach Mai airfield in sight and, even from eight thousand feet, I could see large craters and obstacles on the runways. He dropped to two thousand feet and had the plane's door opened so he could get a better look and prepare for an airdrop. We circled several times, photographing the blocked runways and wondering uneasily why we had been directed to a nonoperational field by the Japanese liaison in China.

Fortunately we had alternative plans for our entry into Hanoi. "Alpha" had been our expected landing at Bach Mai where I was to have been met by a small detachment of Vietnamese Army of Liberation troops and escorted to Hanoi, roughly a mile away. Alternate plan "Beta" was to proceed to Gia Lam, Hanoi's main airport, east of the city on the opposite side of the Red River and near one of the POW camps. "Beta" had been coordinated with AGAS in Kunming in anticipation of possible Japanese opposition, in which case we were to take over the camp, arm the POWs, and hold until the main body of my team arrived from Kunming, perhaps several hours later.

Switching to "Beta" we flew over the swollen Red River and inundated rice fields, followed the Doumer Bridge and Colonial Route No. 1 and shortly had Gia Lam in view. It appeared operational, but there were small tanks and antiaircraft guns mounted on halftracks. I asked my OG leader, Lieutenant Ramon Grelecki, to drop a reconnaissance party. At 2:00 the green light flashed over the open doors and Grelecki and three of his men[4] tumbled into space in sequence. We watched anxiously as they floated gently to the ground. There was no hostile fire from the Japanese.

At 2:06 the last man had landed, and we could see them being picked up in several vehicles. Almost immediately Grelecki radioed the all clear, and four minutes later our landing gear touched the runway.

OFF TO A ROCKY START

The plane taxied to a stop, and a Japanese unit of fifty or sixty men, all fully armed, surrounded the aircraft. The flight crew instantly manned the plane's guns, and we positioned ourselves to fire, while the pilot kept the engines running and turned the nose into the wind, ready for takeoff. I was at the door of the plane, Sainteny close behind, when I spotted Grelecki and his party approaching, followed by several Japanese officers. I ordered my men to hold their fire and hastily deplaned and approached the officers. One was an English-speaking lieutenant.

In the distance I saw a much larger group of men waving British and American flags. They were the British POWs, principally Indian troops captured at Singapore, of whom I had been advised by AGAS and with whom I had been in radio contact when I switched to the "Beta" plan. They had broken out of camp en masse to greet us, but as they came within several hundred yards of our plane a Japanese detachment blocked their advance at bayonet point. In typical British tradition, the POWs then formed ranks and let off three rousing hurrahs, holding their camp-made flags high overhead.

It was a tense moment while we and the Japanese viewed the scene with differing emotions, and for a short time I considered the odds. I would willingly have ignored the bristling weapons of the Japanese armored vehicles to make a rush for the prisoners, but it appeared that any move on our part might well prompt the Japanese guard detachment to open fire on them. In that momentary pause, the situation resolved itself. A small contingent of the POWs, led by a Japanese officer, quietly headed toward me. Lieutenant Commander "Simpson-Jones,"[5] Senior-Captain of Indian POWs at Gia Lam, was coming to "report" that the prisoners were ready to take their place alongside the Allied forces and on conditions at the camp. It was with vast relief that I assured myself that the Japanese authorities would relinquish control of the prisoners to him. I thanked "Simpson-Jones" for his "report" and asked him to provide the AGAS officer with details for the POWs' immediate needs and their speedy evacuation.

Having got through the first few threatening minutes, I turned to my Japanese host who now appeared to be patiently waiting to hear what other demands I might make. I said that we had come to look after Allied prisoners-of-war and to make preliminary arrangements for the Japanese surrender to Generalissimo Chiang Kai-shek. It was evident that the Japanese officers at the airfield had no instructions and were caught completely by surprise. But they made no hostile moves and ordered their men to stand aside. Our pilot, however, continued to maintain radio contact with Kunming as I, with Sainteny, Grelecki, and two OG men, accompanied the Japanese officers to a small building near the runway. The rest of our team under Lieutenant Russell A. Feeback stood by to guard the plane.

Inside the building we were met by a Japanese major, apparently the senior officer, with several subordinates. The two OG men posted themselves outside the door, alongside two Japanese sentries, all within sight of our meeting. After the confrontations we had just had, it may seem incongruous, but we were immediately offered iced towels and cold beer, small civilities customarily observed in the steaming heat of a Hanoi summer, and I was suddenly aware of the contrast to the chills of Kunming's six thousand foot elevation.

The Japanese were correct in their demeanor and very businesslike. I pressed urgently to see the Commanding General but was informed that General Yuitsu Tsuchihashi[6] was in Hué and would not return until late that night. The major suggested we make ourselves comfortable in the city where we would be allowed to circulate freely. But he expressed some doubt that the French officers should remain and suggested it would be best if they returned to China. At this, Sainteny became quite agitated, and I had to think fast since Sainteny and his men were without official status and were risking internment. With those thoughts in mind I informed the Japanese that the French were under my control, that their task was to inquire into the condition of French POWs, and that they would remain with my group. The major cautioned me about strong anti-French feeling in Hanoi and told me the sight of French uniforms in our party would only invite trouble. I took the offensive and reminded him that the Allies looked to the Japanese authorities to maintain public order and that the safety of my group, including the French, was the personal responsibility of the Japanese commander in the area. The Japanese officer abruptly abandoned his stand and arranged our transportation to the city.

Waiting for the transportation to arrive, I reflected on our good fortune that all had gone well so far, considering the surprise landing. I also speculated on what would be in store for us once we reached Hanoi. The Japanese major's reaction to the French in my group highlighted for me the risk of an unpleasant confrontation with the Vietnamese once they were discovered. And the thought of thirty-five thousand armed and belligerent Japanese, still unconvinced that they had lost the war, made me uneasy.

As if to underscore my uncertainties, we did not even get away from the airfield without an incident. The civilian agent, Petris, attempted to elude Japanese surveillance and head for Hanoi to spread the word that the French were coming. It was an unseemly and harebrained attempt, after I had just maintained the correctness of a French mission under my protection. He was caught and unceremoniously dumped in the back of a truck.

More Japanese officers and troops arrived with several sedans, and we made up a convoy led by a small tank. I boarded the lead car with Sainteny and our Japanese officer-escort. Grelecki, Feeback, and the French officers occupied two sedans, and our OG men rode in personnel carriers, with several truckloads of armed Japanese troops bringing up the rear. The convoy crossed the Doumer Bridge and traveled west on Boulevard Carnot, past the Citadel[7] to the *palais du Gouvernement Général* (Governor General's Palace), an elegant structure surrounded by impressive lawns and gardens. There we were met by a Japanese officer who inquired as to the purpose of the French group in Hanoi. I let Sainteny handle the question, hoping he would follow the lead I had given at the airport, but that was not to be. He started well on the humanitarian aspects of his task, and the officer seemed amenable and disposed to accommodate, until Sainteny demanded that the Japanese make available to him the facilities at the Bach Mai radio station to broadcast a "local information program" for the French in Indochina and for communications with his headquarters in China and India. The Japanese made no demur but, with a slightly altered air, informed us that quarters had been readied at the Hotel Métropole in downtown Hanoi and that we should proceed there directly.

Once again we boarded our vehicles. We had been skirting the northern section of the city through thinly populated areas. There had been no evidence of Europeans but we saw Vietnamese in small groups talking animatedly. They appeared interested in our convoy but not necessarily enthusiastic about our presence. Buildings and houses along the route to this point prominently displayed the Viet Minh flag. Our route from the Governor General's Palace to the hotel, along the Avenue Puginier and rue Borgnis Desbordes, showed quite a different aspect. The crowds thickened and there were many streamers in English, French, and Vietnamese stretched across the streets from balcony to balcony proclaiming Vietnamese independence, death to the French, and welcome to the Allies. There were no French flags anywhere—only the red flags with the five-pointed gold star.

We rode in silence for a while, Sainteny being visibly concerned. He stared out in disbelief. I, too, was surprised to see the streets so heavily festooned with Viet Minh flags and hostile placards and speculated aloud that Ho Chi Minh must have reached the city (he had not) and wondered what role the Japanese were playing. Sainteny turned to me and asked what I knew of Ho's plans. I repeated what I had already told him in Kunming—that Ho had a "government" in being and that it was only a question of time and circumstance before his government would be in power. I did not guess then the progress the Viet Minh had already made in taking over the reins of government. Sainteny fell into a depressed silence.

The crowds became more boisterous and hostile as we neared the Métropole. They had learned that "the French have arrived" in an American plane under the protection of the Americans. Japanese soldiers with fixed bayonets were posted every few feet along the route from the Petit Lac to the hotel, and they were hard pressed to contain the surging crowds.

HOTEL MÉTROPOLE

At the Métropole a large group of Europeans came out to greet us. They were mainly French. A few of them started to scuffle with some Vietnamese who had broken through the military cordon, but they were immediately corralled back into the lobby by the Japanese soldiers and Bao An[8] troops. Sainteny had regained his composure at the sight of French faces and was literally mobbed in the lobby. It was, of course, a poignant scene, with tears flowing and endless embraces, but chaotic in the great outpouring of grievances against Japanese and Vietnamese maltreatment. I could not but observe that the Japanese were coolly keeping order and that the French were in a high state of excitement and provocation, which gave me pause.

Several rooms on the second floor had been vacated for us, and I was shown to a large corner room overlooking a small park and the Résidence Supérieure[9] flying a huge Viet Minh flag. I had not been in the room five minutes when Grelecki and a Vietnamese hotel employee escorted in a tough-looking but pleasant Vietnamese, one Le Trung Nghia, representing the Hanoi City Committee. Nghia did not speak French but used the hotel employee as interpreter. He said the Committee had been advised by the Kunming Central Committee of our imminent arrival and had sent a delegation to Bach Mai to escort us into the city, but when the plane had not landed they had returned to Hanoi. Upon learning of our landing at Gia Lam, he had been delegated by the Hanoi City Committee to welcome the Americans to Viet Nam and to offer the hospitality of the city and the protection of the Provisional Government of Viet Nam. I thanked him and asked Nghia to join me in a cold drink which the management had sent up.

Directly I asked the meaning of the crowd outside and their apparent hostility. Nghia said the crowd was not hostile to the Allies but to the return of the French, though quickly assuring me that no harm would come to them if they did not bring in troops or attempt to interfere with the functioning of the Provisional Government. I told Nghia that my mission was to safeguard the Allied POWs and to make preliminary arrangements for the surrender of the Japanese, that there were only five Frenchmen with me and they were on a humanitarian mission to look after the POWs at the Citadel. In response to his questions I assured him that no, I did not anticipate the arrival of French troops; yes, there would be additional Americans coming shortly; yes, it was true that I had met President Ho Chi Minh; and no, the United States did not support colonialism. There was a knock at the door and I was informed that Japanese Lieutenant Ogoshi wished to see me. Nghia excused himself but, in parting, said the City Committee would remain at my disposal, with the employee/interpreter acting as their liaison for the time being.

Lieutenant Ogoshi, in formal military attire, samurai sword included, advised me that the French in my party were creating a serious problem and their presence in the hotel could easily precipitate violence. The General Staff felt that they could not assume the responsibility for the safety of our mission if the French insisted on remaining in the hotel. What did I wish to do with them?

I replied first of all that I could not accept the position that the Japanese authorities could not maintain public order or provide for the safety of the Allied mission of which the French were a part. Secondly, I was operating under the provisions of General Order No. 1 from the Supreme Commander of the Allied Powers and, on his behalf, Generalissimo Chiang Kai-shek expected the Japanese military authorities in Indochina to adhere to the agreement reached in China with the Japanese Imperial representative. I was not quite sure of my ground there, but it had a fine ring and Lieutenant Ogoshi seemed duly impressed at the mention of "Imperial representative." He then proposed quartering the French contingent at the Governor General's Palace where they could be adequately protected and the crowds controlled. I would let him know, I said. He saluted and departed somewhat less majestically than he had arrived.

In the lobby the scene closely resembled Grand Central Station at rush hour. Word had quickly spread that the French military had arrived, and more French were continually arriving. Sainteny extricated himself with some difficulty when I called him aside and suggested it would be in the best interests of all concerned if they quartered themselves separately and preferably within French property. Sainteny jumped at the idea and instantly himself proposed they use the Governor General's Palace. We consulted the senior Japanese officer present who called his headquarters for instructions. He was soon back, bowing and smiling. His superiors had agreed and offered to provide a personal escort and twenty-four-hour security for the French at the Palace. Using the Governor General's Palace fitted neatly into Sainteny's optimistic plans and he was obviously pleased. I was only too glad to be able to pursue my mission without the risk of public disorders or political entanglements.

At the moment of departure the Japanese raised an objection because Sainteny wanted to take along several French nationals to the Palace. The Japanese ruled that out and added that until I had met with the Commanding General and our position in Indochina was formalized the Allied Mercy Team was to consider itself under Japanese "protective and administrative custody." I protested, with Sainteny seconding, but the Japanese were adamant and there was nothing I could do but gracefully acquiesce for the time being. In the interim, there was no objection to our keeping our weapons and radio equipment, communicating with our headquarters in China, and freely receiving visitors. It was late afternoon when Sainteny and his four companions left the hotel with their Japanese escort.

Sainteny's decision to establish himself at the Palace proved to be a serious mistake for him. Instead of making him a colonial authority, it served only to isolate him from the mainstream of events in Hanoi. And the high degree of pride and volubility so noticeable among the French in Hanoi who looked to Sainteny for deliverance made it all too evident to both Japanese and Vietnamese "authorities" that the French were a source of provocation, giving strong reason to hem in Sainteny's party closely. The situation became essentially similar to the indiscreet conduct of the French under Mordant which had brought the March coup down upon them. Sainteny could not have controlled the indiscretions of the French population, but his wiser move would have been to remain within the parameters we had agreed upon and to insist upon remaining with my mission, to be "in on" rather than "out of." Before many days had passed, he would be asking me to remedy his situation, but I was not there to rescue either the French or the Vietnamese from their mistakes.

I returned to my quarters while several of the team circulated among the French in the lobby gathering what information they could. Our radiomen, Eide and Rodzlewicz, went right to work on the top floor setting up a communications center; a top priority was making radio contact with Kunming. Our pilot had returned to China as we left the airfield, so Helliwell knew we had had a safe arrival. Grelecki and Feebach had quickly organized the men into security teams, an intelligence unit, and communications operators. We followed tight security procedures for our own safety and that of our equipment, although no threat to either could be perceived. Everyone worked late into the night getting set for future operations. At about midnight an officer of the Japanese General Staff came to let me know that General Tsuchihashi had returned and would see me at my convenience. We made arrangements to meet at eight the next morning.

GENERAL YUITSU TSUCHIHASHI

Promptly at eight I was met by an English-speaking captain who, from that moment, became my bodyguard-interpreter. The General, he said, had placed a staff car and driver at my disposal and he had been assigned as liaison officer for the General's Staff in all matters concerning our relations with the Japanese. We rode the short distance to the Japanese Headquarters, near the river front and next to the Musée Louis

Finot. There the Captain led the way to the General's office where two
sentries saluted smartly as a third opened the massive double doors. I
have little recollection of the room itself, having been in a state of total
concentration on the armed guards about the headquarters and the
various unknowns which this conference might offer. At the far end of
the room I could see a smallish man at a neatly arranged desk with a
large portrait of Emperor Hirohito hanging on the wall behind and the
Rising Sun draped on the flagstaff nearby. Aligned along the right wall, I
quickly perceived, were ten or twelve senior staff officers standing erect,
almost at attention. A large teak conference table bisected the room.
Three chairs were already arranged, one on each side and the third at
the end nearest the door.

As I entered, the General rose from his desk, stood erect, and bowed
slightly. His officers followed suit, bowing more pronouncedly. I acknowledged their gesture with the customary military salute, and the Captain
introduced me to the General, and then introduced the staff officers to
me. Lieutenant General Yuitsu Tsuchihashi, a man in his late fifties, was
short (perhaps five feet five or six), round of face, apparently of a habit-
ually severe expression, and solidly built. His head was completely
shaved. At the General's invitation I sat on one side of the table, he directly across from me, with the captain-interpreter at the far end. The
other officers remained standing along the wall. Their faces were masks,
impossible for me to read, but certainly not friendly.

I took the initiative and stated that the Japanese government had
surrendered unconditionally to the Allied Powers on 10 August and that I
had been charged by the Generalissimo Chiang Kai-shek to determine the
whereabouts and condition of Allied prisoners-of-war in northern Indochina and to see that they were repatriated as soon as possible. I also informed him that in due course I would be acting as the initial intermediary in arranging for the surrender of the Japanese military forces in
northern Indochina to the Allied Powers. The General did not acknowledge Japanese capitulation but only informed me that on 17 August he
had received orders from the Southern Army Command to cease combat
within five days. On the eighteenth he had ordered the 38th Army to
cease hostilities by 8 A.M. on the morning of the twenty-first. However,
regarding my "mission," he said, he would have to consult with Tokyo. In
the meantime, the Americans were free to circulate at will within the
limits of the city of Hanoi.

I then raised the matter of visiting Allied POWs. The General acquiesced in principle to my demand but wanted to wait for instructions
from Tokyo which, he said, would be forthcoming within forty-eight
hours.

The next item I broached was the question of public order and safety. Tsuchihashi defensively replied that "under the circumstances" and
pending instructions from Tokyo he was gradually turning administrative

authority and tasks over to the "local Vietnamese" authorities. Even though uninstructed on this point, I informed the General that the matter of public order and safety was the responsibility of the Japanese authorities until properly relieved by the Allied Powers. This was not well received, either by the General or by some members of his staff who, for the first time, broke their stony silence to murmur among themselves.

Having established my official status and having placed the burden of responsibility for public order, it was an opportune moment to end the meeting. I stood, saying that I would advise Chungking of the morning's meeting and would communicate with the General later. The General also rose and bowed. I saluted and walked out with my shadow, the Captain, following.

CHAPTER 17

OUR SECOND DAY
IN HANOI

FIRST IMPRESSIONS

After my meeting with Tsuchihashi I drove about the city hoping to size up the local situation. I had not seen much the day before but from the commotion around the Métropole I expected to find the city shut down and the population tense. Instead the shops were open, the outdoor markets crowded with hawking vendors and haggling customers, the public buildings open and busy, and all displaying the Viet Minh flag. In fact, the sea of red flags and streamers was overwhelming. On the busy boulevards the Indochinese walked or biked cheerfully with an air of pride and confidence. Pedestrians and drivers responded in an orderly way to the traffic direction of Vietnamese gendarmes.

As I moved further into the city I became aware of a total absence of Europeans. Except for Japanese patrols and a sprinkling of Chinese, everyone seemed to be Vietnamese. Aside from the red flags, the only symbol of Viet Minh authority was the armed men and women patrolling the streets and guarding the buildings. They were in mixed uniforms but wore armbands of the People's Army of Liberation. However, on close observation I detected a discreet presence here and there of Japanese vehicles filled with armed troops on side streets.

At first I attributed their unobtrusive presence to Japanese precaution against possible disorders, but as my car rounded the Jardin d'Enfants I could see a massive building, heavily guarded by Japanese troops with machine guns mounted at strategic points and protected by barbed wire and sandbags. I was surprised for nowhere else, not even at the General Headquarters, had I seen such protective measures. I asked my captain-escort what it was and he replied, "The Bank of Indochina." The unusual protective measures were necessary, he said, because it was the "only thing of value left in the city."

At the Métropole, we found the area cordoned by armed Vietnamese and a sizeable detachment of Japanese troops at the ready. The triangular park and adjacent streets were jammed with Vietnamese shouting slogans, singing, and at times trying to break the security lines, although their attempts seemed more or less good-natured.

My Japanese captain quickly made his way to the officer in charge, and Sergeant Frederick Altman, a member of my team, came to acquaint me with the situation. Two Frenchmen had stirred up a commotion in the hotel with a rumor that Sainteny and his officers had been taken to the Citadel on a pretext of liberating French POWs and had, instead, been arrested. Some of the French in the hotel threatened the Vietnamese "boys"* and demanded that the Americans organize and lead a "punitive expedition" of French volunteers on a "commando raid" to liberate Sainteny and all the French prisoners. The hotel manager had called in the Japanese, who had quickly restored order. Then the Vietnamese police appeared on the scene, and the French in the hotel taunted them with epithets and obscene gestures. The brouhaha had attracted the crowds.

The police had arrested two Frenchmen known to the kempeitai as agents provocateurs. At my insistence the Japanese captain called the security guard at the Palace and was assured that Sainteny and his officers were in fact there and unmolested. The excitement died down, but I understood better why those trucks of Japanese troops lurked on the side streets. This city of seeming normalcy and peacefulness was seething below the surface, and it obviously did not take much for it to erupt.

Our OSS team had immediately become a center of Allied authority to which everyone with a cause or a desire for prestige brought himself to be heard. The French came to complain, make demands, and play conspiratorial games. The Vietnamese came to be seen with the Allies and acquire status in the eyes of their adversaries, creating an image of "insiders" with the American Mission. Other nationalities came for various self-serving interests.

Among the first to call was the Consular Agent for Switzerland, M. Robert Blattner. He presented his credentials and informed me he would

---

*A pejorative term for Vietnamese house servants, hotel employees, etc.

represent the interests of Germany, Italy, and other nations as required. I thanked him for calling but did not anticipate becoming involved in consular matters. Later, perhaps, I informed him, the Department of State would send a proper representative.

Another early caller was the president of the Bank of Indochina. Visibly upset, he "demanded" that I relieve the Japanese comptroller and guards at the bank and replace them with Allied or French personnel. He was distressed that the Japanese had withdrawn huge sums during the previous week and were demanding more "in payment of expenses incurred in maintaining law and order and for the protection of the French." I expressed my regret that he was having difficulties with his former clients but it was not a matter properly within my jurisdiction. He left in a huff.

HOW HANOI LED THE INSURRECTION

Soon two representatives of the Hanoi City Committee, Vu Van Minh and Khuat Duy Tien, came to establish "cordial relations with the Allies." I wanted very much to hear how the Viet Minh had assumed power in Hanoi, and M. Tien seemed delighted.

His first point was that "the people seized power without bloodshed." And proudly he informed me that "all public utilities and services continue uninterrupted" under the management of local Vietnamese. Everything I saw confirmed his claim. Water was coming out of faucets, lights could be turned on with a flick of a switch, toilets in the hotel flushed, and the telephones worked. The shops and open markets seemed adequately stocked, indicating an ample flow of supplies from outlying districts, and I had even seen a few civilian trucks and buses on the streets, attesting to the availability of some gasoline and public transportation.

Tien then described how everyone in Hanoi had become convinced, after Nagasaki, that the "Rising Sun was about to set" but that in Hanoi the Viet Minh lacked specific guidance. For several days members of the National Salvation Associations had speculated on what action could be taken when Japan capitulated. On 11 August word had reached them that the Party Central Committee was to convene a National Congress, but communications between Hanoi and Tan Trao were slow and insecure, and therefore members of the Viet Minh in Hanoi were in the dark.

On the thirteenth (the day the Party Conference opened at Tan Trao), the Regional Committee met on the outskirts of Hanoi to formulate a course of action. A member of the committee noted that the Viceroy for Tonkin (the Khâm-sai), Phan Ke Toai, had on several occasions expressed a desire to meet with representatives of the Viet Minh. He was known to support national independence but under a Vietnamese monarchical dynasty and Japanese tutelage. The Regional Committee delegated

Nguyen Khang[1] to approach the Viceroy and find out what he had in mind. As might have been anticipated, the Viceroy suggested the Viet Minh join the Bao Dai government[2] and drop its campaign against the Japanese. Khang refused the proposal.

Two days later when Japan announced its surrender, the Hanoi revolutionaries were still without word from Tan Trao. They met again[3] and decided to act on the basis of a 12 March directive from the Standing Bureau of the ICP Central Committee "to launch the insurrection when the situation is favorable." They regarded this as sufficient approval for action, and that night Nguyen Khang took the decision to the Hanoi revolutionaries.

Anticipating a Chinese or, possibly, a French occupation, the Japanese authorities in Tonkin had found it expedient to turn over to the Viceroy the local administration, the Civil Guard, the Central Security Service, the Censorship Service, and other lesser functions. The Tonkin Consultative Assembly in a last-ditch effort to retain power for the defunct Kim Government met in secret session on 16 August at the Résidence Supérieure and, in a bravura performance, voted to rally the people to Bao Dai, eschewed the Communist nationalists, adjourned sine die, and dispersed.

The Hanoi revolutionaries finally received word from Tan Trao that the launching of a general insurrection had been authorized, but they still considered themselves unprepared. They needed to generate popular support and put on a show of force, but how to do it? By a rare stroke of good fortune, their adversaries provided the perfect opportunity. The last, faltering elements of the Kim administration, in a vain effort to salvage their foundering position, had called the 17 August mass meeting of the Central Committee of Civil Servants. Leaping at this providential opportunity, the Hanoi City Committee decided to boldly surface the Viet Minh movement by disrupting the meeting and turning it into a Viet Minh demonstration. They worked feverishly to prepare themselves in the short time available with a plan for positioning specially trained young men and women of the Armed Propaganda Brigade at strategic locations in the crowd and to develop a scenario.

The crowd assembled in front of the Opera House (Théâtre Municipal) to hear anticommunist speakers support national independence under the aegis of Japan. As the first official speaker addressed the crowd, the Brigade agents unfurled their red flags with the gold star and shouted, "Support the Viet Minh." Others took up the cry, and pandemonium effectively broke up the official program. Red flags were everywhere, bouncing and waving wildly over the heads of the crowd, accompanied by chants of "Independence or Death," "Down with the French Colonialists," "Oust the Japanese Imperialists," and the like. The speakers tried to restore order, but it was too late; they had lost control. Then, at a prearranged signal, several members of the Honor Group[4] with pistols drawn dramatically climbed the platform and forced the Baodaist officials into a corner, lowered the imperial flag, and hoisted the Viet Minh colors.

Brigade leaders then took turns in addressing the crowd and shouting slogans, but they were ineffectual and the crowd began to lose interest and grow restless. Finally, Nguyen Khang in an impassioned appeal brought the crowd back in support of the Viet Minh. His theme was that Viet Nam regained its independence from the Japanese, not the French, because France had surrendered Indochina to the Japanese in 1940. Now the Japanese had been defeated by the Allies, and Viet Nam was free. He spoke of independence from all foreigners—Japanese, French, and Chinese; he accused the Kim administration of serving foreign interests and urged the people to rise and overthrow it, to fight for national independence along with the Viet Minh Front and the victorious Allies.

With the crowd now solidly behind him, Khang asked them to form ranks and march to the Governor General's Palace in a display of solidarity and strength. This was a touchy moment for no one knew what the Japanese and Bao An troops would do. But they made no move whatever to interfere. When the march began, the Bao An troops shouldered their weapons and joined ranks with the demonstrators, a tremendous victory for the Viet Minh. Bystanders along the line of march also joined the parade in substantial numbers, and even a heavy downpour did not dampen the crowd's spirit. As a demonstration it was a huge success. Except for the short scuffle on the speakers' platform there had been no violence or bloodshed.

The mass meeting was the first public and unopposed appearance of the Viet Minh as a political force. And it generated enough popular enthusiasm to carry more parades and oratory, along with general celebrations, for three days.

The Hanoi City Committee met that evening in a strategy session and concluded that the time was right to move out. They reasoned that the Kim administration did not dare stand up to them and that, moreover, the security and police forces would join them, weapons and all. They saw no signs that the defeated Japanese would make any move in opposition. Even the apolitical citizenry appeared sympathetic to their cause. Any delay might be fatal. The Japanese could change their minds. Adversary nationalists like the Dai Viet[5] and the Phuc Quoc[6] who had armed units in their ranks might organize opposition. Or the public might become apathetic. The Committee's historic decision was to order an insurrection for 19 August.

Again came a period of feverish preparation. A Revolutionary Military Committee[7] planned the events for the day, beginning with a huge rally to evolve into a massive parade for marching on the Governor General's Palace, the Résidence Supérieure, the Sûreté, the Vietnamese

Security Garrison, the Town Hall, and other targets of opportunity along the way.

In the dawn of 19 August, a Sunday, members of the Armed Propaganda Brigade fanned out to the suburbs and villages, urging the people to join in the rally in front of the Opera House. By nine o'clock great streams of people in family and neighborhood groups were walking or biking in a festive mood toward the city. Many were in Sunday finery and some in regional dress. They were given Viet Minh flags or placards manufactured only the day before and were hastily drilled to respond on signal with appropriate slogans or songs. Almost everyone had to be hurriedly taught the words and tune of their future national anthem, "Marching to the Front."

As they came in such numbers from all directions, converging on the square in front of the Opera House and backing up into all the streets of the area, they were said to form an awesome sight—a mass of humanity capped with thousands of red flags. French corroboration and photographs support the description as not exaggerated. Leading the columns were self-defense units armed with all sorts of weapons from modern Japanese rifles to French *mousquetons,* to old flintlock rifles, and hunting guns.

Toward noon, elements of the rally were organized into assault units and headed in two separate directions. One[8] marched to the Résidence Supérieure surrounded by a high iron fence and guarded by both Japanese and Bao An troops. The demonstrators pressed forward to the fence and called on the troops to lay down their weapons. The troops hesitated, long enough for several members of the self-defense unit to scale the fence. At this, the troops simply stacked their arms neatly on the ground before them and silently withdrew. The demonstrators inside opened the gates and the Residence was "taken." A search soon discovered that the Viceroy and his entire retinue had decamped. The brigade occupied the establishment, hoisted the Viet Minh flag in place of the imperial one, and posted its guards.

This was the first tangible Viet Minh victory, and it had immense symbolic impact. At one stroke, and without firing a shot, the concept of colonial rule was shattered and the whole puppet administration of Bao Dai was publicly unseated.

The Viet Minh self-defense unit found a sizeable cache of modern weapons and ammunition in the armory of the Résidence. Armed with the new weapons and augmented by defectors from the Bao An, the brigade marched on to other public buildings and occupied them with little difficulty.

The second column[9] stormed the Garde Indochinoise (Vietnamese Security Garrison). The commander of the Garrison, a secret sympathizer of the Viet Minh, obligingly opened the gates and handed over the keys of his arsenal. Out of the arsenal they took modern weapons, only to be confronted a few minutes later by several Japanese tanks and truckloads of foot soldiers. This was the moment of truth. The new weapons were of no help to the rebels, as they did not know how to use them, but the Japanese may not have realized that. In any case, the sight of their weapons gave the Japanese cause for reflection. In their momentary indecision, Le Trung Nghia[10] delivered an effective little speech to them, tactfully pointing out that they had been defeated and would soon return to their homeland. The Vietnamese, he said, no longer considered them enemies and, if they did not interfere with the internal affairs of Viet Nam, Nghia would guarantee their security. At this, the Japanese commander withdrew, leaving the field to the Viet Minh.

By evening the entire city, with the exception of the Bank of Indochina, the Governor General's Palace, and several Japanese garrisons, was under the control of the Viet Minh or, more precisely, the Hanoi City Committee.[11]

Certain myths over the years have sprung up about the "taking" of Hanoi. There was no coup d'état, no bloodshed, no reprisals, no French resistance, no secret plot or arrangement with the Japanese, not even substantive Vietnamese aid from outside Hanoi. Even as these events were being described to me by M. Tien, four days after the event, General Giap and his crack troops, with Major Thomas and the "Deer" team, were still battling the Japanese at Thai Nguyen some forty miles from Hanoi. Hanoi, the capital of Tonkin, the seat of French colonial power in northern Indochina, had liberated itself and set the pattern for the liberation of much of the rest of the nation.

Interrupting my inquiry into what had occurred in Hanoi, Lieutenant Ogoshi came with a personal message from General Tsuchihashi: the "Japanese High Command"[12] was concerned about Chinese troop movements in northern Indochina; Japanese outposts on the frontier had reported that three Chinese columns were crossing the border into Indochina at Lao Cai, Ha Giang, and Cao Bang and proceeding southward. Inasmuch as the signing of the surrender had not yet occurred and their only instructions from Tokyo were to "cease hostilities," the crossing was unwarranted and premature. Furthermore it was conceivable that circumstances would compel the Japanese to defend themselves from possible Allied attacks.

Expanding on the note from Saigon, Ogoshi stated that it was General Tsuchihashi's view that the Chinese crossing into Indochina prior to the final surrender would prejudice the political situation in Hanoi, causing possible disturbances and unrest among the Vietnamese and French populations.

I would not accept the note, and I considered its tone arrogant and threatening. I observed aloud that if the Japanese authorities in Indochina wished to violate their Emperor's rescript it was of no concern to the Americans. The Japanese lieutenant took this rebuff very hard. He would have to report to his superiors that he had failed to deliver the Marshal's note to the Allies. I understood perfectly his predicament and could not help but empathize. Through some indirection I was able to suggest that since actual negotiations at our command level had not yet started, perhaps Southern Army Headquarters might want to consider taking the matter up at the Tokyo level. The lieutenant instantly brightened and took his leave.

I notified Kunming immediately of the note and my refusal; within the hour I received a message from Heppner, "Good show."

RUMORS OF AN ABDICATION

During our busy day a UP reporter called to show us his story on our arrival. I asked him about the situation in Hué and Saigon. "Oh, big things are happening in Hué," he said, so I invited him to return in the evening and tell me about it. We had just finished dinner when he arrived.[13] He was a Vietnamese newsman with sources all over Indochina and had been with UP a number of years.

Over coffee and cognac he told us that news of the successful takeover in Hanoi had spread like wildfire. It was too soon to say conclusively that Viet Nam was free and independent, but in his view there was ample evidence that the movement had fired the imagination of the masses and nothing short of an armed force would restore the status quo. Reports from at least seven provincial capitals in Tonkin and five in Annam confirmed Viet Minh claims that the insurrection in those areas had been successful. As in Hanoi, the Viet Minh was in full control of the local administrations. Peoples' Committees from the local citizenry had been set up in cities, villages, and hamlets to man public utilities and courts, maintain public order, etc.

"What happened to Kim government?" we asked. "How could it have completely disintegrated? What about the Japanese? Why didn't they intervene?"

His view coincided with M. Tien's—that the Japanese High Command in Southeast Asia, after the atomic bombs, had made preparations for the inevitable capitulation. He saw the Japanese decision to turn the administration over to the Vietnamese as a result of a warped racist motive. Since early in 1930 the Japanese had promoted a program of racial solidarity against the white man in Asia, especially by jingoists in the army and racist elements in the kempeitai. He thought their pan-Asiatic objective had produced only marginal results among the Vietnamese but, with the war lost, the extremists in Marshal Terauchi's command redirected the program with the intention of presenting the Western Allies with a racial problem to complicate other problems of postwar occupation.

To that end the Japanese in Indochina had turned over most of their administrative responsibilities to the floundering government of Bao Dai immediately after the surrender address of the Japanese Emperor.[14] Bao Dai's prime minister, Tran Trong Kim, had already tendered his resignation and was at the time in Hué waiting for its acceptance. The Viceroy in

Hanoi, Phan Ke Toai, had been attempting to hold his administration together, but after the last meeting of the Consultative Assembly on 16 August (the secret session described by Tien), the Viceroy and most of his ministers and high officials had simply fled to the refuge of the imperial capital of Hué.

The UP man thought that the mischievous racial plan of the Japanese had failed, at least partly, because they had not anticipated contending with the Viet Minh as a third force. Although Asian, the Viet Minh were also communist, adamantly anti-Japanese, and staunchly nationalist; so in his view the racists had lost. His belief was that the Japanese had then chosen the path of discretion, fearing for their own safety and presenting no opposition to the new force.

"But what about Bao Dai?" we asked. "Is there organized opposition to the Viet Minh front?"

Digressing somewhat, the reporter recalled that after the March coup the Japanese had to find others to keep the nation producing for Japan's war machine. They did not want to be accused of perpetuating French colonialism, so they declared Indochina independent and called on Bao Dai to collaborate within the Greater East Asia Co-Prosperity Sphere and in defending the nation against the Allies.

Bao Dai, he thought, had no illusions about the Japanese but nevertheless had accepted and formed a new government acceptable to Tokyo, appointing Kim, an aging intellectual, as his prime minister. The cabinet he described as mostly professors, lawyers, and assorted mandarins of the old school, a weak cabinet and doomed to failure from the start. Four months of fruitless effort had led Kim to resign on 7 August, leaving the administration in a state of limbo at just the time the Viet Minh was ready to come forward.

"But what is Bao Dai doing?" we asked again. Well, he replied, Bao Dai had asked Kim to stay on and Kim had finally authorized a statement to the press on 16 August clarifying his intention of defending the independence of Indochina acquired from the Japanese on 9 March and emphasizing that the Vietnamese would never again subjugate themselves to France.[15] Two days later Kim had attempted to unite various ideological and political groups in support of Bao Dai's effort to save his "empire" by forming a Committee for National Salvation.[16] The next day the Viet Minh had taken over Hanoi.

As we talked into the evening, rumors of Bao Dai's imminent abdication were already making the rounds. The prospect made the French despondent. In their view such an event would end French claims to their former colony. Vietnamese feeling seemed to be mixed. Many, admitting the pro-Japanese bias of Bao Dai's administration, reasoned that it at least was Vietnamese and not pro-French.

As far as I could judge from all the information coming to me from many sources, the Bao Dai government was really finished and the Viet Minh assumption of authority was widespread, although the exact extent of its successes I could not gauge. Our information from Saigon was very fragmentary. And pro-Chinese elements in opposition to the Viet Minh were only now beginning to emerge, probably in the knowledge that Chinese occupation troops were already crossing the border. My team was also getting reports of French provocation and Japanese fifth-column activity.

I was becoming restive, too, about the situation with the POWs and the surrender of Japanese forces. A day and an evening had passed without further word from General Tsuchihashi. Worse than that, I had anticipated that Chungking would set forth its conditions and arrangements for the surrender, but their messages had been entirely silent on that subject. It seemed strange to me that while representing the great victorious nations I was still unable even to see the POWs.

CHAPTER 18

CALLS AND CALLERS

SAINTENY IN "THE GOLDEN CAGE"

I kept an eye out for Sainteny and his party after the false report of their arrest. My staff visited the group at the Palace and not only found them "well and happy" but also prolific: Sainteny's party of five had increased to eleven, the increase coming from Blanchard's group, recently in Haiphong, who with the help of the Japanese had joined Sainteny.

The next morning I visited Sainteny myself, and he complained bitterly that he was virtually a prisoner in the Palace and that I was doing nothing to help him. He then voiced his next grievance, over which he was fuming. The lead story in a local Indochinese paper read: "Viet Minh Fighting with U.S. Troops in Tonkin Will Soon Be Here to Oust the French Oppressors Who Last Year Starved 2 Million People." It was a long headline and one to make Sainteny choke. Worse still, the article mentioned Major Thomas by name, and Sainteny was still seething over the Montfort incident. When he had finished airing his grievances, we laid recriminations aside and reviewed the French situation in Hanoi.

First there were the French prisoners in the Citadel. Some were POWs, some were political prisoners, some were criminals. I asked if there was any one of particular importance for whose release he wanted

171

me to press. Lieutenant Missoffe started to answer, but Sainteny interrupted to say, "Yes, all the French now in prison." I did not believe we
could get the Japanese to open the gates but suggested we make this an
item for discussion with the Japanese. All Sainteny would reply was that
he could do nothing so long as he was held a "prisoner" in the Palace
(later dubbed *"la cage dorée"*).

The second subject Sainteny raised was the condition of the French
in Hanoi. What could be done for them? I suggested their best course for
the moment was to lie low and prevent any incidents which might suggest
reprisals from either the Japanese or the Vietnamese. In my judgment the
volatile situation in all Tonkinese cities made it suicidal for the French to
attempt a confrontation with the Viet Minh, but Sainteny showed his impatience with my unwillingness to endorse a French show of force.

I also described to Sainteny the emergence of a strong pro-Chinese
sentiment among certain segments of the population and a city-wide
display of Chinese flags and pro-Kuomintang posters. He felt that was a
plus for the French, proving that the Viet Minh did not have full control of
the indigenous population. I had to agree but held it was no indication
that they were pro-French. Sainteny kept insisting that we should not
allow the "Annamites" free rein in taking over the country.

We were back on the old kick, but I had no intention of allowing our
mission to become embroiled in his plans. No one will ever know with certainty whether a daring show of force by all the French in Tonkin at that
point might miraculously have toppled the Viet Minh, but the odds were
overwhelmingly against it. And it is worth noting that the French population in Hanoi, who were so eager for our little team of Americans to storm
the Citadel, did not at any time make a move for a French coup, either before or after Sainteny's arrival. In any case, my team was not there to
stage a coup for the French.

Sainteny and I were always in contention about this, but as I was
ready to leave he extended his hand and said, "Well, we are both trying
to do our jobs. I understand your position. Will you do me a favor and send
a message to General Alessandri for me?" I agreed to do so, and this was
the message:

Entire French Military under Major Sainteny have been placed in confinement
within grounds of Governor General's Palace. They may not circulate beyond a certain line of demarcation within Palace grounds nor will they be permitted to see
visitors except Patti.[1]

I could only shake my head in bafflement, but sent the message the same
morning.

The imminent possibility of dangerous confrontations was something
that had to be headed off. The newspaper had said that the arrival of
Thomas, allegedly at the head of the main body of Ho's troops, was to be
the signal for a massive anti-French demonstration. Knowing that demonstrations can sometimes turn into massacres, when I got back to the hotel,

I radioed Kunming of the press report, emphasizing the importance of persuading our "Deer" team to part from the Viet Minh forces and return to Kunming for an airlift to Hanoi. I warned them, too, of the real trouble which could start if even one French uniform should appear in the streets of any Tonkinese city and recommended in the strongest possible terms that our three SO teams operating along the northern borders be returned to Kunming before being airlifted to Hanoi without their French elements. In this way I hoped to disassociate all our Americans from either the Viet Minh or the French causes. But our teams were very loath to submit. Orders and Theater policy seemed to matter little to them. They were in high spirits and the repeated messages ordering them to Kunming had little effect; they wanted to pursue their own paths to victory.

While I was getting these more or less futile warnings off, Sergeant Altman was meeting the plane bringing the second element of our team[2] and several hundred pounds of the most urgent supplies requested by our AGAS agent for the POWs. And our mission was moving to new quarters under Lieutenant Feeback's supervision. The six hotel rooms had proved totally inadequate and insecure, and Grelecki had arranged with the Japanese for more suitable space. He had been shown several residences formerly occupied by the Japanese and had selected the spacious and elegant Maison Gautier with attractive grounds and gardens near the Petit Lac.

Of greater moment, I learned that General Tsuchihashi had received approval for me to visit the prisoners-of-war, although he still refused to release the prisoners until the occupying forces arrived. I immediately arranged with the Japanese to inspect the Citadel and the camp at Gia Lam.

THE PRISONERS-OF-WAR

The Citadel, an old French cantonment in the northern section of Hanoi, was sandwiched between the Sports Arena and the Botanical Gardens. It contained about a hundred buildings of varying size, construction, and age. Many had been barracks for French colonial troops but were then occupied by French prisoners. The most prominent structure at the northeast corner of the compound, formerly the French military prison of ill repute, now held those whom the Japanese considered their most troublesome prisoners, including the de Langlade-Mordant "resistance fighters."

From the outside the atmosphere was martial but not forbidding. French and Japanese troops mingled freely with civilians in what seemed to be a normal garrison complex. The arrival of our car at the gate created a stir, and the streets were quickly cleared of non-Japanese. From our limited perspective the Citadel presented the picture of an orderly military establishment.

We[3] were met at the gate by a surly Japanese major who engaged my Japanese escort in a brusque exchange. Without reading the note from the Japanese General Staff authorizing my visit he announced that there were no American prisoners there. I insisted on touring the compound and determining the condition of the Allied prisoners and the facilities. The Major then led us to an administrative building where a more congenial officer, Lieutenant Colonel Kamiya,[4] came forward to greet us saying he would be pleased to show me the camp. "Where would you like to start?"

I suggested we start with the roster of prisoners by name, rank, serial number, nationality, and category. He looked startled and turned to my interpreter to explain that there were over four thousand inmates and that I should understand it was extremely difficult to maintain current records on all of them. Some, he said, had been transferred to other facilities for medical or administrative reasons, while a few had escaped. However, if the Allied Command required such a list, he would try to have it for me in a week or ten days. I said the Allied Command absolutely insisted and that seventy-two hours should suffice. He promised to do his best.

We first toured the hospital area, a group of barracks converted into wards. They were poorly lit and cluttered with hospital tables, unkempt receptacles, piles of filthy linen and blankets. The aisles between rows of beds were barely sufficient to admit passage. A few droplights from the high ceilings were lit, but many seemed to have burned out long ago.

As we entered the first ward, those nearest the door spied our uniforms and sat up in their beds in startled silence. The reaction was almost instantaneous; all movement on the ward stopped and all heads turned in unison in our direction. Not a sound could be heard except our own footsteps and subdued voices as we proceeded single file down the long aisles.

I stopped at one of the first beds where a cadaverous form tried to raise itself and salute but could only get one leg over the side. I took his hand and told him the war was over. His eyes sparkled for a moment and he feebly asked, "Américains?" "Oui," I replied. All he could say was, "Merci." As I moved from bed to bed to touch each outstretched hand, I could see that they were very sick, probably suffering from many ailments, but all from malnutrition. Even those who were gravely ill and could not move seemed conscious that something important was happening. They had not been told that the war was over. We visited four more hospital buildings, and I saw approximately five hundred patients. Kamiya said there were many more, some ambulatory, but he could not tell me how many.

In each building I had seen only one or two Japanese doctors standing idly around but in plain view for me to notice. From the few patients with whom I spoke I learned that doctors were a scarce commodity. Kamiya explained that at the Citadel most of the medical staff was made up of French army doctors and corpsmen. "Where are they?" They had been directed, he said, to remain in their quarters while I toured the area "to avoid confusion and unnecessary agitation." I asked to see the senior French medical officer, but Kamiya politely refused on the pretext that he needed instructions from the General Staff. Perhaps it could be arranged on a subsequent visit. I was obliged to accept his refusal.

Throughout my observation of the hospital wards, I had the impression that a hurried effort had been made to clean up the really disgusting condition of general filth and sanitation, but there was too much to conceal successfully, and we were appalled and shaken by what we had seen. Inside this miserable hospital, where everyone was in dire need, I heard not one complaint. But in Hanoi their compatriots who had spent the war years in comparative ease and affluence complained incessantly.

Our next stop was at several prison quarters, where we were kept discreetly at a distance from the prisoners. They had been lined up in formation outside the barracks while we toured the inside. It was obvious that the Japanese authorities were not going to let me see much. They had carefully selected the areas for viewing and had the compound under tight security. Despite their rigid measures, I could hear scattered shouts in the distance—"Vive la France," "Vive de Gaulle," "Vive les Américains."

During my initial visit to the Citadel, which lasted about two and a half hours, I learned much, but not nearly enough. The Japanese were still in charge, and I had to have the authority of the Japanese High Command for anything that I wanted. I could only request, not demand. Under all the polite smiles, military courtesies, and diplomatic language, there was strong antagonism between us and I was at the disadvantage. Colonel Kamiya accompanied us to our car and with his seemingly indelible smile turned to my Japanese interpreter and said, "I hope the American captain has found everything satisfactory." I replied, "Not quite," thinking to myself, "Not by a damned sight." We exchanged salutes and my car left for Gia Lam.

We arrived at the POW camp there in the midst of a sudden downpour. The lonely sentry opened the gates of the barbed wire enclosure and we waited while he called on his field telephone. Soon we could see in the distance a vehicle approaching at high speed, dodging potholes and splashing mud in all directions. A Japanese captain and an NCO stepped out. My Japanese escort handed the officer the authorization from the General Staff and asked that we be shown to the Camp Commandant.

The contrast with the Citadel was striking. Gia Lam with its watchtowers and high wire fences, dirt roads and crude barracks, antiaircraft gun emplacements and armored vehicles, gave the appearance of an action unit, while the Citadel had seemed superficially like a peacetime garrison. I had coordinated the time of our arrival with the camp's noonday meal. On our way to the Commandant's office I saw long lines of Indian POWs with mess gear in hand waiting to be served. The rain had stopped as suddenly as it had started, but the mud underfoot was slippery and the men moved along slowly toward the mess hall. They were the Indian troops who had greeted us at the airport. Even at a distance I could see several amputees hobbling along in the mud and some very emaciated figures intent on reaching the serving center, mixed with sturdier men. As we approached, the line stopped and all heads turned in our direction. I waved, and they answered with enthusiastic shouts, making a din with their mess gear, but we hurried on to discourage any further show of exuberance.

Major Oshima[5] was standing at the door, impeccable in full uniform, with cap, ribbons, sword, and spurred boots. I guessed his age at thirty-five. Unlike the smiling Kamiya, his expression was severe and he appeared to feel in full control of the situation. We exchanged courtesies, he and my Japanese escort bowing and I with a military salute. Stepping aside Oshima led us into his spartan office containing only a small field desk and several straight-back chairs.

My first request was again for a roster of the POWs and their physical condition. Anticipating an outright refusal or at the very least a delay, I was completely surprised when without hesitation Oshima handed me several sheaves of paper listing the name, rank, and serial number of each prisoner as of the previous day. It had been prepared and signed by the "Senior-Captain of Indian POWs at Gia Lam"—the redoubtable "Simpson-Jones." The roster listed 287 prisoners, all British subjects.

I was manifestly pleased to have the roster and Oshima noticed it. He relaxed somewhat and asked me how soon it would be before the Allies took over the camp. "As soon as arrangements can be made for their evacuation, a week or ten days." He was not pleased and said that there were a few difficult prisoners who had been creating problems since mid-August. Several days before a delegation of POWs had demanded leave to go into Hanoi for reasons of recreation. He had refused. Another group headed by the same leaders had complained that the guards kept too close a surveillance on their activities. This he had ignored. There were other complaints of a similar character which he could not honor without breaking down the security and safety of the camp and the prisoners.

Oshima wanted me to address the prisoners and discourage them from further agitation. I declined, pointing out that the security of the camp and the safety of the prisoners was his responsibility until properly relieved. However, I suggested he take the matter up with the Senior-Captain, and he said he would. Later that afternoon I spoke privately with "Simpson-Jones" and emphasized the importance of avoiding incidents and pointless violence. The Japanese were armed and still in control and, in my view, postarmistice heroics would be unwise. "Simpson-Jones" understood and assured me he could handle it.

After their lunch the prisoners were formed in front of their quarters for roll call. Oshima suggested I might want to inspect them, and I did, taking the opportunity to observe them at close range and speak with a few. As we approached, the Senior-Captain called them to attention and saluted. I asked them to stand at ease and said a few words, something to the effect that the war was officially over, that the surrender would not be effective for a few days, that we were proud of them, "even the Americans." That brought wide smiles. I asked them to be patient for a few more days and assured them they would soon be evacuated to their homeland. I then walked among the ranks, stopping from time to time to inquire as to their welfare, where they came from, and if they needed anything. Invariably the answer to the last question was, "To get out of here." The prisoners were again called to attention, and the Senior-Captain saluted smartly as we returned to Oshima's office.

It was a strangely emotional experience. The end of a tragic British epic. Those Indian soldiers had been in Malaya in 1942 fighting a British battle to preserve a colonial empire when, against insurmountable odds, they were forced to surrender to the Japanese at Singapore. After three hard years of imprisonment and privation, they proudly retained their British identity before the enemy and Allies alike.

In Oshima's office I noted that the physical condition of the POWs was deplorable. Most seemed to be suffering from malnutrition. Many had undergone amputations and lacked crutches or artificial limbs, being dependent on the help of fellow prisoners to get about. Quite a few appeared to have eye infections and open sores on their faces and arms. Oshima apologetically explained that he had only recently assumed command and had not had time to institute reforms. He was aware of several cases of tuberculosis, beriberi, malaria, and amoebic dysentery and was trying to have those cases admitted to the French hospital in Hanoi. The camp dispensary was limited to twenty beds for emergency cases only and medical care was austere. However, until now, the French doctors at the Citadel and the city hospitals had refused to admit Indian POWs to those facilities. Oshima admitted, however, that after the surrender many of the Japanese doctors and medical personnel had packed up and left. Nevertheless, the Indian POWs appeared to me better off than the prisoners in the Citadel. The organization and size of the camp itself led to good morale and the prisoners were able to help each other to their great benefit.

There was nothing of immediate practical value that I could do to ameliorate the condition of the POWs except to protest to General Tsuchihashi, which I did, and he promised to look into the situation. I also informed Kunming and was advised that they could take no action until the Chinese assumed control after the formal surrender in Hanoi. As frustrating as that answer seemed at the time, there really was nothing to be done without Japanese concurrence and cooperation.

Back at the Maison Gautier, the AGAS agent wanted to see me in private. We walked out in the grounds and he showed me a note in French giving the name, rank, and serial number of an American in the Citadel. It had been passed to AGAS by a Frenchman who had not stopped to identify himself. We were in a quandary as to how to locate the man. We could not ask the Japanese because our man evidently was unknown to them. Furthermore, prisoners had an affinity for getting themselves into untenable situations in prison camps and we did not want to expose him if such was his case. I let our X-2 team see what they could do. The next day a former GBT agent at the Citadel infirmary, one M. Marcel Orthet, identified an American posing as a Hungarian citizen in the French Foreign Legion. He was a flight crewman downed in 1943. On 28 August the Japanese released him to my custody, and several days later he was flown home.

Grelecki had had callers during my absence. One was a young Vietnamese, Le Xuan of the Viet Minh Front. He was persistent in requesting to speak with me personally. President Ho, he said, was on his way to Hanoi and would like to see me. Grelecki suggested he return the next day. This was the first time we had been in contact, even indirectly, since the "Deer" Team had marched out of Tan Trao. Ho's situation had, of course, taken a fantastic leap forward, and I anticipated Le Xuan's return with lively interest.

THE SOVIET REPRESENTATIVE

That night I had a visit from the Soviet representative in Indochina, Mr. Stephane Solosieff. He had called briefly during my first hours in Hanoi, and I had invited him to come at this time for a drink. A pleasant man in his late forties with an open smile and a direct approach, Solosieff was an unusual caller. Unlike the injured French seeking redress, the defeated Japanese masking their inner thoughts behind a façade of correctness, or the Vietnamese pressing for recognition, Solosieff came as an equal in victory, an ally, and a friend. He represented himself as some sort of Soviet liaison to the Japanese political offices in Hanoi, Hué, and Saigon with the task of looking after the interests of Soviet citizens in Indochina who numbered, he said, five or six hundred. Several hundred of these were in the French Foreign Legion, he said, but that still left a quite surprising number of civilians. Undoubtedly many were associated with the large commercial Japanese complex operating in Indochina.[6]

Early in our conversation I discovered Solosieff to be intelligent, worldly, and fluent in several languages, including French and English; doubtless he was proficient in Japanese, too. I had met several Russians of his caliber in Europe and took it for granted that he was also a political agent of Moscow. As the evening wore on, my intuition proved correct and I was pleased that he did not attempt to disguise his role. As for myself, it was common knowledge that I was an OSS officer.

We found common ground in discussing the Viet Minh takeover and speculated on the odds of their success once the French returned. Solosieff believed the French should not anticipate a return to the status quo ante but rather should pursue a course of gradual withdrawal. He thought the Vietnamese not quite ready for total independence and in need of protection from a powerful nation to discourage Chinese and Thai territorial ambitions. I noted that Chiang had already gone on record as claiming no interests in Indochina except where the French were concerned, but Solosieff was not sure that would be the case. He thought the French were the best equipped of the western powers to reconstruct the country and guide the people toward self-government.

Solosieff had heard from the French that Ho Chi Minh and the Viet Minh were under American "protection" and asked if that were true. I told him frankly that we had accepted the Viet Minh's collaboration in clandestine operations against the Japanese but that the United States had made no commitment to interfere in the internal affairs of Indochina.

I asked him about the Soviet position on Indochina, noting that Ho had been groomed by the USSR, for years had been a Comintern agent, and more recently had been a communist delegate instructed by Moscow. Solosieff's answer sounded strangely like an echo of the Roosevelt vision: the days of French colonialism were over, he said. The Indochinese would have to assume a role of responsible nationalism, although they might not be able to handle the reins alone. Perhaps with enlightened French help and American technical assistance they could achieve national independence in a few years. He did not use the word, but his remarks reminded me of the trusteeship concept proposed by Roosevelt and more or less endorsed by Stalin at Yalta.

"What about the Soviet Union?" I asked. He did not believe the Soviet Union would be in a position to interpose itself in Southeast Asia. He took the then-current line that "Mother Russia" after the Nazi onslaught would need time to rebuild. Ho had expounded this same view to me. The communists around the world were, in this vein, to hold the line and maintain their strength while "Mother Russia" recovered. Solosieff moreover felt that Soviet interference in Southeast Asia would create a conflict with the traditional French and British interests which would not be in the best interests of the Soviet Union at that time.

We spoke of events in Saigon, of which I was largely ignorant. His information was that the Japanese had turned over control of the government to a small communist group under the leadership of Dr. Tran Van Giau[7] and that the Viet Minh in Saigon was moving fast. He thought the British would have a difficult time there. He offered to put me in touch with more knowledgeable people, but I declined, pleading limited interest; in fact I was keenly interested but did not want to become identified with his apparatus.

Drinking vodka we talked for several hours in a relaxed atmosphere, a visit I believe we enjoyed equally. As he was about to leave, Solosieff asked me to transmit a message to the Soviet Embassy in Chungking, which I did. In French, it requested the Soviet Embassy to send a representative to Hanoi to deal with the liberation of "certain Russian volunteers" in the Legion imprisoned as POWs and "for many other matters."

As an afterthought, he asked me if I had heard of a Russian subject named Andrei Voskressensky. I had not. His family in Russia had not heard from him since the March coup. About ten days later our X-2 team came across his name during their investigation of the Japanese gendarmerie (the kempeitai) for evidence of war crimes and war criminals. The gendarmerie files revealed that Voskressensky was living in Hanoi and had been employed by the kempeitai since 9 March. His father was Russian and his mother Japanese, although she later became a naturalized French citizen. The father had been at one time a Soviet naval attaché in Tokyo and the son had served as secretary to the wing attaché at the French Embassy in Tokyo. In September 1942 Decoux had requested the son's transfer to Hanoi, where he had worked with the French police until the coup, after which he transferred to the kempeitai. I speculated on why Solosieff wanted Voskressensky, but it was obviously not for humanitarian reasons, and we did not reveal his whereabouts.

I was much interested in Solosieff's allusion to "certain Russian volunteers" in the Legion. The French officer at Ch'ing-Hsi had mentioned that Alessandri had had a number of his Legionnaires court-martialed for communist activities in 1944 but I considered that gossip. Solosieff's admissions gave it more substance, and I set my X-2 team on the lookout for Soviet activities in the Legion. They soon discovered a well-organized communist cell among the Legionnaires imprisoned at the Citadel. They were not all Russians but included German, Belgian, and Hungarian communists, Austrian socialists, and French radicals. Before the coup the cell had infiltrated the de Langlade-Mordant movement and had collaborated with the Viet Minh. During the French retreat to China some had deserted and joined Ho's ranks as intelligence agents and instructors in weapons and tactics.

Interviews with Vietnamese of the Armed Propaganda Brigade in Hanoi and with European members of the cell enabled our investigators to learn the history of the cell. Late in 1944, so as not to overexpose the activities of the ICP, the party's Central Committee founded the Anti-Japanese Democratic Front in Indochina. Ostensibly anti-Japanese and anti-fascist, its members were not readily identifiable as communists and stood a better chance to work within the Decoux administration. Among its objectives, the Front concentrated on proselytizing among foreign elements with antifascist leanings. It established contact with the Foreign Legion and organized a "socialist-communist" group. In November 1944 the group was invited to take joint action against the Japanese and French fascists in Tonkin. It was agreed that Legionnaires associated with gaullism would use their influence with the Decoux administration to stop or reduce the requisitioning of rice, help in the liberation of political prisoners, and secure arms for the Viet Minh. The Chinese sympathizers were to work within the Kuomintang army to assist the Viet Minh outside Indochina. The timid gaullistes failed to carry out their role, but the Chinese "comrades" were more effective. After the coup only a hard core of communists in the Legion remained loyal to the Viet Minh and joined their ranks.

Solosieff was apparently trying to extricate from the Citadel, and perhaps from Indochina, those Soviet agents involved in the Front, before the arrival of either French or Chinese forces. We know, however, that in the French-Vietnamese war Giap's troops had many former Legionnaires in their ranks acting as advisers and political commissars.

During my last days in Hanoi, I asked President Ho the significance of including a provision for the organization of "foreign combat units" in the April 1945 plan of the Revolutionary Military Conference of North Viet Nam. Only half jokingly, he had said, "To take care of our American friends in our struggle for independence." In a more sober vein he explained that those units were made up of French soldiers, mainly Legionnaires, who were "fed up with French colonialism."

During my weeks in Hanoi I was interested to observe Solosieff in the company, variously, of Japanese officials, influential French, Viet Minh leaders, and prominent Chinese. His was the only visible Soviet presence at the time, and he kept his role very low key.

CHAPTER 19

THE TALE OF
TWO CITIES

A PRESS CONFERENCE

M y desire for information on what was happening in Saigon remained urgent. Despite the recently contrived division at the sixteenth parallel, we in OSS looked at Viet Nam as one nation and
were as much concerned with events in the south as in the north. Quite by
chance I found an excellent source of information in the local press corps.
Unbeknown to me, the Saigonese were staging an immense victory parade
on 25 August as we were receiving a group of ten or twelve Vietnamese
representing Hanoi's major dailies and periodicals who had called on the
"Allied Commission" to get editorial and censorship guidance. We invited
them into our large reception room and informed them that we were not a
"commission" and that, as far as we were concerned, there was no censorship and no editorial guidance.[1]

They seemed visibly confused at having a free press but continued
with their formalities. M. Minh,[2] acting as spokesman and interpreter,
asked to read a prepared statement. Opening with a warm welcome, it
lapsed into a listing of French abuses, turned to the Vietnamese desire for
national independence, and concluded with a plea that the United States,
Great Britain, the Soviet Union, and China be sympathetic to their cause.

I thanked them for their kind welcome and invited them to return any time they had questions. Noting their persistent reference to us as a "commission," I explained our nonpolitical role and pointedly reminded them that, although the United States was sympathetic to their aspirations, American policy was one of noninterference in the internal affairs of other nations. In the light of our later war years in Viet Nam, that statement will perhaps startle the reader, but in 1945 it was entirely genuine and clearly reflected settled policy.

They had questions on French and Chinese intentions, Allied attitudes toward Viet Nam, and my reaction to the Viet Minh's success in Saigon. I answered most of the questions, except those on Saigon, and told them I would be grateful for any factual information they might share with me about Saigon and Nam Bo (Cochinchina). Several from the Hanoi dailies offered clippings from their papers, while others offered to sit down with my staff to develop a detailed account. I accepted their offers and assigned Robert H. Knapp[3] to work on the project.

We were in that way enabled to air-pouch on 31 August a comprehensive report on the situation in the south. It was the first information Kunming, Chungking, and Washington received about that area, although three weeks had by then elapsed since the Japanese capitulation. I was able to get a fair picture of events in the south as they unfolded during the time Knapp's report was under preparation, and this was most useful in our day-by-day efforts to prevent outbreaks of trouble in the north.

THE SAIGON "REVOLUTION"

In 1945, as today, the city of Saigon in the heart of Cochinchina differed radically from Hanoi, its sister city to the north. Its geography, climate, social temperament, and political philosophy are all dissimilar. When the Viet Minh in early 1945 assumed control of the Liberated Area in Tonkin, the hegemony of the movement was solidified and unchallenged. And when on 19 August the local committee seized power in Hanoi it was not a totally independent action but in line with a preestablished central directive of long standing. To the south it was quite different.

Cochinchina, that wealthy private domain of French colonial interests, had little in common with the less affluent states of Annam and Tonkin.* The events of August in Hanoi and Hué were only a distant echo in Saigon. Cochinchina was in a state of utter confusion, having been rent by conflicting personal and national interests, and was therefore not quite ready for independence. Not that the torch of independence did not burn brightly in the south, nor that there was a lack of nationalist movements and ardent followers; on the contrary, there were too many movements, all diffusing their efforts in deeply felt ideological and social

*From its inception Cochinchina was administered by the French as a colony, while Annam and Tonkin were given the status of protectorates.

controversies which resulted in interparty struggles. These conditions still obtain today.

Aside from the Communist Party, the most prominent nationalist groups in Cochinchina were the Trotskyites,[4] the pro-Japanese Phuc Quoc and Dai Viet, the political-religious sects of the Cao Dai and the Hoa Hao, and the Advance Guard Youth.[5] And there were many lesser parties. All advocated independence in some form, but only the Communist Party had a well-conceived program and organization.

The Communist Party in Cochinchina was distinctly a product of French political influence. Its membership was small, being drawn from the intelligentsia and petit bourgeoisie, and it was prone to ideological dialecticism rather than assertive action. It almost goes without saying that it had none of the militancy of the ICP in the north. Its leaders in the main were from the professions; they were trained in French schools and were urbanites. Less harassed by the French police, they met openly and casually, unlike their northern counterparts who skillfully operated in a clandestine milieu.

An additional contrast was the parochialism of the southern communists as compared with the wide political participation encouraged by Ho Chi Minh. The Viet Minh under Ho welcomed all political elements, ethnic groups, national minorities, women, and social classes in a democratic front. The southern communists resisted any association with the Trotskyites, Caodaists, the Hoa Hao, and other noncommunist elements. The result was open opposition from its political adversaries and only limited popular support.

Another point worth noting was the autonomous character of the southern Communist Party. Throughout the history of French rule, Cochinchina's administrative and political controls had been entirely separated from those of Annam and Tonkin. After the March coup, the Japanese continued that practice until 14 August, when they allowed Bao Dai to appoint a Khâm-sai (Viceroy)[6] to take over the reins of government in Cochinchina. As a result of this arbitrary geographic separation between the states in Indochina, the Communist Party in Cochinchina was largely isolated from the Central Committee of the ICP in Tonkin and lacked substantive guidance until after the Tan Trao Party Conference of 13 August.

Immediately after the coup the Japanese were hard-pressed to find loyal Vietnamese to replace the French bureaucracy (now mostly in jail) and to protect their rear lines of communications from a threatening Allied sabotage. They found some pro-Japanese sympathizers among the nationalist groups centered in the Japanese-sponsored United National Front,[7] from which they drew the individuals they needed before allowing the Front to languish.

When the leaders of the dormant Front suddenly realized in August that the Viet Minh in Tonkin was moving out to capture control of the independence movement nationwide, they reactivated its membership. On 14 August the Front's Executive Committee moved rapidly into the position the Japanese were about to vacate and took over control of Saigon on 16 August. This has been hailed as the "revolution in Saigon," but it can hardly be thought of as a takeover. The pro-Japanese administration remained intact and no one in Saigon was even aware that a "revolution" had occurred.

The Japanese penchant for intrigue played a crucial role in the "revolution in Saigon." Bao Dai's Viceroy, Nguyen Van Sam, arrived in Saigon on 19 August (as it happened, the same day the Viet Minh seized power in Hanoi). His first move was to arrange with the Japanese for the transfer of large quantities of arms for the creation of a militia under his control. The Japanese gave him the arms.[8]

The United National Front held sway in Saigon for a full week. During that time the news that the Viet Minh had seized power in Hanoi and Hué and that the Emperor had alluded to his probable abdication reached the Saigonese. The masses in the south, who knew practically nothing of the Viet Minh, were impressed.

At Hué the Emperor got word of the proceedings at Tan Trao and of the Viet Minh takeover in Hanoi. With a grim determination to hold on to his precarious position, Bao Dai appealed on 19 August for popular support. To the world he said the people of Indochina were "capable of self-government and have mustered their total strength to consolidate the basis of their independence." Of the people of Viet Nam he asked cooperation, saying "I am prepared to sacrifice myself for the purpose of preserving the independence of the Kingdom and the rights and interests of my people."[9] He had begun to waver, and that was the first hint that he would abdicate if it became necessary.

Despite his title, court, and tenuous authority, internationally Bao Dai's legal position as head of state was subject to question. Six months earlier, on 11 March, he had proclaimed the independence of Viet Nam by publicly abrogating the French-Annamite Treaty of Protectorate of 1884 and by accepting Japan's tutelage. But France had ignored Bao Dai's proclamation of independence and considered Japanese occupation of its colony a "mere incident of war" to be rectified with the defeat of Japan. Legally nothing had changed. As that defeat occurred, Bao Dai's status as head of an independent Viet Nam was in jeopardy. On 20 August, Bao Dai addressed personal messages to President Truman, King George VI, Generalissimo Chiang, and General de Gaulle, seeking their endorsement and formal recognition.

It was at this point that in Hanoi (quite independent of the proceedings at Tan Trao and without coordination with the Central Committee of the ICP), leftist students and faculty held a mass meeting under the auspices of the Association Générale des Étudiants.[10] They adopted a strong resolution calling for Bao Dai's abdication and the institution of a republican form of government under the aegis of the Viet Minh Front, demanded that the Viet Minh Front open talks with all the political parties to form a provisional government immediately and, finally, appealed to the people and the political parties to support a provisional government so that national independence could be achieved. They telegraphed the resolution to the Imperial Palace on the same afternoon.

The pressure was on Bao Dai to act, and to act decisively. The Viet Minh had been urging the city workers and rural farmers to seize power; the intellectuals and university students were agitating for radical changes in the government; and the nationalists had been demanding the overthrow of both foreign and domestic overlords. Bao Dai's reponse to these pressures was not to abdicate, but to hold on just a bit longer by inviting the Viet Minh Front to form a new government to replace Kim's. He shared with his people a desire for independence, having had quite enough of foreign protectorships. He had no personal animosity toward the Viet Minh and would willingly have accepted them into his government after their emergence as a political force. But his gesture was too late: at Hué, Saigon, and Hanoi his ministers were resigning and thus, in effect, he had no government.

Nevertheless, Bao Dai, ever malleable, wired the Viet Minh authorities at Hanoi that he was ready to abdicate and invited the Viet Minh Front to form a national government. His invitation reached Hanoi on 22 August. The Viet Minh had already formed a Provisional Government, had already assumed control of many of the major cities, and had indeed already demanded Bao Dai's abdication in favor of the new republic.

The pressure for change was also being felt by the parties in the south, both the United National Front and the representatives of the Viet Minh. The arms transaction between the Japanese and the Viceroy had not escaped the notice of Ho Chi Minh's trusted friend, Tran Van Giau. It was obvious to Giau that a well-armed opposition would make it extremely difficult if not impossible for the Viet Minh to gain a foothold in Cochinchina. Grasping at straws, Giau arranged to be heard at a hastily called meeting of the United National Front on 22 August.

Tactfully he advanced the premise that the United National Front would be looked upon by the Allies, who were at that very moment landing in Hanoi,[11] as a Japanese-sponsored movement and would therefore promptly be outlawed. Giau, of course, had reference to, although he did not identify them, the pro-Japanese Phuc Quoc, Dai Viet, Cao Dai, Hoa Hao, and lesser groups of similar leanings. He then proposed as an acceptable alternative the Viet Minh—notorious for its vehement anti-French stand, "strongly supported by the Allies with arms, equipment and training," and a recognized front-runner of the national movement.

Giau reminded them that the Viet Minh was also a coalition of many and varied political parties advocating national independence, and he was certain the United National Front would be welcomed and supported in the Viet Minh.

While the meeting was in progress, the astounding news reached them that the Emperor had "instructed the Revolutionary Party of Viet Nam, Left-Wing National Faction, to form a new cabinet . . . to succeed Premier Kim's Cabinet which had resigned en bloc. . . ."[12] Despite the obscure designation, they had no doubt that the charge had been given to Ho Chi Minh and his Viet Minh.

Giau's arguments may not have been wholly convincing to everyone present, but his allegations that the Allies looked with favor on the Viet Minh seemed to be supported by the Emperor's willingness to trust the fate of the nation to its leadership. Just as convincing may have been Giau's allusion to the Viet Minh's armed strength in terms of the alleged Allied support. Another persuasive factor may have been the disposition of the armed Advance Guard Youth[13] to side with the communists.

Throughout the night of the twenty-second and the next day the telephone and telegraph lines between Saigon, Hué, and Hanoi were crowded with priority traffic. The twenty-third proved to be a traumatic one for the sedate imperial city of Hué, the scene of an immense "peaceful" demonstration staged by the Liberation Committee in support of the Viet Minh. They turned out a crowd of more than a hundred thousand (more than double the city's population) articulating their demand that Bao Dai turn over the government to the Viet Minh.

The twenty-third proved also to be the day the United National Front would meet for the last time—to withdraw its leadership in the revolution in favor of a newly-created Provisional Executive Committee for the Nam Bo[14] under the chairmanship of Tran Van Giau. The Committee promptly installed itself in the Government Palace and the City Hall and, within the hour, issued a public pronouncement declaring itself to be the southern section of the Hanoi and Hué government.

In Hué that evening the imperial household received the telegram from the Viet Nam National Liberation Committee demanding the abdication of the Emperor.[15]

If Bao Dai had any reservations about the Viet Minh, the crash of events in Hanoi, Hué, and Saigon had dispelled them. He, with most of the people in Viet Nam, was certain that the Viet Minh had the blessing and support of the Allies and there was no point in resisting the rising tide of "democracy." The next day, the twenty-fourth, following the advice of his personal secretary at the Court,[16] Bao Dai replied to the National Liberation Committee in Hanoi that he had decided to abdicate "so as not to stand in the way of national liberation and the independence of my people." At the same time he asked the Committee to send its designated representative to Hué to legally effect the transfer of powers and authority.[17]

THE MANDATE FROM HEAVEN

It has always seemed to me the greatest paradox that the French, in the closing months of World War II and in their anxiety to subvert the American policy of not assisting a French reoccupation of Indochina, unwittingly led the way to their own undoing. Over and over again they frustrated every request for collaboration with genuine Allied military efforts against the Japanese. Had they worked honestly toward the defeat of the Japanese within the Allied framework, it is most doubtful that there would have been any need to resort to a joint military action with the Viet Minh. The "Deer" team was only an experiment, a trial venture, born out of the frustrations of the French sit-downs, slow-downs, and withdrawals from participation.

And how skillfully Ho succeeded among his own people in pyramiding the little "Deer" team mission into a fantastic psychological factor. First, on the slimmest evidence he convinced the rival leaders of competing parties at Tan Trao that he had American backing and that he was the man and his the party to form a provisional government. In the clinch Bao Dai, observing the Viet Minh's successes in Tonkin and Annam and hearing the widely rumored allegations of American backing, was easily convinced that the Viet Minh was the front to form a national government. In turn, with Giau alleging American military support for the Viet Minh and with Bao Dai inviting the Viet Minh to form a government, how could the nationalist political parties in the south not accept this "American-backed" Viet Minh leadership?[18]

As the unsophisticated masses saw the act of abdication, the Viet Minh inherited Bao Dai's authority by the Emperor's own hand. The perfect order and expedition with which it took place made it clearly the "mandate from Heaven."[19] This aspect of the Viet Minh's assumption of power was not well understood by the Western world at the time and was clearly never understood by the American political and military authorities throughout our later difficulties in Viet Nam. While the world may dismiss the idea of heavenly intervention as mere superstition, it was an important article of faith among the Vietnamese peasantry. The apparent ambivalence of the common soldiery and village leadership in the south through the recent war years is better understood in the context that the Hanoi regime had the "mandate from Heaven" which also brought an encompassing trust in "Uncle Ho."

In the terms of August 1945, Ho parlayed his narrow resources into a legendary success story. It is certainly true, however, that Ho could not have succeeded if his ICP had not been well organized and prepared for seizing power. The many years of preparation did not count for nothing. Nevertheless, without the false aura of American backing, the Viet Minh might very well have failed to achieve the national leadership at any step of their progression from obscurity to preeminence.

So the Viet Minh rose to become the great uniting force and the French nemesis. While Sainteny was fantasizing the political immaturity of the Vietnamese and doubtless expecting their politicians to fall upon each other in a hopeless division of political strength, he himself and his eager DGER associates were in a strange and indirect way a moving force in the Viet Minh's phenomenal rise.

"CITY OF HO CHI MINH"

In Saigon 25 August was the festive day for the Cochinchinese to celebrate the dawning of a new era. Everyone, that is almost everyone, wanted to be a part of it. Viet Minh flags fluttered everywhere. The Nam Ky Party Committee held an unprecedented mass demonstration of over five hundred thousand to witness their new leaders taking office. In their efforts to outdo their compatriots in Hanoi and Hué, the Saigonese paraded past their leaders for nine uninterrupted hours.

In only six days the Viet Minh had succeeded in assuming control in Tonkin, Annam, and Cochinchina. On the surface at least, Viet Nam was finally united and independent. It was to be a short-lived unification as events later showed, but it was a beginning and the Vietnamese were elated.

On the following day the Saigonese and many of their neighbors in the southern provinces heard for the first time the voice of Ho Chi Minh in a broadcast which stirred their somewhat latent spirit of independence. For the first time in modern history they had a sense of belonging, a sense of a larger and more powerful national identity. Sensing the psychological impact of Ho's speech on the Saigonese, Huynh Van Tieng's propaganda machine ground out a new name for Saigon: "City of Ho Chi Minh." Except for the brief period of September-October 1945 the new name was not to be heard again until April 1975 when the cry of "Defend Ho Chi Minh City" was heard once more.

Two days after his assumption of power, Giau was to have his first serious disappointment when he met with Jean Cédile[20] to discuss the role of the French. (It was not until much later that I learned of the circumstances of Cédile's arrival in Saigon, which will be described in its place.) Giau soon learned that the French were only willing to discuss the future of Indochina on condition that French sovereignty first be restored. The Vietnamese took the position that relationships with the French could only be considered if France recognized Viet Nam as a sovereign and independent nation. An impasse was reached very quickly.

HO IS IN HANOI

Le Xuan, the young Vietnamese who had called on behalf of President Ho, was waiting after my meeting with the Hanoi press. Xuan said "Dr. Ho" was staying with friends in Hanoi and hoped I could find the time to meet with him. I said I would, but asked when and where? Xuan explained that "Dr. Ho" wished to stay out of public notice until he was ready to assume office, but he would send a friend to bring me to him. I told him I had a constant Japanese escort and would certainly be followed by the kempeitai, but Xuan was confident that that was not an obstacle. The important thing was that I not let the French, any French whatever, know that Ho was in the city or that I was to meet with him. I reassured him of my discretion and he left, saying he would be in touch.

POLITICAL WARFARE

After his departure I called on Sainteny. The French were operating quite freely within the confines assigned to them by the Japanese. Admittedly they were not allowed to leave the Palace grounds and were restricted to one wing of the Palace, but they were permitted visitors without limit and had their radio communications with the outside. From my casual observations, I could see that Sainteny's group was not just marking time. With the help of Blanchard, who had been a Decoux liaison officer with the Japanese in Saigon and Hanoi, Sainteny was already making long-range plans.

His first request was for passage for Blanchard on one of the shuttle flights to Kunming. Undoubtedly he wanted to report confidentially to Calcutta and Kunming and possibly to obtain some official status for his presence in Hanoi. I arranged the passage the same day.

What troubled me regarding Sainteny's activities was not his effort to establish a French presence in Hanoi but his inclination to agitate the French and create explosive situations. Of course, Sainteny was taking his cues from the SLFEO/Calcutta, but not in every instance. In the early days in Hanoi, when he had no official status or instructions from Paris, he was prone to overplay his role and fly off in several different directions at once. I respected him as a loyal French officer and made allowances for his position as Chief of M.5, but at that particular moment in August 1945 I felt it was unwise to exacerbate the tenuous situation between the French and Vietnamese.

For two days we had had unsubstantiated Vietnamese reports of Frenchmen masquerading as Americans in uniform, creating disturbances among the Vietnamese. Another problem was rumors that the Viet Minh were plotting to assassinate Sainteny and his men, sometimes embellished with the detail that the "boys" at the Palace "would poison their food." The sources of these rumors were the French. They were reported to my men by the French as an actual plot and by the Vietnamese as the work of French agents provocateurs.

Another case in point was Sainteny's exploitation of several news releases originating in Paris, London, and Ceylon. These had been made for reasons of international policy having to do with French-British leadership in Indochina, but Sainteny interpreted them as signals for action, risking a French-Vietnamese confrontation.

After the Viet Minh assumed control in Tonkin, the French, who were concentrated in the major urban centers, maintained a low profile, patiently waiting for liberation from the "insufferable Annamites." Two days before we landed in Hanoi, Reuters had carried the story: "French forces were standing by to reoccupy French Indo-China. A light corps of intervention, one thousand men strong, is ready in Ceylon under its Commander, General Blaizot."[21] The intent of the Paris government in issuing the release was to place Emperor Bao Dai, President Truman, and Chiang Kai-shek on notice that France, too, had a direct interest in Indochina and was waiting in the wings to take its rightful place.[22] But the news that the French were returning had an electrifying effect on both the French and Vietnamese. The French emerged, bold and arrogant, swaggering down the boulevards in pre-Hiroshima fashion. As the days passed without evidence of a French invasion and the Vietnamese remained calm but watchful, the French once more retreated to their less conspicuous role of bystanders.

The day after our arrival Reuters again issued a sensational news release, this time from London. It reported that SEAC had announced it would be responsible for "the military administration of the southern zone of Indochina. The Chinese will take charge in the considerably smaller northern zone. This purely provisional arrangement which follows talks between Britain, the United States, China, and France, will in time be superseded by a French civil administration." To this point the statement would have been reasonably acceptable to France, but it went on: ". . . at the moment France is not in a position physically to take over the territory, it is stated."[23]

The French were outraged. What were the Allies trying to do? Encourage the Chinese to annex French Indochina? Or, worse still, support the "flagrant brigandism" of the Viet Minh to deprive France of its rightful possession? French government circles in Paris, London, Washington, and Chungking all expressed astonishment at the British Foreign Office's comment that France was unprepared to administer its "colony," and countered with the assertion that France was fully prepared to assume its responsibility. French officials said they were unable to understand why the statement was made in London, particularly at a time when de Gaulle was in Washington conferring with Truman.

The French reinforced their argument by emphasizing that there were two completely different problems, one military and one civil. On the military side, they had to admit that there were no French forces on the scene prepared to accept the surrender of any major Japanese forces, although it was entirely possible that some Japanese units might surrender to such French forces as might be there. On the civil side, an

attaché in de Gaulle's office said it was "untrue to say that material difficulties make it impossible for France to administer Indo-China. . . . We
definitely are taking over. . . ."[24]

To stress France's determination to retain absolute control of the
situation, French officials announced that Vice Admiral Georges Thierry
d'Argenlieu, named High Commissioner of France for Indochina,[25] would
leave in a few days and had already sent his deputy, General Jacques
Leclerc,[26] with a military staff. The spokesman added that the Provisional
Government of France contemplated that there would be "no period of
transition between the Japanese surrender and the beginning of the
French civil administration."[27]

World news reached Hanoi via both Radio Delhi and Kunming, and
Sainteny hung on every news item from French official sources for
guidance. These releases provided him with a basis for his belief that
Paris was finally interested in Indochina, that the French government
was ready to move at any moment, particularly from Ceylon, and that
France—not Britain or China—would be in command in Indochina.

By 23 August Sainteny had set his propaganda machinery in motion.
His underground French contacts were instructed to bolster French
morale by spreading the word that the French would be arriving, that
they should be prepared to counter Vietnamese presumption with firm
French action, that the Viet Minh was a "red demon" to be destroyed,
and so on.

It did not take our team long to recognize the fact that Hanoi was a
boiling cauldron of conflicting interests, cultural contradictions, and international intrigues. With a population of nearly one hundred fifty thousand, its people were a mélange of Indochinese of many religions and
political persuasions; of ambivalent Eurasians; of intensely loyal French
colons, bureaucrats, and military personnel; of overseas Chinese with
divided loyalties; and of a sprinkling of non-French Europeans, largely
related to members of the French Foreign Legion. Superimposed on this
mix was the defeated but not defanged Japanese military machine.

From the moment of our arrival we were plagued with the systematic
sub rosa machinations of these diverse groups. Among the most persistent
and effective were the French and the Japanese.

On our second day in Hanoi I had been urgently interrupted by an excited group of indignant Frenchmen who claimed to have word from Haiphong that "Annamites were slaughtering French women and children at
Lang Son and Cao Bang." Within the hour a member of the Hanoi City
Committee came to inform me that French military units were arriving
overland from Lang Son and by boat along the coast, "killing Annamite
women and children." Both reports proved to be unfounded. The French
troops were still in China awaiting General Ho Ying-chin's order to move,
and our agents at Lang Son, Cao Bang, and Haiphong were totally unaware of even minor disturbances. In the course of our investigation we
traced the source of these "reports" to Indochinese elements of the pro-

Japanese Dai Viet and Phuc Quoc at the instigation of the kempeitai. By using Vietnamese agents, the Japanese hoped to undermine the prestige of the Viet Minh administration as impotent in protecting the Vietnamese against the French. At the same time they hoped these agents would agitate the French into local reprisals and create problems for the newly arrived Allied authorities.

But their plan failed. The kempeitai had not counted on the effectiveness of our team nor on my personal reaction. Even before I had word from our field agents on the validity of the reports, I once more placed General Tsuchihashi on notice that he was responsible for law and order everywhere north of the sixteenth parallel.

This relatively mild provocation was only the first in a series produced by the Japanese clandestine services. Another incident, more serious because of its security implications, was the case of an alleged rape attempt on an "American" citizen. A woman living at the Hotel Hanoi on rue Paul Bert lodged a complaint with us against several Japanese who, she said, had tried to rape her. She had come to us because she claimed American citizenship and the Japanese wanted her to infiltrate our OSS mission as an agent of the kempeitai. The woman soon admitted having been born in Paris and married to a lieutenant of Austrian descent in the French Foreign Legion. However, she maintained her claim that her father of French extraction was an American citizen living in Baltimore. The final picture was that she did not enjoy a good reputation and had a long police record of consorting with Japanese soldiers. Given all the facts, we did not discount the evidence that she had been passing herself off as an American and that lately she had become the target of Japanese odium. We suggested she report her complaint to the local police.

There were many other incidents of Japanese mischief aimed at embarrassing the Americans. Japanese military out of uniform robbed the homes of both French and Vietnamese at gun point or set fire to Vietnamese shops. The victims reporting these crimes to the Japanese authorities would be told that the Americans prohibited them from carrying out police duties and to report their complaints to the Americans. I promptly put a stop to that routine by handing the names of the Japanese gendarmes to General Tsuchihashi.

By the time of the formal surrender on 28 September I had protested 142 separate incidents of subversion. They included acts of sabotage, murder, theft, vandalism, provocation, and trafficking in contraband items. During that period our field agents had witnessed and photographed Japanese troops dumping several hundred truckloads of precious rice and foodstuffs into the Red River; setting fire to warehouses filled with Japanese office furniture, clothing, and medical supplies; dismantling heavy machinery, vehicles, communications equipment, and then smashing critical parts with sledge hammers; and on several occasions selling some of the material to the Vietnamese.

When such sales to the Vietnamese were consummated, it was usually at exorbitant prices. If the buyer would not or could not pay the price demanded, the Japanese would berate him and then destroy the property in the presence of the disappointed customer. On other occasions armed Japanese would enter shops, take what pleased them, and vandalize the remaining stock.

Another disconcerting tactic was the transformation of Japanese military to nondescript civilians. Many were given employment by Japanese firms that continued in business in Viet Nam after the surrender. Others banded into groups of "armed pirates" who roamed the jungle trails of Viet Nam and Laos for several years.

The French, the Vietnamese, and the Japanese all tried to involve the Americans in their political traps. My concern was to steer clear of their snares but stay alert for actual trouble if it arose. The team worked well and by constant vigilance we were able to squash many political designs before they could be launched and to stem some of the abuses and most blatant irregularities.

WHO IS IMAI?

My Japanese captain-escort had asked me, when we returned from the Citadel and Gia Lam inspection, if he could call on me during the evening, and I had agreed. Late in the evening he arrived at the villa bringing a bottle of Johnny Walker Red. I was interested in this unusually well-mannered and discreet officer who never seemed to pry but was always well informed, who wore the insignia of captain in the Japanese army but was always treated, I noticed, with deference by Japanese of much higher rank.

I called for glasses and carbonated water. He poured two stiff drinks, sat back in the easy chair across from me and, in a contrite voice, said how sorry he was that Japan had chosen the path of war in 1941 instead of following Prince Konoye's advice.[28] I let him go on. He had known many Americans in Tokyo and still had fond memories of those associations. He hoped he would have the opportunity to renew those old acquaintances. "Maybe they won't want to know me." Things would not be the same in Japan after the surrender and he was grateful for this assignment which brought him once more in contact with the Americans, and so forth.

To get him off that track, I asked him what his assignment was. Without hesitation he replied, "To facilitate the American mission in Hanoi." He must have noticed the look of incredulity on my face and explained that the General Staff had agreed with General Tsuchihashi that it would serve no useful purpose to reject the Emperor's wish to submit to the Allied powers, that Japan had been defeated in war and the Japanese would have to be honorable in their dealings with the victor. I could not believe what I was hearing and suspected some sort of game, or perhaps he had been given another assignment and only wanted to say good-bye. I sat there, drink in hand, waiting for some self-serving request for a favor.

He poured himself another drink and went on to say that he knew about the OSS. Although he could not be sure of my rank, he knew that I was a "senior OSS officer on General Wedemeyer's intelligence staff." And it was obvious to him that my mission was not limited to POW affairs and the coming surrender but covered a wide range of interests.

I had remained noncommittal. Neither his remarks nor his attitude required a reply. He was informative without a trace of hostility. As I reached to refill our drinks, he said that he had been directed by his superiors to "facilitate" my work, "whatever it might be." With that, he handed me his calling card. It read "Ichio Imai" and gave his personal address as 7 rue Pierre Jabouille, Hanoi, and his telephone.

I accepted his card and asked plainly what he was leading up to. Imai answered pleasantly that in a day or two the Viet Minh would be granted full administrative control by the Japanese authorities and that I, in all probability, would want to establish closer contact with them. He was authorized to assist me. It had come to his attention that Le Xuan had called on me and he offered the information that Xuan was a Viet Minh agent. He had been engaged in propaganda work for the Etsumei Army, a revolutionary group of the Viet Minh Front associated with Nguyen Ai Quoc, also known as Dr. Ho, also known as Ho Chi Minh.

I thanked Imai for his interest and asked him to convey my personal appreciation to General Tsuchihashi for his concern and cooperation. For the record I reiterated my earlier position regarding my mission—looking after the POWs and arranging the preliminary surrender talks. However, in view of local French-Vietnamese tensions I would be interested in seeing that no one inflamed the political situation and created a French pogrom. If I needed to consult with the Viet Minh, I would want to do so discreetly without public notice. Imai agreed and said I was at liberty to make any arrangements I wished and that he would remain at my disposal. A few minutes later he left.

It was about eleven, but the staff was still working. I gave Imai's card to our senior X-2 man and told him I wanted to know all he could find out about Imai, but discreetly. No one was to know that I was interested.

Before I left the next day to see Ho, our X-2 gave me the following information:

Summary Brief: IMAI, Ichio, holds the rank of Captain in the Japanese Imperial Navy; former head of the Japanese Naval Mission in Hanoi; in charge of the group's intelligence work. Now on special duty as interpreter for various Japanese Generals in Indochina; seems to hold important assignment and attends all secret conferences of the General Staff.

I had a good laugh in realizing my "shadow" was a top dog in "the game."

Anyhow the kempeitai would be called off. There was nothing to fear from them in seeing Ho and his advisers. The Japanese probably believed all those rumors about American backing for the Viet Minh, too.

CHAPTER 20

A BUSY SUNDAY

AN OFFICIAL WELCOME

On our first Sunday in Hanoi, we were looking forward to a quiet day and were lingering over breakfast when we heard some noise and a band outside our gate. Grelecki got up with "Here we go again—another demonstration," and headed for the door to observe, with Bernique close behind him. At the front steps were four Vietnamese gentlemen asking to see the Chief of the American Mission. It was a delegation from the National Liberation Committee—the new Provisional Government—to welcome the Allies.

Bernique showed them to our main reception room. I immediately recognized Vu Van Minh, and he introduced the head of the delegation, Vo Nguyen Giap, representing President Ho. Giap then introduced Duong Duc Hien[1] and Khuat Duy Tien.[2] They were all dressed somewhat formally in white linen suits, with ties, and, except for Giap who wore an old fedora, wore white pith helmets.

In impeccable French, Giap conveyed President Ho's personal welcome and added his own. Were we comfortable? Did we need anything? We were to consider ourselves guests of the Vietnamese government.[3] They wanted our stay to be a long and pleasant one. I asked Giap to thank President Ho and to say that I was looking forward to seeing him soon.

Two Vietnamese houseboys brought in coffee for our guests and were quietly setting down the trays when Hien spoke to one of them in familiar terms. We were somewhat surprised to learn that the servant, Phat, was a former student and member of Hien's youth movement who had joined Giap's Army of National Liberation. On instructions, Phat had later joined the pro-Japanese Bao An unit in Hanoi to proselyte among the ranks for the Viet Minh[4]. The delegation were teasing him about seeming more at home in Hanoi's French ambiance than on the jungle trails. Although surprised we were not worried as we maintained rigid security on all equipment, codes, and documents and conducted conversations of a sensitive nature outdoors where we were free of bugging and eavesdroppers.

With the formal welcome and courtesy chitchat out of the way, Giap enjoyed his coffee and settled himself for serious conversation. President Ho, he said, was very pleased to learn of our arrival but much concerned that French officers were attached to our mission. He wanted to know from me how it had been possible for the French to arrive in Hanoi before the Chinese. Had there been a change of Allied plans? Were the French to be allowed to occupy Viet Nam?

I assured Giap that Allied plans had not been changed. The Chinese had been designated at Potsdam to temporarily occupy Indochina for accepting the Japanese surrender north of the sixteenth parallel and repatriating the defeated Japanese. The French troops in China would not be allowed to move south until after the Japanese surrender, and then only in small increments. It was my understanding that neither the Chinese nor the Americans had any plan to assist the French to return to Indochina by force.

But what about the group on the plane with me? Why had I brought them? Giap did not understand what was going on.

I could appreciate their bafflement. The Chief of French Intelligence in China was now in Hanoi through the good offices of the Allies, and yet he was confined by the Japanese to the French Governor General's Palace, of all places. The Americans had been the first to enter Indochina, and yet they claimed only the role of observer in disarming the Japanese, leaving the Chinese in charge. The situation in our guests' view was confusing.

I told them plainly that the United States had not until then intended to assist French reentry against the will of the Vietnamese people and would not in the future, to the best of my belief. However, we should all understand that France had been an ally, had suffered greatly in the war against Germany, as had England and the Soviet Union, that France could not be denied our friendship, even though we might disagree with her colonial policies. For that matter, we were not fully in accord with Britain either on that subject. The miniscule team of five Frenchmen had been allowed to accompany our mission on the understanding they would confine themselves to humanitarian work among the French POWs and civilians. So far, they had not been permitted to do even that.

My reference to the Soviet Union aroused particular interest in Giap and Tien. They both wanted to speak, but Tien deferred to Giap who wanted to know why the USSR was not represented in Southeast Asia. My reply came easily: Marshal Stalin had agreed at Potsdam to let the Supreme Commander of the Allied Powers select the Allied representatives who were to accept the Japanese surrender and to designate where the surrenders were to take place. For northern Indochina the Generalissimo had been designated, as the Soviet Union had expressed no preference. The possibility that Marshal Stalin might not be directly concerning himself with the Vietnamese dilemma had evidently never entered their minds. They either ran out of questions or were afraid to ask more for fear of hearing other disagreeable truths.

Giap arose and with a warm smile, which I found as I knew him better to be a rarity, said, "The people wish to welcome you and our American friends. Would you and your staff oblige us by coming to the front gate?" It was then that the background noise brought us to a realization that there was to be an outdoor ceremony of some kind. Bernique assembled the team in the front courtyard as we hurriedly arranged ourselves, with Giap and me leading, followed by the other Vietnamese delegates, who in turn were followed by the rest of the OSS team.

We advanced to the pavement just outside the gate to a colorful and impressive sight. A fifty-piece military band had been formed directly across the street facing us. Waving in the breeze were five huge flags representing the United States, Great Britain, the Soviet Union, China, and the Democratic Republic of Viet Nam. To our left was a military unit of about a hundred men standing at "present arms." In their pith helmets, khaki shirts and shorts, and bearing American and British weapons, they looked very much like the troops described by Thomas of our "Deer" team. To our right were smaller units of unarmed youths in sparkling white uniforms, elements of Hien's youth movement. Framing the scene on Avenue Beauchamp were its arching trees complemented with a profusion of Hanoi's bright flowering plants. Giap pointed with pride to "my troops who have just arrived from the mountains." I had been right.

Within seconds, all flags were dipped except the Stars and Stripes and the band struck up the "Star Spangled Banner," and it was the best rendition I had heard in the Far East. On the last note, all flags were raised and the procedure repeated in succession for each nation, next the USSR, then the U.K., then China, and last the DRV.

After I thanked the delegation, the commander of troops, and the bandmaster, the units passed in review. As the last rank cleared our gate, I noticed a long line of civilians, ten abreast, led by more flags and a variety of placards, some welcoming our mission and others with strong political overtones. Their parade was led by children of school age, followed by teenagers and adults from various sections of Hanoi, singing their new national anthem. Passing our reviewing area, they all executed an "eyes right" and raised their right hands in the clenched fist.

It was almost noon when the last unit marched past and the delegation took its leave. In saying good-bye, Giap in another rare emotional moment turned to me and said, "This is the first time in the history of Viet Nam that our flag has been displayed in an international ceremony and our national anthem played in honor of a foreign guest. I will long remember this occasion."

SEEING HO AGAIN

Indoors I found Le Xuan impatiently awaiting me. He had said he would be in touch, but here he was with an invitation from Ho to luncheon and a car and driver to take me. I took a fast look at the incoming radio messages from Kunming, hoping to find something on surrender negotiations, but there was nothing on that, only more messages from Helliwell to the recalcitrant Captains Conein and Spaulding leading two separate units toward the Indochinese border, again advising them to return to Kunming for airlift to Hanoi sans the French. Le Xuan and I were soon in the back seat of a very old Citroen and on our way. It was almost one and Xuan was beside himself because he had been told I was expected for noon. I was amused but reassured him that I would explain the unavoidable delay and, anyhow, President Ho knew what was happening. Xuan was somewhat mollified but still wished we had started earlier.

Our Vietnamese driver maneuvered his ancient chariot expertly, avoiding the Sunday strollers and streams of bicyclists three and four abreast, talking to each other, oblivious of the vehicular traffic. We dodged down one street, through an alley, up another street, and so on in what seemed to me a very circuitous route. We had been riding almost ten minutes and at a fast clip, but we did not appear to have traveled far. I supposed the driver had been instructed to be sure he was not followed. Finally we stopped in front of a modest two-story house in what I judged to be the old Vietnamese section of the city. Neither Europeans nor Japanese were in sight.[5] A young man standing at the door waiting for us exchanged a word or two with Xuan and led us into the house and up a flight of stairs.

As I entered the upper rooms, a wisp of a man came forward, both hands extended in a warm greeting. I was pleased to see him again but thoroughly shocked. Ho was only a shadow of the man I had met at Chiu Chou Chieh four months to the day earlier. I reached for his hands, and he seemed very unsteady on his sandaled feet. The thin, bony legs supporting his frail frame made a startling contrast with the large head and the radiant smile on his face. His clothes, a high-collared brown tunic and trousers, hung loosely, accentuating his wasted condition.

I started to apologize for being late, but Ho would have none of it, saying he knew it was not my fault, looking straight at Giap with a mischievous smile, and I was inwardly amused to find Giap there, since he had been mum to me about this luncheon. Drawing me toward the other men who stood discreetly apart, Ho introduced me as "our American friend from Washington." Somewhat embarrassed and not wanting a false impression regarding my official status, I corrected, "From Kunming, please!" Everyone laughed, and Ho repeated, "From Kunming." I have tried to recall with exactitude who was present but my only memory is of Ho, Giap, Truong Chinh,[6] and possibly Nguyen Khang.

I inquired into the state of his health, and Ho readily admitted to a bout with malaria and intestinal ailments, but with a wide gesture dismissed the subject by asking me of news from Kunming and Washington. Before I could answer, the young man who had admitted us downstairs came in with a tray of six small glasses and a bottle of Vermouth. The young man poured, and Ho offered me the first. I was anticipating with displeasure a political toast but Ho did not embarrass me and only offered "à votre santé," and I had only to return "à la votre." I noticed without surprise that he barely touched his lips to the glass, as I had heard he was abstemious.

Ho suggested we move into the next room where an attractive table had been laid for six. The meal was simple but delicious: an excellent fish soup followed by bowls of steamed rice and bite-sized pieces of braised chicken and pork, then rice cakes and fruit. My place at the table had been set to Ho's right and was the only one equipped with a European place setting of china and silver. A thoughtful gesture but, having acquired a degree of dexterity in the use of chopsticks and bowl in China, I asked if I, too, could not have them. They were all delighted, the oriental utensils were promptly provided, and it served to break the ice. Everyone relaxed.

Conversation was in French, with occasional English words for clarity. I gathered that only Ho spoke English, and he did most of the talking, keeping the conversation both bland and general. He reminisced somewhat on how his people had worked with AGAS, GBT, OWI, and, of course, the OSS and referred at one point to the American attempts in 1944–45 to recruit him for service with the OWI in San Francisco. He had hoped at the time, he said, that the American project would materialize so that he could meet and talk directly with the UN delegates about his country's aspirations for national independence. In retrospect, he said, he might have been no more successful than he had been at Versailles in 1919.

Lunch over, we moved to the balcony overlooking a courtyard for coffee; the other four excused themselves, and Ho and I were alone. He opened the conversation by saying that he was deeply grateful that I had been able to accept his invitation; he hoped we could review the current situation. I thought it would be useful but noted that my position was extremely limited by my directive and that I had no authority to become involved in French-Vietnamese politics. Ho nodded several times, raised his hands, palms out, and smilingly said, "I understand. I ask for nothing at this time, perhaps later. But today we will talk as friends, not diplomats." I replied with a smile: "Good. Then you don't mind if I report the substance of our conversation to Kunming?" "No," Ho said, "so long as neither the French nor the Chinese know of my whereabouts."

In the next two hours we covered a number of events and issues from the meeting of the "Deer" team to the "uprisings" in Saigon and Hanoi. Ho was eager to bring me up to date and I was glad to learn all I could of the situation.

Recalling with mild amusement the Montfort incident, Ho asked me why the French had ignored his invitations to meet with him in July. At that particular moment he had been interested not only in a clarification of the ambiguous 24 March declaration[7] but also in opening talks with French officials in China. I professed ignorance of French intent except that OSS had passed the messages to AGAS and they had been delivered. Ho had been disappointed and offended with French haughtiness, which he blamed for the French anti-Vietnamese campaign in China. He was particularly irritated with Sainteny. Pointedly he said it was no secret that "Sainteny, the chief of M.5, is de Gaulle's representative." He saw Sainteny's mission as hostile to the Vietnamese and therefore bound to create problems for the Provisional Government.

As for the *"équipe"* at the Palace, he asked, "What did they hope to accomplish? Did they think for a moment they could stop the course of events at that juncture in Viet Nam's history?" I could not speak for the French but only explained that we had brought them to assist us in administering to the large contingent of French POWs and that we had purposefully limited their number to five. Ho was highly skeptical. "That may be your purpose but certainly it is not theirs."

Hoping to alleviate his concern, I suggested that perhaps Sainteny's group could be useful in establishing early contacts with the French, even to induce them to tentatively accept the fact that the Viet Minh was in power. Ho thought not. For the time being he was not disposed to make any further overtures. Later perhaps, when the French perceived their untenable position as pretenders, the situation might change. In the meantime they would be at the Palace where they could be watched. I suggested once more a dialogue with Sainteny, but Ho remained unconvinced that it would produce any constructive results. However, in deference to me, he said I could use my best judgment in the matter.

His concern was not about the French alone; he was uneasy about British and Chinese intentions. He spoke knowledgeably of Franco-British cooperation in Laos, Cambodia, and Cochinchina. Obviously, British interest coincided with French objectives in those areas and with their own long-range goal of reestablishing their prewar colonial sphere in Southeast Asia. As for the Chinese, Ho characterized their interest as "political blackmail." Word from Chungking was that the Kuomintang was already negotiating with the Paris government on several matters of special rights in Indochina and he was convinced the Franco-British-Chinese power play would jeopardize the integrity of the independence movement.

The conversation was depressing and I searched for a change of subject. I inquired into the relationship between the Japanese and the Provisional Government. Ho readily admitted that he had assurances of noninterference from the Japanese; they had been most cooperative. Since the Hanoi "uprising," a silent understanding existed without formal contact or agreement. The Japanese would simply withdraw in an orderly fashion as the Viet Minh authorities took over each government function. But Ho did not know what to expect from the Allies after the Japanese left nor was he certain who would replace them. I said it would be the Chinese, as agreed at Potsdam. Ho was not surprised, he had understood that would be the case, but he had not been sure until that moment. I wondered silently if he had hoped for an American occupation.

Ho was uneasy about the reception the Chinese troops would receive from the Vietnamese and speculated that a large influx of Chinese, added to the Japanese army, would put a terrible strain on the resources of the country. He also alluded, very delicately, to troubles Chinese occupation forces might create if they looted extensively or abused the populace. He asked me to alert the Allied authorities to this possibility and I assured him I would.

These were some of the problems besetting Ho for which there were no ready solutions and over which he could exert little influence.

Except to a handful of close associates and some Chinese, Ho Chi Minh, the man and the name, was still little known to the Vietnamese and even less so to the world leaders molding the shape of Asia. His earlier efforts to achieve American recognition had come to nothing. Ho felt it imperative to find a way to bring his government to the attention of the Allies before the arrival of their occupation forces. He had read Bao Dai's appeal for recognition of Viet Nam's independence sent a few days earlier to the heads of the Allied powers. It disturbed him because the appeal reinforced the Emperor's legal status as head of state but was silent on the existence of the Provisional Government. He was moving swiftly to correct that misapprehension.

According to Ho, Bao Dai was no longer in power; the only legitimate government at the moment was his Provisional Government. I did not dispute his claim with regard to Hanoi or even Tonkin but noted that countrywide Bao Dai was still the head of state. With a knowing smile, Ho informed me that at that very moment a delegation of his government was en route to Hué to accept the Emperor's abdication. Once the abdication was received, he planned to issue a declaration of independence, establish a cabinet, set up a full-fledged government, and attempt to secure international recognition. In a casual tone he asked, "What will the United States do?" I could not speak for our government but gave my opinion that it would have to consider the situation in the light of events. Ho showed his disappointment but did not press me.

It was important to Ho that the United States continue its anticolonial policy regarding Indochina. He was searching for a way to dispel the "misconception" that he was "an agent of the Comintern" or that he was a communist. My willing attention provided him with the only channel to Washington available, and he took full advantage of it. He admitted quite candidly that he was a socialist, that he had associated and worked with French, Chinese, and Vietnamese communists, but added, "Who else was there to work with?" He labeled himself a "progressive-socialist-nationalist" with an ardent desire to rid his country of foreign domination. He spoke eloquently, not making a speech, but with sincerity, determination, and optimism.

As the clock inside struck the half-hour for 3:30, someone came to the door of the balcony and spoke briefly to Ho. Joyfully clasping his hands before his face, Ho turned to me with a beaming smile and announced, "The Khâm-sai of Cochinchina has just cabled his resignation to the Court. He has officially placed the rule of South Viet Nam into the hands of the Executive Committee for Nam Bo." I did not grasp the import of this news. We had heard the day before that the Viet Minh under the direction of Tran Van Giau had already assumed control there. Ho explained that Bao Dai had until now only announced his "intention" to abdicate. But with the last of the three Viceroys out of office there remained no legal obstacle to his actual abdication. It was obviously a matter for jubilation to Ho, and I could hear excited voices within.

I thought his friends were probably waiting to see him and decided to take my leave. Ho walked me to the door and happily said he would long remember our pleasant afternoon and that he would be pleased if I allowed him to stay in close touch. I said I would be seeing him again and very soon. The driver was waiting and within a few minutes I was back at Maison Gautier.

UNDERCURRENTS

I hoped to salvage at least a long evening from my "quiet" Sunday but instead returned to a scene of some tension. Some of our team were standing by to tell me about the latest agitation. It dealt with the apprehension of several agents provocateurs (Vietnamese and Japanese) caught distributing Vietnamese-language propaganda tracts. One leaflet announced the imminent arrival of French paratroopers and administrative officers to take over the "government of Annam." Another expounded the theme that since Japan had to surrender its "rightful place in the East," it was only proper for that role to be assumed by the Vietnamese as the best qualified to rid Asia of "white imperialism, ..." Obviously this anti-French and antiwhite propaganda was intended to create panic and racial discord. Our Vietnamese and French informants attributed the source of this propaganda to the Japanese.

I asked Bernique to call Imai and see that he got copies of the tracts immediately. I wanted Imai to determine the source and to see that those responsible, if Japanese, were restrained. Imai was also to inform the Japanese General Staff that another such incident would be grounds for me to report directly to the Generalissimo without reference to the Japanese in Hanoi.

I also found a message from Kunming of very particular significance, from the Chief of R&A for my personal attention with the comment, "For your guidance only." It was a résumé of a Kuomintang press release to the Chinese Overseas Service in Mandarin and read in part:

> Indo-China not only failed to remain a neutral nation, but was the main base of the Japanese invasion of China from the South, and China suffered heavily as a result of this. However, China has no territorial designs upon the country apart from accepting the surrender of part of the Japanese forces in the northern part of the country.

Accusation of past misdeeds are a traditional Chinese rationale for changing the course of events they do not like. Even today, when China accuses Viet Nam of border violations to justify limited military incursions, their probable aim has little or nothing to do with the border disputes—it lies elsewhere, perhaps in Cambodia and Laos, perhaps in their relations with the Soviet Union. In 1945 this press statement accused Indochina of siding with the Japanese as a rationalization of the Chinese intention to force the French to submit to their demands on other issues—in Shanghai, in the area of special trade relationships and port questions, and so forth.

OSS in Kunming was alerting me to the fact that an accommodation between France and China was in the wind, that the Chinese occupation was to be used only as a device to bring the French into line on several international questions. If an accommodation were reached, the Chinese would withdraw in favor of French reoccupation. Therefore, I was not to overemphasize the past American policy of "self-determination and freedom for dependent peoples."

The message troubled me. It was not yet an official change in Chinese policy; yet it indicated that one might well be in the making. I had no basis to question Kunming and could only let the matter rest until, or if, I heard further. It had been only an hour since Ho had uneasily expressed his fears of Franco-Chinese power plays; well he might fear. And the British had still to be heard from.

SAINTENY WANTS TO MEET HO

Also waiting for me was a message from Sainteny asking me to come to the Palace. I called around six, finding Sainteny in a depressed mood, not angry with me but discouraged with the Japanese attitude and his inability to get about. He had heard over his radio the news that Hué and Saigon had "fallen to the Viet Minh" and despaired that the French in Paris would ever wake up. Nevertheless, he seemed resigned to the fact that there was nothing he could do at the moment.

One of his major concerns, and the reason he had asked me to come, was the security of the French population; if only there were European troops, he said, he would have felt more at ease. He asked whether some arrangement could be made to organize a "small detachment" of French troops from the Citadel to patrol areas of French concentration. I indicated I did not think the Japanese would agree as long as they were in charge. Just for the sake of discussion, I asked Sainteny how many men he thought would be needed. "An even thousand would do," he replied. That was not my idea of a "small detachment." "And what about arming and quartering them?" Sainteny thought the Japanese had the means. I told him he was dreaming, that the Japanese would never agree. To put an end to such an impossible scheme, I jokingly suggested he approach General Tsuchihashi and watch his reaction. Sainteny shot back, "An excellent idea, why don't we both see him?" I was highly amused at his typical eagerness to fasten his outlandish proposals on my shoulders. But I had to be serious and remind him of General Order No. 1, specifying that the maintenance of law and order was a Japanese responsibility. Sainteny became sullen and would only say that he had never seen it. The subject was dropped, but it was to be raised again in the coming weeks.

I told Sainteny about my visits to the Citadel and Gia Lam and the severe limitations under which I had been allowed to see the prisoners, of the overcrowded and unsanitary conditions, the acute shortages in medical staff, services, and supplies. I told him also that I had promptly reported the situation to Kunming and that I had later heard that qualified personnel from the China Theater were on the way to cope with the problem. I also advised him of my official protest to the Japanese High Command in Hanoi and of the little satisfaction I had received.

Sainteny said he understood perfectly well the position he and I were in and wanted me to know how much he appreciated my interest. But the Americans in China, he went on, were not sufficiently concerned with the French plight; if the French had been permitted a free hand, the situation at the Citadel would have been remedied in short order.

In a somewhat acrimonious vein he evinced curiosity about that morning's "noisy affair" in front of the American mission. I explained it had been a courtesy call, a welcoming delegation from the Provisional

Government. His comment was, "At least they have not forgotten French good manners." That brought him back to the subject of protection for the French population. He expressed mild admiration for the Viet Minh's restraint and willingness to avoid violence but added, "Of course the Japanese are still on stage, and it's really too soon to make a judgment."

I told Sainteny that various leading Viet Minh figures had assured me that Ho Chi Minh would not tolerate any unprovoked molestation to the French community. The key word was *unprovoked*, and I told Sainteny that already I had been advised by the Provisional Government that "Captain Blanchard's group" had been actively collaborating with Japanese in instigating minor incidents. Sainteny only shrugged and made no comment.

I did not divulge to Sainteny that I had met with Ho, but he seemed to assume that I was in touch with him and asked me if I could arrange a meeting between them. I assured him I would be glad to find out but reminded him that Ho was unhappy with the negative outcome of his efforts in July. Sainteny protested that he had been prepared to meet with Ho but that "the torrential rains and impassable roads" to Ho's jungle headquarters had handicapped his efforts. I observed that at the time the messages were delivered Ho would have been willing to come to Kunming or even to Chungking. Sainteny answered that it was very important to deal with Ho on "French soil," meaning Indochina, and not "under the nose of the Chinese." He made no mention of having made no reply whatsoever to Ho's invitation, nor did I. At length, I asked Sainteny if he wanted me to pursue the question of a meeting between them, and he replied that it would be useful and he would appreciate it if I could arrange it.

That evening I arranged with Imai to contact Xuan. Xuan came at about nine, and I gave him Sainteny's message for Ho. The answer came right back: Ho would send Vo Nguyen Giap, his Minister of the Interior, to meet with Sainteny *if* I accompanied him. The meeting was to take place the next morning.

CHAPTER 21

FRENCH DIPLOMACY
AT LOW TIDE

TWO ANTAGONISTS MEET

Ten o'clock was the hour appointed for this first meeting between responsible French and Vietnamese contenders, however lacking in official status they both were. I had already sent word to Sainteny that Giap would represent Ho, and I myself arrived beforetimes at the Palace. Sainteny had set the stage in one of the largest and most elegant salons of the Palace suitable for an appropriate display of French sovereignty. His choice of setting could be construed as showing suitable respect for a visitor of importance and a mark of distinction or as exhibiting a not very subtle desire to overawe the Vietnamese. I did not know which.

Sainteny confided to me that I would be surprised to hear the liberal terms France was about to make. It was no surprise, however, for, as I saw it, the French had no alternative at the moment to accepting the Provisional Government.

We watched from a window while Giap and Duong Duc Hien arrived in a shiny black sedan flying the Viet Minh flag from each front fender. They were escorted by a Vietnamese bodyguard armed with a Sten gun who stepped out of the front door and were followed by a second armed guard who opened the rear door for Giap. Giap was dressed in his usual white linen suit and dark tie, wearing his "battle-scarred" fedora which had already become a symbol of his authority as leader of the Viet Minh guerrillas and the Army of Liberation. Dignified, serious, and confident, Giap walked ahead to the front door where he was met by a French officer.

As the guests entered the salon, Giap moved straight toward Sainteny. The French host waited until Giap was at least halfway across the room before he moved toward him, another hint of his inner attitude. I took the lead and greeted Giap, then introduced him and Hien to Sainteny. We walked across the huge room in stony silence to the divan and chairs arranged for the occasion. I broke the silence by commenting on the excitement I had seen in the streets that morning. Giap with a forced smile explained that people were going out to welcome his troops who had "come down from the mountains" after many engagements with the Japanese. They were expected by noon and he himself was going to greet them later.

Sainteny's diplomatic dexterity was certainly at its lowest ebb on what might have become a historic occasion. Despite his efforts to appear civil, he set the tone by cutting Giap short with a paternal lecture on "Annamite" behavior. Brushing aside Vietnamese antipathy to French paternalism, in a well-modulated voice and in benignant terms, Sainteny asked why the Viet Minh had recklessly chosen to "let the world know that French presence in Indochina was no longer welcome." Not pausing for a reply, Sainteny continued that such a declaration had caused the Allies much concern for the safety of the French population in Indochina, leading them to the conclusion that it would be prudent to keep the French authorities out of Indochina for the time being. To emphasize his displeasure, if not his disappointment, with the Viet Minh's behavior, Sainteny cautioned his guests that he "would keep a watchful eye" on the activities of the so-called Provisional Government and judge for himself the worth of its members to rule postwar Indochina.

I expected Giap to stalk out of the room at any moment, but he did not. In perfect French and with absolute self-control, Giap said he had not come to be lectured nor to justify the actions of the people of Viet Nam but had come at the invitation of one he believed to be a representative of the "new French government," and that he was prepared to engage in an amicable "exchange of views." For the first time in his life Sainteny was meeting face to face a Vietnamese who dared to stand up to a Frenchman.

Softening his attitude and with a conciliatory smile, Sainteny announced himself as the personal representative of General de Gaulle. He wanted first of all for the Vietnamese people to know that France was now "a free and liberal nation," that the "old ways" would be discarded, that all undesirable Frenchmen would be repatriated, and that the Annamese would be granted most of their requests. I recalled inwardly Sainteny's admissions to me in Kunming that he was uninstructed but hoped to gain an interim French-Annamese modus vivendi.

Somewhere in his monologue Sainteny must have struck a receptive chord. His conciliatory attitude was not entirely lost on Giap. However, the vague terms of liberality toward the "Annamese," another disliked French colonialist term, appeared to trouble him. Giap asked for specifics, as Ho had wanted to ask the French in July, but Sainteny replied that they would "work out details as soon as the Japanese and Chinese left." That did not satisfy Giap, and he again pressed for specifics. But Sainteny again launched into more generalities. Giap sat stolidly; he was unimpressed with the vague promises.

Noting Giap's obduracy, Sainteny returned to his hard line. I was beginning to feel uncomfortable in the tense atmosphere heavily charged with hostility and distrust. Neither Giap nor Hien seemed willing to concede that France might have any say in Viet Nam's future. Hoping to convince them that in the end Indochina would have to accept outside domination, Sainteny fantasized that only Viet Minh indiscretions had brought about the present untenable situation. The Allies, taking notice of the Viet Minh's opposition to the French, had decided at Potsdam to let the Chinese disarm the Japanese, a fact which would have serious consequences for the Indochinese—for as he, Giap, should well know from past experience, once the Chinese entered Indochina, it would be a long time before they left.

That line of argument seemed to have the desired effect, and Sainteny pushed harder. The Chinese occupation could only mean economic drain, social disorder, and a total loss of freedom. Giap and Hien looked at me for verification, and with a satisfied look Sainteny asked me to confirm his statement. I repeated what they had heard me say the day before—that the Chinese would accept the Japanese surrender north of the sixteenth parallel and the British south of that line, emphasizing my understanding that the Chinese had no intention of remaining in Indochina beyond the period necessary for the Allies to evacuate the Japanese. "And how long will that be?" asked Sainteny, driving his point home. Giap appeared crushed momentarily but soon regained his composure and said it was not the first time the Chinese had come to Indochina but that they would not stay long.

Ignoring Giap's somewhat wavering optimism, Sainteny continued in a matter-of-fact tone that in the meantime the lives of all Frenchmen must be safeguarded "at all costs" and that "the Annamese Provisional Government will be held responsible." The French Government, he said, looked to the Provisional Government to make demands on the Allied authorities to prevent Chinese troops from entering European-populated cities such as Hanoi, Haiphong, Tourane, and Hué, which instead should be policed by Franco-Annamese personnel. Whether this was a calculated maneuver by Sainteny or a Freudian slip, it was impossible to tell, but it instantly registered with the astute Giap. So de Gaulle's representative recognized the "Annamese Provisional Government" as a responsible body! He was asking the Provisional Government to speak for France to the Allied authorities! With aplomb, Giap replied that it would not be necessary to "trouble" the Allies with such matters; his government would see to it that the French would not be molested.

Sainteny had been outplayed and was visibly annoyed but contained himself and immediately changed tack by suggesting this was a family affair, that they could resolve their differences if they worked together, that they had done so in the past to their mutual advantage; perhaps a Franco-Annamite alliance would be the answer. Giap must have decided to cut short the charade. With a very faint smile he said, "Everything is possible."

After a few inconsequential remarks, Giap said he had to go review the incoming troops and with superficial pleasantries, handshakes, and artificial smiles, Giap and Hien left the Palace. After their departure, Sainteny appeared pleased with himself. His casual remarks to me were that he had convinced his guests of their "infantile presumption" of getting along without France. Little did he realize that he had just confronted the one man who would be credited in history with the ultimate dissolution of the French colonial empire in the Far East.

A FRENCH BRIBE FOR THE AMERICANS

I stayed on for a short while, only to receive a shocking surprise. A servant brought in coffee and pastries, and we spoke of the arriving Viet Minh troops and what effect their presence might have in the city. Sainteny seemed worried about them. Then, out of the blue, in a highly confidential tone as if we were conspirators, he informed me that "the French government is prepared to extend a credit of five billion French francs to Americans only, to invest in Indochina, and I [Sainteny] would like to know the right person to contact on this matter and to start negotiations." He urged the utmost secrecy in the matter. I was literally in a rage and incapable of answering—the only time in our often stormy relationship in which I felt anger, contempt, and personal insult. I felt him accountable both as an individual and as a representative of his nation, and it took me some moments to be sure that I could reply without losing control of myself. Finally, I said I would pass his question on to Chungking, which I did that very afternoon. As I had absolutely known would be the case, I received a reply within hours directly from Heppner cautioning me to stay clear of any deals to suborn American officials.[1] No one was having any of that piece of French corruption.

It is also a measure of French unscrupulousness and crudeness in this sort of thing that only a few weeks later the French accused Ho Chi Minh of attempting to bribe me and other Americans in Indochina, an accusation that was an outright lie.

Before I left the Palace, Sainteny, still in a state of mild euphoria, spoke of his plans to set up a "nationwide psychological bureau." He anticipated Vietnamese cooperation in securing the use of the Bach Mai radio facilities to propagandize the Vietnamese. He was waiting for trained propagandists to spread the word of France's new policy emphasizing "greater freedom for Annamese and French alike." I looked at such an undertaking with great doubt but kept my opinion to myself.

Sainteny had one more request. He wanted me to communicate to the "Armistice Commission" (by which I assumed he meant the Allied authorities in Chungking) that the French government, presumably meaning himself, desired transportation for French women and children to points south of the sixteenth parallel to avoid the hazards of a Chinese occupation and asked that a French police force be organized to maintain law and order in Hanoi, Haiphong, Tourane, and Hué. On various occasions he had intimated to me that teams equipped by OSS could eventually be used for police work. So when he again suggested the formation of a French police force, I knew his purpose was to use them as a spearhead for Leclerc's troops, rumored to be enroute to Indochina, rumors widely publicized over Radio Delhi to the great worry of the Vietnamese and particularly the Viet Minh.

With this last transparent deception from Sainteny, I finally was able to get away and returned to the Maison Gautier in a vile humor.

CHAPTER 22

MOVING TOWARD
SURRENDER

THE JAPANESE SUMMONED TO CHINA

T he delay in receiving surrender instructions generated unexpected problems. The Japanese were almost as anxious to surrender as I was to see the Chinese come in and take control. For several days Tsuchihashi had been inquiring of me as to Allied plans and for the same period I had been bombarding Kunming for instructions. Two weeks after Tokyo's capitulation, the free movement of large numbers of Japanese, in and out of uniform, was contributing to a general breakdown of public safety and the orderly pursuit of private affairs. The continued absence of an Allied occupation presence was at the same time not enhancing Allied prestige in the eyes of unsympathetic elements. And hard core racists led by the kempeitai in a last hurrah were exploiting every conceivable weakness in the white man's role in Asia, especially among the Caodaists and the Hoa Hao.

On 27 August I finally received word from the Chinese at K'ai-yuan[1] to set up radio contact between them and the Japanese in Hanoi, which I did. Anticipating an imminent Chinese troop movement, Tsuchihashi became apprehensive of potential incidents between his troops and the Chinese. In a message to the Chinese command at K'ai-yuan he expressed his concern and asked to be told which routes the Chinese would follow so that he could withdraw his troops closer to Hanoi and out of the Chinese line of march.

Instructions to start preliminary negotiations came the next day. They were in the form of a directive to the Japanese commander in Hanoi from, most surprisingly, General Lu Han. This Yunnanese general would accept the Japanese surrender instead of the Kuomintang's favorite marshal, Chang Fa-kwei. The designation of Lu Han clearly presaged more problems for the French and Vietnamese and explained some rather cryptic remarks I had received the day before in a multipurpose message about POWs, Japanese communications, consular matters, and the like. Kunming had wanted me to know that there had been a change in signals by inserting in that message without preamble the following: "Temporarily at least the Chinese want no, repeat no, French to move to Indochina. . . . Some elements Chinese troops move 28 August to Ha Giang and Bac Quang."[2]

My suspicions of Chinese duplicity were being confirmed. With Lu Han in charge of operations in Indochina, Chiang Kai-shek was assuring himself of French tractability in his negotiations on French interests in China. As has been seen, since the March coup Chiang had adopted an unannounced policy of French exclusion from Indochinese affairs. He had refused them arms or reentry into their former colony. Now with Alessandri's troops immobilized in southern China, Chiang planned to use the occupation as a means to force the French to agree to his terms. That unpleasant task he had given to the willing anti-French Lu Han. The French dreaded the choice, while the Chinese hailed it as a wise and well-calculated move.

Lu Han welcomed the opportunity to profit from the occasion and to settle an old score. His deep-seated personal animosity toward the French in general and General Alessandri, in particular, was rooted in an event which had occurred in 1940 after the Japanese occupied Indochina. With French cooperation, the Japanese had closed the old Chinese trade routes and trafficking in contraband between China and Southeast Asia. Governor Lung Yün and General Lu Han had a major interest in keeping those routes open and approached General Martin, commander of the French forces there, with a view to arranging what they thought of as a mutually agreeable accommodation. Lu Han, the negotiator in that particular piece of business, arrived in Hanoi to a cold reception from Alessandri, then Chief of Staff to Martin. The Chinese blamed Alessandri for being the principal opponent to Lu Han's proposals, and Lu Han had never forgiven either Alessandri or the French.

As I read the Chinese directive, I recalled the difficulty Chiang had had with the British over the occupation of Hong Kong and was amused at the trouble the Generalissimo had put himself to in the preamble to let everyone know who was in charge:

By Order of Generalissimo Chiang Kai-shek, Supreme Commander, China Theater, through General Ho Ying-chin, Chinese Field Commander, Lu Han, Commanding General, First Area Command, Chinese Ground Forces, is designated representative for conducting negotiations and receiving the eventual surrender for the Generalissimo.[3]

The directive instructed the Japanese to send a delegation limited to one representative, two assistants, and one interpreter to the remote city of Meng-tzu, deep in the southeastern part of Yunnan, to arrive there on 31 August. It was apparent that Chiang did not want to be overwhelmed by the Japanese in either rank or numbers. Nor did he wish to dignify the occasion by receiving the delegation in Yunnan's capital, Kunming, where Lung Yün would have to participate, or in Chungking where the Japanese might receive undue prominence. The aircraft bearing the Japanese delegation was to be clearly marked with a green cross on both wings and fuselage.

Accompanied by Captain Imai I delivered the Chinese directive to Tsuchihashi. He seemed surprised that the place selected was not Chungking. I explained that this was only a preliminary meeting to arrange the formal surrender and nothing more. At that time no place for the surrender had been fixed and no one knew whether it was to be Chungking, Hanoi, or elsewhere. Reassured, Tsuchihashi said he would appoint a delegation and have an answer for me the next day.

I also brought up the question of the POWs and their need for medical supplies and services. The general replied that on the day before he had ordered additional doctors and ancillary personnel to the POW centers and that I would see an improvement on my next visit, adding that he was embarrassed to have to admit that the Japanese authorities had no money to pay for these needs.

As it happened, I had received several complaints from officials of the Bank of Indochina that the Japanese had withdrawn 60 million piastres[4] in the past eighteen days. The bank officials wanted guidance from the Allied authorities as to what to do about future demands, but Kunming had instructed me: "Do nothing. That is a matter for the bank to resolve."

Nevertheless, Tsuchihashi's plea of Japanese poverty when it came to medical supplies and services for the POWs did not sit well with me, and I told him sharply that money seemed not to be the problem in view of the large sums they had withdrawn in the last eighteen days. He looked completely stunned, and I do not believe he was feigning surprise. I did not care, however, whether his command or some civil branch of the Japanese Imperial government was at work in these dealings, and also informed him that the Yokohama Species Bank of Hanoi[5] which had Japanese assets was also still doing business. The general regained his composure and promised me the POWs would get what they needed.

Tsuchihashi insisted, however, that critical drugs and special supplies were unavailable in Indochina. Prior to 10 August they had come from Japan. Perhaps, he suggested, the Chinese could procure them at Japanese expense and he would see that they were used exclusively for the POWs. I told him to give me a list of requirements, and I would see what I could do. The general promised he would.

Tsuchihashi then raised the subject of the French at the Palace. They were in constant communication, he said, with known agents provocateurs who were creating incidents throughout the city. He asked me to use my influence to restrain them until the "Armistice Commission" arrived. I asked for instances, and Tsuchihashi replied that Imai could provide them. I let the matter drop, so as not to place the United States in the position of policing the French or becoming involved in the maintenance of public order, still a Japanese responsibility.

Late that evening Imai brought me a message intercepted in Saigon. It allegedly originated with the French in Hanoi and was intended for the SLFEO/Calcutta to the effect that the Allies were frustrating French objectives in Indochina and requesting that Paris take action at the diplomatic level. It was a perfectly normal message which Sainteny might send, as he was making no success of his mission on his own.[6] On the other hand, there was a distinct possibility that it was sent by the Japanese in an attempt to create a rift between the French and Americans. If so, they apparently knew nothing of Sainteny's recurring rage at the Allies over their refusal to rearm the French and permit a French reoccupation of the country. Whichever, who could know? I thanked Imai and made no comment.

The next morning Imai brought me the list of the Japanese delegation.[7] I was silently amazed to find Navy Captain Imai, recently reduced to Army Captain Imai, now further reduced to civilian Imai, and so listed in the delegation as "interpreter." It appeared to me that, in fact, he might be the ranking member. If that was the case, I felt that Tokyo had selected a very capable man.

Apologetically Imai asked me to convey to the Chinese that General Tsuchihashi had no plane at his disposal and it would take longer than the two days remaining before the meeting to secure one. Further, the special markings required would increase the time for preparation. Therefore, the general "respectfully requested" that an American plane be sent to Hanoi for the delegation, which would also satisfy the question of arrival time. Imai also brought the list of medical supplies needed for the POWs.

I queried K'ai-yuan on the availability of a plane and was told the Japanese would have to secure their own and I so informed the general.[8] Tsuchihashi did in the end find an aircraft in Saigon. At the last minute the Chinese changed the date of the meeting to 2 September. Four American fighter aircraft were to rendezvous with the Japanese plane over Lao Cai and escort it to Meng-tzu. The delegation would then fly in American L-5s from Meng-tzu to K'ai-yuan for the conference.[9]

Eventually, on 31 August, I was informed that the formal surrender would take place in Hanoi on a date to be specified after the Japanese delegation returned from K'ai-yuan.

CHUNGKING PREPARES TO SETTLE ACCOUNTS

Like a flight of locusts the first elements of "Dragon Cloud's"[10] Yunnanese army swarmed across the Indochinese border on 28 August. They came alone, without the French or the crack troops of Chang Fa-kwei, and the composition of this occupation force gave rise to much speculation. It was a strange mix of Yunnanese and Kwangsi units.[11] Equally baffling was the designation of the Kwangsi general, Hsiao Wen,[12] in the dual role of deputy commander and political advisor to Lu Han. The whole occupation structure seemed odd. Evidently Lu Han did not enjoy the full confidence of the Kuomintang and Hsiao Wen had been given the task of keeping a watchful eye on him to insure that Chungking's interests were protected.

The news of the crossing struck fear and anger in the hearts of French and Vietnamese alike. Sainteny, Giap, and even Imai sought confirmation and information. I had little to offer. Not until I received our OSS analysis did I understand the full political implications of the decisions made in Chungking. With the Japanese out of the way the Communist threat from Yenan had become the Kuomintang's principal concern. Vast areas previously held by the Japanese were now vulnerable to Soviet and Chinese Communist penetration. Chiang had to insure rapid and positive Nationalist control in those areas by redeploying his best and most loyal troops to the key centers of Canton, Amoy, Hankow, Shanghai, Tientsin, and others.

He also wanted to retain among the postwar "Big Five" his position of fourth, willed to him by President Roosevelt. France could be number five. After all, his position above France had been reaffirmed at Potsdam when he had been designated the sole recipient of the Japanese surrender in the China Theater, including northern Indochina. Chiang was quick to perceive a concomitant advantage to his international role of superpower in the benefits that would accrue to China in the occupation of northern Indochina, that is, forcing France to settle on his terms their outstanding differences before she could reenter her former colony.

Chiang's only forces in southern China were the First War Area units in Yunnan under Lu Han and the Fourth War Area units in Kwangsi and Kwangtung under Chang Fa-kwei. Of the two, the Fourth was better equipped and trained and most loyal to the Nationalist government. He would, therefore, use the Fourth for occupation duty at Canton and designate Chang Fa-kwei as his representative to accept the Japanese surrender there. The First he would put to good use in Indochina, and Lu Han could represent him in dealing with the French and Japanese. But at his elbow would be Hsiao Wen to implement the Kuomintang's political policies with the Vietnamese.

During the war years in China (1935–45) the one-eyed warlord governor of Yunnan, Lung Yün, had twice adopted an equivocal attitude toward the communists, first in March 1935 at the Chingsha River when Mao Tse-tung feigned an attack on Kunming and, in later years, when Lung Yün hosted Vietnamese, Hindu, Korean, and other nationalists with communist affiliations. A greedy, cunning, and ruthless man whose family had ruled Yunnan with a heavy hand since 1927, Lung Yün had amassed a vast fortune by trafficking in American Lend-Lease material, opium, and critical and strategic materials from French and Japanese sources. He issued his own currency, maintained a private army to protect his extensive poppy fields along the narrow corridor on the northwest border of Yunnan and Szechwan provinces, and directed his sons' systematic highjacking operations of American Lend-Lease arms, equipment, and rations traveling over the Burma Road to Kunming.[13] At one point in early 1945 his power had so grown that he could brazenly and successfully blackmail the Kuomintang into increasing his "share" of Lend-Lease supplies passing through his province. He had even gone so far as to threaten Chungking with confiscation of Nationalist and American facilities and supplies in Yunnan if his demands were not met.

To remove the troublesome governor from his home base in Kunming, the Kuomintang was hatching a clever plot that rested on an appeal to Lung Yün's greed. Just before the capitulation of Japan, Chiang had offered him "exclusive occupation prerogatives in Indochina" once Japan was defeated, but on condition that he drop his demands for Lend-Lease supplies. In mid-August Lung Yün accepted the offer and recommended his cousin and trusted associate, General Lu Han, as the Generalissimo's representative for accepting the Japanese surrender in Indochina, with the proviso that "no time limit" be placed on the period of occupation. The arrangement also suited Lu Han who during the war years had collaborated with his cousin, the governor, in a lucrative contraband traffic with the Japanese 6th Area Army.[14] The Kuomintang had foreseen that the opportunity for a profitable looting operation in Indochina would be irresistible and would deprive Lung Yün of the protection of his loyal troops who would be marching off to Indochina. The stage was now set for Lung Yün's removal.

Thus, in a well thought out series of moves, the Kuomintang was giving first priority to opposing Mao's forces, its second to forcing France to agree to its economic terms, its third to removing Lung Yün, and its fourth to extracting as much as possible out of Indochina.

While General Tsuchihashi and I had been fretting over the delay in the start of surrender negotiations, Generals Ho Ying-chin, Tu Yu-ming,[15] and Hsiao Wen and Dr. K. C. Wu[16] had been busily setting up the Governor of Yunnan and the French government for the coup de grâce. The same day Lu Han's troops crossed the border, Ho Ying-chin ordered the French troops in China to regroup at Meng-tzu and "await further orders."[17] In

Chungking talks had begun between the Chinese Foreign Office and the French diplomatic representatives regarding France's claims in China. At the same time General Tu Yu-ming, in Kunming, was preparing a coup d'état against Lung Yün.

In Hanoi, word of the Chinese border crossing reached Ho Chi Minh immediately and Giap came to see me, understandably agitated and with more accurate information than I had at the moment. His contacts on the border had telegraphed the arrival of "Yunnanese" troops,[18] and it was that fact which so alarmed the Vietnamese, not the crossing itself. Giap told me that of his own personal knowledge these troops were the "most rapacious and undisciplined of the entire Chinese army." And he was concerned that these Chinese would try to overthrow the Provisional Government and install a pro-Chinese regime.

Unaware of developments in China, Giap blamed Ho Ying-chin for the selection of the Yunnanese. He considered General Ho a "notorious anti-communist and henchman of Chiang Kai-shek," bent on destroying the Viet Minh movement and on annexing north Viet Nam to China. To convince me, Giap told me that the Kuomintang had been grooming several "renegade Vietnamese" (Nguyen Hai Than, Vu Hong Khanh, Nguyen Tuong Tam, and others) to take over the government in Viet Nam after the war. He described them as expatriates without links to the revolutionary movement within Viet Nam, who styled themselves as Vietnamese patriots dedicated to nationalism but were in effect "a group of reactionaries trying to feather their own nests" with Chinese support.

Giap was full of anxiety and wanted to know from me if the Americans knew what they were doing. The same question, for different reasons, had been posed to me on several occasions by Sainteny. I explained to Giap that the Americans were not responsible either for the selection or the control of the Chinese troops and, as a matter of fact, the whole affair of the surrender and occupation was the sole responsibility of Chiang Kai-shek. Looking straight at me, Giap asked if I was not arranging for the surrender. He wanted to understand how it was possible for me, an American representative, to be arranging matters and not be responsible for what was happening. Again, I pointed out that I was not participating in the decision-making process, negotiation of terms, or surrender procedures but was only acting in a liaison capacity. Giap shook his head, unconvinced and worried, and said he hoped things would turn out all right.

Returning again to the Chinese "march south," he expressed concern that Lu Han would bring with him some unsavory Vietnamese elements. He suggested I remind the Allied powers that a Provisional Government was in being in Viet Nam and it would be looking to them for recognition. I could only say that the authorities in Kunming and Chungking were aware of the Provisional Government's existence and that the matter of official recognition would have to await postsurrender consideration.

As Giap left, I could not but reflect that while the nearest and most visible threat to the Provisional Government was the advent of the Chinese troops and their Vietnamese puppets, their most *dangerous* threat was in Chungking. There the Kuomintang and French representatives were negotiating the spoils. There the Vietnamese, as the French at Potsdam, had no voice at all. Nor would the French or Chinese be deterred by the unlikely event of outside recognition of the neophyte Vietnamese government in Hanoi.

CHAPTER 23

CONVERSATIONS

HO LOOKS AHEAD

The message scrawled by Ho Chi Minh on his personal calling card was brief and compelling: "Urgent we meet before 12 noon today. Please come if you can. HOO." I could not imagine what he wanted to see me about.

Since our first visit in Hanoi three days before, there had been considerable excitement about the formation of the new government. The official announcement merely stated that Ho had assumed the offices of President and Minister of Foreign Affairs. Ho Chi Minh? Who was he? Some old-timers suspected he was the "old Communist, Nguyen Ai Quoc," but they were not sure. On direct questioning by journalists, Ho would only add to the mystery by saying he was a "revolutionary" who loved his country and wanted to see it free and independent of foreign domination. The other members of the government were also the object of public interest. Few had ever heard of Vo Nguyen Giap, the Minister of the Interior, or of Pham Van Dong, the Minister of Finance.[1]

In anticipation of the Emperor's abdication ceremony to be held the next day, 30 August, Radio Hanoi kept emphasizing the role of Bao Dai as "supreme counsellor" to the new government but also portraying him as the "humble citizen Vinh Thuy" or M. Nguyen Vinh Thuy. The average

Vietnamese viewed the Emperor in any role as the "heavenly symbol of legitimacy" for any government he endorsed. Ho recognized this trait in his people and exploited it skillfully. He also guided his Minister of Propaganda, Tran Huy Lieu, in the intricate political-psychological game of satisfying the emotional needs of each social, political, and religious element of Vietnamese society. Much was made of the fact that the Provisional Government included Catholics, socialists, moderates, and only a small minority of ICP members. There was little doubt the new government represented a real popular front and at that time enjoyed full support from the people. Further, the leadership was proving itself by the way in which public order and public services were being maintained. There was no interruption of public utilities or transportation and in commerce business was as usual. The almost daily demonstrations were devoid of violence and did not interfere with the life of the city. Everyone seemed happy with the turn of events, even most of the French, and in particular the Japanese authorities. However, word had spread that the Chinese had crossed the border and there was apprehension. Perhaps that was what Ho had in mind to discuss with me.

Ho sent a car to pick me up and by 10:30 I was at the house on Hang Ngang Street. Truong Chinh[2] showed me to Ho's quarters where several people were coming and going in a euphoric atmosphere of busy activity. Ho came in, unhurried and smiling, extending his thin hand in a firm greeting. "I was afraid you would not get my message until later in the day. I want very much to talk with you about some of our decisions and future plans." Chinh pulled up some chairs near the table and we sat down. Except for his emaciation Ho looked perfectly well, was ebullient and talkative, and he could not wait to tell me the news from Hué.

Ho had heard from Tran Huy Lieu, who had been received by the Emperor and had been shown the signed Act of Abdication. It would be read publicly the next day and Bao Dai would turn over the royal seal and sword to the delegation from the Provisional Government. Ho was elated. He viewed this final imperial act as the last vestige of colonialism and the beginning of the new era. Then, as an afterthought, he added—maybe the struggle is not quite over, the Chinese will be coming and the French are already here.

"Oh, yes, the Chinese," he remarked. Reports were filtering in of minor clashes between the Chinese and the people at Lao Cai and Ha Giang. Would it be possible to let him know the route the Chinese would be following? He would send government representatives ahead of the advancing Chinese to restrain the local population should the Chinese become "unruly" or "overenthusiastic" in obtaining war booty. I told him the Japanese had already asked and I had queried the Chinese authorities, but they had not replied. If I received any information, I would gladly pass it on to him.

"And when will Chang Fa-kwei be arriving?" Ho asked. "He won't,"

I replied. "He is sending General Hsiao Wen with the Kuomintang troops, but the senior commander will be General Lu Han, who will receive the Japanese surrender." Ho did not show surprise but after a long and thoughtful pause, he smiled and said, "This is Chiang Kai-shek's way of baiting the tiger out of the mountain. Without Lu Han's troops in Yunnan, Long Van [Lung Yün] will be easily plucked." In a more reflective mood, he expressed concern that the entry of Yunnanese troops would create insurmountable problems. They were not as well-disciplined as Chang's men, and Ho anticipated trouble.

Ho also spoke of the overseas Vietnamese who would soon be riding the Kuomintang baggage train. He referred to them as "pseudo-nationalists" and "lackeys of the Kuomintang" who were out of touch with the people of Viet Nam. Discussing the influence these newcomers might have on the Provisional Government, Ho described them as disorganized, a competing group of opportunists, and remnants of old nationalist parties without a basic program and too many leaders. In his opinion the danger lay in the confusion they might create should the Chinese force them upon the Vietnamese as a puppet government—a possibility he did not dismiss lightly.

Ho reminded me that China's motives regarding Viet Nam's independence were neither honest nor altruistic. Despite Chiang's lofty pronouncements[3] of "no territorial claims in French Indo-China" and his "generous" support of Vietnamese nationalist movements in China, the intent obviously was not in the best interests of the Vietnamese. In his opinion the Kuomintang wanted to frustrate France's will to reestablish itself in Indochina and to prevent a coalition of Vietnamese and Chinese Communist forces in China's sphere of interest. To emphasize his point, Ho noted the Kuomintang's selection of Lu Han and Hsiao Wen as representatives of Lung Yün and Chang Fa-kwei. These individuals were of particular significance to Ho. Governor Lung Yün and his cousin, Lu Han, for fifteen years had harbored pro-Japanese and pro-Chinese Vietnamese nationalists in their province. He regarded them both as spoilers who had jailed and murdered innocent Vietnamese to cover up their nefarious and illicit trade on the Indochina border.

Toward Chang Fa-kwei and Hsiao Wen, Ho was more charitable. They were less crass but equally self-serving. Chang reflected the Kuomintang's anticommunist sentiment, and Ho's memories were still vivid of the suffering and humiliation he had endured in the fifteen months he had spent in Chang's Kwangsi jails. However, he also remembered Hsiao Wen's influence in having him released from imprisonment and giving him a position of influence in the Kuomintang's anti-French nationalist front in China. That temporary collaboration was not because of Chang's or Hsiao's sympathy for Ho or his movement but because they hoped to manipulate and control both. Nevertheless, Ho and his Viet Minh had profited from the short-lived association.

But Ho had not asked me to come to discuss the Chinese, he said; he wanted to acquaint me with his plans for the next few days. He wanted me to be the first to know. I had some misgivings at that preamble but listened without comment. He told me of his first cabinet meeting on 27 August at the Bac Bo Palace where a decision had been reached to formalize the Provisional Government and to fix 2 September as Independence Day. On that occasion he would proclaim the people's independence, would present the members of the Provisional Government to the people, and would outline the government's program for all to hear.

I was surprised and impressed with his thoroughness, although perhaps I should not have been in view of his past performances. I congratulated him and wished him success. Ho modestly accepted my good wishes and went on to say that there was much to be done in a very short time. A committee was working at that very moment on the wording of the oath of office he and the ministers were to take. And the draft of their declaration of independence needed polishing. In fact, he said, that was one of the reasons he wanted to see me just then. He called to someone in the next room for the draft and handed it to me with an air of self-satisfaction. Evidently he had had a major hand in drafting it.

The typewritten document, with many words crossed out and replaced in ink and with numerous marginal notes, was in Vietnamese. I looked at it blankly, then at Ho, who suddenly realized I was unable to read it. Ho called for a young man to translate, and he rendered the first few sentences while I listened carefully. The translator was reading some very familiar words, remarkably similar to our own Declaration. The next sentence was, "This immortal statement was made in the Declaration of Independence of the United States of America in 1776."

I stopped him and turned to Ho in amazement and asked if he really intended to use it in his declaration. I don't know why it nettled me—perhaps a feeling of proprietary right, or something equally inane. Nonetheless, I asked. Ho sat back in his chair, his palms together with fingertips touching his lips ever so lightly, as though meditating. Then with a gentle smile he asked softly, "Should I not use it?" I felt sheepish and embarrassed. Of course, I answered, why should he not? Recovering, I suggested the translator read the passage again from the beginning. He read, "All men are created equal; they are endowed by their Creator with certain unalienable rights; among these are liberty, life, and the pursuit of happiness." Straining to remember, I detected the transposition of words and noted the difference in the order of "liberty" and "life." Ho snapped to the point, "Why, of course, there is no liberty without life, and no happiness without liberty." He entered the correction himself and then pressed me for more, but I pleaded ignorance, which was the truth. I could not remember the wording of our Declaration. And I was becoming uncomfortably aware that I was participating—however slightly—in the formulation of a political entity and did not want to create an impression of participation. I had also noticed, as the translator began, that Mr. Chinh had left the room and I thought I detected, perhaps erroneously, some divergence of opinion among the Vietnamese.

I was particularly interested in Ho's "nationalization program." Giap had referred in a vague way to "conditions in the country" which made it imperative to "nationalize" certain public services and industries. As the "elected Minister for the Interior," Giap felt it absolutely essential that there be no interruption of service in the areas of power, water, sanitation, flood control, communications, transportation, roads, and police and fire protection. The minute he assumed office, it was his intention to bring them under direct government control and to provide those services at a minimal cost to the people. I had observed to Giap that it would take both know-how and money to maintain and operate the services. He had agreed but could see no alternative, as French and Japanese resources would no longer be available. The Vietnamese, he said, would have to go it alone as best they could.

In discussing the program with Ho I again noted that it was not a simple matter of manpower, which was plentiful, but a question of procuring critical items such as generators, cable wire, heavy equipment and vehicles, steel girders and pipes, and the like. Most of these products were imported through French and Japanese commercial outlets. It was going to require foreign credits and national assets to do business with world producers. Ho admitted it, and it was one of his larger concerns. With regret in his voice, he remarked that the war ended too soon and the revolution had to be pushed too fast. Had it been possible to follow a cardinal principal of Marxism—to seize the nerve center of capitalism, that is, the financial structure, in his case the Bank of Indochina—some of the initial economic pressures would have been eliminated. As matters stood, the bank was still under French control and armed Japanese protection. Between the French, the Japanese, and soon the Chinese, the bank would be stripped of all assets. Even if the Provisional Government were to impose taxes to raise revenue, which he had no intention of doing, the people had no money. They could not even withdraw their deposits from the Bank. However, Ho felt it was not the time to be concerned with the economy. After the government was established and functioning, he felt confident it could be worked out.

As I was about to leave, Ho asked if I would do him the honor of attending a brief ceremony with him on Independence Day. I accepted tentatively, and he said he would understand if I did not attend. We left it in that fashion.

PARIS IGNORES SAINTENY

That afternoon I called on Sainteny. The short distance between the house on Hang Ngang Street and the Governor General's Palace was more like going from one end of the earth to the other, and the contrast was that day most noticeable. From the elation of launching a free nation to the anxieties of maintaining an unwanted and dying empire is a long distance to travel.

I had heard from Bernique that the French at the Palace were uneasy on many counts. The Japanese still refused to acknowledge a "French presence" and were keeping Sainteny and his entourage in la cage dorée under armed guard. De Gaulle's representatives were talking to the Chinese in Paris and Chungking while the Chief of M.5 in Hanoi, who had no official status, could talk to no one in authority. Even "l'Annamite" (Ho) had had the audacity to send a subordinate to deal with the "representative of France," only to spurn his magnanimous offer of "greater freedoms." Sainteny's earlier optimism had faded as two days passed with only ominous silence from Ho Chi Minh.

Sainteny received me warmly. His hospitality, as his mood, was unpredictable. It depended on the turn of events and on whether he wanted me to do something for him. That particular afternoon turned out to be the most pleasant visit we had had in quite some time. Sainteny called for coffee and we sat in a corner of the large salon overlooking the Palace gardens. The sun was still high and it was a hot, humid afternoon, but in the recess of the airy room it was very comfortable.

The local radio and press were featuring news on the formation of the new government, and Sainteny and his staff had been following its composition with particular interest. With the exception of Giap and Hien, whom he had met for the first time two days before, Sainteny knew none of them. As he poured coffee from an exquisite silver pot, he asked me if I knew any of them. Yes, I knew Ho, whom I had met for the first time in April but had been in contact with since then. Chu Van Tan had been working with Thomas and the "Deer" team. Pham Van Dong had cooperated with our AGAS people. And, of course, I knew Duong Duc Hien, Giap's friend.

Sainteny pessimistically speculated on the effect the new government would have on future "French-Annamite" relations. In his opinion it was communist in makeup and philosophy. Its Moscow-oriented leadership lacked sophistication and would be unable to cope with the task of governing. Furthermore, if France withdrew its economic base, who would replace it? The Soviet Union, even if willing, at the moment was in no position to help. As for the Chinese, they would only bleed it white. Sainteny's opinion was that sooner or later the French would have to take over, unless the United States intended to replace the French. I declined to be baited.

Unusually candid that afternoon, Sainteny admitted that he was getting no encouragement from either Paris or Calcutta. He confided that he had sent a strongly worded telegram to his government in Paris to the effect that Indochina would be lost to France unless positive steps were taken at the international level. I asked what steps Paris could take. "Well, compel the Chinese to live up to their obligation and release the French troops in Yunnan." He had learned of the Chinese crossing the border without the French and considered it a "Chinese betrayal." If only he had one thousand armed French soldiers in Hanoi, things would be different. I observed that it might also start a bloody war. His answer was that I did not know the "Annamite." They would never attack a Frenchman in uniform; they had too much respect for French authority. I did not comment further. All I could think of was the outspoken determination of Giap and his followers to contest any remaining vestige of French rule and Ho's repeated challenge that he would fight to the bitter end for Viet Nam's independence.

Sainteny found it difficult to accept the apparent apathy of Paris to come to his aid. In his appeal to Paris, he had requested that recognition for his mission be obtained through diplomatic channels in Tokyo so that he could deal directly with the Japanese in Hanoi. So far he had received not even an acknowledgment of his message. As it had been in Paris in July, when Sainteny had tried to interest de Gaulle in Indochina's future, so it was now. "They still do not understand the situation." In his remarks to me Sainteny intimated that if Paris wished to send someone to replace him, he would willingly step aside. It was the first inkling I had that perhaps Sainteny did not enjoy the full confidence of the Paris authorities. However, he was neither replaced nor given official status until October.

It was not until I was about to leave that Sainteny broached two separate requests. He wanted to know if in my opinion Ho Chi Minh was disposed to engage in a dialogue with the French. I thought a moment and ventured my belief that Ho was not a wild-eyed revolutionary. On the contrary, I found him to be a moderate and one of the few pragmatists among the nationalist leaders. From the several conversations we had had, I deduced that he was fully cognizant of his limitations and many liabilities. For example, he recognized that he would be taking over a bankrupt nation, that he had no assurances of outside support, and that his people lacked the technical expertise to govern or establish an economic base. On the other hand, Ho was also conscious of his assets. His followers were disciplined; he had a sound political organization among the peasant-worker-intellectual classes, who were motivated toward a common goal; and the independence movement included 90 percent of the people who, most of all, feared a return to the status quo ante. Having achieved a tremendous psychological and political victory with comparative ease in just ten days and possessing a respectable arsenal, Ho would certainly try to continue the momentum of the revolution. I also saw in Ho a peaceful man who would rather negotiate than fight, although I was convinced that lacking an alternative, he would fight.

Sainteny listened to my remarks and in a reflective mood suggested he ought to talk with Ho directly. Perhaps a personal contact would lead to some concrete understanding for a modus vivendi. Although I had serious doubts about the outcome of a meeting between them because Sainteny had neither official status nor authority to change Paris' inflexible policy of "French absolute sovereignty," I agreed that no harm could come from such a meeting. Sainteny asked if I would arrange it. I promised to try but expressed my opinion that his meeting with Giap and Hien had been counterproductive. Why? he wondered. I told him frankly that he had been not only patronizing but also vague in his offer of cooperation. Sainteny protested that his offer had been made in good faith and for the "good of Indochina." I said I understood and let the matter stand.

I understood only too well that Sainteny could not bring himself to accept the finality of French colonial rule or to recognize the fact that the Indochinese had had enough of foreign domination. He could not grasp the fact that the Indochinese perceived France's weakened state and that, with their goal in sight, they would not hand their country back to the French on the old terms. If the "French representative" could have been less condescending, more diplomatic, and more approachable, perhaps a temporary accommodation could have been reached. But Sainteny was a product of the French empire and part of the colonial system, if only by marriage. He could not forget it. He would repeat to me over and over again, "I just want to see the Tricolor fly over the Governor General's Palace once more." Nothing else mattered.

His other request concerned some of his SLFEO colleagues who, he said, had been airdropped on 23 August from Calcutta into the area of Tonkin north of Hanoi. This was news to me. He feared most of them had been killed or captured by the Japanese or the Viet Minh. Only two days before he had received word from Calcutta that Pierre Messmer and his team had been captured by the Viet Minh. At least they were alive, but where were they? Would I see what I could find out? I told him that I would, of course, but that it would take time. Could he tell me more? He said the SLFEO had sent out several teams of political officers, of whom Messmer was one, and several DGER agents to contact the maquis in Indochina. Most of the teams never reached their targets and little was known of their whereabouts. As for Messmer, he had been designated Commissioner of the Republic for Tonkin and his team included a medic and a radio operator.

It would be several days before I got the least clue on Messmer's team. In the meantime, Sainteny was still the head of M.5 in charge of French liaison for the SLFEO, but he seemed to have abandoned his basic objective, intelligence operations, for more nebulous political warfare activities. He was losing his sense of priorities and indulging in pointless acts of provocation.

CHAPTER 24

PUZZLES

A TEMPEST IN A TEAPOT

The next morning I got up to a blistering radiogram from Helliwell taking me to task for conditions relating to Sainteny's team—their shortage of food, the failure of Sainteny's most recent dispatches to arrive in Kunming, and an alleged threat of Japanese interference with his communications arrangements.[1]

Of greater moment (but less exasperating to me) was Helliwell's news that the French Chargé in an acrimonious confrontation with our Embassy staff had demanded a clarification of what the French called the American "failure to live up to agreement to permit them continued flow of Frenchmen and materials to Hanoi."[2]

It was just another French attempt to exploit the American position in China. There were in fact no agreements or understandings between the Americans and the French regarding the disposition, movement, or other matters relative to the French troops in China. The only agreements in force were between the *Chinese* and the French, American involvement being only incidental to Wedemeyer's role as the Generalissimo's Chief of Staff. To circumvent the Chinese the French were turning to OSS, leaning on the old OSS-DGER operational agreement. Heppner had reminded the French that the OSS-DGER agreement terminated with the cessation of hostilities and that the current embargo was directed by the Chinese government. Heppner had advised them that General Wedemeyer on behalf of Chiang had prohibited the OSS from moving non-U.S. personnel to Indochina for the present and had suggested they approach General Ho Ying-chin.

This tempest had, of course, also been instigated by Sainteny along with his absurd charges against me. He had been bombarding the French at Chungking and SLFEO/Calcutta with alarming messages of a Sino-American conspiracy to keep the French out of Indochina and of OSS plots to replace French control with Ho Chi Minh's communist-sponsored government.

Two typical messages, later revealed by Sainteny,[3] complained:

> We are faced with a joint Allied maneuver aimed at evicting the French from Indochina. Only the Government [in Paris] can, on the international level, protest. . . . It must be understood that at this hour northern Indochina is no longer French.

And another:

> The Allied attitude toward France threatens us with a total loss of face. . . . I must go through Patti for everything. . . . I insist that in fact at this very hour the Allied attitude is more harmful than that of the Viet Minh. . . . Only Leclerc or de Gaulle can and must act.

During the afternoon I called on Sainteny at the Palace, where I found him in his usual sullen mood. This time, however, I was very exasperated. He readily admitted reporting to China that I had not been very cooperative and that he and his team were virtually prisoners in their own land and that the situation was aggravated by the "changing of the guard" from Japanese to the "incompetent and vindictive Annamese."

I asked with some asperity why he was complaining to Chungking about an insufficiency of food, commenting that on the several occasions I had lunched with him the food was not only superior but plentiful. Since we both purchased food on the open market, I could not understand what the problem could be and, if there was a problem, why he had not mentioned it to me before complaining to Chungking? Sainteny exhibited some embarrassment and appeared irritated at being found out in this pettiness. He justified himself by saying that the day before the "Annamese boys" (meaning his domestic staff) had deserted "en masse in the dark of night" and that he and his team were not allowed outside the grounds. I undertook to see that food would not be a problem until he could make his own arrangements. Sainteny asked me not to be too concerned with the French in Chungking as they had no appreciation of the problems he was coping with, surrounded by "hostile Annamese communists" and arrogant Japanese soldiers. He referred to the Chungking "crowd" as "playing the tea and cookie game" while Indochina went down the drain. This was Sainteny's own parochial view, as he certainly knew that the French diplomats in Chungking were being forced to come to terms with Chiang on the important issue of French territorial rights. I could not see that Sainteny's false and inflammatory allegations of mistreatment would help the French position, either locally or in the larger scene.

I ignored his "tea and cookies" sneer at his compatriots. Why, I asked, did he place me in the position of having to explain petty problems I did not create or have any control over? His servant problem, for example. And the mail he had asked me to dispatch to Kunming the previous day was too late for the plane, it having already departed, and the next flight would not depart until the thirty-first. Sainteny claimed he understood, but it was obvious that he had purposely misled the French missions in China to believe I was holding up his dispatches. When I informed him that there was no ground for expecting any Japanese interference with his communications, Sainteny feigned surprise that the subject had arisen.

I was very unsure of Sainteny's motives. Personal pettiness was an obvious possibility. But there was also a possibility that he was attempting to trump up a lack of French logistical support in Hanoi as a basis of pressure for additional French personnel in Indochina. Whatever his true motives, his attempts to discredit American action either in Hanoi or in China would have no influence on the Chinese who were, after all, to be the occupying power.

I told Sainteny that I had seen Ho Chi Minh during the morning and had broached the question of a possible meeting, as he had requested, but that Ho had expressed his unwillingness to meet at that particular time. I softened Ho's refusal, noting that perhaps a meeting could be arranged at a future date. Sainteny shrugged, "It's of no importance; we will do what we have to do, regardless." I asked if he had any reaction from Paris regarding Ho's new government; his answer was evasive and noncommittal. As an afterthought, Sainteny remarked that Paris had its plans and was really not concerned with "red" activities in Indochina.

Our meeting had been exceedingly strained and, as I headed for the door, Sainteny noted that his "Japanese jailers" had been replaced by "Annamese communists." My suggestion that he might want to move to a less conspicuous location close to the American mission only produced the response that he was going to stay where "official recognition of French authority" could be noticed. He still felt very strongly that if there was nothing else he could do, he could at least maintain the "French presence" by occupying the former seat of the French Governor General.

A MESSAGE FOR MR. TRUMAN

If the French were disquieted by Chiang's strategem for French exclusion from Indochina, Ho and his Viet Minh were no less apprehensive about Chinese designs on the future of their leadership. Vo Nguyen Giap had sent me early that morning a note requesting that I transmit the following official message from Ho to President Truman:

In order to guarantee the solution to the problem which the Inter-Allied Commission will be called to resolve in Viet Nam, request that American delegates be made members of said Commission and that these establish relations with our government. We demand for our Govt the only legal body in Viet Nam, and the only one which fought the Japs [sic] (military operations conducted by the Viet Minh League and American officers)[.] the right to have representatives in said Commission.

> Provisional Govt. of the Viet Nam Republic
> President HO CHI MINH
> By the Minister of the Interior[4]

I recognized this as Ho's desperate and probably vain attempt to gain a seat among the nations that would decide the future of Indochina. To have China as the sole occupying power was an intolerable prospect to him. International recognition, if attainable, would strengthen both the movement for independence and his personal leadership. Lacking that, or with it, his desire for an active, decision-making participation by the United States would help offset the exploitative goals of the Chinese, French, and British. Ironically, despite his truthful claims of military resistance to the Japanese, it was only through active Japanese cooperation that his government was functioning. That very day, for instance, the Japanese quietly relinquished all civil police powers to the Vietnamese, except for the protection of the Bank of Indochina and the operations of the kempeitai.

I was unwilling to transmit Ho's message without discussing it with him and called on him in midmorning. With him was a man introduced as Hoang Minh Giam.[5] Without formalities we got right to the point, which was that I could not possibly send his message to President Truman. It was a diplomatic matter beyond the scope of my authority. My remarks did not disturb Ho. With his usual disarming smile and relaxed manner, he said he understood perfectly that I could not communicate directly with the White House but perhaps I could suggest how he could reach President Truman. It was very important that he do so.

Not waiting for me to reply, he turned to Giam and asked him to explain the import of the message. Obviously expecting Ho's request, Giam in fluent French said that the message had a twofold purpose: first to assure the presence of a disinterested party, preferably American, in any negotiations between the Chinese and the French which might jeopardize Vietnamese independence or territorial integrity; and, second, to encourage the Allied Powers to recognize Ho's Provisional Government as the sole and legitimate representative of the Vietnamese people in matters affecting Viet Nam's sovereignty.

Giam's remarks on the second point included a detailed elaboration as to the makeup and roles of various nationalistic parties which were of critical importance to Ho in August 1945 if he was to hold together any sort of legal regime. And, indeed, it cannot be emphasized too much that Chinese overlordship was, to Ho, as much to be resisted as French— perhaps even more. Further, the various Vietnamese parties that present such a confusing jigsaw to us continued to play important dissident roles over the years—under the Provisional Government, after the French return, and throughout the long Vietnamese war. Even today the Socialist Republic of Viet Nam has to take some account of them, and they are not without relevance to the current (1979) disputes between China and Viet Nam.

It was Giam's argument that any delay by the Allies in recognizing the Provisional Government would undermine its position of leadership and lend support to the Dong Minh Hoi and the VNQDD[6] in setting up a pro-Chinese administration. Here Ho interjected that it was imperative for the United States to exert its influence on the Chinese to accept his Provisional Government as a "de facto government before the pro-Kuomintang puppets crossed into Viet Nam."

Without acknowledging any merit in their argument, I reiterated the American policy—that the United States had no plans to interfere in the internal affairs of Indochina, whether on the side of the Chinese, the French, or the Vietnamese; and, further, my understanding was that the only Allied representatives involved in the surrender for northern Indochina would be the Chinese. If American personnel came with the Chinese surrender team, they would be those already attached to the Chinese Combat Forces as military advisers without political assignment or authority to represent the American government in international affairs.

My remarks were blunt, but true. It would have been wrong to raise a hope of American intercession when I knew it would not be forthcoming. The sensitive "old man" understood and with dignified resignation said he appreciated the American position and respected it. However, if I were to oblige him by sending his message, even to Chungking, he still felt it would be helpful. Perhaps there would be someone "in high places" who would understand the plight of the Vietnamese.

In the end, as a concession to a friend, I agreed to bring it to the attention of Ambassador Hurley, but I told Ho I could not predict what action, if any, he would take. In my own mind, I felt the effort would be fruitless, and it proved to be so. On at least one occasion I had heard the Ambassador refer to the Viet Minh as a "hot bed of red Communists."

I also informed Ho of Sainteny's request for a dialogue. Ho was pensive for a moment, then asked to what purpose? I could only guess, I said, perhaps to discuss France's future role in Indochina. Quite gently Ho replied that really there was little to discuss with Sainteny at that point in time unless, he added, it was the return of French forces to Viet Nam and, if that was on his mind, it would be best to wait for such an eventuality before they met. Ho said that if Sainteny had anything constructive to offer in terms of an official communication from Paris, he should send it to the Provisional Government for its consideration. Evidently the matter was closed, and I said no more.

Giam left the room and I, too, was taking leave but Ho insisted that I stay. He had just learned that several important French officials from Paris had arrived in Chungking to negotiate with Chiang on the question of extraterritorial rights in Shanghai, Tientsin, Hankow, and Canton. Obviously such discussions would not be conducted without implications for the future status of Viet Nam. Speculating further, Ho expressed concern for the ownership and management of the Yunnan-fu railway running from Hanoi to Kunming and the operation of the port at Haiphong. He also commented sadly how tragic it was that both at Yalta and Potsdam far-reaching and critical decisions had been made by the Allied Powers without the slightest reference to the will of the people of Viet Nam.

I disagreed with Ho, taking a contrary view. President Roosevelt's main concern regarding Indochina at Cairo, Teheran, and Yalta had been the future of the people of Viet Nam. He had quite forcefully addressed the issue of self-determination for the Vietnamese with both Stalin and Churchill, and separately with Chiang, and had secured the wholehearted support of Stalin and Chiang. In championing the cause of Viet Nam, Roosevelt had clearly indicated his preference for an end to colonialism in Indochina, even at the cost of alienating the British and disrupting U.S.-French relations.

Further, I said, the President had seen to it that Chiang openly stated his position of noninterference and I reminded Ho that Chiang had reiterated that very same position only four days previously by stating,

> . . . in keeping with the provisions of the Allied agreement today, excepting for the dispatch of forces to accept the Japanese surrender in areas north of the 16th degree North Latitude, we have no territorial ambitions in French Indochina. Our hope is that the Vietnamese will gradually achieve *independence through autonomy*, so as to realize the provisions of the Atlantic Charter.[7] [Italics added.]

Ho's only comment was, "Good, we will wait and see." But I knew, of course, that he did not believe the Chinese.

This raised again the matter of the Vietnamese nationalists crossing the border in the wake of Lu Han's occupation forces. Giap and I had discussed the subject several days earlier and concluded that it could lead to serious confrontations. I had already alerted Theater Headquarters and the Embassy to the potential for civil disorders and even armed clashes if the Vietnamese nationalists from China attempted to overthrow the Provisional Government.

As Ho and I were speaking of that, Giam returned with a message. His information was that Chinese troops had moved in on 27 August from Cao Bang and had promptly disarmed a small Viet Minh detachment stationed at Lang Son. Within the hour, Viet Minh reinforcements from the countryside had arrived and counterattacked, forcing the Chinese to withdraw and negotiate for free passage southward. The Chinese had demanded assurance from the Viet Minh that law and order would be maintained in the province through a coalition provincial government. The alternative would be a permanent Chinese military government. After heated discussion, it had been agreed that two representatives from the Viet Minh, two from the Phuc Quoc, and three independents would make up a provincial coalition government.

Shaking his head, Ho protested it was an intolerable arrangement: the Phuc Quoc were Japanese puppets of long standing and were not to be trusted. Giam explained that the Phuc Quoc consisted of three Japanese-sponsored nationalist parties, one of them under the direction of Tran Trong Kim. Ho interrupted to say that the Phuc Quoc had been organized before World War I under the sponsorship of Phan Boi Chau, "an honorable scholar, a well-intentioned nationalist," with visions of a Japanese-Vietnamese entente. In his early teens, Ho said, he himself had considered joining Dr. Chau's pro-Asiatic movement, the Dong Du (Go East). But already imbued with a strong feeling for independence from foreign domination, he had decided to travel west instead—to France.

Ho and Giam provided many details of Phuc Quoc collaboration with the invading Japanese forces, and Ho also dwelt on his personal experiences with the group in exile in China where they carried the role of loyal "Kuomintang lackeys." That enemy collaborators should carry any weight in the new regime was clearly a bitter pill for Ho to swallow.

Before I left, Ho again expressed his urgent hope that I would advise Chungking of what was happening in the north.

A MESSAGE FOR "MR. TAM"

I got my first hint of how Ho intended to approach his problems with the expatriate Vietnamese nationalists through a note I received the next day from Vo Nguyen Giap. As a personal favor he asked me to transmit a message to a "Mr. Tam." The message appeared innocuous and ordinarily I would not have given it a second thought:

> From - Vo Nguyen Giap, alias Van
> To - AGAS for Mr. Tam
> Viet Minh formed Provisional Government Republic. In my own name invite you come Hanoi.

But I felt alerted by Ho's disquietude in discussing the pro-Chinese parties. It momentarily crossed my mind that Giap might be attempting an end play around the Viet Minh. I dismissed the idea for Giap's loyalty to Ho and the Viet Minh was unquestionable. But the request remained unusual. In the past only Ho had asked me to transmit messages and their import had been clear.

What intrigued me was this "Mr. Tam." The only "Tam" with whom AGAS had contact was Nguyen Tuong Tam,[8] the pro-Japanese leader of the Dai Viet associated with the notoriously anticommunist VNQDD and the very same individual with whom Sainteny had secretly consulted in Kunming little over a month ago. It puzzled me that Giap, a principal lieutenant of Ho, would on his own initiative undertake to invite the leader of an opposition party to come to Hanoi. Giap had no assurance that I would not discuss his message with Ho, nor had he asked me to act in confidence. On this reasoning I concluded that Giap must be acting with Ho's knowledge, and I sent the message.[9]

But I remained puzzled as to why the message was being sent. What possible advantage could accrue to the Viet Minh? Was it a trap with arrest or assassination in mind? Not likely. The elimination of Tam would not interfere with the ultimate objective of the VNQDD, that is, the destruction of the communist-led Viet Minh.

Perhaps Ho, a master of conspiratorial maneuvers, was thinking in terms of what we Americans called "if you can't beat them, join them"— a tactic he had been known to use with some success. On reflection I could not see Ho merging his Viet Minh with the VNQDD, but perhaps a key leader among the anticommunist parties could be induced by bribery, coercion, persuasion, or what-not to cast his party's lot with the Viet Minh. I asked Bob Knapp, our political warfare specialist, to help me analyze this new turn of events. We began with the known fact that Ho and Tam had collaborated with Chang Fa-kwei in the Dong Minh Hoi during 1943 and 1944 and reviewed all the circumstances as we knew them.

In the summer of 1943, through OSS contacts with Chinese Communists in the Kuomintang, General Hsiao Wen had met Ho Chi Minh, Chang's political prisoner. Hsiao and Ho had struck a close ideological rapport, and in late July a petition for Ho's release had been forwarded by Chang to the Secretary-General of the KMT. It was approved in late August or early September, with the stipulation that Ho was to be released from imprisonment but retained under Chang's control for political activities among the Vietnamese émigrés. Chang asked Ho to help reorganize the Dong Minh Hoi, ineffective since its inception in the fall of 1942 and torn with interparty dissension. Despite the ICP-VNQDD rivalry, Ho had succeeded in making the Dong Minh Hoi a functioning coalition, satisfying Chang's needs for organization, discipline, and intelligence. By the time Ho left China for the Vietnamese border in August 1944, he had made many enemies, but he had also befriended several disgruntled leaders in the anticommunist bloc embodied in the Dong Minh Hoi. Among them was Nguyen Tuong Tam.

Knapp and I concluded that when Ho learned that Lu Han's forces were bringing his former associates in the Dong Minh Hoi with them, especially the hated VNQDD, he expected a Chinese plan to oust him in favor of a docile and pro-Chinese puppet. If that was to be the game, Ho would know that his government and its very limited military resources could not stand up to the Generalissimo's military strength.

Ho's other nagging problem would be the possibility, or probability, of a Chinese-French "deal"—to remove him, destroy the Viet Minh, and return Viet Nam to the French.

We had available the OSS R&A interpretation of Chiang's statement of 24 August, to which I had alluded in my conversation with Ho, and particularly the KMT's fourteen-point policy on the occupation of Viet Nam. We noted with particular interest that our OSS sinologists believed the Chinese government had no intention of becoming mired in Indochina. Chiang's earlier attitude toward the Vietnamese, expressed to Roosevelt in November 1943 at Cairo, seemed still to be valid. Chiang had said then that the Vietnamese were not Chinese, could not be assimilated into Chinese society, and that he had no territorial interest in Indochina.

The new statement of Chinese policy, however, took no notice of the Vietnamese independence movement or of the establishment of a Viet Minh government. Instead, it recognized French sovereignty over Indochina and implied that China looked ahead to dealing with France at the international level on the disposition of Sino-Franco interests in Indochina.

So it seemed obvious that Ho Chi Minh and his "de facto" government played no part in the Kuomintang's postwar plans. And Chang Fa-kwei's previous support for the Vietnamese nationalists, even though it had had the approval of Chungking, did not now form part of the General-issimo's grand design to move China into a position of preeminence at the peace table vis-à-vis France.

Assuming our analysis to be correct, the invitation to Tam, whose political associates were even then entering Viet Nam from Yunnan, had to mean that Ho was trying to outmaneuver the Chinese. Ho knew that Tam had not been well received by Hsiao in the Dong Minh Hoi, and had been badly abused by the leader of the VNQDD, Vu Hong Khanh. Perhaps it *was* possible that Tam and his Dai Viet could be weaned away from the Dong Minh Hoi. Perhaps he could be persuaded to accept a post in the new government and an acceptable number of assembly seats for his followers. Such a move, if successful, would certainly broaden the base of the Viet Minh government and, to the same extent, weaken the opposition parties from China.

Allied leaders plan OSS operations in China and Burma early in 1945. General Wedemeyer stands behind (left to right) General Sultan, Admiral Mountbatten, and Major General William J. Donovan.

Colonel Richard Pinkerton Heppner, Strategic Services Officer. Director of OSS operations in the China Theater.

Supreme Allied Commanders in Asia inspect the Chinese-American Training Center in China. Left to right: Lord Louis Mountbatten, SAC-SEAC; Mme. Chiang; Generalissimo Chiang Kai-shek, SAC-CT; and Major Chiang, the Generalissimo's son.

Colonel Paul L. E. Helliwell, Chief, Secret Intelligence Branch, OSS, China Theater.

General Stilwell entertains at luncheon. Stilwell is shown with Vice Admiral Yang Hsuan-cheng and General Hurley in Chungking, China.

A rare photo of two Chinese generals who played a major role in delaying a French reoccupation of Indochina in 1945-46. General Ho Ying-chin (second from left) was Chief of Staff to Chiang Kai-shek. General Chang Fa-kwei (third from left) attempted to develop an expatriate government of Vietnamese friendly to China. They are shown on 7 June 1945 in Nanning, China, at Kwangsi Command Headquarters. At left is Major General McClure, commanding the U.S. Army's Chinese Combat Command; at right is Brigadier General Harwood C. Bowman, Commanding General, Kwangsi Command.

Ho Chi Minh (seated) surrounded by his close lieutenants, Pham Van Dong (left) and Vo Nguyen Giap (right). Autumn of 1945.

25 August 1945, Hanoi. Arrival of Giap's troops. The procession continued for several days.

26 August 1945, Hanoi. Ho Chi Minh sends an offical delegation headed by Vo Nguyen Giap to welcome the American OSS mission to Hanoi. While the band plays the American National Anthem, Giap and his delegation join the author and the OSS team in saluting the American flag.

30 August 1945, Hanoi. Anti-French demonstration.

2 September 1945, Hanoi. Ho Chi Minh delivering his declaration of independence.

28 September 1945, Hanoi. Chinese General Lu Han (center) flanked by General Lin (left) and General Ma (right), representing Generalissimo Chiang Kai-shek, SAC-CT, outlines the Allied terms for the surrender of Japanese forces north of the 16th parallel in Indochina.

28 September 1945, Hanoi. Japanse Lieutenant General Yuitsu Tsuchihashi, Command General, 38th Imperial Army (standing center) listens as General Lu Han dictates the terms of surrender. Author (seated right) witnesses the proceedings as an offical Allied representative.

CHAPTER 25

ON THE EVE
OF INDEPENDENCE

BETWEEN SCYLLA AND CHARYBDIS

In the short span of eight days events in Hanoi had overtaken Allied plans for an orderly transition from war to peace. A routine military surrender operation without warning spawned a political maelstrom of international proportions. Conflicting multinational interests surfaced in rapid succession and were promptly deposited with our OSS mission for consultation, arbitration, or resolution.

I attributed this turn of events directly to Chiang Kai-shek's conscious delay in carrying out his occupational role. It contributed to the chaos and state of nihilism that followed. It gave the Japanese time for a final thrust in the futile struggle for ideological supremacy. It provided Ho Chi Minh with the opportunity to install his political structure without external opposition. As to the French, Chiang's procrastination made them more tractable in his negotiations with Paris.

The kempeitai had launched a vicious antiwhite campaign among the Vietnamese and Chinese elements in Indochina, directing its racist venom at the Western Powers in Asia. The French, having lost control over the affairs of their former colony, were in a state of collective frustration, flaying wildly at the Vietnamese, the Chinese, and the Americans. Rumors of a protracted Kuomintang occupation horrified Ho's people and the French colons. They easily envisioned months, even years, of despotic oppression, plundering, famine, and death.

Our position in the OSS was untenable. My authority was limited to matters military, but most of the issues and problems confronting us were political in nature. I kept Kunming and Chungking informed of the complex and explosive situation, but neither the military nor the diplomatic authorities seemed overly concerned. My suggestion to Heppner that he discuss the matter with Ambassador Hurley, urging him to send a foreign service officer empowered to deal with the simmering cauldron that was Hanoi, only elicited the reply, "Refer all matters to the occupation authorities upon arrival." That was well and good, but when would the Chinese arrive? We knew that advance elements had crossed the border on the twenty-seventh, but where were Lu Han and his political staff? Presumably his arrival time depended on Chiang's success in neutralizing the Governor of Yunnan and the progress of his negotiations with the French in Chungking and Paris. That would take time. In the interim we were to cope as best we could, present an image of Allied authority, and maintain a semblance of order.

My persistent requests for policy guidance and assistance in handling the volatile situation in Hanoi had irritated our Embassy and Ho's message to President Truman was the last straw. It proved a vexing problem for Ambassador Hurley who viewed Ho Chi Minh and his Viet Minh as an extension of Mao Tse-tung's "red menace in the East." Compounding the Ambassador's pique were French charges that the American representative in Hanoi was "anti-French and a communist sympathizer." Hurley was furious with Heppner's reluctance to recall me to China and ship me back to the United States.

At Theater level, Wedemeyer's staff was questioning the OSS about my "political activities in Hanoi." Quentin Roosevelt told me later (in October) that Tai Li had complained to Colonel Dickey, China Theater G-2, that I was being too friendly with the Viet Minh and not very cooperative with the Chinese authorities.

On Saturday, 1 September, I received a stern message from Helliwell advising that Wedemeyer's headquarters was "very much concerned about OSS activities in Indochina." The message continued: "Reports coming in that Patti is arranging conferences and mediating between French and Annamites" contrary to Theater instructions and that "Theater wants to avoid [political activities] at all costs since this action puts U.S. in the middle." The message concluded with the admonition: "We are in grave danger of having the entire detachment recalled."[1]

I was annoyed at the attitude of our people in China but not surprised. I knew they were subjected to French and Chinese pressures, but I was also conscious of my responsibility to my mission. Wedemeyer, Heppner, and Helliwell were fully cognizant of my orders from Donovan not to assist the French in their designs for reentering Indochina. They were also well informed that my selection for the mission had been predicated on my understanding of American policy toward "subject people" as stated repeatedly in the past. I felt strongly that if American policy had changed, I should have been so advised and recalled.

Even though the allegations were exaggerated (putting it as kindly as possible), I still wanted OSS-China to know the facts. I radioed Heppner that the only meeting I had arranged since my arrival had been the one between Sainteny and Giap, and that one at Sainteny's insistence. Of political mediation there had been none. We had, however, almost daily intervened with the local authorities to insure the safety of Europeans, in particular the French. And on several occasions we had interceded on behalf of French agents provocateurs apprehended in sundry misdoings.

I also reminded Kunming of my previous exhortations that Headquarters, China Theater, prohibit well-meaning but misdirected Americans from coming to Indochina for sightseeing excursions and urged again that the area be placed "off limits" to all Americans except those with legitimate official business.

Even among authorized personnel I was encountering problems. I had asked Theater and AGAS, soon after my arrival, to send qualified personnel to undertake POW operations and let me get on with OSS business. A small welfare team under the direction of Colonel Nordlinger[2] had arrived on 28 August. Unfortunately Nordlinger had no more success in dealing with the Japanese on POW matters than I had had.[3]

With little to do, Nordlinger and his group soon involved themselves in French-Vietnamese politics. Nordlinger was fluent in French and a World War I francophile and became an easy target of French pressure to release French POWs from the Citadel. The French seized upon the "new Americans," convincing Nordlinger that the French civilian community in Hanoi was in "mortal danger" from the Vietnamese communists and that only the release of French POWs to form "a protective force against Annamite attacks" would save them. This, of course, was hogwash. The Provisional Government had not only assured me that violence toward the French would be avoided at all costs but so far there had been no cause for alarm, despite French provocations.

I briefed Nordlinger on the delicate political balance under which a precarious state of public order was being maintained by the Japanese and the new Vietnamese government and strongly advised him to avoid entanglements with any of the political elements. He agreed that it was a sensitive and highly combustible situation, but I detected an undercurrent of sympathy for the "oppressed French—our former allies." The French with whom he came in contact sensed this, too, and exploited it to the hilt, and at American expense. With the French and Chinese already antagonistic to the OSS mission, the Nordlinger group became a third element in troublemaking. They took umbrage at the restrictions I imposed on their pro-French anti-Viet Minh activities and, for the next months while I was in charge of the OSS mission, their well-intentioned but disruptive tactics were the source of many unpleasant exchanges between Hanoi and Kunming.

A SPECIAL BRAND OF COMMUNISM

While these worries lay heavily on some, the life of the city went on. Grelecki and I toured the city that Saturday morning. The next day, 2 September, was to be the great Independence Day, and there was a festive air everywhere. Except for the weather, hot and humid, it reminded me of Christmas Eve at home. Everyone was busy and cheerful—shopping, walking or biking, talking, and gawking. There was an atmosphere of anticipation, but no one seemed hurried. With the exception of several Japanese military units walking or riding in military formation, we saw only Vietnamese on the streets. At the end of Avenue Puginier we came to a very large parklike area inconsistently and amusingly named *place* Puginier, *rond-point* Puginier, and Ba Dinh square. At the center a work-party was building a raised wooden platform, fifteen or twenty feet high and about twenty feet square, which was to be the focal point of the next day's festivities.

Everywhere we went storefronts were being tidied up and balconies and doorways festooned with red bunting, garlands of flowers, and gay lanterns. Work crews were busily replacing worn streamers across the streets proclaiming "Independence" and "Liberty for Viet Nam," or welcoming the Allies, particularly the Americans. Huge bundles of red Viet Minh flags were being distributed from carts in every neighborhood we saw. Often we had to stop our vehicle to let a formation of boy scouts, a detachment of women guerrillas, or a military unit cross an intersection. Everyone was coming from or going to somewhere. At one point a military band was playing, perhaps rehearsing, right in the middle of one of the small parks which abound in the city.

Our Vietnamese guide authoritatively explained that "tomorrow the people will meet their new government and the French will be gone." I asked him who would head the new government, and he promptly replied, "Ho Chi Minh." He had never seen him, not even a photograph. Nor did he know where he had come from, except that he had heard Ho Chi Minh had been "abroad for a long time," but he did not know where. I asked if he knew Ho's political affiliations. "Oh, yes, he is with the Viet Minh, the people's party." Did he know that the Viet Minh was communist? He seemed confused and embarrassed, then confessed he did not really know what I meant by communist. I did not pursue the point but could not help but observe that in speaking of Ho Chi Minh his answers exuded a proprietary pride, as though Ho were a member of his own family. I was to experience this phenomenon many times in the weeks I spent in Hanoi.

We spoke in French. Our guide, a man in his early thirties, had worked for a French shopkeeper for several years and, before that, at odd jobs gardening and chauffering for French families. His formal education seemed limited to the elementary level. He was quite able to read signs and posters both in French and *Quoc Ngu** but was not conversant with current events or the political scene.

During the morning I took the occasion to speak with a number of merchants. Generally they expressed pleasure at the prospect of an all-Vietnamese government, but some were noncommittal, and a few were not sure it would really make much difference. I often broached the question of what they understood the Viet Minh or communism to be. But only three or four were able to give me any answer at all, and their response was mixed, from "not good," to "wonderful, now the people will be in charge."

During the war I had spent considerable time with giraudistes and gaullistes (including French communists). Those French varied only in degree of loyalty to France, depending on whom they considered capable of returning their country to the prewar status of an established capitalist nation, part and parcel of an economic system suited to the western world complex. In Italy I had worked with the Committee for National Liberation (CNL) which included intellectuals, trade unionists, disillusioned monarchists and fascists, and a very small number of peasants. The action element in the CNL was the Italian Communist Party. Like their French neighbors, the Italians differed slightly from one another in political motivation. But, in effect, both nations were struggling to overthrow an ideological concept imposed on them by Hitler and Mussolini, and not much else. When that had been accomplished, both were prepared to return to the status quo ante, less the concept of nazism or fascism.

I had been led to expect an entirely different attitude in Viet Nam. The Vietnamese would not be satisfied simply with the defeat of Vichy's or Tokyo's fascist rule. They were not willing to return to their prewar status. They wanted change. They wanted to reclaim their country and make it free and independent of foreign domination. That is what I had learned from the political activists during the previous six months in China.

But that morning I did not find this political motivation among the people with whom I spoke. They could not have been the same Vietnamese who just two weeks before had stirred Hanoi to take control of the government. No, these were the city dwellers, urbanites integrated into the French community, accustomed to its affluent and comfortable ways. From their equivocal answers I concluded that they did not object to change. They had not been exactly overjoyed with the French or the Japanese overlords who were, after all, foreigners and not to be trusted.

*Romanized script of Vietnamese writing.

They felt more at ease with their own kind, even if their kind were mandarins or "notables," just so long as they were Vietnamese. It was evident, however, that the real people behind the change were not among the bourgeoisie of Hanoi.

Then I remembered what Ho had said to me in April in the shabby little room on the China border: that Viet Nam was an agricultural country, that 90 percent of its people live off the land, that they are subjected to an evil system of feudalism and mandarinate which reduces them to the level of slaves, and that, unlike the Western world, socioeconomic change in Viet Nam must be initiated among the peasants and also have the support of the industrial worker. But, to succeed, the change must have the full support of the peasant.

Driving back to the Villa Gautier, as I reflected on what Ho had said, I finally and fully understood: the people who effected the revolution were from the countryside, the villages, and the mountains—the peasants.

A visitor was waiting for me at the villa, a M. Buu, possibly in his late twenties, a distinguished-looking Vietnamese. I thought I had seen him before but was not sure. As Bernique and I shook hands with him, he introduced himself as "from the Home Office," and his perfect English and unmistakable Oxford accent startled and intrigued me. He handed me a handwritten note from Giap scrawled on both sides of his personal calling card: the Home Minister sent his compliments, and so on. M. Buu was his personal deputy.[4] He would be grateful to the American mission to facilitate his work, and so forth.

Buu said the purpose of his visit was to acquaint me with a "distressing situation" which gave President Ho much concern. It had to do with French clandestine activities directed from Calcutta. I summarized his account in my report to Kunming:

Several reports have come in from the Viet Minh in the field that French agents have been dropped by parachute at many points and captured by Viet Minh who are now holding them as prisoners-or-war. Latest . . . [carried orders] signed for General de Gaulle by De Raymond, stating that bearer, Captain Dupré Louis, is in charge of mission in Indochina for the Provisional Government of the Republic of France, instructing all civilian and military authorities to assist him . . . and asking all members of French Resistance Group of Interior who have not been in contact with other mission to place themselves at [his disposal] and to follow his directives implicitly. . . . Mission consisted of occupation of all public offices and buildings, civil, civilian and military, and private if necessary. He will represent Provisional Government of Republic of France and will deal with all civil, administrative, and military matters within the region he is assigned. It is well understood that he will relinquish his functions upon arrival of qualified official French representatives.[5]

Buu asked if I was aware of these French activities and if I could enlighten him on what the French were planning. Obviously I was familiar with French intentions, although not privy to their plans, and I candidly told Buu that several civil administrators had been sent to Viet Nam about the time our mission arrived in Hanoi. I explained that, based on past experience in Europe, the French anticipated a period of military-civil government in liberated areas and these teams dropped into Viet Nam seemed to be just that, civil administrators. I mentioned that I had already inquired of Giap about Messmer, but Buu pleaded ignorance. (Giap had not yet responded either.)

In sending Buu, Giap was conveying a tacit message—that the Viet Minh was everywhere, knew exactly what was happening in Viet Nam, and that the Provisional Government would not stand idly by while the French plotted a return in force. I thanked Buu for the information but did not indicate what action, if any, I would take. Nor had he asked that I take any action but assumed (rightly) that I would advise Chungking. Unfortunately, Buu's call gave nothing to reassure Sainteny. I did not learn where the French teams were or the circumstances of their internment.

DINNER AT BAC BO PALACE

Ho had invited Grelecki and me for dinner on independence eve. At exactly 4:30 we entered for the first time the arched gate of the Bac Bo Palace, formerly the Résidence Supérieure. The sentries at the gate saluted smartly, and a young officer escorted us to a room on the second floor. It was large and elegant but only sparsely furnished with a divan, several easy chairs, and a coffee table. Quite a contrast to Sainteny's luxurious salons in the Governor General's Palace.

President Ho, flanked by Giam and Giap, came forward to greet us with alacrity as though he had not seen us in a long time. Of course, we had conferred only two days before at the old house on Hang Ngang Street, but this was the first time in these formal surroundings. He introduced us to the others present,[6] and we moved on to an adjacent room where a table was set for dinner. I sat at Ho's right and Grelecki at his left. Giam was to my right and Giap to Grelecki's left, facing me. The food, as usual, was simple, delicious, and Vietnamese.

It became immediately evident that the occasion would also have political overtones. Ho opened the conversation by saying that my visit on the streets that morning had caused a "small excitement." People were happy to see me show an interest in their preparations for tomorrow's celebration, and he wanted to know what had been said. Was I pleased with what I had seen and heard? He seemed earnestly curious and interested. Not that he did not know what had been said, because someone among the many curious bystanders undoubtedly was a police agent and surely had reported each conversation verbatim. But he wanted my personal reaction because that, he knew, would be reflected in my reports to China. Avoiding political and ideological implications, I remarked on how impressed I had been with the preparations and the openness with which the people spoke. I praised the excellent organizational ability of whoever was directing tomorrow's activities and the cheerfulness of the people going about their tasks.

Our hosts seemed pleased, and Giam enthusiastically interjected that, although the credit for organizing the event belonged to the Hanoi City Committee, it had been the people themselves who actually were defraying the cost of fixing up, cleaning up, and decorating the city. He added that no government funds had been used and that, in fact, they had none. The Bank of Indochina and subsidiary banks were still in the hands of the Japanese and there was no way for the Provisional Government to get at national monies.

I asked what military display was being planned. With disappointment in his voice, Giap replied that he had hoped to have several marching units, but the troops "just back from the jungle" had not sufficient time to train for parades and he had to be satisfied with an "in-place formation." Ho interrupted to say that it really did not matter, the troops would be there for the people to see, and the "People's Army" would also see their new government installed.

We returned to the larger room for coffee. All the Vietnamese but Ho, Giap, and Giam left to attend to chores for the next day. We five clustered around the coffee table, while Ho poured hot French coffee into delicate Chinese demitasses. In a cordial tone he said he had invited us to dinner on the eve of Viet Nam's Day of Independence to express his personal gratitude and that of his colleagues to the government of the United States for the moral and material support his movement had received in recent years. He was particularly grateful to the Office of Strategic Services for its cooperation since 1943[7] and hoped that the same spirit of "fraternal collaboration" would continue in the years ahead. Reminiscing again on his past associations with Americans in China and later in the jungles of Tonkin, he spoke of General Chennault, of Colonel Helliwell, of Glass in glowing terms, and of his "comrades-in-arms," Majors Thomas and Holland and others on their teams.

During a pause, Giam observed that from what could be learned of the proceedings at the UNO San Francisco Conference[8] the Americans did not fully grasp the plight of the Vietnamese. He wondered why the "real" issue of Indochina had not been raised, except in terms of France's role as a colonial power. Was it not obvious that the Vietnamese aspired to what the Americans fought for in their revolution, "liberation from the foreign yoke and national independence?" The Americans, who "in 1776 had led the world into an era of national independence," should most of all appreciate what the Vietnamese were trying to do for themselves. And, obviously for my benefit, he added that "even Italy" had in 1848 taken a page from American history.

While Ho nodded assent and Giap sat stolidly, Giam launched into a

tirade against French wrongs. The French considered them "revolutionaries" and "ungrateful Annamites." Sure, they were "revolutionaries."
They revolted against the French colons, their exploiters and foreign
overlords. As for "ungrateful," what had they to be grateful for? Perhaps
for the privilege of being impressed into forced labor by the *cai** or
perhaps for the excellent roads leading to palatial French villas and
manorial residences on bountiful plantations, while Vietnamese traveled
the dusty or muddy paths to their hovels?

Giap could no longer contain himself and interrupted to say that the
French had built more jails than schools, more prison camps than hospitals, more barracks for their colonial army than houses for the people.
Certainly, the French had provided fine schools for a few privileged Vietnamese, but only to serve their colonial ends. If one wished to improve his
status abroad, one could not freely emigrate, even to France.

His last remarks suggested to me that perhaps he was being unduly
harsh and I noted with some circumspection that he himself was French-
educated and that he, like Giam, Pham Van Dong, Ta Quang Buu, and
many others, were all products of the French educational system. How
could he reconcile that with his charges of French insensitivity in the
field of education? Giap conceded exceptions, noting that some of his colleagues came from more affluent backgrounds, but most did not. Most
were subjected to cruel humiliations and academic discrimination. A student from the peasant or working classes entering the lycée or university
was at a disadvantage from the moment he entered the hall. His unstylish
clothing, his accent and mannerisms set him apart from his "aristo-
cratic" classmates. He became the object of scorn and snobbish attacks
and was accused of bringing down the academic level of the institution.
Only the strong and most persevering succeeded in completing their
schooling. It was not easy, according to Giap. Giam and Ho agreed.

Perhaps sensing that Giap and Giam were getting too argumentative,
Ho said he was sure I was familiar with the French colonial system and it
was pointless to dwell on the past, better to look to the future. Ho voiced
his belief that the coming months would be crucial for Viet Nam: that it
behooved the Vietnamese to demonstrate to the Allied Powers their firm
conviction of purpose; their unyielding determination to rid themselves of
"all foreign control, be it French, Japanese, Chinese, or whatever"; and
that the people of Viet Nam had reached a "level of political maturity"
which had earned them the right to govern themselves. Ho referred frequently to Wilson's "Fourteen Points" and the Atlantic Charter, as
though he were quoting American promises to Viet Nam specifically.

He then brought up the many allegations about his political affiliations, and I listened intently. Ho said he was very aware of French, British, and Chinese charges that he was a "Soviet agent" and the Viet Minh

*Recruiting agent for forced labor crews.

an extension of the "Moscow apparatus in Southeast Asia"; but the United States, which under the "enlightened leadership of the great President Roosevelt" recognized the right of all political parties to coexist, should not be concerned about the communist label given to his movement. He took the position that at that particular moment the Viet Minh was a "nationalist movement, democratically embracing all revolutionary Vietnamese parties." Of course, he admitted, the Indochinese Communist Party was a leading element in the movement for independence, but its members were "nationalist first and party members second."

Giap, who would not be easily silenced, made a most surprising statement: the Viet Minh had adopted communist techniques and disciplinary tactics to organize the various political parties fighting for independence within a social order akin to communism, but nevertheless it had no intention of substituting "another foreign power in Viet Nam for the French." It was on the tip of my tongue to ask if he included the Soviet Union, but it would have been rude and pointless. Giap was not only a doctrinaire communist but also a sincere and loyal Vietnamese.

Ho continued that he wanted the United States to know that his demands for the people of Viet Nam were "few and simple." They desired "limited independence," no more French rule, the right to live in freedom among the family of nations. Here was a change from the hard party line. His reference to "limited," rather than total, independence suggested some doubt in Ho's thinking as to whether he could achieve his goal on the first go-round. Perhaps he was willing to compromise with the French, or possibly with the Chinese. I was in doubt and just listened.

Continuing, Ho said that his people aspired to travel outside Viet Nam, "particularly to America, as I did long ago." They looked forward to the day when France was not the only place to study, when study was not limited to the privileged, when students could also study in the United States.

Ho wanted American technical experts to help establish those few industries Viet Nam was capable of supporting. Ho paused, seeing that Giam was anxious to speak. Giam's view was that what Viet Nam needed and wanted most was the right of free trade, free ports, and foreign capital—even French capital, though he doubted that France could afford it. In his opinion American capital and commerce were most to be desired and Viet Nam, given the opportunity, could develop air and seaports that could take American freight on a regular schedule. Giam continued at some length in this vein, speculating on the future of what Viet Nam could do for itself, if allowed.[9]

Ho then took the floor to raise a matter of urgent importance, the critical food situation. He spoke again of the calamitous famine of 1944, of the huge numbers who had starved to death within the span of a few short months, and of the millions more still suffering the aftereffects of malnutrition.

The food situation in the current year, he said, had not improved greatly because the torrential rains of July and August (the same storm systems that had done so much damage in the Kunming area) had flooded large areas of rice under cultivation. In fact, the reserves of rice held aside for the next sowing were already being consumed. The food situation "at this very moment is absolutely critical." If the Chinese occupation troops expected to subsist on the local market, "everyone will starve." Ho's current reports from the north indicated that the Yunnanese troops were "undisciplined and uncontrolled" and he feared that as they advanced toward Hanoi and Hué the already difficult food situation would become intolerable. Would I, then, call to the attention of the American government that it should "exercise some control over the Chinese occupation forces and request that the Chinese purchase material and food rather than requisition it during their occupation" to avoid "a situation where the Vietnamese will be forced to wage war upon the Chinese to protect livelihood and family?"[10] I agreed to convey his warning.

At 7:30 we felt it time to take our leave as the next day would be a heavy one. At the staircase, Giap took me aside and told me of several French attempts to infiltrate by airdrops some "high-ranking French officials." I asked if they were the same Buu had reported to me earlier. "Yes," he answered, but indicated that there were also others. He referred to "Major Messmer from Calcutta" and two members of his team. Buu would bring me a full report on Monday. Shaking his head, Giap commented, "When will they learn that they are not welcome in Viet Nam under these circumstances?"

CHAPTER 26

INDEPENDENCE DAY

"DO YOU HEAR ME DISTINCTLY . . . ?"

The first Sunday in September was the Feast of Vietnamese Martyrs, observed by over a million Roman Catholics in north Viet Nam alone.[1] Perhaps by a happy coincidence it was also the day selected by Ho Chi Minh as Independence Day. At the Catholic cathedral the feast was marked with solemn high Mass, and the homily had political overtones supporting the new government and independence for Viet Nam. Similar celebrations were held at the Buddhist temple.

From early morning, the crowds in Hanoi were like bees swarming spasmodically in close formation but gradually coming to rest near Ba Dinh square. The boulevards, avenues, and streets were impassable, except by following a slow meandering course, and then only with considerable good-natured jostling. From time to time shrill whistles and orders shouted through megaphones by group leaders opened a narrow passage for formations of sorts.

In several instances these were the entire populations of nearby villages. Men, women, and happy children, decked out in their best, walked toward the square in a tight group led by village elders or party officials. Other groups following the human wave included the distinctive mountain people in their regional dress and peasants in traditional robes, yellow turbans, and several-layered skirts with bright green sashes. Workers' organizations were among the various formations assembling in the streets. They were easily distinguished from their country cousins by their dress, the men in white shirts open at the collar, white shorts or white or dark trousers, no hats. The women were in brightly colored, traditional *ao dai*, a graceful free-flowing garment with panels in back and front, over ankle-length silk trousers, with wide cone-shaped hats hanging over their shoulders.

Toward noon our OSS team was on the streets photographing and noting the various groups, events, and slogans on posters, streamers, and placards. Many of the slogans were in English and French, some in Vietnamese. "Viet Nam to the Vietnamese." "Welcome to the Allies." "Welcome American Delegation." "Woe to the Oppressors." "Independence or Death." *"Le Viet Nam aux Vietnamies."* *"Tha Chet Khong No Le."* *"Tay Tru O'c No Le."* There were also graphics depicting a kneeling Vietnamese bound to a post while being decapitated by a French arm, with the inscription, "Here is French Domination." Another had two black skulls over crossbones and read, "Death to all Domination."

By noon Knapp, Bernique, Grelecki, and I had made our way toward Ba Dinh Square. I had decided not to accept Ho's invitation to the official platform but to view the ceremonies only as an observer in the crowds. We found a convenient spot facing the official platform among some local officials where we could see everything.

Waiting for the arrival of Ho and his entourage, I observed a group of Catholic prelates in dark blue and black cassocks, several with the red piping and sashes denoting ranking church officials. Not far from them I saw Buddhist bonzes in orange and white shrouds and Caodaist dignitaries in their white robes, embroidered turbans, and colored sashes.

The guard of honor and security details had been entrusted to Giap's and Chu Van Tan's troops, theirs being the best trained, equipped, and disciplined. In pith helmets, khaki uniforms, shorts, and knee-high socks, they proudly displayed their new weapons either at the "ready" or at the "trail" position. There were also formations of home guard or "self-defense" units—the people's militia—wearing parts of French or Japanese uniforms, or blue or black jackets and trousers, carrying an equally mixed array of weapons, including ancient muskets, spears, machetes, scimitars tied to long wooden handles, and even bronze clubs. The scimitars and bronze clubs were apparently from village shrines and pagodas. They made a picturesque and awesome sight.

At one the sun was overhead and the temperature hovering in the midnineties, oppressively hot except for an occasional breeze that fluttered the sea of flags in the square. But the large red flag with the gold star high on a huge staff on the platform hung limply.

Suddenly, there were sharp whistle blasts and shouts of military orders from each formation. The honor guard and the military units came to rigid attention as people began to appear on the platform. A few minutes later a second command brought the military to "present arms" and a hush fell over the crowd[2] as the dignitaries arranged themselves behind the white and red bedecked railing. Everyone on the platform seemed to be in white suits with ties and no hats, except for one small figure in high-collared khaki tunic and some kind of headgear—Ho Chi Minh.

Le Xuan, our erstwhile liaison-interpreter, had joined us and had been offering comments, views, and observations. He, too, had been circulating and described the intense curiosity among the crowd and their interest in the "new" leader of the government. Everyone wanted to know who "this mysterious Ho Chi Minh" was. Where had he come from?

The Vietnamese were not the only ones to whom the name was unfamiliar. Even our State Department staffs in Kunming and Chungking had a blind spot in that regard, despite my numerous detailed reports. I was astounded a month later when I read a dispatch[3] from Sprouse, our Consul in Kunming, to Washington, still referring to "HOO Chin-min." One would have thought that he at least would know Ho's name by that time.

The suspense was broken by a voice at the microphone introducing Ho as the "liberator and savior of the nation." The crowd, led by well-placed party members, intoned the chant, *Doc-Lap* (independence), repeated over and over for several minutes. Ho stood smiling, diminutive in size but gigantic in the adulation of his people. Raising his hands in a paternal gesture, he called for silence and began his now-famous proclamation with the words:

All men are created equal. The Creator has given us certain inviolable Rights; the right to Life, the right to be Free, and the right to achieve Happiness.[4]

Ho stopped short and asked his listeners: "Do you hear me distinctly, fellow countrymen?" The crowd roared back: "YES!" It was a master stroke of oratory. From that moment, the crowd hung on every word. My colleagues and I did not understand a word he was saying. Le Xuan made a valiant effort to interpret, but it was difficult. Yet, by listening to Ho's voice, quiet and clear, warm and friendly, and by listening and watching the responses of the crowd, there was little doubt in our minds that he was reaching them.

Ho continued:

These immortal words are taken from the Declaration of Independence of the United States of America in 1776. In a larger sense, this means that: All the people on earth are born equal; All the people have the right to live, to be happy, to be free.[5]

Then turning to the Declaration of the French Revolution in 1791 on the Rights of Man and the Citizen, Ho said "it also states: Men are born and must remain free and have equal rights. Those are undeniable truths."[6]

It was after two when Ho concluded his proclamation and was followed by Vo Nguyen Giap, then Minister of Interior. Addressing himself to the role of the Viet Minh, Giap stressed the work of the party in politico-military affairs, in socioeconomic development, and in the fields of education and cultural programs. In the area of foreign relations Giap singled out the United States and China as special allies and constant supporters of Viet Nam's struggle for independence. Interestingly, no mention was made of the Soviet Union. I never bothered to get a verbatim transcript of Giap's speech, but the next morning the Hanoi press quoted Giap as saying the "United States of America paid the greatest contribution" to the Vietnamese cause for independence and fought with its people "against fascist Japan, and so the Great American Republic is our good ally." At the completion of his speech the newly appointed ministers were presented individually to the people. The ceremony concluded with an oath of allegiance given by the ministers, swearing full support to the Provisional Government of the Democratic Republic of Viet Nam.

Late in the afternoon the local press provided us with a verbatim text of Ho's speech, which we promptly translated and transmitted by radio to Kunming. I also sent by air courier my own paraphrased description and interpretation:

After making his historic declamation and carefully citing the source and explaining the meaning in the context of Vietnamese events, Ho shattered the air of restraint towards the French, so well maintained up to that point. Head high, wisps of hair (he had removed his hat) and beard agitated by the slight breeze, and exerting a powerful emotional delivery, he continued: " . . . for more than eighty years, the French colonialists, abusing the standard of Liberty, Equality, and Fraternity, have violated our Nation and oppressed our fellow citizens. Their acts have gone contrary to the ideals of Humanity and Justice."

In his censure of the French, Ho accused them of having " . . . imposed unhuman laws . . . set up three distinct political regimes in the north, the center, and the south of Viet Nam to wreck our national unity and preclude the union of our people." Ho was relentless in his accusations. "They have built more prisons than schools. They have mercilessly slain our patriots; they have drowned our uprisings in rivers of blood." And specifically: "They have silenced public opinion and fostered political obscurantism. To weaken our race they have forced us to use opium and alcohol." Turning to economic exploitation, Ho charged that the French had " . . . fleeced us to the marrow of our bones, reduced our people to darkest misery and devastated our land . . . robbed us of our rice fields, our mines, our forests, and our raw materials. They have monopolized the issuance of banknotes and the export trade." On taxes: "They have invented hundreds of unjustifiable taxes and reduced our people, especially the peasantry and small businessman, to a state of extreme poverty, . . . hampered the prospering of our national bourgeoisie, . . . mercilessly exploited our workers."

Ho set forth in this public declaration, which he hoped the world at large would hear, his views of the recent history of Viet Nam: that in the fall of 1940, when the "Japanese fascists" violated Indochina's territory to establish "new bases for their fight against the Allies, the French colonialists went down on bended knee and handed over our country to them. Hence from that moment on our people became the victims of the French and the Japanese. Their sufferings and miseries increased. From the end of 1944 to the start of this year [1945], from Quang Tri to north Viet Nam, more than two million of our fellow countrymen died of starvation. On March 9th, the French troops were disarmed by the Japanese. The French colonialists either fled or surrendered, showing that not only were they incapable of protecting us but that, in the course of five years, they twice sold our country to the Japanese."

Ho then went on to say that on several occasions prior to the Japanese coup the Viet Minh League had urged the French to ally themselves with the League against the Japanese. Instead of agreeing to such proposals, the French colonialists had intensified their terrorist activities against the Viet Minh and, before the French fled the country, they had massacred a great number of the political prisoners detained at Yen Bay and Cao Bang.

Addressing himself to the French (completely absent from the crowd) Ho reminded them that, despite all these wrongs, the Vietnamese had always shown a tolerant and humane attitude toward them. Even after the Japanese coup, the Viet Minh League had helped many Frenchmen to cross the frontier, had rescued some of them from Japanese jails, and had protected French lives and property. As though addressing his words to de Gaulle and France, rather than to his immediate audience, Ho concluded that since the autumn of 1940 Viet Nam had in fact ceased to be a French colony and had become a Japanese-occupied territory. He spelled out this point by stating that after the Japanese surrender to the Allies, the people of Viet Nam had risen en masse to recapture its national sovereignty and found the Democratic Republic of Viet Nam. With emphasis, Ho declared, " . . . the truth is that we have wrested our independence from the Japanese and not from the French."

Summing up the state of affairs in Viet Nam, Ho declared: "The French have fled, the Japanese have capitulated, Emperor Bao Dai has abdicated. Our people have broken the chains which for nearly a century have fettered them and have won independence for the nation. Our people at the same time have overthrown the monarchic regime that has reigned supreme for dozens of centuries. In its place has been established the present Democratic Republic."

Then, addressing his remarks to the world powers, [he said,] "For these reasons, we, members of the Provisional Government, representing the whole of the Vietnamese people, declare that from now on we break off all relations of a colonial character with France; we repeal all international obligations that France has so far subscribed to on our behalf; and we abolish all the special rights the French have unlawfully acquired in our territory."

Ho concluded his address with an appeal to the United Nations and, indirectly, to the United States. "We are convinced that the Allied nations which at Tehran and San Francisco acknowledged the principles of self-determination and equality of nations, will not refuse to acknowledge the independence of Viet Nam. For these reasons, we, members of the Provisional Government of the Democratic Republic of Viet Nam, solemnly declare to the world that Viet Nam has the right to be a free and independent country—and in fact it is so already. The entire Vietnamese people are determined to mobilize all their spiritual and material forces, to sacrifice their lives and property, in order to safeguard their right to liberty and independence.

After the formalities ended, it took us at least thirty minutes to squeeze our way a distance of perhaps five hundred yards where we had parked. By cutting across the Citadel reservation we were able to get back to Maison Gautier by dinnertime, although many of the people-glutted streets remained impassable until late evening. I had invited the American contingent in Hanoi to join the OSS staff in a quiet celebration of a Vietnamese "Fourth of July" without fireworks. Alert to the possibility of skirmishes between jubilant Vietnamese and disconsolate French and hoping to keep the Americans out of trouble, I had asked Colonel Nordlinger and Captain McKay, who headed an AGAS team, with their respective groups, to have dinner with us.

BLACK SUNDAY IN SAIGON

All went well until about 9:00 o'clock, when I was handed a note from Imai reporting serious trouble in Saigon. Independence Day in Hanoi had been marked by national pride, native dignity, and commendable restraint, but in Saigon violence and death had lengthened the list of "Vietnamese martyrs." Imai's information was that the Viet Minh leadership in Saigon, either on instructions from Hanoi or in a show of solidarity, had organized a massive Independence Day demonstration. The organizers had been at great pains to insure order and to avoid clashes with the French. The people had been told that British and American representatives were due to arrive in Saigon that day[7] and that it was in the best interests of Viet Nam to show the Allies a peaceful and orderly display of national unity. Nevertheless, to the consternation of the Viet Minh leaders, the various political factions making up the southern coalition paraded down rue Catinat, some two hundred thousand strong, carrying banners and placards displaying party rivalries.

As the demonstrators approached the square in front of the Catholic cathedral, gunshots were heard coming from the French Clubhouse on rue Norodom. Father Tricoire, a Catholic prison chaplain well liked by the Vietnamese, had been felled while standing on the cathedral steps. He lay mortally wounded on the steps, reportedly for several hours.

Word spread like wildfire that the French were attacking and panic ensued. Without further inquiry as to the source of the gunfire, the Vietnamese police arrested several hundred Europeans and French sympathizers. Local hoodlums took full advantage of the confusion and broke into a number of French and Chinese stores and houses, indiscriminately looting as much as they could carry. The orderly demonstration had deteriorated into mass hysteria, mutual suspicion, and an uncertain political future for the newborn nation.

Greatly inflaming the situation was news that had reached Hanoi via Radio Delhi to the effect that General MacArthur (at the Japanese surrender on the USS *Missouri* which had taken place that morning) had urged the French representative, General Leclerc, to use his influence with the Paris government to send troops into the Pacific Theater. As heard in Hanoi, Leclerc recounted that after the signing MacArthur had allegedly taken him aside and said, "If I could advise you, I'd say to you, 'Bring troops, more troops, as many as you can.' " Leclerc's radio address over Radio Delhi together with the trouble in Saigon raised French hopes in Hanoi to new heights. Once more anticipating an early return of French troops flying the Tricolor and with Allied support, they read into the news a rapid collapse of the Viet Minh.

Imai came an hour later to fill me in on information received by the Japanese High Command and told me the Leclerc story had sparked some excitement and minor rebellion at the Citadel. The Japanese command, however, had it under control. In the previous weeks, General Mordant, the "leader" of the gaulliste "resistance"[8] and himself a prisoner in the Citadel, had planned a coup to spearhead, he hoped, a return of French forces under Leclerc. Our information was that Mordant's group had accumulated large stores of arms and ammunition in French homes and warehouses, strategically deployed for the moment of uprising.

I was not the only one aware of Mordant's plans: Giap, too, had his sources. As always, his were more accurate than mine. He knew where much of the French arsenal was cached and the identity of the cell leaders.

There was also the real danger that some Viet Minh hotheads might take it upon themselves to "eliminate" the French POWs in the Citadel along with the known French leaders outside. I discussed my fears with both Giap and Imai, separately. They both assured me that every precaution would be taken, at least until the Allied powers had assumed control. But the events in Saigon offered proof of how easily an inflammable situation could be ignited. Anyone at all could have been responsible for the initial gunfire—the French who stood accused without proof, a warring faction among the Vietnamese feeling abused within the coalition movement, the Japanese themselves or their sympathizers, or a plain madman. Who was to know? I did not like to contemplate the possibilities for Hanoi.

The trouble in Saigon, the unrest among the French in Hanoi, and Leclerc's provocative statement, coupled with Buu's report and Giap's concern about clandestine infiltration of "high-ranking" French officials, made it imperative that American policy vis-à-vis the French be clarified. That night I radioed Helliwell, expressing my concern with external agitation and for the safety of all. I emphasized the dual risk at the Citadel and recommended that special precautions be authorized. I advised against an early release of the French POWs pending repatriation for fear that, if released, they would activate Mordant's "resistance" plans and precipitate civil strife. At the same time I wanted additional protection for the French military and civilian elements in the event the Vietnamese took it upon themselves to effect reprisals for what was happening in Saigon or the threatened return of the French army. These were crucial issues not within the scope of my mission, and they had to be dealt with at Theater level, so I asked for a conference in Kunming for 5 September.[9]

It was well after midnight when things quieted down at the Maison Gautier. However, the lamps were still burning at dawn at the old house on Hang Ngang Street, at the French wing of the Governor General's Palace, and in the homes of many French and Vietnamese political leaders. It was an uneasy night in Hanoi.

CHAPTER 27

AFTERMATH TO BLACK SUNDAY

SPECULATIONS

T he first casualty reports reached Hanoi early Monday morning via Radio Saigon. Unidentified sources claimed a "veritable massacre" had taken place on "Black Sunday" in the Cholon-Saigon area, allegedly "One hundred dead—several thousand wounded." However, the official count on the following day was: three Frenchmen, plus Father Tricoire, and fourteen Vietnamese dead, including one very young girl. Such was the "massacre."

As distorted news stories and rumors swept Hanoi, ugly talk of reprisals against the *"Annamite canards"* could be heard among the French. There were also unfounded speculations that the Viet Minh police in concert with the kempeitai were preparing for a general roundup of known French resistance leaders.

I checked with General Tsuchihashi and he, too, had reports of French agitation, but no overt acts of violence had occurred to his knowledge and he had received no request for assistance from the Vietnamese police. His information from Saigon was that casualties amounted to five dead, several dozen wounded, and some looting. Marshal Count Terauchi's[1] headquarters had indicated that the police in Saigon had arrested some two hundred Frenchmen, "known trouble-makers."

After some discussion on a course of action, I reiterated the previous admonitions that the maintenance of public order was still his responsibility and added that, although I had no authority to dictate to the Japanese commanders south of the sixteenth parallel, it would behoove them to do the same in that sector until the British forces arrived. At that point Tsuchihashi suggested that it would be useful for us both to discuss the situation with Ho Chi Minh. In the meantime he would do what he could to relay my advice to Southern Army Command and assured me that his troops in the north would take every precaution to protect the lives and property of Europeans and Vietnamese.

From Tsuchihashi's headquarters I went to the Bac Bo Palace. Ho received me immediately, and we reviewed the situation in Saigon and the possible consequences nationwide. Ho provided a few additional details on Saigon but nothing significant, until several members of his immediate staff joined us. Among them were Tran Huy Lieu, Propaganda Minister, and Giap. At Ho's suggestion, Lieu gave me an account of what he believed had happened.

According to Lieu it had been understood and agreed to by all the delegates at the 13–16 August meetings at Tan Trao that the revolution would be "democratic" and without violence if at all possible and that an orderly and united front for independence would be presented to the Allies by all political parties. This condition had been met in Tonkin and Annam, but "some southern compatriots" did not quite understand the importance of maintaining "social and economic order," especially during the period of transition.

Lieu made reference to the ambivalent character of some of the political elements in Cochinchina and Cambodia, particularly the noncommunist nationalist groups. He gave, as an example, the Binh Xuyen "bandits."[2] I had not heard of them before and asked for more information. A young man described the group as "pirates" led by a notorious outlaw called Bay Vien. They operated from the village of Binh Xuyen in the swamps south of Cholon, hence their name. He estimated their number to be between one thousand and fifteen hundred "bandits" conducting raids on the Chinese community of Cholon and the wealthy French suburbs of Saigon. He was bitter and of the opinion that Bay Vien had joined the Phuc Quoc after the March coup only to exploit the independence movement for pecuniary advantage and to give the Binh Xuyen an aura of legitimacy, even of official sanction.

I inquired if yesterday's trouble could have been instigated by Bay Vien. "Not likely," was the answer of another staff member. The Binh Xuyen may have joined the fracas after it started, but the real instigators were the French—there was no doubt of it. Then, discounting his own remarks, he explained that other elements had more substantive reasons to create disorder and, specifically, to undermine the prestige of the Viet Minh with whose policy of moderation they disagreed. The Trotskyites who controlled the police were one such element; others included the politico-religious Cao Dai and Hoa Hao groups, all inimical to the Viet Minh.

Seeing my puzzlement at the differences between the Viet Minh and Trotskyite objectives, Lieu explained that both were basically in agreement on the concept of national independence but were diametrically opposed in their order of priorities for achieving a "democratic-socialist" state. The Trotskyites advocated arming the populace, overthrowing all vestiges of foreign rule, resisting all Allied efforts at restoring French sovereignty, and the prompt institution of social reforms. The Viet Minh, which had more or less accepted the old governmental structure, was less radical and disposed to negotiate with the Allies. It favored a gradual transition from democratic-republicanism to progressive-socialism to communism, thereby avoiding the shock of an abrupt socioeconomic change and the ensuing class struggle.

These differences reflected Ho Chi Minh's pragmatism in the light of the tenuous situation in which the Vietnamese found themselves and in the interparty rivalry for political leadership. In fact, Ho's own leadership in September 1945, outside Tonkin, was extremely fragile, and his control of the southern sector could best be characterized as shaky.

Feeling a need to extenuate the lack of party discipline in the happenings in Saigon, Lieu commented that Ho's government in Hanoi had not yet had the opportunity to brace up Giau's administration. It was to be understood, however, that the disorders were not sanctioned by Giau and were of grave concern to everyone in Hanoi. Ho nodded his agreement and, with a mild gesture, dismissed everyone except Lieu and Giap.

Ho seemed to be feeling the strain of the past several weeks. He looked very old and fatigued, with deep furrows at his temples. He was perspiring and coughing unusually hard and often. While the others were talking, he would shut his eyes and gently lean his head against the back of his chair. He was not smoking.

When the others had left, he leaned forward in his chair, clasped his hands, and asked me for my views. In retrospect my remarks sound harsh, even presumptuous, but my immediate concern was to avoid bloodshed. I noted the gravity of the situation (at the time we had no reliable count of casualties) and I feared serious repercussions throughout the country if he did not do something to reassure the French that yesterday's action was not inspired by the Viet Minh. I told Ho that I had talked with General Tsuchihashi who clearly understood his responsibility for public order and safety and that his staff would be in touch with the Provisional Government to coordinate contingency plans. Giap wanted to know whether, if Japanese troops were used, the plan would be coordinated with General Chu Van Tan.[3] I said I did not know but assumed that that would be a proper question to raise with the Japanese.

Returning to the affair in Saigon, Ho wanted the Allied authorities to know that, regardless of which party or group initiated the trouble, the Viet Minh would accept responsibility for ensuring there would be no recurrence. Privately I questioned his ability to carry out that promise, but I made no comment. Ho then asked for more specific recommendations, and I suggested that the first step would be to release the reported "several hundred" French arrested in Saigon and then to initiate an educational program for the Vietnamese on the immediate goals and objectives of the new government, which might dispel many doubts and rumors prevalent among the population. Ho nodded his assent and, smiling for the first time that afternoon, said he had held his first cabinet meeting early that morning and had presented a six-point program which the ministers had approved.

Rapidly he went down the program. It included first, a plan for increasing rice production to stem the threat of famine. During the period of increasing production, he had suggested that every family, starting at once, abstain from rice for one meal every ten days. The rice would be collected and redistributed to the needy. Other parts of his program included a campaign against illiteracy; general elections for a permanent government; a moral reorientation program stressing hard work, economy, integrity, and honesty (to eliminate the bad habits left behind by colonialism); the abolition of head taxes, market taxes, boat taxes, and the smoking of opium; and, finally, instituting complete freedom of religion and interreligious unity.

Somewhat perked up by his own enthusiasm and perhaps pleased that he had anticipated my suggestion, with a patronizing but kindly smile, he asked, "Anything else?" I suggested that he consider delegating some well-known and respected member of the Viet Minh in Hanoi as his personal representative and senior adviser to Giau for the period of transition. I felt it might add prestige to Giau's leadership. My recommendations were well received, and Ho promised that he would see that the French arrested in Saigon were released immediately. Turning to Lieu, Ho asked what could be done right away in terms of public orientation. Lieu replied that he would start in the morning to publish all decrees in an official journal[4] and a public condemnation of yesterday's disorders.

Giap, Minister of the Interior and also responsible for internal security, said he was disturbed by the tone of Leclerc's speech over Radio Delhi. He asked me if I could explain MacArthur's injunction to Leclerc to "bring troops" to Indochina. I pleaded ignorance but surmised that Leclerc's remarks were either out of context or intentionally distorted. However, one had to assume that the French had arrangements with the British who would soon occupy south Viet Nam and undoubtedly Leclerc's troops would follow. Giap showed disappointment at my prognostication but admitted that he, too, was of the same opinion. He felt that if the British allowed the French to reoccupy Indochina a long war lay ahead. His conviction was that the independence movement had come too long a way to abandon it without a struggle.

THE FRENCH COMMISSIONERS

After I left Ho, Giap walked with me to the large conference room on the second floor and told me what had happened to Cédile and Messmer. On the night of 22–23 August after our OSS team had reached Hanoi, two RAF planes (C-47s) from Calcutta had dropped two teams of three Frenchmen each, one team near Saigon and the other north of Hanoi. The team for Saigon landed in a rice field near Bien Hoa, somewhat northeast of Saigon, were picked up by Vietnamese peasants, and were turned over to the Japanese authorities. The team leader was a civilian who identified himself as "Colonel" Jean Cédile, Commissioner for the Republic of France in Cochinchina. He was taken to Saigon and housed by the Japanese, but was released on 24 August. Since then he had been negotiating without much success with Giau and the Provisional Executive Committee for the South. The other team landed near Phuc Yen, about fifteen miles northwest of Hanoi. The leader was Major Pierre Messmer, designated Commissioner for the Republic of France in Tonkin and Annam. His teammates were a pharmacist (paramedic), Captain Brancourt, who had lived in Viet Nam prior to the March coup, and a radioman, Sergeant Marmot, who had accompanied de Langlade on his missions to Decoux and Mordant before the coup. Messmer and his team were detained for several days by Giap's guerrillas and then released near the Chinese border with instructions to join their compatriots in China.

I asked Giap about the Dupré affair; he smiled and said that "Dupré" was the pseudonym of Messmer. When I told Sainteny what Giap had related to me on the fate of the Messmer team, he would not believe it and treated it as a cruel hoax on the part of the "Annamites."

LU HAN'S ADVANCE PARTY

The Sino-Japanese conference at K'ai-yuan ended on 2 September and the delegation, less Imai, returned to Hanoi on the third. Imai had been entrusted with a letter of instructions for General Tsuchihashi and had been flown in on a special courier plane late in the afternoon of the second. With the rest of the Japanese delegation came the advance party of Lu Han's staff.[5] These were the first Chinese of Lu Han's one hundred fifty thousand men to set foot in Hanoi, and they were not to leave Viet Nam until a year later.[6] That evening Colonel Sakai advised me that General Tsuchihashi had received the Surrender Memorandum and asked me to convey to Chungking the general's acknowledgment of receipt, which I did.[7]

In the afternoon still another plane arrived bringing American officers from General Gallagher's[8] staff. They were to contact my mission and arrange accommodations for the U.S. Military Assistance Advisory Group (USMAAG) which would assist and advise General Lu Han. General Gallagher would arrive later in the month.

The next morning Major Stevens of the advance group told me that he was to find suitable quarters for General Gallagher and assist the Chinese advance party in locating an appropriate villa for General Lu Han. I suggested my quarters, a spacious house formerly occupied by the Minister of Finance. However, Stevens, on the suggestion of some unknown person but certainly not anyone on my staff, decided that it would be more fitting for the senior American officer to locate at the Governor General's Palace, and he attempted without my knowledge to requisition it.

After lunch Stevens asked the OSS radio operator to dispatch a message to General Gallagher, which he did. It read:

Have visited Governor's Palace as possible quarters befitting Yank general. Political problems have come up in that French major now in Palace has orders from de Gaulle to remain in Palace. He offered all of the Palace except his room until such time as French High Command arrives to take over. Should I forget about Palace and accept second best?[9]

It was my custom to review all radio traffic at the end of each day, and it came as an unpleasant surprise to discover this gaffe among the day's messages. I discussed the matter with Stevens and strongly recommended he seek other quarters but, of course, Sainteny was already crackling the airwaves protesting the sinister American-Chinese plot to oust the French from the Palace.

MOUNTING TENSION

For two days Hanoi simmered along with a mild display of French optimism and studied constraint on the part of the Vietnamese, but from Saigon the news remained alarming. The excesses of 2 September continued, despite Giau's efforts to prevent them. British and French-controlled radio broadcasts from Delhi and Saigon reported that the Viet Minh administration was losing control of the situation. Conversely, Imai was informing me that the Japanese headquarters in Saigon was of the opinion that the Provisional Executive Committee for the South and, in particular, the local chief of police, Duong Bach Mai,[10] had the situation in hand. I felt that the Japanese were whistling in the dark, merely hoping that it would not become necessary for them to become involved in maintaining order.

We learned from Radio Saigon that all those arrested in the Independence Day disorders had been released. Contrary to expectations, the

French in Saigon and Hanoi reacted to that news with suspicion and fear. They doubted the Viet Minh's motives for the sudden release and feared those released would be prey to Vietnamese reprisals once out of jail. The only justification for this fear might have been a companion news item that Police Chief Mai had attempted to disarm the militant elements of the Cao Dai and Hoa Hao with only limited success. Under those circumstances, the French would have felt safer in jail.

Other unsettling news from Saigon concerned the party (Viet Minh) newspaper, *Dan Chung ("The People")*. It ran banner headlines exhorting the people to remain calm, to restore order, and to show political maturity. The text of the article, however, was plainly divisive and inflammatory, taking to task the non-Viet Minh nationalists for fomenting Sunday's riots and for undermining the cause of independence by attacking "peaceful Vietnamese." We took that to mean "peaceful Viet Minh." It singled out the Trotskyites for selling out to extremist elements.

The anticommunist press in Saigon, joined by the Trotskyites, then counterattacked, accusing Giau and his "cohorts" of pro-French sentiment, conspiring for the return of French rule and acting as traitors to the cause of independence.

The outlook appeared grim. If the intense anti-French fever spread to the north, I was not sure that Ho's government would be able to cope. With these thoughts very much in mind, I stopped at the Governor General's Palace on my way to the airport. Sainteny received me quite cordially and inquired about the "Saigon incident." I told him what I knew, but he was not particularly concerned. His view was that the Viet Minh had lost control and that it was only a matter of time before the whole nation would be in turmoil—not necessarily against the French but among the Vietnamese themselves. Of course, the "poor French" would be caught in the middle, but who was to blame? Certainly not the French who "stood abandoned." Perhaps the situation would be salvaged if the British or the Chinese arrived in time.

I received the impression that Sainteny (perhaps reflecting French sentiment) felt insecure so long as a nationalist movement survived. He felt that it had to be suppressed at all costs. He was not that day the least bit interested in Ho's policy of moderation or cooperation with the French. In fact, I suspected that Sainteny was less concerned with the anti-Viet Minh extremists than with the possibility that Ho might succeed in an accommodation with the Chinese or even with Paris. Such an accommodation might lull the French government into recognizing the Ho regime, granting political concessions, and possibly losing the colony forever.

The calm, unemotional manner displayed by Sainteny was not at all consistent with his previous reactions to the troubles in Indochina and gave me a distinct feeling that he knew more than he cared to tell me. Did he anticipate an imminent arrival of Leclerc's troops? Could he perhaps already hear the bands playing and see the Tricolor flying? Even the misguided attempt to requisition the Governor General's Palace he dismissed as trivial. Because I knew that the American presence in Hanoi would soon terminate with the entry of the Chinese troops, only a few days' march away, I was more curious than concerned about whatever troubles the French might be brewing.

At the airport I found Imai and a Major Miyoshi waiting for me. They had come to apprise me of the Japanese plan in the event of a flare-up in cities north of the sixteenth parallel. The general wanted me to convey to the authorities in China that he was fully prepared to exercise his responsibility for the preservation of order and public safety if the Provisional Government asked for assistance or if, in his opinion, the government was incapable or ineffective. We agreed that responsibility for the maintenance of order rested with the Japanese commander until properly relieved and that, if the Japanese commander wished to avail himself of the capabilities of the Provisional Government, it would be a matter for discussion and agreement with that government and of no concern to the Allies. Again I reiterated that the Generalissimo expected from the Japanese commander full compliance with the terms of the Surrender Memorandum.

I suggested to Imai and Miyoshi that the Japanese authorities formally advise the Provisional Government of their plan. They could, if they wished, mention that it had been discussed with me. In turn, I would report the substance of our meeting to the Chinese Command at Kunming.

We were airborne about 6:30 and landed at Kunming in darkness. Helliwell was waiting for me and in a foul humor. Evidently, Indochina had finally captured the attention of Chungking since the events of "Black Sunday."

CHAPTER 28

IN SEARCH OF
THE TRUMAN POLICY

ANXIOUS MOOD IN CHINA

The August jubilation and joyous excitement of victory in Kunming had, by the first week of September, changed to a pall of anxiety, suspicion, and intrigue. I found the Chinese, French, and Americans despondent, depressed, and in a state of collective nervousness. If Indochina was a tinder box, China was a growling volcano ready to erupt.

There were new faces at the OSS compound. Some were veterans of long field service in the interior of China. Others were newly arrived from the United States, too late for the war but now available for postwar operations.

Helliwell filled me in on all that was happening in Kunming, Chungking, and Yenan. In his curt, spicy, rapid-fire style, he listed the various problems facing the OSS, Wedemeyer, Hurley, and Chiang Kai-shek. Our Mercy Teams were experiencing innumerable difficulties with the Russians, the Japanese, and Mao Tse-tung's troops, as exemplified by the dramatic but much-delayed rescue of General Wainright from a Japanese prison camp in Manchuria[1] and the senseless killing of OSS Lieutenant John M. Birch[2] while he was attempting a similar rescue operation in the Suchow area.

Of quite another nature was the trouble in Kunming where ugly rumors of civil war were circulating. Governor Lung Yün was threatening a coup against the Kuomintang and planning to hold hostage all the Americans and the Allied supplies in Yunnan. Wedemeyer had asked Heppner to help protect American lives and property with OSS resources in the event of trouble, and Lieutenant Colonel (later Colonel) Alfred T. Cox[3], had already been alerted to defend OSS installations, the American Consulate, the American Red Cross, and other American interests.

Topping it all, Wedemeyer and Hurley were being pressured by the French and the British for control of Indochina. Heppner was in Kunming, and Paul and I were to accompany him on the afternoon flight to Chungking to meet with Embassy and Theater representatives to discuss my operations in Indochina and U.S. policy.

In the midst of these pressing problems, OSS-China was being reorganized. There was no longer a need for saboteurs, commando teams, and guerrilla units, and those men were to be returned to the United States. The OSS mission in postwar China was to be exclusively one of intelligence and counterintelligence. Helliwell had already been selected to head the new Intelligence Division.

At lunch we learned from Heppner of still other problems plaguing the Americans. Quentin Roosevelt had seen excerpts of a State Department memorandum prepared by J. C. Dunn.[4] It concerned a meeting between Mme. Chiang Kai-shek and President Truman on 29 August in the course of which the President had indicated that "no decision" had been reached with regard to the future of Indochina during his recent discussions with General de Gaulle.[5]

I was very uneasy about the incertitude of the American position and queried Heppner, but he too was confused. Hurley would have liked nothing better than to see a "democratic Indochina," preferably under the aegis of the Kuomintang. In recent official dispatches to the White House and the Department of State he had on different occasions damned the "imperialist" British, French, and Dutch.[6] He plainly was unhappy, however, with Ho Chi Minh and the communist takeover and would have been glad to have OSS recalled and to let the Generalissimo cope with the problem. Hurley had been clamoring for a clarification of American policy but the only response he received from Washington was a curt "no change." Yet the policy was being modified, at least in execution. Despite President Truman's assertion of "no decision" and the State Department's "no change," the fact remained that we were no longer actively opposing French intentions to take over Indochina by force of arms, if necessary. I noted that perhaps it was time for the OSS to withdraw from the scene. Heppner disagreed. Until we had a clear-cut position from the White House, OSS would ride it out.

SKIRTING THE ISSUES

We landed at Chungking about 2:30 and drove directly to the Chancery. The conference was chaired by Olmsted[7] who opened the session by saying that Indochina had been relatively neglected in the light of more pressing issues. However, recent events made it imperative that Theater address itself to the problems of that area. Heppner expressed agreement and introduced me, suggesting that I report on the current situation.

I outlined the entire Indochina mission, emphasizing my special directive from the White House in April, our operation in China and relations with M.5 in Kunming, and then described the current role of the OSS mission in Hanoi. I gave the conferees a rundown of events since our arrival in Hanoi, describing briefly the conflicting political interests and American-French-Vietnamese relations. I stressed our neutral stance vis-à-vis French aspirations and Vietnamese ambitions for control of Viet Nam. I noted, however, that a point had been reached in the political scene where it was becoming extremely difficult to maintain a neutral position and that a reexamination of that position was in order.

General Olmsted asked what, exactly, my original instructions were and what, if any, the changes in them. I replied that my directive from General Donovan was simply to carry out clandestine operations against the Japanese in Indochina and to set up an effective intelligence network useful to General Wedemeyer. In answer to a question by Paxton[8] regarding my instructions on the use of French forces and resources, I said it was quite proper to use them so long as it did not in any way encourage or assist the French in their objective of reoccupying their former colony by force of arms. I noted that General Wedemeyer and Ambassador Hurley were aware of these instructions and that I had been given full support in my mission by Theater Headquarters and, to a lesser degree, by the Embassy.

Paxton commented that my mission was within the purview of the military and the Embassy had no direct control except for political advice, if requested. We all agreed with that, but the question of American policy was an Embassy matter, and I asked if there had been any change in policy since April. Paxton replied that the last guidance from the Department of State was contained in the 7 June message from Under Secretary Grew.[9] Heppner and I admitted familiarity with the message and asked if we could assume the April directive to me still stood. Olmsted, on the other hand, wanted to know what the June message was about.

Paxton stated that the message provided "no change" in policy but also included ambiguities. Mr. Grew had implied that for all intents and purposes Roosevelt's trusteeship concept for Indochina had been abandoned at the San Francisco Conference. At the same time, the United States insisted on a progressive measure of self-government for all dependent peoples. The question was to be resolved postwar, and Mr. Grew had pointed out it was President Truman's intention, at some appropriate time, to ask the French Government for a "positive response" in that respect. The latest indirect word, he said, was that President Truman had "not reached a decision on the future of Indochina."

Well, Olmsted asked, where does that leave us? Within the week (on 2 September) Ambassador Hurley had discussed with Wedemeyer a harebrained scheme proposed by the French in Washington to treat Indochina as a single surrender area in the British zone under Admiral Mountbatten. An alternate plan proposed by the French was for the Japanese commander, General Tsuchihashi, to surrender himself to the Chinese in Chinese territory but the surrender of his troops to be effected into the hands of the French under the authority of the British command.

Paxton said the French proposals put our Ambassador in an awkward position with the Generalissimo. Fortunately, Washington had not capitulated entirely but had taken the position that if the French could reach an understanding with the British and the Chinese the American government would be glad to act accordingly, provided General MacArthur perceived no objection on military grounds and there was time to give it effect.

Olmsted interrupted to say that obviously it would be difficult for General MacArthur to justify modification of General Order No. 1 by altering decisions made at Potsdam and including the French among the Allied Powers designated to accept the Japanese surrender. Furthermore, he added, the Generalissimo would never agree to allowing a nonparticipatory power in the Pacific-Asiatic war—the French—to accept the surrender of Japanese forces in his theater of operation. Olmsted added that Wedemeyer had discussed the proposals with the Generalissimo and Dr. K. C. Wu,[10] and the Chinese answer would be a resounding "no."

At that point Heppner remarked that the problem of the Indochina dilemma had always been American ambivalence with respect to French interests and American principles of democracy. He had learned in private correspondence with someone in SEAC that as late as 30 August the Department of State had told Bishop[11] in New Delhi that the United States had no thought of opposing the return of French control in Indochina and did not question, even by implication, French sovereignty over Indochina. Yet the State Department repeated its worn-out tune that it was not the policy of the United States to assist France in taking over by force, whatever that meant. Heppner continued: Bishop is told, again by State, that the United States would be willing to see the French resume control on the assumption that their claim has the support of the people of Indochina and that such support is borne out by future events. In other words, our position would be to stand aside and let the French assume control, even by force, as long as we not assist, and then await results.

Helliwell, who had sat quietly throughout, suddenly spoke up, reflecting accurately the bafflement of all of us: so what is the policy? Do we help the French take over control? Do we help Ho Chi Minh set up a "democratic" regime for our Russian ally? Or do we "bug out" and forget all the fancy words of the Atlantic Charter, the Declaration of Independence, and the like?

We all looked to Paxton for the answer. General Olmsted broke the long silence, saying that we could not change old policy nor make new policy, but we certainly should be able to interpret existing policy. Paxton finally suggested we look at one point at a time in the context of announced policy in relation to both the French and the Viet Minh.

As to the French, he argued, we were in the unenviable position of being logistically unable to help them reenter Indochina from the China Theater. That would leave the Chinese as the only ones able, although unwilling, to be of assistance to the French. We need not interpose ourselves between them. So we should do nothing.

As to Ho Chi Minh, he was in place but riding a wild horse bareback and holding only one rein. Since the United States had no official relations with the Provisional Government of the Republic of Viet Nam, it should in no way feel committed to supporting it. There again, we could give him moral support, unofficially and discreetly, but nothing substantive. By the time the Japanese were disarmed and repatriated, we would be out of the picture.

That was Paxton's view and it was all well and good for the Embassy staff by way of advice. But, I asked, where does that leave OSS? Olmsted, sensing some hostility in my question, quickly answered, "Just where you have been right along. Your mission is to work with the Japanese and the Chinese in arranging for the Japanese surrender. Then you have the War Crimes project to get underway, and, finally, your long-range operation. The question of international relations with the French, Chinese, and Vietnamese is a matter for State to work out."

We went on to other matters. The Theater staff had been following my reports from Hanoi with interest, particularly the details of recent events in Saigon. Wedemeyer was concerned that the situation might spill over the sixteenth parallel and wanted to be kept informed. At Heppner's suggestion, I recounted all that had been reported in Hanoi —French fears, Vietnamese reaction, and Japanese concern. I observed that although the troubled area was in SEAC it could easily influence the situation in the China Theater. At the moment the problem was confined to political differences among the Vietnamese seeking control of the government, with peripheral effects on the French and Chinese populations. However, with the imminent arrival of British forces in Saigon for the Japanese surrender and with the French riding the British baggage train, serious trouble could be anticipated. One last important thing I pointed out was that a token group of American OSS-AGAS specialists would be attached to the British advance contingent and, without any doubt, they would be faced with much the same problems I was experiencing in Hanoi.

Olmsted and several other Theater officers present were surprised to hear that an OSS team was scheduled for the SEAC operations, and the General asked for an explanation. I apparently had struck a sensitive nerve, for Heppner instantly stepped in to say that a highly classified operation was involved. He was only at liberty to disclose that the State-War-Navy Coordinating Committee (SWNCC) had authorized the operation and that General Wedemeyer and Ambassador Hurley had been informed.

It was late and Olmsted wanted to end the conference; he asked if anyone had anything more to add. I posed a final question, one we in OSS had agreed upon if American policy was not modified, to wit: was it the sense of the group that I should continue to conduct political warfare activities in Indochina? Olmsted and his staff officers exchanged inquiring glances and sat silent. At length Olmsted asked what I meant by the term political warfare. He said he thought Paxton had answered that question earlier. Paxton, however, was quick to point out that he had not addressed the question of political warfare but had only interpreted publicly announced U.S. policy.

Quite candidly Olmsted admitted he did not understand my question, but that if my instructions were to conduct political warfare and if whatever I did in that political warfare was within the context of U.S. policy, then I should by all means "carry on." Everyone smiled, and the conference adjourned.

As with most conferences at Theater or Embassy level, this one had been pleasant and noncommittal. It seemed to me that the only real purpose of these conferences was to tell the decision-makers that the action people had decided to do this or that, depending on the matters under discussion.

We had been invited to dinner by Walt Robertson[12] and planned to spend the night in Chungking. The OSS office was near the Embassy, and Colonel Willam P. Davis[13] had sent a note to Heppner asking him to stop by for urgent messages from Kunming. Davis had two disturbing pieces of news. One had to do with the evacuation of American POWs from Saigon and the other with Lung Yün's soldiers raiding our American supply installations around Kunming. Major General Henry S. Aurand[14] wanted the OSS to help hold off any further raids on American depots in Kunming.

Heppner put in a call to Aurand and after fifteen minutes of constantly interrupted connections decided to return to Kunming at once. He called Robertson, made our apologies, and we went in search of our pilot. He was at the Officers' Club bar and not happy with the change in flight schedule. It took him two hours to round up his flight crew who, in turn, spent another hour convincing the ground crews to service the C-47 which was to take us back. When we eventually took off, a sharp flight clerk brought us Dixie cups of "operational" scotch and boiled water. No ice, of course.

PROJECT EMBANKMENT

As we relaxed after a wearisome day, I asked Heppner what was so unusual about the OSS operation in SEAC and southern Indochina. I knew little of it, except that Ed Taylor had been operating out of Kandy; that we were involved in supporting a "Free Thai" movement, including negotiations with the Thai Liberation Government; and that Heppner still held a few strings to American interests in SEAC.

Heppner then told Helliwell and me the first part of a story that in less than three weeks was to end in tragedy and produce the first American casualty of postwar Indochina.

In January Secretary Stettinius had alerted Donovan to the State Department's efforts to find out what was happening to American civilian internees (CIs) and prisoners-of-war in Japan and Japanese-occupied areas. The International Red Cross had been providing humanitarian relief where possible, but it was spotty and at the whim of local Japanese camp commanders. Stettinius felt our government should know where the Japanese camps were located, the names and status of American citizens in each camp, their physical condition and morale, etc.

At the same time the Department of State was arranging with Marcel Junod,[15] Francis B. James,[16] and Camille Gorgé[17] to set up an information exchange between the United States and Japan through the Swiss Government. Concurrently, the War Department had established the MIS-X Section under the Military Intelligence Division to help military personnel evade and escape capture. In the China Theater the operation was conducted by AGAS. Civilian internees had no such organization and depended solely on the work of the International Red Cross. Donovan got right on to it and charged SI in SEAC and in the China Theater with locating the camps, obtaining lists of CIs and POWs, and working with AGAS in every way possible. During the war months of 1945 OSS had been extremely successful in that phase of SI operations, culminating in the launching of the MERCY teams.

Donovan had been kept informed by Allen Dulles of Japan's peace feelers through OSS contacts.[18] He also knew of the development of the atomic bomb and something of the test results in New Mexico. During the Potsdam Conference, Donovan anticipated the imminent capitulation of Japan and had alerted Taylor at Kandy and Heppner at Chungking. Concerned with OSS reports of irregularities and abuses in some Japanese camps, Donovan had suggested to the Joint Chiefs that measures be taken to protect American citizens in Japanese camps in Southeast Asia in the event of a sudden Japanese surrender. The State-War-Navy Coordinating Committee did a feasibility study for postwar American participation in

SEAC and their final recommendation was affirmative: American personnel would remain in SEAC at least until American Foreign Service officers were posted to Thailand and other areas. The only Americans available and suited for the assignment were members of the OSS.

Word from Bishop, again unofficially, had reached Heppner that the British Foreign Office was assigning diplomatic and consular officers to various Force Commanders in Southeast Asia to act as political advisers under the direction of Maberly Esler Dening[19] of SOE. Bishop said their function was to report economic and political conditions in areas formerly held by the Japanese. Further, Dening had told Bishop that the British would also address themselves to the problem of "protecting" Allied interests in reoccupied areas and that questions concerning American interests should be channeled through him, Dening, until normal American consular offices were reopened.

This was an unacceptable situation, and Donovan had instructed OSS-SEAC and Heppner in China to quietly follow the British example and set up OSS teams in Southeast Asia to accompany the British occupation forces to Thailand, Indochina, Netherlands East Indies, Malaya, and Borneo. In consequence, by late July Project EMBANKMENT, consisting of about fifty officers and enlisted men trained and equipped for special OSS-AGAS operations, was on standby to move out with the first British "assault unit" for Indochina.

The British SOE Task Force 136 of course viewed the Americans as competitors and the fact that Force 136 was sponsoring the French SLFEO teams for Indochina and Thailand also operated against the American team. The Americans were considered anticolonialist and an anathema to the French, and therefore most undesirable.

In an eleventh hour decision, Major General Douglas D. Gracey,[20] the Commander of the British Occupation Force for Indochina, completely deleted Project EMBANKMENT from the Indochina operation. Heppner had radioed Lord Mountbatten, protesting Gracey's high-handed and arbitrary action, and Mountbatten had obliged his friend by allowing a greatly reduced team, totaling seventeen, to proceed on 2 September well in advance of Gracey's troops.

In charge of Project EMBANKMENT was a remarkable twenty-eight-year-old major (later Lieutenant Colonel), A. Peter Dewey.[21] He had been handpicked by Whitaker to complement my operation in northern Indochina. We had both known Dewey in North Africa and were familiar with his excellent background and splendid record in intelligence and political warfare activities. Heppner, Whitaker, Helliwell, and I all agreed that having Dewey in the south would strengthen our Indochina team, and we therefore requested his appointment.

Dewey had arrived at SEAC headquarters in late July and had immediately put himself in touch with me. We had agreed to coordinate our activities and exchange information and views. Our messages and reports were automatically relayed in a two-way exchange via Kunming.

Although our operational boundaries were limited by the military division at the sixteenth parallel, OSS-SEAC and OSS-CT activities in Indochina were coordinated, with Heppner calling the signals.

Since the Independence Day events I had not kept abreast of Project EMBANKMENT and Heppner brought me up to date. When General Gracey had been overruled by Mountbatten, Dewey's British file had been "flagged" and he had become persona non grata. Gracey had attached the miniscule OSS team to SEAC's Assault Unit Command for Saigon, under British Lieutenant Colonel Cass. Dewey was then told he was on his own and to expect no logistical or military support from the British command. That suited Dewey, leaving him free to carry out his assignment without having to clear with either Cass or Gracey. He was to look after Allied POWs and CIs, determine the status of U.S. property, investigate war crimes against the Allies, and carry out other OSS instructions.

Free to act independently, Dewey wasted no time. While the British methodically prepared themselves for a "proper" entry into Saigon, scheduled for the second week in September, Dewey sent out an advance party of four[22] under Lieutenant Counasse to initiate POW and CI operations. Their C-47 landed about 3 P.M. on Sunday, 2 September, on a Japanese airstrip not far from the main Saigon airport.

After the surprise of my team's 22 August landing at Hanoi, the Japanese must have anticipated the possible arrival of other Allied teams, and they were not caught napping. As the plane hit the tarmac, several military vehicles rushed out to meet the Americans. A Japanese contingent of about thirty officers and men, led by a colonel and his staff, received the team "with respect due rank," as Counasse put it in his official report. To give his team proper status, Lieutenant Counasse had assumed the "Mexican"* rank of major and had bestowed the rank of captain in the same fashion on the sergeants and the rank of second lieutenant on the lowly corporal.

At the time I was boarding a plane in Hanoi for my flight to Kunming on 4 September, Dewey was landing at Saigon with four more members of his team.[23] That evening he radioed his headquarters at Kandy that Counasse had located 4,549 Allied POWs,[24] of which 214 were Americans,[25] at two camps in the Saigon area. Evacuation of the critically ill was to have begun on the fifth, the day of our Chungking meeting; the remainder were to go out on the morning of the sixth. But the message Heppner had received that evening was that the British were competing with the Americans for air space and the American POWs given a low priority. Feeling that our POWs were not to be neglected, General Wedemeyer had ordered three American planes flown from Kunming that afternoon to assist the American evacuation.

---

*Unauthorized, self-appointed title or rank intended to impress or deceive, commonly used in the military parlance.

It was around midnight when we sighted the huge lake near the Kunming airport and well after 1:00 A.M. of the sixth when we rode into the deserted OSS compound. Heppner and Helliwell had to cope with Governor Lung Yün's raids on our installations, while I was mulling over the ambiguities of the so-called "policy" meeting we had concluded in Chungking.

CHAPTER 29

NO ONE'S LISTENING

TOO BUSY TO BE BOTHERED

My trip to China in search of policy guidance had been a failure. We had been talking to people on the action level when we should have been dealing with decision-makers. Wedemeyer and Hurley were preparing to leave for Washington for consultations[1] and would not or could not take the time to see me.

To Heppner's request for help Wedemeyer had responded, "Go ahead and use your best judgment" on matters not covered in current directives—unless overruled by Washington. That was as much as to say, "Whatever you do is all right but do not cross up Washington." Yet no one was telling Heppner what Washington was doing. For three days we spent a good deal of time conferring, cussing, and discussing without reaching a workable conclusion.

One of the issues needing attention was the presence of Dong Minh Hoi leaders in Lu Han's entourage. Their entry into Viet Nam under the Kuomintang's sponsorship was creating public unrest and internal strife. We urged Major General Robert B. McClure[2] to discuss the matter with General Ho Ying-chin and to emphasize the potential risk to Lu Han's mission. I stressed that in a widespread confrontation between the Viet

Minh and the Dong Minh Hoi Lu Han's troops might have the unpleasant task of subduing the Vietnamese by force, resulting in strong anti-Chinese sentiment and delaying the task of disarming the Japanese. General Mc-Clure promised to talk with Ho Ying-chin but was doubtful that any action would be taken; General Ho had more serious problems to deal with. The one overriding concern for the Kuomintang was to cope with the well-planned and smooth takeover of Japanese-held territories in the north by the Chinese Communists. Ho Ying-chin and his staff were devoting all their attention to the reassignment and movement of loyal Kuomintang troops to north China. He had at the same time to contend with the threat of revolt in the south by Lung Yün. And he also had to bear the brunt of the pressure exerted on the Generalissimo by the French and the British for control in Indochina.

Before I returned to Hanoi, General McClure let me know that he had taken up the question of the Dong Minh Hoi with General Ho without success. Ho was not disposed to interfere with Lu Han's arrangements, especially if they were anticommunist. In discussing this matter with Helliwell and the OSS staff I pointed out that from the Allied point of view the question was more of military consideration than of political accommodation, that if civil war broke out—and the elements for one were present—there would be shooting and chaos and a probability that some armed Japanese would take sides. It would be a mess. Yet I agreed with the staff that we had left no stone unturned to alert the powers-that-be and that we could do no more.

SAIGON—THE AMERICAN VERSION

On the seventh Dewey radioed the first American account of what had happened in Saigon on Independence Day. He had pinned down French casualties to three killed and several dozen wounded. The Vietnamese casualties were difficult to assess. The police count totaled nineteen dead and sixteen hospitalized, but many Vietnamese had not sought medical attention for fear of being associated with the demonstrators and therefore subjected to reprisals from opposition groups.

Dewey also air-pouched a comprehensive report clarifying many complex Vietnamese political maneuvers in the south. He confirmed Cédile's landing on the night of 22–23 August and his contact on the twenty-fourth with several left-wing Frenchmen then in Saigon, leading to his meeting with Tran Van Giau[3] on 27 August. By coincidence that meeting took place at the same time Sainteny was meeting with Giap and Hien in Hanoi. In Saigon Cédile had attempted to reach a workable arrangement for coexistence. It failed. As in Hanoi, the Saigon meeting only proved that the French and Vietnamese views on Indochina's political future were diametrically opposed. Cédile had insisted that Indochina's political future could only be discussed after French authority had been restored and within the context of the Declaration of 24 March. Giau and his colleagues maintained that future relationships with France would be discussed only upon condition that the French recognize Viet Nam's independence first. There was to be no common ground.

The Trotskyites were quick to learn of Giau's negotiations with Cédile and of his failure to convince the Frenchman that Viet Nam "was in fact independent." The ICL[4] faction of the Trotskyites promptly accused Giau of selling out to the French and labeled Giau and his followers "traitors to the revolution." During the last week of August the ICL had undertaken a program of social revolution among Cochinchinese workers and peasants. In Saigon order had been maintained until "Black Sunday," but in the rural areas turmoil had been the order of the day. The ICL, joined in many instances by the Hoa Hao, Caodaists, and Binh Xuyen, had encouraged the peasants of the countryside to overthrow the old order—the mandarinate system, the local notables, and public officials—and to set up people's committees instead. Large landowners had been dispossessed of their estates and the lands redistributed to the peasants. In the process many had been killed.

This agitation had been opposed by the Viet Minh, and Nguyen Van Tao was quoted by Dewey as saying, "All those who have instigated the peasants to seize the landowners' property will be severely and pitilessly punished," adding, "We have not yet made the communist revolution, which will solve the agrarian problem. This government is only a democratic government, that is why such a task does not devolve upon it. Our government, I repeat, is a bourgeois-democratic government, even though the communists are now in power."

After "Black Sunday," The Struggle, the Trotskyite party organ, published an editorial on 7 September accusing the Provisional Executive Committee of negligence in failing to provide adequate security measures for the demonstration, even though trouble had been expected.

Dr. Pham Ngoc Thach, one of Dewey's early contacts in Saigon, showed him an appeal to the population of the Saigon-Cholon area from the Provisional Executive Committee and signed by Giau. It blamed "provocateurs" for the disorders and killings of "Black Sunday" and charged: "Now those same persons have organized a meeting" to demand that the population be armed. Dewey interpreted the "persons" to be the ICL Trotskyites and affiliated parties. The appeal went on to state, "The Japanese and Allied authorities, informed of this, fear that new and more bloody difficulties will ensue"; it continued:

According to international agreement, the Japanese Army must assure order up to the arrival of the Allied army of occupation and everyone cannot but know that the Japanese forces here are still intact despite the surrender. Japanese General Headquarters have therefore decided to: (1) Disarm the national troops; (2) confiscate machine guns and other arms; (3) ban all political movements which trouble order and security; (4) ban all demonstrations without prior authorization of Japanese General Headquarters; and (5) disarm the population.

It concluded:

In the interest of our country, we call on all to have confidence in us and not let themselves be led by people who betray our country. It is only in this spirit that we can facilitate our relations with the Allied representatives.

The next day, 8 September, we learned from Dewey that Giau's appeal had forced the issue between the Viet Minh and the opposition out into the open. The ICL Trotskyites who until then had operated more or less sub rosa surfaced to challenge the Provisional Executive Committee. They went ahead with the meeting to demand that the population be armed and to incite their followers against the British troops.[5] The people's committees supported their challenge and a number of clashes occurred in the provinces between the Viet Minh troops and the armed units of the Hoa Hao and the Cao Dai.

At about the same time the news was coming in from Dewey, Quentin Roosevelt discussed with Helliwell several items of British concern which also affected our mission in Indochina. One had to do with a message from Lord Mountbatten to Wedemeyer expressing alarm at the "Annamite agitation and preparation for disorder." Mountbatten had implied readiness to take over sections "within the China Theater."[6]

Another item dealt with a reported Franco-British agreement under negotiation. In early September the French press had leaked the details of the proposed agreement, and Ambassador Caffery had advised Washington that it provided for a "French Civil Administration" as the sole authority in Indochina south of the sixteenth parallel. The only exception was to be the temporary presence of British troops for the exclusive purpose of enforcing the terms of the Japanese surrender and to assure the repatriation of Allied POWs and CIs. French official circles in Chungking and Kandy whispered of the proposed agreement as a fait accompli as early as the first week of September. It was in fact not concluded until 9 October.

These nebulous British machinations posed a serious risk of Anglo-American discord, a risk we in China were not prepared to cope with. With the end of the war the United States found itself in the position of broker between the French and Chinese, between the British and Chinese, and between the French and Vietnamese. If that was to be our role in China, neither Theater nor Embassy had been so instructed. It was everyone's hope that the projected Washington conference to which Wedemeyer and Hurley were going in mid-September would somehow resolve our many problems.

FACTS FOR WEDEMEYER

While in Kunming I prepared a brief for Wedemeyer's "black-book," a synoptic estimate of conditions in Indochina at the end of the war with Japan as viewed by OSS-China.[7] The following portions are of particular interest in the context of subsequent events and decisions pertaining to American involvement in Viet Nam.

Political. The vacuum created in Indochina by the precipitous capitulation of Japan favored the incipient nationalist movement in delivering a new nation in Southeast Asia—the Democratic Republic of Viet Nam. This former French colony no longer looks to France for tutelage and protection and will in all probability resist with all means available the return of the status quo ante.

The new regime, Moscow-oriented but apparently not supported, will probably be unstable for many years. Internal political, religious, and cultural conflict will militate against national unity and may postpone economic development. Despite these obstacles, a strong motivation toward nationalism impels the Vietnamese to resist foreign interference and they will undoubtedly fight if necessary for unqualified independence.

The independence movement and present provisional government are a broadly based political coalition representing some 10 different nationalist parties adhering to political philosophies ranging the political spectrum from extreme right to extreme left. The coalition is called the Viet Minh and is dominated by the Indochinese Communist Party led by an old-line communist, Ho Chi Minh.

The nationalist movement has an active history of popular insurrections supported by the peasantry, workers, and intellectuals since World War I. Popular response to the movement is nationwide and substantially in the millions, indicating that the supporters are neither apathetic nor supine and are willing to fight if interfered with in their ultimate objective—national independence.

Although the Vietnamese do not at this time advocate violence in ousting the French from their present harmless position, there is ample evidence that they will resist, even by force of arms, any French attempt at a military takeover of Indochina. The French authorities recognize the difficulty and appear to be disposed to reach some accommodation in terms of increased autonomy for the "natives" but definitely not self-government.

Encouraged by American statements of anti-colonialism and promises of restoring sovereign rights and self-government to those who have been forcibly deprived of them, the Vietnamese look to the United States for moral support, at least, for "American trusteeship" at most. They interpret the American grant of independence to the Philippines as the model of enlightened democracy and aspire to similar treatment.

Economic. Relatively free to trade with France and Japan and, to a lesser extent, with China, the war has had minimal effect on the area. It can be said that Indochina has suffered the least economically of all the Asiatic countries. American bombings in 1944 and 1945 destroyed lines of communication (roads, bridges, railways, ports and harbor facilities) and many of the principal industrial and power plants. Food and consumer goods shortages can be anticipated throughout the area during the remainder of 1945 and well into 1946, due to violent weather, poor crops, and destruction of plant and transportation facilities.

Pre-1940 French economic policy was based on maximum exploitation of the colony's resources. Indochina was compelled to trade exclusively in the protected French market, buying dearly at prices far above those of China, Japan, and Thailand, but selling cheaply in the unprotected markets of other nations. Recent French pronouncements indicate a probable change in this policy and have pledged "selective" tariff autonomy and equality of tariff rates for other countries. This may be attributed in part to Chinese pressure for postwar markets in Indochina. However, there is no indication at this time that the French intend to pursue an opendoor economic policy.

Japanese demands for payment of administrative costs in Indochina and devaluation of the piaster in favor of the yen have precluded international exchange to the point that the Indochinese financial structure is near bankruptcy. French monopolistic policy at this time actively discourages any American oil and mining interests, as well as sea and air transportation ventures. When approached by American businessmen in Paris and Chungking, the French have preferred not to discuss future economic plans.[8]

International Relations. The most dominant consideration in France's policy toward Indochina appears to be her future role in world affairs. Defeated in war, divided domestically, and divested of her *grandeur* as an imperial power, France has had to rely on the generous support of Britain and the United States. The reassertion of her prestige as a great power depends on regaining control of her former colonies with dignity and honor.

Presently, France lacks the means to retake Indochina from the Vietnamese by force of arms and as an independent victorious partner of the Allied Powers. She will have to resort to tactful persuasion, not demanding but appealing for loyalty to France and promising vague concepts of autonomy and shared responsibilities, which will not convince the Vietnamese.

France appears to be cognizant of her tenuous position and wishes to avoid a direct confrontation with her former subjects, an action which might adversely affect American opinion. In these circumstances, it is believed that France will continue to lean heavily on the United Kingdom, which is almost as anxious as the French to see that no pre-war colonial power suffers any diminution of power or prestige.

Differences between France and China over Indochina will probably continue, even after the outstanding issues of extraterritorial rights have been settled. Despite the Generalissimo's disclaimer of territorial ambitions in Indochina, the Chinese Government is tacitly supporting the Kuomintang-Vietnamese independence movement which is patently anti-French and pro-Chinese. There is evidence in present Chinese plans for the occupation of north Indochina that opportunities exist for a "squeeze" play in which the Chinese will be in an optimum position to extract economic benefits from the Vietnamese and the French.

United States Policy. American policy toward Indochina has consistently been one of non-interference in either French or Vietnamese political ambitions. At times this policy has been construed by some as anti-French and at times pro-Vietnamese.

With State Department concurrence American military operations authorized by the Theater Commander have been conducted in strict conformance with President Roosevelt's injunction that the postwar status of Indochina was a matter for future consideration and that there was to be no American military intervention, and there was none either on behalf of the French or the Vietnamese.

From time to time during the past six months events have made it necessary to provide the French in Indochina and in China with humanitarian support and this was done. Also, military necessity dictated the use of Vietnamese personnel in Allied clandestine operations and this, too, was done. Both French and Vietnamese personnel have been provided with American training and a limited number of arms and equipment for Theater-approved Allied operations against the Japanese.

I was later advised that the brief was delivered to the General's Chief of Staff on 10 September for inclusion in his packet for the trip to Washington. I never knew if the General ever read it or used any portion of it in his meetings, but if it was read by anyone on the policy level its impact must have been lost.

POSTWAR PLANS FOR OSS

While I was in Kunming, Heppner advised me of expected changes in our OSS structure. His information was based on false projections, and we did not foresee the imminent ruin of our entire foreign intelligence apparatus. Nevertheless we operated under the information available to him during the next few weeks. From the Potsdam Conference, Donovan had traveled east to meet with Taylor at Kandy and Heppner at Kunming. Anticipating an early end to the war Donovan wanted to alert his two chiefs in the Far East to postwar intelligence plans. He had stopped at SEAC first, then visited Heppner and told him of his intention to notify the Bureau of the Budget that the OSS was in the process of liquidation and would end its wartime function by the last day of December 1945.

Donovan's plan for an interim reorganization of the OSS was largely based on a memorandum he had prepared at President Roosevelt's request in November 1944 to liquidate OSS at the end of hostilities and replace it with a civilian peacetime organization headed by a civilian director appointed by the President. Domestic political differences and infighting among the military and civilian intelligence agencies had precluded White House action. Nonetheless, Donovan had proceeded on the assumption that the OSS, as such, would cease to function shortly after V-J Day.

The interim organization in our Theater was to have the Intelligence Division[9] forming the core of all OSS operations in China. By the end of September both OSS headquarters and Theater Headquarters were to relocate at Shanghai. The only staff to be left in Chungking pending the movement of Chiang's government to Nanking was intelligence personnel who were to report on political developments.

It seemed to me a logical and normal realignment, but the French seized on the plan to launch another anti-American campaign. Bernique radioed from Hanoi that the French there were gleefully spreading the word that I had been recalled by Washington because of "pro-Viet Minh activities" and that soon the entire OSS contingent in Indochina would be recalled. Helliwell was furious and insisted that I return to Hanoi posthaste and put a stop to that French nonsense.

So on Sunday, 9 September, I returned to Hanoi, still lacking decisive guidance on America's policy but mildly hopeful that Hurley's and Wedemeyer's upcoming appearance in Washington would resolve our doubts and fears.

CHAPTER 30

WARLORDS
AND CARPETBAGGERS

CHINESE CHAMELEONS

F ifteen minutes out of Hanoi flying at about one thousand feet and
following Route Coloniale No. 2, the pilot called my attention to a
long straggling column of humanity heading south. We could distinguish little so we dropped to a few hundred feet and the procession came
into focus. It was a mixture of military vehicles, bicycles, and animal-
drawn wagons, interspersed with scattered clusters of shuffling nondescript pedestrians. Many bore carrying poles or huge bundles slung over
their backs and were leading or prodding livestock. We could make out
flocks of chicken and geese, pigs and piglets, water buffalo, and other
animals being herded along the route. Often the pedestrians would rush
to the shoulders of the road to let vehicles pass, then as quickly as a wave
closes they moved back together to continue the flow southward. It was
Chiang Kai-shek's army of occupation.

Our plane touched down at Gia Lam on Sunday morning, 9 September. That day marked the beginning of a new chapter in the history of
the August Revolution as Lu Han's hordes arrived in Hanoi, unopposed
and unwelcome. These were the Chinese, representing the victorious
European Allies but not truly the Great Powers. To the Vietnamese they
were lackeys of the Western world sent to keep Viet Nam enslaved to

foreign interests. Even thirty years later, Vo Nguyen Giap could not forget Vietnamese antipathy to Lu Han's troops: "Chiang Kai-shek's Kuomintang troops were . . . also the enemy of the Vietnamese people and [the] revolution and our people had a deep hatred for them."[1]

At the airport I saw no Chinese, only Japanese ground crews. I drove across the Doumer Bridge and overtook the rear guard of a Chinese column of the 93d Yunnanese Division. An officer, seeing the small American flag flying from my vehicle, moved the column to the right, saluted smartly, and waved me on. The process was repeated many times along the route of march, which happened to be the same as my route to the Villa Gautier. As I approached the head of the column, the well-disciplined formations had changed from the route step to marching to the tune of a martial band. Accustomed to undisciplined and tattered troops in China, I was impressed with the appearance of that particular unit. They were well clad in blue uniforms and carried their American weapons with pride and military know-how.

All day long the Chinese troops kept coming, marching past the Villa Gautier. By late evening the convoy of trucks and jeeps carrying senior officers and selected staffs had grown into a massive parade. The Japanese soldiery stood in doorways trying to make themselves inconspicuous while the Vietnamese eyed with envious admiration the American arms and vehicles in the hands of the Chinese. The Vietnamese presented the image of curious bystanders, proud but not arrogant, interested, yet neither hostile nor submissive. The Europeans had vanished from view.

SOME FRENCH LIBERALS

Late that evening several "liberal" Frenchmen, not part of Sainteny's entourage, stopped at the villa to bring me news from Saigon and on events at the "Citadel Mordant," as they caustically referred to the French resistance movement in Hanoi. Two were members of the French Socialist Party and one was an active member of the pro-Catholic Mouvement Républicain Populaire (MRP). They had come from Algiers in January 1945 after a stint in the Paris insurrection (August 1944) with the French Forces of the Interior (FFI) to join the faculty at the University of Hanoi. Discreetly active in anti-Japanese conspiracies among the students at the cité universitaire, they had survived the March coup and had collaborated with Dr. Pham Ngoc Thach and Ta Quang Buu in organizing students in Hanoi during the August Revolution. We met often to exchange information and views.

That particular evening they expressed concern over the "formidable" Chinese presence in the city. They feared a clash between the Chinese and Vietnamese would be most unfortunate and might give the gaullistes the excuse they needed to intervene with Leclerc's troops. I observed that after seeing the well-disciplined Chinese units I doubted that French reinforcements would be necessary or tolerated, even if trouble broke out.

M. Gouin,[2] one of the Socialists, turned the conversation to de Gaulle and France, noting that at the moment, despite the loss of Syria,[3] the French empire was still intact. No one in France with the possible exception of de Gaulle seemed much interested in what was happening in Indochina. That, according to Gouin, was understandable. During the winter of 1944–45 living conditions in France had been extremely severe. Shortages of transportation, food, and the bare necessities had made life a matter of survival. Internal politics were in complete disarray, and de Gaulle's image as a world leader had suffered immeasurable damage by his exclusion from the summit conferences at Yalta and Potsdam. It had been a serious challenge to his whole *politique de grandeur* and de Gaulle could not stand the humiliation. Something had to be done to restore France to its rightful place among the world's great powers.

The others nodded agreement, and M. Lebrun,[4] our MRP friend, decried the messianic role which the "Great Charles" had set for himself. Lebrun recalled how unhappy de Gaulle had been with the Americans for refusing under one pretext or another his offer to participate in the Pacific war. He had felt very strongly that it was a point of honor for France to be able to claim having played a part in the Far East. Lebrun thought that de Gaulle viewed the Japanese coup in Indochina not as a catastrophe but as a blessing.

I remembered Lebrun's comments some years later while reading de Gaulle's memoirs, which contain the following passage:

... however painful the immediate results of such issue [the Japanese take-over] I must admit that from the point of view of national interest, *I was not distressed by the prospect of taking up arms in Indochina.* Measuring the shock inflicted on France's prestige by Vichy's policy, knowing the state of public opinion throughout the Union, foreseeing the outbreak of nationalist passions in Asia and Australasia, aware of the hostility of the Allies—particularly the Americans—in regard to our Far Eastern position, *I regarded it as essential that the conflict not come to an end without our participation in that theater as well.* Otherwise every policy, every army, every aspect of public opinion would certainly insist upon our abdication in Indochina. On the other hand, if we took part in the battle—even though the latter were near its conclusion—*French blood shed on the soil of Indochina would constitute an impressive claim.* Since I was certain the Japanese would fight to the very end, *I wished our troops to join battle despite the desperate nature of their situation.*[5]

My French guests asked why we Americans had given Chiang Kaishek a free rein in the occupation of northern Indochina. Why did we divide the country in half? Was it that the United States and Great Britain had political or economic designs on Southeast Asia and wished to keep France out of their plans? They were sympathetic to Vietnamese aspirations, but they were also French and believed France capable of social justice. Once the Socialist-Catholic-Communist bloc in France took control of the government, Viet Nam would be recognized as a sister-nation in the French-speaking community.

I good-naturedly observed that they sounded like Sainteny and his gaulliste friends. They pretended to bristle with indignation and said I knew better. But I responded that I had heard too often the insinuation that the United States was responsible for the division of Indochina and, by extension, the implication that it had dark economic motives. Gouin agreed with me and asked for the real facts: he found it hard to defend the Allied position without knowing the intent.

Minutely I detailed the pre-Potsdam decision of the American Joint Chiefs to realign the command boundaries in the Southeast Asia and Southwest Pacific areas and explained the necessity of releasing American resources for a main thrust against the Japanese homeland. After all, the Americans saw no useful purpose and had no interest in containing or mopping up the Japanese in the British-Dutch-French colonial enclave in Southeast Asia. After considerable discussion among the military leaders a purely military decision had been reached; nothing else. In hindsight it might be said that while the American consideration was military the British may have been more concerned with insuring their colonial interests and had rid themselves happily of the "anticolonial" Americans.

The charge of American manipulation of boundaries for economic reasons was reenforced by Sainteny's propaganda machinery which naggingly referred to a "secret" Yalta agreement to "rob" France of its rightful place in Asia and to the Potsdam decision as one for assuaging Chiang for the loss of Chinese territories to the Russians. Despite my efforts to dispel these false allegations, they have been persistently repeated by French, British, and American writers[6] to the point where the casual reader of history may come to accept them as facts. But they are not true.

A SQUATTERS' ARMY

All through the night Lu Han's troops poured into the city; we could hear their traffic, the racing of motors, the shouted instructions. We awoke next morning to a scene of shocking contrast. The quality of the Chinese "army" had undergone a drastic change. Yesterday's elite corps was today a squatters' army. Crossing town I saw an almost incredible scene of confusion and aimlessly wandering Chinese. Sidewalks, doorways, and side streets were cluttered with soldiers and camp followers hovering over bundles of personal belongings, with household furnishings and military gear strewn everywhere. Many had staked claims in private gardens and courtyards and settled down to brew tea, do household chores and start the laundry. This conglomerate of human derelicts was Lu

Han's Yunnanese rear echelon, resembling a retreating mob of stragglers rather than a conquering army come to disarm the enemy and accept its surrender.

The disciplined troops in their trim blue uniforms marching to bands were no longer visible. They had disappeared into the confines of the Citadel, the grounds of the Governor General's Palace, the former French and Vietnamese barracks. Only the tattered and mixed uniforms of irregular Chinese units could be seen, shod in rubber-soled sandals made from American jeep tires and carrying an assortment of American, French, British, and Japanese weapons. They were all part of the column we had seen from the air.

Standing by, watching this strange migration, were the Vietnamese, including Vo Nguyen Giap, who later remembered seeing

... bands of Chiang's army straggling in. It was hard to believe that this was a recently victorious army. Their faces were puffy and jaundiced, and they looked bewildered. Their yellow uniforms, the shade of turmeric, were ragged and filthy. They lugged baskets full of junky items on poles. Some groups even brought along women and children. Many had difficulty dragging themselves along on legs swollen by beriberi. . . . [7]

The days that followed were for me a study in oriental behavior. The arrival of the Chinese, accompanied by a sprinkling of American advisers, created a mixed atmosphere of detached interest, personal curiosity, and general apprehension. Fraternization between the Vietnamese and the newcomers was kept to a minimum. Only occasional and essential courtesies were exchanged, and the language barrier precluded extensive contact between the two groups. However, American-made vehicles, radios, and military gear in the hands of the Chinese were the object of intense curiosity to the more daring Vietnamese. Storekeepers had changed their inventories overnight. Only inexpensive articles were left on display, and their shelves were largely empty. Doors and windows on the street level were kept securely locked. Neither Vietnamese nor European women ventured on the streets without male escorts, even in broad daylight.

An exception was the Chinese community in Hanoi. At first they came out to greet their compatriots but, as the rear echelon settled in, local enthusiasm waned. Still, with an eye to the future, the leaders of the Chinese community played it safe and requested our mission to dispatch the following message to Lu Han:

Overseas Chinese of Hanoi present you their hearty congratulations and deepest respect for your brilliant career in the final victory and reserve their warmest welcome to your arrival in Indo China. [8]

At that time the Chinese population in the whole of Indochina numbered in the neighborhood of five hundred thousand. By far the largest concentration was in the all-Chinese city of Cholon abutting Saigon and at

Phnom Penh, the capital of Cambodia. Sizeable communities were located in Saigon, Haiphong, and Hanoi. They played a dominant role in the economic life of the nation, controlling vast financial interests in trade and commerce. The Chinese of Viet Nam represented an industrious ethnic group with strong family and political ties to China, to which they still professed their sole national allegiance. As a group they were mainly concerned with their personal and economic safety and welfare.

As the nation's businessmen, merchants, and money brokers they were generally affluent and well able to live the part; instead they chose to gather in middle-class ghettos known as "congregations." The 1935 Treaty of Nanking had categorized these Chinese as "foreigners with privileged status" and as such they were responsible for observing French laws and for the prompt payment of taxes to the Chinese representative in each particular "congregation." Under that arrangement they fared far better than the Vietnamese but not so well as Europeans or Japanese. These Chinese hoped that Lu Han, with plenipotentiary power to govern in the name of Chiang Kai-shek, would free them from French rule and from what they considered an onerous and subservient status. And their hopes were rewarded: just two days after his arrival, Lu Han directed the Provisional Government of Viet Nam to abolish the "congregation system" as demeaning to the Chinese community in Indochina. It was one of the many blows to French prestige during the Chinese occupation and another step in the weakening of the old order.

Two days after my return I learned from M. André Evard[9] of another blow to French prestige. The Chinese had unceremoniously evicted Sainteny and his entourage from the only remaining vestige of French grandeur, taking the Governor General's Palace for the use of General Lu Han when he should arrive. In war it has always been a conqueror's prerogative to locate in the most pretentious and politically significant building of an occupied area. In this case it was desired by the Chinese to make a show of predominance, if not suzerainty, calculated to impress both the French and the Vietnamese. But it was also a means of humiliating the French, reducing their importance, and cruelly placing them in the role of tolerated bystanders rather than victorious participants.

Sainteny relocated on 11 September in a small villa immediately adjacent to the Bank of Indochina. The arrangements, according to Evard, had been made by a SLFEO agent, Colonel Cavalin,[10] with a mutual friend, J. Laurent.[11] I could see that Sainteny hoped to lay claim to the bank for the French. As some local wits put it, if Sainteny could not protect French honor at the Palace, the least he could do was to safeguard its treasury.

The Bank of Indochina had played a major role in all the wartime collaborations of the French and Japanese. The Japanese had turned the entire country over to Ho's government, except the bank, and they still stubbornly kept a firm hold on it and its assets. The French saw the bank as their exclusive property and felt that the Japanese and Vietnamese, having no claim to the bank, could only be regarded as thieves. Any claims on or confiscation of the bank's assets by the Chinese would certainly be resisted by both the French and the Vietnamese. I could not see how the Vietnamese hoped to acquire control of the bank and it really appeared that by the time the Vietnamese were in a position to make a claim all that would be left would be the building itself. I was not far off. The day after Sainteny moved to his new quarters, M. Laurent sent me an official bank announcement. Short and snappy, signed by the bank's president, it stated that "as of September 12, 1945, the Provisional Government is bankrupt."[12] I asked if the bank had any assets left and was told it did, but not to the credit of the government.

HSIAO WEN: THE KMT AGENT

Soon after the advance Chinese came Chang Fa-kwei's trusted agent, General Hsiao Wen, who wore three hats: Deputy Commander to Lu Han; Commander of the 62d (Kwangsi) Army; and head of the political office, Section for Overseas Chinese Affairs.[13] Actually he had still another mission, a secret one to protect Chang Fa-kwei's interests south of the border.

I learned firsthand from Hsiao, late in September, that China could not possibly hope to establish cordial relations with Viet Nam in the postwar era without the active direction of Chang Fa-kwei. Hsiao's opinion, and one which he held until late 1947, was that Lu Han had been the worst possible choice to head the occupation. Hsiao found him ignorant of the Vietnamese "problem," too parochial in outlook, and commanding troops totally unsuited to occupation duty. But Chang Fa-kwei, in Hsiao's view, had long been laying the foundation for a workable Sino-Vietnamese entente which he, Hsiao, had coordinated "with a degree of success." The sudden change of sending Chang and his best troops to Canton instead of Hanoi risked losing Viet Nam to the French and in Hsiao's opinion was a disastrous decision.

Hsiao had arrived during my absence in Kunming, and he and Ho had had several informal meetings. Ho had provided his former jailer and protector with an excellent villa not far from the OSS mission and many other amenities as well, and they had undoubtedly renewed old ties. On the morning of 10 September I attended a meeting at the invitation of General Chu Van Tan, then Minister of Defense, which Ho had called to welcome General Hsiao. After lunch, Ho opened the meeting with a brief welcoming speech in Chinese and then introduced General Tan.

Addressing himself to Hsiao in Vietnamese, the Minister pledged cooperation and assistance to the Allied Forces in disarming the Japanese and in maintaining public order. Tan proposed that liaison be established immediately between the Chinese Command and the "Vietnamese

Armed Forces" so that the role of each nation could be served more effectively. (I could only wonder where Tan was going to dig up the "Vietnamese Armed Forces.") Tan made the generous gesture of "sharing" what food and supplies they had but pointedly remarked that there was not much in Vietnamese larders. After a few general remarks, Tan invited Hsiao to speak.

Hsiao rose slowly with his hand on the hilt of the ceremonial dagger at his side, a gesture of overlordship which was not lost on the Vietnamese, and smiled condescendingly. In Chinese he thanked Ho for his hospitality and understanding and acknowledged Tan's offer of assistance. Right off Hsiao made it clear that the Chinese were well equipped to discharge their responsibilities in dealing with the Japanese. On the matter of public order he said that for the moment the Chinese would look to the "local gendarmerie"; later General Lu Han would decide how the task would be carried out. On rations and quarters for the "Allied troops" he stated that the Chinese Command would provide what was essential from the local economy by a system of requisitioning goods and services with the understanding, of course, that proprietors and merchants would be reimbursed at an agreed fair market value by the Chinese Government.[14] Addressing himself directly to Ho, Hsiao diplomatically suggested that initially it would be appropriate if a qualified Chinese officer were assigned to each one of Ho's ministries as liaison; in that manner the Vietnamese could come to better understand the needs and ways of the Chinese.

As the general's remarks were translated into Vietnamese, Ho and his people dropped their friendly smiles but betrayed no surprise or disappointment. Their faces became stolid and cold as an air of silent hostility overtook the proceedings. Hsiao's voice was sharp and ominous. Listening to the Chinese dicta in the large resounding hall of Bac Bo Palace, one wondered from sentence to sentence what the next desideratum would be.

Suddenly, Hsiao, a master showman and diplomat, broke the tension with a joke which I did not understand but which was obviously appreciated by most. He smiled broadly as he expressed his appreciation for the "warm" welcome the Vietnamese had given the Chinese on their arrival. He eloquently promised that his government would not overlook the fraternal consideration his overseas compatriots had received from the Vietnamese in French Indochina during the past six months of Japanese tyranny. I was not at all sure how to interpret that promise; from what I myself had seen, no love was lost between the "accommodating" Chinese and the antifascist Vietnamese.

The general concluded his remarks with pledges of "eternal friendship . . . common objectives . . . and enduring struggle against foreign imperialism," and so forth. I had a strong impression that Hsiao was trying to set a tone of benevolence as well as overlordship, at least until the Chinese were ready to negotiate more important matters.

Ho led the conferees in a round of applause and invited Hsiao to an adjacent room for tea and a tête-à-tête. Lieu, Giam, Tan, and Giap broke the ice by joining the Chinese officers who had come with the general. Informal conversation, some through interpreters, was carried on until Hsiao and Ho reappeared, smiling, to join the rest. A few minutes later the Chinese left with cordial grins, military salutes, bows, and handshakes. It had been a perfect exercise in oriental diplomacy.

I was about to take my leave also, but Ho insisted that I stay for a cup of tea with him, so we settled in comfortable club chairs in the same room where Ho and Hsiao had talked. Ho asked me if I knew Hsiao Wen. I told him this was the first time I had met him but that I was aware of Hsiao's role in Sino-Vietnamese affairs in China. Ho smiled and chided me good-naturedly, "You can tell me; in fact, I know. He is the newly appointed Chief of Political Secret Services in Hanoi." I did not know this and did not believe it. I knew of Hsiao's role as political officer but did not wish to become involved in Chinese intrigues. I also did not want to divulge to Ho the OSS' role in securing his own release from Chang Fakwei's imprisonment in 1944 and the Hsiao connection. Ho himself, however, alluded to his past association with Hsiao without specifics. He did recount his efforts to reconcile the overseas Vietnamese nationalists at Liuchow in 1943 and the support he had received from Hsiao.

Ho confided that he had just asked Hsiao to intercede with the Kuomintang on behalf of Viet Nam. On reflection, this was not a wise move on his part, he said. He had hoped the Generalissimo, in line with his announced policy of "no territorial ambitions in Viet Nam," would use his influence with the Allied Powers to keep the French military from overthrowing his Provisional Government. Hsiao had been quick to suggest the Kuomintang and the Allies would be more favorably disposed toward Ho's regime if he were to broaden the political base of his government with, for example, the Dong Minh Hoi. Playing his only card, Ho had told Hsiao that it was his intention to "democratize" the government but that it would take time, perhaps not until after the December elections.[15] Hsiao, apparently satisfied with Ho's answer, had reaffirmed the Generalissimo's good neighbor policy and looked forward to mutually beneficial arrangements in which China could count on Viet Nam for preferential treatment in trade and in access to ports in Southeast Asia.

Despite the smiles after their private meeting, I could see that Ho had not won any points. In fact, before we parted, Ho plaintively noted that things would be very difficult but that he had been through worse. In the end, Viet Nam would be free of the French, the Chinese, or any other foreign power. Ho said, "I know that Hsiao has brought along two Vietnamese puppet administrators to organize a Kuomintang-sponsored government at the opportune moment—but he would not openly tell me that. These individuals do not even have the good sense to keep out of sight. If some of my younger people recognize them, I don't know what will happen."

In a prophetic vein, Ho also remarked that he could see bloodshed in the future. If the Chinese presented real opposition to Viet Nam's independence, his people would resist by force of arms. If the Chinese puppets forced the Viet Minh's hand, there would be civil war. And if the French menace became a reality, there would be all-out war.[16] If any of these things came to pass, there would be a "trial by blood." He looked aged. The strain of the joust with Hsiao was telling and, as we walked to the head of the stairs, Ho apologized for his sad and pessimistic mood, remarking that the presence of Chinese troops in his beloved land depressed him.

LU HAN AND THE SPOILERS

Without prior notice Lu Han arrived at the Gia Lam airport on the afternoon of 14 September.[17] I received a hasty telephone call from Hsiao's staff and went directly to the Governor General's Palace to await his arrival. At about 4:30 the general arrived in a small Chinese convoy, and I was among the first to greet him. General Hsiao introduced me as chief of the OSS mission and graciously added that our unit had greatly facilitated his dealings with the Japanese High Command and the Vietnamese government. Lu Han thanked me and asked that I call on him if there was anything he could do, that he would be looking forward to continued close cooperation with our mission, and so forth.

Contrary to the general expectation that Lu Han's arrival would be greeted with considerable fanfare, the general and his senior staff closeted themselves in the sumptuous Palace, which gave rise to wild rumors of the imminent imposition of martial law, military government, execution squads, curfews, and so on. Nothing of the sort happened throughout the period of Chinese occupation. Even so, the occupation was a disastrous and traumatic episode in modern Vietnamese history.

The impact of some fifty thousand[18] troops superimposed on an already shaky economy threatened the very livelihood of every Vietnamese, still unrecovered from the horrendous famine of the previous winter. Yet more pernicious was the systematic, quasiofficial plunder of the nation's resources by the unconscionable warlords and their underlings.

My repeated advisories to the Allied authorities that they provide for the feeding and maintenance of the occupation force went unheeded, and they arrived barefoot and hungry and planning to live off the land. From the very first they took what they needed or wanted from the French, the Vietnamese, and even from the local Chinese, rich and poor alike.

Their leaders were more sophisticated but even more ravenous and predatory. The wildly inflated Central China banknotes commonly known as CNs, which in Kunming were used in bundles for even small everyday purchases, became one of the tools for the financial exploitation of Viet Nam.

Early on, in discussing the southward advance of Chiang's troops, Giap had told me that at Haiphong Chinese troops had forced CNs on local merchants who had refused them because of the unrealistic rate of exchange. At Tuyen Quang, about seventy miles north of Hanoi, the Chinese military authorities had (at least temporarily) fixed the rate at one CN to twenty piastres. In Hanoi, local Chinese merchants were exchanging the CN on a par with the piastre. Giap had been indignant and said to me that his government's position was not to accept any Chinese proposal on exchange rates until the "arrival of the American Commission" when "differences in currency [would be adjusted] through the medium of the American dollar."[19]

The reality was that Ho's first meeting with General Lu Han in Hanoi on 16 September eliminated any hope Ho had of setting exchange rates against the American dollar. When Lu Han "suggested" to Ho that the exchange rate be pegged at fourteen CNs to one piastre, Ho asked that the matter be tabled until a financial committee could be formed.[20] Several days later, without further discussion, Lu Han imposed officially and unilaterally the fourteen to one rate of exchange. This rate for the virtually worthless CN, along with other financial maneuvers, set the stage for a colossal black market which practically destroyed the Vietnamese economy.

With CNs available in China by the ton, Chinese officers in Viet Nam with business connections at home organized themselves into a closely knit syndicate associated with merchants, bankers, and entrepreneurs to buy out at ridiculously little cost every profitable enterprise they could in Viet Nam. They operated not only within the Chinese military structure in Viet Nam but also within the hierarchy in Chungking through the Kuomintang-sponsored Viet Nam Advisory Board.[21] Front companies and trusts were quickly formed to acquire outright ownership or controlling interests in Vietnamese or French-owned plantations, farmland, buildings, factories, mines, port facilities and transportation. Even the small merchant was not spared. Private dwellings, theater houses, hotels and bars, shops, and personal services were sold by their owners for prices incredibly low. If they protested or dared to resist any offer made by the syndicate, the military had ways to persuade.

Many of these Chinese profiteers settled permanently in northern Indochina with their new and prosperous enterprises; and some undoubtedly moved south with their portable assets in 1954 in the great migration away from the Democratic Republic of Viet Nam. But to expect that the thinly disguised expropriation of Vietnamese commercial and real property on a large scale would be soon forgotten would be very unrealistic, just as the carpetbaggers of our country are still remembered with scorn or malice. Reading in 1978 of the expulsion of numbers of Chinese ethnics and of the paid-for-in-gold "escape" of others, one may safely conclude that the properties seized upon so greedily by the Chinese a generation ago are being brought back into Vietnamese ownership. Today's wave of Chinese "escapees" from Viet Nam is not much based on ideology, and their history of economic greed also explains why the present government of China does not lay out a welcome mat for them. They are convenient for drumming up a "grievance" against Viet Nam, but they are not wanted in China.

To return to Ho's first meeting with Lu Han, other matters of extreme difficulty were raised. One was the repair of lines of communications from the border to Hanoi. In the initial days of Chinese occupation in the border provinces, the Viet Minh had responded to Chinese arrogance and disregard for the authority of the Provisional Government by cutting some of the telephone and telegraph lines and destroying some stretches of road leading to Haiphong and Hanoi. Lu Han ignored the cause of the disruptions and "suggested" that they be repaired immediately by the Vietnamese to accelerate the arrival of his forces. Ho countered that it would take time unless the Chinese army undertook the task, but Lu Han was adamant and Ho had to agree to provide the manpower if the Chinese supplied the materials. Lu Han would only say to that that he would look into it.

Lu Han, being unsure of the Viet Minh's strength and the ability of his own troops to cope with Ho's, had first inquired, then demanded of Ho to know the actual troop strength and organization of the Vietnamese army. Again Ho demurred, protesting that the question was irrelevant because Viet Nam was not being occupied but was "in fact part of the Allied Forces." Lu Han still insisted and Ho had to acquiesce to the demand. But Ho had his fall-back positions well thought out. He explained to me later that he had adopted a policy of avoiding any provocation or confrontation which might lead to violence with Chiang's troops as long as Chiang represented the Allied Powers. In pursuance of that policy of rigid abnegation, Ho used the clever subterfuge of redesignating his Liberation Army the National Guard (Ve Quoc Doan) and dispersing his forces to outlying districts, thus giving them a low profile and avoiding clashes with Lu Han's troops.

Ho broached with Lu Han the matter of feeding the army of occupation and at the same time providing for the civil population. Lu Han appeared not insensitive to the problem and accepted in principle Ho's suggestion that the Chinese army find a way of procuring rice from Cochinchina. However, that area was under British control and Lu Han was doubtful that arrangements could be made unless the Provisional Government found a way. Ho replied that with his limited resources, he obviously did not have the authority, the money, or the transportation. It was a frustrating dialogue in Chinese intransigence and Vietnamese impotence.

The other item of great concern to Ho was the probability of Chinese-Vietnamese incidents. Lu Han assured him that the strictest orders had been issued to all his troops to comport themselves properly and to avoid friction, under threat of severe penalties. So as not to lose the initiative and to impress on Ho the authority of the Chinese, Lu Han reminded Ho that harmony was a two-way street and Ho must take steps to cooperate and assist the army of occupation in maintaining order and in particular to see that the people remained calm.

In an afterthought, as their meeting ended, Lu Han informed Ho that, effective immediately, all clocks must be set back one hour to conform to China time, to avoid unnecessary confusion and administrative complications. To Ho this least-damaging of Chinese demands was highly irritating as a general expression of Chinese arrogance and meddling in Vietnamese internal affairs, but of course he agreed.

With the substantive matters of their meeting over, Lu Han attempted a more conciliatory tone and explained that the Chinese presence in Indochina was "purely military and in response to the wishes of the Allied Powers, to disarm and repatriate the Japanese." That done, the Chinese mission in Viet Nam would be completed.[22]

Despite Lu Han's abrasive and lordly manner in laying down his terms, Ho apparently considered the meeting a good omen. Ho himself characterized it as productive and one in which "a cordial relationship had been struck." I found it hard to understand that oriental rationale and said so. Patiently Ho explained it was not so much what had been said but what was implied. For example, Lu Han had tacitly committed himself not to dissolve or interfere with the Provisional Government but instead to work with it so long as it could retain control of the internal administration of the country. Ho also interpreted the commitment to mean that Lu Han would not support or assist the pro-Chinese nationalists from Chang Fa-kwei's clique, the "double Kwang clique" (Kwangsi and Kwangtung) under such leaders as Nguyen Hai Than and Truong Boi Cong.[23] For the first time I detected a split between Lu Han and his political adviser, Hsiao Wen. I could only wonder where it would lead in the days ahead, for I knew that the Dong Minh Hoi, so important to Hsiao's plans for the political future of Viet Nam, was already in Hanoi and anxious to take on the Viet Minh.

CHAPTER 31

DRV: POSTPARTUM PROBLEMS

HO FORGES AHEAD

D espite an uneasy truce, a state of unrest continued in Saigon and the whole of Cochinchina after "Black Sunday." Buu and Lieu both agreed that political rivalries and socioeconomic differences were the basic cause for the unrest. They stressed the lack of communications and coordination between the south and the north. It was Buu, with his excellent grasp of Western mentality, who made it easier for me to understand the southern problem. Saigon and Hanoi, as he pointed out, were almost 800 miles apart geographically, and so were they also separated in political tactics and administrative techniques.

Since its inception on 25 August, the Provisional Executive Committee for the South had instituted government programs and developed political plans without the benefit of Ho's advice or approval from the party's Central Committee in Hanoi. Unlike the north, Cochinchina suffered from an acute case of provincial isolationism and a surplus of political parties. Even the Communists had Stalinists and Trotskyites, while the anticommunists adhered to their racist, pro-Japanese philosophies. Finally, there was the real or imagined threat of communism. The affluent southern society of French colons, Chinese merchants, Vietnamese mandarins, middle class intellectuals, and religious sects made any change in the socioeconomic structure unthinkable. To them communism was the great leveler and an anathema. Prophetically, Lieu observed that it would be a long time before the south would become an integral part of Viet Nam. The southerners lacked drive, initiative, and imagination. They could not visualize a future without a foreign ally—France, Japan, Great Britain, or even more recently the United States.

Despite the weaknesses in the south and the threat of the pro-Chinese nationalists in the north, Ho had decided to move forward with his program of reforms. It was time, he had told me, to fulfill his promises to the Vietnamese for a better way of life. Furthermore, the advent of the British and Chinese occupation forces made it imperative that he forge ahead at once and present the Allies with a truly "democratic" regime. But in pursuing his course he had also to be extremely careful not to alienate the Vietnamese masses or the Allied Powers by overtly espousing communism. The Viet Minh, as a coalition endorsed by a majority of noncommunist groups, was a necessary vehicle. Ho was its founder, as he was also the founder of the Indochinese Communist Party, an equation the French made the most of in their effort to maintain a hold on their empire. But the Viet Minh was seldom equated by the Vietnamese with the Communist Party; the Viet Minh was the people's party, the party which promised independence, freedom from foreign domination, civil liberties, and economic security. Even if it had been openly labeled communist, it would not have mattered because the Vietnamese at large fully supported its aims.

News of the arrival in Viet Nam of the pro-Chinese nationalists in the wake of Chiang's forces made it all the more urgent that reforms be instituted before the arrival of the Dong Minh Hoi, the VNQDD, the Dai Viet, and other expatriate parties. Ho had no intention of being accused of doing nothing by those "Chinese lackeys," as he was so fond of calling them, but wanted to have an ongoing program, clearly identifiable with the Viet Minh and acceptable to the people and Allies alike.

By the time I returned from China, Ho and his Provisional Government had been busily mending fences and plowing new fields. Ho had pressed Giau to broaden the political base of his Committee in the south by including more members of the opposition and to continue negotiations with Cédile, all in the hope that the French and British would recognize the Viet Minh as a de facto political organ capable of national leadership and that armed confrontations would be forestalled.

Nationally, Ho's government had been moving at top speed in instituting reforms and publicizing them. On 5 September Ho did away with the notorious Councils of Notables, replacing them with people's committees (Uy-Ban Nhan-Dan) to be elected locally. The old mandarinate system which had for a long time displayed unmitigated disdain for the common citizenry was abolished.

The long-awaited land reform finally was initiated, but with care not to arouse the enmity of the middle class and substantial Vietnamese landowners. Land redistribution was limited to communal tracts (state-owned), uncultivated land, and French holdings and lands belonging to "fascist collaborationists" which were confiscated and given to landless peasants.

Effective 22 September, all small landowners were to be exempt from real estate and head taxes. This would benefit only those who owned five mu (about two acres) or less. Sales taxes levied at village markets were henceforth to be determined locally by the provincial or municipal authorities. The French-Japanese restrictions on the free trading of grains and cereals were to be abolished. Taxes on business and trade licenses were to be discontinued on 14 September. The odious state monopolies of opium, salt, and alcohol were outlawed. The reforms not only prohibited the use of opium and alcohol but also banned gambling and prostitution. The old and hated practice of forced labor was abolished. Workers were authorized to form unions and encouraged to negotiate with management. An eight-hour working day was to be decreed for all workers.

People's committees were to be elected in each village and province on the basis of new election laws, and a Constituent National Assembly (Quoc Dan Dai Hoi) was to be elected toward the end of the year. The new laws were to provide for universal suffrage for all men and women over eighteen. Minority groups which had previously been excluded from Vietnamese political life were enfranchised. All ethnic groups were to be treated alike and included in a representative government.

Perhaps the most basic reform undertaken, and one very dear to Ho, was for the eradication of illiteracy. Everyone was to learn to read and write. Classes would be compulsory and free. Within one year all Vietnamese over eight were to know how to read and write Quoc Ngu or be fined and lose some privileges of citizenship. The obvious exceptions for reasons of health were allowed for, of course, but Ho wanted a literate society capable of handling the new "independence," capable of benefiting from the schools the government intended to establish, and capable of reaching toward a modern technology.

Lieu was giving all these reforms wide publicity. In addition to the usual radio and press coverage, he was trying to reach the large illiterate segment of the population by using visuals (posters and banners) heavily supplemented by rallies and meetings. The masses, peasants and workers alike, responded with enthusiasm to the government's effort to improve their lot, and the Viet Minh was gaining not only good will but active support. Only a few were alienated, and they did not matter. What mattered was the national welfare, the success of the revolution, and the assurance of the country's independence. For the first time the nation was united in a common purpose and for the moment political differences were submerged—at least in the north.

ADVOCATE OF PASSIVE RESISTANCE,

Despite the outward display of optimism and high spirits, the Hanoi government had its grave concerns. As the foreign occupying forces converged on Viet Nam from the north and the south, it was evident that under the guise of an Allied mission both had ulterior motives. For two weeks the Chinese had shown more concern with looting, pillaging, and despoiling the land than with the Japanese they had come to disarm. Concurrently the British in the south were doing more toward dismantling the Viet Minh government and paving the way for a French reoccupation than in pursuing their declared mission; in fact they were ignoring the Japanese forces which were still fully armed.

Aware of his tenuous position, both militarily and politically, Ho had decided on a policy of passive resistance toward the occupying forces. His government publicly endorsed their mission of disarming the Japanese and offered assistance in getting the job done. On several occasions Ho took the time to explain that policy to me.

Toward the Chinese, clashes were to be avoided at all costs; if Viet Nam's sovereignty was challenged, there was to be no armed conflict; the people would present a united front and, if it became necessary, would refuse to cooperate with Chinese military orders; if necessary, there would be slowdowns of public works, shutdowns of market places, and a gradual dispersal of the population to rural areas. These were to be his tactics.

In the south any disorder would only give the British an excuse to intervene and destroy the revolutionary work of the Viet Minh. Ho had sent word to Giau that under no circumstances was there to be any attack on French persons or property, no violence and no looting. Until the area was clear of the British, the revolution would be "democratic," not "socialistic"; clashes with French troops were to be avoided and French civilians were to be ignored. Toward the British forces, Giau's government was to cooperate in maintaining public order and administrative services, so long as they did not interfere with the operation of the Provisional Executive Committee.

Dewey reported that on 4 September SEAC had severely reprimanded the Japanese commander, Marshal Terauchi, for his inattention to the disorders in Saigon, having already on the second placed him on notice that maintaining order was his responsibility until relieved by the Allied Powers. Further, Terauchi had been ordered to bring into the area several battalions of troops and specifically instructed to disarm the Vietnamese. Evidently that had been the sense of Mountbatten's message to Wedemeyer in which he implied readiness "to take over sections within the China Theater."[1] It also explained Giau's alarm and his warning to the people to remain calm.[2]

At about the time Colonel Cass arrived in Saigon, on 6 September, the Japanese had complied with SEAC's demand and raised their troop strength in the Cholon-Saigon area to approximately seven battalions and had levied a requirement on the Provisional Executive Committee to disarm and disband the Vietnamese militants. In reality the only organized and armed Vietnamese were the Hoa Hao, the Caodaists, and the Binh Xuyen. The Trotskyites and the Viet Minh had only token forces, so the order to disarm applied mainly to anti-Viet Minh groups.

Keeping to Ho's policy of passive resistance and nonviolence, on 8 September Giau had made his strong appeal to the people for cooperation, as already described, and the opposition had immediately charged the Viet Minh with treason. The anticommunists, encouraged by the Trotskyites, had refused to give up their weapons, demanding that Giau step down.

The next day the Viet Minh reorganized the Provisional Executive Committee with a broader base, and Giau stepped aside in favor of an independent nationalist, Pham Van Bach. The new committee reduced the communist membership from six (out of nine) to four (out of thirteen) and brought in one Caodaist, one Trotskyite, one Hoa Hao, three independents, two nationalists, and the bonze (monk) Huynh Phu So, spiritual leader of the Hoa Hao. After examining the list of members, I was not at all convinced that the Viet Minh had relinquished its hold. Pham Van Bach, allegedly an independent, I knew to be a dedicated foe of counter-revolutionaries and a secret admirer of Ho. Then, too, if the Vietnamese were faced with a French occupation and suppression of nationalism, the Trotskyites and possibly several independents would surely side with the Viet Minh. The realignment did not provide the stability needed by the new government in the south; interparty struggles, racist overtones, anti-French sentiment, and fear of the Viet Minh "honor squads"[3] all continued and led to the downfall of the new Committee in less than two weeks.

On 12 September General Gracey's Gurkhas,[4] accompanied by a small French unit of the 5th RIC,[5] arrived at Tan Son Nhut airport (Saigon) from Rangoon for a joint Anglo-French "victorious" entry into "French Indochina." The city was a tinderbox as exaggerated rumors that the French "have landed" spread like wildfire. The Vietnamese were alarmed and the French elated. Dewey's reaction was that the French presence under British protection was "badly timed and ill advised."

The SLFEO agents who had arrived earlier with Cass's Force 136 had met the deplaning French RIC and had led them directly to the ammunition depots, the port facilities, and military warehouses. There the French had brusquely relieved the Japanese and taken control. The Chief of the DGER in Saigon, Navy Captain de Riencourt, had then returned to Cass's headquarters and persuaded Cédile to direct the Japanese prison commander to release a selected number of key members of the "French Resistance" and several hundred Legionnaires, officers, and NCOs.[6] In military formation these French soldiers marched back to the arsenals where they were armed and instructed to scatter throughout the city to contact French civilians and organize them for taking over Saigon.

The French and Vietnamese, seeing armed Legionnaries arrogantly strutting the streets of Saigon, reacted differently but both reacted vehemently. The French savored the first taste of victory and looked forward to the moment they would teach the "ungrateful Annamite" a proper lesson in civility. The Vietnamese were both dismayed and angered and felt betrayed by the Allies and by the Viet Minh. In their tortuous and partisan thinking the anti-Viet Minh factions blamed the return of the French on the "equivocal" attitude of the Viet Minh leadership. As a result the Vietnamese, unlike the French, were disunited and vulnerable.

The French flag was hoisted over several government installations, although not for long. The British ordered it lowered the same day so as not to inflame local feelings. But it was too late.

SOUTHERN OPPOSITION

I was not the only one in Hanoi informed of what was happening in Saigon. Ho, too, had a direct line to Saigon and was deeply worried. The pro-Chinese nationalist factions also knew what was happening and found the French "landing" an excellent propaganda weapon for undermining public confidence in Ho and the Viet Minh. They loudly proclaimed Chiang's position of abiding by the principles of the Atlantic Charter and helping the Vietnamese cause for independence. At the same time, the Viet Minh in the south were negotiating with the French and Ho was making gestures toward France from Hanoi.

The attack on Ho sprang from press reports filed by the first two Western correspondents to reach Hanoi: Serge de Gunzburg, a Chungking-based representative of *Agence France-Presse,* and Phale Thorpe, an American Associated Press representative from Chungking. They both interviewed President Ho, coming away with what they characterized as a "startling" statement, quoting Ho as having said that the "Provisional Government of the Democratic Republic of Viet Nam is ready to accept even French advisers so long as they come to Viet Nam as friends and not as conquerors."[7]

I saw nothing startling in the statement; Ho had repeatedly made the same statement to me and to the French in Hanoi, and I had so reported to Kunming, Chungking, and Washington on several occasions. However, in addressing a French journalist, Ho may have wanted the French public to know that he considered them friends and equals. Whatever Ho's reasons, the statement to the foreign newsmen also appeared in the Vietnamese papers and was immediately pounced upon by Ho's pro-Chinese opposition. Some Chinese read his remarks as leaning toward an accommodation with the French in exchange for political survival, an offer which would not have changed the official Chinese position vis-à-vis the French or the Ho government. The pro-Chinese nationalists, however, were alarmed at Ho's "overture" because an understanding between Ho's regime and the French would leave them out of the arrangement altogether.

Later in the day I spoke with both newsmen who told me they were very much impressed with the "old revolutionary" whom they described as a "very sincere and capable man." De Gunzburg thought that Ho's government could not aspire to the heights it had set for itself "without assistance." I asked if he meant France, but he replied, "Or the United States?"[8]

That evening I called on Ho at his private quarters close to the Bac Bo Palace. He looked extremely tired and depressed. The evening was warm but he had a light shawl over his shoulders and appeared to be cold. Perhaps he was having another attack of malaria, but he assured me that it was nothing, that he was just tired, and asked me to sit next to him. He lit a Chesterfield, inhaled deeply, and stared out the window.

He said something about how peaceful it was outside, then walked to the table where his ever-present rickety typewriter sat with a blank sheet in the carriage. He reached for a circular which he said had been widely distributed all over Hanoi the day before by the Chinese military. It was printed on one side in Chinese, on the other in Quoc Ngu. Ho translated for me. It extolled the courage and personal sacrifices of the overseas Vietnamese nationalists and their dedication to the cause of independence, went on to thank Chiang Kai-shek for his support, and pledged everlasting friendship between Viet Nam and China. After more platitudes, it closed with accusations of Viet Minh collusion with the French and urged all loyal and patriotic Vietnamese to repudiate "Ho and his gang of cutthroats" if they truly wanted independence and freedom. It was signed by Nguyen Hai Than for the Dong Minh Hoi.

Ho turned to me and said, "Now it begins." With a gesture of contempt, which I had never seen before from Ho, he threw the circular back on the table. After a moment, he said, "The Viet Minh before long will have to battle both the Chinese and the Vietnamese."

Ho then asked me what news I had from Saigon. I told him the little I knew and we candidly discussed the implications of the French military presence there. Ho was very much concerned, as well he might be, and remarked that Pham Van Bach's new Provisional Executive Committee would not last long if the events of the past week were any indication, a judgment which proved to be correct. He was deeply disappointed with the British for openly supporting the French and with the Allied Powers for their obvious lack of interest in his cause. He appeared to me to be greatly discouraged.

I tried to bolster his spirits by complimenting him on his announced reforms. For the first time he smiled for a brief moment, but then became serious again. He admitted that his reforms would be hard to achieve without outside aid, but so far no one had come forward to recognize Viet Nam as an independent nation, "not even the Soviet Union."

Land reform, tax reduction, agrarian programs, industrial development—all required more than good intentions and manpower, which he had in abundance. They required money, and the government treasury was bankrupt.[9] Realistically, the economic condition of the nation was critical. Foodstuffs were being depleted hourly by the "Chinese locusts." The fall crop would be insufficient to sustain the people of Tonkin for more than thirty days. And Lu Han's administrators were demanding goods and services in lieu of cash for occupation costs.

It was a dismal picture. I felt sorry for this small man with a large dream but there was no encouragement I could offer, only my usual palliative that I would inform Kunming. It was no substitute for tangible aid. Reflecting on Ho's predicament, I understood the conciliatory tone of his statement to the foreign correspondents. He was dealing from a position of weakness and was in fact making a definite overture to the French in hope of avoiding an armed confrontation and to gain time for his government.

The British and French appearance in Saigon had its repercussions at the Citadel. Sainteny's apparatus wasted no time in passing to Mordant's group within the walls this news as well as the report that General Alessandri in China had sent orders to the French POWs there "to organize into military units" and "to arm one company of Legionnaires to preserve order" when the Chinese assumed command at the Citadel. At the same time the Japanese prison commander claimed to have received instructions from his headquarters to follow the example of Saigon and release all POWs.[10] Colonel Nordlinger had taken over POW operations but consulted with me on both points, and I advised him to countermand Alessandri's order and instruct the Japanese to double the guard to prevent any POW from leaving until otherwise instructed by the Chinese High Command. Nordlinger followed my advice and informed Kunming. The next day we received approval of our action with the notation that Alessandri in Chungking denied issuing any orders to the French in Hanoi.[11]

Northern Indochina was, indeed, a bedlam of unhappy French, incessantly agitating against the "insensitive" Allies and the "ungrateful" Vietnamese; pro-Chinese nationalists actively subverting the Viet Minh government; Kuomintang forces greedily ravaging the countryside; and Japanese secret agents stealthily organizing postwar underground systems. The power center of all these groups was Hanoi.

JAPANESE CLANDESTINE APPARATUS

The Japanese official actions were above reproach, but our counter-espionage team (X-2) had already uncovered an immensely intricate Japanese clandestine network closely interlocked with the economic and cultural complexes of Indochina and still operative. Two very unobtrusive Japanese organizations proved to be the focal points of the Japanese espionage and political warfare systems. One was the Compagnie Indochinoise de Commerce et d'Industrie, known as CICEI; the other was the Centre Culturelle (Bunka Kaikan).

CICEI had evolved in careful stages from the Taitaku, a small Japanese export firm established in Hanoi way back in 1937. The Taitaku at first appeared to do little business, but within six months it opened fifteen branch offices throughout Indochina, all located in modern buildings and all staffed with executive-level personnel. In September 1937 the former Japanese delegate to the League of Nations, Doichi Yamane, opened in Hanoi a second export firm next to the French Consulate on Boulevard Carnot. Six months later a Mr. Bunichi Onishi arrived from Tokyo and established the CICEI. Onishi had connections with the Bank of Formosa, the Yokohama Species Bank, and the Bank of Indochina and, through a series of financial manipulations between those banks, he amassed sufficient capital to buy an interest in the Bank of Indochina and merge the smaller export firms with CICEI. It became then a closed corporation free from outside scrutiny or control.

Initally CICEI concentrated on land exploration, mine exploitation, and the production of high-grade iron ore. Its agents traveled extensively—everywhere taking photographs, making maps and conducting surveys. They called openly on the French civil and military authorities to obtain geological and geographic information; they requested and obtained plans of warehouses and of port and rail facilities; they surveyed waterways, coastlines, navigation channels, and shipping lanes. The more audacious agents even photographed and sketched French military forts, garrisons, and roadblocks.

In the fall of 1938 CICEI expanded its operation to mining high-grade iron ore for Japan in the Thai-Nguyen region. In 1941 when the ore at Thai-Nguyen ran out CICEI took over the mines at Lao Cai to provide the ore needed for Japan's war economy. It also provided excellent French and Chinese intelligence and huge profits for expansion.

Japan was in dire need of chrome and nickel, and CICEI acquired in 1942 through the Bank of Indochina several more mining interests, including a French-owned chrome and nickel company, to form a conglomerate called CROMIC. In 1942–43 CICEI expanded to Saigon, Haiphong, Cao Bang, Lao Cai, Thai-Nguyen, and Thai-Nien. The magnitude of the operation warranted bringing in a high-level financier from Tokyo to take over the financial direction.[12] Allied bombings and submarine warfare during 1944 reduced CICEI's commercial activities, and by 1945 the branch offices were idle. But CICEI kept the staffs intact while accelerating their travel throughout Indochina, along the southern border of China, and between India and Burma. Concurrently, through its banking channels, particularly the Bank of Indochina, the CICEI apparatus corresponded with Tokyo, Berlin, Rome, Bern, Paris, and even Washington, to exchange intelligence information and agents.

The Japanese military in Indochina had its own clandestine operation, Dainan Koosi, which acted as the purchasing channel for the Japanese Army and Navy. Dainan Koosi was under the directorship of a notorious agent named Matusita.[13]

The Navy subsidiary of the Dainan Koosi was the MANWA (or Van Woo) which searched for special ores and metals and procured intelligence related to metallurgic industries. One of its side activities was the exchange of stolen goods and materials for Chinese currency and metals. The currency was used to pay for Chinese intelligence services in China.

The Army subsidiary of the Dainan Koosi was the SYOTU located in Hanoi. Its specialty was buying out or gaining control of gambling dens on the China border to facilitate the infiltration and exfiltration of Japanese agents charged with the procurement of metal coins and intelligence in China. The agents found an excellent barter medium for the much sought after Chinese coins in Indochinese textiles (allegedly stolen from Chinese merchants in Indochina). SYOTU's office records in Hanoi showed that their operation netted an average one hundred tons per month of Chinese copper coins.[14]

By 1944 Dainan Koosi had also acquired nearly four thousand tons of copper from coins containing a mixture of copper and tin. The separation process was done in Indochina and the shipping handled through CICEI and its subsidiary, CATEL. MANWA and SYOTU also procured sizeable quantities of black market antimony, lead, manganese, asbestos, mica, and hides within Indochina.

This incredibly well-organized apparatus had a stranglehold on Indochina's economy and had provided Japan with international assets, Allied intelligence, and strategic materials. Its immediate importance to our mission, however, was that it was serving as a cover for the postwar Greater East Asia Co-Prosperity Sphere program. Defeat at the hands of the Allies did not at all deter die-hard Japanese from pursuing their prewar plans of "Asia for the Asiatics."

Our team had also uncovered solid evidence that the kempeitai was operating out of the Centre Culturelle[15] in Hanoi, Hué, and Saigon. Its agents in large numbers were getting out of uniform and disappearing among the Vietnamese population. We were able to identify former kempeitai personnel as new staff members of old Japanese commercial firms; others had been reported to us by the Viet Minh as "travelers" in the less populous areas of Tonkin and Annam. These Japanese "deserters" had been instructed to "drop out of sight" and organize as business executives, bandits, or pirates for future clandestine activities, especially for agitation and propaganda operations among the anti-French and anti-Viet Minh elements.[16]

One of my immediate concerns was apprehending Ambassador Jean-Marie Yokoyama,[17] the head of the Centre Culturelle, and several of his close associates.[18] Since early in the war Yokoyama had been an OSS target as a leading espionage agent in Southeast Asia with worldwide connections. In 1943 we had located him in Hué where he was operating through the good offices of the Bank of Indochina. He was number two on my "most wanted" list, Subhas Chandra Bose being number one.[19]

It did not take long to discover the whereabouts of these individuals, but we could not apprehend them without Chinese cooperation. Lu Han's security staff was not enthusiastic about confronting old partners in crime and Lu Han himself felt some compunction in renewing acquaintance. Yokoyama and Lung Yün were not strangers. In postwar interrogations, Japanese commanders in southern China readily admitted a long history of contacts with "Chinese warlords and senior officers" dating back to the mid-thirties. Those contacts had been arranged through the Japanese Consul General in Hanoi, Yoshio Minoda, until 1939, when Yokoyama assumed that task.

Before the Japanese came into power in Indochina, their intelligence activities and political agitation had been at times so flagrant as to compel the French on several occasions to expel Japanese diplomats and industrialists, such as Matusita. But the very same individuals returned in 1940 to pick up where they had left off, only with more power and vigor as Japan then dominated the Asian scene.

While in 1940 Japan geared for war in the Pacific and Germany was subjugating France, Tokyo planners were looking far ahead. To accomplish their long-range objective of ending white rule, they expected to oust the British from Burma and Malaya, the Dutch from Indonesia, and the French from Indochina, and they had to convince the Chinese that in their own best interests they should collaborate with Japan. British, Dutch, and Chinese territories were at the time foreclosed to Japan, but Indochina could be a convenient pied-à-terre for their Southeast Asian operations.

In anticipation of the August 1940 military agreement with the Vichy government for preferential treatment in Indochina, Tokyo had selected Ambassador Yokoyama to head the Centre Culturelle in Hanoi, under the cover of consular officer. He was assisted by a deputy, Komaki Omiya,[20] and Mr. Komatsu,[21] a propaganda agent.

Japan's long-range objective of removing all European influence in Asia necessitated a gradual phasing-out of French influence and sovereignty in Indochina. To achieve that, the excellent work initiated by Matusita in the thirties was resumed. It was at that point that Matusita returned to Indochina to direct the Dainan Koosi, after having been expelled by the French in 1938. In 1941 Yokoyama and Matusita became working partners.

Initially Yokoyama's program was oriented to advancing Japanese culture. Soon, however, it degenerated into the openly racist propaganda called the Greater East Asia Co-Prosperity Sphere philosophy. The program had wide publicity and was generally accepted by a large segment of the Vietnamese public, especially among the adherents of the Cao Dai and Hoa Hao sects. But after the March coup and the decisive reverses Japan suffered in the Pacific, Tokyo lost enthusiasm for its racist policy and ordered Yokoyama to concentrate on straight propaganda and espionage. To Matusita and others of the "Asia for Asiatics" bloc, it was a betrayal they attributed to the pro-European element in Tokyo, and they also looked with suspicion on Yokoyama whose mother and wife were both French and Catholic.

As our X-2 team uncovered the complex commercial, political, and intelligence apparatus of the Japanese in Indochina, I found that Matusita's cadres in the Phuc Quoc and Dai Viet were actively pursuing their pro-Japanese racist program, aided and abetted by the kempeitai and racists in the upper echelons of the Japanese Army. And their activities were to continue until well into 1946. After hostilities ended, the kempeitai had assumed the leadership of the anti-European campaign and had added the communist Viet Minh to its hate list.

That was the situation, simply put, when I sought Chinese help. I approached Lu Han's Chief of Staff, General Ma, and suggested the Chinese security agency take over the task of rounding up the known Japanese agents and collecting the vast documentation still available at the Japanese Consulate, the various military headquarters, and at the numerous espionage centers. Ma showed no interest, especially when I mentioned Yokoyama and Matusita. His courteous reply was that General Lu Han had "no instructions from Chungking on counterespionage matters" and that their personnel was "not specialized" in that type of work.[22] The inevitable result was that the Japanese went on their merry way.

Some months later, in my after-action report to the Departments of War and State, I noted the able Japanese convolutions in their wartime relations with the French, Chinese, and Vietnamese. In each case they had secured for themselves the unabashed, almost conspiratorial, collaboration of local elements in carrying out Tokyo's goals, both short and long range.

An excellent illustration of their artful manipulations was the pivotal role played by the French Bank of Indochina in Japan's espionage and commercial ventures. In that instance the success of those operations must unquestionably be credited to the willing collaboration of senior French officials in the banking and political fields, both in Indochina and in metropolitan France. For six full years petainistes and gaullistes alike dealt knowingly with Japanese officials in activities inimical to the Allied cause and detrimental to the best interests of Indochina.

Many Chinese also subordinated their national interest to Japanese objectives in Asia. During the war years they shamelessly traded goods and military advantage for personal gains. Afterward, like the Japanese, the Chinese used the Bank of Indochina as a vehicle to achieve their particular ends by insisting that the Japanese retain control of the bank's assets while the Kuomintang negotiated with the French for favorable terms on the question of extraterritorial rights in China and special privileges in Indochina.

Another useful asset was the pro-Japanese Vietnamese. Encouraged to resist the French colonialists and support Japan's Greater East Asia Co-Prosperity Sphere, these Vietnamese were also skillfully maneuvered. But in 1940 and again in 1945, when they had outlived their usefulness and the chips were down, the Japanese abandoned them to French reprisals and Viet Minh persecution.

As our X-2's work proceeded, it became very apparent to me why the only heavily guarded building in Hanoi was the Bank of Indochina. It also explained why it was the only facility which remained under tight Japanese control until mid-October and why the Japanese wasted no time in withdrawing huge sums before the arrival of the Chinese, leaving a bankrupt account for Ho's Democratic Republic of Viet Nam. The unsavory roles played during World War II of many individuals involved in these subversive operations were never aired publicly, and very few of them were brought to trial.

CHAPTER 32

SOUTH OF THE
16TH PARALLEL

"THE VERY MODEL OF A MODERN MAJOR-GINERAL"

M ajor General Douglas D. Gracey arrived in Saigon the day after his battalion of Gurkhas. A soldier's soldier, highly regarded by his fellow officers and widely respected by his men, Gracey was the traditional British colonial officer. He knew his colonial troops and the natives of India, Burma, and Malaya. He could be counted on to handle the task of accepting the Japanese surrender and General Sir William J. Slim[1] had personally selected him for the job. Furthermore, his 20th Indian Division had fought a long and hard campaign in Burma, and the Indochina assignment would give the troops a well-earned rest. It was to be a relatively routine and pleasant duty.

The British general came to Indochina totally unprepared for the Indochinese "natives" whom he did not know, but he did know that Indochina had been a French colony. Some months later Gracey stated that the sum of his information before leaving Rangoon for Saigon consisted of a one-page summary of the political situation prepared by the French. From the Americans he had nothing. There may have been some substance in his allegation since the British, at de Gaulle's insistence, were not exchanging information on Indochina with the American intelligence services.[2]

Even if Gracey had been informed, it is highly conjectural that his personal convictions would have allowed an alteration in his attitude toward the Vietnamese in the ensuing weeks. The fact that colonial people do not just declare themselves independent without the consent of their rulers was an indisputable axiom in Gracey's book of colonial rule. In accepting the Indochina mission the thought that France might no longer have the "right" to its former colony must not have occurred to him. He equated France's position with that of Great Britain in Singapore, Hong Kong, and elsewhere in the colonial empire. Japan's occupation was a temporary incident of war remedied by the Allied victory.

Before leaving Rangoon, Gracey had been given a dual mission to head the Control Commission for the Supreme Commander, SEAC; and to command the Allied Land Forces in Indochina, south of the sixteenth parallel north.

As head of the Commission, he was directly responsible to Lord Mountbatten for taking control of Marshal Terauchi's Southern Army Headquarters at Saigon; for initiating and carrying out negotiations for the Japanese surrender; for maintaining liaison with the French; and for assisting in the liberation and evacuation of the Allied POWs.

In his role of Commander, he was responsible to General Slim for clandestine operations; securing the headquarters of the Southern Army Headquarters and the Saigon-Cholon area; assisting in the POW-CI operation; disarming and concentrating the Japanese troops; and maintaining law and order. In addition, Gracey would be in command of the French military until General Slim relieved him of this responsibility.

While Gracey was en route to Saigon, on 13 September his orders were amended by General Slim. Here is where Gracey's responsibility became confused. The amendment read, "Do not assume responsibility for law and order outside key areas, unless requested by the French authorities and only with the approval of the Supreme Allied Commander [Mountbatten]; further, until agreement is concluded between the U.K. and France on civil administration in Indochina, designate key areas considered essential to carry out responsibility for disarming and repatriating the Japanese forces."

The amendment clearly relieved Gracey of any responsibility for maintaining law and order anywhere except in very circumscribed areas associated with the operation of disarming and concentrating the Japanese forces for repatriation. In less than ten days he was to violate those orders with far-reaching political consequences.

At the Saigon airport, Gracey was met by Colonel Cass and senior officers who had arrived the day before. There were also Japanese officers and enlisted men who discreetly kept their distance but were on hand, should they be called. They were ignored. Enroute to the city, Cass briefed the general on conditions in Cochinchina, but Gracey did not appear to grasp the import of what he was being told. The soldier-general seemed totally oblivious to the political convulsions in the troubled city. Unquestionably he was ably qualified for the military assignment he had been charged with, but the situation called for a soldier-diplomat, and neither he nor his staff was cut out for that role.

In short order General Gracey learned that, aside from the public utilities and perfunctory police and fire protection, there was no effective government in power. The new Provisional Executive Committee of Pham Van Bach was not in control, nor were the French or the Japanese. The pre-coup French gendarmerie and Sûreté had been supplanted by the pro-Japanese police and kempeitai. Since 25 August these, too, had been replaced with the ineffectual Vietnamese police. Magistrates, courts, and the entire juridical system had been wiped out with the abolition of the mandarinate.

The release and arming of French POWs the previous day had uncorked pent-up passions. Most of the Legionnaires roamed the streets drunk and in search of Vietnamese women. They knocked down doors and looted Vietnamese and Chinese homes and stores, taking what they wanted and vandalizing what they could not carry. The twenty thousand-odd French residents of Saigon, still furious over the rough treatment they had received after the 2 September disorders, became aggressive as the Legionnaires appeared on the streets and indiscriminately took revenge on any hapless Vietnamese who came their way. Compounding the chaos, the Vietnamese began using strong-arm tactics on fellow countrymen who still served French employers.

Through it all the Japanese remained passive, a fact which did not escape General Gracey. Under those circumstances it was not difficult for the colonial-oriented general to decide who was in the right. He viewed the situation as anarchical and called for prompt and firm action. Within hours of his landing, Gracey ordered the Japanese to disarm the Vietnamese, dislodge the Provisional Executive Committee from the Governor General's Palace in Saigon, and then announced that the action "had no political implications." The French lost no time hoisting the French flag over public buildings[3] and displaying the Tricolor on the military vehicles (American-made).[4]

From the moment the British and French troops landed on 12 September, the airwaves crackled with fact and fiction of happenings in Cochinchina. Confused and distorted reports of French excesses, British use of Japanese troops to round up Vietnamese protesters, the imminent arrival of Leclerc's force to reoccupy the whole of Viet Nam, and other rumors made the rounds in Hanoi, exciting everyone and polarizing opposition factions.

By noon of the thirteenth word had been flashed to Hué and Hanoi that the British and the French had taken over and the Vietnamese government run out of office. Even more alarming was the news that Gracey's headquarters had announced that the British would assume the responsibility for maintaining law and order "until [the] arrival of French troops," implying their early return. Our team in Saigon confirmed this report and added that the Provisional Executive Committee while overtly exhorting the population "to remain calm and avoid incidents" was also covertly beginning "to evacuate women and children from the city" to the countryside.[5]

To me the evacuation order was a positive signal that the Viet Minh meant business. I advised Colonel Heppner and General Donovan that in my opinion if the British in the south and the Chinese in the north were running interference for the returning French we had better disassociate ourselves from that maneuver or be prepared to join the colonial interests in the Far East. Dewey in a personal message to Donovan supported my position, adding that he had been admonished by Gracey to stop "consorting with the rebels."

THE ROAD TO MARTIAL LAW

In Saigon Dewey had approached Cédile and found him "an honest and reasonable man, but a *gaulliste*" with instructions to adhere strictly to the terms of the 24 March Declaration. Dewey and Cédile had much in common. They both admired de Gaulle as a French leader and tended to be liberals in their political thinking; and both sympathized with the Vietnamese in their quest for national independence. Their difference lay in national origin. Cédile was a French official bound by France's policy of "gradual independence," while Dewey was an American officer committed to FDR's anticolonialism. Yet they could communicate, and for a while they did.

Dewey's contacts were not limited to the French; he also maintained a close rapport with members of the Provisional Executive Committee, particularly with Pham Van Bach and Pham Ngoc Thach. For almost two weeks Dewey met with the French and Vietnamese in a vain attempt to attain a working arrangement between Cédile and the Committee. His efforts were blocked by an ultraconservative French colonial group headed by Mario Bocquet.[6] The impasse between the French and Vietnamese was not so much a matter of specific demands but of factionalism and vested interests.

Dewey had found a reasonable element among the French willing to accept and negotiate a level of autonomy for the Vietnamese within the context of the 24 March Declaration. Cédile was among those who favored negotiations over the only alternative, armed conflict. But, unfortunately, he was the captive of a powerful moneyed bloc in Cochinchina made up of bankers, plantation owners, shipping agents, mine operators, public officials, and politicians. They were mainly French colons but included a sprinkling of wealthy Chinese and Vietnamese. The latter took the position that there should be no discussions with the Vietnamese and especially no negotiations with the Provisional Executive Committee because they were members of the Viet Minh—all communists—who did not represent the "good and loyal Annamite."

On the other side, the Vietnamese were also divided. The Viet Minh was prepared to talk, even to accommodate to limited French demands provided the French recognized the Democratic Republic of Viet Nam as a point of departure. But they, too, were under attack from opposition factions vying for national leadership and hoping for the collapse of the Viet Minh. The opposition wanted negotiations with Cédile abandoned and open resistance to the return of the French begun.

Mounting pressures and counterpressures exacerbated the tone of the talks and drove the French and Vietnamese further apart. Cédile was attacked by the right wing conservatives for recognizing and discussing French sovereignty with "bandits," while the left-wing liberals condemned him for his obstinacy in refusing to make even minor concessions to the Provisional Executive Committee. Perhaps a less official representative, even a political figure, could have accomplished more under the circumstances. But Cédile was a public official, the High Commissioner of France for Cochinchina, with an ironclad directive which he felt he could not alter, no matter how inadequate. He was not going to exceed his instructions.

Dr. Thach had appealed to Cédile and Gracey for understanding. The Frenchman empathized with him, but the Englishman rudely rebuffed him. Dewey had no influence at Gracey's court and Washington simply ignored his reports. The French felt encouraged by Gracey's refusal to deal with the Vietnamese and sought permission from the British to take over the administration.

By 16 September it had become obvious to everyone that the Cédile-Bach talks were getting nowhere. From the Vietnamese point of view the talks served only the ends of the French, giving them time to solidify their position and to await the arrival of Leclerc. Yielding to intra-party pressure, Pham Van Bach issued a public statement accusing the British of refusing to recognize the only legal government in Cochinchina—the Provisional Executive Committee of the South—and ignoring its proposal for cooperative arrangements to administer the area. Receiving no response, the Committee called a general strike for the following day to protest what it considered a French-British cabal to overthrow the Vietnamese government.

The next morning, 17 September, a Monday, the market place was empty, the trams stood idle at various points along the line, no *pousse-pousses* (rickshaws) were to be found, the "boys" (servants) did not show up, the iron shutters were down and locked over the store fronts. There was no mail delivery and no electric power. Telephone and telegraph service functioned only irregularly and with many wrong numbers and frequent interruptions. Those were the inconveniences. But then started the incidents—arrests of the French, accompanied by ill treatment and some kidnappings of Vietnamese francophiles. The night that followed was an uneasy one.

On Tuesday the situation did not improve. The city was at a standstill. Scattered incidents between the French and Vietnamese were largely in the nature of minor scuffles settled with shouting matches, namecalling, and threatening gestures. More annoying to the French housewife was the lack of fresh bread, milk, and vegetables, as well as a scarcity of water and electricity. Most annoying was the total disappearance of her "boys" who knew where to shop and how to get things done.

During the morning I received the following from Pham Van Bach:

To Allied Mission, Hanoi. British Mission occupied public buildings of Viet Nam Government by armed force in Cochinchina. Expect to be shown the right of Independence of Annamese people. Viet Nam completely independent. The Vietnamese have right to decide their own fate.[7]

The noon report from Dewey's team was unsettling; they had received news which, if confirmed, meant serious trouble. Japanese patrols had apprehended several groups of agents provocateurs identified with the dreaded Binh Xuyen outlaws. They had attacked and severely wounded a number of French military at a cafe and had set fire to two French houses which were completely destroyed for the lack of firefighters and water. By late afternoon similar attacks on both French and Vietnamese became frequent and alarming, and panic began to settle in among the French. The Vietnamese worried mostly about their possessions. Most of the women and children had already been safely evacuated from the city.

Cédile, as France's senior spokesman in Cochinchina, was faced with a dilemma. His original and only orders, issued in Calcutta in August, were to "reestablish order and reinstitute French sovereignty." With armed French and Vietnamese on board bloodshed would be inevitable and Cédile decided to act. He called on General Gracey and pointed to the necessity of protecting French lives and property and proposed that the French POWs be armed. No mention was made of protecting Vietnamese lives and property, according to Dewey's informant who was present at the meeting.

Gracey found Cédile's proposal reasonable and practicable. He would gladly have armed the French, but there were several considerations which gave him pause. For the first time in his military career, Gracey had begun to think in political terms. He had finally come to realize that the Vietnamese were quite serious about independence and that the issue was not negotiable. Also he had begun to relate Indochina to India in an entirely different context. While the British Labor Party in London was debating the future status of India within the British Empire, the Indochinese claimed to have already achieved their independence and without France's consent. And most alarming to the colonial-oriented general was a report from his Field Security Unit that there were low-key grumblings among his Indian troops. Encouraged by agents of the Congress Party of India, several senior NCOs of the Indian Division maintained that British colonial troops should not be engaged in suppressing Vietnamese nationalism.

In assessing his position, the British commander also took into account several factors which favored Cédile's proposal. British troop strength was still dangerously below authorized level, and he knew he could not depend on the Japanese for support. They had already demonstrated their unwillingness to cooperate in disarming the Vietnamese or in curbing their enthusiasm for independence. Should there be a "native" uprising Gracey was not sure his troops alone could cope. In such a case, Gracey feared a bloody massacre, a possibility he felt honor-bound to avoid at all costs.

Under all the circumstances, Gracey concluded that the proper thing to do was to help the French protect themselves, not only because they needed protection but also because he felt strongly they were "in the right." There was no doubt in his mind that sooner or later they would have to be helped. So why not now? But Gracey had official orders, and they did not include arming the French. Like Cédile, he was in a dilemma.

On the morning of 18 September, the decision was taken momentarily out of Gracey's hands. Word had reached Mountbatten that Gracey was not adhering strictly to his instructions, and he had asked Field Marshal Slim to stop at Saigon on his way to SEAC to remind Gracey that he had a single mission—to disarm the Japanese. He was not to become involved in maintaining public order. That was a Japanese responsibility. Further, Gracey was cautioned to steer clear of French-Vietnamese political intrigues.

The warning prompted Gracey to take a different tack and one which today seems strangely out of keeping with his formal orders. He called in the Japanese commander and peremptorily directed him to take immediate and effective measures to restore public order, even if his troops had to fire on the Vietnamese. He also insisted that the Japanese carry out the 6 September order that all Vietnamese military, civil guards, police units, and civilians be disarmed. Gracey reminded the Japanese Area Commander that the surrender had yet to be signed and that, until it was, the Allied Powers would hold the Japanese responsible for the maintenance of public order between the French and the Vietnamese. This was, of course, a scarcely veiled threat that if bloodshed occurred war crimes charges could be instituted, a possibility that did not escape the Japanese commander.

On the surface Saigon and its environs still gave the appearance of qualified normalcy. Incidents between French and Vietnamese and between Vietnamese factions had increased in frequency but the level of violence remained tolerable. There had been no reports of deaths, widespread property destruction, or large-scale disorders. The only open display of weapons was among the military and the local police. Still, sub rosa, the area was an armed camp preparing for a long siege. Quietly both the French and Vietnamese had been procuring and stashing away food and weapons. Cédile, Gracey, and Pham Van Bach were all uneasy, each for his own reasons—all aware that tempers were high and too many were armed.

In an eleventh hour move Cédile asked Dewey to approach the Viet Minh leaders and urge them to call off the strike and help restore order. On the night of 18 September Dewey had a clandestine meeting with Tran Van Giau, Pham Van Bach, Duong Bach Mai (Chief of Police), Dr. Thach (Commissioner for Foreign Affairs), and Nguyen Van Tao (labor leader). They all agreed it was too late for further negotiations or cooperation. The people were outraged at French arrogance and provoked by the French military presence, poised to do away with their hard-won independence. After the meeting, Dewey told Cédile, citing Giau, that "it would be extremely difficult at [this] point in time to control the divergent political factions—not all pro-Viet Minh, but all anti-French."

To Cédile, the Vietnamese reply was loud and clear. No more talks, no hope for rapprochement, no more cooperation—not that there had been before, but Cédile was an optimist. The next morning, the nineteenth, Cédile called a press conference for local and foreign newsmen.[8] From a prepared statement which had not been cleared with Gracey he announced that the Viet Minh did not represent the will of the Indochinese and that the Viet Minh was incapable of maintaining public order. He went on to say that until order was reestablished talks with the Vietnamese were suspended and, when resumed, they would be based only within the context of the 24 March Declaration.

The break was final. The lines were drawn. The foreign press in Saigon which had been highly critical of British policy in south Viet Nam and of Gracey's attitude toward the Vietnamese predicted an imminent uprising and civil war. In reaction to the dispatches of British, French, and American correspondents originating in Saigon, SEAC on 20 September ordered Gracey to "control" the local radio and "screen out" anti-British reports and commentaries. It was a simple order, quite clear, without qualification. But Gracey chose to interpret it otherwise.

The usual practice would have been to place a liaison officer at the predominantly French-operated Radio Saigon to censor anti-British news reports. Instead, Gracey took an extraordinary and unnecessary measure. Without consulting SEAC and on his own authority as head of the Allied Control Commission, Gracey, on the day of receiving SEAC's order, issued Proclamation Number 1 giving himself full authority "to maintain law and order in Indochina south of the sixteenth parallel." Foreign observers and members of the British staff questioned the wisdom of Gracey's action. Granted there had been considerable violence, but even Cédile had characterized it as "tolerable," and the Vietnamese police had managed to retain control of the situation and maintain a semblance of order.

But Gracey, having established his legal position, moved against the Vietnamese press, shutting down all their newspapers but ignoring French-operated Radio Saigon and French newspapers. He instituted a limited screening procedure of the dispatches of the foreign correspondents, which they merely circumvented by filing any critical stories in Kunming, Chungking, or Shanghai. Gracey's other move under the proclamation was to incorporate the Vietnamese police into the British Army as an auxiliary unit under his command.

Cédile's pronouncement, Gracey's arbitrary actions, and the breakdown in communications between the people and the authorities all set the stage for the next phase. In the next twenty-four hours sabotage, plundering, vandalism, and personal assault, even rape, mounted at an alarming rate. These crimes were not exclusive to one side or the other but were shared equally between the French and the Vietnamese. The situation soon became too volatile for Gracey to ignore, and he decided to act again.

The next day, 21 September, Gracey proclaimed martial law. This brought a strict curfew, a ban on all public gatherings and demonstrations, a limit on all nonmilitary traffic to designated sectors, a prohibition on the carrying of weapons of any description, even walking sticks, the institution of military tribunals to deal with crimes against public order, and the death penalty for acts of sabotage or pillaging. Dewey noted with considerable cynicism that although these measures were obviously targeted at the Vietnamese Gracey had the gall to state publicly his "firm intention" to see that the occupation would be conducted under peaceable conditions and "with strict impartiality."

CÉDILE'S COUP

On the night of 21–22 September SLFEO agents advised Cédile that the Vietnamese had consolidated their armed strength under the leadership of the Viet Minh. Cédile knew that Gracey's eighteen hundred-man British-Indian force could not withstand a massive attack from the Viet Minh guerrillas. Once again he called on Gracey and once again he proposed to arm fourteen hundred French POWs quartered since the March coup at the 11th RIC barracks outside Saigon. These men, said Cédile, could be placed under the command of regular French officers and used, if needed, in support of the British contingent. Gracey, still aware of his weak military posture, again found merit in Cédile's proposal.

In the early morning hours of the twenty-second, the British quietly took control of the central prison from the Japanese and released some regular French paratroopers who had been imprisoned during the troubles of the previous week. Those released headed straight for the 11th RIC barracks to organize the fourteen hundred French POWs, mostly Legionnaires, into combat units. As each unit was armed, it was dispatched to a designated rendezvous to await orders. But eager to prove their valor and loyalty to the "new France" the soldiers gravitated instead toward the center of Saigon, where they pounced on any harmless Vietnamese who happened to be within reach.

With armed troops available, Cédile felt committed to securing the city, restoring order, and resuming talks with the Vietnamese, hopefully without violence. His plan was to strike during the night hours of 22–23 September by taking over the administrative complex of the city. He started on the afternoon of the twenty-second, a Saturday, by relieving the Japanese in several Saigon police stations. No one but the Japanese seems to have noticed this action, and the French maintained a low profile during the operation.

That evening Dr. Thach met with members of the OSS Mission. Much to their astonishment, the OSS team learned that in a final and desperate move the Viet Minh were going to stage a mass demonstration of several thousand Vietnamese on the following day. They would march through the city, unarmed, carrying only party emblems, placards, and banners. The Americans cautioned Dr. Thach that such demonstrations were entirely forbidden under Gracey's martial law and that he ran great risk of bloodshed. Dr. Thach replied that it was the Viet Minh's intent to provoke French and British reprisals "causing many casualties, bringing the attention of the world to these 'peaceful freedom-loving martyrs.' "[9]

Within hours, the plight of the Vietnamese in Saigon came to the attention of the world, not through a mass demonstration, but through an orgy of French violence.

Before dawn and according to plan, Cédile's troops swiftly occupied the remaining police stations, the Treasury, the Sûreté, and the post-telephone-telegraph (PTT) offices. Then, somewhat later in the morning, it was the turn of the City Hall, where the Provisional Executive Committee had sat since Gracey evicted it from the Governor General's Palace. (It was a Sunday, the twenty-third of September, exactly three weeks since the first disorders in front of the Saigon Cathedral, undeniably a suitable day for repaying the "Annamites" for their dastardly attack on that "Black Sunday.") Where they stood guard on the steps of the City Hall, Viet Minh sentries were shot down in cold blood by the French. The few occupants of the building, taken by surprise, put up an ineffectual resistance and they, too, were killed or taken prisoner. All the members of the Provisional Executive Committee, except one,* escaped. But Cédile had retaken the city.

*Hoang Don Van, Commissioner for Labor.

As the curfew ended at 5:30 A.M., people emerged from their homes to see the Tricolor flying from the public buildings and French soldiers standing guard everywhere. Both French and Vietnamese first thought that Leclerc had arrived, but that impression was soon corrected as many of the French officers and men were recognized as POWs from the 11th RIC Barracks. The Vietnamese reacted with anger, frustration, and fear.

The French who had lived in fear for three weeks rejoiced. Their moment of victory had arrived, so also their moment of revenge. Instantly they reacted as one savage mob on the rampage. Banding in gangs of three, four, six, and even more, French men and women roamed the streets of Saigon in search of Vietnamese. They found many still unaware of the French coup and set upon them savagely with sticks and fists. In their orgiastic fit the French broke down doors to ferret out cowering "Annamites" from their homes or places of business to administer "a well-deserved and proper thrashing." No one they found was spared —men and women, young and old, even children were slapped around, spanked, and shaken. For most victims the beatings were severe; some were maimed for life. In general, after the beatings, the victims were pushed and shoved into cars or trucks and sent off to the nearest jail for the crime of being Vietnamese. Some with deep gashes and bleeding wounds were just left lying in the streets as being too messy to handle. The number of victims was reckoned, even conservatively, in the high hundreds and probably reached into the thousands.

All this took place before the eyes of the French and British military who stood idly by, apparently enjoying the sport. However, the spectacle was also witnessed by foreign correspondents. Our OSS team, also eye-witnesses, found it just too outrageous and shocking to be ignored. Dewey, as the senior American in Saigon, called on General Gracey to protest the French behavior and British collusion, but Gracey would not receive him. Irritated with Gracey's attitude, Dewey spoke with senior members of the General's staff, mincing no words. He then called on Cédile and Major Buis[10] with no better result. Cédile told Dewey in no uncertain terms that it was none of his business and that without doubt the Americans were to blame for the state of affairs. The next day General Gracey declared Dewey persona non grata and ordered him to leave Saigon as soon as possible. Dewey made his flight arrangements for return to Kandy for Wednesday, 26 September.

Despite Gracey's and Cédile's outward reaction to Dewey's protest, they were both appalled and exasperated by the French behavior. Cédile and Buis tried to intervene by cruising the streets with loudspeakers appealing for order, moderation, patience, and "French dignity." The response from the mob was hostile. Cédile's order to cease and desist from making arrests, except for criminal acts, was ignored. He tried to reason with some of the French leaders that their goal should not be vengeance, but rather a prompt resumption of negotiations within the terms of the 24 March Declaration. The coup had made that possible, he thought. He directed Buis to release all the Vietnamese who had been arrested, which infuriated the French population still further.

Gracey came under different pressure. The foreign newsmen, the most outspoken of whom were British, confronted him with hostility and recriminations. Their critical dispatches hit London, Paris, and Washington within twenty-four hours. Before evening fell Gracey ordered Cédile to disarm the POWs and return them to their barracks and charged the Japanese with responsibility for restoring order in the city.

Releasing the arrestees and getting the POWs off the streets did not, however, settle the matter. The British and the French had overlooked an important factor—Vietnamese reaction to the coup itself. Once released from jail the Vietnamese regrouped under the leadership of the Viet Minh. The Viet Minh which had been the buffer between the French colons and the Vietnamese extremists and had advocated moderation, public order, passive resistance, and negotiation, had then no alternative but to wage war.

COUNTERATTACK

The next day, 24 September, Frenchmen began to "disappear" and a number of factories and warehouses in the port area were sacked and set afire. Electricity and water, which during the strike had been intermittently available, were cut off completely. The Viet Minh self-defense units and workers' assault groups attacked the Tan Son Nhut airport, burned a French ship at the dock, assaulted the prison, and liberated several hundred recently jailed Vietnamese.

Again fear spread in the French community. Without electricity, running water, and transportation, with food supplies running low, and lacking police protection, many French families sought refuge at the Hotel Continental. It was partially occupied by senior Allied officers and several Allied intelligence units, including the OSS Mission, the British Field Security, and the SLFEO. The building and surrounding area were protected by British sentries, and the French felt secure there.

As the day progressed so did the number of incidents. By midday the French-built central market was on fire. Without firemen, equipment, or water, half the stalls were totally destroyed before the Chinese and Indian merchants could bring the fire under control. More windows and doors were barricaded and more people tried to crowd into the Hotel Continental. Gunfire, explosions, shouts and screams pierced the otherwise still and sultry afternoon. For some inexplicable reason few British and French patrols were to be found, only the indifferent Japanese were present. Saigon was in a state of anarchy—no one except the invisible Viet Minh seemed to be in charge.

Reports and rumors circulated among the French that afternoon that groups of armed Vietnamese were gathering in the areas south and east of the city and in the port area. No one could be precise as to who they were or what they were up to. In fact, no one was really sure "they" were there. Once more, the French assumed a low profile, while the British relied for security on the Japanese, who in turn did their utmost to remain neutral. The turmoil of the day subsided temporarily at curfew time. But as people secured their homes for the night, new rumors filtered in that the Vietnamese target was the urban area of Saigon, and the suburbanites felt less threatened.

Tan Dinh, a suburb of Saigon, included the French-Eurasian district of Cité Hérault. Protection of the area had been assigned to the Japanese who made their rounds meticulously and found nothing amiss. The residents of the district must have been asleep several hours when, without warning, a savage force of frenzied Binh Xuyen attacked Cité Hérault. Within the space of two hours they perpetrated one of the most vicious and shocking massacres of the Vietnamese struggle for independence. Three hundred white and Eurasian civilians, including women and children, were taken hostage. Approximately half were returned alive after being tortured and mutilated; the others were brutally slain in the predawn hours of 25 September. The British command did not get word of the attack until one hour after it had been launched. By the time they arrived most of the Vietnamese force had disappeared with their hostages.

Violence continued unabated. Gracey was furious with the Japanese for not cooperating, but there was nothing he could do except threaten the Japanese Commander with charges of refusing to obey Allied orders. That did not solve his urgent problem of restoring order and suppressing the Vietnamese rebels. Still, Gracey did reprimand the Japanese Commander who, in turn, told Gracey that his men were afraid of Vietnamese reprisals if they interfered. Stymied by Japanese obstructionism and the inadequacy of British forces, Gracey once more capitulated to Cédile's demand that he rearm the French POWs of the 11th RIC, but it was too late.

The uncoordinated Binh Xuyen attack on Cité Hérault had already sparked uprisings and violent disorders elsewhere in the area of Cholon-Saigon, south and east to the delta, and north to Phu Cuong and Bien Hoa. The nature of the action alerted Giau that the anticommunist nationalists would attempt to arrogate unto themselves the leadership of the movement. He promptly stepped in and ordered a general strike, the total evacuation of the Vietnamese population, and a blockade of all foodstuffs, declaring Saigon in a state of siege. He threatened to reduce it to ashes if the French did not disarm, withdraw, and recognize the independence of the Democratic Republic of Viet Nam.

During the remainder of the twenty-fifth and on the twenty-sixth, Viet Minh self-defense units erected and manned barricades along the access roads to the city. They turned back all incoming traffic and barred anyone except British and Americans from leaving the city. The very sight of a French uniform at any of the roadblocks was an invitation to shoot, and the French military stayed clear of them. Within the city, Major Buis and his Sûreté searched for arms, explosives, and evidence that Giau and his dreaded Viet Minh were planning a coup. Outside the city limits, in the area patrolled by the Japanese, the insurrection continued.

The terrible struggle for independence which had begun so quietly in the little village of Tan Trao on 13 August had now, in the early hours of 25 September, become a war—a war only in the south but one that would spread northward toward Hanoi and the Tonkin in less than six months and would last with few interruptions for thirty years.

We received our last report in depth from Dewey in Hanoi on the evening of the twenty-fourth.[11] It concluded, "Cochinchina is burning, the French and British are finished here, and we [the Americans] ought to clear out of Southeast Asia." His words were indeed prophetic but went unheeded.

FIRST AMERICAN CASUALTY

Dewey's flight to Kandy was scheduled for 9:30 the morning of 26 September. Captain Herbert J. Bluechel[12] drove Dewey to the airport, only to find that the plane would not leave before noon. They drove to the Hotel Continental to pick up Dewey's luggage. The streets of the besieged city were deserted except for an occasional patrol on the alert. The French were staying indoors and the Vietnamese had left the city or were staying out of sight. At about 11:00 Dewey learned for the first time that a member of his team, Captain Joseph R. Coolidge,[13] had been ambushed and wounded the previous evening. They saw Coolidge briefly at the hospital.

Dewey and Bluechel returned to the airport at 12:15. The plane had still not arrived from Kandy; there would be a further delay. They decided to return to OSS headquarters[14] for lunch, only a ten-minute drive. Dewey was at the wheel of their jeep and they were talking about the unfortunate experience of Coolidge when they came to a roadblock about five hundred yards short of the OSS house. According to Bluechel's official account, they noticed nothing unusual as they neared the roadblock. They were both familiar with it, having negotiated it many times before, the last time that same morning on their first trip to the airport.

The barrier, constructed of tree limbs and brush, was not impassable but it was necessary to slow down. Dewey reduced speed to about eight miles per hour when, without any warning whatsoever, a hidden light machine gun opened fire on them at point-blank range. Major Dewey was struck on the left side of his head and died instantly. The killing occurred at 12:30 P.M. on 26 September, 1945.[15]

The Vietnamese then attacked the OSS headquarters and kept the occupants[16] pinned down with a steady hail of fire until 3:00 P.M., when the Vietnamese called for a truce to retrieve their dead and wounded.

The OSS team agreed and stipulated with the Vietnamese leader that they return Major Dewey's body for the three Vietnamese bodies on the lawn in front of the OSS building. As the exchange was about to be consummated, two platoons of the 31st Gurkha Rifles charged down the road toward the parley, firing at the Vietnamese, who took their dead comrades and fled. Major Dewey's body and jeep went with them and were never recovered.[17]

In a matter of six hours, news of the murder of Peter Dewey flashed around the world, and for several days it seemed that it would assume international political significance.

I first learned of Dewey's death late that afternoon from Captain Imai. Several Chinese staff officers had come to discuss matters of protocol regarding the seating arrangements for the American delegation at the Japanese surrender ceremony (to take place the next day). Bernique broke in to tell me that Imai had some "extremely important and urgent" news for me. I found the usually impassive Imai in a state of much agitation. Composing himself he translated from his Japanese notes a message from Southern Army Headquarters in Saigon to General Tsuchihashi to the effect that the Etsumei army had attacked the American Mission and killed the commanding officer. Imai had no names or other details. The message had come in code and, to his knowledge, no one aside from General Tsuchihashi had been informed. The general felt that I should be the first to be advised.

I asked Knapp to take over the meeting with the Chinese and went directly to see Ho. He had not heard of the affair and was very skeptical of the Japanese report, although he was visibly shaken by the possibility it might be true. He assured me he would personally look into it. By the time I returned to my office it was almost six and I received a message from Helliwell confirming the attack and for the first time learned that it was Dewey who had been killed. My immediate reaction was one of anger at the Viet Minh. It made no sense at all to me. They had murdered their only friend in Cochinchina, and surely the news would not enhance the Vietnamese cause with the American people. I still had no details and wanted to believe that it had not been the Vietnamese who killed Dewey.

In Saigon, after the Gurkha charge and the Viet Minh withdrawal, the OSS team moved into the Hotel Continental. That evening Bluechel called on Cédile and told him what had happened. Cédile wasted no time in informing Gracey who "ordered all forces under their command [British-French] to conduct a complete search for his [Dewey's] body."[18]

Shortly after 6:00 P.M. Colonel John Coughlin[19] notified Washington, and General Donovan set the military and diplomatic cables buzzing. London hounded Mountbatten for details while war correspondents clamored for more specifics and raised ugly and embarrassing questions of plots and counterplots. For a brief time everyone was pointing an accusing finger at his opposite number. The Vietnamese blamed the French on the premise that the Americans were anticolonialist. The French with good and valid reason charged the Viet Minh with cold-blooded murder. A few Americans even suspected the British SOE of plotting the elimination of their OSS competition in Southeast Asia.

The OSS team which conducted an independent investigation of the circumstances surrounding Dewey's death flatly rejected all theories of a "sinister plot" or of malice toward Major Dewey or the Americans. The evidence, largely based on reliable eyewitness reports, pointed to a case of mistaken identity due partially to insufficient national identification. The official report read in part:

... Major A. PETER DEWEY ... was ambushed and killed through being mistaken of a nationality other than American. If the jeep in which he was riding at the time of the incident had been displaying an American flag, I [Bluechel] feel positive that the shot would not have been fired. A flag was not being displayed in accordance with verbal instructions issued by General Gracey, ... [20]

Gracey seemed to be a man without a plan. He merely reacted to events as they occurred, neither anticipating them nor appreciating their impact after the fact. His reaction in the case of Dewey's death was to order the arrest of Field Marshal Count Terauchi, not because the Japanese were responsible for the incident, but because Gracey had to react.

"COCHINCHINA IS BURNING"

Complaints of British partisan conduct, reports of uncontrolled disorders, and the news of Dewey's death had by then gone beyond SEAC and reached London. Mountbatten followed these developments with grave concern, especially at a time when the British Labor government tended to liberalize its policy on India's future status in the Commonwealth. He found Gracey's predilection for becoming involved in Franco-Vietnamese affairs a source of personal embarrassment. From the moment Gracey issued his ill-considered proclamation on 20 September Mountbatten had found himself in the awkward position of having to explain and justify Gracey's highly questionable decisions and subsequent actions. In his report to the Combined Chiefs of Staff on the matter of the proclamation, Mountbatten had explained that although he appreciated the gravity of the military situation in Saigon he felt that the

... proclamation ... was contrary to the policy of His Majesty's Government; and since proclamations of this nature may well appear to be initiated by Government policy, I [Mountbatten] warned Major-General Gracey that he should take care to confine operations of British-Indian troops to those limited tasks which he had been set. [21]

The Admiral's explanations and defense of Gracey's activities continued until the British troops were withdrawn from Indochina on 20 January 1946. At one point Mountbatten told Leclerc that Gracey had overstepped his authority and he intended to relieve him of his command.

Leclerc, predictably, argued that Gracey was doing an excellent job and should be retained. According to Leclerc the disorders of 23–27 September in Saigon were attributable to the work of criminal elements —the Binh Xuyen bandits. H. Norman Brain, Gracey's interim political adviser, disagreed with Leclerc and pointed out that the real problem in Indochina was a legitimate nationalist aspiration which the French should not overlook.

The low-level diplomatic turbulence created by Dewey's death prompted Mountbatten to call Gracey and Cédile to a meeting at Singapore on 28 September. In the presence of Secretary J. J. Lawson,[22] the Admiral reiterated British policy, insisting that British troops were not to interfere in the internal affairs of Indochina, more specifically they were not to be used to fight the Vietnamese. Cédile voiced concern that the French alone could not cope, not until reinforcements arrived, to which Mountbatten urged that he reopen negotiations with the nationalist leaders.

The British position shifted, however, several days later in new orders from London. Mountbatten was instructed to use British-Indian troops to assist the French, if needed, provided this did not prejudice his primary responsibility for Saigon. Mountbatten relayed the instructions to Gracey with the added caveat that his troops were to be used in a preventive role, and not in an offensive one.

On 1 October Gracey took the initiative to reopen talks with the Provisional Executive Committee for the South and succeeded in getting Cédile, Bach, Thach, and Tay to agree on a truce effective on the following day. Mr. Brain participated in the meeting and explained British policy to the Vietnamese representatives. He emphasized British neutrality but explained that by agreement with their Allies the British would not recognize any change of sovereignty of any territory which had taken place by force during the war.

At first glance the policy appeared reasonable and agreeable to both sides, but it did not take long for Bach and Thach to perceive the meaning—prewar sovereignty in the British sense was French and not Japanese, hence Indochina remained French. Regardless of Vietnamese claims that they had fought the Japanese for their independence and that Viet Nam was free and independent, the British still viewed Indochina as a French colony. There could be no peace.

On the second and on the sixth of October two more meetings were held between Cédile and Colonel Repiton Préneuf,[23] representing the French, and the British and the Vietnamese. As a precondition to further discussions, the French demanded the return of the hostages taken during the recent disorders and the body of Major Dewey.[24] The Vietnamese took the position that if preconditions were to be established then the French had to recognize the Democratic Republic of Viet Nam as a free and independent nation.

At the 6 October meeting the French posed the question of maintaining the truce. The Vietnamese agreed to continue the truce on condition that: all civil authority in Saigon be restored to the Provisional Executive Committee as the sole governing body; the local police be returned to the Vietnamese government with the sole responsibility of maintaining public order; all French troops be disarmed and no new French forces be brought in; and all French nationals be concentrated in designated areas where their security and well-being would be guaranteed by the Vietnamese government.

It was quite obvious that the French and the British were not serious in finding a basis for agreement with the Vietnamese. They had entered into negotiations with only one objective in mind—to restore calm to Saigon, lift the blockade, and maintain a truce long enough for their reinforcements to arrive. Their initial demand for the return of all hostages was specious and they knew it. There was no way that the Provisional Executive Committee could have produced the hostages in the hands of the Binh Xuyen or the anticommunist sects. Furthermore, neither the French nor the Vietnamese knew who or how many had been taken hostage during the disorders. The counter-demand for a return to the status quo ante seemed reasonable enough to the Vietnamese, who had nothing to lose, but to the French it was tantamount to capitulation and was therefore unacceptable. It was another standoff.

Although the French and British were only stalling for time and the talks collapsed on 6 October amidst harsh words and threats, the truce held. The SLFEO had advised Cédile that the Viet Minh had deployed its forces around Saigon and at strategic points north and south of the city and also that Hoang Quoc Viet[25] was in close contact with the Party Central Committee in Hanoi, which had advised Giau and Bach to resist any attempt by the Allies to reestablish French control of Saigon. If need be, Hanoi would send military reinforcements on less than twenty-four hours' notice.

Cédile was concerned that the Viet Minh would launch an attack at any moment and asked Leclerc, who had flown in on the fifth, to get Mountbatten to intercede. On the eighth Mountbatten's personal emissary met with Thach and Bach and asked for an extension of the truce for an additional forty-eight hours. The Vietnamese asked to what purpose? There seemed to be no common ground. The French would negotiate only on the premise that they still ruled Indochina, and wished to toss the Vietnamese a bone in the form of promises of future autonomy. Thach reminded the Englishman that Viet Nam had become independent and all that remained to be discussed was the status of the French in Viet Nam's future. The Britisher replied that as long as the door was left open for further talks an accommodation could perhaps be reached. The Vietnamese agreed to the extension.

While the talks were in progress and during the truce, unbeknown to the Vietnamese, Gracey's Indian Division was brought to full strength; the French ship *Triomphant* with Leclerc's 5th RIC aboard had quietly debarked a thousand men (on 3 October), and the Civil Affairs Agreement[26] was signed in London (on 9 October) giving the French full British support in the administration of all of Indochina south of the sixteenth parallel.

The truce did not last past the evening of the tenth. The presence of French troops, quite visible by their number and new American-made equipment, told Giau the whole story. On the night of 10 October Giau's troops attacked the airport and the British troops there. On the morning of the eleventh the Vietnamese confronted French and British troops at every access road out of Saigon. The British called on the Japanese for support, and this time they got it. Leclerc, too, was indebted to the Japanese who helped him break the blockade of the city after two full weeks of combat.

The Vietnamese made one last stand in Saigon on 16 October, but the overwhelming British, Japanese, and French forces compelled them to withdraw into the countryside. The British RAF and the remnants of the Japanese air force were employed extensively in bombing and strafing concentrations of Viet Minh forces.

Later that year General Douglas MacArthur told author-journalist Edgar Snow, "If there is anything that makes my blood boil, it is to see our allies in Indochina and Java deploying Japanese troops to reconquer these little people we promised to liberate. It is the most ignoble kind of betrayal."[27] I find this statement of General MacArthur quite incongruous with the earlier quote attributed to him by General Leclerc, when MacArthur supposedly said to him, "If I could advise you, I'd say to you, 'Bring troops, more troops, as many as you can.' "[28] But, then, we have only the word of a French gentleman whose English may not have been quite adequate.

CHAPTER 33

CONTRASTING SCENES

I n the north the Vietnamese were experiencing a revolution of sorts, basically a change of administration, nothing more than a transition from colonial rule to one of self-government, and without violence. As Ho was quick to remind everyone, it was a time for reassessment, reorganization, and reconstruction. The socioeconomic revolution would come later.

The peaceable Chinese occupation north of the sixteenth parallel was diametrically opposite to the violent British takeover in Cochinchina. Unlike the cavalier expulsion of the Provisional Executive Committee from the Governor General's Palace by the British in Saigon, the Chinese accepted Ho's government at the Bac Bo Palace and collaborated with it throughout the period of occupation. In Tonkin and Annam there had been no need to call on the Japanese to suppress the nationalists or to pave the way for a French return. The Democratic Republic of Viet Nam was in charge. The contrast was striking.

Events in Saigon, however, produced waves of reaction in Hanoi. The news of Gracey's highhanded takeover reached Hanoi at midday on 13 September and rumors began to fly: "The British are the avant-garde of Leclerc's invasion forces!" "The Chinese have agreed to let the French in China reenter Tonkin to join Leclerc's troops!" Talk of "resistance" could be heard everywhere. Ho himself with whom I met that afternoon told me that "steps have been taken to sabotage all lines of communications leading from China and that any such invasion will be resisted by force."[1]

All afternoon and evening Radio Delhi and Radio Saigon poured out a string of stories about the British landing and Gracey's arrival. Naturally they encouraged the French and alarmed the Vietnamese. Radio Delhi at first headlined the presence of Indian troops to "disarm the Japanese," but their subsequent broadcasts zeroed in on Gracey and criticized him for using Indian troops "to suppress Vietnamese nationalism." Indignant at the British action, Ho promptly dispatched a message to Attlee protesting "Mountbatten's undemocratic behavior in Saigon" and directed his Minister of Propaganda to organize an anti-British demonstration for the next day.

Shortly after dawn the side streets of downtown Hanoi came alive with people forming into marching units. By 8:00 they had moved out, waving their Viet Minh flags and chanting anti-British slogans, carrying placards showing John Bull as the overlord of Southeast Asia whipping the Vietnamese into submission. The Union Jack, I noticed, had disappeared from the massed colors in the parade. Some five or six thousand demonstrators made their way from the Municipal Theater to Ba Dinh Square loudly denouncing British "brutality" and "undemocratic" behavior. At the square several party stalwarts made speeches of minor consequence, but no effort was made to arouse emotions beyond the point of controlled indignation. Everything was well orchestrated.[2]

The demonstration reached its climax about noon with a message from Ho on Radio Hanoi (Voice of Viet Nam in Hanoi) to British Prime Minister Attlee. In the name of the "free people of Viet Nam," Ho protested against the British Mission in Cochinchina for the armed eviction of the "legal government" from its seat at the Governor General's Palace. Ho asked the Prime Minister to order the mission to "respect the rights and independence of the people of Viet Nam," adding a veiled threat of avoiding "regrettable incidents in the future."[3]

While everyone congratulated everyone else for a "peaceful and democratic show of political maturity," the French had to have their little indiscretion. At the Citadel several daring young gaullistes succeeded in scaling an almost inaccessible rampart and hoisting the Tricolor. At Colonel Nordlinger's insistence the flag was with great difficulty removed, but not before the word had reached the homebound marchers. I considered the incident a very minor but stupid display of French mischief. Vietnamese agitators, however, pictured it as a "highly provocative act of defiance." Sainteny disclaimed having anything to do with it but seemed pleased with "the boys at the Citadel."[4]

I was ready to drop the matter when local reaction suddenly took on an ugly tone and there was talk in the streets of "storming the Citadel and teaching the French a lesson." Nothing came of the threat, mainly because of my insistence to Ho that I would not fault Chinese or Japanese protective measures, even if they included bloodshed of Vietnamese agitators. It was the first and only occasion on which I had to take a stand with Ho for or against any anti-French measures contemplated by the Viet Minh. Later Ho thanked me for my advice but asked rhetorically how much "French arrogance" he was expected to endure.

BENDING THE TRUTH

The vast confusion created in Hanoi by French propaganda after Gracey's arrival in Saigon is best recaptured by an examination of their themes and tactics.

I received word from Kunming on 13 September that OSS would be moving its headquarters to Shanghai. Within hours Sainteny's "agit-prop" group spread the rumor that the OSS was being withdrawn from China. I personally, according to their propaganda, was being recalled to Washington to face charges of insubordination for failing to assist the French in Indochina "in accordance with Allied orders." The next day Sainteny wanted to know from me when the OSS was leaving for Washington. When I told him there were no such plans, he replied that the word in Kunming, according to his sources, was that OSS was leaving within thirty to sixty days.

A different tack was discovered when the local police apprehended four French POWs in American uniforms ransacking a Vietnamese jewelry store. They had escaped from the Citadel by bribing Japanese guards. Another instance involved two Vietnamese in Chinese clothing arrested by the Chinese military police for stealing auto parts in the Chinese quarter. They, too, were escapees from the Citadel and both were NCOs in the French colonial army being used by Mordant's group to create mistrust between the Chinese and the Vietnamese.

On a different plane the French anti-American campaign voiced strong criticism of American policy in the north vis-à-vis the British in the south. Their themes: the United States betrays its allies; American capitalists have bought Ho Chi Minh with French blood; the Americans are not to be trusted. The most dangerous rumor was that Kunming had ordered the Chinese to release and arm the French POWs at the Citadel for police duty. Such a decision, if true, would have been parallel to the British example in the south. The campaign did impress some Vietnamese and was picked up by anticommunist nationalists as applicable to Vietnamese-American relations.

These rumors were particularly damaging in that each had a small element of truth or appeared logical in the light of what was happening in Saigon. I was asked some truly incredible questions because of them, even by Sainteny, who may at times have fallen victim to his own propaganda machine.

General Hsiao asked me to confirm the rumor that Chungking had authorized Alessandri to order the Japanese Prison Commander in Hanoi to organize POWs into military units to assist the Chinese in maintaining order.

Colonel Stephens of the CCC wanted to know if there was any basis to the story that the Chinese had placed Sainteny in the Bank of Indochina as part of a Chinese-French "deal."

Lieu, the Minister of Propaganda, asked me for any information I could provide on the situation in Saigon regarding the Chinese of Cholon supporting a French military take-over in the south. He also was interested in the role of the OSS vis-à-vis the Sainteny mission and alleged American plans to withdraw from Indochina.

The French propaganda machine also operated abroad—from France, Africa, and India. Typical was a broadcast heard in Hanoi on 17 September purporting to emanate from San Francisco. In Vietnamese it announced that "the presence of Chinese and British troops in Indochina is to maintain law and order pending the arrival of French troops and administrative officers." No mention was made of the basic mission of disarming the Japanese and accepting their surrender. I checked with Kunming and got this prompt reply: the broadcast originated from a clandestine French station ("Brazzaville II" in Africa) and the announcement was a pure fabrication. But it was nevertheless interpreted by Vietnamese and French alike as expressing American intentions for Indochina. For several days the French exploited the broadcast to bolster French morale and to worry the Vietnamese, the Cambodians, the Laotians, and perhaps even the Chinese.

The total effect of the rumors was felt not only among the Vietnamese but also among the French, many of whom had been friendly to me and other Americans in Hanoi. As the climate changed, I radioed Kunming that "since our arrival here the French have changed their attitude toward the U.S. . . . from very friendly to passive. Toward me, particularly, very cool."[5]

Nothing was too small to be used against America. On the morning of the eighteenth Sainteny confronted me with the problem of the "missing dried milk." The French Embassy at Chungking apparently had procured and shipped to Hanoi a thousand kilos of dried milk for distribution to Vietnamese children. The shipment had not arrived and Sainteny wanted me to find out what had happened to it. I referred the matter to Nordlinger who handled all welfare programs and put the matter out of mind. By noon, however, a report was all over town that French food supplies for the "starving Vietnamese," shipped in American transport planes, were being delivered to the Chinese and sold on the black market by the Americans in Hanoi.[6]

Anti-American propaganda was, of course, not the exclusive domain of the French. The Japanese shared the field, and Matusita was still using the propaganda apparatus at the Centre Culturelle in Hanoi, Hué, and Saigon, with some degree of success in influencing sizeable segments of the anti-Viet Minh population. Japanese themes were all based on American "imperialism" as opposed to Asiatic "co-prosperity." Examples: the Japanese had granted the Vietnamese their independence on 9 March 1945; Japan had safeguarded the independence of Viet Nam throughout the period of Japanese occupation; with reference to the Potsdam Conference, the USSR and China had voted for Vietnamese independence, while the United States and the United Kingdom had voted against it; a series of well-placed rumors gave the impression that the Philippines were really controlled by the British who had granted them their independence; a story that Chinese-piloted American planes were used to bomb Hanoi; the entire American war effort in the Far East was an American desire to subjugate the Asian for imperialistic gain.[7]

The Japanese campaign, coupled with the petty French nibbling at the American image, created such an unhealthy atmosphere that I had lately been insisting with OSS-Kunming that we take countermeasures. I was overruled by strong Francophile elements in our Research & Analysis Branch who took exception to my assessment of the French position as too severe. It was the consensus in R&A that the French were being unjustly deprived of their rightful claim to Indochina and that we Americans should be more understanding in that regard. Neither Heppner nor Helliwell agreed and were forwarding my reports without substantive editing to OSS-Washington and to General Wedemeyer.

"LIKE A FLEA ON A DOG"

As the troubles in Saigon worsened and the rumor campaign rose to new heights, the exiled Vietnamese arrived from China. They came with great aspirations of assuming national leadership, but poorly organized and without a viable program. For many years they had concentrated themselves in Kwangsi under the tutelage of Chang Fa-kwei and haphazardly plotted against the French. They hoped to set up an independent Viet Nam with Chinese help. When the war ended everyone had taken for granted that the occupation of Indochina would be delegated to Chang but, with the last-minute switch to Lu Han, confusion had set in among the exiles. The ambitious but fractured Dong Minh Hoi coalition had come apart at the seams. The VNQDD and Dai Viet split from the coalition and each sought national leadership.

The split reduced the effectiveness of the Chinese-sponsored exiles who aligned themselves into two camps. The VNQDD and Dai Viet followed the Yunnanese general Lu Han, while the remnants of the Dong Minh Hoi remained under the leadership of Hsiao Wen, serving Chang Fa-kwei and the Kuomintang. The fragmentation served the Viet Minh well over the next six months, and the pro-Chinese nationalists isolated themselves from the masses, just as Ho had anticipated.

In the last days of August, the Chinese armies had crossed the border in two columns. Chang Fa-kwei's 62d, and 53d armies from

Kwangsi, under the overall command of General Hsiao, occupied Cao
Bang, Lang Son, and key points along the northeast coast to Haiphong,
while Lu Han's 93d and 60th Armies from Yunnan moved to Lao Cai and
down the Red River valley to Hanoi-Vinh-Da Nang.

The Dong Minh Hoi under the feeble leadership of Nguyen Hai Than
followed the Kwangsi Army to Cao Bang and Mong Cai. Anxious to assure
for himself a place of leadership in what he believed would be a Chinese-
sponsored government in Hanoi, Than rushed ahead of the troops to the
capital to seek his sponsor, Hsiao Wen. While Than was en route to
Hanoi, his trusted lieutenant, Vu Kim Thanh, who had raised an army of
fifteen hundred men for the Dong Minh Hoi, formed a "National Provisional Government of Viet Nam" at Mong Cai and "elected" Than president. In Than's absence, Thanh acted in his stead.

On 13 September Than himself entered Lang Son with more party
troops led by Nong Quoc Long.[8] The troops lowered the Viet Minh flag
and replaced it with their own. Than called a mass meeting to which
three or four hundred people came and told the "crowd" that they "must
follow the Chinese [leadership and] policy, even at the cost of their independence."[9] Upon hearing that, the "crowd" left, ran down the Dong
Minh Hoi flag[10] and hoisted the Viet Minh colors. Undoubtedly Viet Minh
agents led the people in the general melee that followed. The crowd, supported by the local militia, attacked Than's followers until Chinese troops
restored order. Than and his party then retired from Lang Son to Kylua
and ordered Vu Kim Thanh's "army" to carry out a punitive raid in the
area from Lang Son to Chu, a town north of Kep.[11]

I learned the same day that the entire Vietnamese population along
the railroad from Lang Son to Kep had left their homes and lands after
several days of plundering and looting by troops of the 62d Army and,
later, by Chinese "pirates." The pirates turned out to be Vu Kim Thanh's
"army." It was not a beginning which endeared the expatriate leaders to
the people, and the shadow government at Mong Cai lasted only until late
October when Hsiao Wen persuaded Nguyen Hai Than to cooperate with
Ho's government in a united front against the French.

While the Dong Minh Hoi was raising havoc along the northeast sector of Tonkin, the forces of Vu Hong Khanh (the VNQDD) and of Nguyen
Tuong Tam (Dai Viet) accompanying the Yunnanese 93d Army were following the same tactics along the northwest corridor from Lao Cai to Yen
Bai to Phu Tho.

As Ho jockeyed with the nationalist exiles from China, I received
from Saigon Pham Van Bach's note of protest[12] and discussed it with Ho.
He concurred in Bach's message with an air of sorrow and resignation
and commented that his worst fears were being realized. "If only there
were a way to stop the inevitable onslaught," he reflected. He confided
that several of Giau's people had arrived the night before with discouraging news. His facts were not substantially different from Dewey's
reports, but I thought his viewpoints and insights of particular interest.

He was highly critical of Gracey's decision on the early release of the French POWs. Ho thought that, aside from resenting their Japanese jailers, the French POWs also despised the Vietnamese who no longer regarded them as their overlords and masters. Ho saw those Frenchmen, as well as many of their countrymen in Indochina, as suffering from a psychological malaise. For four years they had served the Japanese-Vichy cause; then they had become prisoners of those very same masters while their confréres in the north had fought (at least in the POWs' opinion) valiantly for de Gaulle's France. The only way, in Ho's assessment, to ease their conscience was to do something highly dramatic, like a coup de force in Cochinchina. That would be regrettable, Ho added. The French would never return to Viet Nam; before that happened, "the people would destroy the land and then die to the last man, woman, and child."

In Ho's judgment Mountbatten's selection of Gracey for the task in the south had been a poor choice. Gracey was an inveterate colonial officer dedicated to the perpetuation of the old order. The trouble was, said Ho, that neither the French nor their "colonial partners" would accept the fact that Viet Nam was an independent nation, that the French were foreigners, and that the Vietnamese had survived very well without them since 1940.

In a more reflective vein Ho remarked, "I wish the Allies would explain to the newcomers [his term for the gaullistes] the intent of the Atlantic Charter." To him, the passage which read, and Ho could quote it all, " . . . respect the right of all peoples to choose the form of government under which they will live . . . ," meant exactly what it said. "All peoples" included the Vietnamese, who had chosen the form of government they had. To Ho this was the "right of self-determination of people to govern themselves." No matter how you say it, it comes down to whether or not the Allies mean what they say, as Ho put it. He was sure the United States meant it, but did the British? The United States had shown its honest intent in the Philippines. Had the British done the same in India or Malaya? Still in a despondent mood he added that only armed conflict between the people of Viet Nam and their enemies would resolve the future of his country.

Each time I had met with Ho during the previous week I had come away with the feeling that he no longer felt in complete control of the situation. He left with me the impression that events were closing in on him: first the French in the south, then the Chinese in the north, then political dissension and division at home, and always a precarious economic situation. Things were not going well for the Viet Minh and for Viet Nam. Yet there was a lot of fight left in the "old man." His eyes sparkled in pleasure and in anger. He always bounced back.

As the situation in the south deteriorated Ho faced an erosion of his political base in Tonkin. A week after the arrival of Tam and Than, elements of the Vietnamese press which represented the pro-Chinese nationalists ran screaming headlines—"THE FRENCH TAKE OVER IN COCHINCHINA."

Their accounts, though far from factual, were effective for the purpose of picturing the Viet Minh as ineffectual or even traitorous. On the same day, the twentieth of September, the Chinese-language newspaper announced for the first time the arrival in Hanoi of Tam and Than with the blessing of the Kuomintang for the "salvation" of Vietnamese independence.[13]

I was not surprised at the news but puzzled at Ho's apparent calm, almost passivity, at the open belligerence of the pro-Chinese nationalists. He had spoken to me of "a plan to deal with those lackeys," but when would he put it into action? Why did he tolerate their subversive activities when he had the power and force to suppress them? And what gave the pro-Chinese activists the confidence they displayed, aside from their obvious advantage of Chinese sponsorship? I put these questions to Ho.

His answer was that they were an annoyance, not a menace, "like a flea on a dog" that had to be tolerated, if for no other reason than as a sop to the Chinese generals. Ho believed the best short term interests of the Kuomintang were to keep the French out of Indochina and support the nationalist movement until China settled its accounts with Paris. He gambled that as long as the Viet Minh or a Chinese-sponsored regime was in power the French would not attempt a coup de force in the north.

From my first days in China I had come to know the Vietnamese exiles as a group of expatriates seeking national independence. Apart from the Viet Minh element, the group lacked political cohesion and direction. Vehemently anticommunist, they relied heavily on Chinese or Japanese support and American endorsement. Among the members of the Dong Minh Hoi and VNQDD with whom I talked I found a total absence of socioeconomic programs to meet the needs of the masses. They spoke of "assuming power," but no one was really sure what they would do with it. They were hopelessly disoriented politically; after all, many of the so-called leaders, such as Nguyen Hai Than, had been away in China for a very long time. I had to conclude that these Vietnamese were not motivated by a true spirit of independence from foreign domination, but rather purely by desires for personal power and economic gain. Not once did I hear this group say, "We will take over because we have the people with us and we will work for them." That omission was not theirs alone; the French, too, as the Americans later, failed to cultivate popular support.

Ho felt secure. He had told me repeatedly that only the Viet Minh had a workable program and the backing of the Vietnamese people. From my own observations, I had to agree with this boast. However, Ho considered it a problem that in some quarters, particularly among middle class Vietnamese, he and his party were labeled "communists." The pro-Chinese nationalists had no such stigma, and Ho was doing everything possible to divest himself of the label but not of the philosophy.

Early in August at Tan Trao it had been agreed that armed clashes with Chiang's troops or the exiled nationalists were to be avoided at all costs. Toward that end the Viet Minh would underscore the Chinese mission of disarming the Japanese; and if it became necessary to retain control of the government by collaboration the masses would be mobilized in unarmed opposition.

Specifically, Ho's plan was to isolate the VNQDD and the Dong Minh Hoi and bring popular pressure against them. Only as a last resort would Ho's forces engage them in armed conflict. If the Chinese generals came to the support of the opposition, Ho was prepared to compromise while safeguarding the revolutionary objectives.

In the situation at hand, I learned that a secret meeting had been held on the night of 19 September between Ho and Nguyen Tuong Tam in which Tam proposed a merger of his Dai Viet with the Viet Minh.[14] A similar proposal had been made the day before by Nguyen Hai Than of the Dong Minh Hoi. The reason for their sudden willingness to cooperate with the Viet Minh was an abrupt realization that Ho was in and they were out. Ho had a well-organized political machinery, a government in being, and solid support from the people, even from the noncommunists. The only avenue open to them was to merge long enough to discredit Ho and his Viet Minh and assume power with Chinese help. They offered Ho financial backing and the promise of Chinese support in exchange for his organization and popular endorsement.

Giap expressed his flat disapproval when I discussed the proposals with him. In his view the offers were worthless and dishonest. To him they were much the same as substituting Chinese suzerainty for French colonialism. As for financial assistance, the people would manage with what they had, and with less if that was what it took to retain their independence. He would "never agree to sell the principles of the cause for Chinese dollars."

Hoang Minh Giam, the pragmatic socialist-diplomat, took a more realistic view. He thought the proposals had merit as a temporary expedient. A merger of all the nationalist groups would attenuate the opposition and strengthen the Viet Minh, appease the Chinese, and worry the French. But most of all it would present the Allies, especially the Americans, with a picture of a truly "democratic" government.

I myself concluded that Ho would resort to his usually successful tactic of negotiation, delay, playing for time—until the propitious moment for striking back and returning to his own basic objectives.

Giap's young English-speaking understudy, Ta Quang Buu, was sometimes helpful in understanding the nuances of the Chinese puzzle. Buu maintained that despite Chiang Kai-shek's avowal of neutrality there were two separate Chinese forces at play and both were committed to delay as long as possible a return of the French to Viet Nam. The Kuomintang saw the occupation as the opportunity to extract concessions from Paris. The provincial generals, especially Lu Han, saw the occupation as an occasion to plunder in the old tradition, to establish if possible a long-range source and market for contraband operations, and to extend their holdings beyond the Chinese border.

Soon after the Chinese entered Viet Nam these two objectives came into conflict with both the French and the Vietnamese. The French who had been dealing with Chungking since early August found Lu Han unreceptive and, in fact, hostile. Ho, on the other hand, was confronted with a threat of being overthrown by his political rivals groomed in China. Fortunately his opposition suffered from a serious case of divided loyalties.

This conflict of loyalties, according to Buu, transcended Vietnamese nationalist politics because the Chinese generals in Viet Nam were also at odds over occupation policy. Hsiao Wen representing the Kuomintang supported its Fourteen Points policy for the occupation. Of the fourteen points at least four were a constant source of irritation to both General Lu Han and the French: (1) inviting a French representative to the surrender ceremony; (2) keeping the industrial complex and governmental functions operational until after the completion of negotiations between the occupation authorities and the French; (3) requiring the French in Hanoi to call on the "Vietnamese" to provide rations and transportation for the occupation forces (the Chinese Foreign Ministry was to negotiate with the French for agreements on liquidation); and (4) maintaining a neutral attitude toward Franco-Vietnamese relations.

These points, Buu said, did not coincide with the lofty statement attributed to Chiang that "the Vietnamese people would gradually reach independence in accordance with the provisions of the Atlantic Charter." I told Buu there was no evidence that Chiang made the statement. It was my understanding that Hsiao Wen was responsible for it and that it was pure propaganda, without any approval from Chungking. I explained to Buu that we had picked up a circular widely distributed by the Dong Minh Hoi on 10 September, four days before Lu Han arrived in Hanoi. The circular purported to represent Kuomintang policy and by implication to originate with the Generalissimo. Buu had seen it and accepted it as Chinese policy. It read in part:

... the Chinese are supporting the Atlantic Charter, and ... the Allied Powers have no territorial ambitions [in Indochina] ...; The principles of the Atlantic Charter should be [the] basis for an autonomous administration at this time which eventually [could] lead to the independence of the nation, and the principles of [the] Atlantic Charter will be guidance [sic] of Chinese in Indochina.[15]

Our Embassy at Chungking had also been misled by Dong Minh Hoi propaganda and had asked me to verify a statement in the Kunming press attributed to General Lu Han, who was accused of

... having stated in a formal press conference in Hanoi on 5 September that he was sympathetic with the Annamite movement for national independence and with the Annamite demonstrations against British action in "instigating the French to raise the French flag and to take over by force Annamite organizations."[16] General

Lu Han at the same time declared that China had no territorial designs on Indochina but that "the orders of President Chiang Kai-shek were aimed at aiding weak and small nations to achieve their independence and self-government."[17]

My reply to Chungking indicated the obvious. Lu Han could not have held a press conference in Hanoi on September fifth since he was still in China and did not arrive in Hanoi until the fourteenth. However, Hsiao Wen was in Hanoi at the time and had met with several representatives of the press. And if Hsiao Wen made the statements attributed to Lu Han it was conceivable that Hsiao was attempting to insure Lu Han's support of Chungking's plan for a quick settlement of the Franco-Sino negotiations and the prompt return of Lu Han's troops to the mainland.

In looking at Chiang's position, it was clear from his fourteen points that Chiang had no intention of becoming embroiled in the Franco-Vietnamese struggle. He regarded France as a world power with influence among the Allies and did not wish to challenge France's future role in Indochina. Since Roosevelt's death American anticolonialism had deferred to the British and the French will to return to the status quo ante in Southeast Asia, and Chiang found it impolitic to side with the revolutionary Vietnamese against the Western colonial coalition.

Lu Han strongly rejected the KMT's fourteen points and reprimanded Hsiao Wen. He held that the Kuomintang policy was shortsighted and a reversal of China's long-standing position of adherence to the principles of the Atlantic Charter. Hsiao's effort to entrap him into a pro-Kuomintang position had, in fact, backfired. Lu Han advocated a protracted occupation of Indochina, then placing Viet Nam under Chinese trusteeship, with a long-range program for the Vietnamese to achieve self-government without French help. His antipathy to the French, whom he looked upon as not only white but also anti-Chinese, was a constant source of irritation to the Kuomintang. Throughout the period of Chinese occupation Lu Han personally frustrated as much as he was able every French plan to regain control in northern Indochina. General Alessandri had, of course, obtained permission from Ho Ying-chin in early August to accompany the Chinese into Viet Nam, but Lu Han succeeded in barring him until 19 September.

The rift between Lu Han and Hsiao Wen was directly reflected in their Vietnamese nationalist followers: the VNQDD and Dai Viet gravitated to Lu Han's view of a prolonged occupation and friendly ties with the Yunnanese warlord; the Dong Minh Hoi clung to Hsiao's tactic of a quick removal of the Japanese and a prompt withdrawal of Lu Han's armies to China, leaving Nguyen Hai Than in national leadership with Kuomintang backing.

It soon became clear to both factions that they had to contend with Ho Chi Minh and the Viet Minh, regardless of the generals' policies and tactics.

FUNDS FOR GUNS

Ho's problems were not all political. The Japanese first, then the Chinese, made demands of huge sums for the "maintenance of law and order and other administrative expenses." From the first of September, most taxes had been abolished, and there was practically no revenue coming into the national coffers. Then on 12 September the Bank of Indochina had closed the government's account and declared the government "bankrupt." Day-to-day obligations were met from various revenues but long-range programs could not be initiated or carried out. In fact, most of the government's administrative services were donated by party workers, subsisting on their meager resources and by the generosity of more affluent and sympathetic Vietnamese. It was essentially a government of unpaid volunteers.

But one program of the utmost concern to the Ho government was the acquisition of arms and ammunition. The principal source of weapons had been the French and Japanese arsenals. As Lu Han's troops impounded those stocks, the Chinese quietly let the Viet Minh know that Japanese, French, and even American[18] armaments could be acquired through Chinese channels if "conditions" were met: the right price, cash only, and willing cooperation with the pro-Chinese nationalists.

Confronted with the dual threat from the French in the south and the pro-Chinese nationalists in the north, Ho felt that providing for the national defense was of the highest priority. After much soul-searching and on the advice of his close lieutenants, Vo Nguyen Giap and Pham Van Dong, Ho agreed to seek voluntary contributions from the people. On 4 September the government formed the Quy Doc Lap (Independence Fund) under the chairmanship of the Minister of Finance, Dong. The week of 16–22 September was designated Tuan Le Vang (Gold Week), a period when all patriotic citizens, non-Vietnamese included, should donate to the fund for "national defense." Two weeks to the day after the new nation was born the government was appealing for funds to help the country survive.

Pham Van Dong opened Gold Week with an appeal and a personal contribution. Elaborate arrangements had been made in front of the government building, with a speakers' platform on the steps and several tables covered with white cloths to accept and record contributions. At appropriate intervals, interspersed with musical interludes, minor officials and prominent citizens approached the microphone and appealed for contributions. Several well-to-do Vietnamese, some dressed in opulent mandarin longcoats, made their way to the tables to deposit their offerings. However, the first day of the rally was disappointing. A large crowd came to see, but few contributed. The day's effort netted a paltry hundred kilograms of gold and about fifty thousand piastres.[19]

Ho had not been enthusiastic with the idea of asking the people, especially the less affluent, to contribute their meager treasures to a drive for weapons, but it was a desperate situation and his advisers assured him that it was the only solution. After the poor showing, Dong and Giap convinced Ho that only an appeal from him would bring out the people. Ho agreed on condition that he did not have to appear, with Dong delivering the message on his behalf.

On Monday, the seventeenth, Dong read Ho's appeal, which began, "Being busy and unable to come, I send this message to compatriots all over the country." Explaining that the drive was essential "to resist the aggressive intentions of the French imperialists," Ho emphasized that he was addressing "mainly . . . the well-to-do families." On the meaning of Gold Week, he said, " . . . [it] does not only mean a contribution to the finance of national defense but it also conveys an important political meaning."[20] He was trying to say by implication that some of the funds might have to be used to assuage Chinese cupidity.

Ho's message did the trick. During the next six days droves of well-to-do families and humble peasants came to the contribution tables and deposited family heirlooms of gold and silver, pendants, chains, watches, precious gems, earrings, and wedding bands. A week later the local press announced that one hundred twenty-nine kilograms of gold and 1.5 million piastres[21] had been collected. The press termed it a "more than generous" contribution, but I estimated that sum to be very modest in the light of the resources of the wealthy Vietnamese. I had no way then of confirming either the accuracy of the amount collected or the Chinese "take."

Later Ho said to me, "I felt like a traitor" in allowing "the whole farce" to take place, that "every sou" went to the Chinese and that, despite his appeal to the "well-to-do," much of the gold came from wedding bands, rings, and lesser family trinkets donated by poor families, while the wealthy Vietnamese and Chinese merchants and landowners had give only token donations.

After I left Hanoi I learned from our team in Viet Nam that the amount collected had been much higher than the figure given and that at least two-thirds had gone to the Chinese for the purchase of weapons and political favors. This was confirmed by Vo Nguyen Giap who wrote in 1975 that the amount collected was "twenty million piastres and three hundred and seventy kilograms of gold."[22]

Ho's money problems were complicated by other undesirable developments. The arrival of the first Chinese troops gave rise to a black market in American cigarettes, candy, military clothing, and weapons, and it flourished, especially in the Chinese community. A package of American cigarettes sold for 14 piastres. A ten-cent bar of American candy went for 10 piastres. In relation to the U.S. dollar, the going rate of exchange was 14 piastres to one; in the open market it was 20 to one. The

Chinese were offering 200 CN to one U.S. dollar. The official rate fixed in Chungking was 100 CN to one dollar, but it was an artificial rate to favor the Chinese government. In Kunming one dollar fetched as much as 150 to 175 CNs.

Most noticeable in the Hanoi money market in September was the demand for U.S. dollars and Indochinese piastres in exchange for Chinese currency. Although Lu Han's headquarters did not seem particularly concerned with this exchange of China currency, the central government in Chungking was. Orders to American personnel prohibited the exchange of CNs except in officially approved finance centers, and all American personnel were required to have their Chinese dollar holdings declared on personnel records prior to leaving China. That restriction, plus a strong rumor that the Chinese would establish an official rate of exchange, alerted the money changers and led for a time to an inactive money market.

Gold Week also affected the money traffic, mostly in the price of gold which dropped from nineteen hundred to fifteen hundred piastres for one Tael. The drop was attributed to a Chinese-originated rumor that the Vietnamese government would soon confiscate gold, either for its own needs or at the behest of Lu Han for the coffers of Governor Lung Yün.

The Japanese and Chinese demands for money, the traffic in currencies, and fluctuations in money values all had a deleterious effect on the Vietnamese economic and financial structure. But the Ho government staggered along, mainly by the determination of many individuals to provide public services without pay.

WHY WERE THE FRENCH EXCLUDED?

Sainteny called on me on 13 September with one of his many complaints. He was uneasy about the "unnecessarily friendly relationship between the Japanese and the Chinese."[23] What was bothering him was French exclusion from the Chinese-Japanese negotiations dealing with the surrender. Strangely enough, I had the same complaints from Ho later the same day. A feeling of mistrust was unwittingly being engendered by normal exchanges between the representatives of the Allied Powers and the Japanese.

Sainteny just could not accept the fact that the terms of reference of the Potsdam Conference did not include France in the surrender arrangements. Ho on the other hand maintained that his "de facto government" should have some knowledge of what the future of Viet Nam was to be and what the Chinese were concocting. According to Ho, it was not only unfair but even criminal for the Chinese to high-handedly dispose of Japanese assets, which I took to mean weapons and military equipment, and at the same time ship large quantities of Vietnamese food stocks and property to China.

Two days later Sainteny called on me again to discuss the arrival of General Lu Han the previous day and, again, French participation in the Japanese surrender. I admitted frankly that I knew of no plans for French involvement in either disarming or repatriating the Japanese and again told him it had been made clear to me before we left Kunming that this role had been assigned exclusively to the British in the south and to the Chinese in the north.

Sainteny pursued the matter by asking if the French were not to be considered members of the Alliance. I replied affirmatively but remarked that for obvious logistic reasons the French had not participated in the Pacific war and understandably were not actively engaged in the war against the Japanese. Furthermore, the arrangements at Potsdam, which were well-known to General de Gaulle and the French General Staff, specifically delegated the task of dealing with the Japanese in northern Indochina to the Generalissimo. True, the French were excluded but so were the Americans, the British, and the Dutch. This honest and frank reply to an obviously provocative question has been distorted by several writers to imply "callousness" and "hostility" on the part of the Americans and as having long-range consequences in American-French relations.[24]

I knew that Sainteny did not like my answer, and he gave me the distinct impression that he believed the lack of French participation was the fault of the Americans and of me in particular. It was impossible for me to do otherwise when neither Paris, Calcutta, nor Chungking supported his self-imposed role of France's representative in Indochina. On various occasions he admitted to me what he later wrote in his book[25]—that he had absolutely no official mission or directive regarding Indochina and that despite his repeated appeals to Chungking, Calcutta, and Paris for official status in Hanoi,[26] he never received an answer nor the authority he sought.[27]

It was plain that Sainteny and his staff harbored strong feelings of antagonism toward the OSS and the United States, which were from 1945 to 1954 transmitted by implications and innuendoes to official Paris (de Gaulle, Messmer, Massu, Hoppenot, et al.) as American " 'betrayal' of a loyal ally."[28] In occasional remarks of his staff to other French in Hanoi, soon passed back to us, the DGER group attributed all the French troubles in Indochina to an Allied conspiracy to keep France out of Indochina. My assurances to the contrary were to no avail.

Moving on to Lu Han's presence in Hanoi, Sainteny asked me what American reaction would be to a Franco-Sino arrangement for the return of Alessandri's troops to Tonkin. I told him the United States would certainly interpose no objection. This was a Chinese matter. The Generalissimo was in full charge and the Americans, by agreement, were under his military command. I assured Sainteny that if Chiang authorized Wedemeyer to fly American planes with French troops or supplies into

Tonkin, the U.S. Command would do so. But, I emphasized, it would have to be a French-Chinese agreement between the heads of state in Paris, Washington, and Chungking. In my opinion, local arrangements would be fraught with pitfalls and delays. Sainteny did not disagree with my assessment but still hoped to salvage the fast-disappearing French presence in the north single-handedly and at the local level, an impossible task.

As had been his practice of late, Sainteny concluded his visit with a pièce de résistance. This time he confided that he had some apprehension that the Chinese, particularly Lu Han's men, would have him "kidnapped" by the Vietnamese. Their reason, according to him, was his anti-Chinese activities. I assured him he was being melodramatic but that we would keep an eye on him. Coming on the heels of his remarks about a Franco-Sino entente, Sainteny's idea of kidnapping seemed preposterous. I put it down to another of his attempts to pressure us to bring in French troops, but I reported his fear to Kunming, suggesting it be given no weight unless more substantive evidence was discovered.[29]

TILTING—LU HAN VS. THE KMT

Numerous problems surfaced after Lu Han arrived which made my position as senior political officer extremely difficult. The Chinese had come to disarm the Japanese but by September sixteenth I still could not elicit from Lu Han or his staff either a plan or a schedule for doing so. While the Japanese continued their "disinterested" role of conquered spectators, awaiting the pleasure of the Allies, three or four thousand Japanese dropped from sight into the clandestine pro-Asian movement. The news from Saigon was stirring the French into belligerence while Lu Han refused even to talk with them. To complicate every problem in Hanoi, the Vietnamese infighting was wreaking havoc on the local political scene.

When news reached me that General Gallagher was en route to Hanoi I breathed a sigh of relief. Not that the general had any authority in matters of politics, but he at least had rank which could be useful in dealing with the Chinese and Japanese. His mission was merely to assist Lu Han in accepting the Japanese surrender and evacuating the disarmed Japanese.

I met him at the airport on the afternoon of 16 September, and he handed me my first surprise when he told me that Chungking questioned the necessity for a formal surrender ceremony in Hanoi. Factors in question were the French role and the presence in Saigon of the senior Japanese diplomatic representative, Marshal Count Terauchi.

The Kuomintang was sensitive to France's position among the Allies and its presence in Asia could not be totally ignored. To hold a formal surrender ceremony in Hanoi without a French presence could be interpreted in Paris as an affront and Chiang was not willing to risk that.

There was also the question of the Japanese Southern Army Head-quarters in Saigon. Chiang was still smarting over the British Hong Kong affair and did not want to become involved in another jurisdictional dispute with the British. Properly, the surrender of the Japanese forces in Indochina should have been given by Terauchi as supreme Japanese commander, but he was in Mountbatten's theater. It had been suggested that Terauchi surrender to the British in accordance with General Order No. 1 and authorize Tsuchihashi in the north to turn over his weapons to the Chinese, who would also arrange for the repatriation of his troops north of the sixteenth parallel. In principle the arrangement was acceptable to Chungking, and Chiang would have been satisfied with an "administrative" surrender, letting Mountbatten have his formal ceremony in Saigon, where the French would undoubtedly participate. Accordingly, the Chinese memorandum delivered to the Japanese delegation at K'ai-yuan on 2 September would have sufficed to accomplish the task.

But Lu Han was disappointed. He felt he was being relegated to the role of "administrator" vis-à-vis Chang Fa-kwei who was given the military mission and fanfare of accepting the Japanese surrender in Canton. Lu Han had lost face. He protested to General Ho Ying-chin and insisted that a formal ceremony be held in Hanoi. To avoid disturbing the Kuomintang's plans for the removal of Governor Lung Yün from his stronghold in Yunnan, General Ho agreed to reconsider Lu Han's request. But by 17 September no word on the subject had reached Hanoi.

On another thorny subject, Gallagher had been instructed by Theater Headquarters to request from Lu Han air passage for General Alessandri to Hanoi. Again Lu Han raised strenuous objections on the ground that it was understood in Chungking that Alessandri was to proceed to Hanoi only if a surrender ceremony was to be held. Since Lu Han's instructions did not as yet provide for a ceremonial surrender, he saw no valid reason for Alessandri's presence in Viet Nam except to stir up trouble. Gallagher had then observed to Lu Han that the order from Chungking was explicit and one by which he must abide.[30] Lu Han was adamant. But Gallagher told me later that day that arrangements would be made for Alessandri and one other Frenchman to arrive in Hanoi on 19 September.

Gallagher and I discussed the matter of Alessandri's presence in Hanoi, and I had to agree with Lu Han that it would create problems but not in the same sense as Lu Han viewed it. I mentioned the long-standing animosity between Lu Han and Alessandri and my reasons for believing that the Chinese wanted to prolong their stay to systematically despoil the country to Lung Yün's fullest advantage. If Alessandri came now, he might be followed by French troops either from China or from Saigon or he might attempt to secure the release of the POWs at the Citadel. As senior gaulliste, Alessandri would certainly attempt to accelerate a French reoccupation and the prompt withdrawal of the Chinese, in direct conflict with Lu Han's plans. Gallagher was grateful for my views and said he would remain alert to French machinations.

Gallagher inquired into Sainteny's role, and I gave him a rundown on the French team since our arrival in Hanoi. Sainteny was already asking to meet Gallagher, but I advised Gallagher against it at that particular time; it would be better to wait until Alessandri arrived although he, too, was without portfolio of any sort or even a basic political directive from Paris. Gallagher agreed.

AN ARID EXCHANGE

I alerted Sainteny to the request for Alessandri's air passage to Hanoi, and for two straight days the DGER was busy getting ready. The French community was in a state of collective euphoria; they knew the General would come "to take command of the situation." Just at the point that negotiations in the south had broken down and Cédile was giving his hard-line press conference, Alessandri and Léon Pignon[31] arrived at Gia Lam Airport. Without public notice they were whisked away to Sainteny's quarters.

With the arrival of Alessandri and Pignon the relatively low-level operations of Sainteny's group took on a new dimension. The tough stance taken by Cédile and Gracey in Saigon suggested to Alessandri that the time was propitious to open talks with Ho Chi Minh. He authorized Sainteny to send word to Ho that a conference between Ho and a French representative in India would be welcomed. Ho declined; he would not meet with an intermediary, only with de Gaulle. Alessandri would not be put off and pursued the idea further. He convinced Admiral Thierry d'Argenlieu,[32] the High Commissioner-designate for Indochina, then in Calcutta, to meet with a representative of Ho. But Ho had not been consulted. When Alessandri again sent word to Ho that d'Argenlieu would meet with him, Ho was still under the impression that such a meeting would be between the French and his representative. Ho asked ex-Emperor Bao Dai to represent him.[33]

On 22 September I took General Gallagher to meet Ho who asked for our advice on the French proposal for a meeting. We suggested it might be useful to open a direct dialogue. If he did not like what the French had to offer, he did not have to accept. Ho said that he also had discussed the matter with Lu Han because a meeting involved air transportation which only the Chinese could provide. Lu Han had stalled for time but felt he could arrange a plane in ten or twelve days. Gallagher and I still felt that a meeting could do no harm and that Ho should accept. As an afterthought, I added that it would be an indication of French intent to recognize the independent government of Viet Nam if the French went through with their proposed invitation. Ho seized on that idea and decided that instead of sending a representative he himself would go. However, he would go only if the French were willing to meet in China and if an American official also attended as observer.[34]

Very soon thereafter, when the shocking news of Dewey's murder reached me and I went to see Ho, Hoang Minh Giam took me aside and told me about the French invitation for a meeting which had finally materialized. Giam, as Deputy Minister for Foreign Affairs, had received a memorandum from Alessandri referring to the proposed meeting between "the French and the Annamese people represented by the National Revolutionist Party." All references to a meeting between Ho and d'Argenlieu had been omitted and only by implication was Ho invited.

Giam was distressed at the incredible insensitivity of the French. He found it hard to believe that they, of all people, could be either rude or ignorant in naming a defunct element of the VNQDD as the party representing the Vietnamese people. In any case it clearly showed the French intransigence in refusing to recognize the independence of Viet Nam when they failed to invite Ho as President of the Provisional Government of the Democratic Republic of Viet Nam.[35]

This arid exchange left Ho more than ever skeptical of French sincerity and intentions. It appeared to him that the French only wanted to use him, and were not interested in negotiating in good faith. Ho would not even acknowledge receipt of the memorandum, and Alessandri's overtures, such as they were, came to nothing.

UNACCEPTABLE CREDENTIALS

The news of Gracey's Proclamation No. 1 reached Hanoi with the speed of lightning and again stirred the emotions of the French population to a fever pitch. Only Alessandri's strong exhortations to the French community and to the POWs at the Citadel to remain calm contained the explosive situation. General Lu Han became nervous and sent word to the French, officially unrecognized, that he would not tolerate any French display of sympathy with their southern compatriots. The Vietnamese, both communist and anticommunist, kept admirably calm but were nevertheless very wary. The Japanese alone presented a confident neutral posture.

Late in the evening I met with Ho's staff and reviewed the day's events. In the course of our conversation I learned that Ho had received the day before a communication from Mountbatten's headquarters requesting information on Vietnamese troop strength and armaments. To this inept and impertinent demand, Ho had instructed Chu Van Tan[36] to refuse the information and had directed Giam to lodge an official protest with Mountbatten in the name of the Vietnamese government.[37]

That night, 21-22 September, was again one of great unease in Hanoi. Gracey had proclaimed martial law in the south during the day, and all through the night there was unusual activity in Hanoi. There was no violence, but a lot of moving about, meetings, lights on all night at the Bac Bo Palace, and Europeans coming and going at the houses of French resistance leaders. The Vietnamese police, on alert, had stopped Europeans and Vietnamese alike for questioning, but no arrests had been made.

The next morning General Alessandri called on General Lu Han seeking recognition as de Gaulle's representative in Hanoi. Lu Han received him at what had been the palatial residence of the French Governors General but after a minute or so excused himself, leaving his Chief of Staff, General Ma, to treat with Alessandri. General Ma explained that the only French representative accredited to the Chinese government and the only one General Lu Han would recognize as the spokesman for the French government was the French Ambassador in Chungking. In dismissing Alessandri, Ma informed him that Lu Han's mission was to disarm the Japanese and related tasks and he would not become involved in either Franco-Sino politics or Franco-Vietnamese differences. As to the French in Viet Nam, during the occupation they would be treated as any other foreign nationals.[38]

This refusal had to be a bitter disappointment to Alessandri who had clung to a belief that the French would be considered as Allies, not foreigners. How sweet the taste of revenge may have been to Lu Han can only be imagined.

In a situation already deeply humiliating, Alessandri had to bear a further demeaning embarrassment. One of Sainteny's officers had been meeting with a Chinese staff officer to request office space, housing facilities, typewriters, and the like. The requests were refused by the Chinese as "unauthorized," and Alessandri had protested. The Chinese reply was that General Lu Han considered the request "unessential to the French stay in Viet Nam."[39]

After the outright refusal of the Chinese in Hanoi to recognize either Alessandri or Sainteny as officials of France, they both went to see Gallagher who was very sympathetic but not helpful. Again Alessandri was keenly disappointed, as he had hoped for some American support. Finally, Sainteny approached me on the matter of administrative support. I, too, turned him down because I had no instructions to assist the French in setting up a French headquarters in Viet Nam.[40]

Gallagher later told me that Sainteny had requested from him airlift to Kunming and that he had promised to look into it. He asked whether he should accommodate him. I said that although Sainteny's anti-American campaign was damaging to us I would rather have him in Hanoi than in Chungking or Calcutta, where he undoubtedly could continue to misrepresent the Hanoi situation and undermine American prestige. However, I would interpose no objection with OSS-Kunming, if the general wanted to let him go and would endorse the request.[41]

A TACIT AGREEMENT

The day that had brought humiliation to Alessandri and Sainteny was one fraught with worry for the Vietnamese. Radio reports from Saigon brought the news that Gracey had taken over the central prison and released Cédile's paratroopers and, as the day advanced, the further news reported that released POWs on the streets of Saigon were attacking Vietnamese randomly.

Ho feared the Chinese might follow Gracey's example and called on General Lu Han during the afternoon. Their meeting proved to be very cordial. Lu Han told Ho of Alessandri's earlier visit and of his own refusal to recognize the French in Viet Nam as official representatives of France or to grant them any official status.

Ho raised the question of Gracey's Proclamation No. 1 and expressed his hope that it would not be necessary to take similar measures in Tonkin and Annam. Lu Han assured him that he need not fear any interference from the Chinese in the conduct of public administration, with only one proviso: if Ho's administration showed any signs of weakness or inability to cope with the maintenance of public order in all quarters, the Chinese would have to intervene.[42] Ho assured him that he could handle the situation even with minor obstructions from some Vietnamese "enthusiastic nationalists." Evidently they understood one another. Lu Han agreed that "too much" support would not be forthcoming.

That evening Ho admitted to me that he was greatly relieved by Lu Han's assurances of nonintervention. Nonetheless, he was still in a state of anxiety over Cochinchina. He had learned that Leclerc was on the way to Viet Nam with Allied ships and weapons. He asked if his information was correct. I pleaded ignorance, which was a fact, but also gave my view that the British actions and the French self-confidence in Saigon indicated a probability of a French expeditionary force landing in the delta area. No one realized, of course, that while we talked Cédile was already mounting his coup de force and that the next day would find the Vietnamese government ousted from Saigon and the people under violent assault in the streets and the victims of mass arrests.

During the general alarm and excitement of advancing developments, Kunming was not informing me of any progress in the surrender plans, and I therefore checked with Gallagher. He had not heard from Chungking but speculated that the Franco-Sino negotiations were still in progress and that Chungking did not want to expedite the Chinese occupation and let the French in until those issues were settled.

Lu Han was unhappy with Chungking's continued silence and had indicated to Gallagher that if he received no instructions by 25 September he would act on his own initiative. Lu Han had in mind presenting General Tsuchihashi with the surrender terms developed at K'ai-yuan and having the Japanese sign them in the presence of the Americans and then to proceed with implementing the terms.[43]

Ultimately I learned from Gallagher on the twenty-fourth that Lu Han had finally received permission from General Ho Ying-chin to proceed with the surrender ceremony, and I received the same day an engraved invitation in Chinese to attend the ceremony as a "special guest of the Chinese government."

HO'S CONTINGENCY PLANS

Cédile's coup in Saigon sparked a new spirit of national solidarity among the Vietnamese. All factions momentarily set aside their differences and joined the Viet Minh in the struggle against the French. The Roman Catholics of Hanoi had planned a rally in support of the Viet Minh program for national independence which happened, by chance, to be on the twenty-third, the day the news of Cédile's coup was reaching Hanoi. The rally became quite naturally a Catholic protest against British-French intransigence and a demonstration for Vietnamese independence. Vietnamese Bishop Jean B. Tong in the name of all Vietnamese Catholics sent a letter to the Pope asking for his blessing and prayers for the independence of the nation.

I could not ascertain whether this Catholic display of support for the communists was sincere or contrived. But neither could I find any evidence that these Vietnamese were anti-Ho. I was thoroughly impressed with their show of support for the independence cause and, in particular, for their complete faith in Ho. Among the Catholics on the street there was no discussion of communism, socialism, or any other "ism." The issue was national independence and freedom from foreign domination. By supporting the Viet Minh movement the Vietnamese Roman Catholic prelateship hoped to disassociate itself and the Church from the historical fact that it had been instrumental in establishing and fostering French colonialism in Indochina.

And the Viet Minh welcomed the support, if not the religious philosophy, of the two million Catholics and their fifteen hundred clergy—at least they were not for the moment an opposing force. Ho meticulously avoided any display of political partisanship and always stressed the broad national front of the government. He had installed a Catholic, Nguyen Manh Ha, in his first government as Minister of Economics, and he enjoyed the personal support of such prominent Catholics as Tu Ha, the wealthy owner of a large publishing house, and Archbishop Ngo Dinh Thuc, brother of Ngo Dinh Diem.

As news of the day's sad events in Saigon reached Hanoi, our OSS mission was besieged by local and foreign correspondents, officials from Ho's government, Lu Han's staff, and the Alessandri-Sainteny group.

They all wanted news of what was going on or confirmation of radio broadcasts.

Knapp heard a rumor that Ho was seriously considering the inclusion of pro-Chinese nationalists in the government. Of this we had already surmised much, and the pro-Chinese parties were reportedly showing results in other areas of the north, with strong Chinese support for them in Lang Son, Lao Cai, Cao Bang, and Haiphong. The most prevalent rumor was that Ho would step down in favor of Hsiao Wen's protege, Nguyen Hai Than. Sources close to Ho speculated that the Viet Minh would interpose no opposition to Than, provided it retained critical cabinet posts, and that Ho would accept the Vice Presidency.[44] I assumed that the Viet Minh might consummate such a merger on the basis that a Chinese puppet leader would bring financial relief to the bankrupt government and that the ineffectual Than would be the least troublesome of the various possibilities. A further advantage would be that such a compromise would satisfy the Chinese generals' commitments to their Vietnamese followers. My line of reasoning, however, was all wrong.

Ho sent word in the late afternoon that he would like me to have dinner with him late that evening, about nine. Knowing how preoccupied and busy he had been all day, the unusually late hour surprised me and I surmised that he had something important on his mind. I arrived promptly and found several members of his immediate staff, including the Chief of Police, who were also to have dinner with us.

The principal topic was, of course, the situation in Cochinchina and its many ramifications. For the first time the Vietnamese revealed to me their concern with British-French incursions into Laos, at Vientiane and Savannakhet. I knew through our OSS operative[45] that these were SOE operations of the joint British-French Force 136. Ho spoke with concern, expressing his view that the French forces of Leclerc were attempting to infiltrate northern Viet Nam through that rear area. He had ordered General Chu Van Tan to augment his forces in the southern sector along the Mekong and to execute all Vietnamese in the pay of the French who were assisting them. At one point Ho said that as far as he was concerned an "undeclared war" had started between France and Viet Nam and "open hostilities are not far off."[46]

Piece by piece, as dinner progressed, I received more startling information. Ho revealed in hushed tones that his people were "developing a plan of operations for a protracted conflict against the French." Without specificity, Ho suggested that a "Chinese puppet caretaker government" would be acceptable to him. That would permit him and his key lieutenants "to take to the jungle to lead the struggle" while someone like Than and a few Viet Minh representatives remained in a Chinese-sponsored government in Hanoi.[47]

The plan was to have a two-fold objective. It would retain the support of the Chinese and, by implication the Allies; and it would provide Ho and the Viet Minh with freedom of action to combat the French without compromising the Vietnamese cause for independence. I ventured to ask if his absence from Hanoi would not discourage the people and weaken his popular following. Smiling for the first time that evening, Ho said he had no fear of that. He assured me that he had absolute confidence in the people, regardless of political affiliation, and was certain that they were totally with him in their desire for independence. Then with a mild burst of humor, he added, "Even the Catholics." I, too, had to smile at that comment. Did this mean that the new government would abandon its socialist program? As to the form of government, Ho believed everyone was satisfied to wait for that until the Japanese, the Chinese, and the French had left the country.[48]

The conversation then turned to the French, and Ho said he was strongly inclined to exert more control over the French population in all of Annam and Tonkin. He pointedly asked me to suggest a method by which the French could be concentrated in areas away from the high-density centers. I was taken by surprise at the idea. It occurred to me that he meant to use the French as hostages if Leclerc moved northward. I noted that that would be a drastic measure, not only politically but logistically. They would have to be rounded up, transported, housed, fed, and guarded. It would involve not only the men, but women and children, young and old. "Well," he observed, "the French have done the very same thing to the Vietnamese for years and we have learned well from them." I argued that the French would not submit to any form of concentration voluntarily and that would require military manpower. Ho agreed but added wryly, "It would be for their protection, and we have the manpower."

It seemed to me that Ho was quite serious about this concentration plan, and it worried me. I suggested he reconsider his plan and in the meantime might want to discuss it with Generals Lu Han and Gallagher to get Chungking's views. I advised against it for I was certain it would have only adverse political and diplomatic repercussions detrimental to the Vietnamese cause. Ho promised to reconsider.[49]

Ho had been greatly heartened by Lu Han's personal reassurances and by the new political solidarity but he also discussed with me his grave concern with the lack of communications between his headquarters and the Provisional Executive Committee for the South. Giau, Bach, and the Central Committee's delegate, Viet,[50] were either not receiving his instructions or were wilfully disregarding them. In either case, Ho found himself powerless to influence the situation in the south. All that day Ho and his Standing Committee had been busy holding conferences with the Chinese and with the pro-Chinese nationalist leaders. Resistance directives were issued to the Provisional Executive Committee for the South and, more important, individuals from the Central Committee were dispatched to Giau and Bach with personal instructions from Ho.

Before I left Ho took me aside and asked me if there was any truth to the rumor that I would be leaving Hanoi soon. I answered affirmatively, explaining that our intelligence mission was coming to an end and there would be no further reason for me to remain. He wanted to know if other Americans would follow the OSS. I told him that undoubtedly the Department of State would reestablish a Consulate and some kind of diplomatic arrangement. Ho expressed sorrow to see the OSS go but indicated that he understood and, in fact, had anticipated the end of our relationship.

We were moving toward the door as Ho said, "I have something official for President Truman." Without taking it, I gently suggested it would be more proper that he ask General Gallagher to handle it. Ho smiled. "The protocol channel has begun." We said good night and I returned to the villa, wondering if Ho would pass the note to Gallagher.

I had reports that Giam and Giap were meeting with Hsiao Wen and Nguyen Hai Than on a possible merger with the nationalist parties, a move very much in line with Ho's disclosures on the desirability for a time of a puppet government under Chinese sponsorship. In any event, the unusual activity at the Bac Bo Palace and the Governor General's Palace went on far into the night, long after I returned to the Maison Gautier.

Before noon the next day Gallagher came to see me with Ho's message to President Truman and asked me to transmit it to the Department of State. I told General Gallagher I could not send it to Washington directly but would channel it to Ambassador Hurley in Chungking. Gallagher reminded me that Hurley had left for Washington the day before, but I assured him the Chargé would handle it and we transmitted it to Chungking.[51] It read:

From the President of Provisional Government, Vietnam Republic
To the President of the U.S.A., Washington

We beg to inform Your Excellency of following measures taken by Commander in Chief, British Forces in south Vietnam:

Primo, suppression of the press;

Secundo, release of arms and ammunition to French people;

Tertio, disarmament of Vietnamese police forces.

These measures constitute obvious violation of Vietnamese natural rights, direct menace to internal security, and factors disturbing stability and peace in Southeast Asia.

The Provisional Government, Republic Vietnam, therefore lodges most emphatic protest and requests through your intervention the British authorities concerned will cancel those measures.

We shall be very grateful to Your Excellency to urge Britain to stand on basis of principles of liberty and self-determination laid down in Atlantic Charter.

Respectfully yours,
Ho Chi Minh

HANOI—TANGIERS OF THE EAST

Sainteny had given up on me now that he had "found" General Gallagher, but the general would only deal with him through his staff. That morning Sainteny had come to Gallagher's office with a story of an "impending revolt of the Annamese people against the French." He was concerned that "native servants" might poison or attack the French in their homes "either tonight or tomorrow," and that the Viet Minh had instructed its agents "to stand by for the extermination of all French."[52]

I related to Gallagher the facts of my meeting with Ho the night before and my belief that, despite Ho's plans to go underground, Sainteny's fears, dramatic as usual, were unfounded. My opinion was that unless the French initiated hostilities, the Viet Minh in the north would take no action against them. I based my conclusion solidly on Ho's desire to prevent bloodshed and present the Allies with a picture of responsible government. Further, I believed that Ho wished to retain as long as possible control of the government in Hanoi, even with a pro-Chinese "front man." If the Viet Minh took preemptive action, Ho knew that Lu Han would not stand idly by but would use military force to quell any disorders and Ho's position of essential control in the north would be abruptly altered.

The morning had been a quiet one but during the afternoon the news from Saigon came in flash reports and special bulletins—large fires, riots, shootings, arrests, kidnappings—and in Hanoi there were some signs of panic. As dusk fell a few French families were leaving their homes, probably for villas in the country. Merchants were clearing their shelves of any wares of value. The Ministries of Defense and Propaganda had removed their files and much of their communications equipment to a different and secret location. Other government offices were quietly loading equipment into private vehicles and trucks festooned with extra cans of gasoline.[53] But by late evening we concluded that despite the jittery situation there had been no real panic or widespread evacuation. By midnight all was quiet and the next morning the city seemed normal again.

The first thing I did very early the next morning, 25 September, was to assure myself that the Ho government was still at the Bac Bo Palace. It was. The first person I met was Tran Huy Lieu. Before I could even ask where he had moved to, he informed me that Bach had called a general strike in Saigon and that Tran Van Giau would blockade Saigon until the British turned back the administration to the Provisional Executive Committee. He interrupted himself to ask me, with mischief in his eyes, if I had arranged a "safe conduct" for Sainteny. He had just learned that our French colleague was returning to Kunming. As a matter of fact, Sainteny was scheduled to leave on the 9:00 flight, allegedly to close the M.5 office there.

Lieu and I walked together to Giam's office, where news of the Cité Hérault massacre was coming in. Giam was horrified. I had not until then heard of it; it was not even 8:00 in the morning and I had not yet read the night's radio monitor reports. Lieu gave me a quick rundown. Giam assured me that President Ho was both shocked and angered and would want me to know that the Viet Minh neither directed nor participated in the brutal action. Lieu suspected it to be the work of one of the several anti-Viet Minh factions intent on discrediting Pham Van Bach's administration and implicating the communists. It was some time, the reader is reminded, before it was known that the Binh Xuyen was the perpetrator and that "crime for profit" was the basic motive, although lesser political motives were never fully discounted. However, at the time, as the news was trickling in with all the ghastly details it was impossible to know what had prompted the massacre or who to blame.

Throughout the day tension mounted. Sainteny had gone, but his "agit-prop" team was seen among the French, busily bolstering their morale with news that Leclerc was only a few days off the Indochina coast, that the French had reached an understanding with the Chinese government for the French fleet to land at Haiphong, and that the British in the south had ordered the Japanese to clear all Cochinchina of Viet Minh guerrillas, especially in the Cholon-Saigon area. Their stories were accepted by the French community as absolute facts. The Vietnamese, outside the official family, elected to discount them totally, which was also risky. The Chinese were listening and wondering how much of what they heard was fact and how much French fiction. Our French friends were obviously not neglecting their anti-American campaign either, which even intensified after Cédile's coup. I radioed Heppner on the day Sainteny left for Kunming to talk to him and see what, if anything, could be done to persuade them to restrain themselves.[54]

Hanoi had become something of a center of international intrigue and mystery. Journalists had been converging on the city from the United States, Great Britain, France, China, The Netherlands, India, and the Soviet Union. A new war was in the making in the south, and Hanoi was a relatively safe place from which to observe and to gather news and rumors. It was also a hub of French, Chinese, Vietnamese, Japanese, Russian, and American interests.

When Radio Saigon flashed the news of Gracey's order to the Japanese "to shoot the Vietnamese," everyone in Hanoi was shocked and Vietnamese of all political persuasions felt threatened. The Japanese sensed a sudden wave of hatred emanating from the Vietnamese and the "white world" alike. They pleaded innocence in this new role of executioners. The French attempted to rationalize the British order as only a threat that would not be carried out. My Russian acquaintances found it incredibly inhumane and deluged me with messages of protest for transmission to Chungking, Moscow, and London. Even the Chinese were alarmed. General Lu Han sent for me to ask if the report was true, and I told him that OSS-Saigon had verified it.

My old escort, Imai, also confirmed the British instructions to the Japanese in the south but added that it was doubtful the Japanese would go to the extreme directed by Gracey. Imai told me that Marshal Count Terauchi was ill and his Chief of Staff, in consultation with Tsuchihashi, had agreed to comply with Allied instructions "within limits" unless otherwise instructed by Tokyo.

Imai was trying to convey to me without precisely saying so that the Japanese would make every effort to maintain public order but would not assist the French in "eliminating" opposition. He portrayed the thinking of the Japanese High Command as reasoning that the question of Indochina's future status was not clear. No one of the Allied Powers at the "proper level" had ordered the Japanese to turn over Indochina to the French or, for that matter, to anyone else. To become involved in settling the dispute between the French and Vietnamese would not be within the purview of instructions received from Tokyo.

What Imai was not telling me was that the Japanese, at least some powerful pan-Asian elements both in Tokyo and Indochina, still held that any European influence in Asia was undesirable. They preferred Viet Nam to be left to the Vietnamese, or even to the Chinese, as long as European white influence was eliminated. The Japanese anti-American campaign which I had been witnessing lent support to my theory.

I was keeping OSS-Kunming advised but there was little more I could do. As a matter of fact, on the day of the Cité Hérault massacre, both Peter Dewey and I were advised that President Truman had on 20 September signed Executive Order 9620 terminating the Office of Strategic Services effective 1 October, 1945.

TILTING AGAIN—LU HAN VS. THE KMT

Late in the evening of 26 September General Gallagher informed me of an entirely new development. He had received instructions from Theater Headquarters to see that General Lu Han and the Chinese staff assist the French in establishing a French administration in Hanoi. His instructions were not clear as to when or how that was to be accomplished. He had already discussed this with General Lu Han who claimed he had no such instructions and anticipated none. Gallagher's opinion was that Lu Han would not comply, even if ordered by the Generalissimo himself. In such a case, Chiang would be faced with trouble from Governor Lung Yün in Yunnan and from Lu Han in Hanoi. Gallagher asked me to get some clarification through my OSS-Embassy sources, and I radioed Helliwell and Heppner for information[55] but received no answer.

I learned later in Kunming that Lu Han had indeed been instructed to assist the French in setting up a Civil Affairs Administration. He had instead sent a delegation[56] to Chungking to convince the Kuomintang to alter its policy from pro-French to pro-Viet Minh. Before Lu Han's delegation returned to Hanoi, General Ho Ying-chin himself had arrived at Gia Lam airport, by a coincidence just as my plane was taking off for Kunming on 1 October. General Ho had come to Hanoi to personally "discipline" the Chinese army; this was interpreted by the Vietnamese and the French as meaning "to persuade Lu Han to assist the French."

In typical oriental fashion, Lu Han played the perfect host and on the evening of his arrival gave a state dinner in General Ho's honor, inviting as special guests both Ho Chi Minh and General Alessandri. It was the first time that Ho and Alessandri had even been in the same room.

General Ho Ying-chin stayed on in Hanoi for several days meeting separately with the Chinese, the French, and the Vietnamese. Lu Han remained adamant with regard to a French presence and threatened to pull his troops back to Yunnan. In the end, on 4 October, some sort of compromise was reached between the two generals in which Lu Han agreed to:

Complete the disarming of the Japanese by 31 October;

Concentrate for repatriation at designated points all the Japanese troops by 10 November;

Continue informal arrangements with Ho Chi Minh but avoid any formal relations with either Ho Chi Minh or the Provisional Government which could be interpreted as official recognition.

Lu Han was not pleased with the way the Kuomintang wanted to treat the Vietnamese. He obviously preferred an independent Viet Nam under the patronage of China. However, on the very next day (5 October) Chiang Kai-shek pulled his "Kunming incident" and appointed Lu Han governor of Yunnan in place of Lung Yün who, in turn, was "promoted upstairs" to be Director of the Military Advisory Board, an almost powerless role under Chiang's close control in Chungking. From that time Lu Han's interest in the future of Viet Nam diminished as he devoted himself to the problems of Yunnan and delegated his occupation duties to subordinates.

On 8 October, one of Lu Han's delegates to Chungking, Ling Ch'i-han, returned to Hanoi with a new directive. Its essence was: don't interfere with the Viet Minh political structure and administration, but keep a tight hold on the Yunnan-fu Railroad and all port facilities. Return all Chinese troops to China immediately after the Japanese troops are repatriated. Do not occupy (take over) any Vietnamese civilian offices. Do not take over the Bank of Indochina.

I noticed that China's vested interests in Viet Nam were still uppermost in importance and that the Bank of Indochina remained inviolable.

But all those details lay in the future. As I turned in that night my thoughts were on the Hanoi surrender ceremony which would soon take place, eight long weeks after Tokyo's capitulation. It was hard to comprehend or accept that our erstwhile enemies were being goaded by the British in the south to attack and kill the Vietnamese in their own land. Saigon lay that night under siege. I remembered how we had come to Hanoi with such high expectations of a peaceful postwar era. I am glad that I did not know that Peter Dewey would be lying dead in a ditch the next morning.

CHAPTER 34

END OF MISSION

PUTTING OUT BRUSH FIRES

N ews from the south alarmed everyone in Tonkin except the French. They found new hope in Cédile's coup, Gracey's "enlightened" support of French colonial policy, and in rumors of Leclerc's imminent arrival. Sainteny's underground paper[1] fired the French with visions of immediate deliverance. It carried exaggerated news of Cédile's takeover, stories of French heroism in standing up to "Vietnamese pirates," reports of successful military operations in "mopping up pockets of Viet Minh bandits," and false reports of "large forces" landing at Phnom Penh, Cambodia, implying that French troops were enroute to liberate Tonkin via the back door. Although there was little truth in this propaganda barrage, the French in Hanoi and Haiphong chose to believe it and reacted with flagrant displays of confidence and arrogance, giving rise to several minor incidents and a few arrests. The Hanoi government, concerned with French exuberance, wanted to avoid a confrontation at all costs. Ho directed Giap to issue a warning to the French population.

On the morning of 26 September huge posters appeared on the walls of the city, headlined NOTICE TO THE FRENCH PEOPLE. The same warning in pamphlet size was distributed to the French community—stuffed in letterboxes, handed to Europeans on the streets, and included with purchases in Vietnamese shops. It was an official notice signed by Giap as Minister of the Interior for the Provisional Government. It was firm in tone, noting events which had taken place in the south, the maltreatment of the Vietnamese by the French and the British, and the determination of the people to resist all foreign domination and defend their independence, then, reaching its main point, it continued,

Some Frenchmen have voiced their concern for the security of . . . their compatriots residing in Tonkin. The Provisional Government of the Democratic Republic of Viet Nam will not take reprisals against the French here, and once more has ordered the Vietnamese population to remain calm. However, the Government will not tolerate any act of provocation, any attempt to subvert the security and independence of the nation, and will not assume any responsibility for the future reaction of the Vietnamese people to acts of aggression on the part of the French in Tonkin. I [Giap] advise these latter to observe the utmost prudence in their language, as in their attitude, and to abide strictly by the measures which may be taken to insure their own safety.

French reaction to the warning was defiant and contemptuous. Some French POWs "on pass" from the Citadel systematically tore down the posters along Boulevard Gambetta, Boulevard Jauréguiberry, rue Paul Bert, and other main streets, and attacked Viet Minh workers distributing the pamphlets. They were soon joined by French civilians and the situation threatened to get out of hand.

I was quickly apprised of the trouble by Ta Quang Buu's calling to protest the release of POWs by the Americans and letting me know that Giap was very displeased and concerned. Buu said that the disorder might very well force the government to take drastic measures which could lead to bloodshed—a most regrettable matter. I told Buu that to my knowledge no American authorization had been given to the Japanese to release POWs and to inform Giap that I would get back to him within the hour.

I immediately called Colonel Nordlinger and asked him to meet me at Gallagher's office to discuss what was happening. Nordlinger seemed annoyed with my interference but agreed to meet me there in ten minutes. I then alerted Gallagher and told him we were on our way. At the same time our X-2 men had quickly identified several of the involved POWs as leaders in Mordant's resistance.

When I arrived Gallagher and Nordlinger were waiting. Gallagher had already arranged to see Lu Han. On the way to Lu Han's headquarters I learned with surprise that for several weeks Nordlinger had been authorizing the Japanese jailers at the Citadel to issue "one-day passes" to POWs with families in Hanoi. I asked him how many passes had been issued. He did not know precisely but estimated about two to three hundred per day. Gallagher and I were both amazed and dismayed, but Nordlinger merely perceived it as a normal practice in dealing with Allied POWs.

Lu Han received us without delay. He, too, had been made aware of the trouble in the streets and had ordered several patrols to round up the POWs and return them to the Citadel. He then requested that Gallagher withdraw all passes until the situation became calm and that thereafter all passes be screened for merit by an American officer to be designated by General Gallagher. I called Buu from Lu Han's headquarters and asked him to assure Giap that we would "handle" all French POWs but that the local police would have to cope with recalcitrant civilians. Another potential explosion had been thwarted.

Nordlinger pursued his humanitarian mission with real sincerity but as far as I could see never came to realize how he was often used by the French as an innocent front for their political ends. It would be incorrect to categorize him as "pro-French" as some Frenchmen of the epoch have done. He was one of several French-speaking Americans in Hanoi charged with looking after the welfare of the Allied POWs and civilians in the area. As such he was regarded by the French as a father-confessor, protector of the weak, and dispenser of American beneficence. By the time he left Hanoi, in October, he was equally concerned with the plight of the Vietnamese and was instrumental in securing some food stocks for them as well as for the French.

He returned to the United States in December, hand-carrying a letter signed by Ho Chi Minh from the Provisional Government to our Secretary of State, which outlined the difficulties in Indochina and requested recognition of the independence of Viet Nam. The State Department took an icy view of Nordlinger's acting as a channel of communications for an unrecognized "government" and promptly filed the message "without further action."[2]

HO TAKES HOLD

While we were putting out brush fires in Hanoi, Ho was fanning the flames of resistance in Cochinchina. In a nationwide broadcast over the Voice of Viet Nam in Hanoi, Ho adroitly addressed himself to the Vietnamese and French alike. "Dear southern compatriots" was his salutation, but his message was all-inclusive.

His opening remarks excoriated the French for their past traitorous and cowardly behavior and for their continuing effort "to dominate our people once more." Alluding to the French contention that the Cochinchinese supported the status quo ante, Ho said, "I believe and our compatriots throughout the country believe in the firm patriotism of the southern compatriots." And in a clever rhetorical twist he struck at the French ego with, "We should remember the heroic words of a great

French revolutionary, 'I'd rather die as a free man than live as a slave.' "
Pledging national support to "the fighters and the people who are making
sacrifices in their struggle to maintain national independence," Ho assured his listeners that the whole world sympathized with the Vietnamese cause.[3]

Then obliquely addressing his remarks to the French and Vietnamese leaders in the south, he said, "I want to recommend to our southern
compatriots just one thing: as far as the Frenchmen captured in the war
are concerned we must watch them carefully, but we must also treat
them generously. We must show to the world, and to the French people in
particular, that we want only independence and freedom, that we are not
struggling for the sake of individual enmity and rancour. We must show
to the world that we are an intelligent people, more civilized than the
homicidal invaders."[4] These were surely words to keep the door ajar for
renewed negotiations.

We had had no indication that Ho would be addressing the belea-
guered southern Vietnamese, and the message came as a bit of a surprise. It was his first public address to the Cochinchinese since 26
August. Interpreted in the light of recent events the message was a
strong intra-party political pressure play.

Giau and Ho were both products of the same Moscow school for
revolutionary leaders, but they came away with opposing views on tactics and leadership. Ho believed in negotiating, convincing, even compromising, before resorting to violence. Giau was an inveterate Stalinist,
an orthodox communist, and maintained that only through single political
direction, party discipline, and blind obedience to Viet Minh leadership
could the people succeed in their struggle against the French.

After the disorders of 2 September Ho and the Central Committee in
Hanoi had advised Giau to exercise moderation, to open a dialogue with
the French, the Trotskyites, and the noncommunist parties, and to
broaden the political base of his Provisional Executive Committee. But
Giau could not bring himself to share his leadership with Trotskyites and
anticommunists. He had relinquished the chair to Pham Van Bach but
had retained control of the military. He had ignored Hanoi's advice and
carried out a relentless and brutal campaign to exterminate his Vietnamese opposition.[5]

Ho, unable to influence Giau or bring the southern leadership into
line, circumvented the Provisional Executive Committee in his broadcast
by going directly to the people. While unequivocally supporting the people's resistance to the French and British takeover, Ho counseled
moderation and restraint, leaving ample room for negotiation with
Frenchmen of goodwill. The message had the desired effect. Ho had reaffirmed his national leadership and reestablished communications between the south and Hanoi. In the ensuing days an effort was made by
Bach to negotiate with Cédile.

THE JAPANESE SURRENDER

It was on Friday, 28 September, as I was getting ready to leave for the Japanese surrender ceremony, that I received also a personal note of condolence from President Ho on the "untimely death of Colonel Dewey." The bearer was Nguyen Van Luu.[6] I thanked him and said I would be seeing the President at the Palace. He promptly informed me that Ho was not well and would not be at the ceremony. I was surprised and did not know how to interpret his absence. I had seen Ho the previous evening and he seemed well, except for his usual cough. I knew he had been invited and assumed he had accepted, but did not really know.

Elaborate preparations had been made, and the elite Yunnanese Honorable 2d Division[7] mounted guard in and around the Governor General's Palace. These unusually tall Chinese troops (between 5'10" and 6'), in full battle dress, steel helmets, American M-1 rifles with fixed bayonets, were posted along the broad stone staircase leading to the Palace's imposing entrance. Outside, on the Palace grounds, groups of Chinese officers stood about, awaiting the arrival of General Lu Han. They, too, were impressive in their bemedaled blue-gray, high-collared uniforms and Sam Browne belts with ivory handled ceremonial daggers at their sides.

I reached the gate at ten. Unlike previous occasions, security was tight, and the usually relaxed chi'upa (Chinese GI) had been replaced by the crack 2d Division guards. The guard officer carefully verified my official invitation, saluted smartly, and waved me on. When my car rolled to a stop at the foot of the staircase, a sentry opened the door while a junior officer once more checked my credentials. Satisfied, he motioned to another officer nearby, who escorted me to the main reception hall and a reserved place next to the surrender tables.

The room was crowded with several hundred Chinese civilian dignitaries and military representatives and a sprinkling of Americans. I had assisted Lu Han's staff on protocol procedures and was privy to the list of special invitees. It included General Gallagher with senior members of his staff, President Ho and his cabinet, General Alessandri and one representative, myself and five members of the OSS staff, and distinguished guests from the Chinese civilian community. Of all these, the French and Vietnamese were conspicuously absent.

The room had been arranged with about two hundred straight-back chairs facing one end of the hall where a blue-covered table with three high-backed upholstered chairs had been placed for the Chinese to receive the Japanese surrender. On the wall behind their chairs hung a large portrait of Dr. Sun Yat-sen. Facing the Chinese table and about ten feet away was another table covered in white with five less imposing chairs for the Japanese. Four large flags were displayed on the side walls—the American and Soviet on the right, the Chinese and British on the left. The marble columns along the room and over the doors had small clusters of the same four flags. No French or Vietnamese colors were displayed anywhere inside or outside the building.

At 10:30, China time, General Tsuchihashi and four senior Japanese officers (wearing no sidearms) entered the hall and were ushered to the white-covered table. They ignored the chairs placed for them and remained standing, Tsuchihashi in the center. Then, with an almost ritualistic gesture, Tsuchihashi placed his hat on the table with both hands, carefully adjusting it so that the peak pointed toward him. The other officers held their hats in right hands at their sides.

From a separate entrance near the blue table came General Lu Han, General Lin,[8] and General Ma, who seated themselves facing the Japanese. The Japanese barely acknowledged Lu Han's presence by a slight bow.

The official Chinese translator read to the Japanese Commander the Allied terms of surrender. Tsuchihashi and his officers stood rigidly at attention throughout the reading but looked abstracted as though hardly paying attention. The translator then handed the surrender document to the Japanese for signature. Without reading it, General Tsuchihashi signed and returned the document, with a deep bow from the waist toward Lu Han. The Chinese barely acknowledged the bow and summarily dismissed the Japanese without further comment. They left without casting a glance in any direction.

When they had departed, Lu Han read his Proclamation outlining the terms of the surrender and the Chinese responsibilities in Viet Nam. The Chinese translator then read the Proclamation in both French and Vietnamese, although neither nationality was present, and the ceremony ended.

This ceremony which had been so important to Lu Han brought no dramatic changes in Hanoi. Tsuchihashi continued his role as senior Japanese officer in the ongoing task of disarming and concentrating his defeated army at points of embarkation. Japanese soldiers were still assisting Chinese troops in guarding the French POWs in the Citadel, and key Japanese comptroller personnel remained at their posts in the Bank of Indochina.

There was a brief reception in an adjoining room after the ceremony, and I had the opportunity to discuss the absence of the French with General Gallagher. He said that Alessandri had insisted on the display of the French colors with the other Allied flags, which Lu Han had refused to authorize on the grounds that a display of the French flag would surely create an incident. Alessandri had then asked Gallagher to intercede for the French and he had done so, pointing out to Lu Han that the French flag had been flown at both the Tokyo and Manila ceremonies.

Lu Han was adamant, arguing that there was no anti-French resistance in those areas and insisting that in Saigon the mere display of the Tricolor had been the signal for public uprisings and bloodshed. Furthermore, Alessandri's capacity as an official French representative was still "unclear."

I viewed the discord as another symptom of Lu Han's personal antipathy to the French, and he went even further to humiliate General Alessandri on a very personal basis. He had refused to have Alessandri seated in the official section, assigning him instead seat number 115 in the section reserved for nonofficial guests, which appeared to me to be an affront to French prestige generally and to General Alessandri personally.

There was still the other nagging question. Why had Ho not attended? At the reception I noticed several Vietnamese who apparently had witnessed the event in an unofficial capacity. They were in the company of influential local Chinese identified with Than's Dong Minh Hoi. I commented on Ho's absence to Colonel Hsei Chun-yie[9] and he informed me that Ho had been invited personally by General Lu Han as a special guest. However, at the last moment Ho had declined "for reasons of health." Hsei explained that as Ho and his government had no official status in Chungking it was impossible to include him among the Allied representatives.

MERGER IN THE MAKING

I later learned that Lu Han could not openly recognize Ho and ignore the leaders of the other nationalist groups, especially at a time when secret negotiations for a merger of the Viet Minh and the Dong Minh Hoi were under way. Hsiao Wen, under instructions from Chungking, was supporting Nguyen Hai Than, but General Lu Han was not willing to break with Ho and was pressuring Hsiao to effect a merger.

The first step toward a merger took place the morning after the surrender at a meeting arranged by Hsiao Wen between Ho and Than. It was held at the Dong Minh Hoi party headquarters[10] where the party flag was displayed for the first time in Hanoi. A large crowd gathered to cheer both men. Inevitably scuffles broke out between enthusiasts for each faction, and the local police backed up by the Chinese military had their hands full for a short time, but no serious violence was reported.

The meeting lasted about thirty minutes and both men emerged smiling. No public statement was issued, but within the hour two different versions of the talk were circulating on the streets. Than's followers joyfully let it be known that Ho would "step down" in favor of Than and assume the role of "national adviser."[11] My Viet Minh contacts told me that no decision had been reached except that Ho had invited the Dong

Minh Hoi to participate with the Viet Minh in the new government to be elected by the people in a general election scheduled for 23 December.[12]

Spicing the rumors was a story widely circulated, undoubtedly by Than's detractors, that the Kuomintang had given him seven million piastres for organizational purposes but that half the money had been appropriated by Hsiao Wen[13] for his personal use. This had weakened Than's position to the point where he now was prepared to collaborate with the Viet Minh in forming a coalition government.[14] How much truth there was in this story I never knew. But in October, after I had left Hanoi, Generals Lu Han and Hsiao Wen had a serious disagreement regarding the operation of the Dong Minh Hoi and Hsiao Wen was temporarily relieved of his political responsibilities. At one point in the fall of 1945 it was said that Lu Han considered having Hsiao arrested and returned to Chungking in disgrace, but American dispatches from Viet Nam and China from October 1945 to October 1946 indicate that Hsiao Wen was still active in nationalist affairs.

CONFUSION FROM THE MEDIA

The surrender ceremony had been anticlimactic and received only routine coverage in the local press. What captured the headlines were the events in the south in the aftermath of Colonel Dewey's death. For two days the radio and press in Saigon, Hué, Singapore, New Delhi, and Chungking gave the Dewey murder wide coverage, and their differing reports gave rise to general confusion in Hanoi.

The French openly voiced condolences and a show of sympathy for a "friend and ally," while privately finding great satisfaction in the deed. It would surely swing American public sentiment against the "treacherous Annamites." The Vietnamese publicly accused the French and British of a conspiracy to arouse American feeling against the Viet Minh. Some well-placed Chinese agreed with the Vietnamese conjecture but also strongly suspected a British plot to get the Americans out of their theater of operations.

What made the Dewey story attractive to the media was its potential for international repercussions. Great prominence was given in Hanoi to an interview allegedly given in Hué by a wire service correspondent named Phale Thorpe. Speaking on the day after Dewey's murder, he was reported in Hanoi to have condemned "British action in Cochinchina [as] contrary to international law [sic] and that Viet Nam deserved independence."[15] Reportedly, he said he was "returning immediately to Hanoi to inform [the] American Commission there on what was happening in the south to avoid bloodshed in Tonkin . . . [and] that the Franco-Annamese conflict can be regulated either in the U.S. or in China."[16]

Thorpe's remarks, as reported, had not neglected the French role in

Saigon, and the Vietnamese propaganda machine made the most of the opportunity to exploit them. The French, still smarting from official exclusion at the surrender ceremony, countered with propaganda that the "French no longer [are] considered as Allies in the United Nations and that the Americans are contributing to the humiliation of the French in the East as they have in the West."[17] They cleverly reinforced this line by using Thorpe's remarks with minor distortions to make his news story sound like an official American pronouncement.

Radio Singapore featured a detailed account of Mountbatten's dressing down of Gracey in the presence of the British Secretary of State for War, Sir Lawson. The Vietnamese and Chinese press repeated the Singapore report and heavily emphasized Lawson's statement of British policy, "Britain's obligations to her Allies will not involve fighting for the French against the people of Indochina."[18] His statement was apparently prompted by strong opposition within the Labor Government to providing military support for a French suppression of the Vietnamese nationalist movement, coupled with the vehement protest of India's influential Congress Party against the use of Indian troops in aid of de Gaulle's colonialist policy.

Yet, after the Singapore broadcast, Radio Delhi announced that the British had launched two divisions of Indian troops against the Vietnamese guerrillas in Cochinchina. The immediate reaction of the Provisional Executive Committee for the South was to order its military units "to isolate the British and French forces by destroying bridges and roads."[19]

GOING HOME

It was impossible among the confused reports to know in authentic detail what was happening, except that it was abundantly clear that the end of the long hard-fought Pacific war would not bring peace to the Vietnamese. For them a new war had already begun. But it did not involve us. We were going home. Late in the afternoon of 29 September I received the orders I had been awaiting. The OSS was to be "turned over to War and State on 1 October,"[20] and I was to return to Kunming by that date. Captain Bernique and later Lieutenant Commander Swift would close down the installation. By mid-October I would be on my way home. Helliwell would be on his way home only a few days later, and Heppner would return to the United States in mid-November. The CCC was also coming to an end, and General Gallagher and his staff were rapidly winding down, in effect removing themselves from any influential role. OSS in China would immediately become a small phasing-out cadre. Our intelligence operation in the China Theater died a quick death, unnoticed by the American public, who were to pay dearly for the omission.

I spent my last day in Hanoi, 30 September, in busy preparations for departure. I left orders with the staff on the disposition of records and equipment, and we again went over the security plans in the event an emergency evacuation should become necessary. Then came the final conferences and leave-taking calls with General Gallagher, General Lu Han, General Ma, and others. General Gallagher had invited me and some of my staff to lunch with him and his senior staff officers, a pleasant farewell, after which I returned to Maison Gautier to finish my packing.

My last evening I spent with Ho who had invited me to dinner.

CHAPTER 35

A LAST FAREWELL

It was just seven when I was shown into the anteroom of the main reception hall at Bac Bo Palace. Vo Nguyen Giap greeted me and walked with me into the hall where President Ho was waiting with Duong Duc Hein, Nguyen Manh Ha, and Tran Huy Lieu. We all knew one another and there were no formalities. Ho came forward and extended me his frail hand saying, "This is indeed a sad occasion. Let us hope your leaving us is temporary." After I had greeted the others, Ho and I led the group to the dinner table. The conversation, alternating between French and English, was general. It appeared to me that a studied effort was made by everyone to avoid any remark which might have embarrassed me or placed me in a position of defending the Allied (British or Chinese) position in Viet Nam. We sat around the table for ten or fifteen minutes after dinner, when all but Ho and Giap excused themselves, wishing me a pleasant trip and expressing the hope that I would return soon for a visit or to stay.

We three adjourned to a smaller room for coffee. Several minutes later Giap was called out but before he left he shook my hand with warmth. Then in impeccable French he said that if he were delayed and I left before he returned, he wanted me to know how grateful he was for my understanding of the Vietnamese cause. He expressed his personal appreciation and that of his "colleagues in arms" for the "tremendous" assistance the "Americans in Kunming" had provided him "during the early days of the revolution." Giap ended his little speech with expressions of "bon voyage" and the hope that soon Viet Nam would have a friend in Washington.

I was surprised and somewhat moved, as it was a very rare moment indeed when Giap allowed his inner feelings or emotions to show. During the weeks I had dealt with him, he had always been courteous, correct, and businesslike, never revealing any emotion toward the United States or toward me personally. Except for this occasion and on the day of the welcoming ceremony when the DRV flag was dipped to the Stars and Stripes, I would have categorized Giap as a hard-line communist who, in turn, categorized the United States as an imperialist power from which no good could be expected for the Vietnamese cause and whose representative (myself) should be treated with caution.[1] Nor am I sure that he was totally sincere at that moment. As Giap left the room, I thought I detected a glint of assent or approbation in Ho's eyes. Giap's farewell to me may have been encouraged by Ho or perhaps it was his own sincere gesture. I will never know.

When we were alone, Ho asked me for the first time if the United States was going to allow France's return to Viet Nam. Ho was not making conversation. He was apprehensive and wanted to know from me, on an informal basis, what I thought or knew about American policy toward France's obvious intentions.

I told him that American policy as conveyed to me when I was first assigned to my mission was one of "hands off" Indochina, except for intelligence operations directed at the Japanese. I also said that Roosevelt had on numerous occasions stated a policy of no American support for French colonial ambitions and no interference in the internal affairs of Viet Nam. The policy was still operative. I went a step further and told Ho that since Roosevelt's death no official statement by the United States had questioned French sovereignty over Viet Nam, but neither had the United States supported France in its plans for Indochina. As a matter of fact, I knew of no change in policy that required the United States to assist France to reestablish by force its pre-1940 position in Viet Nam. I speculated that the position of the United States could change if the Vietnamese people wanted the French to return under one condition or another. However, that was only speculation.

I also pointed out that my instructions just before departure for Hanoi and repeatedly since then were that American representatives in Viet Nam were to be absolutely neutral. I noted for Ho that irrespective of my personal inclination for or against a particular group or cause I had to adhere strictly to my instructions and perhaps at times my actions may have been misinterpreted by the various interests. Regarding General Gallagher's CCC, the AGAS, and other American elements in Viet Nam, I assured Ho that their role was limited to supporting the Chinese in the only official task assigned to Chiang by the Allied Powers—disarming the defeated Japanese.

We had been over much of this ground many times. However, I felt on this last occasion I should not leave him with any misconceptions or false hopes of American military aid for Viet Nam.

Ho listened very attentively, then shook his head and told me he could not reconcile the United States' position in Washington, Quebec, Teheran, and Potsdam with its passivity in current developments in Saigon. He could not rationally understand the United States, a champion of anti-colonialism, in standing aside and permitting England and even China to assist France in its aim of reimposing colonial rule on Viet Nam. He said one would have to be blind not to accept the fact that French troops, armed and equipped with American supplies, would soon attempt to reenter Laos, Cambodia, Annam, and even Tonkin. "It will cost them dearly," he added darkly.[2]

Once more he expressed the hope that the United States would restrain the French in their colonial obsession. He postulated that if the United States would only exert its influence with de Gaulle a modus vivendi could be reached in Viet Nam in which not only the French but all friendly countries could benefit from Vietnamese independence.

Relaxing in his chair, Ho spoke at length. I was so keenly interested in his personal philosophy that I would not interrupt him, even with a question. He spoke slowly, softly, earnestly, choosing his words carefully.

He was thinking in terms of a pan-Asiatic community consisting of at least Viet Nam, Cambodia, Laos, Thailand, Malaya, Greater Burma (including Bengal), an independent India, a free Indonesia, and the Philippines. These nations, and perhaps others, working together with the United States, Great Britain, and France, would contribute to a peaceful coexistence, developing political and economic programs for the common good. For a brief moment it sounded to me very much like the Japanese concept of a Greater East Asia Co-Prosperity Sphere, except that Ho was talking about interdependence among equal nations as distinguished from a Japanese-dominated regional complex.

Ho regarded the United States as the avant garde of such a movement. He asked, "Has not the United States led the way in the Philippines?" He saw "storm clouds" gathering in the British Parliament to return the lands of India and Malaya to their rightful owners, the people. Ho held that colonialism was a thing of the past. For almost a century the colonial system under any country, even the more benevolent powers, had proved oppressive and regressive. Human dignity had been destroyed and national welfare exploited beyond belief. It was the time for change.

To support his point, Ho again drew on Roosevelt's and Churchill's common principles enunciated in the Atlantic Charter. The United States and Great Britain had assured the world that they sought no territorial gains; nor did they encourage forcible boundary changes against the will of the people, although the British were helping the French in Viet Nam and Thailand; both the United States and the United Kingdom had repeatedly stated they would respect the right of all peoples to choose the form of government under which they would live—and the Vietnamese wanted that privilege. Both the United States and the United Kingdom said they recognized the need to restore sovereign rights and self-government to those who had been forcibly deprived of them. "Is this not applicable to Viet Nam?" he asked.

Ho went on to stress Viet Nam's need for economic development, not under France, Japan, China, or even the United States, but independent of foreign dominance. As proclaimed by the United States and England, Viet Nam looked to a free world trade, not limited as in the past to France or China. Without free trade, Viet Nam could never prosper economically and its people would, as before, be relegated to the menial and artisan occupations and to keeping small shops.

If these were the lofty principles for which the United States and the United Kingdom fought World War II, why then start the new postwar era by reneging on them and in particular by denying them to Viet Nam? Admittedly, the United States had helped Viet Nam in its early struggle and had shown its sincerity of purpose in the Philippines. Why now stand idly by while the French violated the principles of the Atlantic Charter and of the United Nations? I had no answer and Ho did not expect one.

He suddenly came out of his emotional reverie and, smiling, asked me to forgive his impassioned musing. He said it was difficult for him to express his inner feelings with strangers but that he considered me a very special friend with whom he could confide. For the second time that evening I was moved by the personal regard shown me. Both Giap and Ho knew that at best they could only expect from me understanding and sympathy. At the same time I knew they were taking advantage of this last evening to put themselves and their cause in the best possible light. Still, they were isolated from the communist world, they were surrounded by self-interested powers, and the few Americans within their view were the only ones with whom there was a rapport. Americans were the ones who understood the difficulty of achieving and maintaining independence. It was really this intangible rapport that the French in Indochina hated, despised, and fought in every way they possibly could.

I steered our conversation to the recent French proposal for an entente between the Vietnamese and the Paris government. Ho reminded me of the charade of Alessandri's suggestion that he meet with d'Argenlieu. To what purpose? He had followed my advice, but before the meeting could be arranged the French had shown their duplicity and their total disregard for Vietnamese national independence. They followed the "old ways" of the French colonialists.

Ho noted with irony that Sainteny, the son-in-law of Albert Sarraut,[3] not only had refused to talk with him in July but even a month later in Hanoi had shown absolutely no sympathy for the Vietnamese cause when he spoke with Giap. As for Alessandri, what could one say? The French have made him a "hero of the resistance." Which resistance? Against the Japanese? Or the one against the Vietnamese patriots? Surely it was not against the Decoux regime that collaborated with the Vichy and Japanese fascists. Recent history records Alessandri's role in Viet Nam as a leader actively engaged in Decoux's and Mordant's cruel program of repression and subjugation of Vietnamese nationalists. These were the same unreconstructed Frenchmen who wanted to speak for the "new France" about Viet Nam's future. The only future they could or would discuss was the continuation of "old French Indochina," a subject no longer valid.

I asked Ho if he had closed the door to future discussions with the French. No, he said, he was always open to discussions on Viet Nam's problems but such discussions had to be based on mutual trust and honest intent with enlightened Frenchmen willing to talk as equals, and that did not seem to be the case at present.

What about the Chinese? I asked. Ho rose and walked to the window with his back to me. "They are predictable." Returning to his seat, he added, "Once they take all they can carry, they will leave Viet Nam and return to China." They could, however, do immeasurable damage to the country before leaving, not only economically but also politically. The VNQDD and the Dong Minh Hoi would create dissent among the Vietnamese and the Chinese generals would undoubtedly be dealing with the French on terms inimical to the best interests of Viet Nam.

Ho took the instance of Nguyen Hai Than, leader of the Dong Minh Hoi. The day before Than had proposed to him in concrete terms a "unification pact"—a broadly based government consisting of the Dong Minh Hoi, the VNQDD, and the Viet Minh, with minor representation from other nationalist parties. Under it, Ho would step down as President in favor of Than; but Ho would assume the role of Vice President and Senior Counselor. The cabinet portfolios would be allocated one-quarter each to the three principal parties, the remaining quarter distributed among the lesser parties. In return, Ho and the Viet Minh and the new government would enjoy the fullest support from the Kuomintang in resisting French efforts to reoccupy Tonkin.

Ho had received the proposal with reservations but had not rejected it out of hand. Than was not aware that Ho knew of French overtures of Franco-Sino-Vietnamese cooperation made to Than earlier in the week. The French had let it be known that as soon as the Chinese left they would implement the 24 March Declaration and recognize a federal government for Indochina in one guise or another within the French Union and "in terms most favorable to the Vietnamese." If a noncommunist government was in being at that time, recognition by France would be assured. Of course, the Dong Minh Hoi and the VNQDD were anticommunist, hence a major obstacle would be surmounted. The French intention was to see the Viet Minh neutralized and they looked to the pro-Chinese nationalists to do it. The French felt that Than could achieve this and that they could then deal with him, whom they considered "flexible," if not outright feeble, as a leader. The arrangement would not displease General Hsiao Wen or the Kuomintang because what they feared most was the "Moscow-trained" Ho Chi Minh and the "fierce communist-oriented Viet Minh."

When I asked Ho how he felt about Than's proposal, he replied that it was a possible but not probable accommodation. It would postpone the inevitable confrontation with the Chinese and/or French. But he was skeptical of the proposed merger and was almost certain that without Viet Minh leadership the cause for independence would be lost. The Dong Minh Hoi or the VNQDD would perhaps retain the semblance of independent government as long as they were backed by the Chinese. But whatever they set up would still be under French control, and the Chinese would only continue their support as long as it suited their plans to exploit Viet Nam economically. The Chinese would only keep the French out until their negotiations between Paris and Chungking were completed. Then they would leave and the pro-Chinese puppet government would be left impotent to cope with the French forces of Leclerc and Viet Nam would once more be a French colony. Ho could not in conscience allow that to happen. He would find a way to retain control even if he had to take to the jungle, as he had suggested a few nights earlier.

The hour had grown very late and I started to take my leave, but Ho asked me to stay on. So I sat down again. He thanked me for my discretion, for never having pressed for information, and for having respected the confidentiality of his remarks. He was grateful, too, that I had never asked him for information on his background although, he said, he knew I was familiar with several phases of his life. He described briefly his "worldwide" peregrinations and told me he had been on the move since he was ten, perhaps younger. He mentioned two brothers and a sister and referred to his mother and sister with deep affection and as having had considerable influence in his political orientation.

It had been my impression that he was from northern Tonkin, but Ho said he was born in a small village in Annam, Hoang Tru, and was raised in his father's village of Kim Lien, also in Annam. His father had become a minor functionary at the Imperial Court at Hué. Ho was not quite eight when his father had moved his family to Hué where they stayed for several years before returning to Kim Lien. Ho described in some detail the poverty of the peasantry in the small villages under what we would term "the system" and also the formal stultifying life in the mandarin world of Hué.

When Ho was fifteen, his father returned again to Hué. Ho attended school there and was deeply offended by the Western attitude of the headmaster and some of the teachers. They appeared to him arrogant, intolerant, and disdainful of the peasants, workers, and tradespeople. Ho described the school to me as "a lake of Western thought pouring out a stream of colonial philosophy to irrigate and raise a crop of obedient Vietnamese servants useful to France."

In the years that followed his mother's death in 1900, Ho became impatient with French arrogance and Vietnamese passivity and decided to travel to France, the land of *liberté, égalité, fraternité*. He could not remember just when in the winter of 1911-12 he mustered the courage to sign on as crew member on a French ship in port at Saigon. He described to me his first voyage as a seaman and his first glimpse of France at Marseille. The usual seaport derelicts, gamblers, smugglers, and prostitutes disillusioned him, and he wondered why the French did not correct their own evils before they sermonized and "civilized" the Vietnamese. But he also remembered that the French people of Marseille treated him with courtesy, while the French in Viet Nam treated the Vietnamese demeaningly.

He also described later voyages to Portugal, Italy, and Spain, where he never ventured much beyond the port areas. He saw several West and North African ports and at one time visited the Congo and Madagascar. Everywhere he went he observed the attitude of the white man toward the Asiatic or the African black. It was the same as in Viet Nam. His comment to me, "How sad."

I was curious to know what made him decide that communism was the way for him. Ho said that he had not decided directly but had come upon the communist philosophy through socialism. In fact, he still did not consider himself a true communist but a "national-socialist." In England in 1913 he had met a group of Asians, mostly Chinese and Malayans, who were opposed to colonialism (especially British) and spent many hours at the "Overseas Workers" club discussing mutual problems. Their talk centered on the political repressions of the colonials in British, French, Dutch, and Portuguese overseas possessions. Ho said that, for the first time, he realized that something could be done to ameliorate the plight of his people at home and that only by concerted political action would the Vietnamese be treated as anything more than servants of the French. He decided to return to France where some Vietnamese intellectuals were concerned, he had heard, with social-political reforms for the Vietnamese.

After World War I he became involved in politics and joined the French Socialist Party. He wrote articles for the socialist newspaper, *Le Populaire*, on the Vietnamese problem and the total colonial question. Through this first contact in the serious political world he met Jean Longuet, the grandson of Karl Marx and a member of the French Legislature. Longuet had encouraged him to continue his work and, with help from sympathetic liberal French journalists, Ho provided socialist and communist publications with antiestablishment and pro-Vietnamese articles.

Ho admitted to me with an apologetic smile that despite all the political activity he had engaged in he was really following a single nationalist purpose for reforms to better the lot of his own people. At that time he was neither knowledgeable nor interested in international movements or politics. He understood nothing of socialism, communism, trade unionism, or even what a political party could do. He described to me party meetings where heated discussions took place on such questions as participation in the Second International, the Third International, the Workers of the World Movement, and whether the Socialist Party should affiliate with the Bolshevik October Revolution or join Lenin's Third International. For a long time, Ho said, he wondered what had happened to the First International, and we both laughed. The speeches concerned worldwide movements, revolutions of the proletariat, and so forth, but he found they never made any reference to the problem of the colonial world. He had found himself frustrated and at a loss. Everyone was sympathetic with his problem; they treated him as an equal and addressed him as "comrade" or "Monsieur Quoc."* But these new friends treated the colonial question as a minor, merely parochial issue which had to await its turn in their order of priorities. One day when Ho raised the naive question as to which International sided with the colonials, a kind soul whispered, "The Third," and handed him a copy of Lenin's *Thesis on the National and Colonial Questions*.

It was a great turning point for him, Ho said. At last he had found a *point d'appui*. He was greatly moved by Lenin's literary style and depth of understanding. He became a champion of Leninism and participated at one and all party meetings and political rallies, vigorously advocating support for the Third International. He read and studied every writing on colonialism and nationalism he could find. He sought the help of more erudite party members and campaigned for the inclusion of the Socialist Party into the Third International. At the Eighteenth Congress of the French Socialist Party at Tours in December 1920, Ho along with the left-wing element of the party voted to form the French Communist Party and to seek for its admission into the Third International (Comintern). Ho commented to me that there were really so few people in the political ambient interested in the colonial problem that he saw no choice. He also reflected aloud how wrong he had been ever to believe that the French, British, or Russian communists would concern themselves with the Vietnamese problem. "In all the years that followed, no one of the so-called liberal elements have come to the aid of colonials. I place more reliance on the United States to support Viet Nam's independence, before I could expect help from the USSR."

*He was then known as Nguyen Ai Quoc.

Ho said that the Americans considered him a "Moscow puppet," an "international communist," because he had been to Moscow and had spent many years abroad. But in fact, he said, he was not a communist in the American sense; he owed only his training to Moscow and, for that, he had repaid Moscow with fifteen years of party work. He had no other commitment. He considered himself a free agent. The Americans had given him more material and spiritual support than the USSR. Why should he feel indebted to Moscow? However, with events coming to a head, Ho said, he would have to find allies if any were to be found; otherwise the Vietnamese would have to go it alone.

It was by now very, very late, and again I rose to leave. Ho pulled out his old pocket watch to look at the time. Would I stay a minute longer? And again I sat down. Ho asked me to carry back to the United States a message of warm friendship and admiration for the American people. He wanted Americans to know that the people of Viet Nam would long remember the United States as a friend and ally. They would always be grateful for the material help received but most of all for the example the history of the United States had set for Viet Nam in its struggle for independence.

Ho walked me to the front door, thanked me for coming and for listening to his "discourse." He put his hands on my shoulders, "Bon voyage, please come back soon. You are always welcome." As I started my jeep, I looked back at his small silhouette in the door, waving good-bye. It brought to mind our first meeting at the teahouse in Chiu Chou Chieh. He appeared so frail and yet was in fact so indomitable.

PART FOUR

AFTERMATH

"God save thee, ancient Mariner!
From the fiends, that plague thee thus!—
Why look'st thou so?"—With my cross-bow
I shot the Albatross.
                    —Samuel Taylor Coleridge

CHAPTER 36

AMERICA'S
ALBATROSS

I n Washington I found drastic changes in the postwar scene. Most of my former associates had already returned to civilian life, and in the OSS building at the end of Constitution Avenue only a few offices remained open. A striking change to a leisurely pace was clearly noticeable. I arrived in mid-November and was assigned space in a huge office of empty desks where I was to monitor the Indochina project and maintain liaison with the departments of State and War. Wading through the mountain of reports and cables from Saigon, Hanoi, Kunming, Shanghai, and Kandy, a feeling of futility and helplessness came over me. They all presaged a return to the status quo ante in Indochina. Our departure from the scene was being interpreted as official American approval for the French return.

In official Washington the idealistic wartime pronouncements of freedom, justice, and self-determination had quickly submerged in the rush for a return to a prewar America. Of course, we had a new President and a new Secretary of State, both vulnerable to heavy political and economic pressures arising from within and from abroad. The new team in the White House was unbriefed and for the most part had not participated in Roosevelt's vision of a world at peace, free from fear and want. Our domestic and foreign policies were in disarray, beset with doubt, conflict, infighting, and indecision.

War production had come to a sudden halt as the abrupt influx of demobilized manpower produced a mammoth unemployment problem; industry's incapacity to quickly convert its plant to peacetime goods alarmed the national leadership. Compounding the domestic difficulties, world markets were dislocated and bankrupt. The nations of Europe and Asia facing the task of recovery and rehabilitation looked to the unscathed United States for relief and leadership in reconstructing their economic fabric.

Long before World War II American foreign policy had reflected a compulsive expansionism in the field of finance and commerce. This latent policy led to the involuntary establishment of a global network of economic spheres of influence serving the interests of corporate business and its economic elite more than any other sector of American society. Continuity and protection of corporate interests dictated that loyal representatives of large corporations and financial institutions participate in policy formulation and decision-making. Even before World War I, Washington had become the Mecca of powerful lobbies and interest groups quietly dedicated to the proposition eventually articulated by Secretary of Defense Charles E. Wilson after World War II, "What's good for General Motors is good for the country." From this assumption the economic elitists had formed the doctrine that capital rules above all and must be safeguarded at all costs.

The World War II years merely reaffirmed that doctrine and the elitists postulated and fostered the idea that American national security was inextricably linked to the control of foreign markets and resources by a combination of political-military overlordship. Hence, long before the term "military-industrial complex" was coined, the highest levels of our government burgeoned with a corps of corporate-business-banking elitists in uniform and mufti pledged to protecting American worldwide economic interests against socialist encroachment.

With the defeat of the Axis powers, only the Soviet Union and the United States emerged as superpowers, a role that President Roosevelt had planned but President Truman did not want or understand. The wartime cooperation between the two countries ended as Russia reverted to her prewar hostility toward noncommunist nations, especially the United States. Its leaders declared that "warmongers" (economic elite) in America were plotting against the Soviet Union, that the spread of communism was essential for the security of the Soviet Union, and that communism inevitably must triumph over capitalism throughout the world.

In near panic the new administration watched the Soviet Union expand its ideological and economic power into central Europe and Asia. In a desperate attempt to stop the "Red tide" from engulfing additional territories, President Truman announced the policy of containment and economic competition, especially through aid to underdeveloped countries. It immediately set the superpowers and their client nations on a collision course—communism vs. capitalism.

❂ ❂ ❂

Among the first dispatches to come across my desk was a cable dated 5 October from Acting Secretary of State Acheson to our Chargé in China, Robertson, advising him that the United States "neither opposed nor assisted reestablishment of French control in Indochina." However, our "willingness" to see French control "is based on the future outcome of French claims of popular support." This was more diplomatic Jesuitism to allay French fears of American disapproval while stalling for time.

At that point France played a pivotal role in American plans for a viable political and economic realignment in Europe and Asia with Britain in the lead. The major stumbling block was Charles de Gaulle. Truman's antagonism toward the man surpassed Roosevelt's irritation and reflected the official American attitude toward France. The President viewed de Gaulle as petulant, arrogant, and politically unreliable. He was mistrustful of de Gaulle's efforts, in the winter of 1944, to do a balancing act between the East and West by flying to Moscow and negotiating a Treaty of Friendship with the Russians which a year later proved to be a total failure. He was also aware of Stalin's open contempt for the "decadent French" and of his personal objection to inviting France either to Yalta or to Potsdam. Still as 1945 was ending de Gaulle continued to court communist support at home and abroad. But President Truman could not ignore de Gaulle's repeated schemes to isolate the United States from the world with his preachment that the unity of Europe should be built around three poles: London, Paris, and Moscow. Truman was convinced that de Gaulle would tilt toward Russia if it coincided with French interest.

There, too, was the continued question of de Gaulle's insistence on being treated *interpari* with the United States, Britain, and Russia in postwar Europe. In Washington in August 1945 de Gaulle made no secret of his vision of France's assuming the leadership of a West European bloc directed against both the Soviet Union and the United States—mainly the United States. In those talks de Gaulle did not conceal his resentment of American influence in postwar planning which brushed aside French aspirations to rebuild on the ruins of Germany and become Europe's economic and industrial center. Truman was particularly annoyed with de Gaulle's hauteur in demanding for France control of the left bank of the Rhine and internationalization of the Ruhr with France sharing in the production and allocation of its resources. Finally, when the question of American military bases for global defense arose, de Gaulle showed no interest in leasing or cooperating with the United States regarding French territory, a fact that Truman did not dismiss lightly. In this atmosphere of antagonism and distrust Truman was in no mood to offer France any special financial or political support and suggested instead that France would do well to get the communists out of its government and reassess its future course.

De Gaulle came away from the talks with the feeling that the United States was not ready to deal with France as a first-class power, and Truman was left with serious doubts about France's disposition toward the

Soviet Union and communism. It was a dismal start for postwar French-American relations. And, with these major issues in the forefront, the future of Viet Nam was in the American view only a very peripheral matter.

☟ ☟ ☟

In the light of then-current directives I found the reports from our embassies in Paris and Chungking full of inconsistencies. They were not only conflicting with respect to what we were doing in Indochina but also damaging to our national interest, and I could only speculate on how much was known in the White House and whether anyone cared.

Ambassador Caffery in Paris reported on 22 September a conversation he had had with Philippe Baudet of the French Foreign Office. Baudet had described the Viet Minh as being "organized somewhat along communist line[s]" and "in touch with the Soviet Mission in Chungking," but had then expressed the opinion "that the 'Viet Minh' is *not* a communist organization." Baudet said the Communist Party in northern Indochina "has now more or less disappeared as such and appears to have been absorbed in the Viet Minh."[1] After the extensive reports and cables pertaining to Indochina sent to Caffery during the preceding six months I was astonished to read a cable from Paris repeating obvious French obfuscation.

Baudet had concluded his remarks to Caffery by expressing "deep appreciation for shipping the United States has offered to make available in the Pacific" and emphasized the importance of obtaining ships "from the British to send to Indo-China the French military forces necessary to restore order."[2] It was evident these were the ships used by General Leclerc to bring his troops to Saigon. Later, in October and December 1945, they brought more French troops to Haiphong.

On 15 January 1946 the Secretary of War was advised by State that it was contrary to U.S. policy to "employ American flag vessels or aircraft to transport troops of any nationality to or from the Netherlands East Indies or French Indochina, nor to permit the use of such craft to carry arms, ammunition or military equipment to these areas."[3] Still, only three days later, when H. Freeman Matthews who was head of the Office of European Affairs asked Mr. Acheson for guidance on a British request to transfer to the French some eight hundred jeeps and trucks, then in Saigon, and which had been given to the British under Lend-Lease, Acheson replied that "the President thought that we should agree to the transfer" on the grounds that removing the equipment would be "impracticable."[4] These transfers of military resources clearly showed that existing directives were being bent.

From mid-November 1945 to March 1946 copies of several telegrams and letters from Ho Chi Minh to the President, the Secretary of State, the Chairman of the Senate Committee on Foreign Relations, and the United Nations reached my desk. They were earnest appeals for intervention in Viet Nam on the basis of the principles embodied in the Atlantic Charter and on humanitarian grounds. In the main they asked for political support in the Vietnamese quest for independence, citing the example of the United States in the Philippines and expressing the hope that the French would follow the American example. I inquired at State if the letters and telegrams were being acknowledged or at least being seriously considered by anyone in authority and was told that the DRV "government" was not recognized by the United States and that it would be "improper" for the President or anyone in authority to acknowledge such correspondence. Further, the United States was "committed" to look to the French rather than to the Vietnamese nationalists for constructive steps towards Vietnamese independence.

After the 6 January 1946 elections of the DRV's first Provisional Coalition Government, I was approached by Abbot Low Moffat who headed the Division for Southeast Asian Affairs at State. He asked me for background information on Ho Chi Minh, and I provided him with what we had. It was extensive, particularly his career in the Comintern and his association with the Chinese Communist Party. But, above all, I emphasized Ho's nationalist character—that of a Vietnamese patriot first and communist second. I noted that on several occasions Ho had voiced to me his disappointment with both the Soviet government and the communists of the world for not lending his cause for independence even moral support. Only the United States, albeit in vague terms, had spoken out for self-determination, and Ho had responded by dissolving the Indochinese Communist Party (11 November 1945).

Ho was desperately trying to align his newborn nation with the West and he wanted to put to rest the French charges that he and his Viet Minh were tools of Moscow, but we took no notice of his signal. In due time I went on to other assignments unrelated to the Far East as I watched the dénouement in Indochina. It was for me a time of sober observation because I remained totally convinced that no amount of opposition would deflect the Vietnamese from pursuing their independence, whatever the cost or however long it might take. To me it was regrettable that our own nation was not coming to terms with that reality and charting a course which would serve our own best interests—perhaps just staying completely out of it and maintaining a truly neutral stance, both materially and in our planning concepts.

Events in Indochina took their predictable course. The Chinese lingered long enough to get the maximum "squeeze" from the French: between 28 February and 14 March 1946 the French signed a series of agreements with the Chinese yielding their prewar rights and privileges in China. According to the 14 March agreement, the relief of the Chinese occupation army would begin on 15 March and be completed by the thirty-first, but in fact the last Chinese unit did not leave Haiphong until October 1946. Meanwhile Chiang Kai-shek's commercial and financial agents masterfully had laid a solid base in Indochina for an exploitative economic operation that lasted for well over thirty years. We see them now as "boat people."

Abandoned by the United States, ignored by the communist world, pressured by the insatiable Chinese, Ho Chi Minh entered into a tenuous "accord," on 6 March 1946, not with the Paris government but with a lesser official representing the military in Indochina. As Ho was soon to learn, the accord did not bear the imprimatur of the Quai d'Orsay, and the provisions binding the French to recognize the DRV as a "Free State" having "its own parliament, its own Army, and its own finances" was never honored.

Instead, French forces promptly occupied Hanoi on 18 March. A month later Allied occupation was officially terminated and Leclerc's troops (transported, armed, and equipped largely with American Lend-Lease materiel) occupied Viet Nam's major cities. The question of American policy toward Indochina then shifted from the context of wartime strategy to the political-economic arena of America's relationship with France.

The 6 March accord was quickly followed by the Dalat Conference (April-May) where the "Saigon clique" headed by the "French Rasputin," d'Argenlieu, temporarily severed Cochinchina from Viet Nam, and then by the disastrous Fontainebleau Conference (July-September) where Ho signed the short-lived modus vivendi. Ho's willingness to cooperate, at least temporarily, with the French alarmed both the pro-Chinese nationalists and the French colonial interests. The continued survival of Ho and his Viet Minh would undoubtedly spell their eventual demise, and that they wanted to avoid at all costs. Through influential channels in Chungking and Paris another campaign was launched against Ho and the Viet Minh, again employing the old scare tactics of their being the loyal agents of Moscow.

By the summer of 1946 the word had reached Washington, and all official references to Ho were prefixed "communist." On 5 December 1946 Acheson provided Moffat, then visiting Indochina, with departmental guidance in the event he were to meet with Ho. Acheson's lead paragraph in the telegram contained the caveat, "Keep in mind Ho's clear record as agent international communism . . . ,"[5] despite the fact that Kremlin-directed conspiracy was found in virtually all countries *except* Viet Nam. We had no evidence of any Viet Nam-Moscow ties. The Soviet Union not only failed to support Ho through his early struggles for independence but also refused to recognize the DRV until several years later.

Returning from Fontainebleau "empty handed," Ho faced violent opposition from his detractors in the VNQDD and the Dong Minh Hoi. Charges of "betrayal" and "collaboration" were hurled at him and the Viet Minh, along with demands that he step down. To avoid bloodshed and get approval of the Fontainebleau agreement, Ho convened the second session of the National Assembly and secured approval of the modus vivendi, forestalling French opposition. And the Assembly gave Ho a vote of confidence and requested him to reconstitute the cabinet. On 8 November the new cabinet consisted of seven communists, two Democrats, one Socialist, one VNQDD, and one independent. So the Viet Minh was in full control for the moment, but the modus vivendi lasted barely seventy days.

The end began on 20 November when an armed clash took place in the port of Haiphong between the French Navy and Viet Minh shore troops over customs control. The exchange lasted two days before a local agreement ended the dispute. But Admiral d'Argenlieu, then in Paris and indignant at what he deemed Vietnamese effrontery, cabled his deputy in Saigon, Brigadier General Jean Valluy, to "teach those insolent Annamites a lesson." Three days later the French delivered an ultimatum to the Viet Minh authorities demanding the withdrawal of their troops from the area within two hours. When it was ignored, French troops supported by offshore batteries from the cruiser *Suffren* attacked the Chinese quarters in the port city resulting in some twenty-five thousand casualties, including six thousand dead.

Surprised by the ruthless attack, Ho, still the negotiator, tried to avoid a full-scale confrontation and appealed to the French for a cease-fire. The French military, encouraged by d'Argenlieu's disdain for Ho and his DRV government, and looking for an excuse to torpedo the Fontainebleau agreement and to eliminate once and for all the dreaded Viet Minh, ignored Ho's call for moderation and intensified their attacks. On 19 December the local militia (*Tu Ve*) destroyed the Hanoi power station, signaling a general attack on the French. Ho and his government fled into the jungle. Thus the Indochina war, which had been originally sparked by Cédile's coup in Saigon but to some extent contained through French military force and Ho's attempts to negotiate, became a full-scale reality.

۵ ۵ ۵

As the Vietnamese and the French faced off for their protracted war, our decision to assist the French in the form of military aid, which was rooted in economic considerations and European politics, was aired as a simple, ideological decision—an anticommunist one. In 1947 Greece was in economic chaos and under attack from communist guerrillas. Turkey was under pressure from Russia for concessions in the Dardanelles. If successful, these communist efforts would have expanded Soviet influence into the eastern Mediterranean. President Truman therefore announced, in what became known as the Truman Doctrine, that "it must be the policy of the United States to support free people" against direct and indirect communist aggression. The result was that with American economic aid Greece revived her economy and with American military aid Greece put down the communist guerrilla attacks. Likewise bolstered by American economic and military aid, Turkey withstood Russian demands for control of the Dardanelles.

Domestic economic exigencies demanded continued production and outflow of American products, either in the form of trade or aid. In 1947 Secretary of State Marshall offered American economic aid to all European nations, including Russia and her satellites: "Our policy is directed not against any country or doctrine but against hunger, poverty, desperation and chaos." Pragmatically the United States wanted to help Europe, to end the need for the less profitable outpouring of American relief funds, to stimulate a mutually beneficial trade between the United States and Europe, and to lessen the danger of communism in Western Europe, especially in France and Italy. American foreign policymakers feared that if Western Europe came under Soviet domination, together they would constitute an overwhelmingly powerful military and economic bloc and irrevocably endanger American national interests worldwide. In its four years (1948–1951) the Marshall Plan, known officially as the European Recovery Program (ERP), provided Western Europe with $12.5 billion, most of which was spent in this country for foodstuffs, raw materials, and machinery. It sustained our domestic economy and at the same time furthered political stability abroad and reduced communist influence.

Russia condemned the Marshall Plan as an American scheme to gain economic and political control over Europe, which in part it was. She refused to accept any of the aid for herself or her European satellites and initiated her own economic aid program, the Council of Mutual Economic Assistance (COMECON). This competition incited the United States to greater efforts in world domination. In his 1949 Inaugural Address, President Truman reaffirmed America's opposition to Soviet expansion by extending American foreign aid to providing technological skills, knowledge, and equipment to poor nations. The new program, known as the Point Four program, also encouraged the flow of private investment capital to underdeveloped nations with the ultimate objective of winning their support.

The struggle for ideological and economic control between the two superpowers spilled over into the strategic arena in 1948, when the free world nations were shocked by three Soviet-engineered aggressions—the coup d'état in Czechoslovakia, the pressure on Finland to enter the Soviet orbit, and the Berlin crisis. In 1949, the United States led twelve free world nations in forming the North Atlantic Treaty Organization (NATO), a mutual defense pact which insured collective security but also provided an outlet for the production of new strategic material manufactured in the key nations of the organization—the United States, Great Britain, France, and, later, Germany.

Hence, the cycle was completed—from the ideological to the economic (ERP, Point Four), to the strategic (NATO, later ANZUS and SEATO). As in the ideological and economic conflicts, the Soviet Union responded with strategic alliances—the Chinese-Soviet Treaty (1950) and the Warsaw Pact (1955).

It was not until January 1953 that an American leader honestly defined our national interests for what they actually were and still are. In his Inaugural Address, President Eisenhower declared:

We know that we are linked to all free peoples not merely by a noble idea but by a simple need. No free people can for long cling to any privilege or enjoy any safety in economic solitude. For all our own material might, even we need markets in the world for the surpluses of our farms and factories. Equally, we need for the same farms and factories vital materials and products of distant lands. This basic law of interdependence, so manifest in the commerce of peace, applies with thousandfold intensity in the event of war.

Eisenhower clearly stated what most of us know but seldom acknowledge, that our national interests are best served by commercial transactions, especially when these provide the raw materials (foreign resources) needed to produce exportable products manufactured in the United States and sold in foreign markets.

۵ ۵ ۵

American concern for national security manifested itself in active opposition to its principal contender for world spheres of influence, the Soviet Union. This was first expressed on the popular plane solely as an ideological opposition to monolithic communism. The cracks that appeared in that monolith from time to time were not given much play, as for instance the complete break in 1948 between Tito's communist government of Yugoslavia and the Soviet Union, after which Tito stopped his assistance to the communist guerrillas of Greece. There was also the very wobbly position of the strong French communist leadership which abandoned the Vietnamese cause in favor of their own political jockeying in France. The French recognized very early on how well they could put to use the ideological fears existing in America. The threat that France might "go Communist" brought swift results, and labeling Vietnamese nationalism as "Red" or "Moscow-directed" completely forestalled any move by the American government to explore possible avenues with the Ho government. It was a form of blackmail that worked very well over an extended period.

Immediately after the outbreak of French-Viet Nam hostilities, the Department of State on 8 January 1947 instructed Ambassador Caffery in Paris to let the French know that we empathized with the French and were prepared to use our "good offices" to help resolve the dispute. He was to let them know that the United States would approve the sales of arms to France "except in cases which appear related to Indochina."[6] The French wasted no time in replying. On the same day the French Embassy in Washington conveyed France's appreciation for Mr. Acheson's "understanding attitude in discussing the problem of Indochina" and politely turned down our "good offices" with the barb that France would work out its problems without outside help "once it had reasserted its authority." Picking up the old refrain of American culpability for

France's dilemma in Southeast Asia, the French emissary noted that regarding the question of French authority in Indochina the United States must share the responsibility for their delay in asserting that authority because we "had not acceded to French requests in the autumn of 1945, for material assistance."

Concerned with French misunderstanding of our position on Indochina and a possible French defection in Europe, Caffery was instructed in early February 1947 to reassure Premier Ramadier of the "very friendliest feelings" of the United States toward France and its interest in supporting France's recovering economic, political, and military strength. After assuring Ramadier that the United States recognized French sovereignty in Indochina, we moralized on the question of colonies as "outmoded." On Ho Chi Minh, Caffery was instructed to say that we do not lose sight of the fact that he "has direct Communist connections" and it should be obvious that "we are not interested in seeing colonial empire administration supplanted by philosophy and political organizations emanating from and controlled by Kremlin."[7] Thus, the United States chose to remain outside the conflict and yet not censure France for its aggressive role in Viet Nam.

But with the passing weeks American policy began to take shape. On 13 May 1947 our diplomats in Paris, Saigon, and Hanoi were given this official guidance:

> Key our position in our awareness that . . . in southern Asia, we essentially [are] in [the] same boat as French, also as British and Dutch. . . . We should regard close association of France and members of the French Union as not only to the advantage of people concerned, but indirectly [to] our own . . . southern Asia is in a critical phase . . . with seven new nations in process of achieving or struggling for independence or autonomy. These nations include a quarter of the inhabitants of the world and their future course, . . . will be momentous factor to world stability. Following relaxation of European controls, . . . could plunge new nations into violent discord, . . . anti-Western Pan-Asiatic tendencies could become dominant political force, or Communists could capture control. We consider as best safeguard against these eventualities a continued close association between newly-autonomous peoples and powers which have long been responsible for their welfare. In particular we recognize [that] Vietnamese will for indefinite period require French material and technical assistance and enlightened political guidance which can be provided only by nation steeped like France in democratic tradition and confirmed in respect for human liberties and worth of the individual.[8]

Our policymakers in Washington, sensing an inevitable and irreparable loss of critical resources to the West European nations, were buttressing the colonial powers but, with atypical candor and almost panic, the official guidance continued:

> . . . evidence that French Communist(s) are being directed to accelerate their agitation [in] French colonies even [to the] extent [they] might lose much popular support [in] France may be indication [the] Kremlin [is] prepared [to] sacrifice temporary gains with 40 million French to long range colonial strategy with 600 million

dependent people, which lends great urgency foregoing views. . . . Department much concerned lest French efforts find "true representatives Vietnam" with whom negotiations result [in the] creation [of] impotent government along lines of Cochinchina regime, or that restoration [of] Baodai [sic] may be attempted, implying democracies reduced resort [to] monarchy as weapon against Communism.[9]

The specter of communist penetration in areas considered the exclusive fief of Western democracies had compelled our State Department to reassess its position. Although the United States officially regarded the war in Indochina as fundamentally a French problem, the protracted conflict appeared to favor the Vietnamese nationalists—that is, the communists. American suggestions to the French that they make meaningful concessions to the Vietnamese nationalists always stopped short of endorsing the only logical and effective leader, Ho Chi Minh. Accordingly, American policy gravitated with that of France toward the Bao Dai solution—not because he was a nationalist of sorts, but because he was not communist. At that point, the United States was obviously less concerned with Vietnamese nationalism than with stemming the "Red tide."

The American policy of nonintervention came to an end in 1949. Peiping fell to the Chinese Communists in January of that year, and Washington reacted aggressively to French dawdling in granting the Vietnamese the promised autonomy. Following the Elysée Agreement (signed in March 1949), the Department of State instructed the American Consul in Saigon on 10 May to let it be known that the United States desired the "Bao Dai experiment" to succeed "since there appeared to be no other alternative." It also hinted at American willingness to do its part by extending recognition to the Bao Dai government and by providing arms and economic assistance under the proper circumstances. This was the bait dangled before the French to get them moving. Acheson emphasized to our Consul the "urgency and necessity" for a prompt resolution of the differences between the French and the Vietnamese "in view of the possibly short time remaining before Communist successes in China are felt in Indochina."[10] This pattern of day-to-day, country-by-country response to an innate fear of communism plagued the United States throughout the next quarter of a century in our relations with Viet Nam and is still the hallmark of American foreign policy in dealing with the USSR and world communism.

✿ ✿ ✿

Events in China in 1948 and 1949 brought the United States to a new awareness of the vigor of communism in Asia and to a sense of urgency over its containment. American policy instruments developed to meet unequivocal communist challenges in Europe were applied without much modification to the quite different problems of the Far East. Concurrent with the development of NATO, an American search began for collective security in Asia. Economic and military assistance programs were inaugurated, and the Truman Doctrine acquired wholly new dimensions by extension into regions where the European colonial empires were being dismantled. Thus, in the closing months of 1949, the course of American policy was to block further communist expansion in Asia by collective security if the Asians were forthcoming, and by collaboration with major European allies and Commonwealth nations, if possible, but bilaterally if necessary. On that policy course lay the Korean War (1950–53), the forming of the Southeast Asia Treaty Organization (SEATO) of 1954, and the progressively deepening American involvement in Viet Nam.

The French, on 30 December 1949, signed a series of agreements relating to the transfer of internal administration in Viet Nam to Bao Dai's state of Viet Nam, in accordance with the Elysée Agreement of the previous March. By January 1950 Mao's legions had reached Viet Nam's northern frontier, and North Viet Nam was moving into the Sino-Soviet orbit. On 18 January the People's Republic of China recognized the DRV and both signed a trade agreement in Peking for military aid. Twelve days later the USSR recognized the DRV. The Moscow press facetiously explained that Russia was merely recognizing a government France had recognized in 1946. Why Ho and his DRV had not been recognized before was not explained.

Still reacting, Secretary Acheson on the following day (1 February) publicly expressed "surprise" at the Kremlin's recognition of the DRV and said the Soviet action "should remove any illusions as to the 'nationalist' nature of Ho Chi Minh's aims and reveals Ho in his true colors as the mortal enemy of native independence in Indochina."[11] Apparently it had not occurred to Mr. Acheson that only Ho Chi Minh had for over a quarter of a century kept the torch for independence burning in the hearts and minds of the Vietnamese, both communist and noncommunist, that he alone had become the personification of Vietnamese nationalism—a sort of Vietnamese George Washington. While calling Ho another George Washington may be stretching a point, there is no doubt of his being the only popularly recognized leader of the Vietnamese resistance and the head of the strongest and only nationwide independence movement. He had long since become "Uncle Ho" to the poor and humble, with a charisma that successive puppet regimes were never able to overcome. However, these facts escaped our Secretary of State whose experience had been largely associated with the European colonial powers which consistently denigrated indigenous colonial populations. They had stopped calling them "the natives" but the thought remained.

Formal French ratification of Vietnamese "independence" was announced on the second of February. This "independence" when carefully examined is revealed as largely new window dressing behind which the old colonial structure remained intact. However, on the day of French ratification, Acheson in a memorandum to the President recommended official recognition of "the three legally constituted governments of Vietnam, Laos and Cambodia." He described Ho as a "communist agent . . . since 1925" and as one who had "harassed the French ever since" and noted that Communist China [on 18 January] and Soviet Russia [on 30

January) had recognized "Ho Chi Minh as the head of the legal Government of Vietnam. . . ."[12] Here again is reflected the Administration's communist-phobia and an ad hoc reaction to Sino-Soviet moves.

Much can be deduced from Acheson's rationale in recommending to the President immediate recognition of the French puppet governments. In the fourth paragraph of his memorandum, he said that recognition

> appears desirable and in accordance with United States foreign policy for several reasons. Among them are: encouragement to national aspirations under non-Communist leadership for peoples of colonial areas in Southeast Asia; the establishment of stable non-Communist governments in areas adjacent to Communist China; support to a friendly country which is also a signatory to the North Atlantic Treaty; and a demonstration of displeasure with Communist tactics. . . .[13]

Nowhere in his reasoning does one find any allusion to American principles of democracy, freedom, independence, or self-determination. Instead there is a strong endorsement of continued colonialism administered by a European ally, financed by American dollars, and in the interest of the economic elite. The basic cause of the conflict, independence from foreign domination, was cavalierly brushed aside to accommodate "a friendly country" and to secure for ourselves a strategic enclave in Southeast Asia. It was indeed a strange image of American democracy we presented to subject peoples.

Nonetheless, the next day President Truman approved American recognition of Bao Dai and the Associated States of Indochina, and on 4 February our Consul General at Saigon was instructed to deliver to the ex-emperor a congratulatory message from our President and diplomatic recognition of the government of the Republic of Viet Nam.[14]

The French lost no time in asking for American aid. Irritated with American pressure to get on with the "Bao Dai solution" and to grant the Vietnamese greater autonomy, the French entered into the oriental game of "squeeze." On 16 February the French Foreign Office called in our Ambassador in Paris and without mincing words told him that "as a result of recent developments [in China] and the expectation that at least increased military aid will be furnished to Ho Chi Minh from Communist China" the French position had become extremely grave. Further, ". . . the effort in Indochina was such a drain on France that a long-term program of assistance was necessary and it was only from the United States that it could come. Otherwise . . . it was very likely that France might be forced to [consider] cutting her losses and withdrawing from Indochina."[15]

The matter was brought before the National Security Council which concluded on 27 February "that all practicable measures be taken to prevent further Communist expansion in Southeast Asia. . . . Thailand and Burma could be expected to fall under Communist domination if Indochina were controlled by a Communist-dominated government. The balance of Southeast Asia would then be in grave hazard."[16] This was probably the germination of the "domino theory." The action was passed to the Joint Chiefs of Staff who supported the NSC conclusion and recommended to the Secretary of Defense to provide the assistance sought for the French in Indochina. On 1 May the President quietly approved the allocation of $10 million for military items,[17] thus making the first crucial decision regarding American military involvement in Viet Nam.

Acheson, who had traveled to Paris to discuss firsthand the French demands and assure them they would be met, released a public statement on 8 May, saying that he agreed with the Foreign Minister as to the "urgency of the situation" and as to the need for "remedial action." Then, recognizing Viet Nam, Cambodia, and Laos as "independent states" within the French Union, Acheson concluded that the primary responsibility for their security rested jointly with the three separate governments—and France. Accordingly, the United States would grant economic aid and military equipment to the Associated States of Indochina and to France.[18]

No funds had been appropriated by Congress specifically for Indochina, but that fact did not deter the francophiles in the Department of State from jumping into the fray. On 11 May Acting Secretary of State James E. Webb in Washington announced that the Department was working on plans to carry out "at once" a program of economic and technical assistance for Indochina costing in the neighborhood of a "modest $60 million." The monies for the program would come from Economic Cooperation Administration (ECA) China Aid funds, part of which both Houses of Congress had indicated would be made available for the "general area of China." As to the military assistance, Webb circumspectly noted that it was "being worked out by the Department of Defense in cooperation with the Department of State," adding that "the details will not be made public for security reasons." However, Webb did reveal that monies for military items would "be met from the President's emergency fund of $75 million" provided under the Mutual Defense Assistance Program (MDAP) "for the general area of China."[19] Readers will perceive that the era of a fiercely independent American Congress still lay far in the future.

Hence, without further discussion, the United States was irrevocably committed to support a French puppet regime in a war against Vietnamese nationalists and to protect French colonial interests in Southeast Asia in the developing tragedy that was Viet Nam. American assistance, which began modestly with $10 million in 1950, exceeded $1 *billion* in fiscal 1954 *alone,* at which time it accounted for 78 percent of the cost of the French war burden.

ʊ ʊ ʊ

Despite the strong francophile clique in our Department of State, there were also many realists among our Foreign Service officers who were concerned with American interests first. They viewed our involvement, rightly or wrongly, as a necessary means of averting Indochina's sliding into the communist camp, rather than helping France as a colonial power or as a NATO ally. Although the end result was not altered, these individuals joined other policymakers in the Administration in encouraging the French to grant the Associated States full independence.

Unfortunately French objectives still did not coincide with the American goal of decolonization of Indochina and of creating an anticommunist buffer state between Communist China and the states of Southeast Asia. Throughout the period of our assistance to the French military effort (1950–1954) one could plainly hear echoes of 1945 in American-French relations. As in the 1945 experience, the United States was severely constrained in what it could do. Our Military Mission (MAAG) in Saigon was small and limited in its function by the French to a supply-support group. Allocation of all American aid to the Associated States had to be made, by agreement, solely through France. MAAG officers were not given the freedom to develop intelligence information on the course of the war; information supplied by the French was limited, often unreliable, sometimes deliberately misleading. The French resisted repeated American admonitions that the native armies of the Associated States should be built up and until they were they would not constitute a true national Vietnamese army—a lesson which we did not learn even when we were in charge.

It is an historical fact that in each of our ventures to stem the spread of Marxist ideology we became confused and consistently failed to recognize the first cause of the discontent which leads subject peoples to search for a better life. Despite our good intentions, in holding that our form of democracy is the only answer, we fail to accept for other peoples the basic tenet of democracy—the right to self-determination. The inclination of American leadership is to meet the "threat" of communism with economic and military leverage, which in each instance has backfired. And where we have succeeded in imposing our life style for a time, it has often proved thankless, costly, and agonizing.

As the echoes of 1945 still ring clear, we cannot resist speculating: was Southeast Asia important to the security interest of the United States in 1905?. Was the domino theory valid? Could we have won the war without Vietnamese popular support? And could we have fought on the side of France and avoided the stigma of colonialism? Although these questions are still debated, the weight of evidence then and now still says, "No" to each. In the light of our experience in the forties, our alliance with France during the fifties and our subsequent direct involvement with Ngo Dinh Diem and Nguyen Van Thieu were sheer folly. We never paused to listen to the vox populi. Despite our proud heritage of anticolonialism, our Wilsonian principle of self-determination, and Rooseveltian pronouncements of independence for subject peoples, we turned a deaf ear to Vietnamese pleas for liberation from foreign domination and colonial rule.

It would be vacuous to say our government did not know the nature of the problem in Indochina; or that there was no popular leader; or that the Vietnamese were incapable of self-government. Ho Chi Minh, even under various aliases, was known to the Western world since 1919. American officials knew of him and what he had accomplished to unite his people in the cause for independence since 1942 and followed his progress until he died in 1969. The apologists in our Department of State are hard-pressed to justify their supposed ignorance of Ho's nationalist character and the sincerity of his movement for independence. Their own departmental files dating from 1942 reveal that Ho and the Viet Minh were singularly nationalist and without foreign political commitments until 1950.

Even as late as February 1950 the constant and offhand allusions to Ho as a "Commie" or "agent of international communism," without provable evidence, naively influenced our foreign policy and lost us one more opportunity for a peaceable accommodation with the people of Indochina. In May 1949 Secretary Acheson, although lacking the least shred of evidence of Ho's ties to the Kremlin, instructed the U.S. representative in Hanoi to warn the Vietnamese nationalists against any acceptance of a coalition with Ho in the following terms:

In light Ho's known background, no other assumption possible but that he [is an] outright Commie so long as (1) he fails unequivocally [to] repudiate Moscow connections and Commie doctrine and (2) remains personally singled out for praise by international Commie press and receives its support. Moreover, U.S. not impressed by nationalist character red flag with yellow stars [sic].[20]

This was only a prelude to his later and public excoriation of Ho "in his true colors as the mortal enemy of independence in Indochina," which again foreclosed any relations with Ho in February 1950.

Whether Ho was a nationalist or a communist should not have been the issue. The fact remained that he was a nationalist first, a communist second. Ho was more concerned with Viet Nam's independence and sovereign viability than with following the interests and dictates of Moscow and Peking. With American support Ho might have adopted some form of neutrality in the East-West conflict and maintained the DRV as a neutral and durable bulwark against Chinese expansion southward. The Vietnamese had already demonstrated a fear of Chinese domination and continue to do so and have good reasons of their own for acting in a buffer capacity. Were it not for our "communist blinders," Ho could well have served the larger purpose of American policy in Asia.

In the late forties several arguments were advanced in support of Ho's leadership. There were those who maintained that a different American policy could have moved Ho to nonalignment and opposition to Peking; others, this author included, stressed the corollary that Ho was forced into dependence upon Peking and Moscow by American opposition or indifference.

Ho was a communist; he told me so himself and he never denied it when the question was put to him by foreign journalists. But being a communist did not imply that he was unwilling to subordinate communist goals, forms, and international discipline to attain Viet Nam's independence and unity. On more than one occasion Ho and other leaders of the Viet Minh expressed to me serious doubts about communism as a political form suitable for Viet Nam. Ho particularly was not sure that the Vietnamese were sufficiently mature politically to accept communism—perhaps a modified form of democratic socialism was the answer.

But whatever Ho might have preferred in the late forties, neutralism, western affiliation, socialism, or other noncommunist forms, he was offered only narrow options. He had no direct communication with the United States after 1946, and the signals he received from Washington could hardly have been encouraging. By 1947, American military equipment had already been used by French and British forces against the Vietnamese, and the United States had arranged credit for French purchases of $160 million worth of vehicles and industrial equipment for use in the war in Indochina. Marshall's January 1947 public statement on Viet Nam had been confined to a hope that "a pacific basis for adjustment of the difficulties could be found." And the Marshall Plan for Europe definitely threw American resources behind France. Assurances from the Russians were not materially stronger. While the Soviets excoriated colonial powers *other than France*, the imminent possibility of a French Communist government silenced even a verbal backing of Ho, let alone recognition and aid.

As a pragmatist Ho quickly realized that Viet Nam came second to France in American foreign policy and that Viet Nam could not anticipate preferential treatment from Mother Russia while she struggled for preeminence in Europe. In 1946 Ho put his plight in stark terms: "We apparently stand quite alone; we shall have to depend on ourselves." So the military struggle in Viet Nam continued and the French position often appeared to be strong, but huge areas of the countryside remained undefeated. French supremacy was largely confined to the cities and highways.

After 1947 events took a somewhat better turn for Ho. His prospects for American support from 1947 to 1949 were never good and in 1950 vanished completely, but Mao Tse-tung was moving by leaps and bounds in China against Chiang Kai-shek and by 1950 was in a position to come to Ho's assistance across his northern border. Ho no longer was in isolation; he had allies, first China and then the Soviet Union. A new ballgame had begun.   ✪ ✪ ✪

What had happened to the French regime in Indochina since the collapse of the modus vivendi at the end of 1946? In 1947–48 the "Saigon clique" began to admit the possibility of some limited Vietnamese participation in the government of Indochina—but not with the Viet Minh. The imperious d'Argenlieu vehemently maintained that no talks with Ho and his followers were possible but advanced the idea that a return to "the traditional monarchist institution" was the only plausible solution. He sent an emissary to Hong Kong to establish contact with the former emperor. Bao Dai's first reaction was one of distrust, and he was averse to any dealings with d'Argenlieu, the abomination of Viet Nam. Nor was he willing to repudiate Ho Chi Minh whom he admired as a true patriot and whom, in theory, he continued to serve as "Supreme Political Counselor."

Bao Dai was not just the royal playboy, the "Farouk of the Far East" or the *"empereur de boîtes de nuit,"* as the French loved to call him, but was also a cautious and calculating politician. Nor was he a mere French puppet, ready to please the French for favors or money, as can be seen from the fact that they had to court him for over two years before he agreed, as the French saw it, to play their game. Actually, it was Bao Dai's game to rid Viet Nam of French domination for he, too, in his own way, was a nationalist.

It was d'Argenlieu's recall early in 1947 and other events that led Bao Dai to reconsider. D'Argenlieu's recall was instigated by the intense dislike in which he was held by the Vietnamese in Indochina and the Socialists and Communists in France. The Ramadier government in 1947 took the position that France was willing to negotiate a peace settlement with "authentic representatives of Viet Nam." This had a ring of truth but it was an uncomfortable compromise between the Communists and some Socialists of France, who wished to reopen talks with Ho, and the right-wing MRP of France, who would have no truck with Ho. At the same time things were not going well for Ho; he was neither strategically nor politically secure. He was holed up in the jungle and the French had control of the larger cities and towns. On 21 March, Ho made a statement in which he "solemnly declared" that the Vietnamese people only desired unity and independence "within the French Union," and he guaranteed "to respect French economic and cultural interests in Viet Nam." Never were the chances for a settlement better than in that spring of 1947.

At that point a new ingredient emerged. The pro-Chinese VNQDD, the Dai Viet, and the Dong Minh Hoi, encouraged by Chiang's Kuomintang, by the Chinese warlords, and by the United States, formed a new political grouping called the National Union Front. It has been described as a fragile coalition of discredited collaborators, ambitious masters of intrigue, incompetent sectarians, and a smattering of honest leaders without a following. Among the last category was Ngo Dinh Diem who for the first and only time joined a party of which he was not the founder. The National Union Front soon made contact with certain conservative and "separatist" elements in Cochinchina such as the Cao Dai, the Hoa Hao, and the Social-Democratic Party of Cochinchina. The group met in Canton and agreed among themselves to withdraw their support of Ho Chi Minh in favor of Bao Dai. Although these elements were almost wholly discredited among the Vietnamese people, the French found that it suited their interests to encourage them.

D'Argenlieu's successor, the Radical Socialist parliamentarian,

Émile Bollaert, arrived in Saigon on 1 April to face two contending factions, the "legal" government of Viet Nam operating from the jungle and the various groups making up the National Union Front. Off in the background was Bao Dai. Ho's Foreign Minister, Hoang Minh Giam, met with Bollaert on 19 April and made a formal peace offer, but the opportunity for a peaceful settlement again was lost because the French terms were tantamount to a Viet Minh surrender.

Meanwhile the National Union Front, now supported by Vietnamese Catholics, advocated the "Bao Dai solution." The French, fully aware of the "playboy" king's predilection for worldly pleasures, believed they could manipulate him as they had in 1933 when he was a very young man. From their point of view, a united and superficially "independent" Viet Nam under Bao Dai was the lesser of two evils and the only practical answer. They reasoned that his following included the traditionalists and the right-wing nationalists, as well as the affluent mandarin class, a plus for French capitalism and the Bank of Indochina. In America it would conveniently assuage anticommunist elements, and it would also calm anticolonialist prejudice with French promises of gradual autonomy for Indochina.

What was constantly overlooked, however, even by the Americans until 1965, was that militarily Viet Nam could not be "pacified" without an increase of French forces in Indochina by several hundred thousand men. In France, the MRP mistakenly assumed that with Bao Dai on the throne Viet Minh resistance would rapidly vanish, while the Socialists hoped that Bao Dai might somehow act as a mediator and entice the Viet Minh to join the National Union Front.

To put an end to the protracted conflict, the French pressured the National Union Front to appeal to Bao Dai to form a central government. Their delegation called on the former emperor in Hong Kong in May 1947, but still the former emperor hesitated. Bao Dai, the patriot, did not consider the National Union Front representative of the people and he did not want to endorse a French-sponsored government. He would have preferred some accommodation with the Viet Minh which he considered the most vital force in Viet Nam. But Bao Dai, the politician, recognized that the MRP in Paris, which by the summer of 1947 was calling the shots, would never come to terms with Ho. So he decided to take an active role and declared himself against the Viet Minh. It was rumored that he thought his action would encourage American support for himself against the French, just as the United States had used its influence in Indonesia against the Dutch.

With this hoped-for American support at the back of his mind, Bao Dai finally met with Bollaert aboard a French warship in Ha Long Bay.* They both initialed a protocol that promised independence in vague

*Also known as Baie d'Along and Along Bay.

terms, but only after Bao Dai had been assured that the document was purely a "record" of the negotiations and did not commit him to anything.[21] The document obligated the French to a measure of Vietnamese autonomy so minimal that it was promptly condemned by Diem as well as by more opportunistic colleagues in the National Union Front.

Bao Dai's intuition that the United States might look with favor on him was not entirely unfounded. Three weeks after he had initialed the protocol, *Life* magazine published an article by William C. Bullitt, our former Ambassador to France, in which Bullitt argued for a policy aimed at ending "the saddest war" by winning the majority of Vietnamese nationalists away from Ho Chi Minh through a movement built around Bao Dai. In France, Bullitt's views were widely accepted as a statement of American policy and a direct endorsement and promise of American aid for Bao Dai.

Despite what appeared to be an American endorsement, Bao Dai soon panicked over National Union Front condemnation of the meaningless accord he had initialed. Dissociating himself from the developing intrigue, he fled to European pleasure grounds for a four-month jaunt. Still, whether he accepted the Bullitt canard or not, Bao Dai seemed to sense that the United States would inevitably be drawn into Southeast Asia, and he apparently expected American involvement to be accompanied by American pressure on France on behalf of Vietnamese nationalism.

The French, despite the elusiveness of their principal, sent diplomats in pursuit of the royal traveler and publicized their resolve "to carry on, outside the Ho Chi Minh government, all activities and negotiations necessary for the restoration of peace and freedom in the Vietnamese countries"—in effect committing themselves to military victory and Bao Dai.

Bollaert caught up with Bao Dai in Geneva (January 1948) and held a series of meetings with him, in the course of which Bao Dai said that unless the Ha Long protocol was amended he would not return to Viet Nam. He next went to Cannes, then on to Paris to see for himself what was going on. In Paris he found that Indochina was a major and controversial issue among the various ministries, the rival political parties, the financial groups, and the politicians. Strong opposition to the initial accord was spearheaded by the ultraconservative gaullistes who maintained that it gave away far too much. Bao Dai returned to Hong Kong in March, still unwilling to commit himself.

Eventually French persistence and National Union Front pressures persuaded Bao Dai to have another go at negotiation with Bollaert, and they met again in Ha Long Bay on 5 June 1948. This time the protocol was "amended," and France "solemnly recognized the independence of Viet Nam"—but specifically retained control over foreign relations and the army and deferred the transfer of other governmental functions to future talks. No authority was in fact given to the Vietnamese.

The reaction in Indochina was explosive. The Viet Minh cried foul, for Bao Dai had squeezed from the French the magic word, "independence," for which Ho had fought in vain at Fontainebleau and which might now undermine popular support for the Viet Minh. They were wrong to be concerned, for the "Saigon clique" and its horde of colons were seeing to it that nothing significant was given away to the "Annamites." Their press clamored against Bollaert's "surrender" and called for the separation of Cochinchina from the north and turning it into a protectorate. The Paris politicians tried to calm the colons and assured them that nothing would be changed—the war had not ended. The MRP leaders and many people close to the MRP found a prolongation of the war highly profitable and were determined that it not end too soon.

Bao Dai again retired from the scene to Europe, while in Hanoi the French assembled a transparently impotent semblance of a native government. At Saint-Germain, Bao Dai advised Bollaert on 25 August that he would not return to Viet Nam so long as the colonial regime in Cochinchina had not been abolished and so long as he had no guarantee for the independence of Viet Nam. The next day French ministers in Paris were saying, *"Il commence vraiment à se foutre de nous."* It was becoming abundantly clear that Bao Dai ·was far from being the puppet and the "nightclub emperor" everyone had imagined.

Yet in the end (8 March 1949) he caved in and signed the much-acclaimed Auriol-Bao Dai accord, better known as the Elysée Agreement, under which the criticial elements of government were retained by the French and the old colonial structure remained intact. Why did Bao Dai yield to the French? It appeared that if he resisted much longer the French would find a substitute and Indochina would continue indefinitely as a French colony. Viet Minh influence would not abate and the last opportunity for a noncommunist peace would soon disappear. Bao Dai's trip to Paris the year before had convinced him that the hard line right wing was determined to go on with the war as long as it was profitable. To avoid all that, he decided to risk the Elysée Agreement with a view that once in power he could play an international game of his own making. He was banking heavily on American support that, he hoped, would restrain the French and provide Viet Nam with much-needed economic aid.

Once again we see Bao Dai as both a politician and a nationalist. After he signed the Elysée Agreement he tried to find a way to come to terms with Ho. In May word got out that Ho Chi Minh would not be excluded a priori from a new Bao Dai government. For all his fancy footwork with both the French and the Americans, Bao Dai had always believed that a truly representative government could not be had without the participation, or at least the tacit approval, of the Viet Minh which, in spite of everything, he continued to admire. Once back in Viet Nam he refused to declare himself hostile to what he himself called "the resistance."

The first task before the Emperor (he resumed the title "in order to have a legal international position") was to form a government, a task riddled with obstacles: French intransigence, popular indifference, and political opposition. In calculated fashion, the French procrastinated in carrying out the terms of the Elysée Agreement. Their troops remained; their administrators continued to staff every level of government; and no real power or authority was turned over to the Vietnamese. The State of Viet Nam, as it was now called, had become a camouflage for continued French rule.

When Bao Dai tried to force some progressive action from the French, Léon Pignon, the new High Commissioner and a d'Argenlieu man, told him that "French sovereignty would be transferred only to a government in which France had the fullest confidence."[22] But in the summer of 1949 Bao Dai's efforts to form a credible government were frustrated by a lack of confidence among honest men and the venality of the personally ambitious. Upright nationalists refused to serve when their expectations of autonomy proved groundless. In turning down the post of Prime Minister, Ngo Dinh Diem criticized the probity of those who did accept office:

The national aspirations of the Vietnamese people will be satisfied only on the day when our nation obtains the same political regime which India and Pakistan enjoy. . . . I believe it is only just to reserve the best posts in new Viet Nam for those who have merited most of the country: I speak of the resistance elements.[23]

Far from looking to the "resistance," Bao Dai chose his leaders from among men with strong identification with France, often men of great and tainted wealth or with ties with the subworlds of neomercantilism and Vietnamese vice. None commanded a popular following.

The Chief of Staff of the French army, General Georges Revers, was sent to Viet Nam (May-June 1949) to appraise the situation and later wrote:

If Ho Chi Minh has been able to hold off French intervention for so long, it is because the Viet Minh leader has surrounded himself with a group of men of incontestable worth. . . . [Bao Dai, by contrast, had] a government composed of twenty representatives of phantom parties, the best organized of which would have difficulty in rallying twenty-five adherents.[24]

But, in France, the government of Henri Queuille issued a self-congratulatory statement (8 September 1949) claiming to have "solved" the problem in Indochina by setting up the Bao Dai regime. It was idle talk. The "Bao Dai solution" had settled nothing in the long run, and the war in Indochina was continuing, digging deeper and deeper into France's economy and threatening to develop from a war of colonial reconquest into a war of international proportions.

Bao Dai himself did next to nothing to make his government either more representative or more efficient. He divided his time among the pleasures of the resort towns of Dalat, Nha Trang, and Ban Me Thout; for all practical purposes he remained outside the process of government. Perhaps in defense of his attitude and behavior, he characterized the situation in 1950 as follows: "What they call a Bao Dai solution turned out to be just a French solution. . . . The situation in Indochina is getting worse every day."[25] However, by early 1950, the Bao Dai government owed Ho Chi Minh a vote of thanks because Chinese Communist and Soviet recognition of the DRV brought American aid to France and to his regime and internationalized the war in Indochina.

At that juncture, France found its position vis-à-vis the United States awkward. If it were to justify its claim of fighting in defense of the Bao Dai government against the communists, it had little choice but to ratify the Elysée Agreement, to which the Bao Dai government owed its existence. Only then could France ask us for direct military aid for the war in Indochina. Having procrastinated for almost a year, France finally ratified the Agreement on 16 February 1950.

۞ ۞ ۞

While the United States could have exercised a decisive influence in 1945–46 in forcing a settlement of Vietnamese grievances and while France could have advantageously negotiated with the Vietnamese in the spring of 1947, by late 1949 and throughout 1950 a number of circumstances had gradually evolved which had the effect of freezing the course of events in a complex of knotty international issues.

At this period the American economy had witnessed a complete metamorphosis from war production to peacetime demands. The industrial infrastructure had also changed. The labor pool, which had lost its manpower to the armed forces from 1941 to 1945, was replenished with women, formerly independent of outside employment. After the war our greatly expanded productive capacity was utilized to satisfy a backlog of demand deferred in wartime and to provide a higher standard of living for the nation. Unprecedented levels of output for domestic consumer items and foreign economic aid were reached in most industries by 1947–48. But starting in late 1948 and extending into 1949 a readjustment became necessary in the reduction of inventories that were accumulating faster than profitable consumption warranted. Another aspect in the alteration of our postwar economy was the socioeconomic phenomenon of the double-wage earner in American society. With husband and wife working, their buying power increased disproportionately to their normal needs, resulting in sharp inflation and the reduction of the purchasing power of the dollar. These conditions subconsciously suggested a return to a "limited" war economy. Such was the economic state of the nation before the outbreak of the Korean conflict.

As the United States deliberated over whether to provide economic and military assistance to Indochina in early 1950, negotiations opened at Pau, France, between the Associated States and France, to set the timing and extent of granting autonomy to the Bao Dai regime. The talks, originally scheduled for January 1950, did not get under way until 29 June and dragged on to the end of November. Bao Dai, who had gone to France to help get the Elysée Agreement ratified, stayed on as an "observer" throughout the conferences, to the annoyance of the French who preferred him to be more helpful to them in Viet Nam and less interfering at Pau.

Although the Elysée and Pau agreements did produce some tangible results toward self-government, the French again retained control of the military, foreign affairs and trade, the judicial and financial systems. Despite the meager concessions, many Frenchmen viewed the Pau Conference as a disastrous abdication of French authority and as spelling the early demise of France in Southeast Asia. From the Vietnamese delegation's point of view, the results were considered a step forward. They felt that to get anything from the French you had to "nibble" at them, and that required both time and patience. They were wrong, of course, for France lost Indochina without ever giving the Vietnamese their independence. Bao Dai returned to Viet Nam feeling that he had done his utmost to urge France toward keeping its word. He would wait and see; perhaps American prodding would help. After a day in Saigon where the French denied him the use of the Norodom Palace, the seat of French colonial power, he retired to his home in Dalat. The symbolism in this fleeting event speaks volumes on the unchanging situation.

Had the talks led to genuine independence for Bao Dai's regime, the subsequent American-French relationship would probably have been much less complex and significantly less acerbic. Instead, France's reluctance to yield political or economic authority to Bao Dai was reinforced by a proclivity for fielding strong-willed French commanders who were suspicious of Americans, determined on a military victory, and scornful of the "Bao Dai solution." General Marcel Carpentier, Commander-in-Chief when the French applied for aid, was quoted in the *New York Times* (9 March 1950) as saying,

I will never agree to equipment being given directly to the Vietnamese. If this should be done I would resign within twenty-four hours. The Vietnamese have no generals, no colonels, no military organization that could effectively utilize the equipment. It would be wasted, and in China the United States has had enough of that.[26]

The Pleven government finally got rid of Pignon (December 1950) and appointed General Jean de Lattre de Tassigny as High Commissioner and Commander-in-Chief of the French Expeditionary Forces in Indochina, the first and only man to hold both positions. De Lattre electrified the discouraged French forces and regrouped them into a fighting corps. He saw himself as leading an anticommunist crusade that could win a decisive victory in Viet Nam within fifteen months and "save it from Peking

and Moscow." He deprecated the idea that the French were still motivated by colonialism and even told one American newsman:

We have no more interest here. . . . We have abandoned all our colonial positions
completely. There is little rubber or coal or rice we can any longer obtain. And
what does it amount to compared to the blood of our sons we are losing and the
three hundred and fifty million francs we spend a day in Indochina? The work we
are doing is for the salvation of the Vietnamese people. And the propaganda you
Americans make that we are still colonialists is doing us tremendous harm, all of
us—the Vietnamese, yourself, and us.[27]

Moreover, de Lattre was convinced that the Vietnamese had to be
brought into the fight. In a speech entitled "A Call to Vietnamese Youth,"
he declared:

This war, whether you like it or not, is the war of Viet Nam for Viet Nam. And
France will carry it on for you only if you carry it on with her. . . . Young men of
Viet Nam, to whom I feel as close as I do to the youth of my native land, the moment
has come for you to defend your country.[28]

Yet General de Lattre regarded American policy vis-à-vis Bao Dai
with great misgivings. Americans, he held, afflicted with "missionary
zeal," were "fanning the fires of extreme nationalism. . . . French tradi-
tionalism is vital here. You cannot, you must not destroy it. No one can
simply make a new nation overnight by giving out economic aid and arms
alone."[29] As adamantly as Carpentier, de Lattre opposed direct American
aid for Vietnamese forces and allowed the Vietnamese military little real
independence.

Our Minister Counselor in Saigon (from 1950 on), Edmund A. Gullion,
faulted de Lattre on his inability to stimulate in the Vietnamese National
Army either the *élan vital* or *dynamisme* he communicated to the rest of
the French Expeditionary Corps:

It remained difficult to inculcate nationalist ardor in a native army whose officers
and non-coms were primarily white Frenchmen. . . . The Vietnamese units that
went into action were rarely unsupported by the French. . . . Perhaps the most significant and saddest manifestation of the French failure to create a really independent Vietnamese Army that would fight in the way de Lattre meant was the
absence, at Dien Bien Phu, of any Vietnamese fighting elements. It was a French
show.[30]

Gullion erred somewhat with respect to Dien Bien Phu; the record on the
ethnic composition of the defending garrison indicates that as of 6 May
1954, the Vietnamese comprised less than 3 percent of the officers, 16.2
percent of the NCOs, and 39.2 percent of the enlisted men. But Gullion's
main thrust was valid. The Vietnamese army had little or no say in the
making of strategic or tactical decisions and little reason to fight
vigorously in a French-run war.

✿ ✿ ✿

In Washington the major considerations underlying our policymaking from 1950 to 1954 became the growing importance of Asia in world politics, our tendency to view the worldwide "communist threat" in monolithic terms, and the determined attempt of the Viet Minh regime to evict the French from Indochina. The last was construed as part of the Southeast Asia manifestation of the communist worldwide aggressive intent, and it explains the widely held assumption in official Washington that if Indochina was "lost," the rest of Southeast Asia would inexorably succumb to communist infiltration and be taken over in a chain reaction. This strategic concept predated the outbreak of the Korean War in June 1950. It probably had its period of gestation at the time of the Nationalist withdrawal from mainland China (December 1949), after Secretary of Defense Louis Johnson had expressed concern at the course of events in Asia and had suggested a widening of the previous country-by-country approach to a regional plan.

In 1949, Russia, not China, was seen as being the principal source of communist threat in Asia, although it was conceded that China, Japan, or even India might attempt to dominate Asia in the course of time. But in 1949 our National Security Council took the position that the United States, as a Western power, should refrain from taking any lead in Southeast Asia; instead it should encourage the peoples of India, Pakistan, the Philippines, and other Asian countries to take the initiative in stemming communist expansion. The Council particularly pointed to Indochina where "action should be taken to bring home to the French the urgency of removing the barriers to the obtaining by Bao Dai . . . the support of a substantial proportion of the Vietnamese."[31] Indochina was of special importance because it was the only area adjacent to China with a large European army engaged against "communist" forces. Official French sources kept reporting to our diplomats in Paris, Saigon, Hanoi, and Washington that "there were some Chinese troops in Tonkin, as well as large numbers ready for action" against the French on the Chinese side of the border. Both the State and War departments were sufficiently concerned with these (unsubstantiated) reports to ask the National Security Council to examine the situation and consider measures for the protection of American interests in Indochina.

Accordingly, the Department of State developed a paper entitled, "The Position of the United States with Respect to Indochina." The problem as stated was "To undertake a determination of all practicable United States measures to protect its security in Indochina and to prevent the expansion of communist aggression in that area." Following an extensive analysis of the problem based on the assumptions "that the threat of communist aggression against Indochina is only one phase of anticipated communist plans to seize all of Southeast Asia" and that the recent recognition of Ho Chi Minh's government by China and Russia posed a serious threat to the integrity of the French-sponsored regime of Bao Dai in the south, the authors of the paper concluded that "it is important to the United States security interests that all practicable measures be taken to prevent further communist expansion in Southeast Asia." The paper was presented to the National Security Council on 27 February 1950 "for urgent consideration."

The National Security Council in its wisdom agreed with the conclusions of the authors of the paper, particularly with the concept that "Thailand and Burma could be expected to fall under Communist domination if Indochina were controlled by a Communist-dominated government" and that "the balance of Southeast Asia would then be in grave hazard." The paper was then labeled NSC-64[32] and sent to the President with the Council's recommendation "that he approve the Conclusions and direct their implementation by all appropriate executive departments and agencies of the U.S. government under the coordination of the Secretary of State." The document was approved by the President on 27 March 1950 and adopted as American policy.

It should be noted that NSC-64 was prepared and approved by the Truman Administration before the outbreak of the Korean War. Although its concluding statement of what came to be known as the "domino principle" has been thought of as mainly relating to Korea it actually originated in the Indochina struggle. The outbreak of the war in Korea in June only reinforced the administration's belief in the "domino principle," and the Truman doctrine of containment became the national objective.

Both strategists and policymakers came to be of one mind—holding the line in Southeast Asia was essential to American security interests. The French struggle in Indochina came far more than before to be regarded as an integral part of the containment of communism in that region of the world, and we intensified and enlarged our programs of aid to Indochina. Shipments of military aid to the French for their Indochina war acquired in 1951 the second priority, just behind the Korean War program.

❂ ❂ ❂

The news of the outbreak of the Korean War was received in Paris with considerable antipathy and concern. The first reaction was that it was a local affair, a civil war, of no concern to France, and not to be blown up into a major international issue. Many feared that U.S. involvement would distract America's attention from European economic and defense programs. Others suspected American motives as selfish and self-serving, aimed at extending the American line of containment to the west of a "unified" Korea, this to protect American interests in Japan and Taiwan from the "Red menace," an act that could easily bring the United States and the Soviet Union into open confrontation and World War III.

A sampling of French views can be seen in a *Le Monde* article (27 June) which suggested that if Korea were lost, it would at least have the advantage of teaching America a lesson. It would compel us to reassess our Asian policy and see to it that the same thing did not happen in Southeast Asia. It implied that we should cut our losses in Korea and

Taiwan but by all means help France to hold on to Indochina. The article also noted that from the French point of view Indochina was trouble enough; why add to it by becoming embroiled in Korea as well?

In truth, the war in Indochina had become a psychological and economic burden to the French citizen. It had become *la sale guerre* which seemed to go on and on. In 1949–50 only some politicians and big business spoke of a "crusade against Communism" and of defending the "honor of France" in the Far East. The antiwar feeling in France, the victorious Chinese Communists in the north, and the possibility of a French military defeat made a dismal picture.

The general apprehension that the new Korean conflict might get out of hand and place greater demands on French efforts in the Far East for American interests was dispelled on 27 June when President Truman announced that he had directed "acceleration in the furnishing of military assistance to the forces of France and the Associated States in Indo China and the dispatch of a military mission."[33] Although the decision to extend aid had been taken before the Korean outbreak, the announcement coming two days later was a shot in the arm to big business interests which were operating on a grandiose scale in Southeast Asia and wanted the war in Indochina to continue.

With active American involvement in Asia the war in Indochina acquired a new dimension. It was being "internationalized" and becoming a part of America's crusade against communism. It vitalized the Indochina war just when French public opinion leaned toward packing it in. This new dimension served as a powerful incentive to all those political and commercial interests in France which were for continuing the war to "ultimate victory." It also made France more dependent on the United States, even in those areas where she had pursued a shortsighted but relatively independent policy of her own. Consequently, the number of French persons in France who now acquired a financial interest in prolonging the war increased greatly.

At the international level, the war introduced not only the new dimension discussed above but also a sense of responsibility, even culpability, which became the rationale used by the French and Americans alike for leverage in achieving their respective ends. It was argued that while the Indochina war had been, and continued to be, a French war, conducted by the French for a French objective (colonialism), the United Nations' "police action" in Korea was essentially an American war, conducted by American generals, manned and financed by the United States in support of an American objective in Asia (containment of communism). In this inherent incompatibility of objectives ("domino" vs. colonialism) can be found much of the explanation for the differences that cropped up between the United States and France during the 1950–54 period.

✺ ✺ ✺

There is conclusive evidence that France could not have pursued the war in Indochina without American aid, but we failed to use our considerable leverage on the French to force them to take more positive steps toward granting complete independence to the Associated States. An examination of Franco-American relations between 1950 and 1954, however, suggests that American leverage was severely limited and that, given the primacy accorded in American policy to the containment of communism in Asia, French leverage on the United States was the stronger of the two. This is not to imply that if American views had prevailed the problem of communism in Indochina would have been resolved. The Viet Minh struggle for total independence on a socialist plane would have continued, but it might have been more tolerable to Western interests.

Yet, French leverage was formidable. In the first postwar decade France was relatively weak and depended upon the United States through NATO and the Marshall Plan for its military security and economic revival. Neither offered usable fulcrums for influencing French policy on Indochina. Both NATO and the Marshall Plan were judged by our government and public to be strongly in the American national interest at a time when the Soviet threat to Western Europe was clearly recognizable. A communist takeover in France was a real possibility. (The French Communist Party was the largest and most militant political party in France at the time.) Thus, an American threat to withdraw military and economic support from France if it did not alter its policies in Indochina was not plausible and would have jeopardized American interests in Europe more important than any in Indochina.

The only other source of influence was the military aid program for Indochina. There our leverage was severely constrained by the French field commanders. General Henri-Eugène Navarre viewed any function of the US-MAAG in Saigon, beyond bookkeeping, as an intrusion in internal French affairs. Even though it would have been difficult to continue the war without American aid, the French never permitted American participation in strategic planning or policymaking. Moreover, as in 1945, the French suspected the economic aid mission of being oversympathetic to Vietnamese nationalism and insisted our aid be furnished with "no strings attached" and with virtually no control over its use. Underlying this attitude, again as in 1945, was French deep-seated suspicion that the United States wanted to totally supplant them in Indochina, economically as well as politically.

Our consuming fear of the communist specter was our undoing. At no time did we consider the possibility that the Sino-Soviet bloc might have been just as fearful of us as we were of them. Nor had it occurred to our strategists and policymakers that had we set more realistic and attainable goals within given parameters for our economic and strategic development and formulated a national policy based on less than global scope, perhaps coexistence with the communist world might have been less costly and more fruitful. As it was, and to some degree is still today, we merely danced to the Soviet tune, reacting to each "communist threat" but seldom from a position of strength based on preconceived and firm plans. From fear, indecision, and expediency we have been vulnerable to blackmail from both ally and enemy.

In the early fifties French leverage over the United States was made possible by the conviction firmly held in Washington that the preservation of a noncommunist Indochina was vital to Western—and specifically American—interests. The most fundamental fact was that the French were waging a war which we considered, rightly or wrongly, to be essential. Thus, the French were always able, simply by threatening to pull out of Indochina, to win additional concessions and assistance. As the French nation tired of "la sale guerre," this would not have been an unpopular decision within France. When the Laniel government requested in 1953 a massive increase in American assistance, the Department of State representative at an NSC meeting asserted that "if this French Government, which proposes reinforcing Indochina with our aid, is not supported by us at this time, it may be the last such government prepared to make a real effort to win in Indochina."[34]

The upshot of such tactics was that American leverage was minimal. Our aid could be used for little more than to urge greater efficiency and determination on France. We could move Paris to formulate a Navarre-type plan, but we could not influence the way France conducted the war nor move France on political issues in dispute.

The temptation to "go along" with the French until the Viet Minh was defeated was all the more attractive because of the *expectation* of victory which pervaded official Washington. Before Dien Bien Phu, Lieutenant General John W. O'Daniel, Chief of US-MAAG in Saigon, consistently reported that victory was within reach *if the United States continued its support.* In November 1953, General O'Daniel submitted a report on the Navarre Plan stating that the French Union forces held the initiative and would begin offensive operations in mid-January 1954; meanwhile they would attempt to keep the Viet Minh off balance in the Tonkin Delta until October 1954 when the French would begin a major offensive north of the nineteenth parallel. O'Daniel's report concluded that the Navarre Plan was basically sound and should be supported since it would bring a decisive victory.

O'Daniel was not aware that he and our government were being duped. In a secret report to his government in late 1953 (published in 1956 in his memoirs), Navarre himself stated that the war simply could not be won in the military sense and all that could be hoped for was a *coup nul*—a draw. Nor were O'Daniel and our State Department officials aware of the top secret instructions given Navarre by the French National Defense Council on 24 July 1953 directing him to defend Laos, if possible, but "above all else, to ensure the safety of the French Expeditionary Corps" and to prepare the way, as best he could in military terms, for negotiations.

Another important source of French leverage was in European affairs. A primary objective of American foreign policy in 1953–54 was the creation of a European Defense Community (EDC) to "envelope" a new West German Army into an integrated allied force for the defense of Western Europe. France was lukewarm about joining the American-sponsored EDC, in part because France feared an armed Germany and in part because she did not share the American concern for Soviet intervention in Europe. However, French membership in EDC was essential to its adoption by the other five participating nations, and it was up to the United States to convince France. Because of the high priority given EDC in American planning, we had a strong reluctance to antagonize the French in Indochina. Unnoticed at the time was an implicit contradiction in our policy of pushing the French simultaneously on both adopting EDC and on making a greater effort in Indochina which required increased French forces in the Far East. But the French National Assembly would not adopt EDC unless, at a minimum, it was assured that French forces in Europe would be on parity with those of Germany. Thus the French argued that the possible coming into effect of EDC prevented them from putting larger forces into Indochina.

Still another French leverage was demonstrated by their ability to get the Indochina problem placed on the agenda for the Geneva Conference. This occurred at the Quadripartite Foreign Ministers' meeting in February 1954 at Berlin. The Geneva Conference was planned to work out a political settlement for the Korean War. Secretary of State John Foster Dulles did not wish to negotiate on Indochina until there was a marked improvement in the military situation of the French and they could negotiate from a position of far greater strength. But the Laniel government, under mounting pressure from French public opinion to end the Indochina war, insisted despite our objections that Indochina be included on the Geneva agenda. Foreign Minister Bidault reportedly warned that if we did not acquiesce, EDC would doubtless be scuttled.

Putting all these factors together, we really allowed ourselves no latitude in steering a rational course toward Viet Nam from 1950 to 1954. We were locked in by our own "domino principle," by our own optimistic expectations of a French military victory, by our own failure to set realistic parameters in our anticommunist policies based on firm plans, and by allowing our own internal economic needs to play too large a role. The French, in their simultaneous but entirely separate struggle to retain a colonial Indochina, were glad to block any other options by denying the Bao Dai regime any real autonomy, by inhibiting the growth of a real Vietnamese national army, and by exerting their considerable leverage in European difficulties to suppress our anti-French colonial efforts in Viet Nam.

✿ ✿ ✿

Underlying our political failures during those four years lay the deteriorating course of the war in Viet Nam itself. By late 1949 the French army under General Marcel Carpentier had lost the initiative, and in January 1950 General Giap started a series of campaigns against the French. In his first offensive he sealed off part of the strategic Red River delta and pushed on from February to April with even larger-scale operations, securing for the Viet Minh the whole northeastern corner of Tonkin. Through the summer of 1950 while the United Nations forces shuttled across the Korean peninsula, Giap inflicted additional losses on Carpentier's forces in the Lang Son-Cao Bang corridor. Crushed by these military defeats, the French were further demoralized by their government at home which reduced the effective strength of the Indochina army by nine thousand men. The French National Assembly expressed its sentiments by making continued support of combat operations in Indochina contingent on government assurances that no draftees were used there.

After more than three years of unsuccessful campaigns, the French still underestimated the Viet Minh's determination and overestimated their own prowess. As our Marines were landing at Inchon, Korea, in mid-September, Giap launched an attack on the strategic city of Dong Khe (twenty miles southeast of Cao Bang). The French garrison at Cao Bang panicked and fled south, incurring heavy losses on the way. On 17 October Lang Son was abandoned and by the end of the month the whole northern half of North Viet Nam had become Viet Minh territory, into which French troops never set foot again. As one writer put it, "When the smoke cleared, the French had suffered their greatest colonial defeat since Montcalm had died at Quebec."[35]

To the French at home it was an untenable situation. To lose battles was tolerable, but to lose the war in Indochina would have been a disaster for the colons and their war-profiteering sponsors in France. Months earlier France had asked for our assistance on the premise that the war could be successfully prosecuted. Within weeks (May 1950) American funds and a MAAG mission had been authorized by President Truman, and in June we had upped the ante to encourage the French. But in November the war in Indochina had turned into a humiliating rout. It was an unbearable embarrassment for the proud French and raised serious doubts in both France and the United States that the French army could deliver the expected military victory.

For some time the French High Command had been concerned with the way the war had not been progressing; it had in fact become a stalemate. General Georges Revers, after his inspection tour, had recommended certain political and military changes, not all of which were to the liking of the French military establishment and the French government. Portions of his Top Secret report were "leaked" to the French communists and in April 1950, to the consternation of the French, verbatim passages were broadcast over the Viet Bac Radio (the Viet Minh station). Even more damaging, the political portion of Revers's report was also "leaked" and became known as the *affaire des généraux*, a national scandal that reflected adversely on the conduct of some generals.

The scandal and military setbacks suggested another change of command and *la valse des généraux* continued. From Leclerc in 1945, to Valluy, Blaizot, and now Carpentier, de Lattre was added in December 1950, only to be followed by Salan, Navarre, and finally Ely. General de Lattre assumed command from General Carpentier and replaced Pignon as High Commissioner. He arrived to find an army, demoralized, defeated, and decimated, flowing back from the northern sector of Tonkin toward a Hanoi of hysterical civilians ready to flee the Viet Minh onslaught. They had heard on the Viet Bac Radio of the imminent return of the DRV to Hanoi, and the French community was in a state of total panic. It was rumored that Giap had promised Ho Chi Minh that he would be in Hanoi for the Têt, the lunar new year, in February 1951.

The Paris government under public pressure had sent the largest passenger ship available, the *Pasteur*, to evacuate all French citizens from North Viet Nam. But de Lattre, a remarkable man in many ways, would have no talk of retreat, nor would he accept defeat without a fight. He promptly loaded the *Pasteur* with wounded soldiers and returned it two-thirds empty to France, much to the outcry and indignation of the parliament in Paris.

De Lattre, one of France's ablest World War II generals, was highly regarded as a field commander and strategist. Nonetheless, his autocratic personality, often compared to that of Admiral d'Argenlieu, made personal and staff relationships extremely difficult. His hauteur and temperament struck terror in his subordinates who (behind his back) called him "*le roi Jean*." Regardless of his personality traits, de Lattre was a leader and did inspire confidence. When asked why he undertook what many considered a lost cause, he would reply that the cause was not lost, that he was fighting in a crusade against communism. Contrary to the widely held view that the French High Command had appointed him to mollify the critics of the General Staff in the *affaire des généraux* and to preside over the orderly demise of the French empire in the Far East, de Lattre gave every indication he had no intention of withdrawing. As already mentioned, he expected victory in fifteen months.

His first accomplishment was to turn chaos into order, despair to hope, and apathy to initiative—not only among his troops but among the French civilians and noncommunist Vietnamese. He promised little: no improvements, no reinforcements, no easy victories, only more sacrifices. But, addressing his troops, he said, "No matter what, you will be commanded." To the soldiers who rarely understood what they were doing in Indochina, this was the first positive statement from the High Command. He then, as High Commissioner, drafted French civilians in Indochina for guard duty and requisitioned French civilian aircraft as they landed (all unaware) in Saigon and used them to airlift reinforcements to the front.

De Lattre had not been in Indochina a month before Giap undertook the "final phase" of his great offensive to push the French out of the delta and retake the capital city, Hanoi. He launched his attack on de Lattre's forces around Vinh Yen on 16 January. After an initial Viet Minh success, French firepower, supported by aerial napalm bombs, won the day, and when Giap's troops left the battlefield on the seventeenth, they also left six thousand dead and five hundred prisoners behind.

Undeterred by his first failure, Giap regrouped and tried again at Mao Khé (fifteen miles north-northeast of Haiphong). The attack began on the night of 24–25 March and lasted until the dawn of the twenty-eighth. Again Giap failed to breach the French defenses and, withdrawing, left four hundred dead behind; the French lost only forty men and sustained one hundred fifty wounded.

A third less ambitious offensive took place on 29 May on the banks of the Day River, about sixty miles south of Hanoi. In spite of some initial gains, the battle ended on 18 June in another communist defeat. Giap had miscalculated. He was not ready for the "final phase," and the intervening rainy season interrupted his campaign.

But de Lattre knew he was unable to defend the seven million people and the seven thousand square miles of the Red River delta for lack of manpower and hurriedly completed a series of fortified concrete strongpoints from Mong Cai to Vinh Yen (forty-five miles north of Hanoi) and south to the seacoast. This system of fortifications came to be called the "de Lattre Line" and proved no better than the famous Maginot Line. These static defenses were continuously patrolled but the Viet Minh had little difficulty infiltrating them.

Manning the "de Lattre Line," plus the mobile units to patrol it, required approximately ten thousand men, which de Lattre could ill afford if he had to bring the war to the Viet Minh. Although the French General Staff had agreed to establishing the line, originally recommended by Revers in May 1949, it would not raise the troop strength to meet the new requirement. The political opposition in France to sending draftees to Indochina foreclosed any hope of additional manpower from home. There was one other solution: a Vietnamese National Army.

As head of state, Bao Dai could have raised a national army, but he was reluctant to do so. He had no military leaders to run it. The French had already seen to it that no Vietnamese attained any grade above that of small unit commander or acquired any strategic knowledge. Bao Dai had also met strong resistance from the French administrators led by de Lattre's predecessor, Pignon, who followed the MRP and RPF line against a native force not under direct French control. Lastly, Bao Dai was concerned that such a force might defect en masse to the Viet Minh.

It was de Lattre (while still in France) who had broken that resistance and convinced the French that a national army under Vietnamese commanders was essential to ease the French military burden. De Lattre's influence helped to change the French attitude and a Vietnamese military academy was at last opened in November 1950. However, the graduates still had only one army to serve, the French Expeditionary Corps, and were integrated into "yellow" units of the corps which meant they were not Vietnamese but French soldiers. It was not what de Lattre had in mind, and he urged Bao Dai and his Prime Minister, Tran Van Huu, to get on with forming a national force.

Finally in July 1951 the first conscripts were called up, but only a token number answered the call. Neither the national nor the local authorities would press for compliance for fear of unfavorable political repercussions. Many youths, to avoid the draft, joined the Cao Dai or the Hoa Hao militias. Exasperated, de Lattre told a group of conscripts, "to fight for your country . . . like men. If you are Communists, then go and join the Viet Minh. There are people there who fight well for a bad cause."[36]

De Lattre accomplished much during his brief stay in Indochina, although nothing he did actually affected the final outcome of the war. His tour was, of course, cut short by his fatal illness, and this future Marshal of France had also suffered the tragedy of losing his only son, Lieutenant Bernard de Lattre, in the battle of the Day River during Giap's third unsuccessful attempt to capture the delta and Hanoi.

De Lattre valued American aid to the French and stopped in Washington (September 1951) to put in a personal plea for it, as he returned to Paris in failing health. But he considered direct aid to the Associated States "pernicious" and preferred the aid to be distributed by France through French channels. He told Robert Blum, who headed our economic aid program, "As a student of history, I can understand it [American aid], but as a Frenchman I don't like it."[37]

Blum (in 1952) said of the Bao Dai-French-American triangle,

On the one hand are the repeated official affirmations that France has no selfish interests in Indochina and desires only to promote the independence of the Associated States and be relieved of the terrible drain of France's resources. On the other hand are the numerous examples of the deliberate continuation of French controls, the interference in major policy matters, the profiteering and the constant bickering and ill-feeling over the transfer of powers and the issue of independence. . . . There is unquestionably a contradiction in French actions between the natural desire to be rid of this unpopular, costly and apparently fruitless war and the determination to see it through with honor while satisfying French pride and defending interests in the process. This distinction is typified by the sharp difference between the attitude toward General de Lattre in Indochina, where he is heralded as the political genius and military saviour[,] . . . and in France, where he is suspected as a person who for personal glory is drawing off France's resources on a perilous adventure. . . . [38]

On American participation, Blum continued,

It is difficult to measure what have been the results of almost two years [1950–1952] of active American participation in the affairs of Indochina. Although we embarked upon a course of uneasy association with the "colonialist"-tainted but indispensable French, on the one hand, and the indigenous weak and divided Vietnamese, on the other hand, we have not been able fully to reconcile these two allies in the interest of a single-minded fight against Communism.[39]

Blum concluded that

The situation in Indochina is not satisfactory and shows no substantial prospect of improving, that no decisive military victory can be achieved, that the Bao Dai government gives little promise of developing competence and winning the loyalty of the population . . . and that the attainment of American objectives is remote.[40]

His analysis and conclusion did not differ substantially from those of Senator John F. Kennedy who visited Viet Nam in November 1951 and declared:

. . . we have allied ourselves to the desperate effort of the French regime to hang on to the remnants of an empire. There is no broad general support of the native Vietnam Government among the people of that area.[41]

Although de Lattre provided a brief respite for the French from the massive but unsuccessful Viet Minh offensive, Korean armistice negotiations started in July 1951 and both France and the United States became uneasy at the possibility of a large-scale Chinese intervention in Indochina. Such an action would not have been surprising given the large number of Chinese troops massed along the Tonkin border and the material assistance being given to the Viet Minh.

France viewed what was then a new threat with alarm and despondency. Its politicians began hinting at negotiations and compromise with the Viet Minh while the balance of power was, as they believed, in France's favor. But the United States looked at the possibility of Chinese intervention in terms of a continuing deterioration of the French military position, more as a threat of communist expansion and less as a loss of France's colony.

After the Viet Minh debacle in the early part of 1951, Giap reconsidered his strategy and decided to retreat to "phase two" of Mao's principles of revolutionary warfare, reverting to guerrilla tactics, harassing the static French defenses and wearing them down. When de Lattre returned to France (19 December 1951), his deputy, General Raoul Salan, assumed command and tried to bring the war to the Viet Minh, but Giap refused to fight except on his own terms. The French found themselves striking at empty spaces while incurring constant and devastating losses. The Viet Minh fighters would draw the French into the open, strike, then disappear into the jungle. Or they would infiltrate a French position, hit, and run—causing havoc, disrupting communications, and inflicting severe losses without suffering undue casualties to themselves.

In the autumn of 1951 French politicians badly needed a victory in Indochina. The National Assembly was preparing to debate the Indochina budget for 1952–53 and French diplomats in Washington were trying to convince our people to increase America's share in the cost of the war. Thus, a "dramatic victory" in Indochina, contrasting with the stalemate in Korea, would have an impact on the doves in Paris and impress our Congress in Washington.

De Lattre, whose remaining weeks in Indochina were to be numbered, chose for an easy victory the peaceful capital city of the Muong tribe, Hoa-Binh (about forty miles southwest of Hanoi). French troops occupied the city with practically no opposition at dawn on 14 November 1951. Confident that the Viet Minh would not counterattack, the French during the ensuing several weeks poured huge quantities of armor, artillery, and troops into the narrow Black River Valley, expecting to penetrate the heartland of Giap's stronghold in the northeast. It was a bad decision. Giap refused to fight at that particular moment under French rules, but he had not overlooked the potential for whittling away at the French at his leisure.

The French defenses consisted of a series of outposts along the Black River and Colonial Route 6, north and east of Hoa-Binh. Giap attacked the key outpost at Tu Ve (about twelve miles north of Hoa-Binh) on 9 December, and in less than twenty-four hours, his forces drove the French across the Black River.

And the battle of Tu Ve was a portent. The seesaw engagements for control of the Black River continued through December with the French obstinately reinforcing their positions with more men and equipment. But Giap fought by his rules. The Viet Minh vanished in the nearby limestone caves, only to reappear in January 1952 to pursue Giap's tactics of erosion. By the end of the month, finding the effort nonproductive, Salan decided to evacuate the whole Hoa-Binh salient, saving his men and equipment for the forthcoming battle in the delta and the Thai* highlands.

The "dramatic victory" had not materialized; moreover French forces and equipment were badly depleted. The deterioration of the French military position became a major concern to the French government and to American policymakers as well. The contingency of a Chinese intervention dominated the thinking of our Joint Chiefs of Staff and our diplomats.

Early in 1952 our National Security Council concluded that American involvement should be limited to dealing with direct Chinese intervention. In the absence of that contingency, however, and to meet the existing situation, the NSC recommended that we increase our level of aid to French Union forces but "without relieving the French authorities of their basic military responsibility for the defense of the Associated States."

*Also spelled T'ai on French maps. It includes the area of northern Tonkin west of the Red River to the Laos border.

President Truman approved a Statement of Policy on "U.S. Objectives and Courses of Action with Respect to Southeast Asia"* developed by the National Security Council on 25 June 1952 which stated in part:

Carry out the following minimum courses of military action, either under the auspices of the UN or in conjunction with France and the United Kingdom and any other friendly government:

(1) A resolute defense of Indochina itself to which *the United States would provide such air and naval assistance* as might be practicable.

(2) Interdiction of Chinese Communist communication lines including those in China.

(3) *The United States would expect to provide the major forces for task (2) above.* . . . (Emphasis added).[42]

This early French setback in 1952 had so upset our policymakers that they feared communist expansion to the point of committing our forces in a French colonial war. America's albatross had winged its way across the sea.   ☹ ☹ ☹

Indochina by this time had a new High Commissioner, Jean Letourneau. He was a right-wing Catholic and member of the procolonial MRP, who had been Minister of Overseas France and then became Minister for the Associated States. When in April 1952 he succeeded de Lattre as High Commissioner, he retained his ministerial post. The dual function gave him enormous power in "independent" Viet Nam, more than had been wielded by any former Governor General in colonial days. Letourneau's political clout served to inhibit the Bao Dai regime which in June 1952 passed from Premier Tran Van Huu to his former chief of the political sûreté, Nguyen Van Tam. Both were French citizens.

In France, a Parliamentary Mission of Inquiry would later (May 1953) accuse Letourneau of "veritable dictatorship, without limitation or control." The Mission, composed of a Socialist, an Independent, a Popular Republican, and a Radical Socialist, spoke of

"*the Norodom Palace clique*" allowing "itself the luxury of administering *à la française* and of reigning over a country where revolution is smouldering . . .";

Saigon, "where gambling, depravity, love of money and of power finish by corrupting the morale and destroying will-power . . ."; and

Bao Dai's regime, where "The Ministers . . . appear in the eyes of their compatriots to be French officials. . . . "[43]

The Mission report blamed the French for Vietnamese corruption:

It is grave that after eight years of *laisser-aller* and of anarchy, the presence in Indochina of a resident Minister has not been able to put an end to these daily scandals in the life [of the colony] in regard to the granting of licenses, the transfer of piastres, war damages, or commercial transactions. Even if our administration is

---

*In this context Southeast Asia meant the area embracing Burma, Thailand, Indochina, Malaya, and Indonesia.

not entirely responsible for these abuses, it is deplorable that one can affirm that it either ignores them or tolerates them.[44]

An influential French editor, commenting on the Mission's report, blamed "the natural tendency of the military proconsulate to perpetuate itself" and "certain French political groups who have found in the war a principal source of their revenues . . . through exchange operations, supplies to the expeditionary corps and war damages." His conclusion was:

The truth is that the facts now known seem to add up to a lucid plan worked out step by step to eliminate any possibility of negotiations in Indochina in order to assure the prolongation without limit of the hostilities and of the military occupation.[45]

While both the military and political situation in Indochina were going poorly during the latter half of 1952, events in the United States were to deepen our commitment there as the presidential election campaign progressed and the Eisenhower Administration came into office. For a long period the GOP had persistently accused the Truman Administration of responsibility for the "loss" of China to communism. John Foster Dulles's pronouncements during the campaign left no doubt that he regarded Southeast Asia as a key region in the conflict with communist "imperialism," and that it was important to draw the line of containment north of the Rice Bowl of Asia—the Indochina peninsula.[46]

President Eisenhower promised a "new, positive foreign policy" in his first State of the Union message (3 February 1953) and went on to link the communist aggression in Korea and Malaya with Indochina. Dulles, the new Secretary of State, spoke of Korea and Indochina as two flanks with the principal enemy—Red China—in the center. The Republican administration clearly intended to prevent the loss of Indochina by taking a more forthright anticommunist stand.

The prolonged armistice negotiations in Korea created apprehension that the Chinese Communists would turn their attention to Indochina and President Eisenhower warned on 16 April 1953 that any armistice in Korea which merely released armed forces to pursue an attack elsewhere would be a fraud. Dulles later continued this theme (in a speech on 2 September 1953) after the Korean armistice had been signed, noting that "a single Communist aggressive front extends from Korea on the north to Indochina in the south." He continued,

Communist China has been and now is training, equipping and supplying the Communist forces in Indochina. There is the risk that, as in Korea, Red China might send its own Army into Indochina. The Chinese Communist regime should realize that such a second aggression could not occur without grave consequences which might not be confined to Indochina. I say this soberly . . . in the hope of preventing another aggressor miscalculation.[47]

Underlying these warnings to China was the belief that the difference between success or failure in preventing a total Ho Chi Minh victory probably lay in the extent of Chinese assistance or direct participation. Signaling a warning to China was probably designed to deter further Chinese involvement, and implicit was the threat that, if China came into the Indochina war, the United States would be forced to follow suit, preferably with allies but alone if necessary. Furthermore, the Eisenhower Administration implied that in keeping with its policy of massive retaliation the United States would administer a punishing nuclear blow to China without necessarily involving our land forces in an Asian war.

☉ ☉ ☉

Giap, by the time of our elections and new administration, had already found the French Achilles' heel—lack of mobility and cumbersome logistics—and was executing his "war of maneuver" as a prelude to a war of large movement, which was a further prelude to a war of position and eventual victory. His first objective was the conquest of the Thai highlands and the occupation of Laos. On 11 October 1952 Giap moved three divisions across the Red River on a forty-mile front, sweeping before his juggernaut every French outpost in its path to the Black River. On 30 November, the first elements of the Viet Minh reached the Laotian border. Bernard Fall in *The Two Viet Nams* summed it up: "The communist divisions, in the face of French mastery of the air, had covered 180 miles in six weeks of fighting, without using a single road or a single motor vehicle" (p. 119). By 1 December, the French withdrew to the relative safety of the de Lattre Line just north of Hanoi, but not without incurring heavy losses of men and equipment.

During the early spring of 1953 Giap resumed his "war of movement" from the Thai country into Laos, straight to the royal capital city of Luang Prabang. On 30 April 1953 he set up the Resistance Government of Pathet Lao (Free Laotian). He then moved south until the French decided to get out of his way by moving eastward toward the Plaine des Jarres, but Giap pursued and surrounded them. Then, on 7 May, Giap's forces retired to the Viet Bac (northern Tonkin), leaving behind a small force to contain the French and to provide the Pathet Lao under Prince Souphanouvang with political advisers.

May 1953 was also the month when another government crisis in the French Cabinet brought Joseph Laniel, an Independent, into the premiership. Laniel replaced Letourneau with Maurice Dejean as Resident Commissioner General, a new post with different powers. The realignment of the office of High Commissioner eliminated some of the abuses of the previous system but created new ones. The civil functions of the former office were split between the Resident Commissioner General of France in Indochina and the three High Commissioners of the Republic to Viet Nam, Laos, and Cambodia. The military powers formerly vested in the high Commissioner of France were now transferred to the Resident Commissioner General as the sole officer responsible for the defense and security of Indochina. As such, the Resident Commissioner General had full allocation authority for aid given to the Associated States. This arrangement made the civil chief a veritable arbiter over military affairs. It was a carry-over from the era of the Governor General, during which the army had only to assume the minor task of maintaining order.

General Henri-Eugène Navarre was the first and last commander in Indochina to feel the brunt of the new civilian control over military operations. He had developed a plan for a decisive defeat of the Viet Minh projected for 1955 and had obtained American support, particularly from General O'Daniel and Secretary of State Dulles. This Navarre Plan, already referred to, was called the "Navarre Concept for Operations in Indochina" and offered a format for victory which promised success without direct involvement of American troops but predicated on massive American military assistance.

The United States rushed supplies to Laos and Thailand in May 1953 and provided six C-119s with civilian crews for the airlift to Laos. Congress had appropriated $400 million for fiscal 1954, but after the French presentation of the Navarre Plan an additional $385 million was made available. Despite all the aid, General Navarre found himself limited in expanding his operations against the Viet Minh by the Resident Commissioner General's decision on the allocation of these resources. Of course Dejean was following French policy—not to commit any more resources but to stall for negotiations—but Navarre was criticized for the eventual failure of his plan.

The Viet Minh victories of the period highlighted the criticality of France's position; Giap's latest campaigns had proven the Viet Minh's ascending power, partially influenced by increasing Russian and Chinese military aid. French combat levels had fallen dangerously low, and there was no prospect of quick replenishment from France. It was a bleak picture. Rumblings of "an honorable solution" could be heard again in certain political quarters in Paris, to the consternation of official Washington.

The French High Command and the right-wing procolonials saw military victory as the only "honorable solution" and on this point they had the support of the American government, although for different reasons. To achieve a military situation in which "an honorable solution" could be reached it would have been necessary to build up a striking force more powerful than the Viet Minh's and certainly as mobile. That was the lesson General Salan had learned in his year opposing Giap. The search for "an honorable solution" continued.

In Washington Senator John F. Kennedy recognized the vacuity of the Bao Dai solution and the pitfalls of French intransigence on Vietnamese independence as he pointed out:

Genuine independence . . . is lacking in Indochina. . . ; local government is circumscribed in its functions . . . ; the government of Vietnam, the state which is of the greatest importance in this area, lacks popular support . . . ; we should insist on genuine independence. . . . I strongly believe that the French cannot succeed in Indochina without giving concessions necessary to make the native army a reliable and crusading force.[48]

Later Kennedy again criticized the French:

Every year we are given three sets of assurances: First, that the independence of the Associated States is now complete; second, that the independence of the Associated States will soon be completed under steps "now" being taken; and third, that military victory for the French Union forces is assured, or is just around the corner.[49]

Throughout the period of our assistance to the French, American leaders kept in mind the necessity of encouraging them to grant greater autonomy to the Vietnamese. American pressure may well have helped account for the public declaration of Premier Laniel (3 July 1953) that the sovereignty of the Associated States would be "perfected" by transferring to them various functions which had remained under French control, though no final date was set for complete independence. François M. Mitterand (who was politically left-of-center) commented, "We have granted Viet Nam 'full independence' eighteen times since 1949. Isn't it about time we did it just once, but for good?"[50] And Bao Dai said privately, "What do they mean, 'perfect?' What is the matter with the French—they're always giving us our independence. Can't they give it to us once and for all?"[51]

The new Eisenhower Administration on 6 August set down specific conditions for continued American assistance to the French, one being a public French commitment to "a program which will insure the support and cooperation of the native Indochinese." Critical to the French was the $385 million we had promised for implementing the Navarre Plan, and Eisenhower knew it. He instructed our Ambassador in Paris, Douglas Dillon, to tell Premier Laniel and Foreign Minister Bidault that we expected France to "continue [to] pursue [a] policy of perfecting independence of Associated States in conformity with the 3 July declaration."

The United States was uneasy that unless France committed itself to a noncommunist Viet Nam, political pressure within France might impel their government to seek a negotiated instead of a military settlement. It was noted (before Dien Bien Phu) that if the Navarre Plan failed or appeared doomed, the French might negotiate simply for the best possible terms, irrespective of whether the terms offered any assurance of preserving a noncommunist Indochina. This was unthinkable to our strategists and policymakers. Their preference was for France to hold out and to foreclose any attempt by the Viet Minh to take over by any means. In that perception, the Eisenhower administration extended our earlier policy of influencing the French against concluding the struggle in terms "inconsistent" with our basic objectives. In line with the position advocated by the National Security Council on 16 January 1954 the President directed our diplomats to tell the French:

(1) In the absence of a marked improvement in the military situation, there was no basis for negotiation on acceptable terms; (2) we [the U.S.] would 'flatly oppose any idea' of a cease-fire as a preliminary to negotiations because [such a cease-fire] would result in an irretrievable deterioration of the [Franco-Vietnamese] military position [in Indochina]; (3) *a nominally noncommunist coalition regime would eventually turn the country over to Ho [Chi Minh] with no opportunity for the replacement of the French by the United States or the United Kingdom.* [Emphasis added.][52]

This last injunction certainly suggested that our policymakers were already leaning toward an American takeover in Indochina if the French caved in.

The first decade of the cold war had brought us into the Southeast Asian morass little by little, step by step. Our unfortunate stereotype of a monolithic communist expansionary bloc and our emotional approach to the "loss" of China were paths leading into the quicksands. Our Domino Theory pushed us along those paths a little faster. And then our lack of knowledge in depth of the individuality of the states of Southeast Asia and the separateness of their societies disguised the dangers along the paths we had taken. After all, who ever had anticipated we would be called upon to take a position of leadership in these remote areas? Very few could have perceived the deepening involvement.

But as 1954 began, with Dien Bien Phu and the international conferences at Geneva just beyond the horizon, we were already very deep in the morass and on a collision course with both French and Vietnamese objectives. It was to be a year of fateful decisions, and the albatross was circling our ship of state.

〇 〇 〇

By the end of spring 1953, Giap's forces had executed their circular movement from the Red River delta, north to Tonkin, westward over the Thai Highlands, across the Laotian border, then south, positioning themselves in the wide area from the Plaine des Jarres to Central Annam where they successfully harassed Salan's troops. In the process Giap avoided heavily fortified French positions, but overran or occupied many less important French outposts. One of these was the poorly defended airfield and garrison at Dien Bien Phu near the Laotian border which he took on 30 November 1952.

To stand up to the ever-increasing Vietnamese pressure and to develop a military situation in which Paris could find its "honorable solution," Salan concluded he needed additional resources. His plan was to increase the combat effectiveness of his troops by relieving them of their static chores and making them mobile once more. He knew no help could be expected from metropolitan France, but the Associated States could

provide the needed manpower to relieve his troops of the static responsibilities, if Paris would go along with his proposal. It would, of course, involve a sizeable increase in arms and equipment—perhaps the United
States would provide it.

The Paris government had agreed with Salan's plan and had approached the United States for more aid. The request was well timed.
Giap's advance into Laos in April, coupled with the well-publicized war
weariness in France, had already alarmed the administration in Washington which, fearing a total French collapse, had rushed supplies to Laos
and Thailand in May 1953. However, the aid had been given on condition
that Salan's new program produce military successes and that the arms
and equipment be used mainly for troops to be recruited from the
Associated States.

The new aid and revised plan suggested to the French government
that a new military team was in order, and it was at that point that Salan
was replaced by the famous strategist, General Henri-Eugène Navarre,
who assumed command on 20 May 1953. As already noted, the French
National Defense Council instructed Navarre to go slow, defend Laos, and
above all else "insure the safety of the French Expeditionary Corps."
However, once in charge Navarre reviewed the situation on the ground
and formulated his own strategy. He adopted some of de Lattre's and
Salan's concepts to his own use and developed the famous, but disastrous,
plan which bore his name. It was hailed in Washington but damned in
Paris. The plan called for a strong mobile striking force for regaining the
initiative by the fall of 1954. In the interim he would conduct a defensive
strategy (as instructed by Paris) north of the eighteenth parallel but
would aggressively clear central Annam and Cochinchina (contrary to instructions from Paris) during the first half of 1954. In the autumn of 1954
he would launch a general offensive (as agreed with by O'Daniel and
Dulles) north of the nineteenth parallel with the objective of creating the
desired favorable condition for a political settlement of the war.

Meanwhile the Korean armistice had finally been signed on 26 July
after the longest truce talks in history—two years and 17 days, including
575 separate meetings. A political conference was to be held 90 days
after completion of prisoner exchange for discussing "the future of
Korea, and related problems." The prisoner exchange was completed on
6 September. The armistice was praised as an omen of world peace by the
Soviet Union, China, North Korea, and most of the European "Bloc" nations, but not by the DRV. Ho Chi Minh in a message to Chairman Mao (4
August) simply expressed "the boundless delight" of the Vietnamese people that the war in Korea had ended. Were the Vietnamese delighted because they anticipated greater Chinese attention to the needs of the Viet
Minh? Or were they delighted the negotiated peace in Korea would set a
pattern for political settlement of the Indochina war?

Perhaps a bit of both. Certainly China, still geared for war, could with little effort divert its military machinery no longer needed in Korea to Ho's needs, making it possible for him to deal with the French—even the Americans—from a position of strength. The policymakers in Washington and Paris were keeping anxious and watchful eyes on Peking's next move. It was indeed at this period that Dulles signaled China in his St. Louis speech (2 September 1953) of the "grave consequences" of "another aggressor miscalculation."[53]

At his press conference the next day Dulles was asked if his speech implied that the United States was willing to include the question of a possible restoration of peace in Indochina at the projected Korean political conference. Dulles replied:

We have said that the conference as originally set up . . . should be limited to Korea. But . . . [if] the Chinese Communists show a disposition to settle in a reasonable way such a question as Indochina, we would not just on technical grounds say, "No, we won't talk about that."[54]

During the summer Navarre, encouraged by General O'Daniel and Secretary Dulles, had put his plan into effect. For a brief while it seemed to go well, but by the year's end it was a disaster in the field. It was not apparent to the Americans, and the French would not admit, that the French were still stabbing at empty spaces in Indochina. The moment contact was made the enemy dissolved into the jungle, only to reappear elsewhere.

Forced to evacuate the southern Thai country in late September, Navarre turned east to the delta area. With a force of twenty battalions he attempted to clear the Thai Binh province (about fifty miles southeast of Hanoi) of one regiment of Viet Minh regulars. As expected, Giap's forces vanished; nevertheless, the French in late October proudly announced "another victory" to General O'Daniel who was impressed and promptly advised the Joint Chiefs in Washington. Hoping to draw Giap into a trap, Navarre reoccupied Dien Bien Phu with three battalions of paratroopers on 20 November. Giap did not take the bait; instead he watched the French fortify the old outpost and undertook his own preparations for laying siege to Navarre's citadel.

۵ ۵ ۵

Dulles's comments to the press on the third of September regarding possible discussions with the Chinese Communists on Indochina suggested to Laniel a way to deal with Ho Chi Minh. On 19 September Soviet Premier Georgi Malenkov, a strong advocate of détente, stressed the need for the "peace-loving people of the world" to make the Korean armistice a point of departure for "lessening international tension everywhere, including the Far East." On the twenty-first, Andrei Y. Vishinsky, the Soviet delegate to the United Nations, followed suit, proposing "a reduction in armaments and propaganda to avert the threat of a new war." Then Chou En-lai endorsed the Soviet proposal (8 October) and raised the question of a UN seat for the People's Republic of China, repeating Malenkov's theme of easing international tensions so as to consolidate peace in the Far East. The communists in the French National Assembly took up the Moscow-Peking line and clamored for negotiating with Ho Chi Minh for peace, as the United States had done with Kim Il Sung in Korea.

The mood in France, after Navarre's setback in September, had taken on a somber tone. People on the streets and some politicians in the National Assembly were talking of fighting a foot soldier's war for America's anticommunist crusade. They were coming to the grim realization that the war in Indochina was a bottomless pit, that no matter what France did the colony was lost, that for France it was a no-win war.

Laniel, replying to these demands on 27 October, declared his willingness to negotiate. But with whom? Neither Ho Chi Minh nor his "general staff" seemed to want any discussion. Laniel repeated his views to the National Assembly on 12 November, stating his government did not insist on a "military solution" but would settle for a "diplomatic solution," the implication being that the "military solution" was America's, not France's. The debate divided the nation between those who favored negotiating and those who wanted to prolong their profitable arrangements. The latter, generally economic and financial interests, under the influence of the MRP stood proudly for "France's prestige" and found it unacceptable to deal with the communist Ho—at least not until French military superiority gave the French an edge in dictating terms.

While military superiority in the field of battle was nowhere in sight and France debated, Navarre in mid-November was justifying his losses with the old refrain—not enough troops. His request for reinforcements was flatly refused by the Committee for National Defense; he was to make do with what he had. At the same time Laniel, anxious to get on with negotiations for settlement, sent a secret mission headed by Rear Admiral Cabanier to Saigon to find out from Navarre if the time was propitious to open ceasefire negotiations. Navarre told him (on 20 November) that the time was premature, that the French military position would be more favorable in the coming summer (1954).

While Navarre was reoccupying Dien Bien Phu, the Swedish daily, *Expressen*, published (29 November) Ho Chi Minh's reply to a series of questions posed by the Paris-based correspondent, Sven Löfgren. Ho's reply was dated the twenty-sixth and indicated the DRV's willingness to negotiate a cease-fire on condition that the French government recognize and respect the absolute independence of Viet Nam.[55] The French government's reaction was negative. Laniel was interested in pursuing Ho's "willingness to negotiate," but the diehard majority in the government decided to ignore Ho's offer. The government took the position that Ho must make his offer through official channels, not in "classified ads." On 12 December, the DRV news agency repeated Ho's offer for negotiation on the same basis. And, again, on the nineteenth, the seventh anniversary of the war, in a message to the Vietnamese People's Army, Ho broadcast an offer to release several hundred French POWs and once more made his offer to negotiate.

Nothing resulted directly from these peace feelers but, indirectly, they added to the mounting public and political sentiment in France for an end to the seemingly interminable and costly war. At the same time, the optimistic Navarre reports held out the hope that victory was around the corner. Laniel and other French officials told our Embassy people that they considered Ho's offer pure propaganda but admitted that it had produced the intended impact on public and military circles in France and Indochina. Laniel had also mentioned that President Auriol had become so excited by Ho's proposal that he had told Laniel to consult representatives of the three Associated States immediately with the view of seeking the earliest possible opening of negotiations with representatives of Ho Chi Minh. Laniel had flatly refused. American officials were skeptical, and the Embassy reported that a Laniel speech of 24 November left considerable latitude for negotiations, and that Ho's offers had increased the pressure for settlement.

The consistent American policy was to steer the French away from the negotiating table pending substantial military gains on the battlefield. Dulles on more than one occasion told Bidault that the United States felt it inadvisable to have the Indochina war settled on terms favorable to the communists. He wanted the French to continue the war because of his deep conviction that Indochina was a principal link in the line of containment and because we were blinded by French reports on the progress of the war. General O'Daniel was reporting from Saigon that a French victory was likely if our material support was provided, and the Administration willingly poured in more supplies.

President Eisenhower, Prime Minister Churchill, and Premier Laniel, meeting in Bermuda (December 1953), were seriously disturbed by events on the Indochina front. They discreetly indicated their concern in their 7 December communique announcing they had reviewed the situation in the Far East and planned to convene a political conference to reach "a peaceful settlement of the Korean question" and to restore "more normal conditions in the Far East and South East Asia."

While France was preoccupied with finding an accceptable approach to negotiations and Navarre was trying to improve his military posture, Giap was carefully getting ready to spring his trap at Dien Bien Phu. On 22 December, he launched a five-day offensive severing Indochina at its narrowest point and driving across both Viet Nam and Laos. The offensive ended when Giap reached the Mekong River on the border of Thailand.

The Navarre Plan evidently was not working. Prominent officials in Washington led by Vice President Nixon, the "China Lobby," and the entire ultraconservative wing of the Republican Party were vocal in warning the nation of the Chinese Communist threat in Indochina. Nixon, in a radio and television speech on 23 December, cavalierly wrote off the real cause of the Indochina war with the remark, "If China were not Communist, there would be no war in Indochina. . . ."[56] His remark, however, may have been an accurate reflection of public opinion, both then and later. The view "in Peoria" was always that if the communist factor were removed, all would be well in Viet Nam. That American officialdom could be so ill informed remains the puzzle.

Secretary Dulles, at his news conference six days later, referring to the setback in Indochina, said that the military significance of the communist action had been grossly "exaggerated" and that there was "no reason . . . for anybody to get panicky," adding that he had "never thought there was much sincerity" in Ho Chi Minh's peace feelers. And Dulles warned that Chinese Communist intervention in Indochina might set off an American reaction "not necessarily confined to the particular area which the Communists chose to make the theater of their new aggression."[57]

In the autumn of 1953 the United States, England, France, and the Soviet Union had several critical issues to resolve; Indochina was one, but there was also the matter of Germany's and Austria's future. The United States, concerned with communism's expansion, had devised the European Defense Community (EDC) plan which inter alia provided for the rearming of Germany. France strongly opposed an economically and militarily reconstituted Germany but needed the fallout benefits of the American-backed EDC to build up its own position in Europe. The Soviet Union, for obvious reasons, also opposed EDC and supported France's reservations on joining. The United States, hoping to resolve the issue, advanced a proposal for a foreign ministers' meeting, but the USSR stalled. The Soviet counterproposal spoke of the need for a prior renunciation of the EDC by the West and urged the convocation of a meeting of the Big Five, that is, inclusive of Communist China. Finally, the Soviets agreed to a Big Four meeting in Berlin in January 1954.

The conference opened on 25 January in the American sector of Berlin. The chief representatives were Dulles, Eden for the United Kingdom, Vyacheslav Molotov for the USSR, and Bidault for France. The first item on the agenda had to do with Germany's reunification and alliances, but soon other issues crept in. Even before the conference Molotov offered Bidault Russia's help in arranging an armistice in Indochina in exchange for France's withdrawal from EDC. As France's representative, Bidault was firm on EDC and his position was unalterable. With regard to Indochina he had a problem. His personal and political inclination was toward a "military solution," but his instructions were to seek a "diplomatic settlement" even if it meant dealing with the Viet Minh. He needed and actively sought Soviet help. In the days that followed, Bidault met privately and separately with Molotov, Eden, and Dulles, hoping to introduce the Indochina issue on the agenda of the projected Geneva meeting. But Dulles was adamant, even though eventually he had to agree. In the last analysis it was France's war and the Laniel government could not completely avoid negotiations without alienating itself from popular opinion and bringing about its own downfall at the hands of anti-war opposition parties.

The conference ended on 18 February without any agreement on the reunification of Germany or an Austrian treaty. However, before closing, the conferees agreed to accept Molotov's proposal for a Big *Five* Far Eastern peace parley in Geneva on 26 April to discuss ways and means to reach a peaceful settlement of the Korean question and to discuss the problem of restoring peace in Indochina. Dulles had successfully opposed Soviet efforts to gain for Communist China the status of a sponsoring power and insisted that the Berlin communiqué include a statement that no diplomatic recognition not already accorded would be implied either in the invitation to, or the holding of, the Geneva Conference. Even so, when Dulles returned to Washington the next day, he had difficulty convincing Congressional leaders that the seating of the Chinese Communists at the conference table with American representatives would not imply American recognition of the Peking regime.

☺ ☺ ☺

In the meantime (December 1953–January 1954) Giap's forces had begun to position themselves around Dien Bien Phu, while continuing their penetration of Laos. Navarre's efforts to stem the Red Tide were fruitless and resulted in heavy losses and dispersion of forces, particularly in the area of aircraft maintenance. On the sixth of February the Pentagon announced that forty B-26 bombers and two hundred American civilian technicians (to service the planes) would be sent to Indochina. Admiral Arthur W. Radford, Chairman of the JCS, justified the shipment to the House Foreign Relations Committee only a month prior to the siege of Dien Bien Phu by saying that the Navarre Plan was "a broad strategic concept which within a few months should have a favorable turn in the course of the war."[58]

The American press made much of the sixth of February announcement, speculating that perhaps the shipment of "technicians" might be a precursor to sending American combat personnel to Indochina to bail out the foundering French. Senator Mike Mansfield, two days after the announcement, asked on the Senate floor whether if the French could not hold their own in Indochina we would be sending naval and air support to bail them out. Did it mean, he wondered, that if the situation warranted it American combat troops were to be sent? To allay these fears and still support Radford's position, three days later Secretary of Defense Charles E. Wilson said that no American pilots or ground troops would fight in Indochina and added that no aid was planned at "any higher level than now." Wilson denied that Indochina would turn into another Korea for the United States. "From our view and that of the French," he said, "the war is going as well as expected at this stage" with "a military victory . . . both possible and probable."[59]

French demands for more aid and American official reassurances that all was "going as well as expected" did not make sense to the man on the street. At the President's press conference of 10 February, Marvin Arrowsmith of the Associated Press asked Eisenhower if "sending these technicians to Indochina will lead eventually to our involvement in a hot war there." The President would only say that ". . . no one could be more bitterly opposed to ever getting the United States involved in a hot war in that region than I am; consequently, every move that I authorize is calculated . . . to make certain that that does not happen." Daniel Schorr of CBS Radio pressed the point by asking if the President's remarks should be construed as meaning "that you are determined not to become involved or, perhaps, more deeply involved in the war in Indochina, regardless of how that war may go?" The President replied, "I am not going to try to predict the drift of world events now. . . . I say I cannot conceive of a greater tragedy for America than to get heavily involved now in an all-out war in any of those regions, particularly with large units."[60]

The President ended his remarks to Schorr by justifying American involvement "because it is a case of independent and free nations operating against the encroachment of communism."[61] The President overlooked one important point: only France was "independent and free"; Viet Nam, half of it a colony and half engaged in a war for independence, would be neither "independent" nor "free" until the conclusion of the Geneva Conference, still more than five months away.

While the involvement of American forces was heatedly debated in the United States, public opinion in France favored a quick "out" from the endless war. With Laos threatened, Minister of National Defense Pleven wanted to know if it should be defended. The National Defense Committee told him to instruct Navarre to evacuate upper Laos if necessary but to keep in mind that the safety of the Expeditionary Corps remained first priority. Pleven was going to Indochina in February 1954 for a firsthand look at the situation. On the inspection tour were also General Paul Ely, Chairman of the Chiefs of Staff Committee; General Fay, Chief of Staff of the Air Force; and General Clément Blanc, Chief of Staff for the Land Forces. They met with General Navarre, and General Ely expressed concern about the "hedgehog" strategy which only created "game preserves" for the Viet Minh. Navarre defended his strategy as adequate in keeping the Viet Minh at bay and conserving resources. As to Dien Bien Phu, one of the "hedgehog" outposts, Navarre was not sure of the enemy strength encircling it. It looked to him as though the Viet Minh had intended to attack it but gave up because it was too well fortified. Then General Fay questioned the usefulness of the airfield at Dien Bien Phu after several weeks of rain. Navarre replied that no one had mentioned that particular weakness to him but he would look into it.

The inspection party returned to France on the first of March. The military and political reports portrayed a dismal picture. The Generals concluded "that no military solution could be achieved"; not even heavy reinforcements could influence the outcome in any way. Pleven had found the political situation not altogether favorable to the French. He reported that the Viet Minh might not be loved but were feared and respected. The number of villages under the influence of the Bao Dai government was diminishing in direct proportion to the spread of Viet Minh control. Pleven recommended that every effort be made at Geneva to find an acceptable solution. He also advised against dealing directly with Ho because that would be viewed as a betrayal by the Baodaists. Hence the only answer was to use the Geneva Conference as an honorable way of ending the war.

Panic struck the Paris government. It felt that France had no time to lose and must do something drastic to salvage its former colony. After the usual political maneuvering between the doves and the hawks, Laniel placed his conditions for a cease-fire before the National Assembly on 5 March:

1. Evacuation of all Viet Minh troops from Laos;

2. The demarcation of a "no-man's-land" around the Red River delta and controlled withdrawal from the area of all Viet Minh forces;

3. Regrouping of all Viet Minh forces within an area in central Annam to be determined; and

4. The disarming or withdrawal of all Viet Minh troops in Cambodia and Cochinchina.

Even the least informed should have perceived that Laniel's conditions amounted to a Viet Minh surrender and represented only a naive hope of achieving in a desperate, eleventh-hour move all that seven years of war had failed to gain.

Obviously, they were not dealing with the "boys" of colonial days. Ho and his advisers were no longer neophytes in the game of international maneuvering; nevertheless, on 10 March the DRV indicated it was prepared to consider the French proposal. In fact, the DRV considered the French proposal very seriously, not in the context of French objectives but in light of all the implications to the coming Geneva Conference.

For six months Ho and his advisers had been closely following American involvement in the war. Reports from Moscow, Delhi, and Peking pointed to the threat of America's becoming actively engaged on the side of France. The newest Eisenhower statement at another press conference on the tenth of March was very alarming to the DRV as it suggested that American plans for direct involvement had progressed to the point where they could be put into action at any moment. The day before the President met the press Senator John C. Stennis of the Armed Services Committee had demanded that we withdraw our Air Force technicians from Indochina. "We are taking steps that lead our men directly into combat," he said. "Soon we may have to fight or run." This prompted James J. Patterson of the *New York News* to ask the President what we would do if one of those men was captured or killed. The President replied, "I will say this: there is going to be no involvement of America in war *unless it is a result of the constitutional process that is placed upon Congress to declare it*" (emphasis added).[62] This much was public and from it the DRV could easily perceive that the drift was toward active American involvement and that Eisenhower was keeping the option of outright intervention open.

In fairness to all concerned with American involvement in Viet Nam, it should be noted that in late 1953 not everyone was in agreement as to how far we should go into the French-Vietnamese conflict. The Department of the Army emphatically questioned the assumption of some policy-makers that we could continue giving military aid and assistance to the French without eventually having to commit ground forces as well. The Army argued that if the area was as important to American security interests as the NSC maintained, then the issue should be faced squarely in order to make proper arrangements. The Plans Division of the Army General Staff pointed out in most emphatic terms that the Army did not have the capability to commit ground combat troops in Indochina while maintaining ongoing programs in Europe and the Far East. It suggested a reevaluation of the importance of Indochina and Southeast Asia in relation to the possible cost of saving it.

But, with the deterioration of the French position in December and January, the Department of Defense had to consider intervention in Indochina to insure that it did not fall into communist hands. Again, not everyone was of a single mind. Chief of Naval Operations Admiral Robert Anderson proposed to Secretary Wilson (6 January 1954) that we employ combat forces immediately in Indochina on the "reasonable assurance of strong indigenous support of our forces," *whether or not the French government approved*. But Vice Admiral A. C. Davis, Director of the Office of Foreign Military Affairs in the Office of the Secretary of Defense, put his judgment of the matter in cogent terms:

Involvement of U.S. forces in the Indochina war should be avoided at all practical costs. If, then, National Policy determines no other alternative, the U.S. should not be self-duped into believing the possibility of partial involvement—such as 'Naval and Air units only.' One cannot go over Niagara Falls in a barrel only slightly.[63]

Davis continued,

Comment: If it is determined *desirable* to introduce air and naval forces in combat in Indochina it is difficult to understand how involvement of ground forces could be avoided. [Bases would be needed.] Protection of those bases and port facilities would certainly require U.S. ground force personnel, and . . . would need ground combat units to support any threatened evacuation. *It must be understood that there is no cheap way to fight a war, once committed* (emphasis added).[64]

The evident disparity between, on the one hand, our high strategic evaluation of Indochina and, on the other, our unwillingness to reach a firm decision on the forces required to defend the area became the subject of the National Security Council meeting, on 8 January 1954. The representatives of State and Defense were at considerable variance on what should be done on either of two contingencies: first, French abandonment of the struggle and, second, a French demand for substantial U.S. forces. The State Department considered the French position so critical already as to "force the U.S. to decide now to utilize U.S. forces in the fighting in Southeast Asia." The Defense representative refused to underwrite U.S. involvement.

The NSC meeting left open the question of American action in the event troops were indisputably necessary to prevent the "loss" of Indochina. In this regard the JCS kept their options open. The Chiefs thought that the Navarre Plan was fundamentally sound but steadily undercut by the gulf separating the French from the Vietnamese, by Navarre's failure to carry out our recommendations, and by hesitancy in Paris over the necessary political concessions to the Bao Dai government. Yet the JCS refused either to rule out the use of U.S. combat forces or to back unequivocally their employment.

Unable to clearly resolve the basic question of American intervention, the DOD and the JCS came up with a joint "solution"—to rectify French deficiencies. They took the position that an alternative military solution existed within the reach of the French which required no U.S. intervention. The DOD representative argued that the three reasons for France's deteriorating position were their lack of will to win, their reluctance to meet Indochinese demands for true independence, and their refusal to train indigenous personnel for military leadership. The DOD believed that premature American involvement would beg the basic question of whether the United States was prepared to apply the strongest pressure to France, primarily in the European context (EDC), to force the French, both in Paris and in Indochina, to take appropriate measures to rectify their own deficiencies. Only if these measures were forthcoming, DOD held, should the United States seriously consider committing ground forces in defense of the interest of France and the Associated States. The net effect of the DOD-JCS position was to challenge the notion that a quick American military action in Indochina was either feasible or necessary.

Fully aware of the precarious French situation in Indochina, something which the Americans surmised but had no positive knowledge of, Pleven suggested to the Council of Ministers (11 March) that General Ely accept Admiral Radford's invitation to go to Washington. He was to brief the American leaders on the true military situation so they would not go to Geneva thinking that a military victory could be won. Of utmost concern to the French and the Americans was the threat of Chinese intervention. It was no secret that the introduction of Russian-made MIG-15s flown by Chinese pilots could raise havoc with the small and inadequate French air force in Indochina. Pleven was also uneasy that there was no written agreement with the United States as to what action we would take in such an eventuality. Bidault said only a verbal promise had been made by us and that consisting only of a reconsideration of the problem if it came up. However, Bidault reassured the ministers that, in his opinion, the United States would do the honorable thing. Pleven would not be satisfied; he wanted more tangible assurance, and Ely was instructed to do what he could to obtain it.

۵ ۵ ۵

On 13 March the Viet Nam People's Army under the personal command of General Giap began its assault on Dien Bien Phu. This recently reinforced fortress was to take on a political and psychological importance far out of proportion to its actual strategic value because of the upcoming Geneva Conference. The DRV correctly foresaw that a show of decisive force, not to mention a dramatic victory, would markedly strengthen its hand; with the help of the Chinese Communists they had prepared for the siege. The DRV also counted on the psychological effect a defeat of the French Union forces would have on the French nation, sapping the will of the French people and the anticommunist Vietnamese to continue the struggle.

While Laniel was patronizing the Viet Minh with his preposterous conditions for a cease-fire, the Vietnamese were making their final arrangements for the Battle of Dien Bien Phu, arrangements which had begun in late November 1953 when Navarre decided to reoccupy the small outpost and the Viet Minh decided to "liberate" it.

The Viet Minh decision set into motion a tremendous logistic and tactical effort, in some ways comparable to eighteenth century methods but still most effective in the twentieth. The Chinese Communists had provided the DRV with material aid and after the Korean armistice also sent several military advisers. One high-ranking Chinese general was attached to Giap's headquarters; other officers were assigned to various levels of the VPA. They also provided the Viet Minh with about sixty Russian-made 37mm antiaircraft guns, radar installations, and several *Katyusha* (multi-tube rocket launching) batteries manned by Chinese crews to protect the one hundred 105mm howitzers (American-made) positioned on the slopes surrounding Dien Bien Phu. Another useful Chinese contribution was one thousand *Moltova* trucks sent over the secretly constructed road from Meng-tzu, China, to Dien Bien Phu. But the major feat of their mammoth logistic operation was the portage service organized by the Viet Minh from local resources. It kept a steady flow of supplies and men coming to Giap's divisions encircling the French at Dien Bien Phu.

Unquestionably the assault came as a complete surprise to the French. It was preceded by a heavy artillery barrage which proved largely impervious to French counterbattery fire and aerial attack. The French were outnumbered (although they had twelve battalions in garrison) and outgunned. The battle raged furiously from the thirteenth to the eighteenth when the last of the three northern hills defending Dien Bien Phu was abandoned. The first, *Beatrice*, fell on the night of 13–14 March; the second, *Gabrielle*, was overrun on the fifteenth; three days later the third, *Anne-Marie*, had to be abandoned. Full details of the battle have been well described in other works, such as Fall's *Street Without Joy*. Had Giap followed through on his early success, the main post, it is believed, would have fallen in a matter of two weeks, but the final attack did not come until 7 May.

As the battle developed, the optimism that had pervaded Washington statements, both public and private, was replaced with a conviction that unless new steps were taken to deal with Chinese aid the French were bound to go under. General Ely arrived in Washington on 20 March. Dulles and Radford were very much concerned with the sudden turn of events. They wanted to hear from Ely what had happened to the Navarre Plan and how serious the situation was. Ely presented an optimistic view and assured our people that Dien Bien Phu would hold out provided the United States delivered the B-26 bombers. Ely then broached the question of American intervention if the Chinese entered the war, but Dulles said he could not answer that. Ely considered Dulles's answer a change in American position; yet he was not discouraged for Eisenhower had agreed to see him personally.

Ely was received by the President at the White House on the morning of the twenty-second of March with Admiral Radford present. The President indicated that we would honor France's request for more aid and said we would supply as much as was needed to save Dien Bien Phu. General Ely was asked to delay his departure and meet with Radford for further talks. At their meeting on the following day Radford proposed massive night strikes against Viet Minh forces at Dien Bien Phu by aircraft of the U.S. Air Force and the U.S. Navy. This was called Operation Vulture (*Voutur*) and entailed the use of about sixty B-29s from Clark Field in the Philippines, escorted by one hundred and fifty fighters of the U.S. Seventh Fleet.

While Radford and Ely were discussing Operation Vulture, Dulles held a news conference on the twenty-third, at which he optimistically said, "I do not expect that there is going to be a Communist victory in Indochina." He sidestepped questions regarding further aid to France by saying that he did not know if any request had been made, but added, "As their request for material become known and their need for that become evident, we respond to it as rapidly as we can."[65]

By the time Ely was ready to leave, it became evident that he had spoken quite frankly with our officials at the Pentagon and the State Department, for the outward optimism overnight changed to one of serious misgivings. Somehow Ely had let it be known that France was on the verge of negotiating a cease-fire even under the most unfavorable conditions.

The internal debate within the Administration by late March had progressed to the point where it was recognized that: (1) unilateral U.S. intervention would not be effective without ground forces; (2) the use of American ground forces was logistically and politically undesirable; and (3) intervention to save the area would be preferable if it took the form of a collective operation by allied forces. This was the sense of the NSC deliberations, the special reports of Lieutenant General Matthew B. Ridgway and Under Secretary of State W. Bedell Smith, and President Eisenhower's general train of thought. Accordingly, Dulles in his discussions with General Ely went beyond the question of immediate assistance to the garrison at Dien Bien Phu and broached the possible establishment of a regional defense organization for Southeast Asia.[66]

This was the juncture at which the Eisenhower administration began to reconsider its position and back away from unilateral intervention. Any intervention we were going to make would be a part of a collective venture with our European and Asian allies. In a speech to the Overseas Press Club of America on 29 March Dulles warned the public of the alarming situation in Indochina and called for "united action"—without defining further what he meant by this term.[67] This undefined concept alarmed the British and the French, as well as the Chinese. To reduce the risk of an overreaction or a miscalculation, the State Department compounded the confusion with a cryptic "clarification" that any "united action" intervention would not be aimed at the overthrow or destruction of the Peking regime. Then, within the Administration, State recommended: (1) no U.S. military intervention for the moment, and no promise of it to the French; (2) continuation of planning for military intervention; and (3) discussions with potential allies on the possiblility of forming a regional grouping in the event of an unacceptable settlement at Geneva.

The situation at the besieged garrison did not improve, of course. Giap staged a massive attack on 30 March and brought the airstrip under constant fire, rendering it useless to the French. In the next three days Viet Minh forces advanced to within one mile of the center of Dien Bien Phu before withdrawing to regroup.

The President decided, on 3 April, that the United States would undertake no unilateral intervention. Any American involvement would be based on the formation of a coalition force with American allies to pursue "united action," on an open declaration by the French of an intent to accelerate independence of the Associated States, and on Congressional approval (which was to be dependent on the first two conditions).

Despite these policy guidelines, the NSC at its 6 April meeting developed curiously incompatible objectives that the United States "intervene if necessary to avoid the loss of Indochina, but advocate that no steps be left untaken to get the French to achieve a successful conclusion of the war on their own," and also support as the best alternative to U.S. intervention a regional grouping with maximum Asian participation.

Eisenhower accepted the Council's recommendation but decided that from that point on the Administration's primary effort would be directed toward organizing regional collective defenses against communist expansion, getting British support for American objectives in Southeast Asia, and pressing France to speed up its timetable for Indochinese independence. In the meantime, the President would seek behind-the-scenes Congressional support for American participation in a regional arrangement, if it could be put together, and start secret planning for mobilization.

While the President was coming to his 3 April decision against unilateral intervention, General Ely had returned to Paris on 27 March and had reported to Pleven his conversations in Washington, especially the extraordinary offer made by Radford to undertake Operation Vulture. An emergency secret session of top French officials had been called by Laniel to discuss the Radford proposal. The reaction of the participants which, among others, included Pleven, Bidault, and the military service chiefs, was mixed. They felt that American intervention at that point might elicit violent reaction from the Chinese and extend the war (which did not displease Bidault and the hawks) and would further internationalize the conflict, taking the initiative away from France (which Laniel did not want). A liaison officer was sent to Saigon on 1 April to get Navarre's views. His reply was that, by all means, France should accept help to save Dien Bien Phu and "stabilize the situation." In ignorance of Eisenhower's decision against unilateral intervention, another secret session of the top French officials was held on the fourth of April and a French decision was reached to accept Radford's proposal. Laniel called in Ambassador Dillon and made an official request for American intervention. Dillon cautioned that it would take time; the reply from Dulles was prompt enough but not encouraging to the French: America could do nothing without Congressional approval and without the cooperation of its allies, especially Britain, but everything short of a declaration of war would be undertaken. Thus the French request was rejected and Dien Bien Phu had to manage on its own.

When the curtain began to fall on the French effort at Dien Bien Phu and the question of what the United States would do came to a critical point, the Administration had backed away from unilateral intervention.

The DOD remained reluctant in the face of the Army's insistence that air-naval action alone would not do the job and ground forces would be needed. The Korean experience was still vivid and the thought of another Asian land war gave everyone pause. Furthermore, Eisenhower was unwilling to enter into any venture without Congressional approval which, in turn, depended on the participation of allies. Hence, Dulles undertook to persuade Britain, France, and the Asian allies to participate in a coalition for "united action."

Thailand and the Philippines responded favorably to the call for "united action," but the British response was one of caution and hesitancy. Churchill accepted Eisenhower's suggestion that Dulles go to London for further talks. But the British saw danger in pressing for a defensive coalition *before* the Geneva Conference, and Eden was determined not to be "hustled into injudicious military decisions."

Dulles flew to London and on to Paris (11–14 April). In London, he met with strong opposition from both Churchill and Eden. On reflection, Dulles tried to sell the British an ad hoc coalition which might develop later into a Southeast Asian defense organization (SEATO). This, he maintained, would deter China from further interference in Indochina and would strengthen the western position at Geneva through solidarity. Eden was not convinced; he opposed any military action or warning announcement before Geneva. Furthermore, France had not asked for such a coalition. Eden was sure that France wanted to arrive in Geneva with complete freedom of action and without entanglements which would restrain her in achieving peace. Dulles interpreted the British position as one for settlement, lest United States involvement increase the risk of Chinese intervention and an expansion of the war.

Relations between Dulles and Eden after these talks were quite strained. Dulles was irritated at the way Eden wrote off Indochina; Eden on the other hand was highly pessimistic about Dulles's militancy in an area of uncertain value for which the United States had ambiguous, high-risk plans. Furthermore, the British believed that Indochina need not be entirely lost at Geneva in the absence of "united action." They were puzzled by American talk of the "loss" of Indochina, for at 10 Downing Street it was believed that the "French cannot lose the war between now [April 1954] and the beginning of the rainy season however badly they may conduct it."[68]

Dulles fared no better in Paris. The French were seeking quick action to avoid an imminent military defeat at Dien Bien Phu. But Dulles would not be drawn away from a collective allied approach to the war. The French also feared that a coalition arrangement, inherently international, would take control of the war out of their hands; they desired only local assistance at Dien Bien Phu along the lines of Operation Vulture. Another French objection was that efforts toward "united action" would only impede or delay negotiations toward the settlement which they increasingly desired. Our American objective was to keep alive French determination to continue the war.

Premier Laniel reaffirmed to Dulles that his government would take no action which directly or indirectly turned Indochina over to the Communists. But he also reminded Dulles of the strong desire among the French to get out of Indochina at any cost. Laniel stressed that it was necessary to await the results of the Geneva Conference and that the French could not give the impression in advance that they believed Geneva would fail.

In a last-ditch stand, Dulles in Paris and Bedell Smith in Washington tried to convince the French that only by appealing to the British for intervention, as they had appealed to the United States, could the Dien Bien Phu garrison be saved. But the British held fast. Churchill rejected a plea from French Ambassador René Massigli for a statement that Great Britain would join the United States and France in defense of Dien Bien Phu. Dulles returned to Washington (15 April) with only British and French pledges to "examine the possibility of collective defense" for Southeast Asia and the western Pacific, but with no encouragement for concerted action.

Dien Bien Phu was, of course, in extremis in the latter part of April. Giap had dug in around the French and had closed every avenue of escape. On 21 April the French commander, General Christian de Castries, appealed for reinforcements of men and supplies "at any cost." At least 45,000 Viet Minh troops had been added to the original four divisions surrounding the French stronghold which held an estimated 16,500 men. By the twenty-third, Giap's forces had moved to within seven hundred yards of the center of the fortified town.

۞ ۞ ۞

As the desperate struggle at Dien Bien Phu continued, the first part of the Geneva Conference opened on 26 April. It was restricted to Korean questions; but China's Premier and Foreign Minister, Chou En-lai, nevertheless demanded that the United States and other Western powers be excluded from Far Eastern affairs. Dulles argued that the authority of the United Nations was at stake. Chou En-lai replied that Korea was an Asian matter and should be resolved among Asians, "seeking common measures to safeguard peace and security in Asia." Soviet Foreign Minister Molotov supported Chou En-lai and added that "the peoples of Asia have the full right to settle their own affairs."[69]

Dulles returned to Washington on 4 May, and in his public statement of the seventh, said that according to plan he had delegated Under Secretary of State General Walter Bedell Smith to take his place at Geneva. He took the French to task for not giving the Associated States their independence which he observed would have robbed the communists of their claim of leading the fight for independence. Then he foretold the inevitable fall of Dien Bien Phu but reassuringly stated, "the fall of Dien Bien Phu will harden, not weaken, our purpose to stay united." Posing a rhetorical question—"What we should do about the current hostilies in Viet Nam?"—he warned of the risk of a "Communist takeover and further aggression." "If this occurs," he said, "the need will be even more urgent to create the conditions for united action in defense of the area." In the matter of direct intervention or declaring war, Dulles emphasized that Eisenhower would not take any action without Congressional approval.[70]

The last gun fell silent at Dien Bien Phu at about 2:00 A.M., local time, on 8 May 1954. At 4:00 P.M. that afternoon the second phase of the Geneva Conference convened to discuss the Indochina question. It was a meeting of diverse political and economic interests, with France and the DRV in the role of principals but also with a client-patron relationship with the superpowers. The conference got off to a rocky start in an atmosphere of gloom, uncertainty, and suspicion. The Communist Bloc held all the aces.

All the conferees had come with specific motives, none of which was altruistic: France had lost the will to fight and wanted a quick settlement; the United States had failed to keep France in the fight against the spread of communism in Southeast Asia through united military efforts but still pursued containment as a goal; Britain wanted to restore peace and reduce the international tension which adversely affected its interests in that region; Communist China was seizing the opportunity to face the United States on an equal footing in matters of international significance; and the DRV wanted and expected to be recognized as a sovereign entity to be dealt with on its own merit.

Of all the participants, the United States was the most encumbered ideologically. All along we had voiced concern for Indochina's future status as an independent state in various forms and in many forums. With the passing of time the concept of self-determination for the Indochinese became confused and eventually degenerated into mere lip service although remaining an ideological "hang-up."

At Geneva our policy was predicated on fallacious assumptions. While we held that we had been helping the Indochinese to fight communism to assure them freedom and independence, that was not supported by either official American pronouncements or by the realities. First Acheson and then Dulles talked only of "containment of communism," not the freedom from French rule for which the Viet Minh was fighting tooth and nail. Then there was the assumption among our policymakers that the discredited and corrupt Bao Dai government had a strong following among the people. We still failed to accept the fact that it had a history of ambivalence and opportunism, that it had been set up by the French merely as a façade to suppress Indochinese aspirations for self-determination and to safeguard French colonial interests.

The official record of our involvement in Indochina is totally lacking in evidence that our government made any effort to probe into the true nature of Ho Chi Minh and his movement for independence. It perfunctorily dismissed the DRV as "communistic" and willingly joined colonial France in waging a ruthless war against it. At no time did the United States attempt to understand or win the friendship of the Vietnamese people but callously provided the wherewithal for the French government in Indochina to destroy the only grassroots effort to achieve independence.

Almost to the very end, our policy was based on another wholly unfounded assumption—that the French were supportive of American anticommunist objectives and that the French military position was tenable and improving daily. We cannot blame ourselves entirely for this but must share the responsibility. After all, for nearly eight years our diplomats and military leaders had accepted on blind faith all the vagaries and deceptions handed out by the French to obtain American support for their colonial enterprise, never questioning, always willing to oblige. Our officials refused to take a cold, hard look at the Indochina situation; wearing rose-colored glasses was de rigueur. Yet when the end came on 8 May, Dulles, still unwilling to recognize our part in the debacle, unfairly placed the onus on the French. True, the French had been reluctant to admit defeat to the Americans, but we need not have been so obtuse to what was evident all around. The wide gap between France's gravitating toward a negotiated cease-fire and our country's insistence on continuing the war to a "successful conclusion" but without American intervention had already hardened before the discussions began.

Aside from the divergence of motives and America's miscalculated policy, there were other acute differences among the allies as the conference opened. One was with the British. The French had cleverly exploited the American assistance program without having brought in the Americans in full force, yet had been unable to save Dien Bien Phu. But the British were felt in Washington to have been the primary obstacle to "united action" and were accused of having been so blinded by their own self-interest in other areas of Southeast Asia that they failed to appreciate the vast strategic importance to the free world of "saving" Indochina.

The contrasting Communist Bloc unity on the eve of the Conference was more a matter of Sino-Soviet agreement on the desirability of negotiations than of complete accord among the three parties. In the aftermath of Stalin's death, Soviet policy under Malenkov had altered considerably. Domestic priorities no doubt influenced the new regime's proclaimed hopes for a reduction in international tension. Peking, more intimately involved in the Viet Minh cause, stepped up its assistance to Giap's forces between February and April 1954 but also agreed with Moscow on the desirability of convening an international conference, which China would attend, to end the fighting. The limited available evidence suggests that the DRV alone among the three parties considered the call for negotiations premature and urged that they be preceded by intensified military efforts. Ho's much publicized offer of November 1953 to talk with the French was intended more to influence French domestic and official opinion and to demoralize Franco-Vietnamese troops than to evince sincere interest in arriving at an equitable settlement. DRV broadcasts in ensuing months showed a far greater interest in first achieving a clear-cut military victory in the Red River delta and parts of Laos than in engaging in discussions while French forces remained scattered through Indochina.

These developments, in broad outline, provided the backdrop to the Geneva Conference. Strength and weakness seemed to be the respective characteristics of the Communist and Western positions. Yet these labels, as will be seen, are not entirely accurate, for the interaction between and within the two sides was to make clear that the Geneva Conference would not be the setting for a victor's peace.

۵ ۵ ۵

One of the first agreements reached at Geneva occurred in the course of a conversation between Molotov and Eden on 5 May when the Soviet Foreign Minister endorsed Eden's assertion that this negotiation was the most difficult he had ever encountered.[71] Indeed, it seems at first glance somewhat paradoxical that the Indochina phase (8 May–21 July) should have resulted in a settlement within twelve weeks, given the unusual difficulties facing the negotiators.

Key issues were postponed until the eleventh hour while debate wore endlessly on over relatively insignificant matters. Contact between the various delegations was limited by ideological prejudice and political antagonism, forcing some delegates to act as mediators no less than as representatives of national interest; and major agreements were ultimately reached outside the special framework that the conferees had taken a month to build.

Chester L. Cooper, a member of the American delegation and author of *The Lost Crusade: America in Vietnam*, gives a flavor of the absurdities that hampered personal relations among the negotiators:

A certain amount of spice was provided by the attempts of the huge American delegation to pretend that the even huger Chinese delegation did not exist—and vice versa. . . . Many Chinese and Americans had known each other in earlier incarnations. . . . I found myself alone in an elevator with a young Chinese I had known from my college days. . . . Neither of us spoke, but as we looked at each other we began to smile and then to laugh. By the time we arrived at the conference floor we were convulsed. As the door opened we hastily recovered our composures and studiously avoided looking at each other from that moment on. (Pp. 104–105)

The first major roadblock was communist insistence that the Viet Minh-led Free Cambodian (Khmer Issark) and Free Laotian (Pathet Lao) forces were entitled to be seated beside the Royal governments of Cambodia and Laos. Not until 16 June, when Premier Chou En-lai, China's Foreign Minister and its delegate, indicated to Eden that Viet Minh forces would be withdrawn from Cambodia and Laos, was the debate resolved.

The time-consuming exchanges over the authenticity of these communist "resistance forces" in Laos and Cambodia were, interestingly enough, not duplicated when it came to determining the status of the DRV. At the Berlin Conference it had been agreed that invitations to other governments would be issued only by the Berlin conferees, that is, by the Big Four, but not by Peking. Yet, as Molotov admitted at the first plenary session (8 May), Peking as well as Moscow invited the DRV, a move vigorously assailed by France and the United States. No attempt was made, however, to block the DRV's participation. Despite the antagonism of the Bao Dai government, which claimed to be the sole legitimate government of Viet Nam, the DRV was generally considered one of the principal combatants whose consent to a cease-fire was indispensable and therefore its participation required. Moreover, the Soviet Union told the French it would not accept the presence of the Associated States' delegates unless the DRV was admitted to the Conference. By the time Dien Bien Phu fell, all parties were agreed that there would be nine delegations (not states) discussing Indochina.

The nine delegations sat at a round table to exchange views about every second day, obscuring the fact that true bargaining was not taking place. Proposals were, of course, made, debated, and tabled, but actual give and take was reserved for private discussions, usually in the absence of the pro-Western Indochinese parties. Even then, the Geneva talks were hardly dominated by Big Power cabals; political and ideological differences were so intense, particularly between the American and Chinese representatives, that diplomacy had to be conducted circuitously, with Eden and Molotov frequently acting as mediators and messengers for delegates unwilling to be found together. As one example of the American attitude, Dulles told reporters just prior to the first session that the only way he could possibly meet with Chou En-lai was if their cars collided.

The Viet Minh sent a delegation of four, three of whom were no strangers to France. They were led by Pham Van Dong, the principal spokesman for the Viet Minh years before at the Fontainebleau Conference (July 1946) who had risen to Deputy Prime Minister and Minister for Foreign Affairs ad interim. The others were Phan Anh, Minister of Economy; Ta Quang Buu, Vice Minister of National Defense; and Hoang Van Hoan,[72] pro-Chinese, a founding member of the ICP, and the DRV's first Ambassador to Peking. All four were, of course, familiar names from the very earliest days of the Ho regime in Hanoi.

It was not until the latter half of June that high-ranking French and Viet Minh delegates met face-to-face, that Viet Minh military officials conferred with Cambodian and Laotian representatives, and that French and Chinese heads-of-delegations privately exchanged views. Communist and noncommunist Vietnamese refused to talk to one another until the last month of the Conference. Most importantly, the American delegation, under strict instructions to avoid contact with the Chinese, had to rely on secondhand information provided by the British, French, and Soviet representatives, a procedure that was repeated with respect to the Viet Minh.

The problem of contact was acutely felt by the delegation of the State of Viet Nam. Although they finally were granted complete independence by France (4 June 1954), Viet Nam did not gain concurrent power to negotiate its own fate. The French were afraid of upsetting their private and delicate talks with the Viet Minh; they avoided Bao Dai's representatives and sought to exploit close Vietnamese-American relations by informing the Baodaists only after agreements with the Viet Minh had been reached. This French aloofness from the Baodaist delegation continued into July. Although the question of partition had been under discussion in private talks among the French, Viet Minh, Chinese, Soviet, and American representatives, not until late in the Conference did Bao Dai's "government" become aware of the strong possibility that partition would become part of the settlement; on this and other developments the Vietnamese were kept in the dark, a circumstance that would solidify Vietnamese hostility to and disassociation from the final terms. Could this truthfully be considered "independence"?

Between 18 and 21 July the conferees were able to iron out their differences sufficiently to produce the agreements now commonly referred to as the Geneva "Accords." They consisted of separate Military Agreements for Viet Nam, Cambodia, and Laos to fulfill the Conference's primary task of restoring peace to Indochina and a Final Declaration designed to establish the conditions for future political settlements throughout Indochina. Only the Military Agreements were signed.[73] The Final Declaration, consisting of statements by the conferees, was not signed by any nation, but was agreed to by voice vote. As French writers Lacouture and Devillers put it so well, "The Geneva conference had discovered a new form of peaceful coexistence—that which results from tacit agreement among the parties to a negotiation; and a new form of legal obligation between states—an unsigned treaty."[74]

Broadly, the Military Agreements provided for the cessation of hostilities (a cease-fire) which were still in progress; for the partition of Viet Nam along a demarcation line near the seventeenth parallel, with a demilitarized zone five kilometers wide on either side of the line as a buffer zone; for the regroupment of the VPA or Viet Minh forces to the north and the French Union forces to the south of the demarcation line; for movement control of persons across the demarcation line; for the prohibition of troop reinforcements, resupply of arms and war materiel into either side of the demarcation line; for the prohibition of any new bases in

Viet Nam or Laos or of the establishment of military bases by any foreign powers in Viet Nam, Laos, and Cambodia; and for the establishment of an International Control Commission to observe and enforce the terms and provisions of the Agreements.

The political "understandings" contained in the unsigned Final Declaration obligated seven of the nine nations involved (Britain, France, Cambodia, Laos, the USSR, China, and the DRV). The United States and the State of Viet Nam (Bao Dai's government) merely "took note" of the Agreements. Bedell Smith speaking for the United States declared that we would "refrain from the threat or the use of force to disturb" the Agreements. With regard to "free elections in Viet Nam," Smith limited his remarks to express the sense of the 29 June "Potomac Declaration" which had been issued jointly by Eisenhower and Churchill. As included in the Final Declaration it read:

In the case of nations now divided against their will, we shall continue to seek to achieve unity through free elections, supervised by the United Nations to ensure that they are conducted fairly.[75]

The key issues of the Final Declaration pertained to the holding of secret general elections in July 1956: the withdrawal of French forces at the request of the governments of Viet Nam, Cambodia, and Laos; the prohibition of reprisals; the protection of individuals and property; a freedom of choice on which zone one wished to reside in; and respect for the independence of the three States and refraining from interfering in their internal affairs.

✿ ✿ ✿

The wobbly settlement at Geneva put an end to the fighting in Indochina but not to France's obsession to hold on to its "pearl of the East." The humiliation of military defeat at the hands of the Viet Minh and "that miserable Annamite peasant" was more than French national pride could endure. The loss of Tonkin, especially the delta region, was an intense frustration and disappointment to the colon of Viet Nam and the conservative rightist of metropolitan France.

Tonkin represented a century of costly French effort to westernize it and develop it culturally and economically. It was there that the Bank of Indochina stood vigil over France's financial interests in the East, where the University of Hanoi with its French faculty imparted French culture and molded political thought, and where Catholicism flourished among the rural people. Its abandonment under the Geneva settlement represented an irreparable loss. France was demeaned.

Still greater was the humiliation France endured when, in the end and at American insistence, she had to accept withdrawal from Indochina without benefit of a face-saving device of general elections and had to accede to a second, more final abandonment. The supplanting of France by the United States in South Viet Nam and the failure of the

Geneva settlement, both well advanced in mid-1956, denied the French Left its prospects for cooperation with Ho Chi Minh in a precedent-setting experiment at coexistence and disappointed moderates who had hoped to preserve French cultural influence and salvage French capital. It enraged Rightists who interpreted American policies in Viet Nam invidiously. None of these factions was prepared to take a stand for France's staying but all tried to draw political support from acrimonious treatment of the United States.

On the international level the traumatic experience of France's withdrawal heavily strained the Western alliance, which had not been solid even during the Geneva Conference. America's disassociation from the Final Declaration and Dulles's headlong plunge into the formation of the Southeast Asia Treaty Organization (SEATO)—creating a schism in the British commonwealth—was distrusted and resented by both France and Britain. Their worst fears, discreetly voiced in 1944-46, had now come to pass—the United States was taking over in Southeast Asia.

Despite the strong terms of the Accords, all but one of the conferees anticipated continued French presence in Viet Nam. The exception was the State of Viet Nam under its new Premier, the francophobic Catholic mandarin Ngo Dinh Diem. Although he had been appointed by Bao Dai (15 June 1954), Diem wanted full independence for South Viet Nam, free of France and free of Bao Dai. Diem argued that France had just lost a long, devastating, and demoralizing war against Vietnamese communists as well as Vietnamese nationalists. Colonial rule had been tight and previous French promises of independence had been broken. Why believe professions of French good intentions in 1954? Were they any different from those of the past? Added to this skepticism was the problematical relationship of France vis-à-vis South Viet Nam and the DRV. Some South Vietnamese expected France to work actively toward accommodation with the Viet Minh and reunification under Viet Minh direction. Many more felt that continued French presence alone compromised South Vietnamese independence. Diem reasoned, "To convince the people of Viet Nam that the administration was independent, it became a political necessity to be anti-colonial and specifically anti-French."

France's position in Viet Nam had many difficulties. More than Diem, more than the psychological damage done by the colonial years, the United States also made life in Viet Nam difficult for France. At first American policy was directed toward close collaboration, even partnership, with France, looking to a joint sponsorship of the American-backed Diem. We were eager to strengthen Viet Nam and needed and demanded French cooperation but we offered little in return. Our policy insisted upon an immediate and dramatic transformation of French thinking. But we little understood what this meant to France, what problems it created for French domestic and foreign policy, or what American concessions might help effect the transformation.

The United States began revising policy toward Indochina very early, even as the Geneva Conference ended. The exercise was marked by urgency dictated by the belief that Geneva had been a disaster for the free world. The Accords gave Communist China and North Viet Nam a new base for exploitation of Southeast Asia; they enhanced Peking's prestige to Washington's dismay and detriment; and they restricted free world room to maneuver in Southeast Asia. And the grant of Vietnamese territory above the seventeenth parallel to Ho Chi Minh was a painful reminder of the scarifying French defeat, the first defeat of a European power by Asians—Asian communists at that—and a defeat shared by the United States to the tune of more than $1.5 billion in economic and military assistance granted to France and the Associated States.

The first step toward countering the disaster was the establishing of SEATO. It was to be a "new initiative in Southeast Asia" to protect American interests in the Far East and stabilize the "chaotic situation . . . to prevent further losses to communism" through subversion or overt aggression. The pact (concluded on 8 September 1954) proved to be neither the new initiative nor the strong anticommunist shield desired by Dulles. The failure was largely of American making. While Dulles wanted to put the communists on notice that aggression would be opposed, the JCS still stood in opposition and refused to have the United States committed financially, militarily, or economically to unilateral action in the Far East.

As on other occasions, the United States' response to "military urgency" altered its good intentions and moved beyond partnership to primacy in Viet Nam. The EDC proposal, under consideration in Brussels during the Geneva Conference sessions, was finally rejected by France on 30 August 1954, a grave disappointment to the United States. Some have suggested that the French turn-down may have been in part payment for Molotov's support of Mendès-France at Geneva. Then when SEATO came into being Dulles, still on his "stop communism's expansion" kick, pushed SEATO into establishing a line of containment in Southeast Asia and looked to transforming South Viet Nam into a key anticommunist redoubt.

To accomplish this it was essential to insure the loyal support of the Government of South Viet Nam (GVN). The American formula was to convince France to treat South Viet Nam as an independent and sovereign state; urge Diem to organize a representative government, after which the Constituent Assembly would be called and a constitution drafted to herald the dethroning of Bao Dai and the inauguration of democracy; and demand firm French and American support for Diem. Despite his rigidity, his penchant for a one-man show, and his inability to communicate or deal with people, Diem was a nationalist, untainted by past association with either the Viet Minh or the French. This quality, plus full independence and Franco-American backing and encouragement for broad reform ultimately would result in a strong and anticommunist South Viet Nam. Or, at least, so the United States thought.

American determination to back Diem was made with the knowledge that French support for him was hardly enthusiastic. It came at a time when the French nation was plagued with internal political dissension and seriously troubled with the Algerian problem (erupting into open warfare in November 1954) and reluctant in aiding the GVN. Also, opposition to Diem was strong among the followers of Mendès-France's philosophy of "peaceful coexistence." French Union Counselor Jacques Raphael-Leygues, reportedly a member of the Mendès-France "brain trust" on Indochina, told Ambassador Dillon that French contacts in Hanoi had convinced Paris that South Viet Nam was doomed and the "only possible means of salvaging anything was to play the Viet Minh game and woo the Viet Minh away from communist ties in the hope of creating a Titoist Viet Nam which would cooperate with France and might even adhere to the French Union." Raphael-Leygues said France deferred to the United States' wishes over which government to support in Saigon in order to get money for its French Expeditionary Corps and to fix responsibility for the eventual loss of South Viet Nam on the United States.

This thinking alarmed our policymakers and on 23 October 1954 President Eisenhower addressed a letter to Diem announcing that the United States would provide economic aid and military assistance directly to him, his government, and his armed forces.[76] This shifting of our vast financial backing from French channels to the Vietnamese brought doom and gloom to France, and Frenchmen grumbled loudly about the enlarged American role. Nor did France accept being shouldered aside with grace; through the fall of 1954, Franco-American relations worsened. We had shot down the circling Albatross.

Ambassador Bonnet in Washington remonstrated to Dulles that the President's letter gave Diem full rein without requiring as a preliminary condition that he should first form a strong and stable government. He added that the letter might be a violation of the armistice and that the Viet Minh might take advantage of it. Then when Ambassador Dillon suggested at the Quai d'Orsay that French support for Diem had not been all that it might have been, Guy La Chambre (Minister of the Associated States) was inflamed. Not only was it a false allegation, he said, it was a direct slur on General Ely (French High Commissioner in Viet Nam), the government in Paris, and the glory of France. M. La Chambre said he was personally convinced Diem was leading South Viet Nam to disaster but would still support him:

We prefer to lose in Vietnam with the US rather than to win without them; . . . we would rather support Diem knowing he is going to lose and thus keep Franco-US solidarity than to pick someone who could retain Vietnam for the free world if this meant breaking Franco-US solidarity.[77]

Once again military considerations emerged as paramount. The JCS, previously opposed to our assuming responsibility for training the Vietnamese National Army (VNA), finally agreed to sending a training mission to MAAG Saigon but insisted on safeguards against French interference. Since the French Expeditionary Force (about 150 thousand men) was still in Indochina, development of the training and related programs necessitated sending to Viet Nam someone with diplomatic status. General J. Lawton Collins was selected and given the rank of ambassador.

Collins's first serious reservation, perhaps at the suggestion of Mendès-France, was about Diem's ability to stabilize the government and he recommended (16 December 1954) the return of Bao Dai from abroad. If this were unacceptable, he recommended American withdrawal from Viet Nam. The French considered this a drastic measure and asked that Collins and High Commissioner Ely study the problem. Dulles took a contrary view, that Diem was the only suitable leader identifiable, and made it clear that Congress would probably not appropriate funds to a Viet Nam without Diem. Another Franco-American confrontation was coming to a boil, but Collins finally relented and agreed with Dulles, Mike Mansfield, Kennedy, Cardinal Spellman, and others that there was no one in sight to replace Diem. And, perhaps to appease the French, Collins recommended continued American military aid to France. Collins's justification was that "Viet Nam would be overrun by an enemy attack before the Manila Pact Powers [SEATO] could act." And to "encourage the French to retain sufficient forces," Collins urged American financial support of at least $100 million through December 1955. General Ely concurred.

In the meantime events in Viet Nam seemed to support those who, like the JCS, continued to entertain strong reservations about the future of Ngo Dinh Diem and his government. Diem managed to survive attempted coups by army leaders and succeeded in maintaining an unhappy peace with the several armed factions in Cochinchina. But his political future remained questionable at best. At the same time, the French mission in Hanoi pressed hard to preserve economic and cultural prerogatives in North Viet Nam. Echoes of 1945 could be heard again. French political leaders in Paris spoke grandiloquently of a cooperative modus vivendi with the DRV becoming a model for East-West relations—a disquieting message for the American Secretary of State and those in and out of the Administration who shared his convictions. Finally, parallel to these developments, Emperor Bao Dai, in retaliation for Diem's vituperative political campaign against him, actively sought to supplant Diem.

All of these tensions resolved themselves into two central issues between the United States and France. The first was the question of how and by whom Viet Nam's armed forces (VNA) were to be trained. The second, more far-reaching, was whether Diem was to remain at the head of the government or be replaced by another nationalist leader more sympathetic to Bao Dai and France. The first issue was resolved relatively quickly. General Collins struck an agreement with General Ely by which,

despite serious misgivings in Paris, France agreed to turn over the training of the VNA to the United States and to withdraw French cadres. On 12
February 1955, the United States assumed responsibility for training Vietnamese forces and the French disassociation began.

The political controversy over Diem was less easily resolved. Diem
exacerbated matters with increasingly vehement strictures against the
French and Bao Dai. The United States for its part was insensitive to the
impact within France of Diem's militant anticommunism—frequently
directed at the French Left—and of the rancor aroused by American
statements portraying America as the only friend of Vietnamese nationalism. The United States, however, did listen to French warnings that
Diem was categorically incapable of unifying Vietnamese nationalists.
French advice to the United States that Diem should therefore be replaced was seconded by Collins. Throughout the winter and spring of
1955 Dulles and the Department of State in general seemed disposed to
consider favorably suggestions that an alternative leader be placed in
power. However, no one with the requisite qualities (anti-French, anti-Bao
Dai) competitive with Diem's could be found.

But by now the United States and France were caught up in a sweep
of events. The French backed General Nguyen Van Hinh, Chief of Staff of
the VNA, who aspired to the premiership and plotted to unseat the pro-
Catholic Diem. With help from the anti-Catholic sects (Cao Dai, Hoa Hao)
and the Binh Xuyen, Hinh made several unsuccessful attempts at coups
against the Diem regime. Then in September Diem uncovered another
plot, arrested some of Hinh's supporters, removed the general from command, and ordered him out of the country. Hinh refused to leave and continued his machinations against the government. Plans for a coup in October 1954 were dropped when Hinh was told revolt would mean automatic termination of American aid. Another scheduled for 26 October
was foiled when Colonel (later Brigadier General) E. G. Lansdale, our CIA
man on the scene, cleverly diverted the plotters to other endeavors. Finally in November 1954 Bao Dai was persuaded by the United States and
France to intervene on Diem's behalf. He did, by inviting Hinh to Cannes,
and on 19 November the general left the country.

The sects then directly challenged Diem's authority and he responded with force. An uneasy truce ended the first clash in March 1955 and
amid mounting tension in April the United States, France, and Bao Dai all
sought actively to bring about a change in the GVN. On 28 April, Diem,
against the advice of the United States, France, and his own cabinet,
moved again against the sects. When the Binh Xuyen resisted in Saigon,
Diem committed the VNA to battle. Diem's forces won an immediate
military victory while, simultaneously, Diem's brother, Ngo Dinh Nhu,
coopted a committee of nationalist figures who called for Bao Dai's
removal and the transfer of civil and military power to Diem.

Encouraged by Diem's success the United States declared its une-quivocal support for him as opposed to Bao Dai. This presented acute dif-ficulties for France. The French government was convinced that Nhu's "Revolutionary Committee" was under Viet Minh influence and strongly resented a renewed GVN campaign against the French presence.

In May 1955 France, the United States, and Britain met in Paris to discuss European defense, but France promptly made Viet Nam the prin-cipal item on the agenda. France maintained that the United States by backing Diem forced upon France the necessity for withdrawing alto-gether from Viet Nam. French Foreign Minister Edgar Faure held that Diem was "not only incapable but mad. . . . France can no longer take risks with him." Dulles in reply indicated that the United States was aware of Diem's weaknesses but stressed his recent successes as in-dicating redeeming qualities. But Dulles pointed out, "Viet Nam is not worth a quarrel with France" and offered American withdrawal in preference to allied disunity.

No immediate decision was made. During a recess Dulles received advice from the JCS that Diem seemed the most promising avenue to achievement of American objectives and that, while withdrawal of the French Expeditionary Corps was "ultimately to be desired," a precipitate withdrawal should be prevented since it would "result in an increasingly unstable and precarious situation" and the eventual loss of South Viet Nam to communism. Dulles then proposed to the French that they con-tinue to support Diem until a national assembly was elected. British sup-port for Diem seems to have swayed Faure, and he accepted Dulles's pro-prosal. The tripartite meeting ended on a note of harmony, but the under-tones were distinct: the days of American-French collaboration were over and thereafter the United States would act independently of France in Viet Nam.

Backed by the United States, Diem refused to open consultations with the North Vietnamese concerning general elections when the date for these fell due in July 1955. Pressing his military advantage against the sects, he moved to consolidate his position politically within South Viet Nam. In October he won a resounding victory in a popular referendum; it was also a shallow victory because voters were only given a choice be-tween Diem and Bao Dai. As Diem's political strength grew, his relations with Paris deteriorated. In December 1955 Diem suddenly terminated the existing economic and financial agreements with France and called upon France to denounce the Geneva Agreements and break with Hanoi. Soon thereafter Diem withdrew South Vietnamese representatives from the French Union. It should be noted, however, that Diem's political strength did not necessarily represent a large popular constituency. There re-mained discontent in some quarters and a generalized apathy.

On 2 January 1956 general elections in France produced a government under Socialist Guy Mollet, a third of the members of which were communists or avowed neutralists. In early March, Mollet's Foreign Minister, Pineau, declared in a speech to the Anglo-American Press Association in Paris that France would actively seek a policy position bridging East and West and that there was no unanimity of policy among the United States, the United Kingdom, and France. He specifically cited the United Kingdom's Middle East policy and America's support for Diem as contrary to French interests and condemned both powers for stirring up the Moslem world to France's distinct disadvantage in North Africa. A few days later at a SEATO Council meeting in Karachi, Pineau proclaimed the end of the "era of aggression" and called for a "policy of coexistence."

Action followed. France agreed (22 March 1956) with Diem to withdraw the French Expeditionary Corps altogether and the French High Command in Saigon was disestablished on 26 April. On the due date for the general elections agreed to at Geneva, France possessed no military forces in Viet Nam. And the date for the fulfillment of the political portions of the settlement, July 1956, coincided with the inception of the Suez crisis.

As in Coleridge's "Ancient Mariner," the United States was left alone on the foundering ship Viet Nam with the putrefying Albatross around its neck.

☙ ☙ ☙

April 1980

Three decades have passed since these events in Indochina began. In the intervening years the world witnessed the saddest episode in America's history. Castigated and humiliated for its misguided adventurism, the Albatross remains ever present on America's political scene—a scene dominated with an infantile optimism about world capitalist domination that, at best, would isolate the United States and, at worst, precipitate a new world war. It is hardly conceivable that after all that has gone before, our dismal track record in the Far East (China) and Southeast Asia (Vietnam, Cambodia), our national leaders continue to answer the echoes of the past, oblivious to the inevitable consequences. Yet with the dawning of a new decade we are about to embark on a similar but still more perilous course.

The parallelism is striking. The crisis in Iran, attributed by many to American meddling, and the Soviet intrusion into Afghanistan, a by-product of the Iranian upheaval, have suggested a reshaping of our long-range strategy, a strategy in which the United States is once again attempting to provide a defense umbrella for an area where regional rivalries and religious differences are paramount obstacles to any Western influence. In effect, it is a recasting of the former "Truman Doctrine," the 1947 program to stem the tide of communism in Turkey and Greece.

The so-called Carter doctrine, more ambitious than the older model, hopes to cope not only with the classic "threat of Soviet expansionism" but also with complex regional issues related to American corporate control of the oil-producing areas. As in the Truman-Acheson years, the new doctrine is also predicated on the need to "protect American interests." Only this time the area has changed from Southeast to Southwest Asia, as the area of the Middle East, the Persian Gulf, and South Asia is now called. As with the old doctrine the problems are the same—"united action" now called "regional cooperation," with recalcitrant allies; establishment of military bases in politically unstable areas; raising an adequate military force to man and protect those bases; and the potential for open hostilities.

While in the earlier period the United States faced the single issue of "containment of communism" in Southeast Asia, today the issues in Southwest Asia are many and varied, much more difficult to resolve and infinitely more treacherous in outcome. Aside from the Soviet strategic threat, issues such as the Arab-Israel impasse, the India-Pakistan rivalry, the alignment of the oil-producing countries in a pro-Western bloc against Soviet influence, and the ultimate risk of an all-out confrontation with the USSR are insurmountable obstacles to the success of the new Carter doctrine.

In the light of recent experience it is all too obvious that America's interests can best be served by withdrawing from brinksmanship and by reassessing its role in world affairs. The United States no longer has absolute military and economic superiority. Western Europe and Japan no longer need American economic assistance and appear willing to seek independent accommodations with the Warsaw Pact nations and the Soviet Union. The old economic and military strings no longer hold the alliance to America's global objectives. Without resorting to isolationism, the United States would do well to concentrate its efforts on using its national resources for domestic consumption and trading only with other nations on the basis of reciprocity, exclusive of incentives for strategic advantages. Lastly, the United States should strive to achieve essential military parity with, but not superiority over, the Soviet Union. This is the lesson we should have learned from our past history.

APPENDIX I

CHRONOLOGY OF SIGNIFICANT EVENTS

1858–84
France invades Da Nang (1858), occupies Saigon (1859), annexes Cochinchina (1867), attacks Hanoi (1873), and imposes colonial rule throughout Indochina by August 1884.

1890

May 19   Birth of Nguyen Tat Thanh (Ho Chi Minh).

1911

December (?)   Nguyen Tat Thanh, under the name "Ba," sails from the port of Saigon for France.

1919

January   Nguyen Tat Thanh, calling himself "Nguyen Ai Quoc," petitions members of the Peace Conference at Versailles for the emancipation of the Vietnamese people in accordance with President Wilson's "Fourteen Points."

1920

December 25–30   At the Tours Congress, "Nguyen Ai Quoc" opts for the French Socialist Party's joining the Third International (Comintern), thereby becoming a founding member of the French Communist Party and the first Vietnamese communist.

1925

June   Ho founds in Canton the Viet Nam Thanh Nien Cach

Mang Dong Chi Hoi (Association of Vietnamese Revolutionary Youth), an antecedent of the Indochinese Communist Party.

1927

November

Foundation of the Viet Nam Quoc Dan Dang (VNQDD) (Viet Nam Nationalist Party).

1930

February 3

Under instructions from the Comintern (Moscow), Ho Chi Minh at Kowloon (Hong Kong) unifies three splinter communist groups into one official party; and at the first plenum in October adopted the name Dang Cong San Dong Duong (Indochinese Communist Party).

February 9–10

Yen Bay uprisings; VNQDD leadership flees to China.

September

Xo Viet Nghe-Tinh formed in Tonkin.

1931

June 5

Ho Chi Minh arrested by the British police in Hong Kong.

1932

Ho Chi Minh is released from the British prison in Hong Kong and makes his way to Moscow.

1940

June 14

Fall of France.

July 20

Governor General Georges Catroux is replaced by Admiral Jean Decoux.

September 22

Japanese troops occupy northern Indochina with French approval.

December

Ho Chi Minh returns to the China-Viet Nam border and starts a training program for cadres.

1941

February 8

Ho arrives at Pac Bo, Viet Nam.

May 10–19

Meeting of the Eighth Plenum of the Party Central Committee at Pac Bo; the Viet Nam Doc Lap Dong Minh (Viet Nam Independence League or Viet Minh) is founded.

August 14

President Roosevelt and Prime Minister Churchill meet on the high seas, agree on war aims, and produce the Atlantic Charter.

December 7

Pearl Harbor is attacked by the Japanese.

1942

February 15

British surrender Singapore.

March 8

Dutch surrender Java.

April 9

U.S. forces on Bataan surrender.

August 28	Ho Chi Minh crosses the border into China and is arrested by the Chinese authorities.

1943

May 15	Third International (Comintern) dissolved in Moscow.
September 10	Ho Chi Minh is released from imprisonment by Chang Fa-kwei but remains in China to work with the Dong Minh Hoi.

1944

June 6	Allied invasion of Normandy.
August 25	Paris liberated.
September 6–8	General Hurley arrives in Chungking as Presidential Representative to the government of China.
September 12	General Mordant is secretly appointed Delegate General for Indochina.
October 31	Wedemeyer replaces Stilwell as Commander of U.S. Forces in China.
November 1–17	Gauss resigns and General Hurley is appointed American Ambassador to the Republic of China.
December 22	Viet Minh intensifies anti-French and anti-Japanese activities in Tonkin and creates the Viet Nam Propaganda and Liberation Army, the future People's Army of Viet Nam (PAVN).

1945

February 4–12	Yalta Conference.
March 9	Japanese dissolve the French government in Indochina, immobilize French political and military forces, and declare Viet Nam "independent."
March 11	Emperor Bao Dai proclaims independence and cooperation with Japan.
March 24	The Minister of Colonies in the name of the Provisional French Government issues "Declaration Concerning French Policy in Indochina."
April 12	Death of President Roosevelt; Vice President H. S. Truman is sworn in as President.
April 25	United Nations Conference opens at San Francisco.
April 27	First meeting between the author and Ho Chi Minh.
May 8	V-E Day.
July 16	Potsdam Conference opens. OSS' "Deer" Team arrives at Ho Chi Minh's jungle headquarters.
July 24	President Truman at Potsdam approves the military

	decision to divide Viet Nam for operational purposes at the sixteenth parallel.
August 6	First atomic bomb is dropped at Hiroshima.
August 8	The USSR declares war on Japan.
August 9	Second atomic bomb is dropped at Nagasaki.
August 13–15	ICP conference is held at Tan Trao.
August 15	Japan accepts unconditional surrender.
August 16–17	Meeting of the People's National Congress at Tan Trao; Ho is "elected" president of the provisional government.
August 19	Hanoi insurrection.
August 22	The OSS Mercy Team lands in Hanoi. President Truman and General de Gaulle meet in Washington. Commissioners Messmer and Cédile are airdropped into Tonkin and Cochinchina, both captured by Vietnamese.
August 23	Tran Van Giau forms a pro-Viet Minh Provisional Executive Committee for the South in Saigon.
August 24	Chiang Kai-shek publicly declares China has no territorial ambitions in French Indochina.
August 25	Saigon celebrates independence.
August 26	Giap welcomes the American mission in Hanoi. First meeting in Hanoi between the author and Ho Chi Minh.
August 27	Sainteny meets with Giap in Hanoi. Cédile meets with Giau in Saigon.
August 28	Chinese troops cross border into Indochina.
August 29	Mme. Chiang Kai-shek and President Truman meet in Washington.
August 30	Ho's first message to Truman. Bao Dai abdicates.
September 2	The Japanese sign surrender terms on the U.S.S. *Missouri* in Tokyo Bay. Independence Day in Hanoi. Disorders in Saigon. Arrival of first Americans in Saigon.
September 3	Chinese advance staff arrives in Hanoi.
September 4	Colonel Dewey arrives in Saigon.
September 6	First British and French troops arrive in Saigon.
September 9	Lu Han's troops enter Hanoi. Reorganization of the Provisional Executive Committee for the South.

September 11	Chinese in Hanoi evict the French team from the Governor General's Palace.
September 12	Fly-in of advance units of the 20th Indian Division and of the French 5th RIC in Saigon.
September 13	General Gracey arrives in Saigon with the main body of his troops.
September 14	General Lu Han arrives in Hanoi.
September 16	Lu Han and Ho Chi Minh meet for the first time. Opening of "Gold Week." General Gallagher arrives in Hanoi.
September 17	Vietnamese call a general strike in Saigon.
September 19	Cédile suspends talks with the Vietnamese in Saigon. General Alessandri and M. Pignon arrive in Hanoi.
September 20	Gracey imposes press censorship in Saigon.
September 21	Gracey proclaims martial law in the Saigon-Cholon area.
September 22–23	Cédile arms POWs and executes a coup d'etat in Saigon. Ambassador Hurley and Wedemeyer depart for Washington for conferences at the State Department. Gallagher meets Ho. Alessandri calls on Lu Han. Catholics rally in Hanoi.
September 24	Ho's second message to President Truman.
September 25	Massacre at Cité Hérault.
September 26	Colonel Dewey is murdered.
September 28	Gracey and Cédile are called to Singapore by Mountbatten and ordered to reopen talks with the Vietnamese.
September 30	The author meets with Ho for the last time.
October 1	OSS terminated. Gracey reopens talks with Vietnamese. General Ho Ying-chin arrives in Hanoi. Mountbatten is authorized to use Gracey's troops to aid the French.
October 3	5th RIC debark at Saigon.
October 5	Leclerc arrives in Saigon. Governor Lung Yün is removed by Chiang Kai-shek in the "Kunming Incident."
October 6	Talks between Cédile and Bach break down in Saigon.
October 9	British-French Civil Affairs Agreement is signed in London giving the French full authority to administer Indochina south of the sixteenth parallel.

October 10	Viet Minh attack Saigon airport and begin open warfare.
October 16	Viet Minh's last stand in Saigon before retreating to begin guerrilla war.
November 11	Ho dissolves the ICP and sets up the Indochina Association of Marxist Studies.
December 26	Viet Minh, VNQDD, and Dong Minh Hoi agree to unite in a Provisional Coalition Government following national elections.

1946

January 6	First general elections held. Ho Chi Minh (VM) is elected president; Nguyen Hai Than (DMH) is elected vice-president; and Nguyen Tuong Tam (VNQDD-Dai Viet) is appointed Minister for Foreign Affairs.
February 28	Franco-Sino Treaty is signed at Chungking providing for the withdrawal of all Chinese troops from Viet Nam by 31 March 1946, with the French relinquishing all extra-territorial and related rights in China.
March 6	Sainteny signs an agreement in Hanoi with Ho Chi Minh and Vu Hong Khanh in which France recognizes the DRVN as a free state within the Indochina Federation of the French Union; the DRVN agrees not to oppose the re-entry of French troops into Viet Nam to replace the Chinese in repatriating Japanese forces (for a period not to exceed ten months) and to help the Vietnamese maintain order (for a period not beyond 1952).
March 18	Leclerc enters Hanoi. Bao Dai leaves Hanoi for Hong Kong.
April 18–May 11	Dalat Conference (First).
June 1	French announce the formation of an independent state of Cochinchina within the Indochinese Federation and the French Union.
July 6–September 10	Fontainbleau Conference.
September 14	Ho Chi Minh and the Minister of Overseas Territories, Marius Moutet, sign a modus vivendi giving the French unlimited rights in Viet Nam and no hope of freedom or independence for the Vietnamese.
October 28– November 14	The DRVN National Assembly convenes, approves the new government, adopts a constitution, elects a permanent committee, and adjourns.
November 20	Serious armed clashes between the French and Vietnamese occur at Lang Son and Haiphong. French ships shell Haiphong killing six thousand civilians.

December 19 — French demand disarming of the Vietnamese militia (Tu Ve) and turning over all security duties to the French. The Vietnamese reject the demands and large-scale conflict breaks out. Beginning of the Indochina War (1946–54).

1947

The first year of the Indochina War is a period of power struggles and shifting alliances. Frustrated by the Viet Minh's insistence on full recognition of the DRVN and total independence for Viet Nam, the French choose a policy of military victory and exclude meaningful negotiations with Ho Chi Minh. Anticommunist nationalists also clamor for independence and compel the French to seek an alternative focus to Vietnamese nationalism and, from 1947 forward, to advance the "Bao Dai solution."

March — Émile Bollaert replaces Admiral d'Argenlieu as High Commissioner.

May — Paul Mus, Bollaert's political adviser, is told by Bao Dai in Hong Kong that he would ask of France as much as Ho Chi Minh, that he would not rule for France, but if his people wanted him he might reconsider under the right circumstances.

May 11 — Mus meets with Ho Chi Minh who refuses to capitulate to French demands.

July — In an attempt to remove the Communist label from his government, Ho Chi Minh rearranges his cabinet to broaden participation by noncommunists. Dismissed are two close lieutenants, Vo Nguyen Giap and Pham Van Dong, and the only VNQDD minister, Truong Dinh Tri. The new cabinet: three Communists, three Socialists, three Independents, two Democrats, and one Catholic.

September 18 — On the advice of anticommunist moderate nationalists, Bao Dai issues a proclamation that "in compliance" with a request of the Vietnamese people to arbitrate the conflict he would be willing to "talk" with the French.

October — General Valluy launches his Expeditionary Corps' first offensive against Giap's forces in the Viet Bac (northern Tonkin). The massive operation is a colossal failure.

December 7 — First Ha Long Bay Agreement. Bao Dai and Bollaert sign an agreement associating Bao Dai with a French-sponsored nationalist movement.
The French promise in vague terms national independence for Viet Nam.

December 29 — Former U.S. Ambassador William C. Bullitt in an article in *Life* magazine argues for a policy aimed at winning the Indochina War by rallying the Vietnamese away from Ho through a movement built around Bao Dai. His remarks are interpreted in France as U.S. endorsement of the projected "Bao Dai solution."

1948
After signing the first Ha Long Bay Agreement, Bao Dai doubts French sincerity and promptly disassociates himself from it. He flees to Europe for four months with French diplomats in hot pursuit.

March
Bao Dai returns to Hong Kong and further efforts are made by the French to break the stalemate.

May 20
General Xuan with Bollaert's concurrence and the endorsement of many Bao Dai supporters forms a provisional government.

May 27
Xuan presents his government to Bao Dai in Hong Kong, but Bao Dai refuses his approval without French assurances of national unity and independence.

June 5
Bollaert and Xuan in the presence of Bao Dai (acting as witness) hold a second meeting at Ha Long Bay. A new agreement is signed in which France "publicly and solemnly" recognizes the independence of Viet Nam —but specifically retains control over foreign relations and the Army and defers transfer of other governmental functions to future negotiations; no authority is in fact transferred to the Vietnamese.

June 7
Ho Chi Minh denounces the Xuan government as a puppet of France.

July 11
Bao Dai, who on 5 June had hurriedly departed for Europe, advises Bollaert that he disassociates himself from the second Ha Long Bay Agreement.

October
Léon Pignon replaces Bollaert as High Commissioner.

1949
January 31
Peiping falls to the Chinese Communists, bolstering the Viet Minh's hope for a more friendly ally on its northern border.

March 8
Elysée Agreement is signed. France reconfirms Viet Nam's status as an associated state of the French Union and agrees to unifying Viet Nam and placing it under Vietnamese administration. But France yields neither control of Viet Nam's army nor its foreign relations and again postpones arrangements for virtually all other aspects of autonomy.

June 13
Bao Dai arrives in Saigon and takes office as Head of State.

June 14	Cochinchina government tenders resignation to Bao Dai, merging in principle with the new State of Viet Nam.
July 1	Bao Dai officially announces the establishment of the State of Viet Nam. There now are two states, those of Ho Chi Minh (DRVN) and Bao Dai.
September 21– October 1	Chinese People's Political Consultative in Peiping proclaims the People's Republic of China; Peiping is renamed Peking; the People's Republic of China is officially established at Peking with Mao Tse-tung as Chairman.
November	Chinese Communist Army reaches the Sino-Vietnamese border; Lu Han (in Yunnan) surrenders on 9 December to Mao's forces. Thirty thousand Chinese Nationalist troops retreat to Viet Nam and offer to fight "any communist force" alongside the French; the offer is rejected.

1950

January 18	People's Republic of China recognizes the DRVN and both sign a trade agreement in Peking for military material aid.
January 30	USSR recognizes the DRVN.
February 4	United States extends diplomatic recognition to the government of the Republic of Viet Nam (Bao Dai).
February 16	France requests U.S. military and economic aid in prosecuting the Indochina War.
February 21	DRVN decrees "general mobilization."
February	Viet Minh launches first full-scale attack on the French stronghold at Lao Cai and defeats the French.
March 19	Viet Minh demonstrate in Saigon against the presence of two U.S. warships in the harbor, showing support for the Bao Dai government.
May 1	President Truman approves $10 million for urgently needed military assistance items for Indochina.
May 8	United States sends economic and military aid to Indochina administered through France, not the Bao Dai "government."
May 25	Giap's forces attack and take the fort of Dong-Khé on Route 4 (fifteen miles S of Cao Bang).
June 27	Following the outbreak of the Korean conflict, Truman directs acceleration of military assistance to France and the Associated States in Indochina. He also authorizes the dispatch of a Military Assistance Advisory Group (MAAG) to Indochina.

June 29	The Pau Negotiations open in France to arrange the transfer to the Vietnamese of various services and fiscal controls. Talks continue through November.
August 2	USMAAG of thirty-five Americans reaches Saigon.
September 16 –November 2	Viet Minh forces the retreat of the French Army from northern Tonkin.
December 7	General de Lattre de Tassigny replaces General Marcel Carpentier (as Commander in Chief of the Expeditionary Corps) and Léon Pignon (as High Commissioner).

1951

January 13–May 29	Giap launches three unsuccessful major offensives against the French and suffers the loss of nine thousand men and large quantities of weapons and equipment. He retreats to Viet Bac in June to reconsider his strategy and tactics.
February 11–19	At the National Congress of Unification the Viet Minh and the Hoi Lien Hiep Quoc Dan Viet Nam (League for the National Union of Viet Nam, formed in May 1946) merge into one expanded coalition front known as Lien Viet.
March 3	The ICP, dissolved by Ho Chi Minh in November 1945, emerges under a new name, Viet Nam Workers' Party (Dang Lao Dong Viet Nam, abbreviated to Lao Dong).
April	Hoang Van Hoan is appointed DRVN ambassador to the People's Republic of China.
September 7	U.S. signs bilateral economic cooperation agreements with Viet Nam, Laos, and Cambodia, in Saigon.
November	Sen. John F. Kennedy after a brief visit to Viet Nam states there is little support for the pro-French Vietnamese government among the people of Indochina.

1952

April	Jean Letourneau is appointed High Commissioner in place of General de Lattre de Tassigny who had died of cancer on 11 January, 1952. Nguyen Luong Bang is appointed first DRVN Ambassador to the USSR.
June	U.S. becomes heavily committed to supporting the Indochina War and has already borne one-third of the war's cost.
July	The Sino-Vietnamese Goods Exchange Agreement is signed in Peking.
	United States raises Legation in Saigon to Embassy status. U.S. Ambassador Donald Heath presents creden-

tials to Bao Dai. Vietnamese Embassy is established in Washington.

October

Bao Dai, his political support declining, withdraws from politics.

November

Viet Minh pressure forces French to withdraw from the Viet Bac area; large areas formerly controlled by the French are recaptured.

1953

March 5

Death of Stalin.

April 13–30

Giap undertakes a major offensive in Laos, forcing the French to evacuate Sam Neua (13 April), surrounds the area known as the Plaine des Joncs (23 April), captures Luang Prabang (30 April), and establishes the Resistance Government of Pathet Lao.

May 28

General Henri Navarre replaces General Salan as commander and puts into effect the disastrous "Navarre Plan."

July 27

Korean armistice.

July

Chinese military and economic assistance to Ho Chi Minh is accelerated.

August 4

President Eisenhower stresses need to block communist aggression "to save the rest of Asia."

September

Ngo Dinh Nhu (younger brother of Ngo Dinh Diem) unsuccessfully plots to discredit Bao Dai, overthrow the government of Premier Nguyen Van Tam, and openly resist the French.

November 20

French dig in at Dien Bien Phu as Giap begins his famous siege.

November 29

Ho Chi Minh offers for the last time to negotiate a truce with the French.

December 17

Bao Dai replaces Premier Tam with his cousin, Prince Buu Loc.

1954

January 4

In a last ditch stand to break up the military impasse General Navarre puts into action his "plan" to drive Giap's forces from the coastal area of Annam. It fails and Navarre withdraws to his heavily fortified position at Dien Bien Phu early in March.

January 25
–February 19

Berlin Conference (United States, France, United Kingdom, USSR) held to discuss a settlement of the Korean War also agrees to convene in Geneva to seek resolution of the Indochina war.

March 13–May 7	Viet Minh launches a series of full-scale attacks against Dien Bien Phu.
May 8	Fall of Dien Bien Phu. Discussions on Indochina open at Geneva.
July 7	Ngo Dinh Diem is appointed premier of South Viet Nam by Bao Dai who remains the legal, constitutionally recognized Head of State.
July 21	Geneva Accords signed. One provision of the agreements partitions Viet Nam along the seventeenth parallel into North and South Viet Nam, pending reunification elections.
October 9	Last French troops leave Hanoi.
October 24	President Eisenhower offers South Viet Nam direct economic aid.

1955

February 12	United States takes over the training of the South Viet Nam Armed Forces.
February 19	Viet Nam, Laos, and Cambodia are included in SEATO.
October 23	National referendum in South Viet Nam deposes Bao Dai.
October 26	Ngo Dinh Diem proclaims establishment of the Republic of South Viet Nam and becomes President.
December 12	U.S. Consulate in Hanoi is closed.

1956

July 20	Elections promised by the Geneva Agreements fail to materialize.

1957

January 3	International Control Commission reports that neither North nor South Viet Nam has lived up to their obligations under the Geneva Agreements.
October 22	U.S. installations in Saigon bombed by communist elements.

1958

January	Communist guerrilla activities begin in South Viet Nam.
February	International Control Commission moves its headquarters from Hanoi to Saigon.

1959

April–July	Anti-Diem government, aided by communist elements in South Viet Nam, initiates a campaign of sabotage and terrorism. Two U.S. military advisers at Bien Hoa

become second American casualties in a terrorist raid; the first was Colonel A. P. Dewey killed on 26 September 1945.

1960

April 17	Ho Chi Minh's government protests to USSR and Great Britain against USMAAG increases.
May 5	United States announces the increase of USMAAG by end of year from 327 to 685.
June-October	Terrorism in South Viet Nam increases.
November 11–13	A military coup attempt against Diem fails, while United States urges Diem to widen the political base of his government, institute radical reforms, and take positive action against corruption.
December 20	Formation of the National Front for the Liberation of South Viet Nam (NLF), known generally as the Viet Cong.

1961

January 28	President Kennedy approves the Counterinsurgency Plan for Viet Nam.
January 29	Hanoi Radio welcomes the formation of the NLF.
June 12	Chou En-lai and Pham Van Dong meet in Peking and accuse the United States of aggression and intervention in South Viet Nam.
August 2	President Kennedy says the United States will do all it can to save South Viet Nam from communism.
September 25	President Kennedy, addressing the UN General Assembly, warns of war clouds in Viet Nam.
October 18	A state of emergency is declared in South Viet Nam by Diem.
December 14	President Kennedy pledges increased aid to South Viet Nam.
December 31	U.S. military strength in South Viet Nam reaches 3,200.

1962

February 8	United States sets up the Military Assistance Command, Viet Nam (MACV).
February 18	Robert Kennedy in Saigon declares U.S. troops will remain until Viet Cong defeated.
February 24	Radio Peking states that the United States is waging an "undeclared war" in South Viet Nam and demands the withdrawal of U.S. troops and equipment.
March 17	Tass Soviet news agency charges the United States with

	creating "a serious danger to peace" and demands immediate withdrawal of U.S. troops.
April	U.S. forces in South Viet Nam escalate to 5,400.
May 15	President Kennedy sends U.S. forces to Thailand because of deteriorating conditions in Laos.
August 20	Sihanouk asks President Kennedy for guarantee of Cambodia's neutrality or he will ask the Chinese Communists if the U.S. refuses.
December 31	U.S. strength in South Viet Nam reaches 11,300.

1963

January 2–3	Two hundred Viet Cong soldiers badly defeat two thousand ARVN troops at Ap-Bac in the Mekong Delta. Three Americans killed, making a total of thirty from the start of the Second Indochina War.
May 8–June 16	During a Buddhist celebration at Hué the ARVN fire into crowd. Buddhist demonstrations break out at Hué and martial law is imposed (3 June); Thich Quang Duc, Buddhist monk, commits suicide by self-immolation in Saigon (11 June); Diem troops use force to quell riots (16 June).
August 4	Second Buddhist monk burns self to death.
August 20–21	Main Buddhist pagoda (Xa Loi) is raided by Diem's police and martial law is imposed nationwide.
August 25	Students demonstrate in Saigon, several hundred arrested.
August 27	Cambodia breaks diplomatic relations with South Viet Nam.
September 16	Martial law lifted.
October	U.S. troops total 16,500.
November 1	Diem and his brother, Nhu, assassinated in a military coup. Military junta headed by General Duong Van Minh expresses confidence in the United States and promises to prosecute the war against the Viet Cong.
November 7	United States recognizes the provisional government of former Vice President Nguyen Ngoc Tho, now Premier.
November 22	President Kennedy assassinated. President Johnson assures South Viet Nam of continued U.S. support.

1964

January 30	France establishes diplomatic relations with the People's Republic of China.
	Military junta overthrown by General Nguyen Khanh.

February 8	General Khanh appoints deposed General Duong Van Minh Chief of State and himself Premier.
May 2–3	Terrorists in Saigon harbor sink U.S. aircraft transport ship, *Card,* and throw bombs into an American group inspecting the ship.
June 20	General Westmoreland assumes command of MACV.
July 27	U.S. troop level reaches 21,000.
August 2	U.S.S. *Maddox* and U.S.S. *Turner Joy* report attacks by North Vietnamese gunboats.
August 7	At the request of President Johnson, Congress approves the joint "Gulf of Tonkin" resolution (Southeast Asia Resolution).
August 16–September 13	General Khanh ousts General Minh as Chief of State; student demonstrations force the Revolutionary Council to form a triumvirate of Generals Khanh, Minh, and Tran Thien Khiem to lead the nation.
December 21	A serious rift between the military junta and U.S. administration. Khanh declares South Vietnamese forces will not fight "to carry out the policy of any foreign country."
December 24	Viet Cong bombs U.S. BOQ in Saigon, killing two and wounding fifty-two Americans and thirteen Vietnamese.

1965

January 1–February 7	Viet Cong guerrilla attacks and stand-and-fight battles inflict heavy casualties on ARVN and U.S. installations at Binh-Gia and Pleiku air force base. President Johnson orders around-the-clock retaliatory strikes on North Viet Nam.
February 9	United States and South Viet Nam bomb North Vietnamese installations while USSR Premier Kosygin in Hanoi promises increased aid to Ho Chi Minh.
March 30	A Viet Cong raid blows up U.S. Embassy in Saigon, killing twenty, injuring 175.
February-June	In a February Gallup poll sixty percent of those questioned prefer the Southeast Asia problem be dealt with as a UN problem. U.S. troop level in March reaches 27,000. The USSR and North Viet Nam (in mid-April) propose a four-point program for negotiations which includes the withdrawal of foreign troops and reunification of both Viet Nams through free elections. United States responds by increasing its troop strength to 46,500 in mid-May. After a series of coups and counter-coups in which Generals Khanh and Minh struggle for supremacy, General

Nguyen Van Thieu assumes control of the Armed Forces Council (in February). In June (12–18) Premier Dr. Phan Huy Quat is forced to resign; Air Vice Marshal Nguyen Cao Ky becomes Premier, with General Thieu as Head of State, and promptly breaks diplomatic relations with France (24 June).

July 8	Henry Cabot Lodge replaces General Taylor as Ambassador to South Viet Nam.
July 15	Ambassador W. Averell Harriman begins informal Viet Nam talks with USSR Premier Kosygin.
July 28	United States continues to bomb North Viet Nam with particular emphasis on SAM site targets. McNamara urges increased United States ground action in the south.
October–November	Antiwar demonstrations begin in U.S. cities. Washington announces U.S. troop strength in Viet Nam as 148,300 (23 October). Two pacifists burn themselves in front of Pentagon and UN headquarters (2 and 9 November).
December 3	United States intensifies bombing of Laos to curb infiltration along Ho Chi Minh trail.
December 24–25	United States and Viet Cong agree to a thirty-hour Christmas truce and United States suspends bombing of North.

1966

January	Ho Chi Minh declares that Hanoi peace plan must be accepted by the United States if war is to end. A week later, President Johnson announces resumption of bombing after a thirty-seven day pause.
February	President Johnson, Thieu, and Ky confer in Honolulu (6–8 February) and pledge to continue the war.
	General Taylor testifying before Senate Foreign Relations Committee says United States intends to wage limited war on Viet Nam (17 February).
	Senator Robert F. Kennedy suggests Viet Cong be invited to participate in a coalition government in South Viet Nam (19 February).
March 1–5	President Johnson renews peace appeals and again offers aid to Hanoi.
	McNamara announces U.S. troop strength in Viet Nam at 215,000 and recommends bombing petroleum depots in North Viet Nam.
	General Taylor proposes blockading the port of Haiphong by mining the harbor.

March 10–April 6	South Viet Nam government experiences another political crisis. Dismissal of popular General Nguyen Chanh Thi sparks protests and strikes in Hué, Da Nang, and Saigon and demands for civilian government. Premier Ky responds with the use of force at Da Nang, then seeks accommodation with demonstrating Buddhists and agrees to hold referendum on new constitution.
April 12–20	United States initiates B-52 bombing raids over North Viet Nam. McNamara says U.S. forces total 245,000, plus 50,000 naval personnel offshore.
May	Political unrest in South Viet Nam continues with Buddhists and students rioting in Hué and Da Nang against Ky's military rule and U.S. support of his government. USIS library and cultural center in Hué are sacked and burned (26 May). U.S. Consulate and residence in Hué are burned (31 May).
June	United States continues military buildup. President Johnson calls for unconditional peace talks. United States escalates the war by bombing the outskirts of Hanoi and Haiphong.
July	General Thieu calls for more air action against North Viet Nam and proposes invasion of the North to win the war. Reports that Hanoi intends to try POWs as war criminals prompt UN Secretary-General U Thant to urge both sides to adhere to the 1949 Geneva Convention on the treatment of POWs. Ho Chi Minh, responding to telegram from CBS president, declares "there is no trial in view" for U.S. POWs (23 July).
September 1	President de Gaulle, speaking in Cambodia, advises the United States that it must withdraw its forces from Viet Nam before a negotiated settlement is possible and proposes the United States establish a timetable for military withdrawal as a prelude to international negotiations.
September 5	President Johnson replies that he will publish his timetable when the communists offer a similar timetable.
October	McNamara, after a visit to Viet Nam, reports that "pacification has if anything gone backward" and that bombing has not "significantly affected the morale of Hanoi."

November	White House approves expanded list of bombing targets.
	The Viet Cong offers to observe forty-eight-hour holidays at Christmas, New Year and at Tet (8–12 February). South Viet Nam agrees.
December	United States bombers begin massive raids on targets in the immediate area of Hanoi. Concurrently talks begin in Warsaw between U.S. Ambassador Gronouski and Polish Foreign Minister Rapacki in an attempt to establish direct contact with North Vietnamese diplomats in Warsaw. Talks break down after U.S. bombs Hanoi city in mid-December. To salvage the talks, the United States agrees not to bomb within ten-mile radius of Hanoi. Harrison Salisbury of *New York Times*, in Hanoi at Christmas, confirmed the bombing of civilian areas by U.S. aircraft.
	U.S. troop strength reaches 389,000.

1967

January 1–8	Despite McNamara's advice to deescalate U.S. military involvement (October–November 1966), the JCS and Ambassador Lodge urge President Johnson to approve Westmoreland's request for additional troops.
January 10	President Johnson defends (State of the Union Message) U.S. involvement in Viet Nam and says he will persevere in war despite "more cost, more loss and more agony." Embassy officials begin a series of meetings with North Vietnamese Chargé in Moscow.
February 6	USSR Premier Kosygin arrives in London for talks with British officials.
February 8–12	Period of Tet (Vietnamese New Year) ceasefire.
February 14	Kosygin returns to Moscow.
	United States resumes air action over North Viet Nam.
February 15	McNamara again says war cannot be won by bombing alone.
February 27–March 10	President Johnson orders new type of military action to hasten the end of the war and authorizes bombing of North Vietnamese industrial targets previously on restricted list.
March 15	Ellsworth Bunker replaces Lodge as Ambassador to South Viet Nam.
April	Approximately one hundred thousand demonstrate against the war in New York and San Francisco.
May	United States and South Vietnamese forces move into de-militarized zone for first time, and United States bombs Hanoi power plant one mile north of city's center.

June 22	United States military strength reaches 463,000. Communist strength is estimated at 294,000, including 50,000 North Vietnamese regulars.
July 12	General Thieu says his country needs more U.S. troops but rules out general mobilization in South Viet Nam as disruptive to the economy.
August	President Johnson announces increase in ceiling on troops in Viet Nam to 525,000 (3 August). President Johnson approves new bombing targets (8 August). At Senate Foreign Relations Committee hearings, Nicholas de B. Katzenbach, Under Secretary of State, says Tonkin Gulf Resolution gave the President authority to use U.S. forces without formal declaration of war (17 August). McNamara tells Senate subcommittee North Viet Nam cannot be "bombed to the negotiating table" and argues against expanding the war (25 August), but the committee urges the President to intensify the air war (31 August).
September 1	Viet Cong says its political aims are to overthrow Saigon regime and establish a "national union democratic government" composed of representatives of many parties.
September 3	Nguyen Van Thieu is elected President; a peace candidate, Truong Dinh Dzu, runs a close second.
September 29	President Johnson declares United States will end bombing of North Viet Nam "when this will lead promptly to productive discussions."
October 31	Generals Thieu and Ky are inaugurated as President and Vice-President; Thieu appoints Nguyen Van Loc premier.
November 11	President Johnson offers to meet North Vietnamese leaders on neutral ship in neutral waters. North Viet Nam rejects proposal (November 14).
November 16	Senate Foreign Relations Committee approves two "sense of the Senate" resolutions: (1) calling on the President not to commit U.S. troops in future without "affirmative action" by the Congress in accordance with the Constitution; and (2) urging the President to place the Viet Nam issue before the UN Security Council.
November 30	President Johnson nominates McNamara as President of the World Bank. Senate unanimously passes Senator Mansfield's resolution urging the President to bring the Viet Nam issue before the UN.

| December 27–29 | Sihanouk threatens to seek volunteers from China and other communist countries if U.S. troops cross into Cambodia, except where they are in hot pursuit of enemy forces entering Cambodia illegally and in remote areas. China pledges support of Cambodia if the United States extends the war into that country. |

1968

| January 1–2 | Foreign Minister Nguyen Duy Trinh states Hanoi "will hold talks with the United States on relevant questions" after the United States "unconditionally" halts the bombing of North Viet Nam. The United States resumes its air raids over North Viet Nam the next day. |

| January 29–31 | Allies cancel the scheduled Tet truce and the communists launch major attacks on South Vietnamese cities. The Viet Cong temporarily invade the U.S. Embassy grounds in Saigon, and President Thieu declares martial law. |

| April 3 | North Viet Nam offers to meet with the United States "with a view to determining with the American side the unconditional cessation of the U.S. bombing raids and all other acts of war" so that peace talks may start. |

| May 3–13 | United States accepts Hanoi's offer to meet in Paris for preliminary talks. United States and communist delegates hold their first session in Paris (10 May). |

| August 8 | Nixon receives Republican Party's presidential nomination; says he will run on platform of progressive de-Americanization of the war and honorable peace. |

| October 31 | President Johnson announces the United States will cease "all air, naval, and artillery bombardment of North Viet Nam" as of 1 November. President Thieu says the United States has taken the action unilaterally. |

| November 6 | President Richard M. Nixon is elected. |

1969

| January | Henry Cabot Lodge replaces Harriman as chief negotiator (5 January) and enters into the first substantive session of the Paris peace talks (25 January). |

| February 23 | Communist forces launch a general offensive in South Viet Nam. |

| March 6 | Defense Department numbers U.S. forces at 541,000, the peak of U.S. involvement in Viet Nam. |

| June 8 | President Nixon meets with Thieu on Midway Island and announces that 25,000 U.S. troops will be withdrawn by end of August. |

July 23	President Nixon in Guam indicates the United States in future will avoid situations like Viet Nam by limiting its assistance to economic and military aid rather than active combat involvement—"The Nixon Doctrine."
September 3	President Ho Chi Minh dies.
September 16	President Nixon announces a second troop withdrawal of 35,000 men.
November 15	Moratorium against the war draws huge crowds to Washington and other major cities, demanding an end to the fighting and rapid withdrawal of U.S. troops.
December 15	President Nixon announces third troop reduction— 50,000 by April 1970. Current level is 479,500.

1970

March 18	Sihanouk is overthrown as Cambodia's Chief of State in a coup headed by Marshal Lon Nol. All Cambodian ports are closed to the PAVN and Viet Cong forces.
April 13	U.S. troop strength is down to 429,000.
April 30	President Nixon announces he is sending U.S. combat troops into Cambodia to destroy enemy sanctuaries.
June 24	Senate repeals Gulf of Tonkin Resolution.
June 30	Senate passes Cooper-Church Amendment barring further U.S. military operations in Cambodia and aid to Lon Nol without Congressional approval.
October 7	President Nixon proposes plan for cease-fire throughout Indochina.
December	U.S. troop strength is 339,200. Paris peace talks end second full year without progress.

1971

January	Paris peace talks continue on January 7, 14, and 21— the last date marking the hundredth meeting.
June 12	*New York Times* publishes excerpts from secret Department of Defense study, *United States-Vietnam Relations, 1945–1967*, popularly known as the Pentagon Papers.
July 1	North Viet Nam presents a peace proposal to Henry A. Kissinger in secret meeting in Paris, calling for withdrawal of U.S. forces within six months of agreement, release of POWs, and free elections.
October 3	President Thieu "wins" new four-year term in an unopposed, one-candidate election.
December	United States intensifies bombing of North Viet Nam in an attempt to slow down a communist buildup along the Ho Chi Minh trail. U.S. troops in Viet Nam number 160,000.

1972

February 25	Hanoi and NLF delegations walk out of Paris peace talks in protest of continued U.S. bombing of North Viet Nam.
March 23	United States breaks off the formal Paris peace talks, declaring that the communists refuse to negotiate seriously.
April	North Vietnamese begin major offensive in the south, crossing DMZ in force with armor and artillery (2 April). Communists encircle ARVN troops north of Saigon (9 April). U.S. B-52 strike near Hanoi and Haiphong (15 April), ending four-year deescalation of air war against major North Vietnamese targets. United States announces it will resume Paris talks (25 April).
May	Quang Tri falls to North Vietnamese, giving them control of South Viet Nam's northernmost province (1 May). United States and South Vietnamese call off formal Paris peace talks indefinitely. President Nixon orders the mining of Haiphong and six other North Vietnamese ports, as well as a blockade of supplies for North Viet Nam (8 May).
June	U.S. ground combat role in Viet Nam is terminated, leaving a force of less than 60,000 advisers, technicians, and helicopter crews.
July 13	Peace talks resume in Paris.
August 11	United States withdraws last ground combat unit from Viet Nam: ninety-two men of the Third Battalion, Twenty-first Infantry.
September	South Vietnamese troops retake Quang Tri Citadel (15 September). Hanoi releases three American POWs (19 September).
November	President Nixon is reelected. Hanoi agrees to more peace talks, and Kissinger returns to Paris for seven sessions with Le Duc Tho.
December	Peace talks break down (15 December); Kissinger returns to Washington. President Nixon orders renewal of bombing, including B-52 raids in Hanoi-Haiphong area.

1973

January	Peace talks resume (8 January). All offensive operations against North Viet Nam are ordered stopped (15 January).

Accords are signed (27 January) by Secretary of State Rogers, the Foreign Ministers of South Viet Nam and North Viet Nam, and the Viet Cong's Provisional Revolutionary Government.
A cease-fire begins (28 January).

February–March	Five hundred ninety American POWs are released by North Viet Nam. Last U.S. troops leave Viet Nam, officially ending direct U.S. military role (29 March).
July	Graham Martin replaces Bunker as American Ambassador.

1974

January–May	South Vietnamese ARVN conduct offensive operations against the NLF/PAVN bases around Saigon. Cease-fire of January 1973 breaks down but the conflict does not overtly involve U.S. troops. Fighting between North and South Viet Nam intensifies in the Central Highlands and west of Saigon.
June 3	United States withdraws its advisers from Laos, following the formation of a Laotian coalition government (5 April).
August 9	President Nixon resigns from office.
December	Hanoi government (DRVN), anxious to end military operations and to reunite the nation, authorizes the PAVN to launch an all-out offensive against Thieu's forces in 1975.

1975

January 1–7	Communists begin their drive for Saigon and capture the provincial capital of Phuoc Binh, some seventy-five miles north of Saigon.
January 8–April 16	PAVN attacks key cities from Quang Tri (just south of the DMZ) to Phan Rang (160 miles northeast of Saigon).
April 16	Lon Nol surrenders to the Khmer Rouge, ending five years of warfare in Cambodia.
April 20	City of Xuan Loc (thirty miles northeast of Saigon) falls to the PAVN, the last obstacle on the road to Saigon. American helicopters begin evacuation of United States and Vietnamese citizens from Saigon.
April 21	Thieu resigns, turning the government over to the aging Tran Van Huong.
April 27	South Viet Nam Assembly elects General Duong Van Minh ("Big Minh") president with instructions to find a way of restoring peace.

April 28	President Minh is installed and orders the military to "stay where they are" and defend what territory is left.
April 30	President Minh surrenders unconditionally to the communists, and PAVN/NLF enter and occupy Saigon. U.S. military evacuate the remaining 1,000 Americans and begin the evacuation of approximately 130,000 Vietnamese from South Viet Nam.

1976

July 2	Viet Nam formally proclaims its unification as the Socialist Republic of Viet Nam (SRV), with its capital at Hanoi.
December 20	The name of the Viet Nam Workers' Party is changed to the Viet Nam Communist Party.

APPENDIX II

SELECTED BIOGRAPHICAL BRIEFS

This appendix is intended to assist the reader in identifying certain key personalities relevant to the text. It is not a complete biographical history of any individual. Source material has been derived principally from OSS and related official files augmented by data generally available in reference libraries, except where noted.

Alessandri, Marcel, Major General (1893–1968)
Second in command to General Sabattier during the French retreat into China after the Japanese coup of 9 March 1945. Chief of staff to General Martin in 1940, served as commander of Legionnaires in Tonkin in the Catroux and Decoux administrations; joined the Mordant gaullistes in 1944. Anti-American and anti-Chinese. Returned to Indochina on 19 September 1945; appointed commissioner for the Republic of France to Cambodia in October 1945; led French troops into Laos to replace the Chinese in March 1946. Following the debacle of the French attempt to subjugate Giap in the battles for Colonial Route 4, Alessandri was relieved in 1950 as commander of the French Army in Tonkin and recalled to France.

Argenlieu, Georges Louis Marie Thierry d', Vice Admiral (1889–1964)
High Commissioner of France for Indochina by Presidential Decree of 17 August 1945. According to another decree of the same date, the post of high commissioner was defined as "the representative in Indo-China of the Provisional Government of the Republic. . . . He exercises the powers of Governor-General of Indo-China and those of Commander in Chief of land, sea and air forces based in Indo-China. . . ."

Born 7 August 1889, d'Argenlieu had one of the most remarkable careers in the French Navy. He entered the naval service as ensign in 1909, was promoted to lieutenant (jg) in 1910, served as aide to Admiral de Marolles and, as such, in 1911 attended the coronation of King George V. From 1912 to 1914 he participated in the Moroccan campaign under Marshal Lyautey. During the 1914–18 war he saw combat in the Mediterranean aboard torpedo boats, sloops, and patrol ships and played an active part in U-boat warfare. In 1919, as a lieutenant commander he was captain of the *Tourterelle*, a patrol ship, before he was placed on reserve status.

As a civilian d'Argenlieu entered the Roman Catholic priesthood and joined the Carmelite Order of monks under the name of Père Joseph de la Trinité. In 1932 he became provincial president for France of the order.

In August 1939 he obtained a dispensation from the Church and resumed his active status as a regular French naval officer. Assigned to the naval sector of Cherbourg he served on the staff until taken prisoner by the Germans in June 1940. He escaped to England and joined de Gaulle's Free French Navy as a navy chaplain with the rank of lieutenant commander.

Promoted to full commander in July 1940, his rise in rank and influence in de Gaulle's entourage was meteoric. Following the abortive attempt to win over the pro-Vichy Governor General of Dakar, d'Argenlieu participated in the more successful campaign against the Gabon which brought French Equatorial Africa under de Gaulle. His reward was a seat on the French National Committee's Council of Defense of the French Empire and a recall to London for his new duties in 1941.

On 5 August 1941, he was appointed high commissioner for Free France in the Pacific with headquarters at Noumea, Tahiti, with the rank of captain. There he clashed with the U.S. Naval Command and the U.S. Army at New Caledonia where his insistence on maintaining French sovereignty came into conflict with the Allied war effort against Japan. He was also a source of annoyance to the British there and angered the New Caledonians who finally took him into captivity. Advanced to the rank of rear admiral in June 1942, he was recalled to London in September. Enroute he stopped at Washington where he attended a stormy dinner at the home of Assistant Secretary of State Adolf A. Berle at which he is said to have become somewhat strong and unpleasant in his statements.

In May 1943 he was made acting head of the Fighting French Naval Forces with headquarters in London while the French fleet was administered from General Giraud's headquarters in Algiers where it was berthed. This served to split the nominal unity of the French Navy which regarded d'Argenlieu as the "Landlubber Admiral, more a monk than a sailor."

With the liberation of France (1944) d'Argenlieu, newly designated assistant chief of the general staff of the navy and "Admiral Nord," followed de Gaulle to Paris. Instead of establishing his offices in the Ministry of Marine with his immediate superior, Admiral Lemonnier, d'Argenlieu set up a separate headquarters at rue François 1er. This did not enhance his popularity with the traditional navy hierarchy. The post of "Admiral Nord" was terminated early in 1945. D'Argenlieu was not forgotten by de Gaulle, who designated him vice president of the Superior Council of the French Navy, but the Admiral would not give up his separate headquarters.

He has been described as aloof, cold, cynical, and haughty, terrifying to junior officers and reducing government officials to trembling acquiescence. He is said to have been an autocrat who contrived to surround himself with an aura of mysticism and almost religious reverence, unemotional to a certain point but finally giving way to passionate oratory and floods of tears. Many who knew him intimately said that if he were locked in a room for some hours he apparently would agree to anything. Considered by some as "brilliant and a superb diplomat," by others as an "abominable bear and a most foxy man." *Source:* ALUSNA, Paris, Ser. S-14-45. (CIAC)

Bach, Pham Van (1907–   )
President, Provisional Executive Committee of the Southern Viet Nam Republic. A political "independent," Bach was educated in France, receiving a doctorate in law and a diploma in letters from the University of Paris. In 1944–45 he was practicing law in Cambodia when he joined the nationalist movement and the pro-Japanese United National Front. After Tran Van Giau formed the Provisional Executive Committee for the South, Bach was included as committee member without portfolio. In the reshuffle of the Provisional Executive Committee on 9 September 1945, Pham Van Bach succeeded Tran Van Giau as president. Bach continued to participate in Ho Chi Minh's government, and currently (1979) holds the post of president of the People's Supreme Court.

Bao Dai (1913–   )
Emperor of Annam (1932–45). Chief of State of Viet Nam (1949–55). Born Prince Nguyen Vinh Thuy, son of Emperor Khai Din, he succeeded to the throne in 1926 but did not occupy it until 1932. During World War II he collaborated with Vichy's Decoux regime and the Japanese authorities. Forced to abdicate in August 1945 he served the communist-oriented government of Ho Chi Minh as "citizen" Vinh Thuy in the capacity of "Supreme Political Advisor." Following the reoccupation of Indochina by the French, Bao Dai returned in 1949 as head of state for the three *kys* (Tonkin, Annam and Cochinchina). Unable to set up an effective and stable government and after the French defeat and partition of Viet Nam in 1954, Bao Dai appointed Ngo Dinh Diem prime minister and promptly left the country.

Birch, John M., Captain, AUS (1918–45)
A Georgia Baptist missionary, fluent in several Chinese dialects, who left his mission in Hangchou in 1943 and joined Chennault's Fourteenth Air Force. Assigned to intelligence and rescue operations with OSS/AGFRTS, Birch was transferred in mid-1944 to OSS. On 24 August 1945, Birch was posted at Lingchau (Lienyunchiang), situated about 110 miles southwest of the coastal city of Tsingtao. His instructions were to move out on orders to help rescue Allied POWs at a Japanese camp near Suchow (Hsuchou) lying another 150 miles west-southwest of Lingchau. In anticipation of those orders Birch moved toward Suchow on the twenty-fifth. Within thirty miles of his objective, his team was stopped by a Chinese Communist roadblock intended to contain enemy troops in the Japanese-held city. Birch wanted to enter the city but the communist sentries would not let him. Birch was furious and attempted to force his way. Harsh words were exchanged and the Chinese Communist officer ordered his men to disarm the American team. Birch resisted, and he and his KMT interpreter were shot. Two days later General Wedemeyer personally protested to Chairman Mao Tse-tung in Chungking, who said he

knew nothing of the incident but, if a clash had taken place, he hastened to apologize. Mao said he would institute an immediate investigation and, if an American had been killed, those who were guilty would be punished. Nothing further was heard of the promised investigation.

Although Birch was not known to have anticommunist sentiments and had for almost two years cooperated with Mao's forces in gathering intelligence, his name was appropriated years later (1958) by the well-known John Birch Society, an extreme anticommunist group.

Bose, Subhas Chandra (1897–1945)

Hindu nationalist, pro-Japanese, and antiwhite racist. Supported Mohandas K. Gandhi and joined the Swaraj party (c. 1920); advocated militancy and one-man rule to achieve national unity and total independence for India. Jailed on numerous occasions by the British; president of the All-India Trades Union Congress (1929–31); wrote *The Indian Struggle* (1935); led (as president) the left-wing element of the Indian National Congress Party (1938–39) but was forced to resign when his violent anti-British tactics came into conflict with Gandhi's policy of passive resistance. Jailed for the last time by the British for his outspoken Axis sympathies, Bose escaped to Germany in 1941. He arrived in Singapore in 1943 and headed a Japanese-sponsored "Free India Provisional Government" and organized the "Indian National Army." Wanted by the British as a war criminal in 1945, he was rumored to be hiding in Hanoi, but the OSS learned in mid-September that Bose had died in Taiwan in the crash of a Manchurian-bound plane while enroute to Moscow where he hoped to enlist Soviet support for his independence movement.

Buu, Ta Quang (1920–   )

A political "independent," Oxford-educated, taught mathematics and English at Hué. Headed the Decoux-sponsored Vietnamese Boy Scout movement until the Japanese coup when he emerged in the spring of 1945 as assistant to Phan Anh, minister of youth in the pro-Japanese (Dai Viet) Tran Trong Kim cabinet. In August 1945, Phan Anh and Ta Quang Buu merged their Dai Viet youth with the pro-Viet Minh university students staging nationwide demonstrations against the Bao Dai regime and French rule (Hanoi, Hué, Saigon). Buu made available to Giap his paramilitary youth organization and assumed the role of political commissar in the Viet Minh army. After a brief internship under Giap (then Minister of Interior) Buu was appointed in March 1946 vice minister for national defense, a post he held through the 1954 Geneva Accord, except for one year (July 1947–48) when he replaced Giap as minister for national defense. Buu held the military rank of brigadier general (political commissar) in the People's Army.

Catroux, Georges, General (1877–1969)

Governor General of French Indochina (August 1939–July 1940). Recalled by Marshal Pétain and replaced by Admiral Darlan's protege, Admiral Jean Decoux, Catroux went to London and joined de Gaulle's Free French forces. He served in the highest councils of de Gaulle's Provisional Government and was French ambassador to Moscow from 1945 to 1948.

Cédile, Jean (1908–   )
One of several administrators selected by the Ministry of Overseas France to accompany de Raymond's French Colonial Mission to Calcutta for the eventual reoccupation of Indochina. Cédile was designated by d'Argenlieu to be commissioner of the French Republic for Cochinchina. He was parachuted by the SLFEO on the night of 22–23 August 1945, in a blind drop in the area of Tay Ninh (about fifty miles northwest of Saigon). He was picked up by a Japanese patrol and taken to Saigon where he was permitted to contact other Frenchmen. One of his first meetings was with the notorious colon, Mario Bocquet. Unfamiliar with the political situation, Cédile at first accepted Bocquet's version of the "Annamite threat" to France. It did not take him long to see through the colons' anti-Vietnamese line and to realize the seriousness of the independence movement. He contacted the leaders of the Provisional Executive Committee for the South and made a serious effort to come to an understanding with them but was constrained by his official instructions embodied in the "24 March Declaration" of the Ministry of Colonies. Between September 1945 and October 1946 when he finally left Cochinchina, Cédile supported the D'Argenlieu-Pignon policy of frustrating all French and Vietnamese efforts to grant Cochinchina even a modicum of independence outside the French orbit. Cédile's major contributions to French-Vietnamese relations are his famous coup of 22–23 September 1945 in Saigon and his signing of the extralegal convention on 3 June 1946, establishing the Autonomous Republic of Cochinchina with the pro-French President of the Provisional Government of the Republic of Cochinchina, Dr. Nguyen Van Thinh.

Chang Fa-kwei, Marshal (1896–   )
Commander of the Nationalist (KMT) troops in the Fourth War Area (including the western part of his native province of Kwangtung and the whole of Kwangsi). His early contacts with the CCP in Canton (1924–27) included a brief association with a Vietnamese communist on the staff of General Vasili Blyukher (General "Galin") of the Soviet Borodin Mission to China. The Vietnamese acting as "interpreter" for the Mission and using the name of Lee Suei was additionally engaged in Indochinese revolutionary activities and was, in fact, Ho Chi Minh. The two met again under different circumstances in 1942–44. In the mid-twenties during the first KMT-CCP cooperation, Chang Fa-kwei served with many well-known CCP military leaders (Yeh Chien-ying, Lin Piao, Yeh T'ing, Ho Lung, et al.). Although considered left-of-center politically, Chang never joined the Chinese Communists and in 1949 retired to Hong Kong, still supportive of the KMT but at odds with the Taiwanese government as of 1968. Chang visited the United States briefly in the fall of 1960 after attending the Moral Rearmament Conference in Europe. On a speaking circuit (New York, Boston, Washington, Baltimore, and San Francisco) he urged the Chinese to continue the fight against the CCP and restore the Republic of China.

Chinh, Truong (1907–   )
Chinh's real name is Dang Xuan Khu. During his early career he used the aliases Son and Truong Chinh. After 1945 he adopted the name Truong Chinh as his legal name. In 1979, he was Chairman of the Standing Committee of the National Assembly, SRV; member of the Party Central Committee; and member of the Political Bureau. Started his revolutionary career in 1925; joined the Revolutionary Youth

League in 1927 and participated in the founding of the ICP. Arrested by the French in 1930 and sentenced to twelve years' hard labor. Freed by the French in 1936, Chinh returned to his revolutionary activities. From 1941 to 1951, secretary general of the ICP; from 1951 to 1956, secretary general of the Viet Nam Workers' Party. Elected deputy to the National Assembly in 1960. In May 1960 reelected member of the Central Committee and the Political Bureau of the Viet Nam Workers' Party (now changed to the Viet Nam Communist Party).

Cong, Truong Boi (1909–1945)
A Vietnamese nationalist who fled to China in the wake of the 1930 Yen Bay uprisings and joined the VNQDD faction at Nanking. Under the sponsorship of another Vietnamese nationalist, Ho Ngoc Lam, then an officer in the Chinese Army (KMT). Cong was admitted to the Second Class of the Chinese Paoting Military Academy from which he graduated as an officer. He served in the Nationalist Army as regimental commander and senior staff officer of the military academy at Nanning where he came to the attention of Chang Fa-kwei. In 1941 Chang placed Lam and Cong in charge of organizing and training the large number of Vietnamese exiles then fleeing to China. Chang designated Cong commander of the Vietnamese Special Training Class at Ch'ing-Hsi to enlist and train refugees for future Chinese operations in Viet Nam. Ho Chi Minh, then in China, sent Vo Nguyen Giap and several other ICP members to work with Cong who was organizing a united front of the several nationalist groups into the Viet Nam National Liberation League, the precursor of the Dong Minh Hoi of 1942.

Although a nationalist, Cong was pro-Chinese and anticommunist. He collaborated with Ho Chi Minh within the scope of the VNQDD but never accepted Viet Minh leadership.

Decoux, Jean, Vice Admiral (1884–1963)
Governor General, French Indochina (July 1940–March 1945). Commander in chief of the French Far Eastern Fleet in 1939, a protege of Admiral Darlan and pro-Vichy, he succeeded Governor General Georges Catroux. A proud autocratic man with strong rightist views and a temperament similar to that of "Le Grand Charles," Decoux was unable to make his peace with de Gaulle upon his return to France in October 1945. He was tried on charges of collaboration with the Vichy government and in 1949 was pronounced not guilty. Source: Joseph Buttinger, Vietnam: A Dragon Embattled, 2:1222.

de Gaulle, Charles. See: Gaulle de

Dewey, A. Peter, Lieutenant Colonel (1917–1945)
Commanding officer, OSS Project EMBANKMENT. Student of French history at Yale; fluent in French; journalist in the Paris offices of the Chicago Daily News (1939–40); joined the Polish Army in France (spring 1940); after the fall of France escaped to Lisbon and returned to the United States; associated himself with the Office of the Coordinator of Inter-American Affairs; joined the U.S. Army as second lieutenant (fall 1942); served in intelligence operations in Africa and the Middle East. Recruited by OSS in Algiers (1943) and sent on a mission to France

behind the German lines. Returned to OSS-Washington (early 1945) and was reassigned to Hqrs, SEAC in July 1945. Killed by Viet Minh guerrillas outside Saigon (26 September 1945).

Dong, Pham Van (1906–   )
Prime Minister of the Socialist Republic of Viet Nam. Born at Quang Ngai (approximately 130 miles south of Hué) to a well-to-do and scholarly family. His father, a prominent official (mandarin) of the Court at Hué during the brief reign of the boy emperor, Duy Tan (1907–16), saw that Pham Von Dong received a suitable education at Hué and later in Hanoi. As a student he became interested in politics and inevitably came under close scrutiny from the French police for his anti-French activism. He was just under twenty when he traveled to Canton where he met Nguyen Ai Quoc (Ho Chi Minh) and became one of his most promising pupils. A year later (1926) Dong returned to Hanoi and entered the academia to teach history while carrying out Ho's instructions to organize party cells. Arrested by the French Sûreté (1930?) he was sentenced to six years' hard labor at the penal colony of Poulo Condore. After being released in the general amnesty of 1937, at Ho's direction he crossed the border into China in mid-1940 and worked in party organizational and training activities at Ch'ing-Hsi (under the alias Lin Pai-chieh). To escape arrest by the KMT, Dong returned in 1942 to Viet Nam (using the alias Lam Ba Kiet), but in 1944 he was back in China and delegate at the KMT-sponsored reunification conference of the Dong Minh Hoi.

Minister of finance in Ho's first cabinet (1945); led the Vietnamese Parliamentary Delegation to Paris (1946); minister of foreign affairs (1954); headed the DRV delegation at the Conference of Geneva (April–July 1954) after the French defeat at Dien Bien Phu; appointed prime minister in 1955 under Ho Chi Minh and has held that post to date.

Donovan, William Joseph ("Wild Bill"), Major General (1883–1959)
Director of the Office of Strategic Services in World War II.
Lawyer, politician, soldier, diplomat.

Born in Buffalo, New York, Donovan received a Doctor of Laws degree in 1907 from Columbia University and set up in practice in Buffalo. Interspersed with his law practice he involved himself in New York politics and military activities. In 1915 he was appointed to the Polish Commission for the relief of war victims in Poland and the Balkans and for the first time visited Europe (England, France, Germany, and Poland). In 1916 he served in Pershing's Mexican border action. In 1917, as battalion major of the famous New York National Guard 69th Regiment, Donovan went to France and was three times wounded in action. For outstanding leadership and bravery he was awarded the three highest American decorations: the Distinguished Service Cross, the Distinguished Service Medal, and the Congressional Medal of Honor.

At the close of World War I Donovan was appointed to an official mission to Siberia. In 1922 he resumed his law practice until appointed to various posts, from United States attorney (for the Western District of New York) to assistant attorney general of the United States. In 1929 he returned to private practice and tried his hand at state and national politics without success, but his talents were put to use by presidents from both parties. President Roosevelt sent Donovan to Italy and

Ethiopia (1935) and to Spain (1937) to study the rising tide of fascism and European unrest. He reported the changing techniques of warfare, the new weapons and the "fifth column" tactics of the European dictators. In 1940 he was sent to England as Presidential representative to appraise Britain's resources and morale to resist the Nazi onslaught. His report influenced Roosevelt to grant England the historic loan of over-age American destroyers. After a second visit to the Balkans (1941) he was appointed Coordinator of Information (COI) by Roosevelt to assemble worldwide intelligence. After Pearl Harbor the office of COI was reorganized into the OSS with Donovan in charge.

In 1946 he was asked by the White House to work with Justice Jackson in the preparatory work for the Nuremberg trials. After a brief return to private practice Donovan was called once more in 1953 by President Eisenhower to serve as U.S. ambassador to Thailand and in 1956 to organize a fund-raising campaign for Hungarian relief.

In 1957 he suffered a cerebral hemorrhage from which he never recovered. He died 8 February 1959.

Gallagher, Philip E., Brigadier General (1897–1976)
Chief, U.S. Military Advisory and Assistance Group (USMAAG); Brigadier General attached to the First War Area, Chinese Combat Command. Assigned in August 1945 to the Commander of the Chinese Occupation Force for Indochina as adviser in matters of disarming and repatriating Japanese troops in Indochina north of the sixteenth parallel.

Gaulle, Charles André Joseph Marie de (1890–1970)
French general and statesman; head of the Provisional Government of the French Republic (1945); first President of the Fifth Republic of France (1959–69).

A career officer of the French Army and an outspoken critic of the French General Staff's outdated strategy and tactics, he advocated the modernization and mechanization of the French Army. At the outbreak of hostilities with Germany, Colonel de Gaulle was given command of the Fourth Armored Division and promoted to brigadier general. In June 1940 he was appointed under secretary of state for national defense in the cabinet of Premier Paul Reynaud. Strongly opposed to the Franco-German armistice, de Gaulle fled to London (June 1940) to continue the resistance. With British support he rallied Frenchmen in Vichy-controlled areas to his newly organized Free French forces. Under Anglo-American pressure de Gaulle collaborated with General Henri H. Giraud in the French Committee of National Liberation in Algiers until June 1944, when he outmaneuvered Giraud from the post of copresident. De Gaulle then converted the Committee into a provisional government of France under his own leadership. On 26 August 1944, he returned to Paris and installed his provisional government in metropolitan France and was elected provisional president in November 1945. Faced with strong political opposition he was forced to resign in January 1946, temporarily retiring from public life. Following the 1958 crisis (Algerian revolt) he returned to public office as premier. Under a new constitution he was inaugurated president of the Fifth Republic of France in January 1959. After several turbulent terms of office, he resigned once more and went into retirement in 1969.

Giam, Hoang Minh (1912–   )
Socialist party leader and a close personal friend and adviser to Ho Chi Minh. One of the many French-schooled liberals in the early movement for independence, Giam associated himself with Ho Chi Minh's group as early as 1936 when he, Giam, Phan Anh, and other moderates joined the newly founded Socialist Federation of North Indochina, a section of the French Socialist Party in Tonkin. Professor of French and French Literature at the University of Hanoi (1937), Giam was active in the Vietnamese literacy program, directing and teaching the romanized Vietnamese script, *Quoc Ngu*. Although Giam was not included in the official cabinet of Ho's first government, he nonetheless was influential in formulating foreign policy and, in fact, was acting minister of foreign affairs, a post Ho had retained for himself. In the 6 March 1946 government Giam held the post of vice minister of interior; in a reshuffle on 3 November 1946, he was officially designated vice minister of foreign affairs under Ho who had temporarily relinquished the post of minister to Nguyen Tuong Tam in the 6 March realignment; on 30 April 1947, Ho once more relinquished his post of minister of foreign affairs and appointed Giam, who held it through April 1954, when Ho designated Pham Van Dong acting foreign minister to lead the Vietnamese Delegation to Geneva. Since then Giam has held the post of minister of culture.

Giap, Vo Nguyen (1912–   )
Born at An Xa, a village in Quang Binh Province, to a peasant family with a strong nationalist tradition. Giap's father, who had studied Chinese classics, taught his son Chinese characters, Vietnamese history, and particularly his own role in the 1880 resistance to French occupation.

In 1922 Giap entered the *Quoc Hoc (Lycée National)* French language school at Hué, the same school attended several years earlier by Ho Chi Minh, Ngo Dinh Diem, Pham Van Dong, and other prominent Vietnamese nationalists. There Giap was exposed to the writings of Phan Boi Chau and other revolutionaries. At fourteen, Giap joined the Tan Viet (Revolutionary Party for a Great Viet Nam) and participated in student political agitation, leading to his expulsion from the school in 1927. He returned briefly to his native village but was recalled to Hué by the Tan Viet for party work. While in Hué he was taken in by Huynh Thuc Khang, publisher of the radical nationalist newspaper *Tien Dan* (People's Voice). After the unsuccessful uprisings instigated by the VNQDD at Yen Bay (1930) and the subsequent disorders, strikes, and demonstrations at Vinh and vicinity, Giap organized and led a student protest in Hué for which he was arrested and sentenced to three years' hard labor. However, after serving a few months he was released and went to Hanoi where he entered the Lycée Albert Sarraut.

While at the Lycée, Giap earned his living by giving private history lessons at the Thanh Long school (under the direction of Huynh Thuc Khang) and boarded with a well-known Vietnamese writer, Professor Dong Thai Mai, whose daughter he later married. After finishing his studies at the lycée, Giap enrolled at the University of Hanoi, School of Law, from which he received a degree in law (1937) and doctorate in political economics (1938). He had also joined the ICP, met Hoang Minh Giam, a socialist, and the recently released (1936) communist political prisoners Pham Van Dong and Truong Chinh. In 1936 the outlawed ICP needed a legitimate cover for its revolutionary activities and the Indochinese Democratic Front was formed under the joint leadership of Giap and Dong. Concurrently Giap joined the newly-founded Socialist Federation of North Indochina with friends Phan Anh and Hoang Minh Giam.

In 1939, with the collapse of the Popular Front government in France, the ICP and all revolutionary activities in the colonies suffered renewed police repression. Giap and his young bride, Nguyen Thi Minh Giang, became targets of the Sûreté. Giang and her sister, Minh Khai, both ICP members, fled to Vinh with Giap's infant son. In the spring of 1940 Giap and Dong fled to Kunming, China, where they met with Ho Chi Minh. In May 1941 the sisters were captured by the French police, taken to Hanoi, tried by a military tribunal, and found guilty of conspiracy. Minh Khai was guillotined, and Minh Giang was sentenced to fifteen years' hard labor in the Maison Centrale (Hanoi Central Prison). Her infant died, and she herself perished in prison in 1943.

From 1940 on Giap became one of Ho Chi Minh's most trusted lieutenants (the other was Pham Van Dong). Giap was entrusted by Ho to organize the first Viet Minh guerrillas in the pre-DRV period; he was appointed minister of interior in Ho's first cabinet (1945); minister of national defense (1947 to 1980); member of the Party Central Committee, Politburo, National Defense Council; and other leading posts. Generally regarded as the master architect of the Vietnamese victories over the French and the Americans. Throughout his revolutionary career he used several aliases, but the best known are: Yang Huai-nan (in China); Duong Hoai Nam (in Viet Nam); and Mr. Van with the OSS.

Giau, Tran Van (1910–   )
A native Cochinchinese, Giau was educated at Toulouse, France, where he received his doctorate in History; after being repatriated to Indochina in 1931 for participating in protest demonstrations following the trials of the Yen Bay insurgents, he made his way to Moscow and enrolled in the Oriental Workers Institute. He returned to Saigon in 1933 and reconstituted the disorganized ICP and led the dissenting Trotskyites into the "Stalinist" group. In September 1939 the French outlawed all revolutionary activities in Indochina and arrested most of the nationalist leaders, including Giau, who was confined to the penal colony of Poulo Condore. He escaped in 1940 and returned to his clandestine party activities in Cochinchina. He surfaced again after the Japanese coup of 9 March 1945, and successfully launched a coalition nationalist front temporarily uniting the many dissenting nationalist parties under the aegis of the Viet Minh.

In late August 1945 he formed the Provisional Executive Committee for the South and assumed the post of president. Unable to retain control of the dissenting elements within the committee, he stepped aside in favor of Pham Van Bach, retaining for himself the military leadership of the Viet Minh military in the south. In November 1945, after Ho "dissolved" the ICP, Giau participated in the formation of the cover organization known as the Marxist Study Group. In 1950 he was appointed to the important post of director of the Viet Nam Central Information Service and continued to serve the Viet Minh in various capacities.

Gracey, Douglas D., Major General (1894–   )
British; Commander, Allied Land Forces for Indochina, South of the Sixteenth Parallel, North; Head, Allied Control Commission for SAC, SEAC; Commanding General, 20th Indian Division. Arrived Saigon 13 September 1945; departed Saigon 28 January 1946.

Helliwell, Paul L. E., Colonel (1914–76)
Chief, Secret Intelligence Branch, OSS-Kunming; Chief, Intelligence Division, OSS-China. Prominent attorney, banker, and consul general for Thai government in Miami, Florida.

Heppner, Richard Pinkerton, Colonel (1908–58)
Strategic Services Officer, China Theater. Attorney and partner in General Donovan's law firm; entered military service (1940); joined Donovan's staff with the Office of the Coordinator of Information (COI) (1941); attended the British Intelligence School in Canada under Sir William Stephenson and the Commando Training Center in Scotland; was assigned to OSS-London (1942); participated in the planning of OSS operations for the North African landings (TORCH). In late 1942 was invited by Ambassador William Phillips (Presidential Representative) to accompany him to India as his special assistant. Appointed Strategic Services Officer, SEAC (1943); reassigned to the China Theater (December 1944) where he was in charge of all OSS activities under General Wedemeyer until October 1945, when he returned to his law practice. In 1957 President Eisenhower appointed him deputy assistant secretary of defense for international security affairs. He died 14 May 1958.

Hien, Duong Duc (1916–1963)
About thirty years old in 1945, Hien had been active in the first VNQDD. When the Dai Viet was founded in 1941, Hien joined Nguyen Tuong Tam and his brother, Nguyen Tuong Long, in the party leadership. An intellectual and student leader, Hien was elected president of the General Student Association in Hanoi. Drawing from the Association's large membership in June 1944 Hien formed the Viet Nam Dan Chu Dang (Democratic Party) and became its first secretary general. Influenced by his close personal friend, Vo Nguyen Giap, Hien affiliated his party with the Viet Minh League (front), providing both cover for ICP members in times of reprisal and acting as the loyal minority in the Viet Minh League. At the Tan Trao People's Congress Hien was appointed member of the Viet Nam Liberation Committee and he served as minister of youth in Ho's first cabinet. *Source:* OSS-SI Biog file: R&A no. 3336; 25 October 1945. (CIAC)

Ho Chi Minh (1890–1969)
First president of the Democratic Republic of Viet Nam. Born 19 May 1890 in his mother's native hamlet of Hoang Tru, but grew up in his father's village of Kim Lien (commune of Nam Lien, district of Nam Dan, province of Nghe An), now officially designated by Hanoi historians as Ho's birthplace. He left Indochina in 1911 and traveled the world as a seaman and agent of the Comintern, returning to Viet Nam in 1940. He proclaimed Viet Nam's independence from French rule on 2 September 1945 at Hanoi; led a war of resistance to French reoccupation from 1946 to 1954 and a war for reunification from the early 1960s to the day he died. He died in Hanoi on 3 September 1969.

Hsiao Wen, Lieutenant General (c. 1890–   )
Also known among the Vietnamese as Sieu Uan and Tien Van. Political officer in Chang Fa-kwei's Fourth War Area Command. A native of Kwangtung province, Hsiao was considered an expert in Vietnamese affairs. While serving as Chang's

deputy chief, Foreign Affairs Section (early 1943), Hsiao met Ho Chi Minh, then a political prisoner in the Fourth War Area Command, and became Ho's Chinese mentor. Chang delegated Hsiao in January 1944 to oversee the activities of the Dong Minh Hoi and foster pro-Kuomintang sentiment among the Vietnamese. After the war Hsiao was transferred (September 1945) to Lu Han's headquarters in Hanoi and entrusted by the KMT to look after China's interests in Indochina. As head of the newly-redesignated Section for Overseas Chinese Affairs, Hsiao soon came into conflict with Ho and with Lu Han's policies regarding the role of the anti-Viet Minh nationalists in Ho's government.

Over the years Hsiao cultivated many Chinese Communist contacts, including Ho's friend from Yenan, Yeh Chien-ying (Ye Tsin-ying), and displayed left-of-center tendencies, for which he was rewarded in 1950 with a minor advisory post in Kwangtung provincial administration under Governor (General) Yeh Chien-ying.

Hurley, Patrick Jay, Major General (1883-1963)
Born in Choctaw Indian Territory (now Oklahoma). Practiced law in Tulsa (1912-17); a colonel in World War I; under secretary of war (1929); secretary of war (1929-33). He also served on several diplomatic missions. In 1942 he was appointed by President Roosevelt U.S. minister to New Zealand and then (1942-43) presidential representative in the Middle East. Promoted to major general and sent by President Roosevelt to China as envoy (August 1944-January 1945) and ambassador (January-November 1945).

Khang, Nguyen (1919-   )
Joined the Democratic Youth Union in 1938 and the ICP at Hanoi in 1939. Arrested by the French police in May 1941, tried and sentenced to consecutive terms of five and fifteen years' hard labor. Escaped in 1944 and resumed revolutionary activities in Hanoi.

Elected to the Standing Bureau of North Viet Nam Regional Committee and president of the People's Revolutionary Committee for North Viet Nam, Khang was one of the key leaders during the August 1945 Hanoi insurrection. He was a member of the Party Central Committee until at least 1975; however, his name does not appear in the list of members elected in the 1976 Fourth Vietnam Workers Party Congress.

"Leclerc," Jacques Philippe, Marshal (1902-1947)
Born Philippe *vicomte* de Hauteclocque, he adopted the name "Leclerc" in World War II to protect his family during the Nazi occupation of France. Commanded the Free French forces in Equatorial Africa (December 1942-January 1943). Participated with the British Eighth Army in the Tunisian campaign (1943) as commander of the French Second Armored Division. General Omar N. Bradley honored him by designating his division the lead unit to enter Paris (August 1944) to complete the liberation of the city. Appointed by de Gaulle commander of French Forces in the Far East (August 1945), Leclerc represented France at the Japanese surrender in Tokyo Bay. In October 1945 he led the first French troops against the Vietnamese independence fighters in an attempt to reoccupy Indochina. Appointed inspector general of the French Land Forces in North Africa

(1946). Leclerc was killed in a plane crash (1947). He was posthumously elevated to the rank of marshal of France in 1952.

Lee, Duncan C., Lieutenant Colonel (1915–   )
Chief, Japan-China Section, Far East Division, SI, OSS-Washington (1944–45); later, assistant general counsel, OSS. Born in China; educated at Oxford; member of Donovan's law firm. After World War II Lee was vice president and general counsel of C. V. Starr, Insurance Group.

Lu Han, Lieutenant General (1891–   )
A native Yunnanese from the northern district of Chaot'ung bordering Tibet; was generally characterized as a "Lolo barbarian," referring to his origin among the Lolo tribe, a fiercely anti-Chinese, independent people of northern Yunnan. Under the tutelage of his "cousin," Governor (General) Lung Yün, Lu Han graduated from the Military Academy of Yunnan and held many influential military posts. In 1932 as chief of the Military Council Bureau of the Nanking national government. Lu Han facilitated the organization and provided Kuomintang support for Vietnamese revolutionaries (VNQDD) at Nanking.

In the early 1940s Lu Han commanded the First Group Army in the Ninth War Area. In August 1945 he and his troops were designated by Chiang Kai-shek as the Allied Occupation Force for Indochina, with Lu Han as his personal representative to accept the surrender of the Japanese forces north of the sixteenth parallel. On 5 October 1945, Chiang appointed him governor of Yunnan province in lieu of Lung Yün. Eventually (December 1949) Lu Han defected to the Chinese Communists who rewarded him with several honorific posts, such as deputy chairman of the National Commission for Physical Education and Sports. In April 1959 he was reappointed to a powerless post on the National Defense Council in Peking.

Lung Yün (1888–1962)
A native Yunnanese from the northern district of Chaot'ung and a member of the Lolo people. Lung came from a long line of warlords engaged in raising opium poppies and in banditry along the lucrative Tibet-Burma-China trade route. He was appointed (1928) provincial governor of Yunnan and ruled quasi-independently of Chiang Kai-shek's central government. In the early forties Lung Yün commanded three of the five army groups in the central government's Yunnan Force (Y-Force) nominally under the direction of Chiang. During the 1940–45 period Lung Yün's total control of China's section of the Burma Road provided him with large quantities of highjacked American Lend-Lease material intended for Chinese Nationalist forces. His extortionist demands for Lend-Lease supplies in mid-1945 and his flagrant disregard of the central government's authority prompted Chiang to remove Lung from power. On 5 October 1945, during the so-called Kunming incident, Chiang forceably divested Lung of his governorship and military command. He was taken to Chungking and later to Nanking in a face-saving maneuver and given the post of director in the powerless Military Advisory Board. His "cousin," Lu Han, succeeded him as provincial governor and troop commander in Yunnan.

In 1948 Lung Yün fled to Hong Kong and in 1949 to Peking where he joined the Chinese Communists. As a reward for his defection he was appointed to the equally meaningless post of vice-chairman of the National Defense Council, and a vice chairman of the Southwest Military and Administrative Committee, posts he held until 1957, when he was purged during the "Hundred Flowers" period.

Mai, Duong Bach (1904–   )
Vietnamese journalist who received his early political indoctrination in the communist milieu of Moscow (1930–31) and Paris (1936–37); first emerged on the Cochinchinese political scene in 1937 when he was elected to the Saigon Municipal Council. In the 1940 French roundup of revolutionaries Mai was jailed but retained the leadership of the leftist communist element know as "Stalinists." He came to public notice again in August 1945 as commissioner (or inspector) for political and administrative affairs in Giau's Provisional Executive Committee for the South. As Chief of the Vietnamese police in Saigon during the September 1945 disorders, he played a ruthless role in punishing the French and eradicating Vietnamese opponents of the Viet Minh.

At the 1946 conferences of Dalat and Fontainebleau he participated as a Vietnamese delegate. In March 1947 during a policy debate on Indochina in the French National Assembly in Paris, Premier Paul Reynaud accused Mai of being the "criminal" responsible for the many Vietnamese atrocities perpetrated against the French in Indochina. Mai who was sitting in the distinguished visitors' gallery near Émile Bollaert (High Commissioner for Indochina and a radical socialist) was ordered out of the chamber, but he was protected by Bollaert and other communist delegates. However, several days later Mai was arrested and deported to Viet Nam.

Matusita (also spelled Matsushita)
A Japanese secret service agent under the direction of Consul General Minoda in 1930 and subsequently, operating mainly in Cochinchina and Cambodia under the cover of industrialist (director of Dainan Koosi). Expelled from Indochina by the French in 1938 for anti-French and racist activities among southern Vietnamese nationalists, he returned with the Japanese forces in 1941 and resumed his directorship of Dainan Koosi. He established a working relationship with Yokoyama's Centre Culturelle, the Yasu Butai, and the kempeitai. A personal friend and staunch supporter of Prince Cuong De, Matusita (1942) approached the leaders of the pro-Japanese nationalist movement, especially the intellectuals, to revitalize the program. With unlimited funds from the operations of CICEI and Dainan Koosi, Matusita subsidized the Phuc Quoc in the south and the Dai Viet in the north. By 1944 he succeeded in bringing into the pro-Japanese nationalist movement the Cao Dai and the Hoa Hao sects.

Messmer, Pierre (1916–   )
One of several administrators selected by the Ministry of Overseas France to accompany de Raymond's French Colonial Mission to Calcutta for the eventual reoccupation of Indochina. Messmer was designated by d'Argenlieu to be commissioner of the French Republic for Tonkin. He was parachuted by the SLFEO on the night of 22–23 August 1945, in a blind drop near Phuc Yen (about fifteen miles northwest of Hanoi). He was picked up by Vietnamese guerrillas, detained for several days, and released near the Chinese border. He never accomplished his mission and returned first to Saigon and later to Paris. Major Sainteny replaced him as commissioner in Tonkin.

Messmer participated in French-Vietnamese negotiations at the conferences of Dalat and Fontainebleau in 1946. A hard-line gaulliste, he served as chief of cabinet to the minister for overseas affairs and adviser to Governor General Émile

Bollaert in Indochina (1947-48); minister of defense (1960-69) until de Gaulle's resignation as president; and minister of overseas departments and territories (1971-72). In 1972 he was appointed premier by President Pompidou and held that office until 1974 when he was succeeded by Jacques Chirac.

Mordant, Eugène, General (1885-   )
Commander of the French Forces in Indochina from 1940 to 1944. Mordant switched his allegiance from Pétain to de Gaulle in 1943 and secretly offered his services to the Free French in Algiers. De Gaulle accepted the offer and charged him with the task of organizing a Free French resistance movement in Indochina. He was appointed delegate general of the French Government for Indochina and given the powerful post of vice-president of the secret Indochinese Council. His indiscreet operations in 1944-45 alerted the Japanese who executed a coup on 9 March 1945 and jailed Mordant in Hanoi. He was eventually released by the Chinese in late 1945.

Pechkov, Zinovi, Colonel (also spelled Peshkov, Pechkoff, and Petchkoff) (c. 1895-   )
Pechkov was appointed by de Gaulle in 1943 as chief of the French Military Mission in China. Chiang Kai-shek received him with all the honors normally accorded an ambassador and addressed him as "ambassador," but giraudistes in Kunming sometimes mockingly said, "General Pechkov, the French Ambassador in China, who is neither general, nor Pechkov, nor ambassador, nor French." He was, in fact, a colonel in the French Foreign Legion when the title of "general" was bestowed upon him by de Gaulle for the duration of his mission in China. He was, in fact, an adopted son of Maxim Gorki but used the real family name of Pechkov. He was, also in fact, not an ambassador; Vichy was the only recognized French government in 1943, and the title was given him by Chiang, not by the French government. And he was technically not French because he had never been naturalized but he was considered French because of his service in the Foreign Legion.

His famous adoptive father, Aleksei Maksimovich Peshkov, believed by some to be his real father, had chosen the pseudonym Gorki, meaning in Russian "the bitter one." The son, however, was never bitter, although his life had been difficult and unpredictable. After a very poor youth spent in Nijni Novgorod, his birthplace, he followed Gorki to Italy, but the easy life of Capri and Sorrento did not suit him. When World War I erupted, he enlisted in the Foreign Legion and a year later, gravely wounded in combat, lost his right arm. That did not deter him from a military career and twice more he was wounded in Morocco during the Riff War. Extremely clever and the proverbial soul of discretion, Pechkov seemed born with a flair for intrigue common to many Slavs and was entrusted by the French government with many confidential missions during the years preceding World War II.

Pechkov joined de Gaulle after the fall of France and spent some time in America where he had many friends. He was on particularly good terms with Donovan and more than once stayed at the general's Georgetown home. Before leaving for Chungking, Pechkov acted as de Gaulle's representative to Marshal Smuts in South Africa.

In China, his personal charm and wit won him Chiang's recognition and a title he did not hold, thus indirectly increasing de Gaulle's prestige. A grateful de Gaulle placed in Pechkov a confidence he usually bestowed very sparingly. Thanks to Pechkov's restraining influence and his good relationship with Chiang, a modus vivendi between de Gaulle and Chiang would certainly have emerged had not the unexpected arrival of the Meynier mission ignited French rivalries and engendered the opposition of Tai Li.

Pignon, Léon (1908–   )
A veteran *fonctionnaire* of the French Colonial Civil Service during the early thirties in Indochina, Pignon was selected in July 1945 by the Ministry of Overseas France to assist the chief of the French Colonial Mission at Calcutta (Jean de Raymond) in political activities for Indochina. Following the unanticipated Japanese capitulation and the division of Indochina at the sixteenth parallel, de Raymond sent Pignon to China to provide General Alessandri with political guidance. On 19 September 1945 Pignon accompanied Alessandri to Hanoi and opened talks with Ho Chi Minh on 28 September. Appointed director of political and administrative affairs for Indochina, Pignon became Admiral d'Argenlieu's political adviser on 6 October and joined the "Saigon clique" in a relentless effort to reestablish French rule and destroy Ho Chi Minh and his government. Despite Sainteny's and Leclerc's good intentions to reach an accommodation with Ho and his government, d'Argenlieu on the advice of Pignon, representing the procolonial faction, took a hard line toward Ho and obstructed all efforts toward a peaceful settlement. When negotiations collapsed on 19–20 December 1946, and Ho took to the jungle and d'Argenlieu was recalled to France (February 1947), Pignon remained in Saigon as political adviser to the new high commissioner, Émile Bollaert. During Bollaert's term in office (March 1947–October 1948), Pignon helped maneuver Bao Dai into the service of France and prolong the war with the Viet Minh in the interest of the MRP and the war profiteers. Pignon succeeded Bollaert as high commissioner in October 1948. His administration brought to posts of influence not only some of the worst elements of the Decoux era but also the most spectacular development of corruption and racketeering ever recorded in the annals of Indochina. Pignon was eventually dismissed (December 1950) on the heels of the Peyré scandal or the *"affaire des generaux."*

Sabattier, Gabriel, Lieutenant General (1892–   )
Commander of the French forces in Tonkin (1945). After the Japanese coup, he escaped with some two thousand troops to China where he was the senior French military representative of the Provisional Government of the French Republic for about three months.

Sainteny, Jean R., Major (1907–1978)
Chief of M.5, French intelligence unit in Kunming, China, a sub-unit of the SLFEO, Calcutta, and an element of the DGER, Paris (April–October 1945). Son-in-law of twice Governor General Albert Sarraut; associated with banking interests in Indochina (1929–31) and in Paris (1932–39). Landed in Hanoi with the OSS Mercy Mission on 22 August 1945; appointed commissioner of the Republic of France for Tonkin and northern Annam, in lieu of Messmer (1945–47); and delegate general of the Republic of France to the Democratic Republic of Viet Nam (1954).

Sarraut, Albert (1872–1962)
French leader, a Radical Socialist. A member of the Chamber of Deputies from 1902, he was twice Governor General of French Indochina (1911–14 and 1916–19);

and from 1920 to 1940 was almost continuously a member of French cabinets. Briefly Premier in 1933 and again in 1936. Sarraut favored military action against the German occupation of the Rhineland (1936) but was unable to carry out the policy. During World War II he was arrested (1944) and deported to Germany but was freed by the Allies in 1945. After the war he was editor of his late brother's newspaper, *La Dépêche de Toulouse*, and president (1959–60) of the French Union.

Sarraut's governorship of Indochina has been characterized by French and Vietnamese writers as the "years of enlightenment and great reforms." Even Ho Chi Minh in 1945 spoke to me of Sarraut as the "only Frenchman who understood the plight of the Annamese and attempted to do something about it." The truth is that the Sarraut legend of liberalism and benevolent rule is in fact one of unkept promises and token concessions. Albert Sarraut was the father-in-law of Jean Sainteny.

Tai Li, General (1895–1946)
Head of Chiang Kai-shek's secret police and intelligence service. A somewhat legendary figure, said to have been a native of Chiangshan, Chekiang province. Received his early military training under German military instructors in China in the early twenties. Tai Li first came to the attention of Chiang during the student demonstrations of May 1925 in Shanghai. Tai Li, then a junior officer in the Chinese Army Military Police Corps, was also a member of the notorious secret society to which Chiang also belonged, the Ching Hong Pang. He was promoted to captain and assigned to Ch'en Li-fu, Chiang's personal secretary (1925–29). Tai Li was given the task of expanding the Central Bureau of Investigation and Statistics (CBIS) into a more powerful and efficient organization capable of coping with Chiang's military needs. By 1937 Tai Li had established the Military Bureau of Investigation and Statistics (MBIS) and persuaded Chiang to place it under the aegis of the KMT Military Council, giving the director (Tai Li) absolute power to act in the name of the Kuomintang. In the early forties the MBIS was further reorganized as an independent agency directly responsible to Chiang Kai-shek and the name altered to Central Investigation and Statistics Bureau (CISB). Tai Li was powerful, holding the rank of full general, and remained in complete control of the CISB until his death in 1946.

Tai Li owed his awesome power to Chiang's personal endorsement and to his ability to organize and control the multitude of Chinese secret societies. Among the most influential of these was the Triad Society which originated in the nineteenth century, more or less as a mutual aid society in south and central China, extending over the years among the overseas Chinese in India, Burma, Thailand, and Southeast Asia. The character of the Triad was a combination of the anti-Catholic Masonry and the bandit Mafia of Sicily. Its inviolable rule of silence and its secret rituals and recognition signs lent themselves to a closely knit intelligence network principally for "family protection." By the mid-twenties the societies turned from benevolent protective associations to the pursuit of crime, such as in the case of the Green Circle in Shanghai's underworld. In the late thirties the Green Circle was ruled by Tu Yu-sung, a clever man who made his home and headquarters in the French concession beyond the reach of Chinese police. Tai Li enlisted his services in organizing his anticommunst and pro-KMT intelligence system.

Another society useful to Tai Li was the south China group under Ming Teh called the Red Circle and operating in the Canton-Hong Kong-Kweilin area. Its

main enterprise was smuggling, and Tai Li used it as a source of revenue and guerrilla operations against the Japanese.

A third group of which Chiang Kai-shek was the titular head was known as
the Ko Lao Hui under the direct control of Feng Yu-hsiang, dubbed "the Christian
general." Tai Li put this group to spying on the Chinese Communists and the Russians. The character of Ko Lao Hui was fascistic.

A fourth group of secret societies in Tai Li's apparatus was the Blueshirts, a
European-oriented fascist organization composed of approximately ten thousand
elite, mainly Whampoa Academy graduates, modeled after Hitler's "brown
shirts." They were used by Tai Li in conducting Gestapo-type interrogations, anticommunist assassinations, and sabotage operations against both the Chinese Communists and the Japanese.

This widespread network of agents gave Tai Li unlimited flexibility and the
power of life and death over Chiang's enemies. What originally was intended as an
intelligence organization against the common enemy by the end of World War II
had become a secret state police to control the Chinese people. At one point in
1944–45, on Chiang's instruction, Tai Li established secret contact with Japanese
commanders in China, Burma, and Southeast Asia, and provided personal protection for Koruda, the head of the Japanese Secret Service, in Chungking.

Tai Li met an untimely death on 17 March 1946 while in flight from Tsingtao
to Shanghai when his plane "vanished" in mid-air near Nanking.

Tam, Nguyen Tuong (c. 1910–1963)
A writer-journalist in Hanoi, Tam was a member of the Viet Nam Nationalist Party
(Viet Nam Quoc Dan Dong), the first VNQDD. This party looked to China as an ally
in achieving independence but resisted any Chinese efforts at national control.
When the influence of the Japanese began to dominate the Indochinese scene
(1940), Tam turned to Japan for aid against France and founded the Great Viet
Nam Democratic Party (Dai Viet Dan Chin), Dai Viet for short. The French
promptly clamped down on its activities and jailed its leaders. Tam escaped to
China in 1942 and joined Vu Hong Khanh's Viet Nam Nationalist Party (Viet Nam
Quoc Dan Dong) at Kunming. This was the second VNQDD. Although Tam main-
tained a low profile in China, he and his party (Dai Viet) became identified as pro-
Japanese nationalists. Chang Fa-kwei decided to have him jailed for a brief period
in 1944 "to teach him a lesson." Shortly before the second congress of the Dong
Minh Hoi (March 1944) Chang released Tam and invited him as a delegate to the
Congress of Liuchow where he met Ho Chi Minh, Vo Nguyen Giap, and Pham Van
Dong. In the fall of 1945 Ho solicited Tam's support and later gave him the post of
minister of foreign affairs in the Provisional Coalition Government of January
1946. As minister of foreign affairs Tam headed the disastrous conference at
Dalat (April–May 1946). When asked to head the Fontainebleau Conference he
pleaded illness and, with Vu Hong Khanh, fled first to China, then to Hong Kong.

In February 1947 Tam, Khanh, and other Dong Minh Hoi leaders participated
in the conferences of Nanking and Canton where they formed a United National
Front to withhold all further support from the Ho government and to persuade Bao
Dai to act as their spokesman. Their efforts were frustrated by the French and by
Bao Dai's inclination to play both sides—the Viet Minh and the French. In October
1947 Tam withdrew from the pro-Bao Dai movement and from active politics but
continued to write articles from abroad against the French and American involve-

ment in Viet Nam. During the 1963 Buddhist rebellion Tam committed suicide (July 1963) in protest against Ngo Dinh Diem's oppressive regime.

Tan, Chu Van, Lieutenant General (1909–   )
A member of the Nung minority mountain people, Tan was born into a poor peasant family in the village of Phu Thoung (in the Tonkinese province of Thai Nguyen). His formal education was limited to a few years of primary schooling from which he had to withdraw at the age of ten for lack of tuition money. After the Yen Bay uprisings many revolutionaries concentrated in the Thai Nguyen region and Tan joined (1934) the leading group, the ICP. Given the task of organizing the revolutionary movement in the Vu Nhai area of the province, Tan led numerous protest demonstrations and strikes and formed several self-defense units (1934–40). In the fall of 1940 Tan was assigned to the military staff of Bac Son War Zone and the next year (1941) was given a field command in the newly-created Army of National Salvation. For eight grueling months Tan held out against French military raids but in March 1942 he withdrew to the China border. As the French relaxed their reprisals and returned south, Tan returned with his forces to the old Bac Son-Vu Ninh base (February 1943). During 1943–44 Tan expanded his base of operations, built his forces, and linked up (March 1945) with the forces of Vo Nguyen Giap in the Cao Bang area to form the Viet Nam Army of Liberation.

In 1945 Tan was elected to the ICP Central Committee, a post he retained until the mid-seventies. During the 1945 revolution Tan was appointed to the influential Leadership Committee and named minister of national defense in Ho Chi Minh's first cabinet. In recent years Chu Van Tan has continued to occupy key posts in the leadership of the DRV: vice chairman of the Standing Committee of the National Assembly, member of the National Defense Council and of the Lao Dong Party Central Committee, secretary of the Viet Bac Regional Bureau of the Lao Dong Party and commander of the armed forces in the Viet Bac. Until 1970 he held the additional post of chairman of the Administrative Committee of the Viet Bac Autonomous Zone. Tan is now in semiretirement but continues to write articles on the Viet Bac minorities covering a wide range of topics. *Sources:* General Chu Van Tan: *Reminiscences on the Army for National Salvation,* pp. v, 1, and 2. In August 1979 the Hong Kong-based *Far Eastern Economic Review* reported that General Tan had been placed under house arrest in Hanoi.

Tao, Nguyen Van (1905–1970)
French-educated journalist; in the late twenties and early thirties an active member of the French Communist Party and member of its Central Committee. His interest lay mainly in French labor unions and he was identified as a "syndicalist." In 1932 Tao was repatriated by the French and settled in Cochinchina where he organized a trade union movement among the industrial workers of the Cholon-Saigon area. The dire economic situation of the workers and peasants in the early thirties favored his election as a communist delegate to the Saigon Municipal Council in 1933. Popular support reelected him in 1937, and he remained in office until 1939. During his period of tenure he edited a radical newspaper and collaborated with other communist leaders (Nguyen Anh Ninh, Tran Van Giau, Duong Bach Mai, et al.) in opposing the Trotskyites and strengthening the ICP in Cochinchina. Tao's efforts on the Council produced appreciable results

in bettering working conditions and wages. After the French outlawed the Front Populaire (1939), the police clamped down on radical elements in Saigon, arresting Tao and sentencing him to five years' hard labor at the Poulo Condore penal colony. Released by the Japanese after the 1945 coup, Tao returned to Saigon and his party activities.

In August 1945 Tran Van Giau appointed Tao secretary-general and commissioner of the interior in the Provisional Executive Committee for the South. His long background in the labor field prompted Ho Chi Minh to appoint him minister of labor in his October 1946 cabinet, a post he held through 1968. Since his retirement, Tao has been secretary of the Communist Party Committee of Phu Tan District, An Giang Province. *Source:* (1) OSS-SI Biog file: R&A no. 3336, 25 October 1945; (2) U.S. Joint Publications Research Service. (CIAC)

Terauchi, Field Marshal, Count Hisaichi *(Juichi)* (1879–1946)
Born in Yamaguchi prefecture, Japan; the son of Lieutenant General Count Masataki, former Minister of War (1902) and prime minister of Japan (1919). Hisaichi graduated from the Imperial Military Academy (1900), the Japanese Military Staff College (1909), and received further training in Germany. Major general (1924); held major commands in Chosen, Manchuria, and Taiwan (1932); promoted to full general (1935); served as minister of war (army) (1936–37); commanded Japanese forces in North China (1937–38); appointed member of the Supreme war Council in 1938; represented the Imperial Japanese Army at the Nazi Convention of Nuremberg (1939); commander in chief, Japanese forces in the Southwest Pacific (December 1941–August 1945). During World War II his command (Southern Army) comprised four armies numbering one million men charged with the defense of the southwest Pacific area ranging from Burma to New Guinea. Terauchi's Southern Army Headquarters was established at Saigon on 6 November 1941, moved to Singapore in May 1942, to Manila in late 1942, and back to Saigon on 17 November 1944, where it remained until the Japanese surrender to the British on 30 November 1945.

Hisaichi Terauchi was best known for his autocratic, xenophobic, racist character. His uninspired harsh disciplinarian spirit contributed in part to the decline of the Samurai chivalry during the war years. With help from a prominent anti-KMT Chinese banker-financier, Wang Keh-min, Terauchi set up Japan's puppet "Provisional Government of the Chinese Republic" at Peking in December 1937. Terauchi's occupation of North China was marked with the wanton execution of thousands of pro-KMT and Communist Chinese. During World War II Terauchi openly encouraged and supported the "unauthorized" xenophobic activities of the infamous Lieutenant Colonel Masanobu Tsuji, responsible in part for the atrocities committed against Australian and Indian POWs (at Singapore) and American and Filipino POWs (on Bataan). After the fall of Corregidor, Terauchi was incensed with his senior commander in the Philippines, General Nasaharu Homma, and Homma's liberal policy toward the Filipinos and Americans. Terauchi sent an adverse report on Homma's attitude to Tokyo from his headquarters in Saigon. Subsequently, he had Homma relieved of his command, returned to Japan, and forced into retirement in semidisgrace.

Than, Nguyen Hai (1879–1955)
Son of a mandarin; born in Ha Dong, near Hanoi; a follower of Phan Boi Chau; participated in the Tonkinese nationalist movement (1907–09); emigrated to China

(1912) where he made his residence until 1945. Elected to the Executive Committee, and secretary of the Dong Minh Hoi at its founding conference (August 1942). Than proved ineffectual in unifying the divergent political parties and unreliable as a leader; after embezzling party funds he left Liuchow, the center of Dong Minh Hoi activities, and did not return until the second Dong Minh Hoi conference in March 1944; he was elected then a "control" member in the reorganized Dong Minh Hoi.

In September 1945 Than returned to Viet Nam with Hsiao Wen's troops, hoping to assume the reins of government but ran into conflict with Ho Chi Minh and his Viet Minh. After a series of negotiations with Ho, Than was "elected" vice-president of the Provisional Coalition Government (January 1946); unhappy with the "honorific" office, Than resigned and left Hanoi for Canton. He surfaced again in March 1947 at Hong Kong to form a new anti-Viet Minh and anti-French coalition, the United National Front, advocating the return of Bao Dai to Viet Nam. Failing to achieve popular support or to obtain military support from Chang Fa-kwei, his old mentor, Than's movement collapsed. Returning to Canton in the fall of 1947, Than retired from active politics.

Tsuchihashi, Yuitsu, Lieutenant General (c. 1885–   )
Commanding General, 38th Imperial Japanese Army. Tsuchihashi assumed command of the newly reconstituted French Indochina Garrison Army from Lieutenant General Kazumoto Machijiri on 4 December 1944. Tsuchihashi graduated from the Japanese Military Staff College (1920), spoke fluent French and served concurrently as Military Attaché to France and Belgium (1937–40). In early 1939 Tsuchihashi went to Hanoi to discuss with Governor-General Jules Brevié the possibility of interdicting American supplies routed through Indochina for Chiang Kai-shek's army. The French demurred. In March 1945 Tsuchihashi carried out a coup against the French administration and immobilized all French forces in Indochina. He surrendered his forces north of the sixteenth parallel to the Chinese at Hanoi on 28 September 1945.

Viet, Hoang Quoc (1905–   )
Born in Bac Ninh province; attended the Practical School of Industry in Haiphong (1922); expelled (1925) following a strike; worked in factories and mines; joined the Thanh Nien Party (1928); was arrested (1930) as a labor agitator and sentenced to the penal colony at Poulo Condore; released in 1936. Became a member of the ICP Central Committee (1941–77); Chief Procurator (1964); member of the Presidium of the Central Committee of the Viet Nam Fatherland Front (1977); President of the Viet Nam General Federation of Trade Unions (1977); member of the Presidium of the Congress of the Viet Nam National United Front (1977).

Wainwright, Jonathan Mayhew, General (1883–1953)
American general. Graduated USMA (1906); served in France (1918); major general (1940); stationed in the Philippines when the Japanese attacked (December 1941); commanded northern front until he succeeded General MacArthur as commander in chief; gallantly defended Bataan and Corregidor (1942); prisoner-of-war (1942–45); awarded the Congressional Medal of Honor and promoted to full general (1945); commander of the Fourth Army (1946); retired (1947).

General Wainwright, the highest ranking Allied prisoner of the Japanese, was rescued by an OSS Mercy Team (Mission CARDINAL) led by Major Robert F. Lamar.

The team landed on August 16 outside Mukden and made their way on foot toward the Hoten prison camp where they expected to find Wainwright. Intercepted by a Japanese patrol unaware of Japan's capitulation, they were disarmed, stripped, and beaten. At the Japanese headquarters in Mukden, Lamar was informed by the officer in charge that he had just learned "that the war is over." Lamar and his men were restored to dignity with profuse apologies and then told that Wainwright was at a smaller camp in Sian (Liao-yuan) about 110 miles northeast of Mukden. The Japanese said that Soviet permission had to be obtained before the team could proceed because Sian was in communist-controlled territory. After much delay, the Russians authorized the team to travel on, and they reached Sian (19 August) where they found Wainwright and a distinguished group of prisoners, including General Edward M. Percival, former British commander at Malaya; Sir Benton Thomas, former governor of Malaya; Sir Mark Young, former governor of Hong Kong; A. W. L. Tjarda van Starkenborgh Stachouver, former governor general of the Dutch East Indies; C. R. Smith, former governor of Borneo; Major General Callaghan of Australia; and others of high rank. After more delays, on 24 August a senior Soviet officer offered to escort the prisoners to Mukden provided General Wainwright procure his own transportation, which he did with the help of the Japanese camp commander. Three days later, at 1:30 a.m. of the twenty-seventh, the exhausted group boarded a train at Mukden for the 1,200-mile ride to Hsian. From there they were flown to Chungking and, later, to Tokyo Bay, where General Wainwright stood next to General MacArthur on 2 September during the surrender ceremony aboard the battleship U.S.S. *Missouri.*

Wedemeyer, Albert Coady, Lieutenant General (1897–   )
Commanding General, U.S. Army Forces, China Theater, and concurrently chief of staff to Generalissimo Chiang Kai-shek (October 1944–April 1946). Graduated USMA (1919); served in China, the Philippines, and Europe (1920–35); graduated from the Command and General Staff College, Leavenworth (1936); attended the German War College, Berlin (1936–38); member of the WDGS Plans Division (1941–43); deputy chief of staff (SEAC) to Lord Mountbatten (October 1943–October 1944). Promoted to lieutenant general (1945). Presidential survey mission, China and Korea (1947–48); commander of the sixth U.S. Army (1949–51); retired from active service (1951).

Whitaker, John Thompson, Colonel (1906–1946)
Chief, OSS-SI, China Theater, at Chungking (1945). Author, journalist, war correspondent. Born in Chattanooga, Tennessee; graduated from the University of the South at Sewanee, Tennessee (1927); began his journalistic career with the *Chattanooga News* (1927) and later wrote for the *New York Herald Tribune,* the *Chicago Daily News,* the *Washington Star,* and the *New York Post.* As a reporter and war correspondent covered the critical sessions of the League of Nations at Geneva (1931–32); was in Vienna and Berlin during the putsch and Hitler purge (1933–34); reported the exploits of Italy's troops in Ethiopia and was the first correspondent to reach Eritrea (1935); covered part of the Spanish rebellion (1936–37); narrowly escaped execution as a Czech spy when the Germans invaded Czechoslovakia (1938). Whitaker's antifascist articles in 1940 displeased Mussolini who expelled him from Italy (1941).

Throughout his journalistic career Whitaker saw the development of World War II from Geneva to Pearl Harbor and wrote in-depth analyses in the press and in his several books, *We Cannot Escape History* (1943), *And Fear Came* (1936), and *Americas to the South* (1939). He demonstrated the depth of his passion against Mussolini's and Hitler's fascism when the United States became involved in the war by undergoing two painful operations to qualify himself physically for military service. General Donovan invited Whitaker to join the OSS (1942); he accepted and served as a civilian intelligence officer with front-line units throughout the North African and Sicilian campaigns, earning the praise of Generals George S. Patton and Mark Clark. Commissioned in the field a lieutenant colonel of infantry (1943), Donovan designated him chief, psychological warfare (OSS-MO). Reassigned to the China Theater to head the OSS Secret Intelligence Division (1944), Whitaker directed covert intelligence for China, Japan, and Korea. In the summer of 1945 Whitaker suffered a relapse of past injuries and was evacuated to the United States for hospitalization. Awarded the Legion of Merit (twice), the French Croix de Guerre and Legion of Honor, and lesser decorations. Whitaker died 11 September 1946.

APPENDIX III

POLITICAL PARTIES

This appendix describing only the principal political parties involved in the history of Viet Nam during the 1940s is included for the ready reference of the reader in identifying the political elements mentioned in this book. No attempt has been made to present a concise, chronological, historical account of the complex evolvement of the numerous Vietnamese political parties, fronts, and movements. The political parties listed are in alphabetical order using the generally accepted name, followed parenthetically by the official Vietnamese name and English translation.

Sources: OSS-SI and R&A reports (1943–45); SSU-WD files and material assembled and analyzed by the Department of State, Office of Intelligence Research (1946–48), much of which is incorporated in OIR Report no. 3708, dated 1 October 1949 (PAOVN).

ADVANCE GUARD YOUTH (Thanh Nien Tien Phong)
Under the Decoux administration, in the early 1940s, a youth and sports program was created to safeguard French values and assure a pro-French attitude among the youth of Viet Nam. While the program proved effective in developing physical culture and good living habits, it also heightened the social consciousness of the youth and trained them in organization and group discipline. After the Japanese coup, the Dai Viet government of Tran Trong Kim entrusted the Minister of Youth, Phan Anh, with reorienting the program toward political and military objectives. Anh's assistant, Ta Quang Buu, was made responsible for the program in Annam and Tonkin; Dr. Pham Ngoc Thach, a secret communist, was placed in charge of the Cochinchina sector which was the training ground of the Japanese Yasu Butai guerrillas. On 2 July 1945, Dr. Thach's group converted its activity into the Thanh Nien Tien Phong, the core of a local paramilitary force which played a decisive role in the August revolution in Cochinchina and continued its guerrilla operations against the French reoccupation. In the north, Phan Anh and Ta Quang Buu

merged their Dai Viet youth with Giap's forces in Tonkin. The students at the University of Hanoi set the stage for the demonstration of the General Association of Students on 21 August 1945, which called for Bao Dai's abdication and the formation of a government under the Viet Minh.

ANNAMESE COMMUNIST PARTY (Annam Cong San Dang)

At the Thanh Nien national congress of the Viet Nam Revolutionary Youth League, held at Hong Kong between 1 and 9 May 1929, some Tonkinese delegates proposed the formation of an Indochinese Communist Party. The proposal, supported principally by delegates from Tonkin and Annam, was aimed at obtaining recognition from the Moscow Comintern as a party apart from the Chinese Communists. Under the guidance of Ho Chi Minh the émigré faction of the Youth League in China strongly opposed the proposal. The Youth League was unwilling to deviate from the political line previously set by Ho, which aimed at building a revolutionary nationalist party with socialist tendencies.

After several heated debates one delegate from Annam and two from Tonkin proposed the adoption of the name "Indochinese Communist Party" for the organization. When they were turned down by the congress, the dissidents split from the Youth League and returned to Indochina where they won over a large number of the Youth League membership in their own regions and in Cochinchina and set up the Indochinese Communist Party (Dong Duong Cong San Dang). By November 1929 the new organization was sufficiently strong to rival the Viet Nam Revolutionary Youth League which had upheld the émigré leadership in China. For fear of losing its militant members to its rivals within Indochina, the émigré leadership secretly adopted the name Annamese Communist Party (Annam Cong San Dang).

The split in the Viet Nam Revolutionary Youth League resulted in the formation of three separate parties—the Annamese Communist Party, the Indochinese Communist Party, and the Indochinese Communist League or Alliance (Dong Duong Cong San Lien Doan). All three asked Moscow for official recognition and relations between them were bitter. Not until Ho Chi Minh returned to Hong Kong on instructions from Moscow in January 1930 was a fusion arranged. From February to October 1930 the fused organization was known as the Viet Nam Communist Party (Viet Nam Cong San Dang). The Central Committee of the party was transferred from Hong Kong to Haiphong.

A congress held in Hong Kong in October 1930 formalized the actions of the preceding period and adopted for the new party the name Indochinese Communist Party (Dong Duong Cong San Dang) to conform to the rules of the Comintern, because that title included all of Indochina, not solely the three kys. The Central Committee was then transferred from Haiphong to Saigon. (See Indochinese Communist Party).

BINH XUYEN (Lien Khu Binh Xuyen)

This group originated from the fusion of a number of bandit gangs, some of whose members had been released from the penal colony of Poulo Condore by the Japanese. It derived its name from the village in the marshy lowlands south of the Saigon-Cholon region where the Binh Xuyen maintained its headquarters and refuge from the law. Apolitical at first, concerned only with river piracy, banditry, and murder for pay, the Binh Xuyen entered the political arena late in 1944. Under the leadership of several strongmen, such as Le Van Vien (alias Bay Vien) and

Duong Van Duong, the several gangs were organized into a well-disciplined paramilitary organization. The "politically oriented," principally for personal gain, Le Van Vien, with the concurrence of his associates, offered their services to the pro-Japanese nationalist Viet Nam Phuc Quoc Dong Minh Hoi (Viet Nam Restoration League), shortened to Phuc Quoc. Having legitimized the criminal Binh Xuyen and given it a political label, Le Van Vien proceeded to gain the confidence of the kempeitai and promoted himself into a position of influence in the Saigon police from which he was able to protect his cohorts from police harassment and obtain amnesty for many. After the August 1945 revolution in Saigon, Tran Van Giau placed Vien in command of the Saigon-Cholon troops and for a brief period the Binh Xuyen collaborated with the Viet Minh in resisting the French. During the 2 September disorders in Saigon and the 24–25 September attack on Cité Hérault, the Binh Xuyen figured prominently in anti-French activities. Vien's opposition to Viet Minh leadership made him unreliable to Giau and, early in 1946, to his successor, Nguyen Binh, who put a price on Vien's head. Vien then joined alternatively the Hoa Hao and the Cao Dai which in 1946 were fighting the French, at times alongside the Viet Minh. But Viet Minh insistence on unquestioned leadership led the sects and the Binh Xuyen to abandon the uncoordinated effort by the end of 1947. Vien threw his support in the fall of 1947 to Bao Dai, then in Hong Kong being considered by the French to head a French-sponsored government for Viet Nam. Vien entered into an arrangement with the French in which the Binh Xuyen would hunt down their former Viet Minh allies in return for special privileges in Saigon-Cholon to exploit the vice market in prostitution, gambling, opium, etc. By mid-1951 Vien had established himself as a close financial partner of Bao Dai and his Binh Xuyen was the operating organization for the vice market. Le Van Vien was made a general and owner of *Le Grande Monde,* the most fabulous gambling establishment in the Far East. In 1955 Ngo Dinh Diem attempted to eliminate the sects and the Binh Xuyen. He made the Binh Xuyen his first target and, after a seven-month siege, Vien's troops gave up and General Vien fled to France to a life of leisure, enjoying the fortune amassed in the service of the French and Bao Dai.

BUDDHIST HOME CONTEMPLATION (Tinh Do Cu Si)
A religious social movement with a large Chinese membership whose principal tenet was that "profound contemplation at home" is superior to the use of priests and pagodas. Its adherents in the late 1940s were estimated at five hundred thousand and they strongly opposed the Viet Minh. It had no hierarchy of command and offered only uncohesive passive resistance to the DRV government.

CAO DAI (Dai Dao Tam Ky Pho Do)
Dai Dao Tam Ky Pho Do or "Third Amnesty of God," popularly known as Cao Dai, was initially a religious-social movement which later expanded into an influential politico-military party. An amalgam of many religions, whose creation proceeds from spiritism, Cao Dai draws heavily on both Christianity and Buddhism. Its ritual shows the strong influence of Vietnamese folk religion and French Catholic practices.

Nguyen Van Chieu, prophet and founder of the Cao Dai movement, first declared in 1919 that he was in communication with God, who was speaking to him through an adolescent medium. Chieu believed Him to be the One True God, the Jehovah of the Jews and Christians, the Supreme Being of the Buddhists, the Brahma of the Hindus. Later, in Saigon, Chieu announced that God had granted mankind what he described as the Third Amnesty for sin. According to Chieu, the First Amnesty was proclaimed to the West through Moses and Jesus, the Second Amnesty to the East through Buddha and Lao-tzu. The Third Amnesty, unlike the others, was not transmitted through an inspired prophet but was derived through table-tapping spiritualistic seances. Chieu claimed only that he was the first recipient of a new series of divine revelations. Indeed, in 1926, when the Cao Dai sect first began to organize in earnest, Chieu stepped aside as leader in favor of a recent convert and Cochinchinese notable, Le Van Trung.

Trung, a capable organizer, within a year increased the membership from a few hundred to over twenty thousand, including among the converts some high officials of the French colonial administration, students, and landowners. Trung became the first Giao Tong or "Pope" and established his holy see at Tay Ninh (about fifty miles northwest of Saigon on the Cambodian border). There he erected the High Altar, a cathedral expressing in structure and décor the background of the sect. The church towers are European in inspiration; the open sweep of its floor suggests a mosque; and its wall decorations of plaster cobras and dragons are reminiscent of a Buddhist pagoda. Statues of Confucius, Jesus, Buddha, Lao-tzu, Brahma, Siva and Vishnu are prominently displayed. Dominating the great nave is a single staring eye—"the eye of God"—the supreme symbol of the religion, similar to the Masonic eye. The Cao Dai claims several spiritual "fathers" or "saints" believed to guide the sect through mediums. Among these are Sun Yat-sen; Trang Trinh Le, a Vietnamese divine; Victor Hugo; and Joan of Arc. The hierarchy and ritual are closely patterned after the Roman Catholic Church, whose clergy promptly labeled the Cao Dai the "religion of Satan."

Appealing largely to the uneducated and essentially superstitious masses, the Cao Dai mushroomed in size to over five hundred thousand by 1930, giving the French authorities cause for concern. A schism took place in 1933 when Pham Cong Tac, one of the original founders, organized a secret sect known as Pham Mon to exploit political objectives. With the death of Pope Le Van Trung in 1936, Tac seized control of the temple at Tay Ninh and proclaimed himself "interim Pope." From this point on the Cao Dai split into several distinct sects but retained in all of them a rigid rightist political philosophy, conservative in nature and vehemently anticommunist and promonarchical.

From 1934 to 1941 the Cao Dai maintained secret relations with the Japanese agent, Matsushita, and with Prince Cuong De in Japan. With the Japanese entry into Indochina (1940) the Cao Dai movement emerged as an extremely powerful force in Vietnamese politics. Aware of the Caodaist relationship to Japan as a cover for the return of Cuong De and for promoting the Greater East Asia Co-Prosperity Sphere program, the French authorities closed all the temples and pagodas and deported Pham Cong Tac to the islands of Comore, Madagascar, in August 1941. The movement went underground and did not surface again until the 9 March coup, when it provided the Yasu Butai with espionage agents and manpower for the Japanese guerrilla units. In Cochinchina, Tran Quang Vinh, a principal subordinate of the "pope," was the commander in chief of the "Cao Dai Army." The Japanese furnished Vinh with arms and used his troops as an auxiliary police force.

After the August 1945 revolution the Cao Dai was temporarily neutralized by the Viet Minh interim government in Saigon. The Cao Dai attempted to collaborate with the Viet Minh, but Tran Van Giau's intransigence and Nguyen Binh's repressive tactics (he held Tran Quang Vinh prisoner for several weeks) convinced the Cao Dai that its only hope was to come to terms with the French. In June 1946 a few joined the French forces against the Viet Minh guerrillas. The French released Pham Cong Tac from exile in the Comore and more Caodaist military units joined the French. By the end of 1946, Nguyen Binh's attack on Tay Ninh was the last straw and Pham Cong Tac committed the Cao Dai "army" to full collaboration with the French.

From 1945 to mid-1955 the political power of the Cao Dai played an important role in Vienamese affairs. It literally constituted a state within a state, administering and controlling a sizeable area northwest of Saigon and maintaining its own army which received support first from the Japanese and then from the French. In 1955 this political power was broken by President Ngo Dinh Diem through a combination of negotiation and force. In February 1956 Pham Cong Tac fled to Cambodia and Vietnamese national troops took over Tay Ninh. With the surrender of its armies and the death of Pham Cong Tac the sect lost most of its temporal power but none of its religious fervor. In South Viet Nam the sect supported, at least outwardly, the Diem government. In Cambodia the sect reached a working agreement with the NLF (Viet Cong) and continued its fight for unification and independence.

CAO DAI LEAGUE (Doan The Cao Dai)

A political auxiliary of the Caodaist religious movement in Cochinchina, headed by the "Pope" of the order, Pham Cong Tac (see Cao Dai, above). There were twelve sects in all, with a total membership in 1947 estimated at from one to four million. The League claimed to have had from one to two million adherents who allegedly supported the Mat Tran Thong Nhut Quoc Gia Lien Hiep (see National Union Front, below). While this claim was undoubtedly exaggerated, the League was important, primarily because it had a number of armed troops (estimated twenty-five thousand) at its disposal, some of whom were used in 1944–45 in the Japanese Yasu Butai (see n. 18, chap. 5), first against the Allies and in late 1945 against the Viet Minh in the south. The principal military leader of the Caodaists was Tran Quang Vinh, commander in chief under the authority of the "Pope."

Politically the League was divided on the issue of cooperation with the French, and a good deal of rivalry was generated among its leaders for positions of authority within the DRV and the Bao Dai governments. During World War II under Japanese domination Caodaism was used as a vehicle for Japanese propaganda for a Greater East Asia Co-Prosperity Sphere (see Viet Nam National Independence Party, below). With the fall of Japan, some elements of the League came into conflict with the Viet Minh in Cochinchina, whose conciliatory policy toward the Allies they opposed. There was also a strong current of xenophobia within the League and many members favored the return of Cuong De to the throne of Annam.

In October 1947 a large section of the League withdrew its support from the French-sponsored Cochinchina government, but the differences among the Caodaists were soon reconciled and they jointly supported the Nguyen Van Xuan government and accepted Bao Dai as Viet Nam's negotiator with the French. Several months later, on 27 January 1948, the League signed a pact of alliance with the other religious sect, the Hoa Hao, to eliminate the fratricidal struggle between the two religious orders. The pact provided among other things an agreement to support "Bao Dai in his negotiations with France," and in July 1949 the "Pope" openly aligned himself with the Bao Dai government.

COCHINCHINESE DEMOCRATIC PARTY (Parti Democrate Cochinchinois)
Founded in 1946 by Nguyen Tan Cuong, it was a separatist party favoring a completely autonomous Cochinchina to be administered by France. It was replaced in 1947 by Nguyen Van Tam's Cochinchinese Front. Cuong formed the Popular Front of Cochinchina, still advocating separatism within a French federation.

COMMUNIST PARTY—see Indochinese Communist Party

CONSTITUTIONALIST PARTY
Formed in 1923, the Constitutionalist Party was the first legal political organization to be organized in Indochina. Its prominent leaders were Nguyen Phan Long, a former functionary in the French administration; Duong Van Giao, a Saigon lawyer; and Bui Quang Chieu, a professor and educator. This party attempted, within the framework of French sovereignty in Indochina, to mitigate some of the more illiberal aspects of French rule. It campaigned for French citizenship, equality before the law, the transformation of the Colonial Councils into genuine legislative bodies, agricultural credit to improve the lot of the peasant, and other moderate reforms. The whole program was placed by its sponsors within a context of French-Vietnamese political collaboration which alone, they declared, could guarantee France's remaining in Indochina; any other course would abet revolutionary attempts to oust the French completely.

The party gained some influence in Cochinchina among intellectuals, the wealthier Vietnamese landowners, and government officials. It waged a particularly successful campaign against a proposal to turn the port of Saigon over to a financial consortium that would operate it as a monopoly. In 1925 the party was successful in electing a bloc of its candidates to the Colonial Council. The French colonial authorities tolerated the movement, particularly since it managed to establish some connections with liberal forces in metropolitan France.

However, when the reform movement failed to realize its major objectives and the administration did not act on its program, a number of its adherents gave up the political struggle and turned to the new religion, Caodasim. Others found their way into the clandestine revolutionary groups.

After 1934 the Constitutionalist Party regained a certain amount of influence and participated in the electoral struggle for the municipal council of Saigon. But it never achieved any real measure of success; by then the activities of the legal organizations of the revolutionary movement far eclipsed its activities. With the advent of World War II, a number of its followers, sensing the increasing influence of Japan in Indochina, helped form a new revolutionary nationalist party, the *Viet Nam Cach Menh Dang* (see Viet Nam Revolutionary Party), and the Constitutionalist Party disappeared from the political scene.

DAI VIET (Dai Viet Dan Chinh) Great Viet Nam Democratic Party, (Dai Viet Quoc Dan Dang) Great Viet Nam Nationalist Party, (Dai Viet Quoc Dan Hoi) Great Viet Nam Nationalist Association

A pro-Japanese faction of the Viet Nam Nationalist Party (Viet Nam Quoc Dan Dang) known as the VNQDD broke away from the parent organization in 1940. The faction was led by Nguyen Tuong Tam and became the Great Viet Nam Democratic Party (Dai Viet Dan Chinh), commonly called the Dai Viet. After the Japanese entry into Indochina (September 1940) the Dai Viet gained influence and strength. The French clamped down on its activities and, in 1941, arrested Tam and other leaders, but Tam succeeded in escaping to China. At the same time Nguyen The Nghiep, leader of the VNQDD in Kunming, returned to Indochina and formed the Great Viet Nam Nationalist Party (Dai Viet Quoc Dan Dang), leaving the leadership of the VNQDD in China to a former school teacher, Vu Hong Khanh. Nguyen Tuong Tam joined the VNQDD in China and led the Dai Viet Quoc Dan Dang until his return to Viet Nam in the fall of 1945. Tam kept the Dai Viet in China in the forefront of the nationalist movement by bringing it into the Chinese-sponsored Viet Nam Revolutionary League (Viet Nam Cach Menh Dong Minh Hoi) known as the Dong Minh Hoi in October 1942 and, again, in the reorganized Dong Minh Hoi of March 1944.

In Indochina the remnants of the original Dai Viet Dan Chinh and the re-formed Dai Viet Quoc Dan Dang were merged and reorganized in 1942 by a xenophobic young student, Truong Tu Anh, into an anticommunist, antimonarchical, ultranationalistic party rivaling the pro-Japanese Phuc Quoc. Both parties were driven underground by the French police until late 1944. In February 1945 many pro-Japanese organizations emerged, among them the newly formed Great Viet Nam Nationalist Association (Dai Viet Quoc Dan Hoi), which brought together:

1. The Great Annam People's Party (Dai Viet Quoc Dan Dang);
2. The Great Annam Democratic Party (Dai Viet Dan Chinh);
3. Several other groups including the Youth Patriots (Thanh Nien Ai Quoc), a terrorist party violently anti-French, and the Servants of the Country (Phung Xa Quoc Gioi).

In the north, associated with the Viet Nam Restoration League (Viet Nam Phuc Quoc Dong Minh Hoi), was the National Socialist Party (Dai Viet Quoc Xa) with a membership of about two thousand. This party was directed by Tran Trong Kim, premier of the Bao Dai pro-Japanese government and closely associated with the kempeitai in the Yasu Butai recruiting efforts among the Vietnamese for the puppet military forces. Participating in the League in the south was the Great Viet Nam Nationalist Party (Dai Viet Quoc Dan Dang), mainly pro-Japanese elements from Cochinchina.

In the fall of 1945 the Dai Viet returned to Viet Nam under the protection of the Chinese occupation forces and attempted to assume a leading role in the Hanoi government. The best it could achieve was a cabinet post for Nguyen Tuong Tam and several seats in the Assembly of Ho Chi Minh's Provisional Coalition Government of January 1946. Several months later Tam, who had been appointed Minister for Foreign Affairs, abandoned the government and fled to China. In 1946 the Dai Viet, aware of American interest in Bao Dai and hoping to replace Ho Chi Minh with the ex-Emperor, adopted a pro-American attitude and initiated a violent anticommunist campaign. In February 1947 Tam, in China, joined his former colleagues of the VNQDD and the Dong Minh Hoi in forming the National Union Front (Mat Tran Thong Nhut Quoc Gia Lien Hiep) in Nanking to support Bao Dai as spokesman for Viet Nam. The Dai Viet limped along through 1950 but never attained a leading political stature.

DEMOCRATIC LEAGUE (Lien Minh Dan Chu)

The Democratic League was a component of Le Van Hoach's Viet Nam National Assembly (Viet Nam Quoc Gia Tap Doan) of Cochinchina. He also organized the Viet Nam Quoc Gia Lien Hiep (see Viet Nam National Rally) in December 1947. The Democratic League was a republican-oriented organization. It was opposed to the Viet Minh but fought with it against the French. Its representative in negotiations with other nationalist groups was Do Du Anh.

DEMOCRATIC PARTY

The party was founded in Saigon in 1937 by a Cochinchinese lawyer, Trinh Dinh Thao, closely associated with the Caodaist "Pope," Pham Cong Tac. One of the key party leaders was Dr. Nguyen Van Thinh who became in 1946 the first president of the French-sponsored Republic of Cochinchina. The party favored a dominion-type status for Indochina and it was the forerunner of the Indochinese Democratic Party (see below) which emerged after the war in Cochinchina.

DEMOCRATIC-SOCIALIST PARTY—see Viet Nam Democratic Socialist Party (Viet Nam Dan Chu Xa Hoi Dang)

DONG MINH HOI (Viet Nam Cach Menh Dong Minh Hoi) Viet Nam Revolutionary League

A coalition of Vietnamese political parties sponsored by the Chinese Kuomintang in the early forties in southern China. From 1911 Vietnamese nationalists found refuge from French repression in China. The 1930 uprisings at Yen Bay and the ensuing French reprisals swelled the ranks of the politically-oriented Vietnamese community in China and the migration continued throughout the forties. After the Japanese occupation of Indochina (September 1940) political consciousness among the Vietnamese émigrés, spurred by the communist movement for independence and the Chinese government's interest in postwar Indochina, coalesced.

In the fall of 1940 a committee led by seasoned revolutionaries associated with the VNQDD put together the "Viet Nam National Liberation League" (Giai Phong Hoi) which was launched in the spring of 1941. The League included the VNQDD, the Viet Minh, the Dai Viet, and lesser parties. Its objective was to bring their assets together toward achieving their common goal, that is, ousting the Japanese and the French from Indochina and forming a free and independent Vietnamese government. This early League fumbled along for several months while interparty rivalries, lack of organizational discipline, failure to win popular support from the Vietnamese in China, and charges by the old revolutionary (Nguyen Hai Than) that several members of the Viet Minh were communists led to the League's dissolution. Than's charges alarmed the KMT and uncovered Pham Van Dong, Vo Nguyen Giap, and Hoang Van Hoan as members of the ICP. After they fled to Viet Nam in January 1942, the League ceased to function and most of its members moved to Liuchow.

The Chinese Nationalist government, in a move to control Vietnamese political activities for possible future advantage, asked the VNQDD liaison to the KMT, Nghiem Ke To, to invite all the Kunming revolutionary groups to send representatives to Liuchow for negotiating a merger of all exile groups. There were three Vietnamese organizations then operating in Liuchow: (1) the Viet Nam Restoration League (Viet Nam Phuc Quoc Dong Minh Hoi), known as Phuc Quoc, comprising some seven hundred members, led by Hoang Luong; (2) the Viet Minh; and (3) a group of Vietnamese nationalist exiles from the Viet Nam Nationalist Party (Viet Nam Quoc Dan Dang), known as the VNQDD, and from the Great Viet Nam Nationalist Party (Dai Viet Quoc Dan Dang), known as the Dai Viet. In May 1942 Nghiem Ke To returned to Yunnan with a mandate from Chungking to liquidate existing disagreements between the parties by creating a coalition organization. On 10 October 1942 the Viet Nam Revolutionary League, popularly known as the Dong Minh Hoi (DMH), was formed at Liuchow with official recognition from the Area Commander, Marshal Chang Fa-kwei, and a monthly subsidy of one hundred thousand Chinese dollars. The principal leadership was provided by the VNQDD, which dominated the organization. The Viet Minh and ICP had been purposely excluded. The program was modeled broadly on that of the Chinese KMT, including the Three People's Principles of Dr. Sun Yat-sen. It sought the liberation of Indochina from the French and Japanese and envisaged close cooperation between Viet Nam and China. Organizationally, the Dong Minh Hoi was set up as a paramilitary formation to work in close liaison with the Chinese Nationalist Army. It also maintained an espionage network in Tonkin.

The Dong Minh Hoi fared no better than its predecessor. It was riddled with inefficiency, corruption, and embezzlement (Nguyen Hai Than had absconded with some money from the DMH fund) and suffered from poor leadership and stiff opposition from the ICP and Viet Minh. When the Dong Minh Hoi made no progress in its first year, Chang Fa-kwei was called to account by the KMT and decided to shake up the organization. In March 1944 he called a meeting of the "Congress of Overseas Revolutionary Groups of the Dong Minh Hoi" at Liuchow for the purpose of "reunification" and widening its political base. The reorganization returned Nguyen Hai Than to a place of respectability on the Executive Committee, added three ICP members—Le Tung Son, Pham Van Dong, and Ho Chi Minh (released from Chang's jail in September 1943)—and expanded the role of the Phuc Quoc which represented a sizeable number of Vietnamese military in training with the Chinese army.

The coalition character of the Dong Minh Hoi came to an end in late 1944 when Ho Chi Minh, with Chang's approval, returned to Viet Nam and the leadership reverted to party lines. Vu Hong Khanh heading the VNQDD clashed with Nguyen Hai Than, who pretended to lead the Dong Minh Hoi, and with Nguyen Tuong Tam of the Dai Viet. But from March 1944 to September 1945 the Dong Minh Hoi played an important role in China as a tool of the KMT in dealing with the French and in counterbalancing the communist influence of the Viet Minh in Viet Nam. After the war the Dong Minh Hoi lost control of the VNQDD and a schism emerged among the pro-Chinese Vietnamese. Only as the Dong Minh Hoi served as an adjunct to the Chinese occupation troops in Indochina did it have even minimal influence. Neither the Dong Minh Hoi nor the VNQDD was able to cope with the Viet Minh; they participated in Hanoi political affairs only at the pleasure of Ho Chi Minh.

In 1946 dissident leaders of the Dong Minh Hoi and the VNQDD temporarily allied themselves with the Viet Minh, but the alliance was short-lived. In February 1947 Nguyen Tuong Tam (Dai Viet), Vu Hong Khanh (VNQDD), and Nguyen Hai Than (DMH) formed a National Union Front in Nanking and threw their support to Bao Dai in opposition to Ho Chi Minh. The effort foundered and by 1948 the Dong Minh Hoi was slowly fading away while its members joined the multitude of splinter groups and sects.

GREAT RELIGION OF THE THIRD AMNESTY (Dai Dao Tam Ky Pho Do)
A Caodaist sect led by Tran Quang Vinh, the military leader and spiritual deputy to the "Pope." This sect had been furnished arms by the Japanese and was used as an auxiliary police force under the supervision of the kempeitai throughout Cochinchina. (See Cao Dai, above.)

HOA HAO (Phat Giao Hoa Hao)
A political religious sect based on Hinayana Buddhism, founded in 1939 by Huynh Phu So, in An Giang province on the Cambodian border west of Saigon. Hoa Hao derives its name from the home village of its founder. One evening in May 1939 Huynh Phu So was "seized by supernatural powers" which cured his several ailments and inspired him with a modified version of Buddhism. He went out to preach his new religion to the peasants and the poor in simple language and without complicated ritual, stressing that the faithful could communicate with the Supreme Being anytime and anywhere, needing no temples to offer their prayers. The new prophet soon extended his religious teaching to social and political matters, much to the alarm of the French authorities. They called him the "mad Bonze," while his followers saw him as the "living Buddha." His religious rallies threatened to turn into anti-French demonstrations and in August 1940 the French confined So to a psychiatric hospital. After a thorough examination by French doctors, who declared So sane in May 1941, the French were compelled to release him, but they exiled him to the town of Vinh Loi on the southern coast of Cochinchina.

Despite So's absence from the center of political activities the sect continued to win adherents and became politically important during the Japanese occupation. It was effectively used by the Japanese to foster antiwhite, xenophobic tendencies in line with the Greater East Asia Co-Prosperity Sphere program. In October 1942 the French tired of the nationalist activities of the Hoa Hao and attempted to remove So to Laos, but the Japanese agent, Matsushita, with the help of Hoa Hao agents in a dramatic coup kidnapped So and brought him to Saigon where he lived for several years under the protection of the kempeitai.

In mid-1945 So returned to Cantho province and set up the independent state of Can-tho Quoc and demanded a voice in the government of Tran Van Giau. Tolerated at first, in late September 1945 with Japanese help Giau dismantled the "new state." Even so for a time the Hoa Hao collaborated with the Viet Minh guerrillas in Cochinchina but in 1946 split away. Having acquired a supply of arms and ammunition it formed its own combat units and the Viet Nam Democratic Socialist Party (Viet Nam Dan Chu Xa Hoi Dang). So's refusal to submit to Viet Minh control led to his capture and execution for treason in June 1947.

After So's death the Hoa Hao offered its services to the French who eventually armed twenty thousand from the sect to fight their common enemy, the Viet Minh. But without So's leadership the sect gradually degenerated into armed bands of terrorists directing their hatred toward the white French and their Vietnamese collaborators. The extensive region southwest of Saigon where the Hoa Hao were concentrated broke up into a number of so-called Hoa Hao "baronies" ruled like feudal states. In the spring of 1955 Ngo Dinh Diem asserted control over Hoa Hao territory, outlawed its leaders, and in July 1956 arrested and executed its most powerful leader, Ba Cut. Since then the sect as a group has been virtually inactive politically.

INDEPENDENTS

The several National Assemblies of the Vietnamese government included a sizeable number of independents. They represented many political viewpoints, including that of the conservative mandarin hierarchy. The leader of the independents in 1946 was Hoang Minh Chau, and the influence of the independents in the Viet Nam government was strong. The first cabinet of the DRVN (1945) recognized their importance and assigned three posts to "nonparty" individuals. In his second cabinet (January 1946) Ho reserved two posts at ministerial level for independents. In the second session of the National Assembly (October–November 1946), of the 291 delegates present, 90 or thirty-one percent were independents. They included political personalities who were quite capable of creating political organizations should the occasion have arisen. In a sense they were the political weather vane of the Viet Nam government. Their willingness to support the resistance movement against the French was the outward sign of national unity under the DRVN government.

INDOCHINESE COMMUNIST (LEAGUE) ALLIANCE (Dong Duong Cong San Lien Doan)—see Indochinese Communist Party (below) and Annamese Communist Party (above)

INDOCHINESE COMMUNIST PARTY (Dang Cong San Dong Duong)*

The Indochinese Communist Party was founded on 3 February 1930 at Kowloon (Hong Kong), China, by Ho Chi Minh, but its seeds were planted in June 1925 at Canton, China, when Ho founded the Viet Nam Revolutionary Youth League (Viet Nam Thanh Nien Cach Mang Dong Chi Hoi). It was made up of Vietnamese students, professionals, and workers, some of whom were members of the Chinese Communist Party. From June 1925 to April 1927 the League published a weekly paper called *Youth (Thanh Nien)*, containing primarily appeals to nationalist sentiments and material on the history of Viet Nam. Only in 1926, after a preparatory period of educational activity such as translations of Marxist terminology into Sino-Annamite, did Ho finally write that "only a communist party can [ultimately] insure the well-being of Annam."

During the early years of the League Ho made no attempt to form a Vietnamese communist party; he only laid the foundations. He selected members of the League for enrollment in the Whampoa Military Academy, where the future leaders of both the Chinese Nationalist and the Chinese Communist regimes were being trained under the Kuomintang. Ho also developed and directed programs for teaching young émigrés; preparing written propaganda and issuing the weekly paper; creating and maintaining liaison with nationalist and communist organizations in the interior of Indochina and sympathetic organizations abroad; and establishing

*Vien. The Long Resistance (1858–1975), p. 66.

Canton as the center of the émigré movement, with authority over the interior movement in Indochina as well as over the training of new recruits from Indochina.

The split in the Kuomintang between the Communists and Chiang Kai-shek's
followers forced Ho to leave Canton in April 1927 for Hong Kong and then
Moscow. Some members of the Youth League were imprisoned, but the League's
work went on. The Kuomintang authorities were basically anti-French and were
willing to allow it to exist as long as it directed its agitation, even of a communist
nature, against the French. In December 1928, following the arrest of some Youth
League leaders who were also members of the Chinese Communist Party, the
center of the organization was transferred to Kwangsi and then to Hong Kong.

Despite difficulties, it was estimated by May 1929 that Ho's program had
been reasonably successful. League-trained revolutionaries sent into Indochina
had established regional committees in Tonkin, Annam, and Cochinchina, with city
committees in Hanoi, Haiphong, Saigon, Mytho, and Cantho, each controlling a
number of provinces. The majority of Tonkinese members came from the peasant
and laboring classes. In Annam and Cochinchina, the composition was mixed and
included workers, teachers, students, and peasants. The leadership was composed
predominantly of teachers and intellectuals, and the important functions were carried out by graduates of the Canton emigration.

Under Ho's leadership the communist members of the Viet Nam Revolutionary
Youth League had assumed control of that organization. A congress of the Youth
League, held in Hong Kong 1–9 May 1929, revealed that the émigré leadership in
Canton was out of step with the new trend developing in the interior (Indochina)
organization. This was demonstrated particularly when the one delegate from Annam and two delegates from Tonkin proposed adopting the name, "Indochinese
Communist Party," and split away when they were not upheld. The émigré leadership of Canton conceded the necessity of organizing a communist party but maintained that the congress had no authority to take action until the Youth League
itself had adopted a communist program. In reality, the leadership was unwilling
to deviate from the political line previously set by Ho Chi Minh which had aimed at
building a revolutionary nationalist party with socialist tendencies. The congress
continued its work and adopted statutes bringing the organization into line with
the decisions of the Sixth World Congress of the Comintern (Moscow) while still
maintaining its quasinationalist character. It also aligned the Youth League with
the New Viet Nam Revolutionary Party (Tan Viet Cach Menh Dang) (see Phuc Viet
and VNQDD), opposed the Viet Nam Nationalist Party (Viet Nam Quoc Dan Dang),
and addressed a letter to the Comintern (Moscow) requesting recognition of the
Viet Nam Revolutionary Youth League.

Meanwhile the dissident delegates, having returned to Indochina, succeeded
in winning the support of the Tonkin and Annam regional organizations of the
Youth League to their point of view and setting up a new organization which they
called the Indochinese Communist Party (Dong Duong Cong San Dang). Emissaries
to Cochinchina also succeeded in establishing a section in that region and by
November 1929 the so-called Indochinese Communist Party was sufficiently strong
to rival its parent organization, the Youth League of Cochinchina, which continued
to uphold the émigré leadership in Canton. By that time the émigré leadership had
secretly adopted the name, Annamese Communist Party (Annam Cong San Dang)
for fear of losing its militant members to its rivals within Indochina. The so-called
Indochinese Communist Party also had its effect on the other nationalist groups.
On numerous occasions the New Viet Nam Revolutionary Party had unsuccessfully

undertaken fusion negotiations with the Youth League, but it only kept losing members to the League in the process. To hold its losses, it too created a communist affiliate in 1929 and called it the Indochinese Communist League or Alliance (Dong Duong Cong San Lien Doan). There were, then, three splinter groups among the communist members of the Youth League but none was recognized by the Comintern (Moscow). Both the Annamese and Indochinese Communist Parties sought recognition from the Comintern without success. The leadership attempted to locate Ho Chi Minh to help in this task, but Ho was in Thailand and could not be reached.

Finally, in January 1930, Ho returned to Hong Kong and presided over a conference of delegates from the three groups and on February 3rd the three factions were fused into the Viet Nam Communist Party (Viet Nam Cong San Dang). During the following eight months the Party adopted rules to conform to the Comintern standards and formed trade unions, peasants' cooperatives, communist youth organizations, and relief organizations. To conform to the rules of the Comintern, at its first plenum held in October 1930 the Central Committee of the new party adopted the name, "Indochinese Communist Party" (Dang Cong San Dong Duong), to include all of Indochina and not solely the three Vietnamese Kys. The Central Committee was transferred from Haiphong to Saigon. In April 1931, at its Eleventh Plenum, the Central Executive Committee of the Comintern recognized the Indochinese Communist Party (ICP) as a national section.

The events of 1930–32 in Indochina, which were highlighted by a strong wave of nationalist unrest and subsequent demonstrations, trials, executions, and insurrections, augmented the ranks of communist sympathizers. The ICP membership, a meager 1,000, was no measure of its true influence; it was estimated that some 100,000 peasants followed the leadership of the ICP during that period. The party played a leading role in the strikes and demonstrations as well as in actual insurrectionary attempts. It also attempted to create peasant soviets called Xo-Viets at Ha Tinh and Nghe An. The violent methods employed by some insurrectionists were censured even by the Comintern which regarded unfavorably activities that smacked of terror and pillage on the part of individuals as not in consonance with the "organized violence" of Marxist doctrine. It should be noted that neither Ho Chi Minh nor the ICP approved of terrorism undertaken mainly by the VNQDD and other nationalist groups although some ICP individuals did participate. Ho Chi Minh maintained additionally that the time was not right for an uprising, that the ICP was too young, inexperienced, and unarmed to undertake such a task. He was proved right, for the French authorities not only were able to suppress the communist movement but also publicly tried many of its leaders and members as common criminals. The entire apparatus of the ICP was smashed. The party suffered a final blow when its international connections were severed with the detention of Ho Chi Minh by the British in Hong Kong.

In 1933 some effort was made to reconstitute the ICP, an effort augmented by the release of many of the political prisoners who had been jailed. However, it was not until 1935, at the Communist Congress held in Macau, that the real reorganization of the ICP was accomplished. This conference also ushered in the new policy of the Seventh World Congress of the Comintern and one which was very difficult for the Vietnamese to accept. The new policy was to abandon the anticolonial struggle and substitute the objective of obtaining democratic rights, to allow for collaboration with the mother country (in Viet Nam's case, France) against the menace of Fascism. Perhaps to assuage the ICP this congress reaffirmed the adherence of the ICP to the Communist Third International and established the organizational form of the party parallel to all other national sections of the Comintern. With the inauguration of the Popular Front government in France and the application of the New World Communist policy adopted in Macao, the ICP in 1936 and 1937 promised to collaborate with the French authorities. The Trotskyists violently disagreed with the new direction and maintained that the communist faction was betraying the Indochinese to please the French communists and ultimately the Soviet government which had signed a mutual defense pact with France (2 May 1935). Nevertheless, from 1936 to 1939 the ICP collaborated with the French Communist Party and to a lesser degree with the French administration in Indochina. Strong opposition came from the Trotskyists and other nationalist parties. However, the ICP survived.

The outbreak of war and events in France radically changed the situation. A decree of 26 September 1939 pronounced the dissolution of the French Communist Party. It was applied vigorously in Indochina, where the French police used it to destroy all the extremist organizations, both Communist and Trotskyist. The ICP was again driven completely underground but, unlike the situation in 1932, it had a functioning, tightly knit organization that was to demonstrate shortly that it was capable of serious action against French authority.

The ICP Central Committee (presided over by Nguyen Van Cu, ICP's Secretary General) met 6–8 November 1939, and adopted a new line to bring the party into step with the antiwar position of the Comintern and the USSR as it developed after the Stalin-Hitler Pact (23 August 1939). The resolution called for replacing the old "Democratic Front" with a "United Front of anti-Imperialist Indochinese Peoples." This new front would, with the help of the USSR ("the fortress of world revolution"), carry on a struggle against the "imperialist war," overthrow "French imperialism and the native feudalists," recover the independence of Indochina, and install a republican regime. The practical effect of this resolution was to oppose all measures designed to aid the French war effort, such as sending Indochinese troops abroad, raising hours of work to increase production, or increasing taxes to meet war costs. The colonial authorities acted with dispatch. Application of a decree of 21 January 1940 led to the arrest of "120 agitators and their incorporation into a special work formation" and to the detention of 184 others. It had little effect on the ICP which was already strengthening its underground apparatus in preparation for an overt attempt to take power.

The fall of France in June 1940 led Ho Chi Minh to take over the reins of the ICP. He had been in Kweilin to set up the ICP External Bureau in Kunming but arrived at the Vietnamese border in December 1940 and instituted a training course for cadres that were to lead the insurrection. Under Ho's direction the ICP prepared and circulated literature in Vietnamese, Chinese, and French calling on the masses to struggle against French imperialism and Japanese Fascism and constitute a unitary government of Indochinese democratic countries with the help of the Chinese Communists and the USSR. These appeals were addressed to all sectors of the population—wealthy landowners, government functionaries, military personnel, workers, and intellectuals. The literature emphasized the weakening of the colonial regime occasioned by the defeat of metropolitan France and warned against an alliance of French imperialism and Japanese Fascism. To proprietors and planters, the ICP stressed the raising of taxes, the seizure of property, and high prices of goods as the consequence of such an alliance. The ICP warned the

Caodaists to beware of Cuong De as a Japanese puppet and to abandon their pro-Japanese sentiments as they would be the first to suffer the consequences of Japanese victory. To the students, teachers, and white-collar workers the ICP held up the example of the Soviet and Chinese youth and their struggle against capitalist domination. The women of Indochina, as mothers, wives, and sisters of men called up for military duty in the service of France and Japan, were reminded of the heroic Trung sisters and Joan of Arc, who had delivered their countries from foreign invaders. All this propaganda ended with a pressing call to rally to a Soviet regime and to install it after driving the French from Indochina. To the Chinese the pamphlets extolled the Sino-Japanese conflict and the Chinese revolution. They outlined the desire of the ICP to link its struggle with Mao Tse-tung's forces and called for the creation of a volunteer Chinese corps to help in the defense of Indochina. And to the French the ICP inveighed against its policy of making concessions to the Japanese and appealed for solidarity of the French and Indochinese against reaction and Japanese Fascism.

The Franco-Japanese negotiations for the occupation of Tonkin were concluded on 22 September 1940. On the same day the Japanese crossed the border from China at Dong Dang and Lang Son. They clashed with the French garrison at Lang Son. Dong Dang fell on the twenty-third and Lang Son on the twenty-fourth. The incoming Japanese also bombed Haiphong. With the Japanese troops came a large contingent of Vietnamese nationalists, followers of Prince Cuong De, belonging to the Phuc Quoc. These Vietnamese, taking advantage of the French defeat, started an uprising at Lang Son hoping for Japanese support. But the Japanese and French quickly settled their differences and on 5 October the Japanese returned Lang Son to the French who swiftly dealt with the insurrectionists. The Phuc Quoc and other nationalist supporters fled back to China. Taking advantage of the temporary French defeat and the elated mood of the people, the ICP wasted no time and encouraged the communist leaders in Indochina to form their first guerrilla unit in the area of Bac Son.

In the south, the French were faced with demands from Thailand for Laotian and Cambodian border territories. Against this second front in Cochinchina, the French moved Vietnamese colonial troops and mobilized civilian Vietnamese. The ICP instigated a mutiny among the Vietnamese troops in Saigon to signal a local uprising meant to spread throughout Cochinchina among the worker-peasant elements. The insurrection broke out on the night of 23 November 1940, but the French were ready and the plan failed in Saigon. In the other provinces of Cochinchina the insurrection lasted several days but in the end was quelled by the French. The usual murderous repressions followed, in which several key members of the ICP Central Committee, including Le Duan and Le Hong Phong, were arrested, practically decapitating the ICP in Cochinchina.

On 8 February 1941, Ho Chi Minh crossed the border into Indochina, set up his headquarters in the caves of Pac Bo (Cao Bang province) and convened the Eighth Plenum of the ICP Central Committee (May 1941) which decided to prepare an armed insurrection, set up guerrilla bases, and fight with the Allies against French and Japanese Fascism. Truong Chinh was appointed Secretary General of the ICP and the Viet Minh Front (Viet Nam Doc Lap Dong Minh) was formed. Throughout the period to 11 November 1945, the ICP continued to guide the political affairs of Viet Nam. The ICP was dissolved in name only in 1945 and replaced with the Association for the Study of Marxism. Its members in the National Assembly were known as the Marxist Group and included well-known communists—Vo Nguyen Giap, Nguyen Van Tao, Nguyen Khanh Toan, Tran Huy Lieu, and others. Sub rosa the Party never ceased to exist; it used several names until it adopted the name of Viet Nam Workers' Party (Lao Dong) in 1951. At the Fourth Congress of the Viet Nam Workers' Party held on 20 December 1976, the name was changed once more to the Viet Nam Communist Party (Viet Nam Cong San Dang), the original name chosen on 3 February 1930, in Hong Kong.

INDOCHINESE DEMOCRATIC PARTY (Parti Democrate Indochinois)
This party was founded in 1937 by Dr. Nguyen Van Thinh, who later became the first premier of the "Republic of Cochinchina" (1946). He was a large landowner in the south holding French citizenship, politically moderate, and favoring collaboration with France.

Being pro-French in orientation, the party accepted the French declaration of 24 March 1945, which envisaged an Indochinese federation composed of five autonomous states—Tonkin, Annam, Cochinchina, Laos, Cambodia—forming a part of the French Union.

The party favored a hierarchal system of indirect elections for village councils, provincial councils, and a Cochinchina council; strong ties with France; and French representation with a strength of one-third in the Cochinchina government. In 1946 it advocated complete separation from Tonkin and Annam.

Disillusioned by French duplicity regarding Vietnamese independence and particularly the French role in Cochinchina under Admiral d'Argenlieu, Dr. Thinh committed suicide on 10 November 1947.

LEAGUE FOR THE NATIONAL UNION OF VIET NAM (Hoi Lien Hiep Quoc Dan Viet Nam)—see Lien Viet

LIEN VIET (Hoi Lien Hiep Quoc Dan Viet Nam)—League for the National Union of Viet Nam
An expanded front of political parties which eventually replaced the Viet Minh. Founded on 27 May 1946. The twenty-seven founding fathers led by Ho Chi Minh and including prominent representatives of all the political organizations as well as independents, jointly pledged "to safeguard our autonomy. . . ."

Ho Chi Minh's decision to dissolve the ICP on 11 November 1945 (replaced sub rosa by the Indochina Association of Marxist Studies), left only the communist-led Viet Minh to shepherd the anti-French nationalists. After the departure of the Chinese occupation forces in mid-1946, the Viet Minh was faced with disruptive opposition from the Dong Minh Hoi and the VNQDD. To resolve the problem and to achieve a degree of national unity, Ho decided to regroup the divergent nationalists into one homogeneous bloc, the Lien Viet. The new front was packed with former Viet Minh communists, except for one VNQDD member. Ho was elected Honorary Chairman, while the septuagenarian Huynh Thuc Khang was appointed Chairman, Directing Committee.

The agreement was short-lived. One of the planks in the Lien Viet platform was the unification of the administration of the army, a point strongly opposed by the Dong Minh Hoi and the VNQDD which feared the Viet Minh would take control of the anticommunist nationalist forces. They were right. Using their refusal as a pretext, Giap attacked the nationalist forces and defeated them by mid-June 1946. He then proceeded to eliminate all opposition in Hanoi (while Ho Chi Minh was in France), and by August 1946 the DMH and VNQDD were no longer factors. With the formation of the Dang Lao Dong Viet Nam (Viet Nam Workers' Party) in March

1951, the Viet Minh was absorbed into the Lien Viet and disappeared from future official references.

MONARCHIST PARTY (Bao Hoang Chinh Dang)

One of the principal constituents of the Viet Nam Rally in Annam, formed in September 1945 by *Commandant* Lang, a Mandarin Superior of the Court of Hué. Its membership, estimated at ten thousand, was from the conservative mandarinate and the royal family.

In February 1949 the party broadened its activities and adopted a new name—Tan Viet Nam Dang (see New Viet Nam Party)—with headquarters at Saigon. Its main leader was Nicholas Truong Vinh Tong, a supporter of the Provisional Viet Nam Central Government of Nguyen Van Xuan.

NATIONAL UNION FRONT (Mat Tran Thong Nhut Quoc Gia Lien Hiep)

The first group of nationalists to support Bao Dai in 1947. It was established at Nanking, China, on 17 February 1947, primarily by Dong Minh Hoi and VNQDD leaders who had fled to China to gain the support of a number of nationalist political groups in Cochinchina. The orientation was anti-French and included elements known for a hostility to the French that bordered on xenophobia. The National Union Front was also opposed to the DRV, which at that time adhered to a settlement "within the framework of the French Union" and sought no more than an alliance between Viet Nam and France. However, the National Union Front would have been quite capable of uniting with the Ho Chi Minh government if by so doing it could help achieve an independent Viet Nam.

The leadership of the Front was shared by:

1. Tran Trong Kim, formerly the premier of Bao Dai's puppet government under the Japanese and leader of the defunct National Socialist Party. He represented elements of the conservative mandarinate.

2. Nguyen Hai Than, who had been vice president in the Ho Chi Minh coalition government and was a leader of the Dong Minh Hoi. He was representative of the old intellectual-scholar group.

3. Nguyen Van Sam, an influential Cochinchinese who led the Viet Nam Democratic Socialist Party. He had formerly been the imperial delegate of the Court of Annam to Cochinchina.

4. Nguyen Tuong Tam, who had been foreign minister of the Ho Chi Minh coalition government and was a leader of the Viet Nam Nationalist Party (see Dai Viet and VNQDD).

The National Union Front brought together the following parties and groups:

Viet Nam Revolutionary League (Viet Nam Cach Menh Dong Minh Hoi)
Viet Nam Nationalist Party (Viet Nam Quoc Dan Dang)
Viet Nam Democratic-Socialist Party (Viet Nam Dan Chu Xa Hoi Dang)
Viet Nam Nationalist Youth Alliance (Viet Nam Quoc Gia Thanh Nhien Doan)
People's League (Doan The Dan Chung)
Cao Dai League (Doan The Cao Dai)
Buddhist Group (Doan Do Cu Si)
Viet Nam Catholic League (Viet Nam Lien Doan Cong Giao)

Organized as a counterforce to the communist-led Viet Minh, the Front was fraught with dissension from its inception. Its leading spokesmen, tainted with questionable past associations, contributed to the Front's ineffectiveness as a vehicle to national unity and to its early dissolution.

French efforts to undermine Ho Chi Minh through Bao Dai were initiated in the fall of 1947. The French High Commissioner, Émile Bollaert, in a speech at Ha Dong, outside Hanoi, on September 10th, defined the basis on which France was prepared to settle the conflict in Indochina. The limited concessions France offered only served to discredit Bao Dai's pro-French supporters and strain the relations between monarchists and republicans in the Front.

Two of the Front's leaders, the pro-Chinese Nguyen Hai Than and the pro-Japanese Dai Viet leader Nguyen Tuong Tam, both former members of Ho Chi Minh's cabinet, failed to inspire confidence among the nationalists, who wanted no foreign support. Frustrated by the influence of the pro-French element led by Nguyen Van Sam, Tam retired from the movement at the end of October 1947 and Than returned to Canton seeking aid from his old friend, Chang Fa-kwei, who politely refused to become involved. Sam, a former collaborator in Bao Dai's wartime puppet regime, was assassinated by Viet Minh terrorists in October 1947, putting an end to the Front's effectiveness.

A new coalition emerged in December 1947, called the Viet Nam National Rally, which detached the support of the Caodaist and Hoa Hao political formations from the National Union Front. On 16 December 1947, the National Union Front in Annam announced its adherence to the Viet Nam National Rally, leaving the Front depleted of strength. Its dissolution in April 1948 to give "each party in the Front liberty of action" was a mere formality.

NATIONALIST FRONT (Mat Tran Quoc Gia)
A new Front formed in China by some leaders of the Dong Minh Hoi and the VNQDD, including Nguyen Hai Than, Nguyen Tuong Tam, and Vu Hong Khanh, who fled to China and then to Hong Kong after troops under their control were defeated by the Viet Minh forces acting in conjunction with the French army in 1946. The Front was organized to group nationalists disaffected with the Ho government. This split weakened the nationalist cause vis-à-vis French opposition and enhanced the Bao Dai movement.

NEW VIETNAM DEMOCRATIC PARTY (Tan Viet Nam Dan Chu Dang)
The southern component of the Viet Nam Democratic Party, founded in Cochinchina by Huynh Van Tieng in 1945. In October 1945, Pham Ngoc Thach, a leader of the Viet Minh in the south, described them as the "party of patriotic students completely won over to the republican and democratic ideas of the West. These students are the radical socialists of Viet Nam, but radicals of the Turkish variety" (see Viet Nam Democratic Party, below).

NEW VIET NAM PARTY (Tan Viet Nam Dang)—see Monarchist Party

NEW VIET NAM REVOLUTIONARY PARTY (Tan Viet Cach Menh Dang)—see Phuc Viet

PHUC QUOC (Viet Nam Phuc Quoc Dong Minh Hoi) Viet Nam Restoration League
The origins of the League can be traced to the early Hoi Viet Nam Quang Phuc

(Society for the Restoration of Viet Nam) founded by the Vietnamese patriot Phan Boi Chau in 1912 at Canton, China. From 1885 to the turn of the century Phan Boi Chau spearheaded a promonarchical nationalist movement in Viet Nam. After the French invasion of Saigon (1861), Hanoi (1883), and Hué (1885), many Vietnamese emigrated to China, Japan, Formosa, and Thailand where they dreamed of some day returning to a free and independent Viet Nam.

Phan Boi Chau, on the advice of the veteran resistance leader Nguyen Thanh, in 1903 sought the backing of Prince Cuong De to organize a resistance movement in Indochina and among the émigrés abroad. Cuong De, a linear descendant of the royal house of King Ham Nghi (exiled by the French to Réunion Island in the Indian Ocean), was the leading pretender to the throne of Annam and agreed to assume the leadership of the movement. Under the auspices of the Japanese Constitutional Party and the tutelage of the East Asia Popular Culture Society (Toa Dobun Kai), Cuong De moved from Hué to Tokyo and established his headquarters for the resistance movement there.

Following a series of conspiratorial moves, demonstrations, and uprisings in Viet Nam, the French in 1909 persuaded the Japanese government to withdraw its support of Cuong De, but he was permitted to remain in Japan. Phan Boi Chau continued to operate from China and in 1912 organized the Society for the Restoration of Viet Nam, later changed to Viet Nam Restoration League (Viet Nam Phuc Quoc Dong Minh Hoi), generally referred to as the Phuc Quoc. The League became involved in insurrectionary attempts in 1913 leading to further French reprisals and the exiling of the young Emperor Duy Tan in 1916. Since then the name of the League has been connected with every major political upheaval in Indochina.

After the unsuccessful insurrection of 1913, the League was primarily an association of older-generation political prisoners and exiles favoring the restoration of Cuong De. In July 1925 a group of young men met at Ben Thuy and reformed the League within Indochina and established contact with émigrés in Canton. They called the reformed League Tan Viet Cach Menh Dang (New Viet Nam Revolutionary Party). In the meantime Phan Boi Chau was arrested (June 1925) by the French, condemned to death, then reprieved and freed. By 1930 Chau had withdrawn from political activities.

A small group of Vietnamese nationalists using the name Phuc Quoc Quan (Viet Nam Restoration Army) emerged in 1931 in northern Tonkin under the leadership of Hoang Luong, a former employee of the Yunnan-fu Railroad, but it was not until 1940 that they achieved a measure of success when the group won several hundred followers from among the Indochinese colonial troops who participated in a revolt attendant upon the entry of Japanese troops in Indochina. A "provisional government" was set up at Dong Dang in the border region. It was short-lived, however, because the Japanese soon came to agreement with the French authorities, and Hoang Luong and his soldiers had to flee to China. There Hoang Luong was regarded as pro-Japanese, was arrested, and was placed in a concentration camp by the KMT. His troops were incorporated into the Chinese National Army to be used in the "future invasion" of Indochina.

The Phuc Quoc was to become the principal organizing agency of pro-Japanese Vietnamese nationalists in the Japanese occupation of Indochina during World War II. In 1943 the kempeitai used the Phuc Quoc to recruit Vietnamese soldiers for their puppet military force and the Yasu Butai. As the military position for the Japanese worsened, they encouraged Vietnamese nationalists to support the Greater East Asia Co-Prosperity Sphere program and turned their attention to Prince Cuong De, then in Japan. He was to replace Bao Dai, the French puppet emperor.

The pro-Japanese nationalist movement (Phuc Quoc) began to take a legal character in 1945 during a period of political maneuvering and jockeying as support for Cuong De's candidacy for the throne increased. In anticipation of the Japanese dismissal of the French government in Indochina on 9 March 1945, several underground organizations emerged in February to function legally under the Japanese regime after the coup. The League (Phuc Quoc) soon absorbed the others as affiliates and became the central organization, e.g., in Cochinchina the Phuc Quoc provided the Cao Dai with political orientation and became the political arm of the religious sect.

Nine days after the Japanese coup the Phuc Quoc held the first Japanese-sponsored demonstration for independence in Cochinchina. While at first many of the nationalist groups had believed in a final Japanese victory, later events proved them wrong and a marked change began to take place in the ranks of the parties. Many began to lose confidence as the underground anti-Japanese revolutionary nationalists increased their agitation.

The general toleration by the Chinese of Vietnamese political exiles in China against French rule in Indochina expressed a permanent Chinese interest in northern Indochina. To this was added in 1941 the immediate problem of the extension of Japanese strength into Indochina which closed a valuable channel of supply from the port of Haiphong to southern China. Thus it became a matter of direct military concern to the Chinese KMT to strike a blow against the Japanese in this area; the utilization of Vietnamese for espionage and the creation of a local military force became a necessity. The remnants of the nationalist parties and groups in exile began to reform their ranks and vie for Chinese support. Two competing leagues were formed: the Viet Nam Independence League (Viet Minh) and the Viet Nam Revolutionary League (Dong Minh Hoi), the latter not to be confused with the earlier 1927 group. The Viet Nam Restoration League (Phuc Quoc) was also included as one of the parties in the Chinese-sponsored Viet Nam Revolutionary League (Dong Minh Hoi) and, with the Dai Viet, represented the principal pro-Japanese elements in China.

The Viet Nam Restoration League lingered in limbo until 1945 when it virtually disappeared from Indochinese politics after the defeat of Japan and the accession to power of the Viet Minh in September 1945. The bulk of its former supporters became partisans of the DRV government and joined the various parties represented in that government. Its leadership, apparently discredited for having gambled on the success of the Japanese, was eclipsed, disappearing for a time from the political scene.

After the outbreak of fighting between the French and Vietnamese in December 1946, Cuong De, in a letter to President Truman dated 9 June 1947, attempted without success to solicit American aid for the Vietnamese. Later, on 7 October 1947, emissaries were reported to have made contact with Bao Dai, then in Hong Kong, in an effort to set up a rival government to the DRV, but Cuong De later disavowed responsibility for that move, adding that his only plans were to visit Chiang Kai-shek, "an old friend." As for supporting Bao Dai, Cuong De indicated that the struggle for independence took precedence over the question of leadership and that he was in favor of agreement between Bao Dai and Ho Chi Minh.

Cuong De's unwillingness to associate himself too closely with Bao Dai was attributed, apart from his own personal desire for leadership, to his intransigent advocacy of Vietnamese independence. This attitude marked the subsequent activities of the Viet Nam Restoration League (Phuc Quoc) which had tried to play the role of an intermediate third group in Vietnamese nationalist politics. Although opposed to the communist leadership of the DRV, the Phuc Quoc refused to identify itself with the Bao Dai government because it considered such French concessions as had been made inadequate.

Cuong De elaborated on his position and that of the Phuc Quoc in a December 1947 letter to the Vietnamese press in which he stated that the struggle for independence was favorably regarded by the democratic countries of the world but that the communist leadership of the DRV was a complicating factor perpetuating the conflict. Cuong De appealed to Ho Chi Minh, "whose sincerity and patriotic sentiments are unquestionable, to look carefully into the international situation and to give way to other persons who can be accepted by the democratic countries." Later in May 1948 he again appealed to the United States without success to assist in negotiating a French-Viet Nam agreement for independence.

The League established its headquarters at Canton in 1948, but Cuong De was unable to leave Japan for China where he wanted to make contact with the KMT and Vietnamese nationalists. According to Cuong De, permission to leave Japan was denied by American occupation officials. By March 1949 Cuong De felt that the situation in Viet Nam had become more critical and renewed his attempts to go to Canton and "direct actively the campaign for freedom." He made the exaggerated claim that the Phuc Quoc had a membership of "180,000 effectives" and 10 million supporters. Significantly, he indicated willingness to accept aid from the USSR or the Chinese Communists and to collaborate with Ho Chi Minh in a united front. In April 1949 the Phuc Quoc formed a party in Kwangsi, China, and in July Cuong De declined an invitation from Bao Dai to participate in the Bao Dai government, an action that underscored Cuong De's continued unwillingness to accept the concessions made by the French thus far. With the death of Cuong De in 1951, the Viet Nam Restoration League faded from Vietnamese political life.

PHUC VIET (Tan Viet Cach Menh Dang) New Viet Nam Revolutionary Party—see chart 1

The origin of this party can be traced to the Viet Nam Restoration League (see Phuc Quoc, above). It is of particular interest because the Phuc Viet was the meeting ground of a wide variety of nationalists ranging from reformists to communists and the scene of unending quarrels between these elements up to the time of its dissolution in 1930.

After the failure of the 1913 insurrection, the Phuc Quoc was relegated to an association of older-generation political prisoners and exiled individuals favoring the restoration of the monarchy under Prince Cuong De. It was not until July 1925 that a group of young men met at Ben Thuy and reformed the organization within Indochina and renamed it Phuc Viet (Restoration of Viet Nam). Devoid of real political acumen but agreed on the major aim of independence for Viet Nam through revolutionary action, they resolved to establish contact with émigrés in Thailand and China. They found the Vietnamese residents in Thailand disinclined to engage in political activity. Subsequent efforts in Canton were more successful, and the organization's representatives established liaison with what was then a lively functioning center of émigré activity looking to the creation of revolutionary organizations in Indochina.

In March 1926 the abbreviated name was changed once more to Hung Nam (Viet Nam Restoration League). The program was modified also by abandoning the avowedly revolutionary monarchical principles of the Phuc Viet. The new program called for independence through peaceful revolution; republican principles to be supplemented by communist theories; moral, intellectual, and economic reawakening; party reorganization; and elementary military training for all party members.

The envoy who had made contact with the émigrés in Canton returned to Viet Nam in 1926; he, as well as other members of the Hung Nam, had been won over to support Ho Chi Minh's (communist-directed) Viet Nam Revolutionary Youth League, and the envoy was anxious to fuse the two organizations. After discussion, the name Hung Nam was provisionally changed to Viet Nam Revolutionary Party (Viet Nam Cach Menh Dang) to facilitate the fusion. The moderates of the Hung Nam were not happy with the democratic-socialist orientation of the communist-directed youth organization; nevertheless, when the new "Progressives" headed by Pham Quynh appealed for support, many of the moderates became immediate partisans of the new organization, only to have their hopes dashed by its failure to win favorable recognition from the French. The remaining members of the Viet Nam Revolutionary Party decided to continue building their own "revolutionary party." The name Viet Nam Restoration League (Hung Nam) was definitely dropped, and the organization moved steadily to the left.

By 1927 the Viet Nam Revolutionary Party began to look for allies. In April 1927 fusion was attempted with the New Viet Nam Party (Tan Viet Dang), a minor political group in Annam which numbered only about sixty members. The fusion was partially successful and some new members were won. When the Canton émigré committee made renewed efforts (July 1927) to persuade the Viet Nam Revolutionary Party to merge with the Viet Nam Revolutionary Youth League, the response was favorable.

To facilitate fusion, the Viet Nam Revolutionary Party accepted the program of the Viet Nam Revolutionary Youth League and formally adopted a new name, Viet Nam Revolutionary League (Viet Nam Cach Mang Dong Chi Hoi). The statutes of the organization were clearly communist, calling for national and world revolution, and the party structure was patterned after the cell structure of communist organizations. This program, however, belied the true state of affairs within the newly formed Viet Nam Revolutionary League. A considerable number of the members were not inclined to accept their newly found communist allies. Aggravated by personal and political differences, the fusion negotiations foundered. A period of tactical shifts and feints began in which the Viet Nam Revolutionary League or "Party of the Interior" vied with the Viet Nam Revolutionary Youth League or "Émigré Party" for support and adherents.

The active influence of the Viet Nam Revolutionary League was confined to Annam. The bulk of its membership (150 to 200) were petty functionaries within the administration. Because the organization had scant success in winning adherents in Tonkin, where the communist-directed Viet Nam Revolutionary Youth League and the Viet Nam Nationalist Party were the center of attraction for young nationalists, the Viet Nam Revolutionary League decided to send agents to Cochinchina in an attempt to recruit adherents.

In February 1928 a meeting of the Central Committee revealed that the party was steadily losing ground to the Viet Nam Revolutionary Youth League. Agents in Cochinchina reported the existence of a rival nationalist association led by Nguyen An Ninh (see ICP, above) and were commissioned to prepare a definitive report on it. In the interim new efforts to contact the émigré center in Canton were authorized to facilitate fusion. The reply was a stunning blow to the leaders of the Viet Nam Revolutionary League: they were urged to liquidate their organization and join the Viet Nam Revolutionary Youth League.

In July 1928 a convention was held to recognize the weakened Viet Nam Revolutionary League. At the convention its name was changed to the New Viet Nam Revolutionary Party (Tan Viet Cach Menh Dang). The convention was not disposed to take any action designed to link the party's destiny with that of other organizations because of continuing difficulties with the Viet Nam Revolutionary Youth League. It turned down proposals for fusion with the Nguyen An Ninh association in Cochinchina and the Viet Nam Nationalist Party in Tonkin in favor of a general policy of observing the development of other parties, looking neither to alliance nor to combat with them.

The New Viet Nam Revolutionary Party fared badly. Leftwing members continued to defect to the Viet Nam Revolutionary Youth League, a process that reinforced the more conservative leadership in control of the organization. A meeting in February 1929 witnessed another reorganization of the already weakened party and the adoption of a new program that tossed overboard the communist-inspired doctrine that had been officially adopted during the fusion negotiations. This action was a prelude to virtual dissolution. As a result of police suppression in 1930 and the desertion of members who formed a separate communist group—the Indochina Communist Alliance (Dong Duong Cong San Lien Doan)—preliminary to fusing with the Indochinese Communist Party, the New Viet Nam Revolutionary Party was completely disorganized by 1930.

POPULAR MOVEMENT (Doan The Dan Chung)

According to the history of the National Union Front, the Popular Movement was "organized in December 1945 as a reaction to the policy of terror and treachery of the Viet Minh. Originating in Hanoi, it had its echoes notably in Hung Yen, Thai Binh and Hai Duong, the three most populous provinces of Viet Nam." It repeatedly advocated "overthrowing the DRV government" of Ho Chi Minh and establishing a "truly democratic government . . . with Bao Dai as president of the Republic." The National Union Front further reported: "After the establishment of the sham coalition government, in which the representatives of all the political groups participated in principle, the Movement ceased to be violent in order to direct its activities into social and more suitable political channels." The platform of the Popular Movement called for liberation of political prisoners held by the DRV government and organization and education of the masses. Leaders of the movement were Nguyen Gia Tuong, Nguyen Gia Tru, Luu Duc Trang, and Phan Huy Dan. Except for its nominal participation in published manifestos, it fell into oblivion.

SOCIALISTS—See also, Viet Nam Socialist Party

No separate Socialist organization existed among the Vietnamese in the period between World Wars I and II. However, there was a branch of the French Socialist Party in Indochina. It was known as the Cochinchina-Cambodia Socialist

Federation. It embraced Vietnamese, a number of whom acquired French citizenship, as well as French citizens. It was recognized by the directing committee of the French Socialist Party in 1936, having a small membership in Hanoi as well as in Saigon.

The Socialist organization attempted to ameliorate the colonial regime in Indochina and favored extension of the metropolitan regime to Indochina and a policy of French-Vietnamese association. Some of its Vietnamese members became well known individually but, as a party, it did not become an important factor in Vietnamese political life.

TROTSKYIST MOVEMENT—see chart 2

The central political doctrine around which the Trotskyist groups in Indochina were organized was the "theory of permanent revolution" and its application to the colonial world—a theory first advanced by Leon Trotsky in the period preceding the 1905 revolution in Russia. It was Trotsky's contention that only the proletariat, although a weak and embryonic class in colonial countries, could successfully lead the struggle for national independence as well as solve the tasks of the democratic revolution, e.g., land division, separation of church and state, and the granting of democratic rights. This was because modern imperialism gave rise to a corrupt and comprador bourgeois class in the backward colonial lands, a class that was unable to play the progressive role of the rising industrial and commercial classes of western Europe during the period of bourgeois revolution.

In line with this conception, the Trotskyists bitterly attacked the official Comintern policy of alliance between the communists and Chiang Kai-shek during the period 1924–27. They predicted defeat for the young Chinese Communist Party at the hands of its reactionary Nationalist allies who, the Trotskyists claimed, would behead the revolution. Following the rupture of relations with Chiang Kai-shek, the Trotskyists attacked the creation of "soviets" by the communists, claiming that this policy would isolate the Chinese Communists from the nationalist movement. In fact the policy led to their suppression by the KMT in the large cities and forced the communists to evacuate their forces to the countryside.

These developments were closely studied by the Indochina communists and led to the creation in 1931 of groups opposed to the official party line and the policy of the Communist International (Comintern). The groups formed at that time were:

> Left Opposition (Ta Doi Lap)
> October Left Opposition (Ta Doi Lap Thang Muoi)
> Indochinese Communism (Dong Duong Cong San)

These were reinforced by returning students from France, among whom was Ta Thu Thau, the most prominent leader of Indochinese Trotskyism. These students had received their education under the direction of French Trotskyists. By 1932 a small Trotskyite organization comprising these elements was formed in Cochinchina. It was in the throes of an internal schism over the issue of cooperation with the communists when some thirty of its leaders were arrested by the French colonial police in August 1932. The Trotskyists, in common with all the other nationalist organizations, had to rebuild after the repressions of 1932.

The split in the movement that existed in 1932, exacerbated by regional particularism, was to be a permanent feature of Indochinese Trotskyism, except for a short period in 1939. One group, called the "Bolshevik Leninist Group" or the "International Communist League" (ICL) but popularly known as the "October" group because of its illegal publication of that name, existed principally in Hanoi under the leadership of Ho Huu Tuong. The other group, led by Ta Thu Thau, centered mainly in Saigon and was known as "The Struggle" group since it functioned within a united front organization with socialists and communists and, with the communists, published the joint paper called *The Struggle (La Lutte)*.

The "October" group criticized "The Struggle" group, primarily on the grounds that the latter collaborated too closely with the Indochinese Communist Party, and independently issued the underground newspaper *October (Thang Muoi)* from 1931 to 1936. At the end of 1937 the legally published weekly, *The Militant (Le Militant)*, appeared, only to be suppressed. In 1938 *October* again appeared as a semilegal paper but it was superseded by the legal publication, *The Spark (Tia Sang)*, published weekly at first, then daily.

The "October" group carried on active agitation in Hanoi, Haiphong, and Vinh among the numerically small laboring class. Its immediate objective was the creation of a legal trade union movement. Action committees set up with Trotskyist participation were successful in backing many strikes in the period 1936 to 1940. When "The Struggle" group was recognized as an official section of the newly constituted Fourth International (Trotskyists) toward the end of 1939, the "October" group was disbanded and its members joined the unified party.

In Cochinchina the major efforts of the Trotskyists centered around "The Struggle" group. In 1933 the Trotskyists attempted to build a united front organization in order to rally the disoriented and disorganized nationalists after the French repressions of 1930–32. This projected organization, to be called the Indochinese Revolutionary League (Dong Duong Cach Menh Dong Minh Hoi), was to embrace all revolutionary nationalists agreeing on a minimum program of revolutionary demands. By May 1933 their efforts were rewarded with the actual creation of the organization known as "The Struggle."

Ta Thu Thau was able to play an increasingly important role in the political life of Cochinchina during 1935–37. In this period "The Struggle" group, which had been a united front of Trotskyists and communists, gradually came under his sway. When Thau was certain of support by "The Struggle" group, he published an article attacking the French Popular Front government. It led to a two-year jail sentence but made him a popular martyr.

During the 1939 elections for the Colonial Council of Cochinchina the Trotskyists began publishing *The Struggle* in the vernacular with the same title, *Tranh Dau*. They won a smashing victory and gained many adherents. They were temporarily successful in overcoming the split in their own ranks by unifying the two existing organizations, "The Struggle" and the "October" groups.

In contrast to the official line the Comintern had adopted at its Seventh World Congress in 1935, the political line of the Fourth International in 1939 was clearly antiimperialist. It did not accept any programmatic alliances with other groups, albeit progressive, but favored united action on specific issues. It further warned its supporters against any approval of national defense, "even against the Japanese" on the grounds that the coming war was equally reactionary on both sides. In the given situation in Indochina, the Trotskyist propaganda was successful in attracting many who were thoroughly dissatisfied with both French colonial rule and the menace of Japanese domination.

In 1939 the political situation in France indicated that the French colonial authorities would soon resume their traditional policy of repression. The Trotskyists, who had, thus far, relied for the most part on their legal organizations, began to construct an illegal apparatus. An underground organization limited to the Saigon-Cholon working class was set up. In September 1939 the expected blow fell. The legal organization was dissolved and its leadership jailed. The activities of the Trotskyists were effectively curtailed by the repressions; the total number arrested by the French police in this period was six thousand and included practically all the leaders of the clandestine nationalist movement. The reemergence of the Trotskyist movement in Indochina awaited the end of World War II.

It was in August 1944 that the first regrouping of adherents of the Fourth International took place in Saigon. These elements were partisans of the former "October" group. Aided by several supporters of the movement from the north, they reconstituted the International Communist League (ICL). Apparently the unification of the Trotskyists into one party in 1939 had not been effective because the differences between "The Struggle" and the ICL (revolving mainly around the question of relations with the Communist Party) were still not reconciled. In general, however, there was programmatic agreement between the groups and they were known popularly as the Fourth Internationalist Party (Trang Cau De Tu Dang).

Shortly after the 9 March 1945 coup the ICL called on the "revolutionary Saigon masses" to prepare for the coming revolution. A manifesto of 24 March declared:

The future defeat of Japanese imperialism will set the Indochinese people on the road to national liberation. . . . [Those] who cowardly serve the Japanese rulers today, will serve equally the Allied Imperialist states. . . . Only the working class . . . under the flag of the Fourth International, will . . . accomplish the . . . task of the revolution.

The Stalinists of the Third International have . . . [allied] themselves miserably with the "democratic" imperialisms. . . . If today they march with foreign capitalists, in the future, they will help the classes of national exploiters to destroy the revolutionary people. . . .

The program of the Trotskyists called for opposition to imperialism and for support of world revolution, a worker-peasant united front, the creation of people's committees (soviets), establishment of a constituent assembly, arming the people, seizure of the land by the peasants, nationalization of the factories under workers' control, and the creation of a workers and peasants' government.

"The Struggle" group played an influential role in the events of August and September 1945. Its attitude toward the Japanese was summed up in a statement made by Ta Thu Thau:

We must never have confidence in them [the Japanese]. However, at this time, we must clutch their shoulders to lift ourselves up. As soon as we are capable to keeping our footing, we must use our shoulders to throw them over.

During the August 1945 meeting of the United National Front in Saigon, "The Struggle" group amalgamated with the Viet Minh and refused unity with its counterpart, the ICL, in order to support the Viet Minh in the establishment of a Viet Nam republic. However, the political line of "The Struggle" and the ICL was similar in most respects and brought them in conflict with the communist Viet Minh leadership.

In the ensuing struggle for independence the Trotskyists maintained an un-compromising opposition to French rule under any guise and charged both Ho Chi Minh and Bao Dai with betraying the cause for independence. They complicated the war against the French by their continued hostility toward the Viet Minh, who followed a policy of exterminating their Trotskyist opponents.

UNITED NATIONAL FRONT (Mat Tran Quoc Gia Thong Nhut)

A coalition organized on 14 August 1945 of pro-Japanese parties and Trotskyists of "The Struggle" group. It comprised:

National Independence Party (Viet Nam Quoc Gia Doc Lap Dang)
Advance Guard Youth (Thanh Nien Tien Phong)
Intellectual Group (Nhom Tri Thuc)
Federation of Functionaries (Lien Doan Cong Chuc)
Buddhist League (Tinh Do Cu Si)
Hoa Hao Buddhist Sect (Phat Giao Hoa Hao)
"The Struggle" group (Tranh Dau)
Cao Dai League (Doan The Cao Dai)

This Front was strongly influenced by Trotskyist doctrine and called for the overthrow of the Tran Trong Kim government and the repudiation of Nguyen Van Sam, the Imperial Resident appointed by Bao Dai after the 9 March coup. Ten days after the formation of the Front (25 August) the Viet Minh leader in Cochinchina, Tran Van Giau, convinced the members of the Front to unite with the Democratic Republic of Viet Nam and let the Viet Minh lead the country to freedom and independence. The Southern Executive Council of the United National Front formed the Provisional Executive Committee of the Southern Viet Nam Republic and left the leadership to the Viet Minh.

VIET MINH (Viet Nam Doc Lap Dong Minh) Viet Nam Independence League—see charts 2 and 4

The Viet Minh was a coalition of political groupings comprised at first (1941) of the Indochinese Communist Party, the New Viet Nam Party, the Viet Nam Revolutionary Youth League, sections of the Viet Nam Nationalist Party, and various "National Liberation Associations"—including workers, peasants, youth, women, soldiers, and officers.

The dominant political group in the Viet Minh was the Indochinese Communist Party (ICP) whose membership in northern Indochina functioned exclusively within the League and formulated the policy of the organization. The program of the Viet Minh was built around the concept of collaboration with the Allied nations to defeat Japan and liberate Indochina from French colonial rule. In Cochinchina the Viet Minh was little more than an appendage to the ICP. It appeared as a legal organization in Saigon in August 1945 with the emergence of the underground Communist Party under the leadership of Tran Van Giau and Nguyen Van Tao.

Ho Chi Minh, who in 1940 had been operating in China, was authorized by the Comintern to proceed with planning for an insurrection in Indochina. On 8 February 1941, he crossed the Indochina border and established his headquarters in one of the limestone caves of the hamlet of Pac Bo (Cao Bang province). As the Comintern representative he convened and presided over the Eighth Plenum of the Party Central Committee from 10 to 19 May 1941. Ho instructed the plenum, "For the time being, section [regional], and class interest should be subordinated to the vital interests of the nation: should we fail in this moment to liberate the country, to recover independence and freedom for the whole nation, not only would the country and the people remain enslaved for ever, but also the section [regional] and class interests could never be restored." The plenum agreed with Ho and accepted his proposal to change the name of National United Front Against the French and Japanese Fascists (adopted previously in line with Comintern directive) into the more particular name, Viet Nam Independence League. The plenum outlined a program of social and military action and scheduled a period of preparation including military organization and training.

In August 1942 Ho Chi Minh in an attempt to interest the Allies in Chungking in his cause for independence crossed once more into China and was arrested by the Chinese as a "French spy" and jailed for a period of thirteen months.

During the period 1941–45 the Viet Minh carried out a well-disciplined program of organization and training culminating in the formation of a provisional government in August 1945, formalized in Hanoi on 2 September 1945 as the Democratic Republic of Viet Nam.

The Viet Minh continued as a front until 1946 when it sponsored the League for the National Union of Viet Nam (Lien Viet) as a super-Viet Minh. With the formation of the Viet Nam Workers' Party in March 1951 the Viet Minh was absorbed into the Lien Viet and disappeared from later official references.

VIET NAM CATHOLIC LEAGUE (Viet Nam Lien Doan Cong Giao)
Organized in December 1945 by the Bishop of Phat Diem diocese, Le Huu Tu, as the official political organization of Catholics in Indochina. Indochinese Catholics numbered almost two million in the late 1940s, mostly concentrated in the province of Annam. There were reportedly fifteen hundred native clergy. At the time of its organization the League was headed by Nguyen Manh Ha who was appointed minister of economy in Ho Chi Minh's first cabinet. He remained in Hanoi after the outbreak of hostilities in December 1946 and never opposed Ho's objectives for independence.

After the outbreak of the fighting, political control of the League passed into the hands of Ngo Dinh Diem, a conservative nationalist who was vehemently anticommunist and violently opposed to French control of Viet Nam. Bishop Le Huu Tu favored a monarchical form of government and collaborated with the French. It was under the aegis of Ngo Dinh Diem and Bishop Le Huu Tu that the Viet Nam Catholic League became a component of the Mat Tran Thong Nhut Quoc Gia Lien Hiep (see National Union Front, above).

VIET NAM COMMUNIST PARTY (Viet Nam Cong San Dang)—see Annamese Communist Party and Indochinese Communist Party

VIET NAM DEMOCRATIC PARTY (Viet Nam Dan Chu Dang)
The origins of the party date back to the General Students' Association of the University of Hanoi, founded in 1940. The Association was not a political party but served as a vehicle for nationalist penetration during the period of Japanese occupation. With Japanese approval the Association held a mass meeting of some fifteen hundred students on 16 May 1943, at which a resolution was adopted calling for a "Viet Nam National United Movement." From that students' organization emerged the Viet Nam Democratic Party founded in June 1944. The president of

the General Students' Association, Duong Duc Hien, was a leading organizer of the new party and its first representative on the Tong Bo, the directing committee of the Viet Minh League.

The Viet Nam Democratic Party served to unite moderate elements among the students, intellectuals, middle class, and Catholics who, committed to democratic ideals, would not readily accept communist ideology. The Party was no sooner formed than it entered the Viet Minh Front. Its members held Ho Chi Minh in high regard and under no circumstances would oppose him on any fundamental issues.

The Party in the late 1940s had a total of forty-five members in the National Assembly, led by Do Duc Duc and Ton Quang Phiet. It controlled important posts in the DRV. During the "August Insurrection" Duong Duc Hien and Cu Huy Can were members of the "People's Liberation Committee." In Ho's early governments (2 September 1945 to 6 March 1946) the Democratic Party controlled four ministries —Youth under Hien, Agriculture under Cu Huy Can, Justice under Vu Trong Khanh, and Education under Vu Dinh Hoe.

Before the breakdown of negotiations with France in 1946, the Viet Nam Democratic Party played a leading role in warning the French against further encroachments on the sovereignty of the Viet Nam Republic. After the outbreak of fighting in December 1946, the Party was a loyal component of the Viet Minh coalition in the fight against the French.

VIET NAM DEMOCRATIC SOCIALIST PARTY (Viet Nam Dan Chu Xa Hoi Dang) Founded in September 1946 under the leadership of Nguyen Van Sam to regroup resistance elements in Cochinchina. It was described by the National Union Front, of which the Viet Nam Democratic Socialist Party was a participating element, as the "union of a number of political, religious, labor, and disunited groups resisting French aggression, among them notably the Viet Nam Independence Party. . . ." Another co-founder of the Viet Nam Democratic Socialist Party was the principal leader of the Hoa Hao, Huynh Phu So. In fact, the party was primarily a coalition of socialist-minded elements in Saigon and part of the leadership of the Hoa Hao movement.

The party's program called for the fight for the independence of Viet Nam; establishment of a democratic regime and opposition to all forms of dictatorship; and realization of a socialist society in which there would be no exploitation of man by man, in which each man would have the right to compensation for labor, and in which there would be no class struggle. The Party's newspaper, *The Masses (Quan Chung)*, was edited by Nguyen Van Sam and Tran Van An.

The vigorous participation of this party in the National Union Front and its opposition to the communist leadership of the DRV government brought it into sharp conflict with the Viet Minh-directed administrative committee of Nam Bo (South Viet Nam), which ordered the dissolution of the party on 18 April 1947. A special tribunal of 25 April 1947 condemned Huynh Phu So to death for his refusal to obey the authority of the DRV in the south. On 20 May 1947, Nguyen Van Sam was condemned for his refusal to obey the April order. Huynh Phu So was executed in June 1947, and Nguyen Van Sam was assassinated in Saigon on 10 October 1947. The deaths of its two most prominent leaders were accompanied by clashes within the organization between provincial Hoa Hao adherents and the Saigon leadership. These led to a split in the party, one faction controlled by Saigon, the other by the provinces. Differences became manifest early in October 1946 over the question of participation in the local Cochinchina government which was being reshuffled.

Tran Van An participated in the government set up on 6 October 1947. Bao Dai disavowed support of this government and was echoed by the Hoa Hao leader, Nguyen Phuoc Hau, who declared that the Hoa Hao would not participate in a separatist or autonomous government. The Saigon Committee indicated on 19 October 1947 that it desired Tran Van An's participation inasmuch as the new government under President Nguyen Van Xuan did not favor autonomy or separatism. Further, the Saigon Committee claimed that the Hoa Hao sect had been dissolved by Huynh Phu So (already executed) when he joined the Viet Nam Democratic Socialist Party. The breach between the Hoa Hao leaders and the Saigon Committee widened and, by November 1947, became irreconcilable.

Deprived of its principal leaders through assassination and split by contending groups, the Viet Nam Democratic Socialist Party became practically defunct. The Executive Committee of Southwest Viet Nam issued a manifesto on 7 December 1948, calling for speedy negotiation of an agreement between France and Bao Dai. No further indications of activity on its part have been noted.

VIET NAM INDEPENDENCE LEAGUE {Viet Nam Doc Lap Dong Minh)—see Viet Minh

VIET NAM NATIONAL ASSEMBLY (Viet Nam Quoc Gia Tap Doan)—see Viet Nam National Rally

VIET NAM NATIONAL INDEPENDENCE PARTY (Viet Nam Quoc Gia Doc Lap Dang)
An element of the Viet Nam Restoration League (see Phuc Quoc, above) in the southern area, founded by Tran Van An, Nguyen Van Sam, Ho Van Nga, and Ngo Tan Nhon. Some of the elements of the dissolved Viet Nam Revolutionary Party which had been founded in 1939 joined the new organization. The party was markedly pro-Japanese in orientation and favored collaboration with the Japanese Army and the adherence of Viet Nam to the Greater East Asia Co-Prosperity Sphere.

VIET NAM NATIONAL RALLY (Viet Nam Quoc Gia Lien Hiep)
An outgrowth of the National Union Front, developed after the break-up of the Front because of internal differences between monarchist and republican elements. The Rally came into existence officially on 23 December 1947, at Hanoi, after a period of maneuvering and negotiations between various political groups opposed to Ho Chi Minh's DRV.

In line with the National Union Front's mandate to convoke an elected national assembly that would form a provisional government to negotiate agreements with France, Le Van Hoach approached the various political groups in Saigon in an effort to group them together. Le Van Hoach had been forced on 1 October 1947 to relinquish his post as President of the Cochinchinese government to Nguyen Van Xuan. It was not until 11 December 1947 that Le Van Hoach succeeded in forming a new organization, called the Viet Nam National Assembly, in Saigon. He left the south and traveled to Annam and Tonkin to win adherents. Using the Assembly as incentive, he organized the Viet Nam National Rally on 23 December 1947, in Annam and Tonkin. In a speech for the new organization (Rally), Le Van Hoach for the first time declared himself a monarchist and pledged the support of the Cao Dai, Hoa Hao, Catholics, and Protestants in Cochinchina who, he claimed, comprise "more than three million of a population of four million inhabitants who are monarchists."

The Viet Nam National Assembly in the south then changed its name to conform on 25 December 1947, "because the national groups from the north to the south always desire to form themselves in one bloc." The southern bloc comprised:

The southern branch of the Viet Nam National Rally
Cao Dai Tay Ninh
Hoa Hao
Catholics (Cong Giao)
Protestants (Tinh Lanh Hoi)
Democratic League (Lien Minh Dan Chu)
VNQDD

On 2 February 1948, the various components of the Viet Nam National Rally held a national meeting at Saigon for the election of a central committee, drawing up a plan of joint action and the formulation of the political objectives to be attained. At that meeting it was decided to convoke a national congress in conjunction with the existing administrative committees of Tonkin and Annam and the provisional government of Cochinchina. The congress was held under the auspices of Nguyen Van Xuan in Saigon on 20 May 1948; it established a "Provisional Viet Nam Central Government" with Nguyen Van Xuan as its president.

The rally was closely associated with the Bao Dai restoration movement from its inception and with the government that Bao Dai subsequently created. It held another national congress at Hanoi in December 1948 and a regional meeting of the North Viet Nam (Tonkin) organization in May 1949. One of the principal constituents of the Rally in Annam was the Bao Hoang Chinh Dang (see Monarchist Party, above).

Despite its imposing array of constituent organizations, the Viet Nam National Rally was a minor political organization whose influence was severely limited as it represented mainly the small monarchist elements of Tonkin, Annam, and Cochinchina.

VIET NAM NATIONAL UNITED MOVEMENT—see Viet Nam Democratic Party

VIET NAM NATIONALIST PARTY (Viet Nam Quoc Dan Dang)—see VNQDD

VIET NAM NATIONALIST YOUTH ALLIANCE (Viet Nam Quoc Gia Thanh Nhien Doan)
One of the many groups claimed as a constituent of the National Union Front. It was reported in 1949 as having "17,000 members, most of whom were intellectuals and peasants; 1,200 to 1,500 of them fighting in the ranks of the Viet Nam Nationalist Party (VNQDD) among the guerrillas of the Tonkin Delta." French sources opposed to the DRV government lumped the Alliance together with the Democratic Socialist Party and the Popular Movement and placed their total membership at five thousand. DRV government sources claimed the Alliance was a "pure French invention." If it existed as an operating body it was undoubtedly of little significance.

VIET NAM RESTORATION LEAGUE (Viet Nam Phuc Quoc Dong Minh Hoi)—see Phuc Quoc

VIET NAM REVOLUTIONARY LEAGUE (Viet Nam Cach Menh Dong Minh Hoi)—see Dong Minh Hoi

VIET NAM REVOLUTIONARY PARTY (Viet Nam Cach Menh Dang)
In 1939 a regrouping of nationalists took place in Cochinchina with the formation of the Viet Nam Revolutionary Party. It embraced Duong Van Giao and other leaders of the Constitutionalist Party, the pro-Japanese Nguyen Van Nha, the revolutionary youth leader Tran Van An, the ex-Trotskyist Dao Duy Phien, and intellectuals such as Phan Khac Suu, Nguyen Van Thoi, and Ho Van Nheet.

The organization had planned an insurrection in Cochinchina for September 1940, to have been synchronized with the Japanese invasion of Tonkin. Nguyen Van Nha conspired with the Trotskyist leader, Ta Thu Thau, in an effort to effect common action, but the plan failed when the Japanese and French reached an agreement. A similar effort was made with Duong Van Giao in an effort to assist the Thais in an attack on the Indochinese western border. However, as in the case of Japan, Thai demands were granted and the French obtained a free hand in dealing with their internal opposition.

The conspirators were discovered and arrested. Duong Van Giao, Phan Khac Suu, and Dao Duy Phien were each sentenced to five years' imprisonment. Nguyen Van Nha was aided in his defense by the Japanese Consul. He, Tran Van An, and Nguyen Van Thoi were interned until July 1941, following the Japanese occupation of Cochinchina. All played prominent roles in the later pro-Japanese independence movements.

VIET NAM REVOLUTIONARY YOUTH ASSOCIATION (League) (Viet Nam Thanh Nien Cach Mang Dong Chi Hoi)—see Indochinese Communist Party

VIET NAM SOCIALIST PARTY (Viet Nam Xa Hoi Dang)
The party was founded at Hanoi in July 1946 under the joint leadership of Phan Tu Nghia and Nguyen Xien and the political sponsorship of Vo Nguyen Giap. With twenty-four seats in the DRV National Assembly the party represented the Socialist bloc in the left wing of the Assembly. In staunch support of Ho Chi Minh's socialist-democratic philosophy, the party was allowed to openly voice dissent on issues with the assurance that in the end it would endorse the Viet Minh party line. It soon gained the reputation of being the government's "loyal opposition party" in the National Assembly.

The formation of the party was announced by a manifesto issued on 27 July which identified the organization as the Viet Nam equivalent of the European Social-Democratic parties of the Second International. The manifesto, addressed to the "Workers of Viet Nam, Fellow Countrymen," stated that its efforts would be finished "when the country is free, . . . when socialism is victorious." It equated the realization of its ideals with "the task of national liberation" and welcomed "all enlightened patriots, all sincere democrats, all men who love liberty."

Before World War II there had existed in Indochina a Socialist Federation, which included both Vietnamese and French among its members and was part of the Metropolitan French Socialist Party. Phan Tu Nghia, Phan Anh, Hoang Minh Giam, and Vo Nguyen Giap had been part of that group in the 1930s and, in 1936, had formed the Socialist Federation of North Indochina. The Viet Nam Socialist Party disassociated itself from the old organization which was "ruptured in the ordeal of war" (a reference to the hostility shown by certain French Socialists in Indochina to the Vietnamese struggle for independence) but called on all those who had "remained faithful to socialism" to join the "new socialistic organ on Vietnamese soil, formed by members of that old Federation and by new militants recently come to Socialism."

When the National Assembly convened in October 1946, the party's most prominent representative was Hoang Minh Giam, who later became minister of foreign affairs when President Ho relinquished that office. Also prominent was Phan Anh, who was appointed minister of national economy in January 1947 and also served in several other leading posts, including that of minister of national defense. In addition, socialist Nguyen Van Huyen, a long-time associate of Giap, was appointed minister of national education. The vice minister of communications and public works, Dong Phuc Thong, was also a Socialist.

Although it is difficult to assess the influence of the party in Vietnamese affairs, it can be said that it served as a link between the extreme left and the moderates in the DRV government.

VNQDD (Viet Nam Quoc Dan Dang) Viet Nam Nationalist Party (see chart 4)
The VNQDD was the most significant noncommunist, pro-Chinese, revolutionary nationalist organization that emerged in the 1920s. As with the Phuc Quoc, it traced its origin to the teachings of Phan Boi Chau and to the student movement that developed at the end of World War I. It reflected the impact of Chinese culture on Vietnamese life as expressed in the doctrines of Dr. Sun Yat-sen and maintained throughout the years links with KMT elements in China.

At the outset the differences between the Viet Nam Nationalist Party and the New Viet Nam Revolutionary Party (see Phuc Quoc and Indochinese Communist Party) were not very great. An obstacle to unity was the particularist character of the two organizations brought about by regional differences in temperament and outlook. The VNQDD's strength lay primarily in Tonkin, that of the New Viet Nam Revolutionary Party in Annam. The issue of communism was the bar on which unity foundered.

The VNQDD was formed in November 1927 by a group of young intellectuals associated with a political-commercial publishing venture called the Nam Dong Thu Xa (Annamese Library). Its publications dealt with such matters as the Chinese revolution, the life of Dr. Sun Yat-sen, nationalism, and world revolution. Although the commercial business was suppressed, it succeeded in establishing a circle of interested friends who under the influence of Nguyen Thai Hoc became the organizers and leaders of the VNQDD.

The party was modeled directly after the Chinese KMT and its name, "... Quoc Dan Dang," reflects the Vietnamese pronunciation of "Kuomintang," that is, National Party. It was organized to fulfill the functions of a government with a central section composed of three branches—executive, legislative, and judicial. Attached to those branches were departments of propaganda, finances, economic affairs, army, espionage, foreign affairs, and so forth. It included Vietnamese of both sexes. Its doctrine was democratic-socialism. It favored the establishment of a democratic-republican regime that would help other downtrodden peoples in their struggles against colonial oppression (the Canton section of the

VNQDD collaborated with the League of Oppressed Oriental Peoples; see chart 4). This orientation toward the Chinese KMT was not accompanied by a desire for Chinese influence in Indochina; on the contrary the VNQDD counted on aid from the KMT as an ally but not as a "liberator" that would replace French domination by Chinese.

The party was clearly revolutionary in its approach. It envisaged the use of violence to obtain funds for operations; assassination of opponents and traitors; military training for its membership; and so forth. It carried on intensive work to win supporters among the Vietnamese enrolled in the French Army in Indochina but failed to unite with other revolutionary groups at home and abroad. The VNQDD remained virtually confined to Tonkin.

In mid-1928 attempts were made to solidify the party and intensify its activities. By early 1929 the VNQDD had succeeded in winning to its ranks students, functionaries, and some military, but this burst of activity also aroused the interest of the French police. In February 1929 the assassination of a Frenchman engaged in recruiting Vietnamese laborers for work in Cochinchina and New Caledonia resulted in the arrest and indictment of some 225 members out of a total membership of fifteen hundred. It was a severe blow, but under the direction of its most prominent young student leader, Nguyen Thai Hoc, the party soon recovered.

The organization was reformed on the communist cell pattern to give it the security needed against police action and it undertook a program to manufacture bombs and small arms, raising the necessary funds by banditry. A new program of action was elaborated which envisaged four phases of activities: (1) a secret period of organization; (2) a semisecret period of preparation; (3) an open period of revolution; and (4) a period of reconstruction under the direction of the party. To recoup the losses brought about by traitors who had confessed to the police, the VNQDD decided to punish several of them as an object lesson and as a public display of organizational strength. The bodies of the victims were marked with inscriptions, "for not having kept the blood oath."

Popular feeling against the French administration had become so strong by 1929 that Nguyen Thai Hoc believed an armed uprising would be successful because it could gain the support of the mass of dissatisfied Vietnamese. A minority in the party disagreed, holding that a longer preparatory period was needed. Nevertheless, 10 February 1930 was set as the date for insurrection. It started at Yen Bay. There were also attacks on Lam Thao and Hung Hao in Phu Tho province. Bombs were thrown in Hanoi, and disturbances spread to a number of other cities. But the entire movement was vigorously suppressed by the French police. The leaders of the VNQDD were arrested. Nguyen Thai Hoc was executed. Other leaders fled to China.

The removal of the majority leaders gave the minority a chance to assume the party's leadership. The new leaders sought to invigorate the movement by decreeing the deaths of high French functionaries and their mandarin supporters, but their immediate concern was to gain funds. The party degenerated into a collection of bandit gangs attempting to extort money from unwilling victims. The French police continued to track down the members; one after another, the main sections of the party were discovered and the leaders arrested.

The activities of the VNQDD within Indochina came to a halt at the end of 1932. The center of the movement shifted to China, where earlier émigrés had maintained the organization and prepared for its eventual reconstruction within

Indochina. Unlike the VNQDD in the interior of Indochina, the émigré organization in China had been badly split. Its unification came about as a result of pressure from the new elements in flight from Indochina. The two major émigré groups were the Viet Nam Nationalist Parties of Canton and Yunnan (see chart 4). Both groups could trace their genealogy back to Phan Boi Chau. Like the "Interior Party," these two groups were modeled after the Chinese Kuomintang.

The VNQDD of Canton had been formed in 1925 by anticommunist Vietnamese who were repelled by the influence of the Viet Nam Revolutionary Youth League created by Ho Chi Minh (see Indochinese Communist Party, above, and chart 1). The Canton government extended material and moral aid to this group. The first step envisaged was building a "League of Oppressed Oriental Peoples" (see chart 4) which would include Chinese, Vietnamese, Hindu, and Korean sections. (This organization had no relation to the organization of the same name created by Ho Chi Minh; see Indochinese Communist Party, above). Lack of sufficient Hindu and Korean members led instead to the establishment in 1928 of a party called the Viet Nam Cach Menh Dang (Viet Nam Revolutionary Party). Another group formed a rival party called Viet Nam Quoc Dan Cach Menh Dang (Viet Nam Nationalist Revolutionary Party) which vied for support from the Kuomintang. When the Viet Nam Nationalist Revolutionary Party began to receive a regular subsidy from the KMT, it became the more important of the two organizations and absorbed the membership of the first group. On 28 October 1930, it was officially recognized by the Canton government under the name Viet Nam Nationalist Revolutionary Party.

At the end of 1931 and toward the beginning of 1932 relations were established with the Viet Nam Nationalist Party in Yunnan (see chart 4). The Canton organization thereupon dropped the word "revolutionary" from its title and began fusion attempts. These were not successful until 1933.

Meanwhile, in 1932 the organizer of the Canton party, Lenh Trach Dan, decided to establish a "Provisional Indochinese Government," a project that permitted him to enlist the aid of wealthy Chinese in exchange for honorific titles. This led to internal difficulties within the group and representations to the Chinese government. The KMT, keeping in mind its diplomatic relations with the French government, invited the Canton party to dissolve its "provisional government."

The Canton party in April 1932 held a congress for the purpose of reorganizing the Viet Nam Nationalist Party. During that congress dissident members objected that Chinese KMT delegates were playing too prominent a role. This had its effect, for the KMT officially withdrew its subsidy from the party and then dissolved the party for not having obeyed in full the previous order to disband the "provisional government."

The officials of the Canton party made their way to Nanking where they successfully reconstructed the party. Contact was established with Lu Han, then chief of the Military Council Bureau of the Nanking Chinese National Government. This led to direct relations with the Central Executive Committee of the KMT and important sections of the Chinese government. Authorization was obtained to establish the party officially at Nanking and a monthly allocation of funds was secured. Following this, efforts were made to effect fusion with the Yunnan organization.

The origin of the Yunnan group, like the others, can be traced to Phan Boi Chau and Cuong De. Le Phu Hiep, a supporter of their movement, had become politically active in Yunnan. He had achieved the rank of colonel in the Chinese administration and was a leading figure in the Vietnamese community of Yunnan. In 1928 he was instrumental in forming the Trung Viet Cach Menh Lien Quan (Revolutionary Sino-Viet Nam Military League). That organization soon foundered, but its members later joined the émigré Viet Nam Nationalist Party created by Nguyen The Nghiep, who had escaped from Indochina where he had been sentenced to a ten-year jail term in early 1930 after the Yen Bay insurrection. He established a number of party cells in Yunnan where membership may have reached three hundred.

The party (VNQDD) was a section of the Chinese KMT—its units corresponded to units of the KMT and depended upon them. The arrangement served the VNQDD quite well as it gave them protection from the Chinese authorities. And protection was necessary because the organization was constantly raising funds through extortion and robbery along the length of the railroad from Yunnan to Tonkin. Conditions became so bad that the Chinese authorities were finally forced to put a stop to the illegal activities of the party. In September 1930 Nguyen The Nghiep left to establish the party in Burma at Bhamo, an unsuccessful venture. He returned to Yunnan and was arrested following the murder of a political rival.

The party nevertheless fared well. It obtained military training for its members by enrolling them in the Yunnan Military School. Some fifty-odd partisans were enrolled in the Chinese army. Still others worked in the arsenal at Yunnan, where they were trained in the manufacture of grenades and explosives. The party engaged in a number of business and agricultural enterprises to augment its finances. By the end of 1932 it tried to solidify its position still further by fusing with the Canton and Nanking organizations.

From 15 to 24 July 1933, the fusion proceedings were in full swing and both parties were finally amalgamated under the leadership of the "Overseas Bureau" of the VNQDD in Nanking. For the next seven years the VNQDD maintained a low profile but profited from its association with the Chinese KMT.

Then in 1940 when the influence of the Japanese began to dominate the Indochinese political scene, the VNQDD underwent internal schisms. Some of the nationalist elements looked to Japan as they had previously looked to China for aid against the French. A pro-Japanese faction under the leadership of Nguyen Tuong Tam adopted the name Dai Viet Dan Chinh (Great Viet Nam Democratic Party) (see Dai Viet, above). At the same time Nguyen The Nghiep returned to Indochina and formed the Dai Viet Quoc Dan Dang (Great Viet Nam Nationalist Party) (see Dai Viet, above). The leadership of his group in exile in Kunming, Yunnan, bearing the name VNQDD was taken over by Vu Hong Khanh, a former school teacher. It was Vu Hong Khanh's group that was to become a factor of political importance within Indochina with the resurgence of the nationalist movement at the end of World War II.

Under KMT instructions General Chang Fa-kwei in Kwangsi province attempted to organize and put to use for the Chinese the many Vietnamese political groups then in southern China. In October 1942 at Liuchow, China, he organized the Viet Nam Cach Menh Dong Minh Hoi (Viet Nam Revolutionary League) (see Dong Minh Hoi, above). The VNQDD, under the leadership of Vu Hong Khanh, played the leading role in manipulating the Dong Minh Hoi for the Chinese KMT.

Later, when the Chinese occupied Indochina (September 1945) the VNQDD followed the Chinese troops into Hanoi and acted as a counterforce to Ho Chi

Minh's communist Viet Minh and the DRV government, but it kept its identity separate from the Dong Minh Hoi. After considerable VNQDD opposition to the DRV and the Viet Minh, Ho, in the interest of national unity, in the fall of 1945 struck a deal with the VNQDD and promised Vu Hong Khanh fifty seats in the National Assembly of the Provisional Coalition Government to be elected in January 1946 and two cabinet posts—foreign affairs and economy. Vu Hong Khanh was given a seat on the all-important Military Council. The entente was short-lived, and the VNQDD continued its opposition to the communist regime and for a while, after the December 1946 hostilities between the French and Vietnamese erupted, some elements of the VNQDD in Cochinchina sided with the French army.

As one of the oldest nationalist parties in Viet Nam the VNQDD had considerable prestige, but also poor leadership and opportunism in individual leaders striving for personal power, plus dependence for support on various foreign powers, particularly Japan and China—all of which contributed to its ultimate disintegration.

While Bao Dai was trying to form a coalition government in 1947, the VNQDD participated in founding the Mat Tran Thong Nhut Quoc Gia Lien Hiep (National Union Front). However, its strong republican principles made for conflict with other forces supporting Bao Dai who were desirous of restoring some form of monarchy and more willing to come to terms with France. VNQDD relations with the monarchist elements were further exacerbated by its repeated demands for Chinese, American, and United Nations intervention in the Indochinese conflict. These difficulties finally led to a split, and the VNQDD faded into oblivion, occasionally issuing party literature in Hanoi and mildly collaborating with other political elements for the return of Bao Dai. Vu Hong Khanh was reportedly living in Hong Kong in 1949, no longer interested in party activities.

DEVELOPMENT OF COMMUNIST ORGANIZATIONS IN INDOCHINA, 1921–31

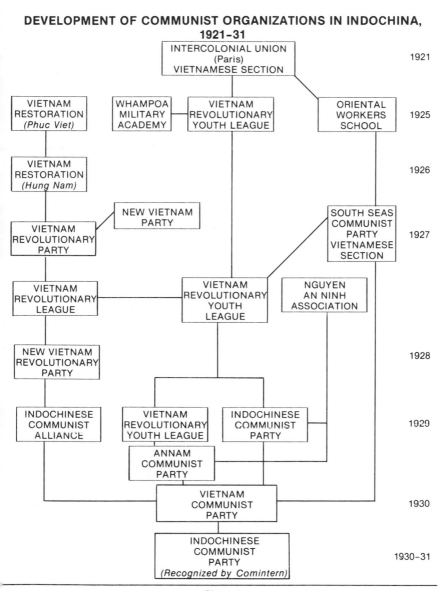

Chart 1

DEVELOPMENT OF COMMUNIST ORGANIZATIONS IN INDOCHINA, 1931–45

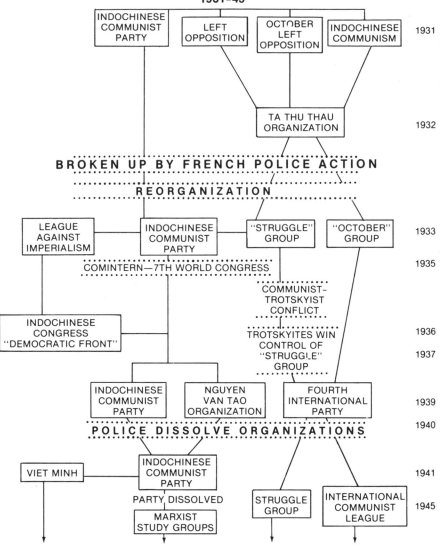

Chart 2

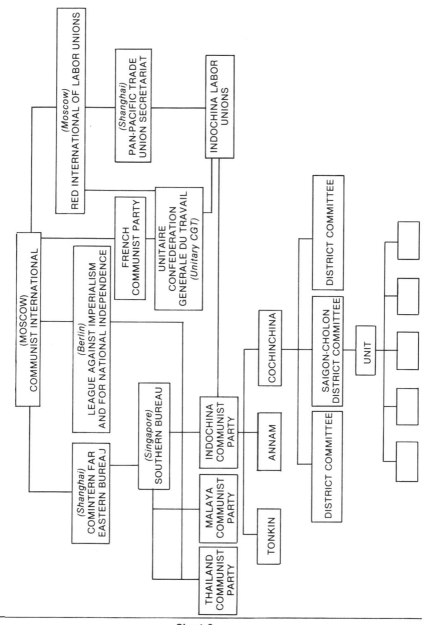

Chart 3

HISTORY OF THE VIET NAM NATIONALIST PARTY (VNQDD), 1925–49

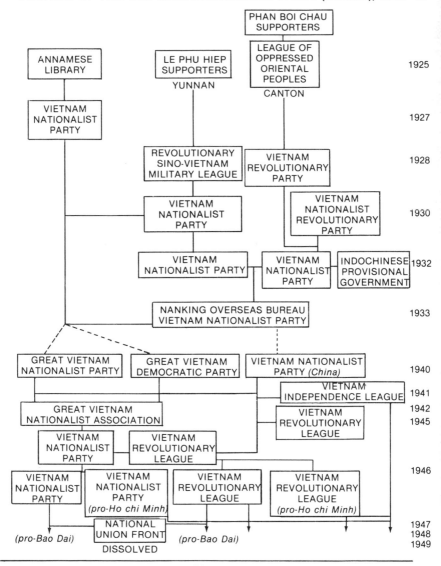

Chart 4

NOTES

PART ONE: WASHINGTON

1: The Beginning of an Era

1. Conservatively estimated at 6,000 French, 56,000 Americans, and 1,500,000 Vietnamese.
2. See Appendix II.
3. Concurrently Wedemeyer was also Chief of Staff to Generalissimo Chiang Kai-shek. See Appendix II.

2: ". . . if China goes under . . ."

1. Chief, Secret Intelligence Division, OSS-CT. See Appendix II.
2. Elliott Roosevelt, *As He Saw It*, p. 53.
3. Ibid., p. 54.
4. 25 February 1942.
5. Marshall's first choice had been the Army's senior-ranking officer, Lieut. General Hugh A. Drum, but for political and personal preferences, he was not selected.
6. Arthur Bryant, *Triumph in the West*, p. 26.
7. Joseph W. Stilwell, *The Stilwell Papers*, arranged and edited by Theodore H. White, p. 230.
8. Maj. General Thomas T. Handy, Chief, Operations and Plans Division, War Department, General Staff.
9. WD: Radio WAR-3243, Marshall to Stilwell, 26 August 1943; Item 759, Book 2, in JWS Personnel File. (Record Center, Kansas City, Mo.)
10. Presidential Emissary, whose mission was to present SEAC to the Generalissimo and secure formal assent to the new Allied command structure for Southeast Asia.
11. See Appendix II.
12. WD: Radio CFB 28167, Wedemeyer to Marshall for JCS, 4 December 1944; Item 6, Wedemeyer Data Book. (Italics added.)
13. DOS: Diplomatic Files, no. 851 G.00/7–2644; Telegram, In-message no. 1293, 26 July 1944, Section one, from Chungking (Gauss) to Washington (SecState). (CIAC)

3: Indochina: Pressure Point

1. Elliott Roosevelt, *As He Saw It*, p. 115.
2. *The Memoirs of Cordell Hull*, 2:1595.
3. Ibid.
4. Ibid., p. 1597.
5. FRUS (1942), 2:561.
6. Ibid., p. 416.
7. Ibid., p. 453.
8. Lieut. General Émile-Marie Béthouart, Chief, French Military Mission in Washington, established by General Giraud in December 1942 to negotiate and expedite the arming of French troops with American materiel.
9. Supreme Headquarters, Allied Expeditionary Force.
10. Special Operations Executive, the British counterpart to OSS.
11. Head of the Office of Far Eastern Affairs, Department of State.
12. DOS: Memorandum from Ballantine to Stettinius, dated 16 December 1944; File: 851 G.01/11–2744, CS/MAN. (CIAC)
13. DOS: Letter, dated 22 December 1944, from Stettinius to Donovan. (CIAC)
14. The second Quebec conference (code-named OCTAGON), 10 September 1944.
15. DOS: Letter, dated 20 October 1944, from Hull to Donovan. (CIAC)
16. FRUS (1945), 6:293. (Italics added.)

4: The Unintelligible Intelligence Community

1. Secret Intelligence and Special Operations.
2. The official name of BIS was the Central Investigation and Statistics Bureau (CISB). The short form BIS was commonly used by American intelligence agencies in China.

5: OSS: The French Indochina Desk

1. Major Austin O. Glass, former director of the Haiphong office of Standard Oil Company of New York.
2. Major Duncan C. Lee, Chief, Japan-China Section, Far East Division, SI-OSS. See Appendix II.
3. Edmund L. Taylor, Lieut. Commander, USNR, Deputy Head, "P" Division, but then "Acting Head" in the absence of Captain G. A. Garnon-Williams, R. N. (British).
4. SEAC: Memorandum-P/1114, Hqrs SEAC, dated 21 July 1944, from P Division to Deputy Chief of Staff (Thru: Director of Intelligence). (CIAC)
5. SEAC: Record of Meeting held in the Supreme Commander's Room on Monday, 24 July 1944. (CIAC)
6. 20 June 1940.
7. Charles de Gaulle, *War Memoirs: The Call to Honour, 1940–1942*, translated by Jonathan Griffin, p. 104.
8. General Henri Giraud, High Commissioner for North and West Africa, and Commander-in-Chief of all French armed forces, including naval units.
9. Bureau Central de Renseignements et d'Action (BCRA) (Central Bureau of Intelligence and Action), the Free French counterpart to British SOE and American OSS. Later renamed the DGER.
10. Colonel Pechkov was appointed by de Gaulle in 1943 as Chief of the French Military Mission in China. See Appendix II.

11. Charles de Gaulle, *War Memoirs: Unity, 1942-1944*, translated by Richard Howard, p. 321.
12. M. François was a director of the Banque Nationale pour le Commerce et Industrie. The American Consul at Kunming in mid-December 1943 had mistakenly reported to Ambassador Gauss that a French "industrialist," Mr. François, had been sent to North Africa "on a mission by Admiral Decoux." (Disp. no. 7, 14 December 1943, from Ringwalt to Gauss.) (CIAC)
13. Charles de Gaulle, *War Memoirs: Unity, 1942-1944*, p. 322.
14. Pieced together from conversations with British opposite numbers in SEAC and, in part, by OSS-Europe.
15. French Liaison Section in the Far East. An element of the Direction Générale des Services Spéciaux (DGSS), later reorganized as the Direction Générale des Études et Recherches (DGER), a clandestine organization comparable to SOE and OSS. The SLFEO (Calcutta) was under the direction of Commandant Léonard (code-named "Lion"), an associate of de Langlade.
16. OSS: based on my interview with Colonel Tateki Sakai, senior staff officer, Hqrs, 38th Imperial Japanese Army, at Hanoi, on 31 August 1945. (CIAC)
17. OSS: "Counterintelligence Report-Hanoi, OSS/X-2"; and my interrogation of senior staff members of the 38th Imperial Japanese Army, September 1945. (CIAC) Some of the more obvious indicators of Japanese intentions, aside from the conversion of the Indochina Garrison Army into the tactical 38th Imperial Japanese Army, were the several clandestine operations undertaken by the kempeitai. These were not totally unknown to the Allied intelligence services, including the SLFEO. One such operation was Project Yasu Butai. After the Allied landings in France (June 1944) Ambassador Kenkichi Yoshizawa, later replaced by Ambassador Matsumoto, asked Tokyo for instructions regarding Japanese policy in Indochina should Vichy capitulate. There was no immediate reply to the political question; instead the Imperial General Headquarters (IGHQ) authorized the kempeitai to create a political warfare unit in Indochina with the objective of eliminating the French military and destroying French influence. At the same time it was to organize and support local anti-French movements for independence. On 10 January 1945 the Southern army *tokumu kikan* (intelligence agency) created the Yasu Butai (Annam Unit). Under the direction of Staff Intelligence, Lieut. Colonel Ishida Shoici, with headquarters in Saigon, operational units were established at Hanoi, Haiphong, Hué, and Phnom Penh. Enlisting the support of French civil and military individuals of known pétainiste leanings, pro-Japanese Vietnamese nationalists among the ranks of Phuc Quoc, Dai Viet, and Phuc Viet parties, the religious sects of the Caodaists and Hoa Hao, the criminal bands of the Binh Xuyen, Shoici organized a "native" paramilitary unit for guerrilla operations. The Yasu Butai activities were coordinated with military operations of the Southern army and the political requirements of the Japanese Embassy utilizing the clandestine apparatus described in Chapter 31, below. After the 9 March coup, the Yasu Butai paramilitary units engaged French and British units (Force 136) in skirmishes on the Annam-Laos border. Later in July and August the Japanese units were attacked by the Viet Minh in the Tonkin mountains.
18. Military police organization with functions similar to those generally associated with the secret police of totalitarian governments. The kempeitai was normally attached to a major military command but answerable only to the Imperial General Headquarters in Tokyo. It exercised extraordinary authority

over military and civilians in Japan and in Japanese-occupied areas in matters of state security, espionage, counterintelligence, surveillance of foreigners, and thought control. Its methods of operation included kidnapping, torture, and murder.

6: The Americans Discover Ho Chi Minh

1. The China unit of MIS-X (Washington) responsible for the escape and evasion of downed airmen and POWs in enemy areas. Its British counterpart in China, with which AGAS cooperated, was BAAG (British Army Aid Group), an element of MI-9 (London).
2. OSS: Letter Report, dated 18 January 1945; subject, "FIC Intelligence Report by GBT Group, dated 17 January 1945"; from Hqrs, AGAS-China. (CIAC)
3. DOS: Telegram no. 116 (sent via Naval Radio), dated 26 January 1945; subject, "Situation in Indo-China"; from Ambassador Hurley to SecState. (CIAC)
4. DOS: Telegram no. 1293 (sent via Naval Radio), Section ONE, dated 26 July 1944; from Ambassador Gauss to SecState. (CIAC)
5. The New York office of the OSS was located with the British Security Coordination Office at 630 Fifth Avenue (International Building). Principally a Secret Intelligence Branch office, it was also responsible for the supervision and direction of the activities of other OSS branches (MO, X-2, SO, R&A, etc.) in the New York City area and for liaison with the intelligence services of the various United Nations representatives operating from the United States.
6. The famous "Churchill's man called 'Intrepid,' " then operating secretly and with official American sanction out of New York City.
7. Colonel Morris B. DePass, Jr. (U.S. Army).
8. Director of the Bureau of Foreign Affairs of the National Military Council, and Director of Chinese Military Intelligence.
9. Chinese province adjacent to the NE border of Tonkin, Indochina, with easy access routes across the frontier.
10. A branch of OSS engaged in one aspect of propaganda ("black") which if not outright mendacious, which it may be, is intended to subvert by every possible device. Its source is disguised and is disowned by the government using it.
11. A Marine Corps Reserve officer, trained by OSS in MO for duty at Stilwell's base in Assam, Burma.
12. DOS: Telegram no. 1576 (Sections ONE and TWO), dated 31 December 1942, from Ambassador Gauss to SecState. (CIAC)
13. Central Committee of the Indochinese Section of the International Anti-Invasion Association. DOS: Disp. no. 1955, dated 23 December 1943; subject, "Continued Detention by the Chinese Authorities of the Delegate of the Indochina Section of the International Anti-Aggression [sic] Association"; from Ambassador Gauss to SecState. (CIAC)
14. William R. Powell, OWI Air Liaison Representative in Kunming.
15. I kept my pledge for 33 years. Since most of the files have been declassified, I feel at liberty to disclose their contents.
16. Third Secretary at the American Embassy at Chungking.
17. Again from an unidentified "Annamite."
18. The Chinese Foreign Office explained to our Embassy staff that the suppression had been necessary "so as not to create unfavorable reaction from the Vichy Government."

19. Then Second Secretary at the American Embassy at Chungking.
20. Commander of the Fourth War Area. See Appendix II.
21. Head of the Chinese Organization Board of the KMT Central Executive Committee.
22. Then Chief of the Division of Far Eastern Affairs, Department of State.
23. Vincent's reference was to the Viet Minh.
24. Boncour had been Counselor of the French Embassy at Chungking when Vincent held a similar post at the American Embassy there.
25. DOS: Telegram no. 838, dated 30 June 1943, from Hull to AMEMBASSY, Chungking. (CIAC)
26. Colonel Jacques de Sibour and Major Austin O. Glass, then assigned to OSS/AGFRTS, were also in touch with SACO.
27. This attitude was later reflected in General Blaizot's secret instructions to his staff based on de Gaulle's policy decision "to continue to supply the British with all types of information . . . with the following restriction: (I) If the British reproduce or use any of the French material they must not make this information available to any American agency." *Source:* Military Attaché, New Delhi, India; Report no. R-160-45, dated 27 March 1945, p. 2. (CIAC)
28. Ho Chi Minh had gained notoriety only the previous two years (1940–42) as a leading communist revolutionary. See Appendix II.
29. An abbreviation of the Viet Nam Cach Menh Dong Minh Hoi (Viet Nam Revolutionary League). See Appendix III.
30. DOS: Disp. no. 1955, n. 13, above.
31. Ibid.
32. Arthur R. Ringwalt.
33. DOS: Disp. no. 126, dated 5 August 1944; subject, "Democratic Party of Indochina"; from American Consulate at Kweilin, Kwangsi, China, to AMEMBASSY, Chungking. (CIAC)
34. Sprouse had been reassigned to the Department of State in Washington.
35. At the Versailles Conference in 1919, Ho Chi Minh had tried unsuccessfully to petition President Wilson on behalf of Indochina.
36. British Ambassador to the United States, 1941–46.
37. Cairo, 22–26 November, and Teheran, 28 November–1 December 1943.
38. DOS: Memorandum of Conversation, dated 3 January 1944; subject, "Status of Indochina After the War"; participants, Secretary of State Hull and the British Ambassador, Lord Halifax. (CIAC)
39. DOS: Memorandum, dated 5 January 1944, from S. K. Hornbeck, Adviser on Political Relations, to SecState. (CIAC)
40. In return for his freedom from Chinese detention in August 1943, Ho agreed to cooperate with Chang Fa-kwei by taking an active role in reorganizing the Dong Minh Hoi. However, factional disputes and charges that Ho was using his position to advance his communist aims led Chang, in March 1944, to ask Ho to step aside as one of the leaders of the Dong Minh Hoi but to remain as a member. He was given the post of Minister in the newly-formed "Provisional Republican Government of Viet Nam." Ho also promised to collaborate with the Chinese in intelligence-gathering activities.
41. As the war effort shifted from Europe to Asia, the OSS and OWI staffs were being rapidly augmented.
42. De Sibour and Glass of OSS and Powell of OWI.
43. The letter, dated 18 August 1944 at Kunming, China, was signed by three

members of the Executive Committee of La Ligue de l'Independance de l'Indo-chine: Pham Viet Tu, chairman; Vuong Minh Phuong, member; and Tong Minh Phuong, member.

44. DOS: Enclosure no. 1 to Dispatch no. 77, dated 9 September 1944; subject, "Memorandum of Conversation"; from Wm. R. Langdon, American Consul General, Kunming, China, to SecState. (CIAC)

45. A close associate and trusted lieutenant of Ho Chi Minh. See Appendix II.

46. Viet Nam Tuyen Truyen Giai Phong Quan, generally translated in Hanoi publications as "Armed Propaganda Brigade for the Liberation of Viet Nam" and also "Viet Nam Propaganda and Liberation Army."

47. See Appendix II.

48. These were under the command of Lieut. General Gabriel Sabattier, Commander of French Forces in Tonkin, and Maj. General Marcel Alessandri, a Legionnaire officer.

49. In April and May 1945 I interviewed many French officers and enlisted men who attributed their safe passage into China to the "valiant and generous assistance of the Annamite locals."

50. OSS: Letter, Hqrs USFCT, dated 20 March 1945; subject, "Intelligence Activities and Aid to Resistance Groups in French Indo-China"; from Mervin E. Gross, B/Gen., GSC, Act'g C/S, by command of M/Gen. Chennault, to OSS-CT, APO 879. (CIAC)

51. Charles Fenn, Ho Chi Minh—A biographical introduction.

52. Ibid., p. 76. I learned in September 1945 from Pham Van Dong that it was he who had accompanied Ho on this first meeting with Fenn.

53. Ibid., p. 77.

54. Ibid., pp. 78 and 79.

55. The most flyable eastern section of the Himalayan range between India and China, used by Allied planes in World War II for ferrying men and supplies at altitudes of 15,000 to 25,000 feet.

PART TWO: KUNMING

7: What Washington Did Not Know

1. Chief, Secret Intelligence Branch, OSS-Kunming. See Appendix II.

2. WD: Radio WARX-55402; dated 19 March 1945; subject, "14th Air Force Operations Against Japanese in French Indo-China"; from War Department to Chennault, Info Gross and Weart, signed "Marshall." (CIAC)

3. WD: Radio WARX-56286, dated 9 Apr 1945, from [General] Hull to Wedemeyer. (CIAC)

4. OSS: Letter file no. SI-005-304; OSS-Hqrs CT; dated 4 March 1945; subject, "Policy in French Indo-China"; from Heppner to Helliwell. (CIAC)

5. DOS: Telegram no. 116, n. 3, ch. 6, above.

6. Assistant Chief of Staff, Operations Division, War Department.

7. WD: Personal Note (hand-carried by Colonel George A. "Abe" Lincoln), dated 9 February 1945, from General J. E. Hull (at Yalta) to Wedemeyer at Chungking. (CIAC)

8. DOS: Telegram no. 266, dated 16 February 1945; subject, "Indochina"; from Grew (Acting) to AMEMBASSY, Chungking. (CIAC)

9. OSS: Memorandum from the Board of Military Operations-KMT; dated 10 March 1945 at 1100 hrs. CT; Reference no. 61; to General Gross, subject, "Questions raised by General Ho Ying-chin and Wedemeyer to His Excellency, The Generalissimo." (CIAC)

10. Claire Lee Chennault, *Way of a Fighter*, p. 342.

11. OSS: Letter, dated 20 March 1945; subject, "Intelligence Activities and Aid To Resistance Groups in French Indo-China"; from Hqrs. USFCT, to OSS, CT, APO 879. (CIAC)

12. OSS: Letter, dated 20 March 1945; File: AG no. 311; subject, "Establishment of Intelligence Radio Net in FIC"; from Hqrs, USFCT to CO, OSS-CT; by Command of Maj. General Chennault. (CIAC)

13. With the arrest of Aymé and Mordant, Sabattier automatically assumed command of the French forces in Tonkin and Mordant's responsibility of Delegate General for Indochina.

14. A Chinese border town about two miles E of Mong Cai. Also spelled Tunghsing.

15. A Vietnamese coastal city at the extreme eastern end of Tonkin near the China border.

16. Another Vietnamese coastal town, 40 miles SW of Mong Cai.

17. OSS: Radio Msg, dated 22 March 1945, from Mykland, Repo and Opso, Chungking, to Bird, Kunming. (CIAC)

18. An area of approximately 2,000 square miles, about 75 miles N of Hanoi in the mountainous area of Tonkin.

19. In early March Helliwell authorized the issuance from OSS stock of six new Colt .45 automatic pistols and several thousand rounds of ammunition to an AGAS representative for delivery to Ho Chi Minh.

20. An ancient city (Fuhsingchen) about 200 air miles SW of Kunming in Yunnan province. Estimated population in 1945, 25,000. Also spelled Ssu-mao.

21. This was a misnomer. The only French Military Mission accredited to the Chinese government was at Chungking under "General" Pechkov. The M.5 in Kunming was a unit of the SLFEO/Calcutta and responsible to it for clandestine operations in Indochina.

22. A province in Central China. Chungking is one of its principal cities.

23. Educated in Switzerland, Tong was employed by SI, OSS-CT, to assist in the penetration of "Free Thais" into Bangkok.

24. Major (later Lieut. Colonel) Harley C. Stevens, OSS representative at the American Embassy in Chungking.

25. Annamite Society of Mutual Assistance in Yunnan, and the Annamite Sporting Club.

26. President Roosevelt had died on 12 April 1945.

27. In the context of the conversation, Ho hoped to discourage American recognition of other Vietnamese nationalist parties, but did not intend to preclude limited collaboration with the gaullistes.

28. Hurley had succeeded Gauss in January 1945 as Ambassador to China. See Appendix II.

29. Deputy SSO-CT. Formerly an executive of Sears, Roebuck and Company. After the war, he settled in Bangkok as an exporter.

30. Chief, American Observation Group (the DIXIE Mission), at Chinese Communist headquarters in Yenan.

8: The New French Problem

1. *Domei* in English, 10 March 1945; FIR no. 5, item 5, p. 16. (Italics added.) (CIAC)
2. Radio Saigon in Annamite, 9 March 1945, 0345 G.M.T.; FIR no. 5, item 49, p. 26. (CIAC)
3. *Domei* in English, 11 March 1945; FIR no. 5, item 48, p. 25. (CIAC)
4. *Domei* in English, 13 March 1945; FIR no. 5, item 51, p 26. (CIAC)
5. OSS: French strength in March 1945 consisted of nearly 74,000 regulars of the Colonial Army, including some 19,500 Europeans, mainly officers, NCOs, and Legionnaires. There were approximately 25,000 auxiliary (militia) and security troops, including about 360 Europeans. The French forces were grouped into two divisions and one brigade: the Tonkin Division under Sabattier in the north, the Annam Independent Brigade deployed in the Central Annam and Laos district, and the Cochinchina Division located in Cochinchina and Cambodia. The main strength was in the north. The French Naval Fleet consisted of about 16 warships of the escort class and an undetermined number of motorized junks in the Saigon-Cape St. Jacques waters. The air fleet was minimal: approximately 20 older-type reconnaissance planes, all in northern airfields.
6. OSS: of these only 2,100 were Frenchmen; the remainder were Indochinese military of the Colonial army.
7. Radio Tokyo in Japanese, 11 March 1945, 1030 G.M.T.; FIR no. 5, item 52, p. 26. (CIAC)
8. OSS: based on statements made by Pechkov and members of the French Military Mission (Chungking) that these installations had been generously supplied since early 1943 with arms and equipment, first by British airdrops from India, and later by the American Fourteenth Air Force.
9. DOS: Disp. no. 159, dated 13 March 1945; subject, "Neutralization of French Forces in Indochina"; from American Consulate General, Kunming, to AMEMBASSY, Chungking. Substance of this dispatch cabled to Washington. (CIAC)
10. Ibid., p. 1.
11. Ibid., p. 3.
12. Founded after World War I. See Appendix III.
13. Founded early in 1939 by Huynh Phu So. See Appendix III.
14. DOS: Disp. no. 159 (see n. 9, above), p. 3, 7th para.
15. Border town in northern Tonkin on the Hong (Red) River, 155 miles NW of Hanoi. Also spelled Lao Kay and Laokay.
16. United Nations Relief and Rehabilitation Administration.

9: A Tour of the China Border

1. Manned by the 19th Liaison Air Group, Fourteenth Air Force.
2. Commandant Jacques de Laborde de Monpezat, leader of M.5's Operation Poitou, an intelligence-gathering unit in the border area of Cao Bang.
3. OSS operative later transferred to a coastal watch operation at Pakhoi.
4. At Ha Giang, Cao Bang, and Lang Son.
5. OSS: Letter, Hqrs CCC (Prov) USFCT, Office of AC/S, G-2; dated 27 April 1945; subject, "G-2 Requirements for OSS in Connection with Future Plans CCC (Prov) Operations"; from Colonel George R. Hayman to CO, OSS-CT. (CIAC)
6. This initial meeting between Ho Chi Minh and me occurred on 27 April 1945.

7. An influential member of the Central Executive Committee of the League for the Independence of Indochina (Liuchow-1944) and also member of the Kunming Board (1944). Although in his early forties, he appeared much younger. At twenty as a student at Yen Bay he participated in the violent insurrection there led by the Annamite Nationalist Party in 1930. Forced to flee to China, he became Ho's key organizer in Yunnan. Considered a hard-core Marxist.

8. These warehouses stored rice to be collected by government officials for the provisioning of the French and Japanese armies.

9. In May 1945 I received a copy of the "Black Book" from Ho Chi Minh and a set of photographs which were forwarded to the American Embassy at Chungking for transmission to the Department of State, as attachments to my report of the meeting with Ho. A search of the S.S.U.-W.D. files in 1975 and the Department of State archives gave no clue as to what became of the material. Duplicate copies of the photographs are in my collection of documents.

10. The exact location was in one of the several limestone caves of the Pac Bo region. Pac Bo, a small hamlet approximately one mile south of the Chinese border and 30 miles SW of Ch'ing-Hsi, is within easy reach of Cao Bang, Bac Can, and Lang Son. The area is sparsely populated by the Nung people.

11. The OSS-SO team, code-named "Gorrilla," consisted of Majors John W. Summers and Nelson E. Guillot, Captain Shirly R. Trumps, and First Sergeant Donald A. Spears.

12. Commander of the 9th RIC.

13. Mountain people scattered throughout the highlands on both sides of the Red River in northern Tonkin. Generally referred to as a tribe of the montagnard ethnic minority.

14. *New York Times*, 27 March 1945.

15. *Domei* in English, 9 April 1945.

16. OSS: Out-Msg no. 74, dated 6 May 1945, from Helliwell to Patti. (CIAC)

17. Commander of the Chinese Occupation Forces in Indochina, north of the sixteenth parallel. See Appendix II.

18. Brig. General Philip E. Gallagher, Chief of the U.S. Military Advisory and Assistance Group to the Chinese occupation force in northern Viet Nam.

19. The term used by de Gaulle to describe Mordant's arrest and imprisonment following the Japanese coup. See Charles de Gaulle, *War Memoirs: Salvation, 1944-1946*, translated by Richard Howard, p. 190.

20. Gabriel Sabattier, *Le destin de l'Indochine: Souvenirs et documents, 1941-1951*, pp. 192-93.

10: A "Think Tank" Session

1. OSS: Letter, Hqrs USFCT, dated 10 May 1945; subject, "Demolition Operations"; from E. O. Shaw, Col AGD, by command of Wedemeyer, to Chief, OSS-CT. (CIAC)

2. Major (later Lieut. Colonel) Quentin Roosevelt, OSS liaison officer to Chiang Kai-shek.

3. Maj. General Robert B. McClure, Chief of Staff, China Theater, and Senior American Field Commander in China.

4. A major theater command consisting of troops and supplies to support combat units in the field with rations, ammunition, transportation, housing, administration, etc.

5. French Military Attaché with the French Embassy at Chungking.
6. The appeal was prepared in both Vietnamese and English. The open letter was in English and Chinese. Copies delivered to other nations may have used other languages. (CIAC)

11: The Reluctant Ally

1. Lieutenant de vaisseau Flichy, deputy chief, M.5.
2. Commandant Jean Sainteny, Chief, M.5. See Appendix II.
3. Colonel Emblanc, Squadron Leader Milon, Lieut. Commander Flichy, and several others.
4. Pakhoi (Peihai), treaty port, SW Kwangtung province, in SE China on the Gulf of Tonkin, approximately 350 miles W of Hong Kong and about 60 miles E of Mong Cai on the Indochina border.
5. I designated Captain Bernique and Lieutenant Ettinger for OSS; Sainteny designated Lieutenants Louis Fouchier-Magnan and François Missoff for M.5.
6. Head of an OSS-SO team code-named "Chow" located at Poseh (Paise), China, approximately 275 miles SE of Kunming and 60 miles N of Ch'ing-Hsi.
7. OSS: Memorandum for Record, dated 23 May 1945; subject, "Agreement between Generalissimo and General Sabattier"; prepared by Brig. General M. E. Gross, Act'g C/S. (CIAC)
8. OSS: Extract of "Plan of Operations for FIC"; dated 25 May 1945; agreed to by SLFEO and OSS. (CIAC)
9. In Kwangtung province, about 120 miles E of Pakhoi and 50 miles NE of Fort Bayard.
10. USN, attached to AGAS for OSS coastal intelligence activities.
11. The French group consisted of 8 officers, 40 European Legionnaires, and 60 Annamite enlisted men.
12. Deputy Chief of Staff (Rear Echelon) USFCT at Kunming.
13. Present at the meeting were Generals Weart and Alessandri, Colonel Heppner, Captain Patti, and Lt. Commander Flichy.
14. Minutes of Meeting. (CIAC)
15. Code name of André Dewavrin, Head of the DGER in Paris, successor to the wartime French resistance organization, BCRA.
16. Chief, SLFEO-Calcutta, the operating arm of the DGER in the Far East. His code name was "Nestor."
17. OSS and Theater G-2 maintained excellent Order of Battle sections and Photo Interpretation units; in addition, the U.S.-Chinese (CCC) intelligence system, although cumbersome at times, produced excellent material on Japanese troop dispositions, unit identifications, and target information. French "intelligence" reports, disseminated without processing (analysis) to Allied agencies were often vague and unconfirmed, more in the nature of local gossip and always from unidentifiable sources.
18. A small island of approximately 10 square miles in the NE sector of the Gulf of Tonkin, 25 miles S of Pakhoi.
19. A small island of approximately 3 square miles in the Gulf of Tonkin, 100 miles S of Mong Cai and 80 miles SE of Haiphong.
20. Deputy Chief of Staff, USFCT.
21. Assistant Chief of Staff, G-2, USFCT.
22. Chief of Staff, USFCT.

23. OSS: Letter Report, dated 13 June 1945; subject, "Summary of Activities and Developments in China Theater during the Month of May"; from General Wedemeyer to General Marshall. (CIAC)

24. Also present were General Gross, Colonels Heppner and Roos, Major Sainteny, and I.

25. A special commando-type operation against the Japanese 22d Division headquarters in the Lang Son area. The unit comprised one hundred French officers and men led by one American officer and four enlisted men of the OSS-OG Branch.

26. A three-man team, one American OSS or British SOE officer, one French officer, and one radio operator, parachuting into France, Belgium, or Holland to help organize and arm a large part of the resistance movement in Europe in advance of D-Day.

27. Brig. General George H. Olmsted, AC/S, G-5 (Civil Affairs), U.S. Army Headquarters in China.

28. OSS: Minutes of Meeting with General Alessandri, 17 July 1945, "Equipment and Arms for French Troops under Lend-Lease: Use of French Troops in China Theater." (CIAC)

29. The criticality of the logistic problem was a very old one to the Americans and, ironically, was one cause of President Roosevelt's irritation toward the French "cave in" in Indochina in 1939 and 1940. The first Japanese demand had been to close the northern ports of Indochina to China-bound military supplies, as well as the rail facilities to the China border. Getting military supplies into China had been a wracking problem ever since.

30. Sainteny was in Paris attempting to gain official support for his M.5 mission.

12: "Trusteeship" Redefined

1. UN Conference on International Organization held at San Francisco from 25 April to 26 June 1945.

2. *Bulletin d'Information publié par le Service Français d'Information en Chine*, no. 64, 28 April 1945. Also DOS: Disp. no. 191, dated 17 May 1945; subject, "Indochina Situation"; from American Consul General, Kunming, to SecState. (CIAC)

3. Then Acting Secretary of State. For text of statement see Note dated 13 April 1942, Welles to Henri-Haye, FRUS (1942), 2:561.

4. Held in Washington, D.C., 21 August to 29 September 1944, with representation from the U.S., U.K., and USSR. The conferees held a separate session, 29 September to 7 October 1944, between the U.S., U.K., and China. The Conference laid the foundation for the United Nations Organization for joint security and to maintain the peace. Inter alia, it discussed the trusteeship system applicable only to: (a) territories then under mandate of the League of Nations, (b) territories taken from enemy states as a result of the war, and (c) territories voluntarily placed under the system by states responsible for their administration.

5. FRUS (1945), 6:307 and 312.

6. Ibid., p. 312.

7. Ibid. pp. 308–9.

8. DOS: Press Release, dated 18 May 1945; published in DOS Bulletin of 20 May 1945, p. 927.

9. FRUS (1945) 6:310.
10. DOS: Telegram no. 750 (sent via Naval Radio), dated 11 May 1945; subject, "French Indochina"; from Ambassador Hurley to SecState. (CIAC)
11. DOS: Telegram no. 749 (sent via Commercial Radio), dated 19 May 1945; subject, "Indochina"; from Grew (Acting) to AMEMBASSY Chungking. (CIAC)
12. DOS: Telegram no. 873 (sent via Naval Radio), dated 7 June 1945, from Acting Secretary Grew to AMEMBASSY Chungking. Only portions of this message were printed in FRUS (1945) 6:307–8, and 7:120. Copy of complete text in my collection.

13: The "Deer" Team at Kim Lung

1. Village about 50 miles NW of Hanoi, deep in the densely forested province of Tuyen Quang. A communal center for several small hamlets, selected for the capital of the revolutionary stronghold known as the "Liberated Zone." Its approximate location is 13 miles ESE of the provincial capital of Tuyen Quang and 25 miles NW of the provincial capital of Thai Nguyen, N of highway 13.
2. The six provinces comprising the "Liberated Zone" or "Area" were Cao Bang, Bac Can, Lang Son, Ha Giang, Tuyen Quang, and Thai Nguyen.
3. Member of the Kunming Branch of the Central Executive Committee.
4. Leader of the pro-Japanese movement, Dai Viet. See Appendix II.
5. I had cautioned Majors Davis and Thomas that the area was under Viet Minh control and French personnel would be unwelcome, but Thomas was being counseled by the French in the field that only they could be trusted to fight the Japanese, that the "Annamite" would only cache any arms supplied them for a confrontation with the French and, furthermore, that the travel time from Ch'ing-Hsi to the interior was being grossly exaggerated, etc.
6. These men were under the command of General Chu Van Tan, leader of the "Army for National Salvation" (AFNS). See Appendix II. Tan's mission was to provide security cover for the "Deer" team while it operated with the Viet Minh.
7. OSS: After Action Report no. 1, dated 17 July 1945 (Kim Lung, Tonkin); received at Kunming 27 July 1945; from "Deer" to "Chow"; part II, "The Reception." (CIAC)
8. A village 16 miles SW of Thai Nguyen and 28 miles NW of Hanoi.
9. DOS: Telegram no. 1448 (sent via Naval Radio), dated 26 March 1945; subject, "Transmittal of translated text of declaration published in the *Journal Officiel de la République Française, Ordonnances et Decrét*, 25 March 1945"; from Ambassador Caffery, Paris, to SecState. (CIAC) It was a broad noncommittal declaration on the future of Indochina issued by the Ministry of Colonies on 24 March 1945, based on the premise that after the war the "five countries which make up the Indochinese federation" (Tonkin, Annam, Cochinchina, Cambodia, and Laos) would be returned to France and form with France and the other members of the commonwealth a "*Franunion*." The declaration made no mention of independence but outlined a series of "reforms" and promised Indochina a "special place in the organization of the *Communante Française*" (French Commonwealth).

14: Historic Decisions

1. General Charles de Gaulle, Head of the Provisional Government of the French Republic. See Appendix II.

2. Jean Sainteny, *Histoire d'une Paix Manquée—Indochine 1945–1947*, p. 59; hereafter *Histoire*.
3. Babelsburg, Germany, about 12 miles SW of the city between Berlin and Potsdam.
4. In May 1941 the Comintern representative, Ho Chi Minh, then traveling under the pseudonym "Old Thu," presided over the 8th plenum of the Party Central Committee at Pac Bo which founded the Viet Nam Doc Lap Dong Minh (Viet Nam Independence League) or Viet Minh, for short. See Appendix III.
5. A system of forced labor in which male villagers were conscripted by local mandarins and turned over to plantation owners, mine operators, and public works contractors. Usually indentured for a period of three years, these laborers worked under conditions akin to slavery: under constant armed guards, the food minimal, housing conditions intolerable, and medical care grossly inadequate.
6. The Committee consisted of Party Secretary General Truong Chinh (chairman), Vo Nguyen Giap, Tran Dang Ninh, Le Thanh Nghi, and Chu Van Tan.
7. "Tien Quan Ca" (Marching to the Front).
8. The Standing Committee was composed of Ho Chi Minh, Tran Huy Lieu, Pham Van Dong, Nguyen Luong Bang, and Duong Duc Hien.
9. Nguyen Khac Vien, *The Long Resistance (1858–1975)*, p. 100.
10. *Our President Ho Chi Minh*, p. 124.
11. OSS: "Report of DEER Mission"; dated 17 September 1945, from A. K. Thomas to Chief, SO Branch, OSS-CT; sec. VIII, p. 10. (CIAC)

15: Unscheduled Peace

1. DOS: Telegram no. 1348 (via U.S. Army Signal Corps), dated 13 August 1945; subject, "Use of French Troops for Occupancy of French Indo-China"; from Ambassador Hurley to SecState and AMEMBASSY, Paris. (CIAC)
2. Ibid., p. 3.
3. DOS: Telegram no. 1257 (via U.S. Army Signal Corps), dated 15 August 1945; subject, "Instructions Japanese Surrender in Indochina"; from SecState Byrnes to AMEMBASSY, Chungking. (CIAC)
4. Copies of Telegram no. 1257 were also sent to the American Ambassadors in Paris and London with the notation, "Ambassadors Winant [London] and Hurley are being instructed to support any representations which their French colleagues may make to this end."
5. DOS: Directive by President Truman to the Supreme Commander for the Allied Powers in Japan (MacArthur), dated 15 August 1945. *Source*: FRUS (1945), 7:530.
6. The British claim of not having seen GO No. 1 was in conflict with Prime Minister Attlee's note no. 6 of 18 August 1945, in which he thanked President Truman for his "personal and Top Secret telegram No. 4, containing general order number one . . . ." *Note*: Truman's telegram no. 4 was not found in the Department of State's files, but Telegram No. 6935, 16 August 1945, 6 P.M., to Ambassador Winant in London stated, "General Order No. 1, was sent out from Washington last nite [15th] by the White House directed for delivery to Prime Minister." (740.00119 PW/8-1645). *Source*: FRUS (1945), 7:504.
7. FRUS (1945), 7:511.
8. Each team included an agent who had been in contact with certain prison

camps, a Japanese-English interpreter, a radio operator, a doctor or paramedic, and support personnel from SI and SO Branches of OSS.

9. French plans had anticipated a French reentry into Indochina in late 1946 at the earliest to mid-1947 at the latest.

10. OSS: Radio Msg no. 1740 (WAY–2189, WLUP–587, JHKE–790), Hqrs OSS-CT, dated 18 August 1945, from Helliwell to 109 (Donovan) et al. at Washington, Chungking, and Kandy, p. 5. (CIAC)

11. Member of the Kunming Committee; owner of the Quang Lac restaurant and tailor shop in Kunming.

12. Prime Minister in the pro-Japanese administration of Bao Dai's government following the March coup.

PART THREE: HANOI

16: Uninvited Guests

1. An auxiliary field 75 miles NE of Kunming.

2. First Lieutenant (later Captain) Ramon Grelecki; Second Lieutenant Russell A. Feeback; 1st Sergeant Frederick Altman; T/Sergeant Alvin Toso; Staff Sergeant Guillaume M. Trequier; Sergeant Robert C. Roos, III; T/5 August O. Aubrey; T/5 Raymond J. Barriault; T/5 Helmer A. Lund; T/3 Eide; and Privates Henry F. Rodzlewicz and Gerard A. Lariviere.

3. Lieutenants Louis Fouchier-Magnan and François Missoffe, Communications officer Lieutenant Casnat, and civilian agent Roland Petris.

4. The others were Feeback, Aubrey, and Eide.

5. An alias used by the POW camp leader working with the British Army Aid Group (BAAG).

6. Commanding General, 38th Imperial Japanese Army. See Appendix II.

7. A former French military cantonment containing a large prison area, several hospital wards, and barracks. In 1945 it was manned by the Japanese military command in Hanoi to house French POWs, criminal inmates, and political internees.

8. Indochinese security troops (police) organized by the pro-Japanese administration. A vast majority of the Bao An were Viet Minh sympathizers and agents for the Armed Propaganda Group in Hanoi.

9. The official residence of the Khâm-sai (Bao Dai's Viceroy for Tonkin). Under French rule it had been the residence of the French Résident Supérieur (Governor of Tonkin). Later renamed by the Viet Minh Bac Bo Palace or Palace of Independence. After 2 September 1945 Ho Chi Minh made this building his place of work and residence.

17: Our Second Day in Hanoi

1. Then Chairman of the Hanoi Revolutionary Military Committee. See Appendix II.

2. After the 9 March coup the Japanese had installed Bao Dai as head of an "independent Viet Nam." The Japanese rejected the Emperor's first choice for prime minister, Ngo Dinh Diem, and insisted on the appointment of Professor Tran Trong Kim, a distinguished but aged man of letters. The new cabinet was made up largely of elderly mandarins, men of wealth and position, generally associated with Japanese interests, and interspersed with pro-French sympathizers.

3. The 15 August meeting took place in the village of Van Phuc, just outside Hanoi. Present were Le Liem, Dong Kim Giang, Nguyen Khang, Tran Tu Binh, and Nguyen Van Loc.

4. A "punitive squad" selected from members of the National Salvation Association (Union), under the direct supervision of the Regional Committee. The "Honor Group" was charged with the elimination when necessary of spies, traitors, and enemies of the Viet Minh.

5. Shortened from Dai Viet Quoc Dan Dang (The Great Viet Nam Nationalist Party). See Appendix III.

6. Shortened from Viet Nam Phuc Quoc Dong Minh Hoi (Viet Nam Restoration League). See Appendix III.

7. The committee consisted of Chairman Nguyen Khang; Le Trung Nghia, the delegate who had welcomed us to Hanoi the day before; M. Quyet, Secretary of the Hanoi City Committee; and a M. Than. They established their headquarters at 101 Boulevard Gambetta in the palatial home of a pro-French mandarin "temporarily" out of town.

8. Under the joint command of Le Trung Nghia and Nguyen Khang.

9. Under the command of Quyet, Secretary of the Hanoi City Committee.

10. Member of the Hanoi Revolutionary Military Committee.

11. These installations not taken under Viet Minh control were probably all occupied by Japanese forces. Even when Sainteny and his party took up quarters in the Governor General's Palace, a considerable part of it was still in use by the Japanese.

12. The note was from the Southern Army Headquarters at Saigon, under the command of Field Marshal Count Hisaichi Terauchi. See Appendix II.

13. My notes failed to record the reporter's name.

14. Broadcast by Radio Tokyo on 15 August.

15. OSS: Broadcast over *Domei* in English, 17 August 1945; FIR no. 16, item 10. (CIAC)

16. Comité de Salut National, composed of intellectuals, students, professionals, workers, and ethnic minorities. (Not to be confused with the Viet Minh National Salvation Association.)

18: Calls and Callers

1. OSS: Radio Msg no. 11 (M/C-11), dated 24 August 1945, from Hanoi, Patti for Sainteny, to INDIV for FMM, info Alessandri. (CIAC)

2. Captains Roger P. Bernique and Aaron Bank, Sergeants Robert H. Knollin and Maisonpierre, T/5s William Chidekel and Frank I. Seigel, Corporal Otto Dobrovolny, and two X-2 agents.

3. With me were my AGAS agent and the Japanese escort officer whom I knew only as "the captain."

4. I speculated whether this Kamiya might be the Kamiya who had collaborated with Blanchard in Haiphong and was described in Kunming as a former liaison officer between the Japanese Military Headquarters in Hanoi and the Decoux administration. Later investigations confirmed that Kamiya was not a member of the hospital staff but head of the Japanese Army Liaison Section in Hanoi.

5. Oshima had been the head of the Japanese Gendarmerie at the infamous Shell Building in Hanoi from February 1944 to 15 August 1945.

6. The USSR entered the war against Japan on 10 August 1945.
7. See Appendix II.

19: The Tale of Two Cities

1. Throughout Vietnamese history the media in all forms had been subject to varying degrees of censorship and editorial guidance. This had been particularly true during the Decoux regime and the Japanese occupation.
2. Vu Van Minh, a member of the Hanoi City Committee and head of the Provisional Government's Office of Information.
3. Civilian political warfare specialist assigned to our MO Section.
4. See Appendix III.
5. See Appendix III.
6. Nguyen Van Sam, a co-founder of the pro-Japanese Viet Nam Quoc Gia Doc Lap Dang (Viet Nam National Independence Party). See Appendix III.
7. Mat Tran Quoc Gia Thong Nhut (United National Front), established on 14 August 1945, composed of the following organizations: (1) Viet Nam Quoc Gia Doc Lap Dang (Viet Nam National Independence Party); (2) Thanh Nien Tien Phong (Advance Guard Youth); (3) Nhom Tri Thuc (Intellectual Group); (4) Lien Doan Cong Chuc (Functionaries Federation); (5) Tinh Do Cu Si (Buddhist League); (6) Phat Giao Hoa Hao (Hoa Hao Buddhist Sect); (7) Tranh Dau ("The Struggle" group); and (8) Doan The Cao Dai (Cao Dai League). The Front was strongly influenced by Trotskyist doctrine and excluded the Viet Minh communists.
8. The bulk of this arsenal went to the Cao Dai and Hoa Hao "armies" and was used later against the French, the British, the Viet Minh, and later perhaps even against Ngo Dinh Diem.
9. OSS: *Domei* in English, 21 August 1945; FIR no. 16, item 8. (CIAC)
10. General Association of Students. They met in Hanoi at the *cité universitaire* under the direction of Phan Anh and Ta Quang Buu, former leaders of the youth movement during the post-coup regime of Admiral Decoux.
11. A telephone call from Nguyen Khang in Hanoi had alerted Giau that an "Allied Armistice Commission" was expected momentarily in Hanoi. The so-called "Commission" was, of course, our OSS Mercy Team.
12. OSS: only Giau and his close associates knew of Bao Dai's action until he announced it at the meeting. The Japanese had suppressed the news for six days, releasing it for the first time on 28 August. *Source: Domei* in English, 28 August 1945; FIR no. 16, item 11. (CIAC)
13. The Thanh Nien Tien Phong (Advance Guard Youth) was one of two major armed forces in the United National Front, the other being the Caodaist "army." See Appendix III.
14. Also known as the "Provisional Executive Committee of the Southern Viet Nam Republic." Its members were Tran Van Giau, President (Communist); Dr. Pham Ngoc Thach, Commissioner for Foreign Affairs (Viet Minh); Nguyen Van Tao, Secretary General and Commissioner for the Interior (Communist); Huynh Van Tieng, Chief for Propaganda (Democrat); Duong Bach Mai, Commissioner for Political and Administrative Affairs for the East (Communist); Nguyen Van Tay, Commissioner for Political and Administrative Affairs for the West (Communist); Hoang Don Van, Commissioner for Labor (Viet Minh); Pham Van Bach, member (Independent); Ngo Tan Nhong, member (National In-

dependence Party); and Huynh Thi Oanh, a woman member (Independent). Source: OSS and PAOVN-OIR Rpt. no. 3708, 1 October 1949. (CIAC)

15. The Viet Minh demand for abdication, telegraphed on 23 August from Hanoi, and Bao Dai's message to the Viet Minh, inviting it to form a new cabinet and sent from Hué on 22 August, crossed in transmission without coordination.

16. Pham Khac Hoe.

17. On 25 August the Party Central Committee appointed Tran Huy Lieu (vice-president of the National Liberation Committee) to head the Provisional Government's delegation to receive the Emperor's abdication. The other members of the delegation were Nguyen Luong Bang and Cu Huy Can. On the same day Bao Dai, in the privacy of his imperial council, executed the Act of Abdication at the Palais Kien-trung. The Hanoi delegation arrived at Hué on 28 August and was received by Bao Dai in private audience—and perhaps for the first time in Vietnamese history an Emperor of Annam shook hands with one of his commoners. On the following day in the imperial throne room Bao Dai handed the Act of Abdication to Tran Huy Lieu. Late the next afternoon (30 August) Bao Dai appeared in ceremonial robes before a huge crowd assembled at the Ngo Mon gate (the palace's southern gate) and read the Act of Abdication. The imperial colors were struck and the red flag of the new Viet Nam hoisted. The ceremony was concluded by handing over to the delegation the symbols of royal authority—the gold seal and the gold sword with the gem-encrusted handle—while the crowds shouted praise to citizen Vinh Thuy, lately the Emperor. Source: Nguyen Luong Bang, as related to me in September 1945 at Hanoi.

18. As recently as September 1977 General Tran Van Don, reportedly one of the group responsible for the fall of the Ngo Dinh Diem regime in November 1963, in an interview with BBC Radio stated, "We knew at that time that this organization [the Viet Minh] was backed by the Americans." Later in the same interview General Don added, ". . . even Bao Dai . . . , when he knew that this group led by Ho Chi Minh was backed by the Americans, said that is the best way to get independence. And he resigned very fast. He said there is nothing to say against these people [the Viet Minh] because they are fighting for independence and the Americans are supporting these people." In a parallel BBC interview in 1977, General Edward G. Lansdale (who was in north Viet Nam for a brief period in 1954 on behalf of the CIA) had this to say about the influence of American activities in 1945 under my direction: "The people up in the North whom I talked to . . . were positive that the Ho Chi Minh group were alright because of US support and as such could be trusted entirely. . . ." Source: Michael Charlton and Anthony Moncrieff, *Many Reasons Why—the American involvement in Vietnam*, p. 15.

19. Derived from Confucius's philosophy and loosely interpreted as fate, destiny, or divine decree. To the Confucian it meant the celestial order or will of Heaven. The Vietnamese called it *Tiên minh*. Hence, the disintegration of French rule, the Japanese capitulation, the Emperor's abdication, and Ho's assumption of power were signs from above—the will of Heaven.

20. Commissioner of the French Republic for Cochinchina. Clandestinely parachuted in the environs of Saigon on the night of 22–23 August by the SLFEO/Calcutta.

21. OSS: Reuters, 20 August 1945; FIR no. 16, item 7. (CIAC)

22. Bao Dai's regime was foundering, de Gaulle was in Washington meeting with President Truman, and Chiang Kai-shek was preparing to occupy Indochina under the terms of the Potsdam Agreement.
23. OSS: Reuters, *Statesman*, 23 August 1945; FIR no. 16, item 1. (CIAC)
24. OSS: Associated Press, 24 August 1945; FIR no. 16, item 6. (CIAC)
25. OSS: Vice Admiral Georges Louis Marie Thierry d'Argenlieu. See Appendix II.
26. General Jacques Philippe (Leclerc) de Hauteclocque, Commander of French Forces in the Far East. See Appendix II.
27. OSS: Associated Press, 24 August 1945; FIR no. 16, item 6. (CIAC)
28. Prince Fumimaro Konoye (1891-1945), three-time prime minister of Japan and considered by many to have opposed Japan's entering the war against the United States.

20: A Busy Sunday

1. See Appendix II.
2. Secretary of the Hanoi ICP.
3. I observed the *politesse* despite the fact that we owed nothing to the Vietnamese for our position. We were housed appropriately by the Japanese military authorities regardless of any Vietnamese or French political situation.
4. When the Japanese assigned the Maison Gautier to our OSS team, they had selected Phat from among the ranks of the Bao An to act as informer for the kempeitai. After clearing with the Hanoi party cell, Phat undertook the Japanese assignment, but he was not given any instruction or contacted further by the kempeitai.
5. I later learned that the house was located on Hang Ngang Street in the NW section.
6. See Appendix II.
7. Alluding to the declaration of the Ministry of Colonies described in chap. 13, n. 9, above.

21: French Diplomacy at Low Tide

1. OSS: Radio Msg no. 027 (Reg. no. 626), dated 27 August 1945, from Hanoi (XUF), Patti, to INDIV for Heppner. And reply Radio Msg no. 16 (M/C 5651) and WLUP (Chungking) 958, dated 28 August 1945, from INDIV to Patti, info Chungking. (CIAC)

22: Moving toward Surrender

1. Chinese city approximately 100 air miles S of Kunming, the location of General Lu Han's First War Area Command.
2. OSS: Radio Msg no. 5, dated 27 August 1945, from PARROT, K'ai-yuan, to INDIV and Patti. (CIAC)
3. OSS: Radio Msg no. 8, dated 28 August 1945, from PARROT, K'ai-yuan, to Patti. (CIAC)
4. The first withdrawal on 10 August had been for 21 million piastres; the second a few days later for 29 million piastres; and a third demand for 30 million piastres was partially honored (10 million piastres) a few days prior to my discussion with Tsuchihashi.
5. On rue Paul Bert.
6. It was in fact an authentic message from Sainteny to the SLFEO/Calcutta. Several years later Sainteny gave the full text in his *Histoire*, p. 102, n. 7.
7. OSS: The delegation consisted of Lieut. Colonel Sakai, staff officers Major

Miyoshi and Captain Takahashi, and Mr. Imai, interpreter. Japanese-English. *Source:* OSS Radio Msg no. 39 (M/C 39), dated 29 August 1945, from Patti, Hanoi, to INDIV for relay to PARROT.

8. A great difficulty in addition to securing a plane was finding paint of the specified shade of green for its markings.

9. OSS: Radio Msg no. 30 (M/C-31), dated 31 August 1945, from COMGEN-CCC to Patti. (CIAC)

10. Governor Lung Yün's popular appellation.

11. Lu Han's forces comprised the Yunnanese 60th and 93d Armies, the KMT troops from Kwangsi, the 53d and 62d Armies, and three separate reinforced units, the 23d, 39th, and 93d Divisions, plus the Honorable 2d Division, an element of the 52d Army (IX Group Army).

12. See Appendix II.

13. It was common knowledge while I was in China that in 1944-45 the governor's highjacking operations netted him several thousand American jeeps and ten times that number of tires. The tires were sold to owners of small carts. In all my experience worldwide I never heard quieter carts.

14. As later attested to by the Commander of the Japanese "China Expeditionary Army," General Yasuji Okamura, he and Governor Lung Yün corresponded throughout the war. *Sources:* (1) History of IBT, 1:191-92; (2) Japanese Officers' Comments, Okamura, p. 6, OCMH; and (3) Romanus and Sunderland, *Time Runs Out in CBI,* p. 141, OCMH.

15. Formerly commander of the V Group Army (Reserve) under Stilwell in the Burma-India campaign. Appointed in the fall of 1945 to head the Chinese Reserve Command in Kunming.

16. Vice Minister of Foreign Affairs of the KMT government.

17. OSS: Radio Msg no. XUF-23 and BUD-11 (M/C 5870), dated 29 August 1945, from INDIV to Patti and PARROT. (CIAC)

18. The troops involved in the border crossing were not "Yunnanese" but elements of the 62d Kwangsi Army, formerly of Chang Fa-kwei's II Army Group Command of the Fourth War Area, now reassigned to Lu Han's occupation force under the political control of General Hsiao Wen.

23: Conversations

1. The other members of the Provisional Government:

Minister of Propaganda	Tran Huy Lieu (Communist)
Minister of National Defense	Chu Van Tan (Viet Minh)
Minister of Youth	Duong Duc Hien (Democrat)
Minister of National Economy	Nguyen Manh Ha (Catholic)
Minister of Social Welfare	Nguyen Van To (non-party)
Minister of Justice	Vu Trong Khanh (Democrat)
Minister of Health	Pham Ngoc Thach (Viet Minh)
Minister of Public Works and Communications	Dao Trong Kim (non-party)
Minister of Labor	Le Van Hien (Communist-Viet Minh)
Minister of National Education	Vu Dinh Hoe (Democrat)
Minister without portfolio	Cu Huy Can (Democrat)
Minister without portfolio	Nguyen Van Xuan (Viet Minh)

Source: PAOVN, OIR Rpt. no. 3708, 1 October 1949. (CIAC)

2. See Appendix II.
3. Ho's reference was to Chiang Kai-shek's address of 24 August before the joint meeting of the Supreme National Defense Council and the Standing Committee of the KMT. *Source:* Chinese Overseas Service in Mandarin, 25 August, 0930 G.M.T.; FIR no. 16, item 4. See *Statements and Speeches of Chiang Kai-shek,* p.12.

24: Puzzles

1. OSS: Radio Msg no. XUF-25 (M/C-5958), dated 30 August 1945, from INDIV & Swift, OSS-CT, to Patti. (CIAC)
2. OSS: Ibid.
3. Jean Sainteny, *Histoire,* p. 102, n. 7.
4. OSS: Radio Msg no. 47 (OUT-6021), dated 30 August 1945, from Patti for Provisional Government, Hanoi, to Heppner for Hurley, info INDIV. (CIAC)
5. Socialist Party leader and close personal friend of Ho Chi Minh. See Appendix II.
6. The Viet Nam Quoc Dan Dang (Viet Nam Nationalist Party), the most significant noncommunist nationalist group. See Appendix III.
7. The Chiang statement had been published in Kunming by the Central Daily News (*Chung Yang Jih Pao*) of 25 August 1945.
8. Leader of the Dai Viet. See Appendix II.
9. OSS: Radio Msg no. 52 (M/C-52), dated 31 August 1945, from Vo Nguyen Giap (alias Van), Hanoi, to AGAS for Mr. Tam, Kunming. (CIAC)

25: On the Eve of Independence

1. OSS: Radio Msg no. 34 (M/C-37), dated 1 September 1945, from INDIV, Hqrs OSS-CT, to Patti, Hanoi. (CIAC)
2. Stephen L. Nordlinger, Colonel, G-5 Section, CT Staff, headed an American humanitarian and welfare unit to assist Allied POWs in Hanoi.
3. OSS: Radio Msg no. 54 (M/C-6114), dated 31 August 1945, from Nordlinger, thru Patti, Hanoi, to INDIV for Aurand and G-5. (CIAC)
4. Ta Quang Buu, a political independent. See Appendix II.
5. OSS; Msg no. 73 (M/C-73), dated 2 September 1945, from Patti, Hanoi, to INDIV. (CIAC).
6. Three or four gentlemen whose names I cannot recall.
7. Alluding to OSS-Chungking's efforts in 1943–44 to have him released from Chang Fa-kwei's jails.
8. Referring to the UN Conference on International Organization which met from 25 April to 26 June 1945.
9. The popular legend, repeated many times by authors and historians (P. Devillers, B. Fall et al.) that either Ho or I ever discussed postwar economic concessions or arrangements in exchange for an American guarantee of Viet Nam's independence, beyond the scope of this and similar conversations, is pure fiction, invented by French writers such as Pierre-Maurice Dessinger in *Le Monde,* 14 April 1947, pp. 1 and 2.
10. OSS: Msg no. 60 (M/C-61), p. 2, dated 1 September 1945, from Patti, Hanoi, to INDIV. (CIAC)

26: Independence Day

1. Roman Catholics in north Viet Nam numbered roughly over one million, about ten percent of the population. The hallmark of Ho's popular following was his

appeal to all Vietnamese minorities, including the various religious groups. It was rumored in 1945 that in deference to the Roman Catholic Vietnamese, Ho had appointed a prominent Catholic layman, Nguyen Manh Ha, as Minister of Economy in his first cabinet. The Catholic Church in Viet Nam supported Ho's nationalism until December 1946 when the fight against the French began. Prior to that, in March 1946, Monsignor Le Huu Tu, the Apostolic Vicar of Phat Diem, was made Supreme Advisor to Ho's government in lieu of Bao Dai who had fled to Hong Kong.

2. Estimated to have been between five and six hundred thousand, as determined from U.S. aerial photographs taken that day.

3. DOS: Disp. no. 21, dated 27 September 1945; subject, "Situation in Indochina; Activities of the Viet Minh League"; from American Consul P. D. Sprouse, Kunming, to DOS and AMEMBASSY, Chungking. (CIAC)

4. This is a literal translation of Ho's words. It may be at variance with that of many historians who were not present to hear Ho's delivery, but it is the agreed translation of Vietnamese linguists on my staff and that of English-educated Vietnamese translators present on that occasion.

5. Ibid.

6. Ibid.

7. This may have had reference to the OSS-AGAS team under Lieutenant Emile R. Counasse, USA, which landed on 2 September at the Saigon airport to liberate Allied POWs, among whom were 214 Americans.

8. In this account the term "resistance" will be retained as used by the French. However, it should be noted that with the cessation of hostilities with Japan, the French action became a counter-insurgency movement aimed at overthrowing the Vietnamese Provisional Government.

9. OSS: Msg no. 63 (M/C-22956), dated 2 September 1945, from Patti to INDIV, Relay to Gallagher for info; and Msg no. 64 (M/C-22934), dated 2 September 1945, from Patti to PARROT, info INDIV. (CIAC)

27: Aftermath to Black Sunday

1. Field Marshal Count Hisaichi Terauchi, Commander in Chief, Japanese Southern army. See Appendix II.

2. *Lien Khu Binh Xuyen (Binh Xuyen)*. See Appendix III.

3. Minister of Defense in the Provisional Government. See Appendix II.

4. These were published several weeks later in the *Viet Nam Dan-Quoc Cong-Bao*, shortened to *Cong-Bao*, a type of official register or gazette.

5. OSS: Radio Msg no. 39 (M/C-44) dated 3 September 1945, from Gallagher, First War Area Command, to Patti, Hanoi. (CIAC)

6. The Franco-Sino agreement of 28 February 1946 called for the complete withdrawal of Chinese forces no later than 31 March 1946, but the Chinese failed to meet the deadline. The last Chinese unit (Honorable 2d Division) left Haiphong in October 1946.

7. OSS: Msg "unnumbered" (M/C-76), dated 3 September 1945, from Patti to Gallagher, Kunming. (CIAC)

8. Officers on this flight included Lieut. Colonel J. H. Stodter, staff intelligence; Major Stevens, administrative officer; and Lieutenant Reginald Unger, aide-de-camp to General Gallagher.

9. OSS: Radio Msg no. 76 (M/C-80), dated 3 September 1945, from Stevens to CG-1, Kunming, for relay to K'ai-yuan. (CIAC)
10. An old-line communist. See Appendix II.

28: In Search of the Truman Policy

1. Lieut. General Jonathan M. Wainwright. See Appendix II.
2. Lieutenant (later Captain) John M. Birch. See Appendix II.
3. OSS officer in charge of the Chinese Commando Training Center at Kunming.
4. James Clement Dunn, Assistant Secretary of State.
5. President Truman had met with General de Gaulle at the White House on 22 August 1945 and later told Mme. Chiang that de Gaulle had assured him that steps would be taken immediately by France to give Indochina its independence. The President also indicated to Mme. Chiang that there had been "no discussion of a trusteeship" as far as he was concerned.
6. See chap. 12, p. 119; also FRUS (1945), 7:113–114, 545, 546.
7. Brig. General George Olmsted, AC of S, G-5, U.S. Army Headquarters in China (representing Wedemeyer's headquarters at the conference).
8. John Hall Paxton, Second Secretary, American Embassy at Chungking (representing the Embassy at the conference).
9. See chap. 12, n. 12, above.
10. Chinese Vice Minister for Foreign Affairs.
11. Max W. Bishop, Secretary of the American Commission at New Delhi.
12. Walter S. Robertson, Minister-Counselor of Economic Affairs, American Embassy in China.
13. Colonel William P. Davis, Jr., Deputy Strategic Services Officer, OSS-CT.
14. Commanding General, US, SOS-CT.
15. Chief of the Delegation to Japan of the International Committee of the Red Cross.
16. Special Representative of the American Red Cross at Geneva.
17. Swiss Minister in Japan.
18. Since 7 May 1945, first in Lisbon and then in ensuing months in Bern, Stockholm, and Wiesbaden.
19. Maberly Esler Dening (later Sir Esler), British Political Adviser to the Supreme Allied Commander, SEAC (Mountbatten); also Chief of SOE operations in SEAC.
20. Maj. General Douglas David Gracey. See chap. 32 and Appendix II.
21. See Appendix II.
22. The advance party consisted of First Lieutenant Emile R. Counasse, Sergeants Nardella and Hejna, and Corporal Paul.
23. The four members of Dewey's party were Captain (later Major) Herbert J. Bluechel, Captain Leslie S. Frost, Lieutenant Konrad Bekker, and T/5 George Wickes. On the following day three more members of Dewey's team arrived: Captains Frank M. White, Joseph R. Coolidge, and Herbert W. Varner.

24.

	Camp POET (Saigon)	Camp 5-E	Totals
British	920	1,394	2,314
Dutch	592	1,164	1,756
Australian	164	101	265
American	5	209	214
	1,681	2,868	4,549

25. | | |
|---|---|
| 131st FA, 36 Division | 120 |
| Cruiser *Houston* | 86 |
| VPB-117 | 3 |
| VPB-25 | 2 |
| 308th Bomber Group | 3 |
| Total Americans | 214 |

29: No One's Listening

1. They left Chungking on 19 September 1945.
2. Maj. General Robert B. McClure, Chief of Staff to the Commanding General, U.S. Army in the China Theater (Wedemeyer); and Deputy to the Generalissimo's Chief of Staff (Ho Ying-chin).
3. Also present at this meeting were Dr. Pham Ngoc Thach and Nguyen Van Tao.
4. International Communist League, the left-wing faction of the Trotskyist party. See Appendix III.
5. Lieut. Colonel Cass (British) had landed at Saigon on 6 September with a small advance unit of Indian troops of the 20th Indian Division and Force 136 with a handful of SLFEO agents.
6. FRUS (1945), 7:543.
7. Assistance in the preparation of this brief was provided by OSS's R&A and members of the American Embassy, Chungking.
8. The Economic Section was provided by the Economic Counselor of our Embassy at Chungking.
9. Formerly the Secret Intelligence Division (SI).

30: Warlords and Carpetbaggers

1. General Vo Nguyen Giap, *Unforgettable Days*, pp. 33–34.
2. Marcel Gouin, Professor of Architecture at the U. of Hanoi.
3. A French attempt to reestablish prewar colonial status over Syria (contrary to Allied assurances given earlier to the Syrian government) was frustrated by Churchill's ultimatum to de Gaulle ordering his troops withdrawn from the Middle East and sent to fight with the Allied forces in North Africa and Italy.
4. Rev. André Lebrun, a Trappist priest, had been active in the Résistance until he was transferred to Saigon in January 1945. He made his way to Hanoi in February to join his radical friends in the youth movement for independence, using his cover as chaplain at the Citadel to help the Vietnamese during the insurrection.
5. Charles de Gaulle, *War Memoirs: Salvation, 1944–1946*, p. 187. Italics added.
6. Jean Sainteny, *Histoire*, pp. 59–60. Philippe Devillers, *Histoire du Viêt-Nam*, pp. 149–50. Bernard B. Fall, *The Two Viet Nams*, p. 55.
7. Vo Nguyen Giap, *Unforgettable Months and Years*, translated and with an Introduction by Mai Van Elliott, p. 23.
8. OSS: Radio Msg no. 26 (M/C-6729), dated 7 September 1945, from Patti for Chairman of Committee of Overseas Chinese in Hanoi to PARROT, thru Gallagher, for General Lou [sic] Han. (CIAC)
9. André Evard, informer for OSS in Hanoi, of undetermined loyalty, had been at one time a United Press correspondent and also assistant manager for Air France in Hanoi.
10. The colonel had successfully evaded the Japanese dragnet following the 9

March coup and had continued to maintain contact with the French underground. Mme. Cavalin, his wife, also collaborated with Mordant's resistance under the direction of Mme. Sarraut (sister-in-law of Sainteny) and in August had unsuccessfully attempted to penetrate the OSS Mission in Hanoi. (OSS: Radio Msg no. 94 [M/C-98], dated 10 September 1945, from Patti to INDIV.) (CIAC)

11. Jean Laurent, Director-General of the Bank of Indochina.
12. OSS: Radio Msg no. 98 (M/C-102), dated 11 September 1945, from Patti to INDIV for relay to Chungking and Washington. (CIAC)
13. Formerly the Foreign Affairs Section, Fourth War Area.
14. Actually the cost of occupation was levied on the French by the Chinese government's extracting monthly advances (40 million piastres) from the Bank of Indochina "for urgent military needs." The account was to be liquidated by "future Sino-Franco negotiations."
15. The elections ultimately took place on 6 January 1946. The Dong Minh Hoi won twenty seats out of three hundred in the new government, and Nguyen Hai Than was "elected" Vice-President in the Provisional Coalition Government.
16. OSS: Radio Msg no. 98 (see n. 12, above).
17. Lu Han's arrival has been reported variously on dates from 9 to 18 September. The exact date is as given, officially reported in OSS: Radio Msg no. 119 (M/C-123), dated 14 September 1945, from Patti to INDIV. (CIAC)
18. Various writers have fixed the number of Chinese troops in Lu Han's army of occupation at 180,000 men. This high figure represents the approximate total that transited during the period of occupation (September 1945 to October 1946). The Chinese government claimed a figure of 150,000 to account for the cost of the occupation to be charged to the French. Actually there were never more than 50,000 troops in garrison at any one time.
19. OSS: Radio Msg no. 111 (M/C-115), dated 13 September 1945, from Patti to INDIV and Washington. (CIAC)
20. OSS: Radio Msg no. 140 (M/C-144), dated 17 September 1945, from Patti to INDIV. (CIAC)
21. Its membership consisted of Shao Pai-ch'ang (Military Administration), Ling Ch'i-han (Foreign Affairs), Chu Hseieh (Finance), Chuang Chih-huan (Economy), Cheng Fang-heng (Communications), Ma Ts'an-yung (Food), and Hsing Shen-chow (Kuomintang).
22. OSS: Msg no. 140 (see n. 20, above).
23. Truong Boi Cong fled to China in the wake of the 1930 Yen Bay uprisings and joined the VNQDD faction at Nanking. See Appendix II.

31: DRV: Postpartum Problems

1. FRUS (1945), 7:543. Telegram from Hurley to SecState, dated 31 August 1945, 5 P.M.
2. See chap. 29, pp. 276–77, above.
3. Paramilitary units adept at kidnapping, torture, and assassination.
4. One battalion of the 16th Cav. Regiment, 20th Indian Division (Gurkhas).
5. One company of the 5th Régiment d'Infanterie Coloniale (Colonial Infantry Regiment). This was a reconstituted element of the original French forces assembled and trained in Africa for General Blaizot's Corps Légèr d'Intervention (CLI) for the reconquest of Indochina. See chap. 3, p. 20.

6. The Dutch, Australian, and British POWs were being repatriated. The American POWs had already been evacuated by Dewey's team.

7. OSS: Radio Msg no. 105 (M/C-109), dated 12 September 1945, from Patti to INDIV. (CIAC)

8. Ibid.

9. Pham Van Dong told me that on 3 September the new government had found less than 1.5 million piastres in the national treasury.

10. OSS: Radio Msg no. 99 (M/C-103), dated 12 September 1945, from Nordlinger to CG-SOS-CT for Mayer. (CIAC)

11. OSS: Radio Msg no. 80 (M/C-86), dated 13 September 1945, from Mayer to Nordlinger. (CIAC)

12. Masumi Yaghiou, son of the president of the Bank of Formosa, had been entrusted by the Japanese government to oversee and control all financial transactions of the industrial-commercial complex in Indochina associated with clandestine operations. He was the sole authorized liaison between the civil and military segments of the apparatus and high-level Japanese officials everywhere.

13. Also spelled Matsushita. See Appendix II.

14. In 1944 the Chinese government cracked down and decreed that anyone found with "excessive amounts of copper coins on their persons or of textiles not obtainable in China" would be summarily executed. Postwar interrogation of Japanese officers of the Dainan Koosi revealed that a considerable amount of the traffic in coins and textiles involved "certain warlords" in Yunnan, Kwangsi, and Kwangtung.

15. A nationwide political warfare center organized in Hanoi by Jean-Marie Yokoyama. The center ran a Japanese school system for children of Japanese families in Indochina and conducted courses in Japanese cultural and political philosophy for Vietnamese youths. It was also an agent-recruiting center for anti-French and anti-Viet Minh nationalists. The center worked in tandem with CICEI.

16. OSS: Radio Msg no. 111 (see chap. 30, n. 19, above).

17. A career diplomat, Yokoyama had been a Minister to Spain until recalled in 1939 for the Indochina post. His mission was to organize and direct espionage and political warfare operations and to act as counselor to the Imperial Court at Hué. His French Catholic mother and wife opened many doors for him in French circles in Saigon, Hué, and Hanoi. He collaborated with his industrial counterpart, Matusita. On 10 March 1945 Yokoyama went to the Kien Trung Palace to advise Emperor Bao Dai to collaborate with Japan in the Greater East Asia Co-Prosperity Sphere program and succeeded in getting Bao Dai to recognize the racist program while "saving face" by declaring Viet Nam "free of foreign rule" and his readiness to collaborate with the Japanese in consolidating Viet Nam's independence.

18. Komaki Omiya, Doichi Yamane, Komatsu, and, of course, Matusita.

19. Indian nationalist leader. See Appendix II.

20. Arrived in Indochina in 1939 under the sponsorship of Doichi Yamane, the former League of Nations delegate and member of the Japanese Secret Service. Komaki Omiya was appointed to the Board of Directors of a CICEI affiliate, the CIDIM. He collaborated for a brief period in 1942–43 with the Viet Minh in an effort to turn the Vietnamese against the white race but had little success because of the anti-Japanese sentiment in the Viet Minh.

21. A former newspaperman for the Japanese army paper, *Yomiuri*. He headed the popular culture aspects of the Centre Culturelle.
22. OSS: Radio Msg no. 160 (M/C-164), dated 20 September 1945, from Patti to Helliwell. (CIAC)

32: South of the 16th Parallel

1. Lieut. General (later Field Marshal) Sir William J. Slim, Commander-in-Chief, Allied Land Forces, Southeast Asia Command.
2. See chap. 6, p. 49 and n. 27, above.
3. Removed later in the day at British behest.
4. OSS: Radio Msg no. 111 (see Chap. 30, n. 19 above).
5. Ibid.
6. Member of the French resistance and an influential southern planter; had collaborated with the GBT in gathering Japanese intelligence for AGAS. He was the most outspoken member of the bloc against Vietnamese independence and was actively anti-Viet Minh.
7. OSS: Radio Msg no. 142 (M/C-146), dated 18 September 1945, from Patti to IN-DIV. (CIAC)
8. Since 6 September SEAC had authorized British, American, French, Dutch, and Indian correspondents to cover the occupation and related news in its area of jurisdiction.
9. OSS: Memorandum, File MLB-2739-A, dated 30 September 1945, from Branch Hqrs, OSS-Det 404, Saigon, to CO, OSS-Det 404, Hq., SEAC, APO 432. (CIAC)
10. A close associate of Leclerc and his advance man in Saigon. Buis had taken over the Sûreté and was in full charge of Vietnamese political intelligence under Cédile.
11. I have pieced together events following the twenty-third of September from spot reports received in Hanoi and Kunming from OSS-Saigon and OSS-Kandy, from information made available to me in Hanoi by the Viet Minh, and from newspaper accounts released in China. (CIAC)
12. (Later Major), OSS-SI attached to SEAC and Dewey's deputy in Saigon.
13. Captain Coolidge had been returning from Dalat with a number of Allied officers, including some French, and young Vietnamese women. Ten miles outside Saigon the convoy ran into a Viet Minh roadblock. The mixed group of officers, all speaking French belligerently, tried to dismantle it. Mistaking them for Frenchmen, the Vietnamese tried to stop them. A scuffle followed, shots were fired, and Coolidge was hit. He was hospitalized at the British 75th Field Ambulance Hospital, Saigon, with a severe neck wound and was later evacuated to the United States where he spent the next eight months in Army hospitals.
14. At the Villa Ferier, north of the city adjacent to an unused golf course.
15. Extracted from affidavit made by Major Bluechel on 13 October 1945. OSS Doc. no. MLB-2739-B. (CIAC)
16. Captain Frank M. White, OSS; T/5 George Wickes, OSS; Major François Verger, French army, attached to E Group, Saigon Control Commission; James McClincy and William Downs, both American war correspondents.
17. Extracted from affidavit made by Captain White on 13 October 1945. OSS Doc. no. MLB-2739-B. (CIAC)
18. Extracted from affidavit made by Major Bluechel on 13 October 1945. OSS Doc. no. MLB-2739-B. (CIAC)

19. Commanding Officer, OSS-SEAC.
20. OSS Report, Doc. no. MLB-2739-A, dated 30 September 1945, to CO, OSS Det. 404, Hqrs SEAC, APO 432. (CIAC)
21. Vice Admiral The Earl Mountbatten of Burma, *Post Surrender Tasks—Section E. Report to the CCS by the SAC-SEAC, 1943-1945*, p. 287.
22. The Rt. Hon. J. J. Lawson, Secretary of State for War.
23. Head of Leclerc's Deuxième Bureau (Intelligence).
24. Ho Chi Minh had ordered the Viet Minh to find Dewey's body so that he could return it to the American authorities. On 12 October 1945, in a continuing effort to find the body, leaflets offering a reward of five thousand piastres for the major's body were found by French troops. The body was never recovered.
25. Ho's personal representative to the Provisional Executive Committee for the Nam Bo. See Appendix II.
26. See chap. 29, p. 277.
27. Edgar Snow, *The Other Side of the River—Red China Today*, p. 686.
28. See chap. 26, p. 254.

33: Contrasting Scenes

1. OSS: Radio Msg no. 111 (see chap. 30, n. 19, above).
2. OSS: Radio Msg no. 119 (M/C-123), dated 14 September 1945, from Patti to INDIV. (CIAC)
3. OSS: Radio Msg no. 139 (M/C-143), p. 1, dated 17 September 1945, from Patti to INDIV. (CIAC)
4. OSS: Radio Msg no. 119 (see chap. 30, n. 17, para. 2, above).
5. OSS: Radio Msg no. 111 (see chap. 30, n. 19, above).
6. OSS: (a) Radio Msg no. 149 (M/C-153), dated 18 September 1945, from Nordlinger to CG-SOS-CT for Wadelton G-5; (b) Radio Msg no. 171 (M/C-175), dated 23 September 1945, from Patti to INDIV; (c) Radio Msg no. 19252 (M/C-149), dated 26 September 1945, from Ellis, signed CG-SOS-CT, to Nordlinger; and (d) Radio Msg no. 126 (M/C-176), dated 27 September 1945, from INDIV & Swift, to Patti. (All CIAC)
7. OSS: Radio Msg no. 151 (M/C-155), dated 19 September 1945, from Patti to INDIV. (CIAC) See chap. 31, pp. 301-306 passim.
8. Son of Nong Kinh Du, a leader in the Dong Minh Hoi, and a close friend of Nguyen Hai Than.
9. OSS: Radio Msg no. 111 (see Chap. 30, n. 19, above).
10. Ibid.
11. Ibid.
12. OSS: Radio Msg no. 142 (see Chap. 32, n. 7, above).
13. OSS: Radio Msg no. 159 (M/C-163), para. 2, dated 20 September 1945, from Patti to INDIV. (CIAC)
14. Ibid.
15. OSS: Radio Msg no. 98 (see chap. 30, n. 12, above).
16. The first British unit, Colonel Cass's, did not arrive in Saigon until 6 September, and there is no evidence of British-sanctioned French action against the Vietnamese until 22 September.
17. DOS: Disp. no. 21 (see chap. 26, n. 3, above).
18. Chinese Nationalist (KMT) troops, in large numbers, were equipped during the war with American weapons and thus readily available in making a "deal."
19. OSS: Radio Msg no. 139 (see n. 3, above).

20. Ho Chi Minh, *Selected Works*, 3:26–27.
21. OSS: Radio Msg no. 201 (M/C-208), p. 1, para. 4, dated 29 September 1945, from Patti to INDIV. (CIAC)
22. General Vo Nguyen Giap, *Unforgettable Days*, p. 76.
23. OSS: Radio Msg no. 111 (see Chap. 30, n. 19, above).
24. Bernard B. Fall, *Street Without Joy*, pp. 69–70. Joseph Buttinger, *Vietnam: A Dragon Embattled*, 1:628–30, passim.
25. Jean Sainteny, *Histoire*, p. 84.
26. Ibid., p. 102, n. 7, and p. 106.
27. Ibid., p. 109.
28. Bernard B. Fall, *Street Without Joy*, pp. 69–70.
29. OSS: Radio Msg no. 122 (M/C-126), dated 15 September 1945, from Patti to INDIV. (CIAC)
30. OSS: Radio Msg no. 141 (M/C-145), p. 1, para. 5, dated 17 September 1945, from Patti to INDIV. (CIAC)
31. Colonial administrator detailed as political adviser to General Alessandri. See Appendix II.
32. See Appendix II.
33. OSS: Radio Msg no. 159 (see n. 13, above).
34. OSS: Radio Msg no. 197 (M/C-204), dated 28 September 1945, from Patti to INDIV. (CIAC)
35. Ibid.
36. Minister of Defense. See Appendix II.
37. OSS: Radio Msg no. 170 (M/C-174), p. 2, para. 6, dated 23 September 1945, from Patti to INDIV, Chungking, Washington. (CIAC)
38. OSS: Radio Msg no. 167 (M/C-171), dated 22 September 1945, from Patti to INDIV. (CIAC)
39. OSS: Radio Msg no. 169 (M/C-173), dated 22 September 1945, from Patti to INDIV and Chungking. (CIAC)
40. Ibid.
41. Ibid.
42. OSS: Radio Msg no. 167 (see n. 38, above).
43. Ibid.
44. OSS: Radio Msg no. 170 (see n. 37, above).
45. Captain Aaron Bank was in the border area investigating war crimes and had reported British-French Force 136 (SOE) activities. OSS: Radio Msg no. 14 (M/C-121), dated 23 September 1945, from Bank to INDIV and Swift. (CIAC)
46. OSS: Radio Msg no. 173 (M/C-177), dated 23 September 1945, from Patti to INDIV. (CIAC)
47. Ibid.
48. Ibid.
49. OSS: Radio Msg no. 176 (M/C-180), dated 24 September 1945, from Patti to INDIV. (CIAC)
50. Hoang Quoc Viet. See Appendix II.
51. OSS: Radio Msg no. 172 (M/C-176), dated 24 September 1945, from Patti to Helliwell, info Heppner. (CIAC)
52. OSS: Radio Msg no. 176 (see n. 49, above).
53. Ibid.
54. OSS: Radio Msg no. 184 (M/C-188), dated 25 September 1945, from Patti to Helliwell and Heppner. (CIAC)

55. OSS: Radio Msg no. 185 (M/C-189), dated 25 September 1945, from Patti to Helliwell, info Heppner. (CIAC)
56. The delegation consisted of Shao Pai-ch'ang (Military Administration) and Ling Ch'i-han (Foreign Affairs).

34: End of Mission

1. *L'Entente*, a four-page French-language newspaper, was published clandestinely by Sainteny's group for the French communities in Hanoi and Haiphong. Outlawed at first, it was allowed to publish openly toward the latter part of 1945, subject to Viet Minh censorship.
2. DOS: Memorandum for the Record, dated 5 December 1945, prepared by J. C. H. Bonbright, Div. of European Affairs; File: FW 851 G.01/10–2245 CS/LE. (CIAC)
3. Ho Chi Minh, *Selected Works*, 3:30–31.
4. Ibid., p. 31.
5. This factor ultimately culminated in his recall to Hanoi in November 1945. See Appendix II.
6. Secretary General of the Foreign Office, a close associate of Hoang Minh Giam, who was then Deputy Minister for Foreign Affairs. The post of minister was retained by Ho Chi Minh.
7. An element of General (Governor) Lung Yün's Yunnan-Indochina Force, under the command of Major General Chao Yao-ming, Commander of the 52d Army. The Honorable 2d Division was the last Chinese unit to leave Viet Nam in October 1946.
8. Commander of the 60th Chinese Army.
9. Head of Lu Han's Secretariat and Chief of Protocol.
10. 23 Avenue de Grand Buddha.
11. OSS: Radio Msg no. 199 (M/C-206), p. 1, para. 1, dated 29 September 1945, from Patti to INDIV. (CIAC)
12. The elections were held on 6 January 1946.
13. The Vietnamese called Hsiao Wen *Tien-Van*.
14. OSS: Radio Msg no. 201, p. 1, para. 6 (see chap. 33, n. 21, above).
15. Ibid., para. 7.
16. OSS: Radio Msg no. 196 (M/C-26294), dated 28 September 1945, from Patti to INDIV. (CIAC)
17. OSS: Radio Msg no. 201, para. 7 (see n. 14, above).
18. Ibid., para. 2.
19. Ibid., para. 3.
20. OSS: Radio Msg no. 136 (M/C-187), dated 29 September 1945, from INDIV to Patti. (CIAC)

35: A Last Farewell

1. Thirty years later Giap still seemed perplexed by my sympathy and support of the Vietnamese struggle for national independence. In his book *Unforgettable Days* he noted, "While the French were frantically trying to return to Indochina, the American officer by the name of Patty [sic], for some reason we didn't know, showed sympathy for the Viet Minh's anti-Japanese struggle" (p. 19).
2. In 1945 the question of Laos and Cambodia as separate political entities was never at issue. In the context of the struggle for Vietnamese independence the

three nation-states complex was interwoven in the French concept of the French Indochina "federation." On two separate occasions I asked Truong Chinh and Hoang Minh Giam to clarify the apparent contradiction in terms between Viet Nam as a nation and Indochina as used in the name of the Indochinese Communist Party. They both held that the terms were compatible since the three nation-states, under French rule, had developed a commonality of geographical, political, and economic interests. Hence Viet Nam, the name of the three *kys* (regions of Tonkin, Annam and Cochinchina) was also applicable to the French "federation" of Indochinese states.

3. Former Governor-General of Indochina. See Appendix II.

PART FOUR: AFTERMATH

36: America's Albatross

1. DOS: Telegram no. 17 (sent via U.S. Army Signal Corps), dated 22 September 1945; subject, "French and Indo-China"; from Caffery (Paris) to AMEMBASSY (Chungking). pp. 1, 2. (CIAC)
2. Ibid., pp. 2, 3. (CIAC)
3. DOD: *United States-Vietnam Relations 1945-1967*. Study Prepared by the Department of Defense (House Committee on Armed Services [Print]. Washington: U.S. Government Printing Office, 1971. Book 1 of 12, Part I, A., p. A-24. *NOTE:* Hereinafter cited as *US-VR, DOD Study*.
4. DOS: Memorandum dated 18 January 1946, from H. F. Matthews to Acheson. National Archives, Diplomatic Files. Doc. no. 856E.00/1-1846. (CIAC)
5. DOS: Telegram no. 305, dated 5 December 1946, from Acheson to American Consul (Saigon) for Moffat. National Archives, Diplomatic Files. Doc. no. 851G.00/12-346. (CIAC)
6. DOS: Telegram no. 75, dated 8 January 1947 (7 P.M.), from Byrnes to AMEMBASSY, Paris (Caffery). National Archives, Diplomatic Files. Doc. no. 855.24/1-347. (CIAC)
7. DOS: Telegram no. 431, dated 3 February 1947 (8 P.M.), from Marshall to AMEMBASSY, Paris (Caffery). National Archives, Diplomatic Files. (unnumbered)
8. DOS: Telegram no. 1737, dated 13 May 1947 (8 P.M.), from Marshall to AMEMBASSY, Paris (Caffery). National Archives, Diplomatic Files. Doc. no. 851G.00/5-1347.
9. Ibid.
10. DOS: Telegram no. 77, dated 10 May 1949, from Acheson to AMCONSUL (Saigon). National Archives, Diplomatic Files. Doc. no. 851G.01/5-649. (CIAC)
11. *US-VR, DOD Study,* Book 1 of 12, Part I.A., p. A-59.
12. DOS: Memorandum dated 2 February 1950, from Acheson for the President; subject, "U.S. Recognition of Vietnam, Laos, and Cambodia." National Archives, Diplomatic Files. (unnumbered) (CIAC)
13. Ibid.
14. DOS: Telegram no. 59, dated 4 February 1950, from Acheson to AMCONSUL (Saigon). National Archives, Diplomatic Files. (CIAC)
15. DOS: Telegram no. 837, dated 22 February 1950, from AMEMBASSY, Paris (Caffery) to SecState. National Archives, Diplomatic Files.
16. *US-VR, DOD Study,* "Conclusions of NSC 64," dated 27 February 1950. Book 1 of 12, Part II.A.2., p. A-36.

17. DOS: Telegram no. 2049, dated 3 May 1950, from SecState to AMEMBASSY (London). National Archives, Diplomatic Files.
18. *US-VR, DOD Study,* Book 1 of 12, Part I.A.3., pp. A–60 and A–61.
19. DOS: Press Release no. 485, dated 11 May 1950. National Archives, Diplomatic Files.
20. DOS: Telegram no. 14, dated 11 May 1949, from Acheson to AMCONSUL (Hanoi). National Archives, Diplomatic Files. Doc. no. 851G.01/5–11–49.
21. The Protocol was signed on 7 December 1947.
22. Devillers, *Histoire du Viêt-Nam de 1940 à 1952,* p. 445.
23. *US-VR, DOD Study,* Book 1 of 12, Part II.A.1., p. A–7.
24. Ibid., p. A–8.
25. Ibid., p. A–7.
26. Ibid., p. A–18.
27. Ibid., p. A–19.
28. Ibid.
29. Ibid.
30. Ibid., pp. A–19 and A–20.
31. NSC: Doc. no. 48/2, dated 30 December 1949, *"The Position of the United States with Respect to Asia,"* para. 3.h. to *Conclusions of the NSC Report on.* National Archives, White House Papers.
32. NSC: Doc. no. 64, dated 27 February 1950, *"The Position of the United States with Respect to Indochina."* This document established the basis for American policy regarding U.S. involvement in Viet Nam. National Archives, White House Papers.
33. WH: White House Press Release dated 27 June 1950, "Statement by the President." National Archives, White House Papers.
34. *US-VR, DOD Study,* Book 1 of 12, Part II.A.2., p. A–39.
35. Fall, *Street Without Joy,* p. 33.
36. Fall, *The Two Viet-Nams,* p. 116.
37. *US-VR, DOD Study,* Book 1 of 12, Part II.A.2., p. A–27.
38. Ibid.
39. Ibid., pp. A–27 and A–28.
40. Ibid., p. A–28.
41. Ibid., p. A–26.
42. NSC: Doc. no. 124/2, dated 25 June 1952, *"Statement of Policy by the National Security Council on United States Objectives and Courses of Action with Respect to Southeast Asia."* Section: *Courses of Action,* para. 10c. National Archives, White House Papers.
43. *US-VR, DOD Study,* Book 1 of 12, Part II.A.2., p. A–21.
44. Ibid.
45. Ibid.
46. Dulles, *War or Peace,* p. 231; and Gurtov, *The First Vietnam Crisis,* pp. 25–26.
47. Speech before the American Legion, St. Louis, Missouri. DOS, *Bulletin* XXIX (14 September 1953), pp. 339–342.
48. *US-VR, DOD Study,* Book 1 of 12, Part II.A.2., pp. A–26 and A–27.
49. Ibid., p. A–27.
50. Fall, *The Two Viet-Nams,* p. 221.
51. Shaplen, *The Lost Revolution,* p. 93.
52. *US-VR, DOD Study,* Book 1 of 12, Part II.A.3., p. A–51.
53. Text of speech is in DOS, *Bulletin* XXIX (14 September 1953), pp. 339–342.

54. DOS: *Bulletin,* XXIX (19 September 1953), pp. 342–343.
55. Ho Chi Minh, *Selected Works,* 3: 408–10.
56. DOS: *Bulletin,* XXX (4 January 1954), p. 12.
57. DOS: *Bulletin,* XXX (11 January 1954), p. 43.
58. *US-VR, DOD Study,* Book 1 of 12, Part II.B.2., p. B–18.
59. *China and U.S. Far East Policy, 1945–1966* (Congressional Quarterly Service, Washington, D.C., 1967), p. 67.
60. National Archives, *Public Papers of the Presidents of the United States: Dwight D. Eisenhower, 1954.* Washington (USGPO, 1960), pp. 250, 253.
61. Ibid.
62. Ibid., p. 306.
63. *US-VR, DOD Study,* Book 1 of 12, Part II.B.1., p. B–6.
64. Ibid.
65. DOS: *Bulletin,* XXX (5 April 1954), pp. 512–513.
66. *US-VR, DOD Study,* Book 1 of 12, Part II.B.2., p. B–20.
67. DOS: *American Foreign Policy 1950–1955: Basic Documents* (2 vols., USGPO, 1957), II:2373–2376.
68. *US-VR, DOD Study,* Book 1 of 12, Part II.B.2., p. B–25.
69. *China and U.S. Far East Policy, 1945–1966* (Congressional Quarterly Service, Washington, D.C., 1967), p. 68.
70. DOS: *American Foreign Policy 1950–1955: Basic Documents* (2 vols., USGPO, 1957), II: pp. 2383, 2386–2390.
71. A valuable source for details of the conference is Eden's *Full Circle: The Memoirs of Anthony Eden* (Boston: Houghton-Mifflin, 1960).
72. Hoang Van Hoan was part-Chinese, Mandarin-speaking, and the DRV's Ambassador to Peking from 1951 to 1958. He was dropped from the Politburo and other positions of authority in 1976 and defected to Peking on 3 July 1979 while en route to Berlin.
73. At Geneva at 2400 hours, 20 July 1954, by Brig. General Henri Deltiel for the Commander in Chief of the French Union Forces in Indochina, and by Ta Quang Buu, vice-minister of National Defense of the DRV.
74. Devillers and Lacouture, *End of a War: Indochina, 1954,* p. 300.
75. DOS: *American Foreign Policy 1950–1955: Basic Documents* (2 vols., USGPO, 1957), I: p. 1707.
76. Ibid., II: pp. 2401–2402.
77. *US-VR, DOD Study,* Book 1 of 12, Part IV.A.3., p. 17.

SELECTED BIBLIOGRAPHY

Because this book is principally a firsthand account of a brief period in the history of Viet Nam the following bibliography is limited mainly to works cited in the text and notes. The author has diligently avoided repeating facts, opinions and interpretations stated by other writers except where these were essential to the text for clarity, generally supported by official American documentation and the author's personal involvement. To recapitulate in this bibliography the several thousand items in current work on Indochina and Viet Nam would be redundant. The reader concerned with Vietnamese history, culture, economics, etc., both colonial and contemporary, will find many excellent bibliographies in the works of other authors. To mention only a few: Joseph Buttinger's bibliographies are prolific and discriminating. Bernard B. Fall, drawing widely from French sources, provided an invaluable group of bibliographies for a better understanding of the French view on Indochina. Conversely, King C. Chen's *Vietnam and China 1938–1954* (1969) is replete with rare and useful source material, including Chinese documentation and works of Chinese and Vietnamese writers, while Frances Fitz-Gerald's *Fire in the Lake* (1972) offers an expanded bibliography which includes sources indispensable to a clear understanding and appreciation of Vietnamese social practices and moral conduct. Finally, the books of Foreign Languages Publishing House in Hanoi have proved to be good control sources for time, place, and people in reconstructing the history of the period.

☙ ☙ ☙

Bator, Victor. *Viet-Nam: A Diplomatic Tragedy.* Dobbs Ferry, N.Y.: Oceana Publications, 1965.
Bodard, Lucien. *The Quicksand War: Prelude to Vietnam.* Translated and

with introduction by Patrick O'Brien. Boston: Atlantic-Little, Brown & Co., 1967.

Bryant, Arthur. *Triumph in the West: A History of the War Years Based on the Diaries of Field Marshal Lord Alanbrooke, Chief of the Imperial General Staff.* New York: Doubleday & Company, Inc., 1959.

Bullitt, William C. "The Saddest War." *Life,* December 29, 1947.

Buttinger, Joseph. *Vietnam: A Dragon Embattled,* 2 vols. New York, Washington, London: Frederick A. Praeger, Publishers, 1967.

Cameron, Allen W., ed. *Viet-Nam Crisis: A Documentary History, Volume I: 1940–1956.* Ithaca and London: Cornell University Press, 1971.

Catroux, Georges, *Deux actes du drame indochinois.* Paris: Librairie Plon, 1959.

Charlton, Michael and Moncrieff, Anthony, eds. *Many Reasons Why: The American Involvement in Vietnam.* London: Scolar Press, 1978.

Chen, King C. *Vietnam and China, 1938–1954.* Princeton, N.J.: Princeton University Press, 1969.

Chennault, Claire Lee. *Way of a Fighter.* Edited by Robert Hotz. New York: G. P. Putnam's Sons, 1949.

Chi, Hoang Van. *From Colonialism to Communism: A Case History of North Vietnam.* New York: Frederick A. Praeger, Publishers, 1964.

Chiang Kai-shek. *Statements and Speeches: Volume I, August-October, 1945.* Shanghai: International Publishers, 1945.

Cole, Allan B., ed. *Conflict in Indochina and International Repercussions: A Documentary History, 1945–1955.* Ithaca: Cornell University Press, 1956.

Cooper, Chester L. *The Lost Crusade: America in Vietnam.* Greenwich, Conn.: Fawcett Publications, Inc., 1972.

Crozier, Brian. *Southeast Asia in Turmoil.* London: Penguin Books, 1965.

Decoux, Jean. *A la barre de l'Indochine: Histoire de mon gouvernement général, 1940–1945.* Paris: Librairie Plon, 1952.

De Gaulle, Charles. *War Memoirs, Volume One: The Call to Honour, 1940–1942.* Translated by Jonathan Griffin. London: Collins, 1955.

_____. *The War Memoirs of Charles de Gaulle: Unity, 1942–1944.* Translated by Richard Howard. New York: Simon and Schuster, 1959.

_____. *The War Memoirs of Charles de Gaulle: Salvation, 1944–1946.* Translated by Richard Howard. New York: Simon and Schuster, 1960.

Devillers, Philippe. *Histoire du Viêt-Nam de 1940 à 1952.* Paris: Éditions du Seuil, 1952. The most accurate French account of the period; barring several omissions and minor inaccuracies generally attributable to his sources and to the lack of American documentation, it is by far one of the more reliable histories.

Devillers, Philippe and Lacouture, Jean, eds. *End of a War: Indochina, 1954.* New York, Washington, London: Frederick A. Praeger, Publishers, 1969.

Dong, Pham Van, and the Committee for the Study of the History of the Viet Nam Workers' Party. *Our President: Ho Chi Minh.* Hanoi: Foreign Languages Publishing House, 1970.

Drachman, Edward R. *United States Policy Toward Vietnam, 1940-1945.* Rutherford, Madison, Teaneck: Fairleigh Dickinson University Press, 1970.

Ducoroy, Maurice. *Ma trahison en Indochine.* Paris: Les Éditions Internationales, 1949.

Dulles, John Foster. *War or Peace.* New York: The Macmillan Company, 1950.

Duncanson, Dennis J. *Government and Revolution in Vietnam.* New York: Oxford University Press, 1968.

Eden, Sir Anthony. *Full Circle: Memoirs of Sir Anthony Eden.* Boston: Cassell, 1960.

Ely, Paul. *L'Indochine dans la tourmente.* Paris: Librairie Plon, 1964.

Fall, Bernard B. *Street Without Joy: Insurgency in Indochina, 1946-1963.* 3rd ed. Harrisburg, Pa.: Stackpole Books, 1963, and *Street Without Joy.* 4th ed. London and Dunmow: Pall Mall Press, 1965.

——————. *The Two Viet-Nams: A Political and Military Analysis.* 2d rev. ed. New York, Washington, London: Frederick A. Praeger, 1968.

——————. *Ho Chi Minh on Revolution: Selected Writings, 1920-66.* Edited and with introduction by Bernard B. Fall. New York: The American Library, Inc., A Signet Book, 1968.

——————. *Viet-Nam Witness, 1953-66.* New York, Washington, London: Frederick A. Praeger, Publishers, 1966.

Fenn, Charles. *Ho Chi Minh, a biographical introduction.* New York: Charles Scribner's Sons, 1973.

FitzGerald, Frances. *Fire in the Lake: The Vietnamese and the Americans in Vietnam.* Boston, Toronto: Little, Brown and Company, 1972.

Ford, Corey. *Donovan of OSS.* Boston, Toronto: Little, Brown and Company, 1970.

Gelb, Leslie H. "Vietnam: The System Worked." Reprint 206, The Brookings Institution, Washington DC, 1971. New York: *Foreign Policy*, Number 3, Summer 1971, pp. 140-67.

Gettleman, Marvin E., edited with an introduction. *Viet Nam: History, Documents, and Opinions on a Major World Crisis.* New York: Fawcett World Library, 1965.

Giap, Vo Nguyen. *The Military Art of People's War: Selected Writings of General Vo Nguyen Giap.* Edited and with an introduction by Russell Stetler. New York and London: Monthly Review Press, 1970.

——————. *Unforgettable Days.* Hanoi: Foreign Languages Publishing House, 1975.

——————. *Unforgettable Months and Years.* Translated and with Introduction by Mai Van Elliott. Southeast Asia Program Data Paper no. 99. Ithaca: Cornell University, May 1975.

Gurtov, Melvin. *The First Vietnam Crisis: Chinese Communist Strategy and United States Involvement.* New York: Columbia University Press, 1967.

Hammer, Ellen J. *The Struggle for Indochina.* Stanford, Calif.: Stanford University Press, 1955.

Hertrich, Jean-Michel. *Doc-Lap! L'independance ou la mort.* Paris: Vigneau, 1946.

Ho Chi Minh. *Selected Works,* 4 vols. (1922–1960). Hanoi: Foreign Languages Publishing House, 1960, 1961, and 1962.

Hull, Cordell. *The Memoirs of Cordell Hull,* 2 vols. London: Hodder & Stoughton, 1948.

Indochinese Communist Party. *Breaking our Chains: Documents on the Vietnamese Revolution of August 1945.* Hanoi: Foreign Languages Publishing House, 1960. An excellent compilation of documents.

Isaacs, Harold R. *No Peace for Asia.* New York: Macmillan, 1947.

Isoart, Pierre. *Le phénomène national viêtnamien: De l'indépendance unitaire à l'indépendance fractionée.* Paris: Librairie Général de Droit et de Jurisprudence, 1961.

Kahin, George McTurnan and Lewis, John W., eds. *The United States in Vietnam,* Revised Edition. New York: The Dial Press, 1967.

Lacouture, Jean. *Vietnam: Between Two Truces.* New York: Random House, 1966.

—————. *Ho Chi Minh.* New York: Random House, 1968.

—————, and Devillers, Philippe, eds. *End of a War: Indochina, 1954.* New York, Washington, London: Frederick A. Praeger, Publishers, 1969.

Lancaster, Donald. *The Emancipation of French Indochina.* New York: Oxford University Press, 1961.

McAlister, John T., Jr. *Viet Nam: The Origins of Revolution.* New York: Doubleday & Company, Inc., 1971.

MacDonald, Elizabeth P. *Undercover Girl.* New York: The Macmillan Company, 1947.

Mansfield, Mike. "Reprieve in Vietnam." *Harper's Magazine,* January 1956.

Mordant, [Eugène] General. *Au service de la France en Indochine: 1941–1945.* Saigon: Imprimerie Française d'Outre-Mer, 1950.

Mountbatten of Burma, Vice-Admiral the Earl. *Post Surrender Tasks—Section E of the Report to the Combined Chiefs of Staff by the Supreme Allied Commander, South-East Asia, 1943–1945.* London: Her Majesty's Stationery Office, 1969.

Mus, Paul. *Viet-Nam: Sociologie d'une guerre.* Paris: Éditions du Seuil, 1952.

Porter, Gareth. *A Peace Denied: The United States, Vietnam, and the Paris Agreement.* Bloomington & London: Indiana University Press, 1975.

Raskin, Marcus G. and Fall, Bernard B., eds. *The Viet-Nam Reader: Articles and Documents on American Foreign Policy and the Viet-Nam Crisis.* New York: Random House, 1965.

Romanus, Charles F. and Sunderland, Riley, eds. *United States Army in World War II, China, Burma, India Theater: Time Runs Out in CBI.* Washington, D.C.: Office of the Chief of Military History, U.S. Army, 1959.

Roosevelt, Elliott. *As He Saw It.* New York: Duell, Sloan and Pearce, 1946.

Sabattier, G[abriel]. *Le destine de l'Indochine: Souvenier et documents, 1941-1951.* Paris: Librairie Plon, 1952.

Sainteny, Jean. *Histoire d'une paix manquée: Indochine 1945-1947.* Paris: Fayard, 1953.

Schaller, Michael. *The U.S. Crusade in China, 1938-1945.* New York: Columbia University Press, 1979.

Shaplen, Robert. "The Enigma of Ho Chi Minh." *The Reporter,* January 27, 1955.

_____. *The Lost Revolution.* New York: Harper & Row, Publishers, 1965.

Smith, R. Harris. *OSS: The Secret History of America's First Central Intelligence Agency.* Berkeley, Los Angeles, London: University of California Press, 1972.

Snow, Edgar. *The Other Side of the River: Red China Today.* New York: Random House, 1962.

Stilwell, Joseph W. *The Stilwell Papers.* Arranged and edited by Theodore H. White. New York: Schocken Books, 1972.

Tan, General Chu Van. *Reminiscences on the Army for National Salvation.* Translated by Mai Elliott. Southeast Asia Program Data Paper no. 97. Ithaca: Cornell University, May 1975.

Thorne, Christopher. *Allies of a Kind: The United States, Britain and the war against Japan, 1941-1945.* New York: Oxford University Press, 1978.

Tuchman, Barbara W. *Stilwell and the American Experience in China, 1911-45.* New York: Bantam edition, The Macmillan Company, 1972.

United States Department of Defense. *United States-Vietnam Relations 1945-1967: Study Prepared by the Department of Defense.* (Books 1 to 12) Washington, D.C.: U.S. Government Printing Office, 1971.

United States Department of State. *Foreign Relations of the United States, Diplomatic Papers, 1942 (vol. II) and 1945 (vols. VI and VII).* Washington, D.C.: United States Government Printing Office, 1956, 1969.

_____. *Political Alignments of Vietnamese Nationalists: Report No. 3708.* Office of Intelligence Research, Division of Research for Far East. Washington, D.C., 1949.

Vien, Nguyen Khac. *The Long Resistance (1858-1975).* Hanoi: Foreign Languages Publishing House, 1975.

Vigneras, Marcel. *United States Army in World War II, Special Studies: Rearming the French.* Washington, D.C.: Office of the Chief of Military History, Department of the Army, 1957.

Wedemeyer, General Albert C. *Wedemeyer Reports!* New York: Henry Holt & Company, 1958.

INDEX

A

E

O